CW01083523

PORTSMOUTH TROLLEYBUSES

David R.H. Bowler

Cover captions

Front

The majority of Portsmouth Corporation's trolleybus services started and terminated on The Hard outside the Main Gate of HM Dockyard. Four AEC661T trolleybuses, from left to right 298, 230, an unknown vehicle, and 295, await their departure times to various parts of the United Kingdom's sole island city.
(Online Transport Archive [photographer M. Eavis])

The coat of arms of Portsmouth, featuring a golden star between the horns of a crescent on an azure shield, has medieval origins and may have been adopted at the time Portsmouth was granted its Charter by King Richard I in 1194 as there are obvious connections to the arms of the King and his crusades.

The style of the coat of arms applied to Portsmouth trolleybuses adopted the motto 'Heaven's Light Our Guide', entirely appropriate in view of the maritime connections, and dates from 1929 when the town was granted City status and was replaced by a more complex version featuring a crest, supporters and heraldic badge in 1970.

Rear

(Upper)
By now 26 years old, Portsmouth AEC661T trolleybus 250 pulls away from the Eastney Depot stop. It will pass the depot entrance and head north along Eastney Road before continuing along Goldsmith Avenue to Fratton Bridge and then onwards to Guildhall Square and the Dockyard on circular service 17.
(Tony Belton)

(Lower)
At the historic Hard in the latter days of the Portsmouth trolleybus system 1936 AEC661T 233, equipped with a Cravens 52 seat body, waits at the kerb prior to departure on Eastney circular service 18 whilst BUT9611T 301, dating from 1950, stands towards the middle of the road before departure to Southsea South Parade Pier on a service 5 journey. In the distance the masts of HMS Victory, Nelson's flagship, can be seen through the Main Gate of HM Dockyard.
(Tony Belton)

Published in 2014 by Adam Gordon Books
ISBN 978-1-874422-96-9

Designed, Typeset & Printed by Henry Ling Limited, at the Dorset Press, Dorchester DT1 1HD

CONTENTS

2. Network Development

3. Service Developments

AUTHOR'S ACKNOWLEDGEMENTS

In 1969 the Reading Transport Society, forerunner of today's British Trolleybus Society (BTS), published a duplicated booklet chronicling the relatively short life of trolleybuses in Portsmouth written by Roger Funnell and David Janes. I was brought into contact with these gentlemen by BTS stalwart John Whitehead and was instantly provided their generous and unflinching support. I cannot speak highly enough of their combined efforts to ensure that little known facts were put at my disposal and in endeavouring to unravel the undoubtedly complicated operating practices of the undertaking, particularly in view of the absence of a large proportion of the erstwhile transport department's records. Free access to Roger's findings and research has greatly expedited the appearance of this volume and but for the continual advice and support of David, who has chronicled the development of public transport in Portsmouth since its inception, this book would be very much the poorer. It is saddening to record that Roger Funnell passed away in September 2010 and will never have the opportunity to see this detailed record of Portsmouth's trolleybuses.

David Janes sketched the many maps based on a wide variety of sources, including my inputs, and these were prepared electronically by Rodney Funnell, the son of Roger Funnell, and by Patrick Leidenberger, a colleague in Switzerland, to whom I extend my sincere thanks.

The staff of the Portsmouth City Council Records Office has been extremely helpful throughout my six years of research, however, as touched on above, it is evident that a large percentage of the erstwhile City of Portsmouth Passenger Transport Department's records were never entrusted to their care. Whether this is due to their loss in wartime or excessive enthusiasm for salvaging paper at some stage in the past is a matter of conjecture – privatisation and takeovers have tended to result in the archives of many municipal operators being lost. Furthermore financial constraints have meant that not all the records that have survived have been properly catalogued, a situation that has been exacerbated by the recent cuts in central government funding leading to the closure of the Search Room at Portsmouth Museum and redundancies. Amongst the staff, Mrs Diana Gregg stands out for her efforts in identifying information of interest and her encyclopaedic knowledge of the City!

Unsurprisingly, my efforts to contact Transport Department employees from the trolleybus era almost fifty years after it ended met with little success, thus I am most grateful to Gordon Ferguson, a former driver, for his recollections.

A large number of trolleybus enthusiasts have also provided willing assistance, whether in respect of complicated enquiries into very specific points or in the provision of photographs, namely: David Barber, David Beilby, Tony Belton, Ashley Bruce, Geoff Burrows, Roger Funnell, Bruce Gould, Philip Groves, Dave Hall, Robert Hall, David Harvey, Ed Humphreys, David Janes, Martin Jenkins, David Lawrence, Stephen Lockwood, Geoff Lumb, Roy Marshall, John Mawson, Alan Oxley, David Packer, Colin Page, Malcolm Pearce, Bob Rowe, Tim Runnacles, Peter Smith, Robert Smith (including access to the records of the late Les Bern and George Tucker), Robin Symonds, Hugh Taylor, Malcolm Wells and John Whitehead. Special mention should also be made of the efforts made by an earlier generation of enthusiasts, specifically Les Bern, Sam Harrison and George Tucker. My sincere apologies to anybody I may have inadvertently omitted.

Finally my thanks to the publisher Adam Gordon and his team for having patiently produced another of my trolleybus system histories to his customary high standard and for ensuring that a generous proportion of the proceeds will benefit the trolleybus preservation movement.

David Bowler
Pfungen, Switzerland

INTRODUCTION

My first visit to Portsmouth must have been in the mid-1960s, some years after the last trolleybus had run in the city, when I spent some time based at RAF Thorney Island nearby. However, the catalyst for this history must be laid squarely on our son's shoulders. He was firmly set on a career in the Royal Navy from about six years of age; this ensured regular pilgrimages from home in Switzerland to Portsmouth for 'Navy Days', and other naval events, until he entered university in Portsmouth. The fact that, despite all odds, our son is now a Marine Engineering Officer in the Royal Navy will ensure our links with the city for years to come!

During that visit one could not fail to be impressed by the clean and smart buses, admittedly motorbuses, operated by the City of Portsmouth Passenger Transport Department and providing a genuine service to the population in co-operation with Southdown Motor Services, the 'country' or suburban operator.

In the 1930s the Department had been notable in purchasing a considerable number of experimental trolleybuses for comparison purposes before deciding upon which type to standardise. The system coped so successfully with the tribulations of the Second World War that there were calls for the conversion of many motorbus services to trolleybus operation and extensions to the east and west of Cosham. However, both before and after the war, any thoughts of expansion were hampered by the city's island location and possibly one of the most aggressive suburban operators in Britain who was determined to ensure itself a portion of the off-island traffic although within the city boundaries. Nonetheless, it is fallacy to believe, as some commentators suggest, that all Portsmouth's trolleybuses looked the same and that every service ran between Cosham, immediately to the north of Portsea Island, and the main entrance to HM Dockyard at The Hard!

Turning to operational matters, it is interesting to note that although both Portsea Island and those parts of the mainland once foreseen for trolleybus routes are virtually flat, many of the experimental vehicles, and all the AECs selected as the preferred type of trolleybus upon which to standardise, were equipped with regenerative control. The General Manager and Engineer of the period, Ben Hall, insisted at industry conferences that the decision to employ regeneration had proved financially worthwhile although this type of control was normally more associated with trolleybus operators in hillier areas.

Notwithstanding the national decline in passenger journeys, much has happened to public transport in the United Kingdom's sole island city since the last trolleybus ran on Saturday 27 July 1963. Political *diktat* required that the erstwhile City of Portsmouth Passenger Transport Department became an 'arms-length' company which immediately suffered predatory competition from neighbouring operators, including Southampton Citybus, the by then privatised Southampton City Transport. In 1988 the Portsmouth undertaking was sold to a consortium of its employees (25%) and Southampton Citybus, and renamed Portsmouth Citybus, thereby ending municipal involvement in an important service to its citizens after 87 years. The latter's holding passed briefly to Stagecoach and then to the Transit Holdings Group trading as Blue Admiral which was itself acquired by First Bus in April 1996.

Traffic congestion in Portsmouth today must be amongst the very worst anywhere in the United Kingdom but in a country which associates car ownership and the production of on-street emissions as signs of civilisation and prosperity this is hardly a surprise. The retention of trolleybuses and their extension into the distant suburbs alone would not have prevented this but such a policy might have contributed to a better situation than currently exists. Britain has a gigantic challenge ahead if it is ever again to offer its citizens the urban mobility and environmental-friendliness that only electric public transport can provide.

David Bowler
Pfungen, Switzerland

NOTES FOR GUIDANCE

Terms and expressions

For the benefit of non-enthusiast the more obscure terms used in connection with trolleybuses, and in particular the trolleybus overhead line installations, are explained:

Bracket arm — A tubular steel support bolted to the upper section of the *traction pole* at right angles and projecting over the road, from which to suspend the *trolley wire* as an alternative to a *span wire*. They were usually employed where the length of *span wire* between traction poles would be unduly long or along straight stretches on narrow roads to reduce the number of traction poles. They are also referred to as a single bracket arm to differentiate from a *gantry* or double bracket arm.

Cantrail — The horizontal length of metal or wood above the upper saloon windows on a double-deck vehicle that supported the roof.

Composite (body) — In this form of bodywork, the main framework constructed from hardwood, reinforced as necessary with steel flitches, supports and brackets, and panelled in metal.

Converter — Rotating electromechanical device, like a motor or a generator, used to convert alternating current (AC) into direct current (DC).

Curve segment — The special curved fitting which replaced several separate *pull-offs* in the *running wire*, and thus gave a smoother passage for the *trolleyheads* on sharp curves.

Dress ring — See *wheel trim*.

Drop light — A type of opening side window employed in the main side bays of the lower and upper saloons of bus bodies, whereby the entire pane of glass dropped downwards into a recess within the side panels below.

Frog — The overhead line equipment equating to railway points where one pair of trolley wires left or joined another, known as facing or turnout frogs where the lines diverged, and trailing or junction frogs where the lines converged. Facing frogs were operated either by hand (the conductor leaving the vehicle and pulling an operating handle, connected by cable to the frog mechanism, on an adjacent *traction pole*) or automatically by the *trolleyheads* of a trolleybus energising a solenoid through a contact fitted to the overhead line a short distance before the frog. The direction of the frog could be changed by the trolleybus drawing power as the *trolleyheads* passed beneath the contact.

Gantry — A tubular steel support joining the upper section of two *traction poles* on opposite sides of the roadway, from which to suspend the *trolley wire* as an alternative to *span wire*; also referred to as a double bracket arm.

Half-drop — A type of opening side window employed in the main side bays of the lower and upper saloons of bus bodies whereby the window was divided horizontally into two; the upper pane of glass dropped downwards outside the fixed lower pane.

Hanger — The attachment which, by use of soldering or a mechanical grip, also known as an 'ear', and a porcelain insulator, supported the *trolley wire* beneath a *bracket arm* or *span wire*.

Metal framed (body) — In this form of bodywork, a steel or aluminium frame was built with timber packers and wooden inserts to accept the many screws needed to hold the interior finishers and exterior panels; also referred to as an 'all metal' body.

Motor generator — An electric motor using the traction power supply as its source of energy, driving a generator to produce power for a vehicle's low tension lighting.

Pull-off — A *span wire* or wires providing additional support or securing a correct alignment of the trolley wires on bends under the correct tension, creating a curve consisting of a series of short straight sections.

Quarter light — A separate, roughly triangular, side window situated between the driver's cab door or main cab side window(s) and the front pillar.

Railless — See *trolleybus*.

Rake — The slope from the vertical at the front and/or rear of a body.

Rectifier — A device for converting alternating current (AC) into direct current (DC).

Reversing triangle — An arrangement in the overhead line to enable vehicles to turn by means of a three-point reversing procedure into and out of a side turning.

Rosette — An anchor fitting, rag-bolted or otherwise fixed to the face of a building, used instead of a *traction pole* to which a *span wire* (or wires) was attached.

Route — The way or series of roads and streets between two points.

Running wire — See *trolley wire*.

Section insulator — An overhead line assembly containing a short length of non-conductive material of the same profile as the *trolley wire* to break the route up into electrically isolated half-mile sections as required by law in the United Kingdom.

Service	The timetabled frequency of vehicles identified by a service number along a stipulated *route*.
Span wire	A load-bearing wire erected across the width of the roadway (usually between opposite or diagonally opposite *traction poles*, but sometimes anchored to buildings by a wall *rosette*) from which the trolley wires were suspended.
Trackless	See *trolleybus*.
Traction pole	A steel tubular pole used to support bracket arms, gantries and span wires, usually about 31ft long, set 6ft into the ground at the roadside at a 5° rake away from the road (to compensate for the weight supported) and embedded in concrete. There were four grades of pole, light, medium, heavy and extra heavy, varying in girth and used according to the weight and/or strain they were expected to carry.
Trolleybase	The point at which the *trolleypoles* were attached to the roof or a roof-mounted gantry of the vehicle. The trolleybase enabled the *trolleypoles* to move laterally and vertically, whilst large inclined springs latterly more or less parallel to the *trolleypoles* provided the tension necessary to keep the under-running wheel in contact with running wires.
Trolleybooms	See *trolleypoles*.
Trolleybus	A public passenger transport vehicle with rubber tyres which travels along ordinary roads and is powered by electricity that is collected from a pair of conductor wires hung above the road by means of a under-running wheels or skids attached to sprung *trolleypoles*. Contrary to a tramcar, a trolleybus does not require tracks laid in the road surface and was accordingly initial known as a *railless* or *trackless*.
Trolleyhead	The retention and swivel device at the extreme end of each *trolleypole* which held the under-running current collecting wheel or sliding slipper.
Trolleypoles	The roof mounted tubular booms which, by means of a sprung base permitting lateral and vertical movement, kept the under-running wheel in contact with the running wires in order to draw current to propel the vehicle.
Trolley vehicle	The official term used in legislative documents for a *trolleybus*.
Trolley wire	The copper alloy conductor wire along which the under-running wheels ran. The pair of wires was kept laterally apart and suspended about 20ft above the surface of the road. The wire nearest the centre of the road had positive polarity and that nearest the edge of the road had negative polarity.
Twin line hanger	A spacer assembly designed to clamp the two *trolley wires* the correct distance apart (generally 2ft) when supported by a *bracket arm* or *span wire*. The *trolley wire* itself was held by 'ears' bolted to and insulated from the hanger assembly.
Turning circle	An arrangement in the overhead line to turn vehicles back along the route by means of a U-turn.
Vent panel	The panels immediately above the lower saloon windows but below the upper saloon floor-line which could contain ventilation louvres.
Wheel trim	An ornamental pressed steel ring, normally chromium plated, fitted over the exterior face of the wheel hub; also referred to as *dress rings*.

Abbreviations

The following abbreviations are used in the text:

AA	Anti-Attrition Metal Co. Ltd.
AC	Alternating current
AEC	Associated Equipment Company Ltd.
AEU	Amalgamated Engineering Union
ARP	Air Raid Precautions
BET	The British Electric Traction Co. Ltd.
BICC	British Insulated Callender's Cables Ltd.
BoT	Board of Trade
BR (SR)	British Railways (Southern Region)
BS	British Standard
BTC	British Transport Commission
BTH	British Thomson-Houston
BTS	British Trolleybus Society
BUT	British United Traction Ltd.
CEB	Central Electricity Board
CPPTD	City of Portsmouth Passenger Transport Department
DC	Direct current
ER&TCW	Electric Railway and Tramway Carriage Works
FP	Feeder pillar
GPO	General Post Office
H&D	Hants and Dorset Motor Services Ltd.
hp	Horse power
LBSCR	London Brighton and South Coast Railway
LPTB	London Passenger Transport Board
LSWR	London and South Western Railway
MCW	Metro-Cammell-Weymann
MCCW	Metropolitan-Cammell Carriage, Wagon and Finance Company
MoS	Ministry of Supply
MoT	Ministry of Transport (known as the Ministry of War Transport between 1939 and 1946, and the Ministry of Transport and Civil Aviation between 1946 and 1959)
MoWT	Ministry of War Transport
MP	Member of Parliament
MPTA	Municipal Passenger Transport Association (known as the Municipal Tramways and Transport Association between 1926 and 1939, and as the Municipal Tramways Association prior to that)
MTTA	Municipal Tramways and Transport Association
NFVT	National Federation of Vehicle Trades
NJC	National Joint Council

NJIC	National Joint Industrial Council
OAP	Old age pensioner
OMO	One-man operation
p.a.	*per annum*
PCT	Portsmouth Corporation Tramways
PHLR	Portsmouth and Horndean Light Railway
PSV	Public Service Vehicle
RTC	Regional Traffic Commissioner
SEB	Southern Electricity Board
SMS	Southdown Motor Services Ltd.
SR	Southern Railway
swg	Standard Wire Gauge
TGWU	Transport and General Workers Union
TMS	Tramway Museum Society
UK	United Kingdom

At various points in the text use has been made of a standard code (which will be familiar to enthusiasts) when referring to the type of body and seating capacity of a particular type of trolleybus. The code usually consists of two figures separated by an oblique stroke to indicate, respectively the upper and lower-deck seating capacity. Letters are prefixed to indicate body type and suffixed to indicate doorway positions. The elements of this code used in connection with Portsmouth's trolleybuses are as follows:

Prefix letter(s):	H	Highbridge double-deck layout, i.e. with centre as opposed to side gangway in upper saloon.
Figures:		Indicate the number of seats in the upper and lower saloons respectively.
Suffix letter(s):	R	Rear doorway with open platform.

For example, AEC661Ts 25–100 (RV8307–336, RV9106–154) were H26/26R, i.e. highbridge bodywork with 26 seats upstairs, 26 seats downstairs and a single rear doorway with open platform.

Conversion Factors: Units and Currency

During the period in which the trolleybuses operated, Britain used Imperial units of measure and pre-decimal currency. These traditional units are used throughout this book as no useful purpose would be served in providing conversions in the text. The following table will be of use to readers wishing to convert any figures quoted to metric units and decimal currency.

Length:	1 inch (in.) = 25.4 centimetres (cm)
	1 foot (ft) = 12 inches = 30.5 centimetres (cm)
	1 yard (yd) = 3 feet = 91.4 centimetres
	1 chain = 22 yards = 20.1 metres (m)
	1 furlong = 10 chains = 22 yards = 201 metres
	1 mile = 8 furlongs = 1.6 kilometres (km)
Area:	1 acre = 4,840 square yards = 4,046.86 square metres = 0.4047 hectares
Weight:	1 pound (lb) = 0.45 kilogram (kgs)
	1 quarter (qtr) = 127 kgs
	1 hundredweight (cwt) = 4 quarters = 50.8 kgs
	1 imperial ton = 20 hundredweights (cwt) = 1.02 metric tonnes
Currency:	1 penny (d) = 2.4 pence (p)
	1 shilling (s) = 12d = 5 pence (p)
	1 pound (£) = 20 shillings (s) = 240d = 100p

To Trudy and Thomas
Thank you for your patience!

CHAPTER ONE

HEAVEN'S LIGHT OUR GUIDE

Most of the conurbation that we now know as the City of Portsmouth is located on Portsea Island, a flat land area about 4 miles long and 2½ miles wide which at no point rises more than 20ft above sea level, bordered on the south by the Solent, on the west by Portsmouth Harbour and on the east by Langstone Harbour. A tidal channel running between the Portsmouth and Langstone Harbours separates the island from the mainland at Cosham. The geography of Portsmouth is typical of the submergent coastline found along the length of England's south coast. Chichester Harbour, Southampton Water and Poole Harbour are further examples nearby, known as *rias* or drowned river estuaries resulting from a fall in the coastline or a rise in sea level. Typically the resultant large estuary is at the mouth of a relatively insignificant river (the River Wallington in the case of Portsmouth Harbour) carrying small volumes of fluvial sediment which would otherwise soon fill the *ria*.

The geology, white plastic soil or clay resting on chalk, is that of the Palaeogene Hampshire Basin, comprising the area between the South Downs and the Isle of Wight and dipping beneath the Solent. Portsdown Hill (447ft high) is a chalk mound, detached from the South Downs, extending for about 7 miles between Fareham and Havant, along the shores of Portsmouth and Langstone Harbours. The hill dominates the skyline to the north and rises up just 1 mile to the north of Portsea Island.

The deep sheltered estuary, entered through a narrow mouth nowhere more than 225 yards wide, made Portsmouth Harbour, strategically located on the south coast just 70 miles from London and with the Isle of Wight as a natural defence, an ideal naval base. The harbour extends over about nine square miles with sufficient depth throughout to float the largest warships even at low tide.

Little is known about Portsmouth's history prior to the twelfth century although there is evidence of Bronze Age habitation in the Milton area whilst in about AD 300 the Romans built a fort at the northern end of the Harbour at Portchester. The Anglo-Saxon Chronicles record that in AD 501 two ships of invaders led by *Porte* landed at *Portes Mutha*. The Saxons inhabited the area for the next 500 years. Following their conquest the Normans recorded their gains in the *Domesday Book*. Reference is made to there being three villages on the island in 1087: Frodintone (Fratton) in the centre of the island; Copenore (Copnor) to the north-east and Bocheland (Buckland) to the north-west.

Portsmouth became a trading port for ships from Normandy. In 1194 Portsmouth was granted a Royal Charter and construction of a dock began in 1212. The union between England and Normandy was fragmented with the death of King William I and there followed a series of wars with France during which the French made several attempts to land on the Hampshire coast. Portsmouth was sacked on three occasions in the fourteenth century decimating its population and it remained a small town until the reign of King Henry VIII (1509–1547). Previous monarchs had only taken opportune interest in naval matters and the majority of fighting ships were chartered from merchants as and when required. But during Henry's reign a standing fleet of over 50 purpose-built warships were constructed and the world's first dry dock opened in Portsmouth. Henceforth the prosperity and growth of Portsmouth was closely interwoven with that of the Royal Navy and the expansion of possessions abroad.

By the eighteenth century the town had outgrown the walls of Old Portsmouth and new homes were built in Portsea, although much of the island was still used for farming. At the time of the first census (1801) housing had reached the new airier suburbs of Southsea which began to develop as a sea bathing resort and the population had reached 32,166. The rest of the island continued to be covered in housing and by 1914 little empty space remained. The population grew to 94,799 in 1861, 190,281 in 1901, and to 250,000 in 1931. Slum clearances began in the 1930s whilst housing estates began to spring up on the mainland; nonetheless it was primarily the bombing and evacuation of the Second World War which pushed the population into decline. The estimated population in 1939 was 260,000 but this fell to 233,545 in 1951 and to 214,000 in 1961.

The important road access between Britain's premier naval port and the capital, the Portsmouth Road, follows ancient trackways running south-southwest through Kingston upon Thames, Guildford and Petersfield then across the South Downs and through the Forest of Bere. As the amount of wheeled traffic grew during the seventeenth century local rates were levied to pay for road repairs, but small parish councils were unable to maintain the roads in a suitable state to cope with the inordinate amount of heavy naval traffic. In 1711 one of the first Turnpike Trusts in the country was founded by Act of Parliament to maintain the road between Petersfield and Portsmouth for which service the trustees were entitled to collect tolls related to the type of traffic.

The journey time between London and Portsmouth began to markedly decrease. The fastest stage coaches took about 16 hours in 1770, but by 1805 they took about 9 hours and by the 1820s there were 80–100 coaches running along the road every week. Their monopoly was short-lived as railway mania spread across the country.

Rather than risk the vagaries of the roads, goods were transported to and from Portsmouth by coastal shipping but after almost continual Anglo-French conflict through the eighteenth century the ascendancy of Napoleon Bonaparte put vital supplies increasingly at risk. Despite Britain's naval supremacy, the need to defend colonial possessions throughout the world left few resources for protecting slow moving coastal vessels.

This prompted proposals for an inland waterway between London and the South Coast. In 1743 the River Wey had been made navigable upstream as far as Shalford, just south of Guildford whilst in 1787 the opening of the Arun Navigation permitted coasting vessels to reach Billingshurst about 5 miles southwest of Horsham. In 1813 parliamentary approval was given to link the two navigations with the 23 mile long Arun and Wey Junction Canal which opened in 1816. In the meantime a westwards extension into Chichester Harbour, then through a 13-mile long dredged channel around the south of Thorney Island and the north of Hayling Island to Eastney Lake and thence by canal across Portsea Island to Portsmouth Harbour, was promoted. Construction of the Portsmouth and Arundel Navigation began in 1818. The Portsea section comprised a 2½ mile long cut from Eastney Lake in the southwest corner of Langstone Harbour, where locks provided access to the sea at high tide. It then headed west to the site of Milton 'White House' public house before following the course of Goldsmith Avenue to Fratton Bridge and thence the route of today's railway to a terminal basin between Lower Church Path and Arundel Street (just off Commercial Road). It never reached the proposed and more practical destination of Portsmouth Harbour.

The Portsea section opened on 19 September 1822 and was navigable by vessels of up to 150 tons. The route to London opened throughout in May 1823. Traffic was never great as the risks to coastal shipping disappeared with the end of the Napoleonic Wars in 1815. There were soon problems with sea water in the canal contaminating Portsmouth's wells and this led to the canal's early closure, part being purchased in 1845 for use by the railway. The rest of the canal was filled in during the 1890s.

The first mainline railway in Southern England was the London and Southampton Railway. Construction began in 1834 with through trains from Nine Elms, Battersea to Southampton starting to run in 1840 by which time the company had been renamed the London & South Western Railway (LSWR). The citizens of Portsmouth, annoyed that Southampton had beaten them into the railway age, then opposed a parliamentary bill for a branch line from the Southampton mainline at Eastleigh to Portsmouth insisting on a direct route to the capital. In November 1841 the LSWR opened their branch line but to Fareham, a market town and small commercial port with a growing brick and tile industry, at the northwest end of Portsmouth Harbour, and continuing due south to Gosport. Their prime commercial goal was now just a short ferry crossing away.

On 14 June 1847 the London Brighton and South Coast Railway (LBSCR) opened an extension of their coastal route, which had reached Chichester in June 1846 and Havant in March 1847, to Cosham and onto Portsea Island with intermediate stations at Hilsea and Fratton to a terminus at Portsmouth Town, today's Portsmouth and Southsea station. The LSWR extended their line from Fareham to Portcreek Junction, Cosham, where a connection was made with the LBSCR line which opened to goods on 1 September 1848 and to passengers on 1 October 1848.

Although trains now reached Portsmouth the journey to London was either via Brighton or Southampton. Financed by local businessmen and civic leaders, construction of a direct route from an end-on junction with the LSWR at Godalming to Havant was completed in December 1858. Services were operated by the LSWR but the LBSCR objected to LSWR trains running over their tracks into Portsmouth and following an interruption of services at the junction it was necessary to seek a legal solution, running powers being granted in January 1859. The Portsmouth Direct Line was purchase by the LSWR in 1859.

The LBSCR and LSWR jointly extended the railway from Portsmouth Town station to Portsmouth Harbour station, the line opening on 2 October 1876, and on 1 July 1885 along a ¼ mile long branch from Fratton to East Southsea station, near The Strand road junction. This latter line could not compete with the trams, closing in 1914 since when much of its route has been built over.

Urban passenger transport in Portsmouth is believed to have commenced in 1840 when the Portsea Island Conveyance Co. introduced a horse bus service between North End and Southsea, Grove Road via The Hard and Old Portsmouth. By 1857 services were running hourly from Southsea, Grove Road to Portsea and Landport, and from Portland Street, just off Queen Street, to Portsmouth Town railway station connecting with each scheduled train. Further services connecting North End to the Cambridge Hotel, Palmerston Road, and from the Dockyard to the Royal Marine Artillery Barracks at Eastney were operating by 1860.

In 1863 the Landport and Southsea Tramways Co. (L&ST) was authorised by Act of Parliament to build and operate a horse tramway between Portsmouth Town station and Clarence Pier, primarily to connect the railway with steamer services to and from the Isle of Wight. The line was built with step rails protruding above the road surface to 4ft 7¾in. gauge enabling railway wagons to run on their flanges along the tramway although there is no evidence of a connection between the railway and the tramway or that such transfers ever took place. Services began on 15 May 1865, however it was only in spring 1875 that the line was re-laid with conventional grooved tram rails.

In 1872 the Provincial Tramways Company Ltd. was registered to operate tramways in various towns including Cardiff, Portsmouth and Plymouth. In September 1874, their subsidiary, the Portsmouth Street Tramways Co. (PST) opened a line from North End, Gladys Avenue via London Road, Kingston Crescent, Commercial Road, Cambridge Road, High Street and Broad Street to the Floating Bridge, Old Portsmouth. Their trams ran over L&ST lines between Portsmouth Town station and Cambridge Road. The PST had depots and stables at Gladys Avenue and Broad Street.

The General Tramways Company of Portsmouth Ltd. (GTC) opened a line on 18 March 1878 between the Queens Hotel, Osborne Road and High Street, Old Portsmouth via Western Parade, Southsea Terrace, Jubilee Terrace, Kings Terrace and Alexandra Road. At the beginning of February 1878 the Provincial Tramways Company Ltd. purchased both the L&ST, which since October 1876 had lost much of its Isle of Wight traffic with the opening of the railway extension to Portsmouth Harbour station, and the GTC, thereby solving any difficulties of running through services over L&ST lines between Southsea Terrace and Alexandra Road, or over PST lines along High Street and Broad Street to Floating Bridge, Old Portsmouth. On 17 June 1878 the line along St George's Road and Ordnance Row was opened and a service introduced between the Queens Hotel, Osborne Road and The Hard via Alexandra Road. In autumn 1879 further lines planned by the GTC opened, namely the Southsea route was extended from the Queens Hotel along Clarendon Road to The Circle; Pembroke Road between Southsea Terrace and High Street; and along Edinburgh Road, Lion Terrace and Park Road to Ordnance Row and The Hard. On 30 May 1880 the GTC's Southsea line was extended east along Clarendon Road to The Strand and on 24 July 1880 further along Clarendon Road to the South Parade Pier which had opened a year beforehand. At the end of December 1880 a branch was opened from Commercial Road along Lake Road to a terminus at the junction with Fratton Road and Kingston Road, Buckland. An extension of the North End line, first to Hilsea 'Coach and Horses' on 4 July

1881 and then through Hilsea Arches and across Ports Bridge, the swing bridge connecting Portsea Island to the mainland, as far as Cosham Railway Gates opened on 31 July 1881. In August 1889 the Edinburgh Road and Lion Terrace line was closed and replaced by a direct line in Park Road.

The GTC, L&ST, PST and Gosport Street Tramway Co., all subsidiaries of the Provincial Tramways Company, were amalgamated in August 1883 as Portsmouth Street Tramways Co., operating some 42 trams and carrying 1.7 million passengers annually.

The final company formed to build horse tramways was the independent Portsmouth (Borough), Kingston, Fratton and Southsea Tramways Company (PKFST) whose initial service, between Fratton Bridge and Southsea, Granada Road via Victoria Road North, Albert Road, Festing Road and St Helen's Parade, commenced on 26 November 1885. Their line continued north along Fratton Road and Kingston Road but due to the gradient over Fratton Bridge it is not known when services were extended over this section. There had obviously been negotiations with the PST as in early 1886 the PST's Lake Road line and the new PKFST line along Fratton Road and Kingston Road was connected. The PST extended their Lake Road service over PKFST tracks to Powerscourt Road, about 150 yards south of Kingston Crescent (Kingston Cross), on 22 February 1886. A branch along Victoria Road South and Marmion Road as far as the junction with Lennox Road opened on 19 April 1886. However, there are indications that the line along Albert Road and Festing Road to Southsea, Granada Road soon ceased to be regularly used. In 1892 the creditors of the PKFST took the company to court as its shares had ceased to be quoted and in due course the company was acquired by the PST. The Provincial Tramways Company Ltd. was now operating all the tramways in Portsmouth, a network of some 14 miles with a fleet of 58 trams and around 250 horses.

Until the opening of the tramway in 1881 the PST had run a horse bus between North End and Cosham. The five redundant buses were now put on to other services and by 1885 horse buses were running between Cambridge Junction and Havelock Park via Green Road and Cottage Grove, and between Commercial Road, Bedford Hotel, just north of the station and Dockyard via Queen Street. On 14 February 1887 the former was re-routed via Elm Grove and had been extended to the dockyard. On 15 August 1887 it was extended eastwards to Eastney 'Highland Chief' via Alexandra Road, Kings Road, Elm Grove, Albert Road and Highland Road. At some stage in the mid-1890s the two horse bus services were combined to provide a through service from Commercial Road to Eastney, although not all journeys ran from end to end.

In 1872 the Welsh bus and tramway *entrepreneur* Solomon Andrews started to operate horse buses in competition with the Portsmouth trams in retaliation for the Provincial Tramways Co. subsidiary Cardiff Tramways Co. Ltd. expanding into his perceived area of interest in Cardiff. At the end of 1887 Provincial purchased Andrews' buses in Portsmouth and Cardiff, the services were amalgamated and direct competition eliminated, and Solomon Andrews joined the company Board.

In August 1895 a delegation of Portsmouth Corporation Road and Works Committee accompanied Mr A. W. White, PST General Manager, on a visit to Bristol where another private concern, the Bristol Tramways and Carriage Company, had started to electrify their tramways. In February 1896 Portsmouth Council appointed a Tramways Committee to consider purchasing the PST lines, electrifying them and leasing them back to the company. On 13 July 1897 the Council unanimously decided under the provisions of the Tramways Act 1870 to compulsory acquire those PST lines whose powers were 21 years old and purchase the other, more recent lines.

Agreement was reached between the company and the Corporation in May 1898 and an unopposed parliamentary bill was passed a month later as the Portsmouth Corporation Tramways Act 1898. The PST was given 12 months' notice of the Corporation's intent to acquire their undertaking which, by agreement, was deemed to be on 31 December 1899. The company immediately started a programme of track relaying in an effort to secure the maximum financial compensation, submitting a claim of £306,450 18s 6d in April 1899. The Tramways Committee informed PST that they would only be acquiring the company's tramway operations and not their horse bus and carriage activities whereupon the Provincial Tramways Company refused to finalise the sale. A compromise was reached whereby a new Provincial subsidiary, the proposed Portsmouth and Horndean Light Railway (PHLR), would benefit from a link to the Corporation's tramways at Cosham and a traction power supply, as well as a non-competition agreement. The entire PST tramway undertaking, just over 15 route miles, passed to the Corporation on 31 December 1900 at a sum, after arbitration, of £185,633.

Tenders were invited for electric tramcars and trackwork, Dick, Kerr & Co. being selected to supply 80 double-deck open-top four-wheel electric trams equipped with reversed stairs and for the construction of the permanent way. The PST horse tram depot at Gladys Avenue, North End was enlarged and rebuilt to provide covered accommodation for up to 113 electric trams whilst in October 1900 work started on the construction of a tramways power station in Vivash Road, Fratton, to provide traction power independent of the municipal power station in Gunwharf Road, Old Portsmouth.

Test runs and driver training commenced between North End and Hilsea at the end of July 1901 and these journeys were progressively extended to Clarence Pier. Following the Board of Trade (BoT) inspection electric tram services were progressively introduced on the following dates:

24.09.01 Hilsea – North End – Kingston Crescent – Commercial Road – Town Hall – Clarence Pier
(Hilsea – North End reverted to horse trams on 27 October 1901 due to delays in the delivery of the new electric trams and because of a dispute with the military authorities on strengthening Portsbridge)

28.10.01 Floating Bridge – Cambridge Road – Town Hall – Commercial Road – Lake Road – Fratton Road – New Road – Copnor Railway Gates
(Conversion of the existing horse tram routes Floating Bridge – Lake Road and new extension)

28.10.01 North End – Fratton Road – Fratton Bridge – Victoria Road – Southsea *The Circle*
(Horse tramway conversion and abandonment of Marmion Road)

28.10.01 Town Hall – Bradford Junction – Rugby Road – Fawcett Road – Southsea *The Strand*
(Horse tramway conversion Town Hall – Bradford Junction and new electric tram route Bradford Junction – Southsea The Strand)

28.10.01 Dockyard – St George's Road – Alexandra Road – Clarence Pier
(Horse tramway conversion)

06.11.01 North End – Fratton Road – Fratton Bridge – Victoria Road North – Rugby Road – Fawcett Road – Southsea *The Strand* – Southsea *South Parade Pier*
(Horse tram conversion Victoria Road North and Southsea *The Strand* – Southsea *South Parade Pier)*

06.11.01 Dockyard – Park Road – Town Hall – Blackfriars Road – Bradford Junction – Rugby Road (junction with Fawcett Road)
(Horse tram conversion Dockyard – Town Hall)

As can be seen, the vast majority of the conversion programme was completed in less than 2 months. Additional new electric tram routes were subsequently built as shown:

29.01.02 Victoria Road South – Albert Road – Highland Road – Eastney 'Highland Chief'
(Horse bus conversion, operated by horse trams as far as Festing Hotel until 1898)

09.04.03 Hilsea, north side of Portsbridge – Cosham, PHLR Interchange Platform
(Passengers had to walk across the bridge until 15 April 1903 when through running commenced)

The last horse bus service Commercial Road – Queen Street – Dockyard – St. Georges Road – Alexandra Road – King's Road – Elm Grove – Albert Road 'Bold Forester', is believed to have been withdrawn on 31 March 1904.
The following electric tram services were in operation by 1905:

A Portsdown Hill – Cosham, PHLR Interchange Platform – Hilsea – North End *Junction* – Kingston Crescent – Commercial Road –Town Hall – Royal Pier Hotel – Clarence Pier

B North End *Junction* – Fratton Bridge – Bradford Junction – Victoria Road – Southsea *The Circle* – Southsea *The Strand* – Southsea *South Parade Pier*
Extended North End – Hilsea – Cosham, PHLR Interchange Platform – Portsdown Hill as required

C Dockyard *Main Gate* – Alexandra Road – Royal Pier Hotel – Osborne Road – Southsea *The Circle* – Southsea *The Strand* – Southsea *South Parade Pier*

D Copnor Railway Gates – New Road – Lake Road – Commercial Road – Town Hall
Extended to Clarence Pier on Sundays and bank Holidays, weather permitting

E North End *Junction* – Kingston Crescent – Commercial Road – Town Hall – Royal Pier Hotel – Osborne Road – Southsea *The Circle* – Southsea *The Strand* – Waverley Road – Fawcett Road – Fratton Bridge – Fratton Road – North End *Junction*
Outer Circle

F Copnor *Railway Gates* – New Road – Lake Road – Commercial Road – Town Hall – Park Road – Dockyard *Main Gate*

G Dockyard *Main Gate* – Park Road – Town Hall – Blackfriars Road – Bradford Junction – Fawcett Road – Waverley Road – Southsea *The Strand*

H Town Hall – Royal Pier Hotel – Osborne Road – Southsea *The Circle* – Victoria Road – Bradford Junction – Blackfriars Road – Town Hall – Commercial Road – Lake Road – Fratton Road – Fratton Bridge – Blackfriars Road – Town Hall
Inner Circle 'Figure 8'

J Copnor Railway Gates – New Road – Lake Road – Commercial Road – Town Hall – Cambridge Road – Old Portsmouth – Floating Bridge

K Eastney 'Highland Chief' – Highland Road – Albert Road – Victoria Road – Bradford Junction – Blackfriars Road – Town Hall
Extended to Clarence Pier as required

L Eastney 'Highland Chief' – Highland Road – Albert Road – Victoria Road – Bradford Junction – Blackfriars Road – Town Hall – Cambridge Road – Old Portsmouth – Floating Bridge

M Eastney 'Highland Chief' – Highland Road – Albert Road – Victoria Road – Bradford Junction – Fratton Bridge – Fratton Road – North End Junction – Hilsea – Cosham, PHLR Interchange Platform

All services ran in both directions, the alphabetic designations, although used internally within the Tramways Department from the early days, were not displayed on the trams themselves until June 1914.

ER&TCW open top tram 44 pauses at the Marmion Road stop whilst heading south in Victoria Road South, Southsea, on a service X journey to Southsea *South Parade Pier* and then back to the Town Hall and Twyford Avenue in 1916. (O.J. Morris [David Bowler collection])

CHAPTER TWO

ELECTRIC TRAMS AND A RAILLESS FUTURE

The electric trams proved a tremendous success, earning a net profit of £21,426 7s 6d in 1904–1905 and paying £3,500 in rate relief the following year. During the summer of 1906 it proved necessary to increase the power station's output whilst 16 more trams were ordered from Dick, Kerr and Co., to essentially the same design, except for direct stairs, as cars 1–80.

When Provincial Tramways were granted their Light Railway Order to construct the Portsmouth and Horndean Light Railway (PHLR) between Cosham and Horndean, Portsmouth Corporation Tramways (PCT) received running powers for about 1 mile over the southern end of the line as far as Portsdown Hill, Widley Lane, where in summer a fairground was set up on the downs. The line opened on 2 March 1903 and PCT cars commenced running to Portsdown Hill or the Cosham Interchange Platform, just to the south of the later Cosham Compound terminus, in May 1903; however, due to a dispute about the cost of traction power supplied by Portsmouth Corporation to PHLR and poor passenger loads between Cosham and Portsdown Hill in winter, PCT ceased running beyond the Cosham Interchange Platform on 30 June 1907. A tramway junction was laid in Portsmouth Road at the end of the PHLR private track (just south of the junction between Portsmouth Road and today's Chatsworth Avenue), the horse tram tracks still *in situ* in Portsmouth Road were re-laid and electrified, and henceforth all PCT cars to Cosham terminated in Portsmouth Road immediately to the south of the level crossing at Cosham railway station. From 6 July 1907 the PHLR ran as far south as the end of their private track about 200 yards beyond the Interchange Platform.

On 1 August 1924 a through service of PHLR cars between Horndean and Portsmouth Town Hall via Kingston Crescent and Commercial Road commenced. Following Christmas extensions to Palmerston Road in 1924 and 1925, and to Clarence Pier on summer bank holidays, the 1926 Christmas extension continued until 19 April 1927 when cars were further extended to Southsea South Parade Pier on a permanent basis. The PHLR cars were re-routed between North End and the Town Hall via Kingston Road and Lake Road on 30 March 1931.

The following route extensions were constructed during the lifetime of the tramways, the network finally reached a total of 17.56 route miles:

Fratton Bridge – Goldsmith Avenue – Milton 'White House' 20 July 1909

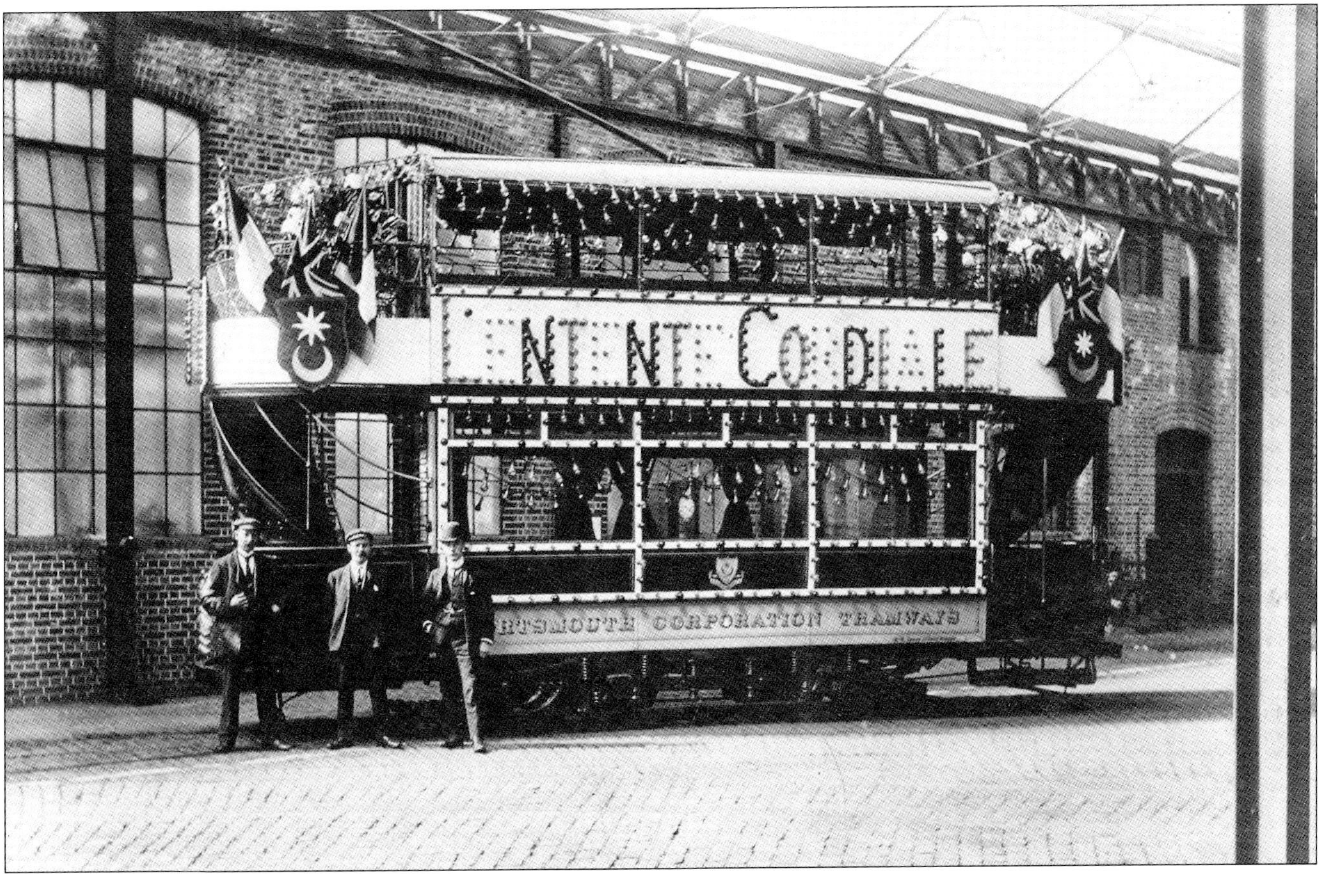

No. 80, the last of the first batch of electric trams, was experimentally equipped with a top cover in February 1904 at a cost of £65. It is seen here on the tram track access fan at North End Depot especially decorated and illuminated for the visit of the French Fleet to Portsmouth in August 1905. The top cover was removed again in 1907. (Charles Hall Archive [Paul Fox collection])

Commercial Road (Kingston Crescent) – Twyford Avenue – Northern Parade – Alexandra Park 4 July 1913
Albert Road 'Festing Hotel' – Festing Road – St Helens Parade – Southsea South Parade Pier 31 July 1913
Milton 'White House' – Eastney Road – Eastney 'Highland Chief' 22 September 1913

There were numerous changes and re-routings over the years in an endeavour to find the optimal pattern of services. By 1914 the following services were in operation:

A Cosham Railway Station – Hilsea – North End *Junction* – Commercial Road – Town Hall – Royal Pier Hotel – Clarence Pier

B Twyford Avenue – Commercial Road – Town Hall – Blackfriars Road – Bradford Junction – Victoria Road North – Albert Road – Festing Road – Southsea *South Parade Pier* – Southsea *The Circle* – Victoria Road – Bradford Junction – Fratton Bridge – Fratton Road – North End – Hilsea – Cosham Railway Station
Unidirectional service worked in conjunction with service X.

X Cosham Railway Station – Hilsea – North End – Fratton Road – Fratton Bridge – Bradford Junction – Victoria Road – Southsea *The Circle* – Southsea *South Parade Pier* – Festing Road – Albert Road – Victoria Road North – Bradford Junction – Blackfriars Road – Town Hall – Commercial Road – Twyford Avenue
Unidirectional service worked in conjunction with service B.

C Dockyard *Main Gate* – Alexandra Road – Royal Pier Hotel – Osborne Road – Southsea *The Circle* – Southsea *The Strand* – Southsea *South Parade Pier* – Festing Road – Highland Road – Eastney – Milton *White House* – Goldsmith Avenue – Fratton Bridge – Bradford Junction – Blackfriars Road – Town Hall
Extended to Dockyard Main Gate or Clarence Pier as required.

D Copnor Bridge – Lake Road – Commercial Road – Town Hall – Royal Pier Hotel – Clarence Pier
Sundays and Bank Holidays only, weather permitting.

O North End *Junction* – Kingston Crescent – Commercial Road – Town Hall – Royal Pier Hotel – Osborne Road – Southsea *The Circle* – Southsea *The Strand* – Waverley Road – Fawcett Road – Fratton Bridge – Fratton Road – North End *Junction*
Circular service, formerly E Outer Circle. Weekdays only.

F Copnor *Railway Gates* – New Road – Lake Road – Commercial Road – Town Hall – Park Road – Dockyard *Main Gate*

G Dockyard *Main Gate* – Park Road – Town Hall – Blackfriars Road – Bradford Junction – Fawcett Road – Waverley Road – Southsea *The Strand* – Southsea *South Parade Pier*

H Fratton Bridge – Victoria Road – Southsea *The Circle* – Osborne Road – Royal Pier Hotel – Clarence Pier.

J Copnor Railway Gates – New Road – Lake Road – Commercial Road – Town Hall – Cambridge Road – Old Portsmouth – Floating Bridge

L Floating Bridge – Old Portsmouth – Cambridge Road – Town Hall – Blackfriars Road – Bradford Junction – Victoria Road – Albert Road – Highland Road – Eastney *Highland Chief* – Milton *White House* – Goldsmith Avenue – Bradford Junction – Blackfriars Road – Town Hall
Unidirectional, anticlockwise service worked in conjunction with service Z.
Extended to Clarence Pier as required.

Z Town Hall – Blackfriars Road – Bradford Junction – Goldsmith Avenue – Milton *White House* – Eastney *Highland Chief* – Highland Road – Albert Road – Victoria Road – Bradford Junction – Blackfriars Road – Town Hall – Cambridge Road – Old Portsmouth – Floating Bridge
Unidirectional, clockwise service worked in conjunction with service L.
Commencing at Clarence Pier as required.

M Eastney 'Highland Chief' – Highland Road – Albert Road – Victoria Road – Bradford Junction – Fratton Bridge – Fratton Road – North End Junction – Hilsea – Cosham Railway Station
Sundays and Bank Holidays only, weather permitting.

– Cosham Railway Station or North End – Kingston Crescent – Commercial Road – Town Hall – Royal Pier Hotel – Clarence Pier
Undesignated extra.

– Cosham Railway Station or North End – Fratton Road – Fratton Bridge – Fawcett Road – Waverley Road – Southsea *The Strand* – Southsea *South Parade Pier*
Undesignated extra.

On 16 December 1918, with 'the war to end all wars' finally over, the General Manager Mr Spaven, presented a review of the undertaking recommending reconstruction and early extension of the tramway system. Essential maintenance was outstanding and the trams were heavily loaded, carrying 14 million more passengers than in 1914 (+17.7 per car mile). There were 100 passenger trams in the fleet of which 92 were in daily service, too few to permit regular overhauls and repairs. Assuming that the high ridership levels would continue, there would be insufficient trams to meet traffic demands in summer 1919. He felt it impossible to purchase additional tramcars and suggested that motor buses be bought to run on alternative routes into town and provide temporary replacement services as the tramways were repaired.

In January 1919 the Tramways Committee resolved to put the tram track into good order and increase the engineering staff. They recommended purchase of 25 additional double-deck cars to be equipped with open-balcony top covers and drivers' vestibules, as well as the conversion of six of the existing fleet to open toast rack. These subsequently materialised as 12 totally enclosed top-covered double-deck cars 105–116 and just one single-deck open toast rack purchased second-hand from Southampton Corporation Tramways. Tramway extensions were planned from Milton 'White House' to Hilsea 'Coach and Horses' via Milton Road, Baffins Road and Copnor Road; from North End to Alexandra Park along the length of Gladys Avenue; and the track layout at Bradford Junction was to be improved. These were included in the Portsmouth Corporation Act 1920 which extended the Borough boundary but only the latter was carried out. The enlarged tram fleet required additional depot accommodation and the search began for a suitable site in Eastney, a location at corner of Eastney and Bransbury Road being identified, although test bores proved the land to be unstable.

In March 1919 ten Thornycroft 40 hp J-type motor buses equipped with open-top double-deck bodies were ordered. Delivery began in July 1919 and they were used to supplement trams to North End before being allocated to a new service

In April 1930 Portsmouth & Horndean Light Railway 9 waits at the start of the private reserved track on its way to Horndean whilst Portsmouth Corporation Tramways 95, with a most detailed indicator display of intermediate points (used from 1911 until phased out from about 1932), heads south along Portsmouth Road, Cosham, towards Palmerston Road. A Southdown Motor Services Tilling Stevens Express with Short Bros. single-deck body disappears towards Cosham Railway Station. (National Tramway Museum)

between Devonshire Avenue and Milton Road (St. Mary's Road) via Elm Grove, Dockyard, Edinburgh Road and Arundel Street. Seasonal services to the top of Portsdown Hill and an experimental service between Eastney and Cosham were tried in 1921 but operations were hampered by insufficient spares, breakdowns and the unsuitable road surfaces.

In August 1922 the Tramways Committee decided not to build the Milton – Hilsea tramway extension for at least the next 10 years and proposed a motor bus service instead. In view of complaints about vibration and damage to the road surface from the Thornycrofts, seven lighter Dennis 50 cwt equipped for one man operation (OMO) were ordered. On 24 August 1923 the local press referred to the double-deck trackless trolley vehicles in Birmingham which had successfully replaced the trams on the Nechells route in that city on 27 November 1922, the first conversion of a tram route to railless electric traction in the UK, and suggested that this form of transport could successfully operate along Milton and Copnor Roads. Portsmouth and District Motor Services Ltd. was running a motor bus service over this route and it was felt that the Corporation's only chance of recapturing the route was by offering a comfortable ride. The Birmingham manager asserted that the trolleybus ran smoothly, was practically noiseless and that for ease and comfort no other vehicle could compare with it. The article concluded by urging the Tramways Committee to show their progressiveness by considering the possibility of such a service linking Milton, Copnor and Cosham.

The Portsmouth Tramways Committee set up a subcommittee in September 1923 to consider ways of linking the various districts with the tramways by use of either railless trolleybuses or petrol buses.

The Sub Tramways (Traffic and General) Committee considered a report from the General Manager and the Engineer on 16 October 1923. They recommended:

1. Milton 'White House' to Hilsea, London Road 'Coach and Horses' tramway extension should be proceeded with as soon as possible in accordance with the 1920 Parliamentary Powers received.
2. Powers should be sought for a short line between Grosvenor Hotel and Clarence Pier following the existing footpath and crossing the Common between these two points.
3. Power should be sought for a line from Gladys Avenue to Alexandra Park linking up with the Twyford Avenue and Northern Parade tramways.
4. a. Obtain Parliamentary Powers (or sanction of the MoT) to equip the present motor bus routes with trackless trolley vehicles and overhead lines.
   b. Upon the adoption of 'a.' some of the present omnibuses to be converted into OMO saloon body type.
5. Provide and run 20-seater OMO petrol buses along the seafront between Clarence Pier and Fort Cumberland or alternately between Clarence Pier and the Eastney tramways at Henderson Road.
6. Provide and run 20-seater OMO petrol buses along, say, Chichester Road, Laburnum Grove, or preferably Stubbington Avenue to deal with cross traffic between the new tramways and the existing tramways in London Road, and also to act as a feeder to both lines.
7. Seriously consider purchasing the Portsmouth and Horndean Light Railway.

8. Obtain powers to connect the existing tramways in London Road (by means of a railless system along the new Western Road and Southampton Road) and the market square at Fareham and the present tramway terminus at Cosham, through Cosham along Havant Road, and terminating for the time being at Havant.
9. A new bus and tram depot in the eastern part of the borough.
10. Improvements to deal with tram traffic at Southsea *South Parade Pier* and Clarence Pier.

After consideration the Subcommittee recommended Clauses 1, 3, 5, 6, 10 (Clarence Pier loop) for action; a fuller report into Clauses 7, 8, 9 at the next Tramways Committee Meeting and no action on clauses 2, 4. On 23 October 1923 the Tramways Committee adopted all the recommended extensions (including 8) but rejected Clause 4 (trackless trolley equipment).

There were no further discussions about the use of trolley vehicles until late 1929.

In December 1923 the Tramways Committee considered a letter from the motor manufacturer Straker-Squire Ltd., Edmonton, London N18, which was considering opening a factory in Portsmouth. In addition to a similar assurance about motor buses it was resolved that 'In the event of the Committee deciding at any time to put down a railless system of buses they would be prepared, all things being equal as to price and quality, to give preference to the Straker-Clough system'. Straker-Squire ceased trading in 1926.

The Portsmouth Watch Committee was the licensing authority for motor buses and services within the borough until the Road Traffic Act 1930, and from around 1920 they required that all private operators charged a minimum fare of 6d to all passengers picked up and set down within the boundaries as a condition of their licence to avoid competition with the tramways. The Ministry of Transport (MoT) prohibited PCT from running beyond the boundaries; however, there were no restrictions on the private operators running outside the borough. In the summer of 1925, for reasons that remain obscure and without consulting the Tramways Committee, the Watch Committee abandoned this policy. Southdown Motor Services (SMS) immediately reduced their fares and the Corporation promptly retaliated by introducing a motor bus service to Drayton, New Inn, beyond the borough boundary. By the end of 1925 some 232 private motor buses were licensed in Portsmouth, in addition to the Corporation's 32 motor buses, and they plied for hire throughout the borough without restriction.

A period of severe competition, during which proposals and counterproposals for the re-introduction of minimum fares were discussed under MoT arbitration, only came to an end in June 1927. In brief, SMS agreed to re-introduce a 6d minimum fare for all passengers picked up within the city boundaries and set down south of Cosham railway station and vice versa. However, in return PCT gave up the right to operate motor bus or tram services within the boundaries north of Cosham railway station.

Discussions were continuing as to the take-over of the tramways traction power supply by the Electric Lighting Committee and (closure of) the tramways power generating station at Vivash Road, just northwest of Fratton Bridge. As Mr Spaven's retirement was approaching, the Tramways Committee began to consider an amalgamation of the posts of General Manager and that of Engineer. This put the Engineer, Mr V.G. Lironi, in a difficult position and he asked for early retirement with a 'golden handshake'. In October 1925 he was offered eight years' salary and arrangements were made for him to retire on 31 December 1925. It was decided to buy all traction current from the Electricity Committee, although steam was initially kept available at Vivash Road at busy times and holidays in case of any emergencies. The steam and electrical plant at Vivash Road was finally disposed of by tender in October 1926, and the power station buildings were sold by auction in July 1933.

The advertisement for the combined position of General Manager and Engineer to the Corporation Tramways undertaking attracted 33 applications. On 19 January 1926 a special committee short-listed: Mr Walter T. Young from Dundee Corporation Tramways, Mr Ben Hall (Halifax), Mr T. P. Sykes (Rotherham), Mr G. T. Craven (Reading), Mr Charles O. Silvers (Wolverhampton), Mr J. A. Bromley (York), and Mr John F. Cameron (Northampton). All seven were interviewed on 12 February 1926, the worthiest candidates being considered to be Messrs Bromley, Hall and Young. Deputations visited Dundee, Halifax and York to see how the undertakings were managed. On the basis of their reports Mr Ben Hall was appointed at a salary of £1,000 p.a. rising by four annual increments to a maximum of £1,200. On Halifax's request his starting date was put back and Mr Spaven remained until 31 July 1926.

Mr Lironi's application for retirement was also deferred until October 1926. Possibly to his frustration, Mr Hall stated that he could continue to use his services as Engineer with the additional responsibility of supervising the rolling stock, workshops, etc. Although it seems that Mr Lironi initially had some difficulties in coming to terms with the new management structure he remained with the undertaking until reaching his normal retirement age in 1931.

A further potential site for a depot in the eastern suburbs had been found at the junction of Highland Road and Eastney Road, Eastney, and negotiations for its purchase started in November 1925. By February 1927, the valuers had warned of a restrictive covenant on the site, limiting use of the frontage onto Methuen Road immediately to the north to housing. The purchase of additional land fronting into Highland Road was also discussed, the owner being prepared to sell the plot of land already being negotiated for and a 45ft frontage to Highland Road for £1,550. By summer 1927 it was evident that the plot at Eastney would cost £7,350 plus costs and the decision was taken to purchase this as well as the additional land.

On 18 July 1927 a new service numbering system was introduced to replace the alphabetical codes which had been displayed on the trams since June 1914 although used internally since 1902. The service numbers were allocated in consecutive pairs, one for each direction of travel, whereas the alphabetical codes were applicable to the service between named points in both directions of travel. This principle would be applied to all trolleybus services. A system of consecutive alphabetical pairs of letters was introduced to designate motor bus services.

1 Cosham Railway Station – Hilsea – North End *Junction* – Guildhall – Royal Pier Hotel – Clarence Pier
Unidirectional southbound service, formerly tram service A.

2 Clarence Pier – Royal Pier Hotel – Guildhall – North End *Junction* – Hilsea – Cosham *Red Lion*
Unidirectional northbound service, formerly tram service A.

3 North End *Junction* – Fratton Bridge – Fawcett Road – Southsea *South Parade Pier* – Albert Road – Bradford Junction – Guildhall – Alexandra Park
Unidirectional clockwise service, formerly tram service X.

4 Alexandra Park – Guildhall – Bradford Junction – Victoria Road North – Albert Road – Festing Hotel – Southsea *South Parade Pier* – Fawcett Road – Fratton Bridge – North End *Junction*
Unidirectional anticlockwise service, formerly tram service B.

5 Dockyard *Main Gate* – Royal Pier Hotel – Southsea *South Parade Pier* – Festing Hotel – Eastney – Milton *White House* – Fratton Bridge – Bradford Junction – Guildhall – Dockyard *Main Gate*
Unidirectional circular service (anti-clockwise) worked in conjunction with service 6, formerly tram service C.

6 Dockyard *Main Gate* – Guildhall – Bradford Junction – Fratton Bridge – Milton *White House* – Eastney – Festing Hotel – Southsea *South Parade Pier* – Royal Pier Hotel – Dockyard *Main Gate*
Unidirectional circular service (clockwise) worked in conjunction with service 5, formerly tram service C.

7 Copnor Bridge – Fratton Bridge – Guildhall
Extended to Palmerston Road or Clarence Pier as required.
Unidirectional southbound service, formerly tram service D.

8 Clarence Pier or Palmerston Road – Guildhall – Fratton Bridge – Copnor Bridge
Extended to Clarence Pier or Palmerston Road as required.
Unidirectional northbound service, formerly tram service D.

9 Cosham Railway Station – Hilsea – North End *Junction* – Fratton Bridge – Victoria Road North – Victoria Road South – The Circle – Royal Pier Hotel – Guildhall – Kingston Crescent – North End *Junction*
Unidirectional clockwise service worked in conjunction with service 10, formerly tram service O.

10 North End *Junction* – Kingston Crescent – Guildhall – Royal Pier Hotel – The Circle – Victoria Road South – Victoria Road North – Fratton Bridge – North End *Junction* – Hilsea – Cosham Railway Station
Unidirectional anticlockwise service worked in conjunction with service 9, formerly tram service O.

11 Copnor Bridge – Lake Road – Guildhall – Dockyard *Main Gate*
Unidirectional southbound service worked in conjunction with service 12, formerly tram service F.

12 Dockyard *Main Gate* – Guildhall – Lake Road – Copnor Bridge
Unidirectional northbound service worked in conjunction with service 11, formerly tram service F.

13 Dockyard *Main Gate* – Guildhall – Bradford Junction – Fawcett Road – The Strand – Southsea *South Parade Pier*
Unidirectional southbound service worked in conjunction with service 14, formerly tram service G.

14 Southsea *South Parade Pier* – The Strand – Fawcett Road – Bradford Junction – Guildhall – Dockyard *Main Gate*
Unidirectional southbound service worked in conjunction with service 13, formerly tram service G.

15 Copnor Bridge – Lake Road – Guildhall – Old Portsmouth – Floating Bridge
Unidirectional southbound service worked in conjunction with service 16, formerly tram service J.

16 Floating Bridge – Old Portsmouth – Guildhall – Lake Road – Copnor Bridge
Unidirectional northbound service worked in conjunction with service 15, formerly tram service J.

17 Floating Bridge – Old Portsmouth – Guildhall – Bradford Junction – Festing Hotel – Eastney – Milton *White House* – Bradford Junction – Guildhall
Unidirectional circular service (anti-clockwise) worked in conjunction with service 18, formerly tram service L.

18 Guildhall – Bradford Junction – Milton *White House* – Eastney –Festing Hotel – Bradford Junction – Guildhall – Old Portsmouth – Floating Bridge
Unidirectional circular service (clockwise) worked in conjunction with service 17, formerly tram service Z.

At its maximum the tramcar fleet comprised:

1–80	Open-top cars built in 1900/01 by the Electric Railway and Tramway Carriage Works mounted on Brill 21E 4-wheel trucks.
81–84	Open-top cars built in 1880 as horse cars by G. F. Milnes mounted on Brill 21E 4-wheel trucks.
85–100	Open-top cars built in 1906/07 by the United Electric Car Co. mounted on Brill 21E 4-wheel trucks.
101	Water car built in 1904 by Portsmouth Corporation Tramways mounted on Brill 21E 4-wheel truck.
102	Water car built in 1919 by Portsmouth Corporation Tramways mounted on Brill 21E 4-wheel truck.
103	Water and rail-grinding car built in 1919 by Portsmouth Corporation Tramways mounted on Brill 21E 4-wheel truck.
104	Single-deck open toast rack car ex-Southampton mounted on Brill 21E 4-wheel truck.
105–116	Totally enclosed top-covered cars with platform vestibules built in 1920 by English Electric mounted on English Electric 21E 4-wheel trucks.
1	Totally enclosed top-covered car with platform vestibules built in 1930 by Portsmouth Corporation Tramways mounted on Peckham Cantilever truck.

A number of cars in the series 1–80, 81–84 and 85–100 were rebuilt by the Corporation from 1929 onwards but they retained their dated open-top layout. By the time that the reconstruction programme ended in 1935 the following cars had been rebuilt: 3, 7, 9, 10–12, 17, 19, 24, 29, 36, 40, 43–45, 48, 49, 51, 55–57, 64, 69, 73, 80, 85, 99. The work carried out on each car varied widely including new rocker panels, staircases and improved seating but no effort was made to provide top-covers. The last two cars to be rebuilt 10, in 1934, and 11, in 1935, received driver's vestibules, whilst toast rack tram 104 received a canopy roof in 1930 and a boat body in 1933.

On 3 August 1927 two additional but short-lived tram services were introduced:

19 Fratton Bridge *Orchard Road* – Fawcett Road – The Strand – Royal Pier Hotel – Clarence Pier
Unidirectional southbound service worked in conjunction with service 20, formerly tram service T.

20 Clarence Pier – Royal Pier Hotel – The Strand – Fawcett Road – Fratton Bridge *Orchard Road*
Unidirectional northbound service worked in conjunction with service 19, formerly tram service T.

They were withdrawn again on 10 October 1928 and replaced by motor bus services K and L respectively which were subsequently extended at both ends.

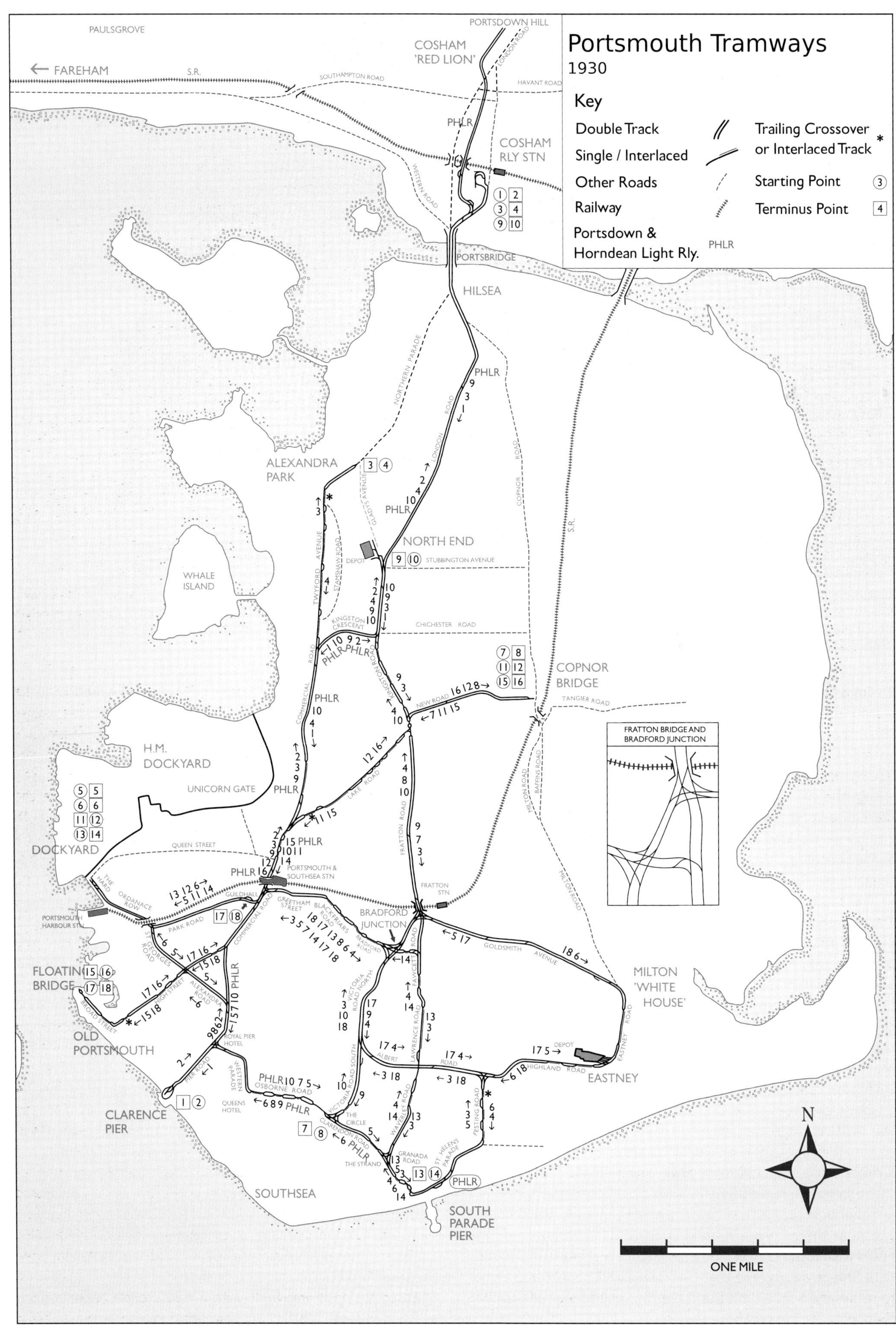
Portsmouth Tramways
1930
Key
Double Track
Single / Interlaced
Other Roads
Railway
Portsdown & Horndean Light Rly.
PHLR
Trailing Crossover or Interlaced Track *
Starting Point
Terminus Point
PORTSDOWN HILL
COSHAM 'RED LION'
PAULSGROVE
FAREHAM
COSHAM RLY STN
PORTSBRIDGE
HILSEA
ALEXANDRA PARK
NORTH END
WHALE ISLAND
H.M. DOCKYARD
UNICORN GATE
DOCKYARD
COPNOR BRIDGE
FRATTON BRIDGE AND BRADFORD JUNCTION
BRADFORD JUNCTION
PORTSMOUTH & SOUTHSEA STN
FRATTON STN
PORTSMOUTH HARBOUR STN
FLOATING BRIDGE
OLD PORTSMOUTH
MILTON 'WHITE HOUSE'
EASTNEY
CLARENCE PIER
SOUTHSEA
SOUTH PARADE PIER
ROYAL PIER HOTEL
QUEENS HOTEL
THE CIRCLE
THE STRAND
ONE MILE
N

In its original livery, tram 111, one of the 12 totally enclosed English Electric cars on Brill 21E trucks delivered in 1920, stands at the Royal Beach Hotel, Southsea, where South Parade joins St. Helens Parade in 1925. Once considered the resort's premier residence, the Royal Beach Hotel housed many civic meetings following the destruction of the Guildhall in 1941 and enjoyed an enviable reputation for its dinner dances in the post-war period. (National Tramway Museum)

On 8 October 1929 a renegotiated agreement between the Corporation and SMS was announced effective from 1 January 1930. The undertakings agreed to co-ordinate their timetables with SMS motor buses charging the applicable tram fare and issuing tickets printed by the Corporation. All revenue earned within the city boundary passed to the Corporation: SMS was paid an agreed amount per bus mile operated reflecting the company's working expenses. Transfer and season tickets were to be continued and the fares charged on Southdown buses fixed by the Tramways General Manager.

The topic of railless electric traction next appeared on the Tramways Committee agenda in 1929 when a new Corporation Bill was discussed. The Parliamentary Agents handling the Bill, intended in the first instance to acquire land for a municipal aerodrome, recommended a number of additional items to bring local legislation up to date including the acquisition of powers to operate trolley vehicles and abandon the tramways (although there were no plans for either). On 25 November 1929 the Tramways Committee recommended that such powers should be acquired.

Once prepared, the draft Bill sought provision whereby the MoT might authorise new routes for trolley vehicles on any road either in the city or within a direct line distance of 5 miles from the Guildhall. SMS withheld their approval of the renegotiated agreement with the Corporation due for introduction on 1 January 1930 pending consideration of this clause as the agreement encompassed the operation of SMS buses within the City boundaries. In preparation for a meeting with SMS it was agreed that the Town Clerk should endeavour to retain the 5 mile limit but if this was not acceptable to SMS then as far as the city boundary.

By the beginning of February 1930 it was learned that the PHLR had withdrawn their objections to the 5 miles clause but that SMS had requested a change failing which they would oppose the Bill. SMS remained intransigent and the Portsmouth Corporation Act 1930 granted solely authority to operate trolley vehicles along any street or road in the City for which the Corporation was already authorised to construct or operate tramways. Although this resulted in a successful outcome to the joint agreement negotiations any future Corporation trolley vehicle system had been effectively restricted to the limits of the prevailing tramways.

In November 1930 the Tramways Committee again considered introducing trolley vehicles. A route between the Dockyard Unicorn Gate and Southsea *South Parade Pier* via Unicorn Road, Commercial Road, Guildhall, Greetham Street, Bradford Road, Rugby Road, Fawcett Road and Waverley Road was proposed. There had been talk of a tramway extension to Unicorn Gate in the past but it had only been served by special motor bus services.

At the end of October 1929 tenders were invited for the different components of the new Eastney Depot, that of Messrs A. and J. Main and Co. Ltd., London, for steelwork, Robertson maroon coloured protected metal sheeting, Mellowes wired glazing, Robertson ventilators and roof drainage and roller shutters, totalling £16,193, being accepted on 3 December 1929. The tender of the London Plenium Heating Co. Ltd. of £2,723 for the installation of heating apparatus was also accepted. However, this company was subsequently declared bankrupt.

Eastney Depot was built with a reinforced concrete floor and administrative office accommodation, the architect being

Mr H. J. Dyer of Portsmouth, but without fire protection sprinklers. Tramway trackwork was supplied by Hadfields. MoT loan sanction was sought for £39,646, the estimated cost of the new depot. Work was completed towards the end of 1931, being considered as ready for occupancy from 1 January 1932. The new facilities were formally opened by the Lord Mayor on Thursday 21 January 1932.

In their search for new motor buses a deputation of the Sub Tramways (Omnibuses) Committee visited works of The English Electric Co., Leyland Motors Ltd., Park Royal Coachworks Ltd. and Short Bros (Rochester) Ltd. in January 1931. They were much impressed by a demonstration of a three-axle trolleybus and in view of the possibility that the tram track along Fawcett Road and Waverley Road between Fratton Bridge and The Strand would be the first section to come up, suggested that the full Tramways Committee might be interested in their report. Their report on trolley vehicles was read to the Tramways Committee on 3 February 1931 who discussed the matter in depth before considering the question of removing the tram track in Fawcett and Waverley Roads. They resolved to leave the matter with the Subcommittee with instructions to report at an early date on the question of trolley vehicles generally and especially with regard to running trolley vehicles or motor buses along Fawcett and Waverley Roads.

The Sub Tramways (Omnibuses) Committee stated on 17 February 1931 that trackless trolley vehicle running costs were 1½d per mile less than those of a petrol bus of the same passenger carrying capacity. The use of the electricity generated by the Corporation would be a considerable advantage whilst the MoT granted a loan period of 8 years for trolley vehicles compared to 5 years for petrol omnibuses.

Mr Hall, now titled General Manager and Engineer following Mr Lironi's retirement, responded that he had, in the meantime, inspected Crossley's latest heavy oil engines, i.e. diesel, and suggested that it might be desirable to replace the trams with diesel buses. He felt that trackless trolley vehicles should only run through Greetham Street after the planned road widening had been completed. Six trackless trolley vehicles would be required to operate a service between South Parade Pier and the Dockyard through Fawcett and Waverley Road, at a cost of £2,000 each. It was estimated that the cost of converting the overhead line would be £3,400. In comparison six Crossley diesel buses would cost £1,900 each or petrol buses £1,800. Crossley were prepared to replace their diesel buses with petrol buses should they prove unsatisfactory. The Subcommittee agreed that the tram service should be discontinued and the track lifted but there was much debate as to the replacement vehicles. Having compared the running costs of petrol, diesel and trolley buses, the original motion to purchase diesel buses was carried and recommended to the full Tramways Committee. The Roads & Works Committee was

Portsmouth's last new tramcar, domed-roof car no.1 designed by General Manager & Engineer Mr Ben Hall was built in the undertaking's North End workshops on a Peckham Cantilever 2-axle truck in 1930. It is seen here at the passenger waiting shelter and loading island in Guildhall Square prior to departure to Clarence Pier. (National Tramway Museum)

The conductor stands contently in front of 1901 ER&TCW open top tramcar 57 at the Dockyard terminus on The Hard. The preceding car has been rebuilt and carries a brighter livery of crimson and white introduced in 1929 whereas 57 retains the 'maroon and cream' (officially referred to as scarlet lake and Oxford ochre) colours. It was a quantum leap from such a tramcar to the latest trolleybuses of the mid-1930s. The Dockyard Main Gate is just out of sight to the left behind the gentleman wearing a trilby hat and carrying an umbrella. The pub on the corner of Queen Street is a Gales of Horndean house, their brewery was half a mile beyond the outer terminus of the PHLR. (National Tramway Museum)

to immediately remove and retain the setts, and the Tramways Department remove and retain the rails and contribute the sum of 5s per square yard towards the cost of the work. The overhead equipment was to be left in place for possible use by trolley vehicles at a later date.

The Tramways Committee approved the recommendation on 3 March 1931; however, the proposal was turned down by the City Council on 17 March 1931 and referred back to the Committee. There was no further mention of trolley vehicles for almost 12 months, the Tramways Committee and the undertaking itself being fully committed to renewing the agreement with SMS and the £5,107 13s 10d deficit on operations in the year ending 31 March 1931. It was necessary to rename the Reserve and Renewals Fund as the Renewals Fund as this loss absorbed all the reserves!

It was decided to seek fare protection from the Regional Traffic Commissioners (RTC) rather than continue negotiations with SMS. A special subcommittee was established to review the situation. Their proposals, at the first meeting on 8 July 1931, were based on the Corporation operating its own bus services within the City Boundaries and SMS charging a higher fare than that prevailing on the Corporation's trams and buses for travel on their vehicles within the City and within a distance of a quarter mile from the City Boundaries.

At a meeting on 17 July 1931 Mr A. D. McKenzie of SMS stated that the suggested protective fares south of Cosham Railway Station Gates were acceptable with but one exception. However, should the Corporation insist on running beyond Cosham Railway Station to the City Boundaries, SMS would seek a ruling from the RTC.

Portsmouth's Town Clerk pointed out that extensions to the City Boundaries were likely and asked if SMS would accept the Corporation running buses to a reasonable distance from the new boundaries based on the same mileage which the Company suggested they should now be allowed to run within the city boundaries. SMS agreed to consider this option. In fact the boundary extension took place on 1 April 1932, the point where they crossed main roads becoming Portsdown Road, Portchester on Southampton Road and Rectory Avenue, Farlington on Havant Road. There was no change on the London Road where the boundary remained a short distance beyond the summit of Portsdown Hill at 'Boundary Oak'.

As Mr Hall considered it would be uneconomic for the Corporation to run services to the city boundaries negotiations with SMS continued on the basis of protective fares within the city south of Cosham Railway Station Gates but with a payment in respect of passengers carried on SMS vehicles or bus miles run between Cosham Railway Station Gates and the City Boundaries. The Corporation was prepared to commit not to operate their services beyond Cosham Railway Station Gates for the time being subject to reasonable fares and services being offered to residents of the City north of Cosham Railway Station. The existing agreement was to continue until the RTC had heard the licence applications from both the Corporation and SMS.

SMS agreed on 14 August 1931 to protective fares at 2d higher than those on Corporation vehicles but would not agree to make a payment to the Corporation to ensure that the Corporation did not introduce services in the area

Guildhall Square in the tramway era looking south (photographed from the Portsmouth and Southsea Station railway bridge). The tramway passenger waiting shelter and loading island is situated in the middle of the Square between the Queen Victoria Statue and the Guildhall steps. The Southdown double-deck motor bus closest to the camera has an opening roof. (National Tramway Museum)

Rebuilt with platform vestibules, new rocker panels, direct staircases and improved seating in 1934, tramcar 10 was the penultimate car to be modernised. The tram is standing at the passenger waiting shelter and loading island in Guildhall Square for service 15 to Old Portsmouth and Floating Bridge on 2 August 1935. The Guildhall is on the left, beyond the waiting shelter. (National Tramway Museum)

already worked by SMS, i.e. the company effectively secured a monopoly north of Cosham Railway Station.

Having blocked each other's licence applications, a compromise was reached, effective 14 December 1931, whereby no PCT motor buses ran north of Cosham Railway Station Gates although SMS made no special payments for this pseudo-monopoly, whilst the Corporation removed their objections to SMS working within the city on condition that protective fares, on a sliding scale of 1d–2d in excess of the Corporation fares, were re-introduced. This gave the Corporation a degree of protection and reduced the risk of SMS's long-distance passengers being crowded-out by short stage passengers in Portsmouth. Despite a protracted argument in 1934, this arrangement remained in force until 1946.

On 25 August 1931 Councillor Pugsley successfully proposed a resolution that the Subcommittee consider the advisability of acquiring trolleybuses.

At the 6 October 1931 Tramways Committee Meeting it was agreed that the Roads and Works Committee should discuss the reconstruction of the tram track between St Mary's Road and Kingston Cross with the MoT in connection with road reconstruction. Due to the lack of traffic in Old Portsmouth it was decided to divert tram services 17, 18 (the Eastney, Milton circular) to operate from the Guildhall via Park Road to the Hard instead of along Cambridge Road and High Street to Floating Bridge.

On 18 March 1932 the General Manager reviewed the first months of service of the AEC and Crossley diesel buses. Interestingly, he commented: 'In service no objectionable exhaust is noticeable from either engine, and the smell of the exhaust, whilst it can be distinguished from that of the petrol engine by smell, is no more noxious. Unlike the smell from the petrol engine, the exhaust from the oil engine is non-poisonous and is not injurious to health'!

On 20 September 1932 the Tramways Committee adopted the recommendation of its Sub Tramways (Passenger Vehicles) Committee that the Subcommittee should be immediately instructed to consider the question of the desirability of acquiring trolley buses and report to the Full Committee at the next meeting.

The Subcommittee considered the General Manager's suggestion that an experimental trackless trolley route should be built to evaluate their performance as a new medium of transport within the city. They were convinced that the time had come for a gradual replacement of tram services as and when the tracks needed renewal. The Kingston Road tram track was now life-expired and on 27 October 1932 they recommended that trolley vehicles should be introduced on a route between South Parade Pier and Cosham Railway Station, via The Strand, Waverley Road, Fawcett Road, Fratton Road, North End, Kingston Road, London Road and Portsmouth Road, rather than the Dockyard Unicorn Gate route suggested in 1930. This had been the route of the tram services 3 and 4 until 20 April 1931 when it had been diverted to run via Victoria Road North, Victoria Road South and Clarendon Road, instead of Fawcett Road and Waverley Road. The tramways along Kingston Road between the junction with New Road and Kingston Cross would be abandoned. The entire cost of the conversion was estimated as £7,000.

The Tramways Committee resolved on 20 December 1932 that the principle of gradual replacement of the tramcar services by trackless trolley vehicles be adopted, and asked the Subcommittee to prepare a comprehensive scheme for the full Committee prior to a report being made to the Council.

1930 domed-roof tramcar 1 stands at the passenger waiting shelter and loading island in Guildhall Square prior to departure on service 2 from Clarence Pier to Cosham Railway Station. The Sussex Hotel in the background is on the corner of Greetham Street. (National Tramway Museum)

CHAPTER THREE

THE CONVERSION PROGRAMME

Mr Hall reported in January 1933 that continued tramway operation would require capital expenditure of some £204,000 to cover track reconstruction and new rolling stock over the next 10 years. He recommended tramway abandonment and pointed out that now was the moment to experiment with trackless trolley vehicles, again suggesting the Southsea South Parade Pier and Cosham Railway Station route. Trackless trolley vehicles should replace the tramways as the tracks became due for renewal or as the outstanding debt thereon was redeemed. He estimated that the cost of replacing the tramway network with a trackless trolley vehicle system would be £21,240 for overhead line adaption, £200,000 for 100 trolley vehicles, and £37,041 to reinstate the roads once the track had been removed; a total sum of £258,281. His recommendations were adopted.

In May 1933, members of the Tramways Committee accompanied by the General Manager, visited Birmingham, Bradford and Wolverhampton to observe trolleybus operations, and the English Electric factory at Preston. To emphasise the planned break with the past in July 1933 the former tramways power station was sold for £6,700, the amount being credited to the Tramways Capital Account.

The department's detailed route plan was completed by mid-July 1933 and the vehicle specifications followed by the end of the month. Fifteen vehicles would be required and Mr Hall suggested that in order to make a comparison as to size, etc., five 3-axle vehicles carrying 60 passengers and ten 2-axle vehicles carrying 50 passengers should be obtained. Two of each should be equipped for regenerative control and the remainder for augmented field control. The vehicle proposals were referred back by the full Tramways Committee to the Tramway (Passenger Vehicles) Subcommittee for further consideration. First they suggested 15 2-axle trolley vehicles and then 11 2-axle and four 3-axle trolley vehicles. Further discussion on the type of control included series parallel in addition to augmented field and regenerative.

The road at Southsea South Parade Pier tram terminus was considered unsuitable for a trolleybus turning circle and in August 1933 it was suggested that a terminal loop should be constructed from the south end of Waverley Road (The Strand) along Granada Road, St Helen's Parade, South Parade, Alhambra Road and back to Granada Road. As an alternative in November 1933 the Parks and Open Spaces Committee were asked if they would give up some land at the west end of the Canoe Lake Grounds upon which a roadway for a turning circle would be built. A 50-foot roadway was pegged out to the east of the Emanuel Fountain which had been donated to the City by its first Jewish mayor. Despite 115 objections it was decided in March 1934 to build a 60ft wide road through the Grounds about 300ft from the Emanuel Fountain providing sufficient space for three trolley vehicles. This decision was upheld by an MoT enquiry on 15 May 1934.

It was intended that the turning circle would be limited to use by trolley vehicles only but to enforce this it was necessary for the City Council to make an Order under Section 46 of the Road Traffic Act 1930 and Section 29 of the Road and Rail Traffic Act 1933. For operational convenience it was decided to seek permission for its use by Corporation motorbuses too. Pending confirmation by the MoT 'Trolley Vehicles Only' signs were set up.

In July 1934 the MoT responded that under the terms of the Instrument of the Minister of Health authorising the appropriation of a part of Canoe Lake Gardens for highway purposes, the Corporation had no power to restrict use of the new road to tramways department vehicles. A renewed application was made to the Ministry of Health for approval to appropriate part of the Canoe Lake Gardens solely for the use of vehicles of the Corporation's Tramway and Trolley Vehicle Undertaking, and sanction was received in November 1934.

When calls for tender for trolley vehicles were issued in September 1933 the Portsmouth Trades Council asked, without success, that the Corporation seek powers to build the fleet by direct labour. Tenders were received towards the end of October 1933 and Mr Hall recommended that only firms which had experience in building trolleybus chassis and bodies be considered. He suggested that the following companies be considered for the chassis:

Associated Equipment Co. Ltd.
Guy Motors Ltd.
Karrier Motors Ltd.
Leyland Motors Ltd.
Sunbeam Motor Co. Ltd.

As it was anticipated that the Corporation would build up a large trolleybus fleet, it was felt that by ordering a selection of chassis and bodies, it would be possible to assess which type and combination was most suited to the local conditions.

The following chassis and control equipment were selected (Guy's tender was not accepted):

50-seater 2-axle Regulated Field Control		
AEC661T	2 at	£1,069
Karrier E4	2 at	£1,073
Leyland TBD2	3 at	£1,047 10s
Sunbeam	2 at	£1,065 each.
50-seater 2-axle Regenerative Control		
AEC661T	2 at	£1,069 each
60-seater 3-axle Regulated Field Control		
AEC663T	1 at	£1,230
Sunbeam MS3	1 at	£1,187
60-seater 3-axle Regenerative Control		
AEC663T	1 at	£1,230
Sunbeam MS3	1 at	£1,208

On 27 October 1933 the Tramways Committee resolved to place orders with the English Electric Co. Ltd. for nine 50-seat double-deck composite bodies at £785 each and two 60-seat double-deck composite bodies at £838 each; and with Metropolitan Cammell Weymann Motor Bodies Ltd. for two 50-seat double-deck all-metal bodies at £833 and two 60-seat double-deck all-metal bodies at £887 each.

They selected the following combination and sought the full Council's approval:

4 AEC661T (£1,069 each) with English Electric H50R bodies (£785 each)
3 Leyland TBD2 (£1,047 10s each) with English Electric H50R bodies (£785 each)
1 Sunbeam MF2 (£1,065) with English Electric H50R body (£785)
1 Karrier E4 (£1,073) with English Electric H50R body (£785)
1 Sunbeam MF2 (£1,065) with MCCW H50R body (£833)
1 Karrier E4 (£1,073) with MCCW H50R body (£833)
1 AEC663T (£1,230) with English Electric H60R body (£838)
1 Sunbeam MS3 (£1,187) with English Electric H60R body (£838)
1 Sunbeam MS3 (£1,187) with MCCW H60R body (£833)
1 AEC663T (£1,230) with MCCW H60R body (£833)

The entire matter was vigorously debated at the 13 December 1933 City Council meeting. Councillor Lay opposed the tenders' acceptance and complained of the proposal to buy so many different types of chassis. Several manufacturers were converting motorbus chassis into trolley bus chassis by changing the power units and he did not think the chassis would stand the strain of a trolleybus traction motor with long propeller shafts. He suggested that 3-axle vehicles suffered from more running repairs and higher maintenance charges than those with two axles and added that the variety of electrical equipment meant the purchase of at least seven spare motors. He moved an amendment that the tenders be considered further.

Councillor Hickson seconded the amendment recalling how the Corporation had experimented with seven or eight different types of petrol bus. Some were continually breaking down. Trolley buses had been running in Britain and elsewhere for a quarter of a century and the Tramways Committee and the Manager should have been able to advise the Council to take, at the most, two types enabling them to be run efficiently with a small number of spare parts. Instead the Committee proposed to get buses from four makers and to buy five different types of chassis rather than select a standard type. Councillor Stokes asked why the various types were suggested. He thought the Committee could have investigated the matter and found out what was the experience of other corporations as to the best type. Councillor Lane also asked why out of 15 chassis the Committee should recommend nine different types, which meant holding nine different sets of spares.

Alderman Sir John Timpson, JP, Chairman of the Tramways Committee, stated that the Committee had fully considered the matter under the Engineer's advice. The Council should appreciate that in respect of spares the trolley bus could not be put in the same category as the petrol bus but rather in the category of the trams, which only required a small stock of spare parts. By putting into service a variety of makes the Corporation would only be emulating what had been done up and down the country. Councillor Prince maintained that the recommendation was sensible. The Engineer had gone into the question thoroughly and the Committee had carefully considered the matter for months. There was no question about the reputations of the firms concerned. The chassis were special ones that could be fitted to trolley buses to take the extra half ton of weight involved. Alderman Avens, replying to the discussion, urged the Council to trust the Tramways Committee and enable them to get on with their work. Only the mover and seconder voted for the amendment, which was lost, and the recommendation was adopted.

Traction poles had been deliberately omitted from the calls for tender for overhead line work. In October 1933 Messrs Clough Smith and Co. Ltd. pointed out that their contracts normally included the supply and erection of new poles, as well as the removal, re-planting and reinforcement of existing poles. The company feared divided responsibilities in respect of the satisfactory completion of the contracts and any delays that might occur should their tender be accepted. They agreed to carry out the pole work for an estimated £4005, the same figure as if carried out by direct labour. As Clough Smith's tender for the overhead equipment was the lowest at £3,997 7s 10½d, it was resolved to accept both this and the pole work tender at £4,005, in February 1934. Soon afterwards special alloy trolley wire, at an additional cost of £329, was added to the specifications, whilst the Canoe Lake turning circle cost a further £314 14s 3d. Clough Smith also supplied the following spare traction poles: ten 31ft medium weight and ten 31ft heavyweight poles for £112 and 28 extension sleeves at £28 1s 9d. It was recorded that this was the company's 27th trolleybus overhead equipment contract.

The firm started their work at Portsbridge on 26 February 1934 by planting additional traction poles to support the increased weight of the trolleybus overhead equipment, continuing thence to various other points along the route, particularly junctions with tramway overhead equipment, requiring additional support.

Many of the existing poles were strengthened by filling them with concrete and steel rods and the opportunity was taken to improve the city's street lighting, by placing lamps every 40 yards. In order to achieve this, each alternate traction pole was lengthened by removing 4ft from each pole and welding on about 8ft of tube to take the lamp bracket. When this was completed, the existing lamps on the tramway cross spans were removed. Wooden balls replaced some of the cast iron finials previously used on the top of the poles and some of the cast iron bands, which covered the welded joints on the strengthened poles, were chipped off, so that they resembled the new poles. The ornamental wrought iron brackets on the tramway traction poles in Kingston Road were removed by 15 March 1934 and only the bare brackets with the stay rods remained. The erection of the additional poles was also completed at this time and work began on stringing the overhead wires between North End and Cosham. A turning circle on the undertaking's property between the PHLR and Portsmouth Road, immediately to the south of the railway, officially referred to as Cosham Railway Station or Railway Gates but widely known as Cosham Compound, was strung but this consisted only of an extra pair of wires hung from the existing tramway cross spans. The five additional poles planted at the terminus were made of reinforced concrete.

The first span wires were strung from North End to Kingston Crescent by May 1934 and during this month the junctions were inserted at North End and the short section of Gladys Avenue to the depot was wired.

Property demolition in Kingston Road between Lake Road and Buckland Street for road widening resulted in some traction poles being relocated. In view of the planned street widening, on 20 March 1934 the Tramways Committee approved the reconstruction and realignment of the tram track between St Mary's Road, Fratton and New Road, at a cost of £5,840. Although Portsmouth's trams were still expected to survive another 10 years, by now the Tramways Committee was considering replacing them in Twyford Avenue by trolleybuses and at a Special Joint Committee Meeting held on 12 April 1934 it was agreed that any road widening should be carried out in conjunction with the removal of the tram tracks. The Council was recommended to purchase those properties necessary for road widening and within 3 months it was decided to limit the track relaying to the section between Lake Road and New Road used by tram services 11, 12, 15, 16.

In June 1933 SMS applied to the Traffic Commissioners for licences to operate from the Victoria Hall, a cinema in the apex of the junction between Cambridge Road and Hampshire Terrace, to Southsea South Parade Pier. The Tramways Committee resolved to object to the extension to the Pier.

Only in late September 1933 did the Tramways Committee consider applying to the Area Traffic Commissioners for licences to extend bus services north of Cosham Railway Station Gates. The proposal was amended to seek licences to extend services to Portchester, Waterlooville and Farlington, and seek protection for bus services in the city. It was hoped that the applications would be heard by the Traffic Commissioners for the Southern Area before they went out of office at the end of the year; however, by November 1933 it was evident that, due to the number of objections, this would be impossible and that the matter would be considered by the new South Eastern Traffic Commissioners in Portsmouth on 23–25 January 1934. The Town Clerk asked if the applications should be amended to permit operation to the city boundaries, but it was resolved that this matter be left to the Chairman, Vice Chairman, Town Clerk and General Manager to take such steps as felt necessary. At the beginning of February 1934 the RTC rejected the applications to run bus services to the city boundaries. Legal advice suggested that no further action be taken for the time being.

In February 1934 it was calculated that a deficit of £31,168 was anticipated for 1934–35 and the Tramways Committee suggested a full report from the General Manager on the state of the undertaking. Somewhat vulture-like, SMS enquired if, in view of the deficit, the undertaking was for sale! The key points of this report in respect of trolley vehicles were:

PART III

Alternative Forms of Transport

The City Council at their meeting on the 14th March, 1933, decided upon the principle of the gradual replacement of the tramcar service by trackless trolley vehicles and the route from the South Parade Pier to Cosham, via Fratton Road was then decided upon.

The Corporation have power under the Portsmouth Corporation Act 1930 to operate trolley vehicles along any route over which they have power to operate tramways, but a Provisional Order will be necessary to operate trolley vehicles over other routes.

In considering this question attention must be given to the amount of the outstanding debt on the tramways undertaking.

The outstanding debt on the undertaking amounts to £117,719 and the annual loan charges amount to £23,293. Of this sum of £117,719 the sum of £19,977 is in respect of the portion of the new depot used for tramway purposes. It this is deducted, the balance of the debt on the tramways undertaking to be provided for if the tramcars were displaced would be £97,742. This amount consists of loan sanctions having varying periods to run not exceeding ten years

The Tramways General Manager reports as follows:

The outstanding debt on the tramway track to date is	£95,143
The annual Capital Charge on this debt	£18,924
Of the outstanding debt, £1,261 will be redeemed by 31 March 1936, reducing the annual charge then to	£18,253
This figure, £18,253, will be the annual charge to March 1940, when a further £38,403 will be redeemed, reducing the annual charge to	£5,379
At March 1941, a further £8,719 will have been redeemed, reducing the annual charge to	£3,815
At March 1942, a further £9,076 will be redeemed, leaving the annual charge on the outstanding balance of debt £17,499, which will be cleared entirely by the end of March 1944	£2,364
The outstanding debt on Tramway Rolling Stock to date is	£2,598
The last charge on the loan for this rolling stock, which is	£2,992
will be made during the current year.	
The position generally is that for Tramway Track, during the next six years, the Department will require to meet an annual Capital Charge averaging	£18,365
After 1940 and to the date of the clearance of the debt, 1944, the Annual Capital Charge will average	£3,481
If the tramways were abolished, the Department would be relieved of some £9,000 per year, the cost of permanent way repair and road maintenance,	£9,000
and some £4,000 per year being the rate charge on Tramway Track. This total would to a large extent meet the outstanding debt on tramway track.	

In the event of the tramways being abolished, however, your Committee would be called upon to find the sum of £37,000 being the cost at the agreed rate of 5s per super yard for the reinstatement of the road surfacing; against this would be set the scrap value of the rails, etc., which at current rates is approximately £3,600.

Being relieved of the rate and road maintenance charges above referred to would represent approximately 1d per tramcar mile.

To replace the whole of the original 17.7 miles of tramway with a Trackless Trolley Vehicle System, it is estimated would cost for overhead line construction £28,300, and for one hundred Trolley Vehicles £200,000, a total of £228,300.

The Annual Capital Charge on the Overhead Line at 15 years' life would be approximately £2,695 and on vehicles at 10 years' life would be £25,946 – a total of £28,641.

It is believed owing to the less cost of operating, and the possibility of the Trolley Bus being more attractive than the Tramcar, a trolley bus system in substitution of the Trams would well support this charge.

With regard to the cost, £37,000 – your Committee's responsibility for road reinstatement – it might be possible for the payment to be spread over a long period of years, and it is the opinion again expressed that a contribution towards the cost should be sought from the Ministry of Transport and the Road Fund.

If the tramways were replaced by trackless trolleys, it would be possible to properly co-ordinate the two remaining media, trackless services and bus services, and effect very considerable economies thereby, and again it is the opinion expressed, that by this modernisation and co-ordination the additional standing charges, and the obligation in respect of road charges would be covered by revenue.

Full consideration should be given to the possibility of an early substitution of your tramways by the more modern method – the Trolley Bus, there being every reason to believe economies which would be effected by the change-over would ensure for the community the cheapest and most efficient transport service possible, with every prospect of the undertaking meeting its financial obligations in the entirety and the Manager recommends that in view of the fact that the tramway track in Kingston Road is to be abandoned at an early date, consideration should be given to the matter of the further development of the new medium to be introduced, and the reorganisation of the services as they will continue for the time being. He points out that the withdrawal of the tramways in Kingston Road will affect two established tramway services, that is – the 3 and 4 North End, South Parade Pier and Twyford Avenue, and the 9 and 10, Cosham, Fratton Road, Palmerston Road, Guildhall and North End. This matter was referred to in the report to your Committee of October 14th, 1932, and possible alternative routes for the continuation of these two tramway services were suggested, but in view of the circumstances that it appears difficult to induce more revenue to the Tramways (indeed the reverse condition seems to become more acute), the fact that these two tramway routes are covered in part by alternative services, and the recent rather strongly voiced agitation for the removal of the tramways from Twyford Avenue following the growth of other traffic through this road it is with confidence submitted that the proposals as follow would form a safe basis for the further development of the trolley bus system in substitution of tramways, and allow of the better co-ordination of the services to the public convenience.

The trolley bus route at present being equipped as your Committee are aware, is a direct connection between Cosham and South Parade Pier via North End, Kingston Road, Fratton Road, Fawcett Road and Waverly Road, which previously was provided by the No. 3 and 4 service operating in this length. If the overhead trolley bus line were extended from the South Parade Pier through Festing Road, Albert RoadBradford Road to the Guildhall, and on to Twyford Avenue, this extension of the trolley bus service would in its entirety replace the 3 and 4 tramway service. Whilst Blackfriars Road cannot be considered an ideal route for trolley buses, the arrangement above proposed would remove one tram car service from this road and reduce the number of tram cars passing through by 25%. At a later period, ifthe Greetham Street improvement and extension is carried out, and itwas considered necessary or desirable, the trolley bus route then could be transferred from Bradford Road and Blackfriars Road to the new road.

This trolley bus route in its entirety – Cosham, South Parade Pier and Twyford Avenue, could be operated at 10 minute intervals with eleven trolley bus vehicles, and for the 5 minutes service as isrequired during the summer months, double this number of vehicles would be necessary.

With the development of building of residential property about Northern Parade, this trolley bus route could then be extended at little cost through Northern Parade to Cosham, and so complete a circular route – Cosham to Cosham. The suggested extension South Parade Pier to Twyford Avenue is approximately 4½ miles in length, and the cost of equipping the overhead trolley bus lines over this route is estimated to be £9,000. The length between Alexandra Park and Cosham via Northern Parade is approximately 1.477 miles, and the estimated cost of the trolleybus lines connecting Alexandra Park with London Road is £2,100.

If this construction (South Parade Pier to Twyford Avenue) could be authorised, and completed by October next, the 15 trolley bus vehicles at present on order would suffice to replace the 3–4 tramway service and provide a circular route with a service atten minute intervals Cosham to Cosham. The E and F bus service, Eastney to Alexandra Park, could be extended from Alexandra Park to Guildhall or Clarence Pier as required, and so provide a five minute service Alexandra Park to Guildhall, and allow of the tramways in Twyford Avenue being wholly withdrawn. If this be agreed to, nine additional trolley bus vehicles would be required for the extended route before the next summer season.

With the opening of the trolley bus route through Fawcett Road, the I and J bus service now operating will be diverted via Victoria Road, Palmerston Road, Guildhall to North End.

With the lay-out of the trolley bus route extension above, it would be easily possible then by connecting the trolley line through Kingston Crescent and from the Guildhall to Clarence Pier, to complete the wiring for trolley bus services over the main routes of the City.

With the withdrawal of the 3 and 4 and 9 and 10 tram car services, the 1 and 2 tram service, which is also affected by competitive bus operation and not remunerative could be replaced at once by an extension of the A and B special bus service front the Victoria Hall to the Clarence Pier; thus a ten minute service of vehicles between Clarence Pier and Cosham, and the five-minute service between Kings Road and Cosham would be maintained.

These substitutions would allow of the withdrawing of 24 tram cars from regular service on the roads, and as you are aware, the three tramcar routes in question cover for considerable lengths and so compete with the routes served by your omnibuses.

We recommend that the suggestions of the Tramways General Manager be adopted and that:

(a) the trolley bus route be operated from the South Parade Pier, through Festing Road, Albert Road, Bradford Road to the Guildhall and on to Twyford Avenue and that tramcar service No. 3 and 4 be withdrawn.
(b) application be made to obtain a Provisional Order to operate trolley buses from Twyford Avenue along Northern Parade to enable the circular route to be operated from the South Parade Pier via the route mentioned in (a) continuing by Northern Parade to Cosham.
(c) the E and F bus service, Eastney to Alexandra Park, be extended from Alexandra Park to the Guildhall.
(d) the I and J bus service be diverted via Victoria Road, Palmerston Road, Guildhall to North End and that the 9 and 10 tramway service be withdrawn.
(e) the 1 and 2 tram service be withdrawn and replaced by an extension of the A and B special bus service from the Victoria Hall to the Clarence Pier.

The Tramways General Manager also suggests that when the Provisional Order is applied for to authorise the construction and operation through the Northern Parade, an application be made at the same time for a Provisional Order to construct and operate a Trolley Bus Service from Ports Bridge through the Northern Road to the foot of Southwick Hill, with a turning circle via the 'Red Lion' and Spur Road, This would open up a new service, and cater directly amongst other things, for the Municipal Housing Estate at Wymering.

We recommend that this suggestion be adopted and application be made for the necessary Provisional Order.

With the completion of the conversions above referred to, there would remain a total of approximately 8.4 miles of the original tramway system to convert for trackless operation, i.e.,

Goldsmith Avenue to Festing Hotel, via Milton and Eastney.
The Strand to Guildhall, via Osborne Road and the Terraces.
The Royal Pier Hotel to Clarence Pier
King's Road to the Dockyard, via St. George's Road.
The Guildhall to the Dockyard, via Park Road.
The Victoria Hall to Floating Bridge, via High Street.
Lake Road, from Commercial Road to Fratton Road.
New Road, from Kingston Road to Copnor,
Fratton Bridge to Bradford Road Junction and Rugby Road, and Albert Road Police Station to Circle.

We recommend that these lengths be converted within the next two years.

We have also considered the advisability of making application to the Minister of Transport for a Provisional Order to enable the Corporation to operate trolley vehicles to the City boundaries.

We recommend that the necessary application be made to the Minister of Transport for a Provisional Order to operate trolley vehicles to the City boundaries.

With the exception of a recommendation that contributions to the motor insurance fund should be reduced by one third, the Tramways Committee passed the report to the City Council for adoption.

The *"Evening News"* reported on the Tramways Committee's recommendations as far as the travelling public were concerned in their 9 July 1934 editions:

- Reduce 1d fare stages from 1.22 miles to 0.9 miles; 1½d stages from 1.68 to 1.35 miles, and 2d stages from 2.2 to 1.8 miles.
- Workpeople boarding vehicles from any terminus up to 8 a.m. should pay 1½d for return journeys over a 1d stage; 2½d for return journeys over a 1½d stage; 3d for return journeys over a 2d stage; 4d for return journeys over a 2½d stage; and 5d for return journeys over a 3d stage.
- Reduce the 3½d fare to Cosham 'Red Lion' to 3d.
- Oppose Southdown Motor Services Ltd.'s application to renew their stage carriage licences to operate within the City with a view to obtaining adequate protection for the services of the Corporation.
- Obtain a new valuation of the undertaking for rating purposes.
- The Finance Committee should be requested to consider the incidence of central administration expenses.

In April 1934 the Tramways Committee Chairman, Ald. Sir John Timpson; Councillor W. S. R. Pugsley and the General Manager inspected a trolleybus chassis presumably intended for Portsmouth and presumably at AEC Southall.

On 11 and 12 June 1934 trolleybus wires were erected in Kingston Road and on 26 June 1934 a start was made on the construction of the South Parade Pier turning circle.

By now there had been a number of letters to the press from the Milton and Southsea Ratepayer's Association about the Corporation's inability to run motorbuses to the city boundaries and on 18 May 1934 the Tramways Committee discussed the alternative of running trolleybuses instead. It was resolved to make an application for a Provisional Order.

The Tramways Committee were eager to move forward and implement their policy of replacing the tramways by trackless trolley vehicles. On 9 June 1934 they resolved to replace tram services 3 and 4 by the construction of a trolleybus route between Southsea South Parade Pier and Twyford Avenue, Alexandra Park via St Helen's Parade, Festing Road, Albert Road, Victoria Road North, Bradford Road, the Guildhall, Commercial Road and Twyford Avenue.

They also resolved to apply for a Provisional Order to operate trolley vehicles on the following routes beyond the existing tramway network:

Twyford Avenue – Hilsea via Northern Parade
(creating a circular route between Cosham and South Parade Pier replacing motorbuses).
Portsbridge – Cosham 'Red Lion' via Northern Road to the foot of Southwick Hill, thence as a turning circle via London Road and Spur Road.
Cosham – city boundaries at Portchester Cross Road, Widley and Farlington Rectory Avenue.

They also recommended that the remaining tram routes should be converted to trolley vehicle operation within the next 2 years. Tram services 1 and 2 should be withdrawn and replaced by an extension of motorbus services A and B from Victoria Hall to Clarence Pier. Solely the tram track between Lake Road and New Road would be re-laid at an estimated cost of £1,953.

On 12 June 1934 the City Council approved all the recommendations and on 18 July 1934 the General Manager was authorised to invite tenders for the overhead equipment including the necessary traction poles and pole work. Clough Smith agreed to prepare a list of requirements for a trolleybus route between Southsea South Parade Pier and Alexandra Park via Festing Road, Albert Road, Victoria Road North, Bradford Road, the Guildhall, Commercial Road and Twyford Avenue.

On 10 July 1934 the first trolleybus, 3-axle Sunbeam MS3 14, was towed to Portsmouth and put to use for driver training between North End and Cosham Railway Station (the only section of overhead wiring completed) the next day. It experienced difficulties in turning at North End as the southbound wiring from London Road into Gladys Avenue

The first trolleybus to be delivered to Portsmouth, Sunbeam MS3/MCCW and F 14, was presented to the Tramways Committee on 17 July 1934. They were photographed at Cosham Railway Station terminus on their first journey. Identifiable amongst the personalities are Sir John Timpson, Chairman of the Tramways Committee (fourth from the left with a watch chain visible), and Mr Ben Hall, General Manager and Engineer (immediately to the rear of the trolleybus wearing a light coloured suit, bow tie and dark hat). The girder bridge in the background carried the PHLR on reserved track over the railway line from Cosham to Fareham. (David Harvey collection)

had not yet been erected and the trolleybus had no traction batteries. The Milton and Southsea Ratepayers Association suggested that consideration should be given to sunshine roofs on trolley buses! By the end of July 1934 the entire route had been wired and trials were carried out throughout.

On Wednesday 1 August 1934 Colonel Woodhouse of the MoT inspected and approved the route between Southsea South Parade Pier and Cosham Railway Station which was slightly less than 5 miles long. Public services commenced at 9.05 a.m. on Saturday 4 August 1934:

3 Cosham Railway Station – Hilsea – North End *Junction* – Fratton Bridge – Southsea *South Parade Pier*
Unidirectional southbound service

4 Southsea *South Parade Pier* – Fratton Bridge – North End *Junction* – Hilsea – Cosham Railway Station
Unidirectional northbound service

The two unidirectional services ran every 10 minutes, requiring seven trolleybuses, the first day's service being provided by Nos 5, 6, 7, 10, 11, 14 and 15, the run out sequence of the first five vehicles being 14, 5, 10, 11 and 15.

The trolleybuses replaced trams in Fratton Road between St Mary's Church, Fratton and New Road, Buckland, resulting in tram services 3, 4, 7, 8 being curtailed as follows:

3 Guildhall – Bradford Junction – Victoria Road – Clarendon Road – Southsea *South Parade Pier* – Festing Hotel – Albert Road – Victoria Road North – Bradford Junction – Guildhall – Alexandra Park
Unidirectional anticlockwise service

4 Alexandra Park – Guildhall – Bradford Junction – Victoria Road North – Albert Road – Festing Hotel – Southsea *South Parade Pier* – Clarendon Road – Victoria Road – Bradford Junction – Guildhall
Unidirectional clockwise service

7 St Mary's Church, Fratton Road – Fratton Bridge – Guildhall – Clarence Pier
Unidirectional southbound service

8 Clarence Pier – Guildhall – Fratton Bridge – St. Mary's Church, Fratton Road
Unidirectional northbound service

Tram services 9 and 10 were also withdrawn and replaced by extended motorbus services I and J operating Cosham 'Red Lion' – Copnor Road – Stubbington Avenue – North End Junction – Fratton Bridge – Victoria Road – Osborne – Road – Guildhall – North End. However, to supplement the trolleybuses in Fawcett Road a tram service ran between St Mary's Church, Fratton and Southsea South Parade Pier via Victoria Road for the rest of summer 1934. This service may have been undesignated or displayed service numbers 9 and 10. The service reappeared for summer 1935 (9 June 1935 – 2 September 1935) and was advertised as the 9 and 10.

Tram services 1 and 2, which followed Commercial Road and Kingston Crescent, rather than Fratton Road and Kingston Road, were withdrawn on 1 October 1934 and replaced by motorbus services O and P, extended to Cosham 'Red Lion'. These were the last regular Portsmouth Corporation Tramways services to operate to Cosham although it is known that works cars continued to run for some months whilst, curiously, trams

Leyland TBD2/English Electric 5 and Sunbeam MF2/MCCW and F10 pass in Portsmouth Road, Cosham, at the Ports Bridge public house in 1934. Please notice the inset panel mounted centrally beneath the lower beading to the white waist band below the rear platform window on No. 5 which illuminated to show STOP when the brakes were applied, and the position of the registration number plate in the vent panel immediately above the offside upper corner of the rear platform window. (Transport World)

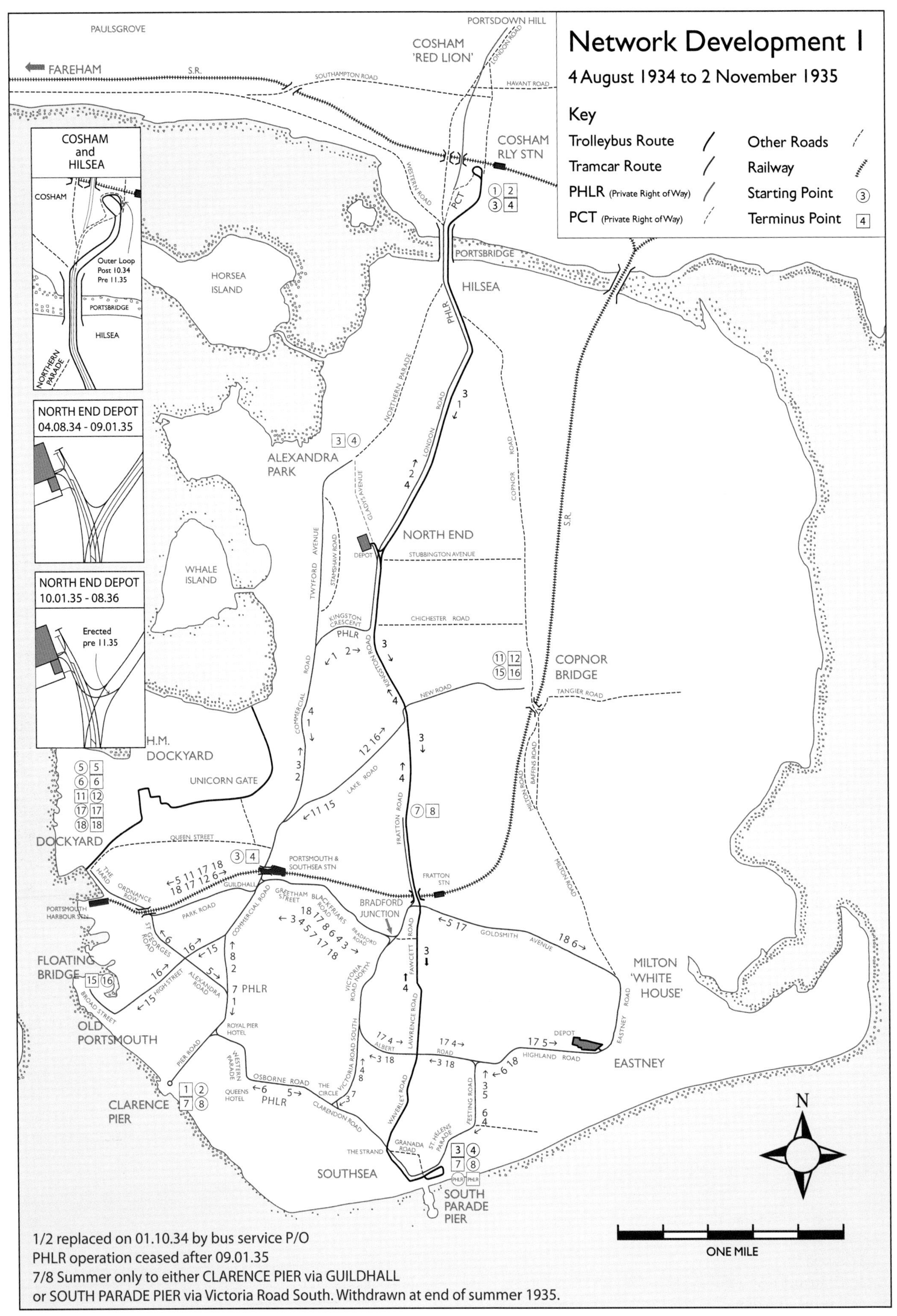

Network Development I
4 August 1934 to 2 November 1935
Key
Trolleybus Route
Tramcar Route
PHLR (Private Right of Way)
PCT (Private Right of Way)
Other Roads
Railway
Starting Point
Terminus Point
COSHAM and HILSEA
COSHAM
Outer Loop Post 10.34 Pre 11.35
PORTSBRIDGE
HILSEA
NORTHERN PARADE
NORTH END DEPOT 04.08.34 - 09.01.35
NORTH END DEPOT 10.01.35 - 08.36
Erected pre 11.35
PAULSGROVE
FAREHAM
S.R.
SOUTHAMPTON ROAD
PORTSDOWN HILL
COSHAM 'RED LION'
LONDON ROAD
HAVANT ROAD
COSHAM RLY STN
WESTERN ROAD
PCT
PORTSBRIDGE
HILSEA
PHLR
HORSEA ISLAND
ALEXANDRA PARK
NORTHERN PARADE
LONDON ROAD
COPNOR ROAD
GLADYS AVENUE
TWYFORD AVENUE
STAMSHAW ROAD
NORTH END
DEPOT
STUBBINGTON AVENUE
WHALE ISLAND
CHICHESTER ROAD
KINGSTON CRESCENT
KINGSTON ROAD
COPNOR BRIDGE
TANGIER ROAD
NEW ROAD
COMMERCIAL ROAD
LAKE ROAD
H.M. DOCKYARD
UNICORN GATE
FRATTON ROAD
BAFFINS ROAD
MILTON ROAD
DOCKYARD
QUEEN STREET
PORTSMOUTH & SOUTHSEA STN
FRATTON STN
THE HARD
ORDNANCE ROW
GUILDHALL
PORTSMOUTH HARBOUR STN
PARK ROAD
GREETHAM STREET
BLACKFRIARS ROAD
BRADFORD ROAD
BRADFORD JUNCTION
GOLDSMITH AVENUE
ST GEORGES ROAD
FLOATING BRIDGE
HIGH STREET
ALEXANDRA ROAD
VICTORIA ROAD NORTH
FAWCETT ROAD
MILTON 'WHITE HOUSE'
BROAD STREET
OLD PORTSMOUTH
ROYAL PIER HOTEL
LAWRENCE ROAD
EASTNEY ROAD
DEPOT
PIER ROAD
WESTERN PARADE
ALBERT ROAD
HIGHLAND ROAD
EASTNEY
OSBORNE ROAD
QUEENS HOTEL
THE CIRCLE
VICTORIA ROAD SOUTH
WAVERLEY ROAD
FESTING ROAD
CLARENCE PIER
CLARENDON ROAD
ST HELENS PARADE
GRANADA ROAD
THE STRAND
SOUTHSEA
SOUTH PARADE PIER
N
ONE MILE
1/2 replaced on 01.10.34 by bus service P/O
PHLR operation ceased after 09.01.35
7/8 Summer only to either CLARENCE PIER via GUILDHALL
or SOUTH PARADE PIER via Victoria Road South. Withdrawn at end of summer 1935.

1934 AEC663T / MCCW & F trolleybus 15 and 1920 English Electric tram 103, the latter in the crimson and white livery introduced in 1929, at Cosham Railway Station terminus. It is likely that this photograph dates from the first few days of trolleybus operation; in any case, tram service 1 was withdrawn on 1 October 1934. The PHLR crossed the railway line from Cosham to Fareham using the girder bridge in the background to the left of the trolleybus. (National Tramway Museum)

Two of the four 3-axle vehicles in the experimental trolleybus fleet, Sunbeam MS3 14 and AEC663T 12, pass in London Road, Hilsea, in 1934. Both tram tracks and overhead wiring remain in place. Note the bands and bus stop signs on the nearest traction poles. (National Tramway Museum [Transport World])

were reintroduced on these services at the height of the summer season in July 1935 in connection with the visit of HM King George V!

On 15 August 1934 a trolleybus overran the limit of its trolley booms at the junction of London Road and Northern Parade, Hilsea, resulting in a de-wirement that pulled the conductor wires out of their hangers for about 100 yards leading to a short circuit that brought tram and trolleybus traffic to a halt. At one time seven trams and six trolleybuses were marooned whilst other traffic was dislocated for about an hour.

Leyland TBD2/English Electric H26/24R No. 5 travelling south in London Road, 30 September 1934. (D.A.P. Janes [photographer G.A. Tucker])

During their first four weeks of service (4 August–1 September 1934) the trolleybuses carried 404,210 passengers who paid £2,577 4s 8d in fares. They ran 30,110 revenue miles and earned 20.54d per mile compared to the motorbuses' 14.94d and trams' 16.1d. The average fare per passenger was 1.53d. The trolleybuses earned an operating profit of £173 up to 31 August 1934. The August Bank Holiday Monday fell on 6 August 1934 and the Corporation had 103 tramcars, 90 motorbuses and seven trolleybuses out on the road. By the end of 12½ weeks trolleybus operation the profit had increased to £1,043. This was considered a very satisfactory return. In those 12½ weeks 1,143,449 passengers were carried and the revenue per mile for the 99,912 miles run averaged 16.83d.

In October 1934 short workings were introduced between Southsea South Parade Pier and North End, where they used the reversing triangle installed in July 1934 at the entrance to North End Depot enabling trolleybuses to reverse out into Gladys Avenue, providing a 5-minute headway on this part of the route. A month later, it was decided to construct an additional doorway at the northeast corner of North End Depot at a cost of £180 including doors, the original southern doorway being used henceforth as the entrance and the new doorway as the exit. The work was completed in March 1935 and trolleybuses terminating at North End ran through the depot building.

It was found that the reinforced traction poles between St Mary's Road and Fratton Bridge were tending to bend under the increased weight of the overhead equipment, the estimated weight of four trolleybus and two tram wires exceeded 350 lb at each 40 yard point of suspension. This made it difficult to maintain the minimum height of 20ft between the points of suspension. Clough Smith fitted tubular gantries across the road between the upper parts of the traction poles at a charge of £221 19s 7d. Throughout 1934 Hants Wireless Relay Ltd., were fixing their wires to the traction poles for which privilege they paid 1s per pole p.a. rent. During September 1934 the positive wire suspension ears were painted red.

The undertaking's advertising contractor Messrs Griffiths and Millington pointed out in August 1934 that there was less advertising space on trolleybuses than on trams or motorbuses and asked for changes to the contract if it was to be extended to the trolley vehicles. Their offer of £25 p.a. per trolley vehicle or 60% of the receipts from advertisers, whichever sum was the greater, the existing agreement to be extended for 5 years from 31 December 1935 with no change to the terms for trams and motorbuses, was accepted.

The continuing economic depression and requests for reduced fees from their customers due to the gradual reduction of tram services led Griffiths and Millington to request even less onerous conditions in January 1935. They asked that the guaranteed amount per vehicle be suspended retrospectively from 31 December 1933 and that they pay 50% of the receipts from advertisers to the Corporation until the tramway conversion programme was completed. There would be no change to the conditions of the motorbus and trolleybus contract; however, when tramway operations ceased, they asked to lease the advertising rights on all vehicles for a period of 7 years.

On 8 October 1934 Hampshire Light Railways (Electric) Ltd. gave 3 months notice of their intent to end their through-running agreement with the Corporation in respect of the PHLR trams. SMS immediately applied to the Traffic Commissioners to run four additional motorbuses on the Horndean route to replace the trams and the Corporation took steps to oppose the application. The Traffic Commissioners granted SMS a temporary licence to increase their services to replace those run by PHLR trams until 31 March 1935. This was intended to enable the Corporation to consider if they wished to take up their powers in the Horndean Light Railway Order to acquire that part of the Light Railway within the City Boundary. In principle, these powers would only pass to the Corporation 3 months after the abandonment. The Council adopted the Tramways Committee's recommendation not to exercise its option and decided not to oppose the SMS applications to operate replacement buses, subject to SMS continuing to grant fare protection to Corporation services.

The last PHLR tram ran between Southsea South Parade Pier and Horndean on 9 January 1935. As the PHLR service had been rerouted along Commercial Road and Kingston Crescent when trolleybuses were introduced on Fratton Road on 4 August 1934, the frequency of the curtailed Corporation tram services 3 and 4 between South Parade Pier and Alexandra Park was enhanced to compensate for the absence of PHLR cars as far as Kingston Crescent. It was soon found that they ran at a loss and the former timetable was re-introduced until the summer season.

Probably in the autumn of 1934, Sunbeam MF2 8 waits at Southsea South Parade Pier prior to another departure for Cosham Railway Station. In the left background a Portsmouth and Horndean Light Railway open-top tram waits at its terminus during the last 6 months of the line's existence. (D.A.P. Janes Collection [Roy Marshall])

The first moves towards converting the Southsea South Parade Pier – Alexandra Park, Twyford Avenue tram route were made on 18 July 1934 when the General Manager was instructed to invite tenders for the overhead equipment including the necessary traction poles and pole work, as detailed by Clough Smith, together with 5 miles of trolley wire. Four tenders were received by 30 August 1934:

Estler Bros.	£9,020 16s 2d
Clough Smith and Co.	£10,203 18s 3d
British Insulated Cables Ltd.	£11,230 3s 1d
Transmission Lines & Cable Construction Co. Ltd.	£12,201 5s 8d

The lowest tender, that submitted by Estler Bros., plus an additional £124 18s 9d for *'Duo-Met'* trolley wire was accepted on 11 October 1934.

It was calculated that nine more two-axle 50-seat vehicles would be required for the South Parade Pier – Alexandra Park conversion and its extension along Northern Parade to Hilsea. Tenders were invited on 11 October 1934 and that from English Electric Co. Ltd. for AEC 661T chassis equipped with English Electric all metal bodies at £1,908 8s each complete was accepted in January 1935. A lower tender was received from Cravens Railway Carriage and Wagon Co. Ltd. at £810 for all metal bodies but Mr Hall found no evidence of the firm's experience in building double-deck trolleybus bodies. The Tramways Committee agreed that this tender was not suitable for the Department's requirements. In November 1934 advertisements were placed for the disposal of 30 disused tramcars.

On 18 September 1934 the Tramways Committee reviewed the terms of a Draft Provisional Order to enable the Corporation to extend their trolley vehicle system to the City Boundaries. It was passed to the City Council who on 23 October 1934 agreed that application should be made to the MoT for a Provisional Order under Section 32 of the Portsmouth Corporation Act 1930. The routes requested were:

Route 1	Twyford Avenue, Alexandra Park along Northern Parade to Hilsea, London Road, 6 furlongs 8.18 chains.
Route 2	Junction of Portsmouth Road and Northern Road, Cosham along Northern Road, to its junction with London Road at the foot of Southwick Hill, then along London Road to its junction with Spur Road, and along Spur Road to its junction with Northern Road, 7 furlongs.
Route 3	Cosham Railway Gates (existing trolleybus terminus), along High Street, Cosham and Havant Road to Rectory Avenue, Farlington, 2 miles 1 furlong 5 chains.
Route 4	From Northern Road, Cosham along London Road to the city boundary at the top of Portsdown Hill (Widley), 7 furlongs 2.73 chains.
Route 5	From Northern Road, Cosham at its junction with Southampton Road, proceeding along Southampton Road to the City boundary at Paulsgrove (junction of Portsdown Road near Portchester), 2 miles 1 furlong.

Opposition was anticipated and the Town Clerk warned that it would be necessary to convince the MoT that there was a need to operate trolley vehicles to the boundaries. He suggested engaging an independent expert, e.g., Mr Arthur Fearnley, the recently retired General Manager of Sheffield Corporation Tramways and Motors, to support Mr Hall. He reported that the MoT would first hold a local inquiry for which it would be desirable to engage a member of the Parliamentary Bar at a fee of about £200 per day. If, after the inquiry, the MoT decided to make the Provisional Order, it would have to be included in a Parliamentary Bill which, in view of the expected opposition, would be referred to the Standing Committee. The Town Clerk emphasised that supporting documents should estimate the receipts per mile and the working expenses, and that the Committee should then decide whether the application was to be based on the need for the services or the right of the Corporation to provide their own services to the boundaries.

Mr Hall stated that in his view services were essential in the interests of the City's ratepayers, a large number of whom when travelling to a point north of Cosham Railway Station had to change to SMS services. He suggested that the support of the authorities immediately adjoining the City and the County Council should be sought.

It was proposed to borrow £36,000 for a period of up to 10 years, for the necessary additional trolleybuses and £18,000, for 15 years, for the provision of equipment along all five proposed routes and any necessary construction works. During November 1934, statutory notices of the proposals appeared in the press and notice boards were set up along the routes.

On 11 December 1934 application was made to the MoT for sanction to borrow £10,795 15s 4d for the construction of the Southsea South Parade Pier – Festing Road – Albert Road – Bradford Junction – Guildhall – Twyford Avenue, Alexandra Park – Hilsea – Cosham 'Red Lion' route:

Estler Bros. tender	£ 9,020 16s 8d
Estimated cost of pavement reinstatement at foot of poles by direct labour	£ 400
Estimated cost of painting poles, etc. by direct labour, 580 poles at 12s 6d each;	£ 362 10s
124 tubes at 5s each.	£ 31
Total	£ 9,814 6s 8d
10% contingencies	£ 981 8s 8d
	£10,795 15s 4d

This figure was reduced to £8,645 in January 1935 by excluding the portion of the route along Northern Parade which the Corporation was not yet authorised to construct. Application was made to the MoT for sanction to borrow £1,908 8s per vehicle for just nine complete trolley vehicles from English Electric. The tramway conversion programme combined with the global economic depression meant that the Department had a surplus of employees; indeed Mr Hall informed the Tramways Committee in September 1934 that it would be necessary to dismiss 40 traffic employees. Estler Bros. agreed to delegate certain work to the Department thereby ensuring that otherwise redundant employees could be retained.

By 12 March 1935 it was learned that objections to the granting of a Provisional Order had been made to the MoT. The Southern Railway (SR) objected to the Farlington route as it would result in trolley vehicle overhead wiring being placed over the railway at Cosham Railway Station level crossing. Six Paulsgrove residents considered a trolley vehicle route unnecessary as they felt that SMS services already adequately served the district. SMS objected to the extension along Northern Road to the foot of Southwick Hill and all routes to the city boundaries on the grounds that the routes were already adequately served.

At an informal meeting with SMS the company suggested that they would withdraw their opposition to Route No. 2 and raise no objection to trolley vehicles operating along Northern Road to the foot of Southwick Hill and Cosham 'Red Lion' if the Corporation did not proceed with their application to operate trolley vehicles to the city boundaries, provided that the Corporation would agree to maintain the existing fare stage of 3½d from the 'Red Lion' on the trolley vehicles.

The Tramways Committee accordingly recommended agreement with SMS bearing in mind the Traffic Commissioners' view stated in January 1934 that there was no public need for additional services on the routes to the city boundaries. Alderman Sir John Timpson felt that it would be a waste of money to proceed with the application whilst Councillor Rogers stated that the Council would be 'closing the door' for all time by passing this recommendation. Routes 3, 4 and 5 were deleted from the Draft Provisional Order. The legal obstacles thus removed, the somewhat reduced Portsmouth Corporation (Trolley Vehicles) Order Confirmation Bill covering just Routes 1 and 2 referred to above was given an unopposed third reading in the House of Lords during June 1935.

Estler Bros. agreed to start work on the conversion of the Southsea South Parade Pier – Alexandra Park route on 3 November 1934. Tram service frequencies were reduced from 10 to 12 minutes for the winter as usual but in addition services 1 and 2 Clarence Pier – Cosham were withdrawn entirely on 1 October 1934 and replaced by motorbuses thereby reducing the number of trams along Commercial Road between the Guildhall and Kinston Crescent to aid the conversion work. It also meant that the tram route beyond North End to Cosham

Victorian villas provide the backdrop for Karrier E4/MCCW and F11 as it heads south along London Road on a service 3 journey to Southsea South Parade Pier on 16 September 1934. Smith and Vospers was a well known local baker with branches in the city and surrounding area. Their Green Road Bakery was bombed in 1941. In 1961 they were acquired by the Mothers Pride Group and in 1962 baking was moved to Manor Park at Eastleigh. (D.A.P. Janes [photographer G.A. Tucker])

was now only regularly used by PHLR cars. This left the following tram services in operation:

3 Southsea *South Parade Pier* – Festing Hotel – Albert Road – Victoria Road North – Bradford Junction – Guildhall – Alexandra Park
Unidirectional northbound service worked in conjunction with service 4

4 Alexandra Park – Guildhall – Bradford Junction – Victoria Road North – Albert Road – Festing Hotel – Southsea *South Parade Pier*
Unidirectional southbound service worked in conjunction with service 3

5 Dockyard *Main Gate* – Royal Pier Hotel – Southsea *South Parade Pier* – Festing Hotel – Eastney – Milton *White House* – Fratton Bridge – Bradford Junction – Guildhall – Dockyard *Main Gate*
Unidirectional circular service (anti-clockwise) worked in conjunction with service 6

6 Dockyard *Main Gate* – Guildhall – Bradford Junction – Fratton Bridge – Milton *White House* – Eastney – Festing Hotel – Southsea *South Parade Pier* – Royal Pier Hotel – Dockyard *Main Gate*
Unidirectional circular service (clockwise) worked in conjunction with service 5

7 St Mary's Church, Fratton Road – Fratton Bridge – Guildhall – Clarence Pier
Unidirectional southbound service, summer only

8 Clarence Pier – Guildhall – Fratton Bridge – St Mary's Church, Fratton Road
Unidirectional northbound service, summer only

11 Copnor Bridge – Lake Road – Guildhall – Dockyard *Main Gate*
Unidirectional southbound service worked in conjunction with service 12

12 Dockyard *Main Gate* – Guildhall – Lake Road – Copnor Bridge
Unidirectional northbound service worked in conjunction with service 11

15 Copnor Bridge – Lake Road – Guildhall – Old Portsmouth – Floating Bridge
Unidirectional southbound service worked in conjunction with service 16

16 Floating Bridge – Old Portsmouth – Guildhall – Lake Road – Copnor Bridge
Unidirectional northbound service worked in conjunction with service 15

17 Dockyard *Main Gate* – Guildhall – Bradford Junction – Festing Hotel – Eastney – Milton *White House* – Bradford Junction – Guildhall – Dockyard *Main Gate*
Unidirectional circular service (anti-clockwise) worked in conjunction with service 18

18 Dockyard *Main Gate* – Guildhall – Bradford Junction – Milton *White House* – Eastney –Festing Hotel – Bradford Junction – Guildhall – Dockyard *Main Gate*
Unidirectional circular service (clockwise) worked in conjunction with service 17

The conversion was expected to take 16 weeks, however, work only began in the first week of February 1935 due to difficulties in obtaining traction poles and Estlers were granted an exception to the penalty clause in their contract. A start was made towards the end of December 1934 on clearing the trees from around Queen Victoria's statue in Guildhall Square, so that a trolleybus turning circle could be constructed, although it was, in fact, never built. Estlers continued by planting new traction poles at Bradford Junction and along Bradford Road, Blackfriars Road, Greetham Street and Festing Road.

On 12 December 1934 the first fatal accident involving a trolleybus took place in Lawrence Road near the junction with Fawcett Road when a Royal Marines Pensioner was killed.

Only now was it discovered that there would be a clearance problem beneath the railway bridge over Commercial Road immediately to the west of Portsmouth and Southsea Station. Although the surface had been lowered on the west side of the road in 1901 to enable electric trams to pass under the bridge nothing had been done on the east side where the girder bridge was 16ft 6in. above the road. The trolleybuses were some 15ft 9in. high, leaving insufficient clearance for the vehicle's trolley equipment and protective troughing beneath the bridge. Rather than restrict the Commercial Road services to low-bridge bodied vehicles it was decided to lower the road surface on the east side despite the obstacle of a sewer beneath the surface. In view of the disruptions that this would entail it was decided not to start work before the last week of August 1935 to avoid any clash with the Naval Review Week and a visit to Portsmouth by H.M. King George V on 15 July 1935. Subject to satisfactory weather, it was expected that the work would be completed by 16 September 1935.

Throughout March, April and May 1935 Estlers planted new traction poles where required and lengthened others for street lights along the line of route between St Helen's Parade and Alexandra Park terminus. At the end of March 1935, the first gantries or double bracket arms were assembled in Festing Road, the southern end of Northern Parade used by trams and the northern end of Twyford Avenue. On 5 June 1935, following approval of the Portsmouth Corporation (Trolley Vehicles) Order Confirmation Bill, Estlers began planting traction poles along Northern Parade between Alexandra Park and London Road, Hilsea.

Mr Hall told the Tramways Committee on 5 July 1935 that the new trolley vehicles were now unlikely to be delivered before the end of August and that the overhead equipment would also not be completed until then. He was pressing Estler Bros. to complete their work as soon as possible; however, a delay in starting services was inevitable due to the road work necessary beneath the railway bridge over Commercial Road. Proposals to operate a short-working between Southsea South Parade Pier and the Guildhall were not implemented.

The first trolley wires along the extension were hung along both sides of St Helen's Parade, and connections made with the existing wiring at South Parade in early July 1935. These were immediately followed by trolley wires along the westbound route in Bradford Road, Blackfriars Road and Greetham Street, and the eastbound wiring was completed by the end of the month. Wiring was completed from Greetham Street and along Commercial Road to just north of Lake Road by 16 August 1935. Wooden troughing beneath the railway bridge over Commercial Road and the trolley wires on the east side of the road were in place by 22 August 1935. Work on lowering the road at this point started on 26 August 1935 as scheduled, and was completed by 20 September 1935 at a cost of £1,600. The amount was divided equally between the Roads, Works and Drainage Committee and the Tramways Committee.

All wiring was aloft above Commercial Road by 2 September 1935, although no frogs were yet in place at the junction with Kingston Crescent. Although not yet foreseen for passenger

A pre-war view of Karrier E4/English Electric 9 at Southsea South Parade terminus (Canoe Lake turning circle). (D.A.P. Janes collection [photographer's name not recorded])

services, wiring along Kingston Crescent soon followed with connections at both ends thus providing a direct route to North End Depot although no passenger-carrying depot journeys used it at this stage. The Northern Parade wiring was connected to that in London Road on 6 October 1935 whilst the overhead along Festing Road, Albert Road and Victoria Road North had been completed in the meantime thereby completing Estler's work.

Trolleybuses 1, 3, 6 and 8 were partially illuminated 3–12 May 1935 for the City's celebrations of H.M. King George V's Silver Jubilee. The undertaking budgeted up to £500 to buy suitable decorations, enough to decorate 200 vehicles. Jubilee Day, 6 May 1935, was declared a National Holiday and employees were paid at time and a quarter with those men having to work being granted an extra day's holiday with pay. The King visited Portsmouth on 15 July 1935 and a number of tram services withdrawn previously were especially reintroduced. He remained for the Silver Jubilee Fleet Review the next day, an integral part of the Naval Review Week, and which proved to be the second busiest day in the Tramways Department history with takings of just under £2,000.

The Corporation were obliged by the Portsmouth Corporation Act 1930 to offer workmen's fares on the trolleybuses, although there was no such obligation for motorbus and tram services. It was suggested that they should be introduced on 1 April 1935; however, after discussion the matter was referred to a Subcommittee who, in their report on the tramway deficit, made it clear that the question of reduced fares for workmen would have to be linked to a re-arrangement of the fare stages and thus an increase of ordinary fares. The question of increasing ordinary fares was to a large extent dependent on the result of the Corporation's application for further protection from the services of SMS. As this application was unsuccessful, the effect of reducing the fares stages would reduce the protection between Cosham and North End to just ½d and as SMS were running 22 buses per hour on this section against the Corporation's 18 it was feared that the Corporation would lose a considerable number of passengers.

Mr Hall reported that notwithstanding major increases in operating costs, the undertaking's fares were no higher than before the First World War and that taking into account the reduced fares for the maximum distances, the average fares were even lower than pre-1914. If workmen's fares on the basis of a return journey for a single fare were introduced, he expected revenue to fall by £15,800. Any workmen's reductions would have to be compensated by increases in normal fares and in view of the SMS situation this increase could only be achieved by penalising short-stage riders. Fuel oil tax would increase by 7d per gallon in August 1935 (costing an additional £4,250 p.a.), there had been applications for increased salaries from the Department's senior officers, and there had been a recent loss in revenue from advertising contractors.

It was decided not to introduce workmen's fares as the trolleybus network was still too small and to reconsider the situation when the tramways replacement programme was complete. This provoked a letter from the MoT, dated 30 September 1935, pointing out that Section 31 of the Portsmouth Corporation Act 1930 required that reduced fares should be available to 'the labouring classes' travelling on trolley vehicles, and that it was necessary to implement these provisions on any new trolleybus service. Despite this, the Tramways Committee adhered to their previous decision and no action was taken.

It was decided in March 1935 to fit an improved differential braking system to the trolley vehicles on order at an additional cost of £15 per vehicle. The General Manager was instructed to submit a report as soon as possible as to the number of trolley vehicles required to replace all remaining tram routes and tramcars. There was still about £50,000 in the Renewals Fund for tram track renewals; however, as the tramways were now being abandoned it was decided that part of these monies should be used for road reinstatement upon tram abandonment. The cost of the work in Kingston Road would be charged to the fund during the current financial year. On 9 April 1935 Milton and Southsea Ratepayers Association asked if the trolley vehicle service could be extended from Fawcett Road along Rugby Road to the Guildhall. Mr Hall responded that this was already under consideration. At the beginning of May 1935 he submitted a report on the expedited substitution of the tramways by trackless trolley vehicles and was instructed to proceed forthwith with the preparation of estimates and plans.

In May 1935 English Electric asked if the Corporation would permit them to display a trolley vehicle of the same design as those on order in Portsmouth livery at the Commercial Motor Show in the autumn. They would then be prepared to sell it to the Corporation at the same price as those on order. Instead the Tramways Committee suggested that they display one of the nine vehicles on order and that the vehicle display advertising for holidays in Southsea. AEC 661T No. 24 accordingly appeared. Mr Hall was authorised to visit Preston to inspect the trolleybuses which were now nearing completion.

In spring 1935 St Paul's Advertising Service placed a sample sign on a traction pole in front of the old Tramways Office at the Guildhall. In June 1935 their offer for permission to place advertisements on up to 50 traction poles for a fee of £7 p.a. in business centres and £5 elsewhere, with an option to increase the number if the advertising medium proved successful, was accepted.

On 29 July 1935 the Tramways Committee discussed conversion of further tram routes to trolleybus operation, trolleybus route extensions and the purchase of more vehicles, specifically:

1. Specifications of 76 2-axle trolleybus chassis suitable for 52-seat double-deck bodies.
2. Specification of 76 – 52-seat normal height double deck all-metal trolleybus bodies suitable for 2-axle trolleybus chassis as standardised by such trolleybus manufacturers.
3. Specification of the required overhead equipment for the following existing and new routes viz:

Conversion of Existing Tramway Routes

Guildhall to Clarence Pier	0.94 miles
Highland Road, Eastney Road, Goldsmith Avenue and Victoria Road North from Fratton Bridge to Bradford Road Junction	2.21 miles
Rugby Road	0.11 miles
Clarendon Road, Osborne Road and Western Parade	1.13 miles
Victoria Road South from The Circle to Albert Road	0.40 miles
Park Road	0.53 miles
Cambridge Road, High Street and Broad Street	0.93 miles
Alexandra Road, St Georges Road and the Hard	0.76 miles
Lake Road	0.61 miles
New Road	0.62 miles
Total	8.24 miles

New Routes

From the junction of Northern Road and Portsmouth Road, Cosham to Cosham 'Red Lion' via Northern Road and Spur Road returning via High Street and Northern Road.	0.872 miles

The Committee agreed to an amendment to Specification 1 to provide for contractors being asked to quote for 'one

Three axle AEC663T/English Electric 12 heads south, probably in London Road, Hilsea, towards Southsea South Parade Pier. (Photographer's name not recorded)

chassis and for numbers up to 76 chassis'. Three-axle vehicles were not discussed.

On 4 September 1935 the Tramways Committee considered the tenders received. There were eight tenders for the supply of the chassis: Leyland Motors Ltd., £1,054 11s; Crossley Motors Ltd., £1,057 11s; Karrier Motors Successors Ltd., £1,057 11s; English Electric Co. for AEC, £1,058 11s; Sunbeam Commercial Vehicles Ltd., £1,059 11s; Associated Equipment Company, £1,060 11s; Guy Motors Ltd., £1,060 11s; and Ransomes, Sims and Jefferies Ltd., £1,062 11s.

First of all it was decided to standardise on 76 vehicles of the same type. Mr Hall had prepared a report on the four types of trolley vehicle which had been on extended trial. This showed that 2-axle vehicles were more suitable than 3-axle vehicles for the narrow roads with sharp bends common in Portsmouth whilst conductors had found it impossible to check and collect all fares, and efficiently discharge their duties, within a stage length during peak hours on the larger 3-axle trolleybuses. The greater earning capacity of the 60 seat vehicles did not justify the higher running cost during the much longer off-peak periods of light loading. He considered that the 2-axle chassis with regenerative equipment was the most economical in operation, the current consumption for the seven months ending 31 July 1935 being 1.69 units per mile as against 1.95 units for vehicles with augmented field control. In addition to the lower current consumption due to the use of regenerative braking, the mechanical braking equipment was subjected to considerably less wear and tear, whilst deceleration was noticeably smoother.

The eight months ending 31 March 1935 showed the following average costs per mile for repairs and maintenance, cleaning and oiling, labour and material, electrical energy and maintenance of the overhead line for the different chassis in service:

AEC 661T	2.715d per mile
Leyland TBD2	2.862d
Sunbeam MF2	2.910d
Karrier E4	3.128d

For four months ended 31 July 1935:

AEC 661T	2.360d per mile
Leyland TBD2	2.804d
Sunbeam MF2	2.434d
Karrier E4	2.993d

It was stated that a reduction of one-tenth of a penny per mile on the fleet of vehicles would result in a saving of £800–£1,000 a year. This factor was considered by the Tramways Committee in recommending the AEC661T chassis at £1,058 11s each, including £5 for a 48 volt ironclad battery. Although not the lowest tender, the undertaking wished to standardise their fleet and with a difference of just £8 between the highest and lowest, the choice depended upon the maintenance costs.

Mr Hall wished to equip the new vehicles with traction batteries in order to be able to run short-workings to locations without overhead wiring rather than for emergency use. Although the specification called for a 48 volt battery, only Crossley and Leyland had quoted for such a battery, the remainder quoting for a 60 volt battery. Having carried out trials with 48 volt units, experiments with 60 volt 60 ampere-hour batteries had shown that the battery power operating range was almost 2½ miles and that by allowing the battery to recover for 6 minutes a further 1¹/₁₆ miles could be run at an average speed excluding stops of 3 mph. He considered this a distinct improvement. It was agreed to consider the tenders as submitted and ask Crossley and Leyland the additional charge for 60 volt batteries, both firms replying that there would be no additional cost.

There were 12 tenders for the bodies, varying between £768 and £933 per body, seven companies, including English Electric

Leyland TBD2/English Electric 5 in Albert Road at Festing Road Junction heading west. Again, the recessed window above the offside windscreen has already been added to improve the driver's view of the overhead line above. There is a semaphore arm illuminated traffic indicator on both front corner pillars but only an offside driver's rear view mirror. (Omnibus Society)

having submitted the same figure of £915. The second lowest, from Cravens Railway Carriage and Wagon Co. at £780 per body was accepted, despite an amendment that the tried and tested product of English Electric be ordered. The report stated that Cravens' specification fully satisfied the Corporation's requirements, and the general design indicated that the detail of the structure and assembly was almost identical to the earlier order for 16–24 placed with English Electric. In retrospect, the poor experiences as to the durability of the Cravens bodies, which were not limited to Portsmouth, makes one wonder if this was a good decision.

There had been five tenders for the supply and erection of overhead equipment along the remaining tram routes, as authorised by the Portsmouth Corporation Provisional Order, and the extension from Portsbridge to Cosham 'Red Lion' along Northern Road:

British Insulated Cables Ltd.	£20,731 5s 9d
Clough, Smith and Co. Ltd.	£19,619 18s 1d
District Transmission Lines Ltd.	£19,130 13s 5d
Estler Brothers Ltd.	£22,924 3s 2¾d
Eve Construction Co. Ltd.	£25,329 6s 9d

It was noted that District Transmission Lines Ltd. had no previous trolleybus experience. The Tramways Committee recommended Clough Smith's tender at £19,619 18s 1d although not the lowest received, as it was considered as offering the best value, and recommended that application be made for MoT sanction to borrow the entire sum.

The City Council considered tenders totalling £159,249 14s 1d, as recommended by the Tramways Committee, on 10 September 1935:

Overhead Equipment	£19,619 18s 1d submitted by Messrs Clough Smith and Co. Ltd.
Chassis:	£1,058 11s each submitted by the English Electric Co. for AEC chassis.
Bodies:	£780 each submitted by Messrs Cravens Railway Carriage and Wagon Co.

The meeting came to no conclusion following debate on the principle of accepting the lowest figure tendered and various accusations as to certain chassis details not being disclosed. At their next meeting on 17 September 1935 the Lord Mayor called upon Alderman Sir John Timpson, Chairman of the Tramways Committee, to move the adoption of the recommendation. This led to Councillor Prince proposing that the matter be referred back for further consideration, arguing that as the AEC661T chassis with English Electric equipment had shown the best results of all the vehicles tested, the General Manager should have given precisely its specifications in inviting chassis tenders. If that had been done they would now be considering a tender exactly in accordance with his needs. He added that the lowest tender, that of Leyland, fulfilled the specifications as laid down by the General Manager who was now stating that an additional £17 would have to be added to the tender price to reach his requirements. He believed there was an attempt to mislead the Council! The whole thing had been rushed through and the General Manager had not had the time to give the Committee the true facts of the tenders received. When Councillor Hickson pointed out that every month's delay would add a deficit of £2,000 to the trams, the amendment was lost and the recommendations were carried.

By 10 October 1935 AEC 661T/English Electric trolley vehicles 16–23 had been delivered with No. 24 to follow after the Commercial Motor Show. The first test runs were made along the new route between Southsea South Parade Pier and Cosham Railway Station via Festing Road, Bradford Junction, the Guildhall and Northern Parade in the early morning of Friday 11 October 1935. The railway bridge on Commercial Road, where the road had been lowered on one side, was negotiated with ease. In order to provide sufficient clearance beneath telegraph wires crossing the new trolleybus overhead wiring in Northern Parade without increasing the height of their supports, the GPO had substituted insulated wires in place of guard wires at a cost of £57 to the Corporation.

After their 15 October 1935 meeting the Tramways Committee inspected the new route. Joining a trolleybus at the Guildhall they journeyed to Cosham via Commercial Road and Northern Parade and returned by the same route before continuing to South Parade Pier. Alderman Sir John Timpson told the newspapers that the trial run was 'entirely satisfactory' and that when the changeover was complete 100 trolley vehicles would replace 120 tramcars.

On 3 November 1935, the extension between Southsea South Parade Pier and London Road, Hilsea came into use. There was an 'end-on' connection to the existing wiring at South Parade Pier, a right-angled crossing with it at the junction with Waverley Road and Lawrence Road, and finally a junction with the existing wiring at Portsbridge. Service 3 vehicles, upon reaching South Parade Pier, continued to Cosham Railway Station via Festing Road, Albert Road, Bradford Junction, Guildhall, Commercial Road, Twyford Avenue and Northern Parade as service 3A, thereby introducing a 'figure eight' routing. The existing service 4 was renumbered 4A and the new southbound service Cosham Railway Station – Southsea South Parade Pier via Northern Parade, Twyford Avenue, Commercial Road, Guildhall, Bradford Junction, Albert Road and Festing Road numbered 4. Trolleybuses on the new service 4, upon reaching Southsea South Parade Pier, continued to Cosham Railway Station via Fratton Road and North End as service 4A. The introduction of the 'A' suffix to the service number followed a decision to subsequently extend these services to Cosham 'Red Lion' and, in anticipation of this 'short workings' to Cosham Railway Station carried an 'A' suffix. The service number indicator blind on the first 15 trolleybuses did not include 3A or 4A and displayed 3 or 4 on these journeys.

3 Cosham Railway Station – Hilsea – North End *Junction* – Fratton Bridge – Southsea *South Parade Pier*
Unidirectional southbound service operated in conjunction with service 4A

3A Southsea *South Parade Pier* – Bradford Junction – Guildhall – Alexandra Park – Hilsea – Cosham Railway Station
Unidirectional northbound service operated in conjunction with service 4

Services 3 and 3A provided a unidirectional circular service (clockwise) Cosham Railway Station – Hilsea – North End *Junction* – Fratton Bridge – Southsea *South Parade Pier* – Bradford Junction – Guildhall – Alexandra Park – Hilsea – Cosham Railway Station (the anti-clockwise service was provided by services 4 and 4A).

4 Cosham Railway Station – Hilsea – Alexandra Park – Guildhall – Bradford Junction – Festing Hotel – Southsea *South Parade Pier*
Unidirectional southbound service operated in conjunction with service 3A

1935 AEC661T/English Electric 16 loads at St Mary's Church Fratton Road. The open windows, driver's dustcoat and white top to the conductor's cap indicate that, despite the ladies' hats and long coats, this must be summer. Leyland Titan TD4/English Electric motorbus 124 on service K approaches the stop on its way to Clarence Pier. (David Beilby collection [English Electric])

4A Southsea *South Parade Pier* – Fratton Bridge – North End *Junction* – Hilsea – Cosham Railway Station
Unidirectional northbound service operated in conjunction with service 3

Services 4 and 4A provided a unidirectional circular service (anti-clockwise) Cosham Railway Station – Hilsea – Alexandra Park – Guildhall – Bradford Junction – Festing Hotel – Southsea *South Parade Pier* – Fratton Bridge – North End *Junction* – Hilsea – Cosham Railway Station (the clockwise service was provided by services 3 and 3A).

The two new services brought the amount of trolleybus overhead in use up to 9.4 miles. During the first day of operation the tower wagons of Estler Bros., stood by at Bradford Junction in case of any mishaps. Tram services 3 and 4 were withdrawn and the tramways in Commercial Road north of Lake Road, Kingston Crescent and Twyford Avenue abandoned.

On 7 November 1935, trolleybus 10 collided with the 'Morning Star' public house, at the corner of Blackfriars Road and Greetham Street. The accident, in which seven persons were injured, occurred late at night and resulted in considerable damage to the vehicle. In September 1936 the claim from Brickwoods Brewery for damage to the public house amounting to £151 was settled for £100.

Brighton Corporation Tramways asked Mr Hall if he would loan them a 2-axle trolley vehicle as a part of their evaluation of trolleybuses as successors to their tramways. AEC 661T 20 ran beneath temporary overhead wiring making an anticlockwise loop round the Level for a week commencing 11 December 1935 although formal Portsmouth approval was only granted on 12 December 1935. The vehicle must have made a positive impression as Brighton subsequently also ordered AEC661T trolleybuses, indeed it is quite likely that the loan was facilitated by AEC, who were certainly involved in the demonstration the following month of London Transport AEC663T No. 61.

Mr Hall submitted his proposals for trolleybus turning points at The Hard; Copnor Bridge, New Road; and Guildhall Square in mid-September 1935. The Tramways Committee accepted the first two but was not in favour of the last and delegated the matter to a subcommittee to discuss the best road layout. Tentative proposals for the improvement of Clarence Esplanade, and plans for loading bays and a turning circle at Clarence Pier were discussed in December 1935. Progress with the latter was slow, indeed in May 1936 Mr Hall instructed Clough Smith to proceed with the overhead line based on the tram track layout. Work only started at the beginning of 1937, the loading bays being completed in February 1937.

During February 1936 a subcommittee considered how the undertaking might comply with the Finance and General Purposes Committee instruction that all estimates must be revised to avoid any losses falling on the rates. The Tramways Department's estimated deficit of £12,801 for 1936–1937 was related to the cost of the tramway conversion programme. Having considered the prevailing fare structure, Mr Hall was instructed to submit proposals for increasing some fares and amending certain fare stages.

Leyland TBD2 5 crosses Guildhall Square heading north. Just ahead can be seen the Portsmouth and Southsea Station railway bridge across Commercial Road whilst the goods warehouse is on the other side of the road behind the tram! (D.A.P. Janes collection)

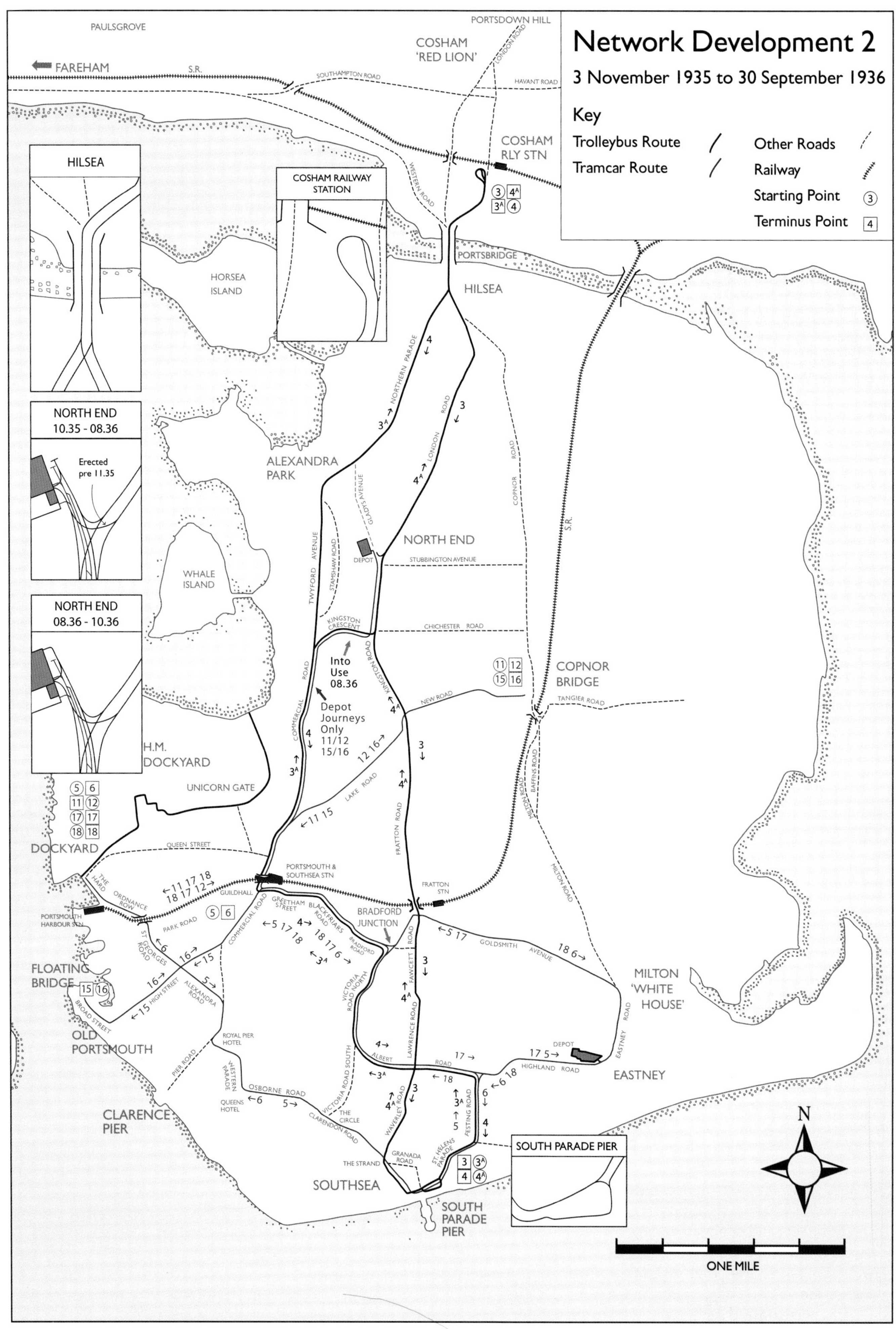

Network Development 2
3 November 1935 to 30 September 1936
Key
Trolleybus Route
Tramcar Route
Other Roads
Railway
Starting Point
Terminus Point
PAULSGROVE
FAREHAM
S.R.
SOUTHAMPTON ROAD
PORTSDOWN HILL
COSHAM 'RED LION'
LONDON ROAD
HAVANT ROAD
COSHAM RLY STN
WESTERN ROAD
HILSEA
COSHAM RAILWAY STATION
PORTSBRIDGE
HORSEA ISLAND
NORTHERN PARADE
LONDON ROAD
ALEXANDRA PARK
NORTH END 10.35 - 08.36
Erected pre 11.35
NORTH END 08.36 - 10.36
WHALE ISLAND
GLADYS AVENUE
COPNOR ROAD
NORTH END
DEPOT
STUBBINGTON AVENUE
TWYFORD AVENUE
STAMSHAW ROAD
KINGSTON CRESCENT
CHICHESTER ROAD
KINGSTON ROAD
COMMERCIAL ROAD
Into Use 08.36
Depot Journeys Only 11/12 15/16
COPNOR BRIDGE
TANGIER ROAD
NEW ROAD
H.M. DOCKYARD
UNICORN GATE
LAKE ROAD
FRATTON ROAD
BAFFINS ROAD
MILTON ROAD
DOCKYARD
QUEEN STREET
PORTSMOUTH & SOUTHSEA STN
FRATTON STN
THE HARD
ORDNANCE ROW
GUILDHALL
PORTSMOUTH HARBOUR STN
PARK ROAD
GREETHAM STREET
BLACKFRIARS ROAD
BRADFORD JUNCTION
GOLDSMITH AVENUE
ST GEORGES ROAD
BRADFORD ROAD
FAWCETT ROAD
FLOATING BRIDGE
HIGH STREET
ALEXANDRA ROAD
VICTORIA ROAD NORTH
MILTON 'WHITE HOUSE'
BROAD STREET
OLD PORTSMOUTH
ROYAL PIER HOTEL
LAWRENCE ROAD
EASTNEY ROAD
DEPOT
ALBERT ROAD
HIGHLAND ROAD
EASTNEY
PIER ROAD
WESTERN PARADE
VICTORIA ROAD SOUTH
OSBORNE ROAD
QUEENS HOTEL
THE CIRCLE
CLARENDON ROAD
WAVERLEY ROAD
FESTING ROAD
CLARENCE PIER
SOUTH PARADE PIER
THE STRAND
GRANADA ROAD
ST. HELENS PARADE
SOUTHSEA
SOUTH PARADE PIER
N
ONE MILE

1935 AEC661T/English Electric all-metal H26/24R No. 24 stops outside St Mary's Church, Fratton Road, on its way to Southsea South Parade Pier. The tram track crossover remains in situ but the separate overhead wires have gone. Trams continued to run between Southsea South Parade Pier and the crossover at St Mary's Church via Victoria Road until 2 September 1935. Trolleybus 24 only entered service on 9 April 1936 having been displayed at the 1935 Commercial Motor Show at Olympia London, 7–16 November 1935. (City of Portsmouth Archives)

On the Subcommittee's recommendation it was decided on 12 March 1936 to put into effect the General Manager's proposals for a revision of fare stages on 1 April 1936. A meeting with SMS was arranged to discuss the position of fares stages from Cosham to North End. There were immediate protests to the new fare stages from a number of trades unions.

Costs began to rise when in May 1936 the National Union of Vehicle Builders and the National Federation of Vehicle Traders informed the Tramways Committee that there had been a change to the national agreement and the abolition of the agreed system of wages for vehicle workers. These employees had now been placed in one grade with an immediate advance of ½d per hour with a further ½d per hour increase on 1 October 1936. The initial award meant an increase of 1½d per hour for employees in Corporation service. Alderman Sir John Timpson informed the Committee that the TGWU were endeavouring to obtain uniformity for all tramway employees and suggested deferring the matter pending a union decision. A decision was reached by the Joint Industrial Council for tramways employees in mid-June 1936, effective from the first full pay period in July 1936, the increases being 2s 6d per week for adult drivers and conductors, 1s per week for juniors, and 1s per week for all others.

Mr Hall asked the Tramways Committee to consider changing the undertaking's name in view of the fact that the trams were fast disappearing. On 16 June 1936 it was decided to change the name from 'Portsmouth Corporation Tramways' to 'City of Portsmouth Passenger Transport Department' (CPPTD) with the name of the Committee altered accordingly.

At their 16 June 1936 meeting the Passenger Transport Committee considered a solicitor's letter seeking their commitment to introduce workmen's fares on trolley vehicles by 1 October 1936, failing which he would open a test case. The Committee resolved that as the delivery of trolley vehicles would be almost complete by the end of September, the following workmen's fares, approved by the City Council on 19 June 1934, would be introduced from 1 October 1936:

Return journey for	1d stage	Fare 1½d
	1½d stage	Fare 2½d
	2d stage	Fare 3d
	2½d stage	Fare 4d
	3d stage	Fare 5d

It seems likely that a trolleybus short-working operated between St Mary's Church, Fratton and Southsea South Parade Pier during the summer seasons of 1936–39 in the same manner as the trams. The trolleybuses turned at St Mary's Church by use of their traction batteries.

In early February 1936 AEC advised that the first of the 76 trolleybus chassis was now ready for delivery to the body builders and suggested that members of the Tramways

AEC661T/English Electric 22 on service 4A heading north in London Road, North End. The building in the apex of the junction of Gladys Avenue (to the left) and London Road (to the right) served as a booking office for Southdown Motor Services for many years. (David Beilby collection [English Electric])

Committee might wish to visit the works and test the new chassis. A delegation travelled to Southall in the Department's Daimler car used for the airport service. Mr Hall pointed out that the loan application for the trolley vehicles and overhead equipment was currently based on the figures submitted to the Council on 10 September 1935 and totalling £159,249 14s 1d. A deduction of £2,300, representing the cost of the extension along Northern Parade, needed to be made as this had already been provided for in the Portsmouth Corporation Act 1930. However, £2,140 for reinstating paving and the Clarence Pier turning circle had not been included in the loan sanction and a supplementary loan application for this amount was made.

In March 1936 Mr F. H. Peacock, Rolling Stock Superintendent, Southend-on-Sea Corporation Electric Light and Light Railways Department was appointed Assistant Engineer.

During March 1936 additional traction poles to support the increased weight of trolleybus overhead equipment were planted in the vicinity of Bradford Junction, Fratton Bridge and Rugby Road. Surviving ornate iron scrollwork on the original poles was removed throughout. In April pole planting continued between Guildhall Square and Clarence Pier, and between the Royal Pier Hotel and Clarendon Road. A turning circle was constructed at the north end of The Hard immediately before the right-angle corner into Queen Street, the additional supporting poles being planted outside the Dockyard Main Gate. In May 1936 work began hanging trolley wires in Rugby Road whilst further traction poles were planted in High Street, Broad Street and East Street, Old Portsmouth (the latter to support the reversing triangle at Floating Bridge).

Portsmouth's trams were equipped with fixed trolley heads as, until now, the single overhead conductor wire had been hung immediately above the tracks. Initially the trolleybus overhead wiring was strung about 12in. above the tram wires, ready to be lowered into use. However, as the conversion programme progressed it was increasingly desirable for the trams to use the positive trolleybus conductor wire once it was in place and this deviated considerably from the position of the tram tracks. In early May 1936 each tram was accordingly equipped with a swivelling trolley head which could follow the alignment of overhead wiring at some distance from the centre line of the tram tracks, and a bamboo retrieval pole, carried in brackets on the rocker panel. The retrieval rope which had previously hung from the end of the trolley pole was removed as it could have fouled other vehicles or pedestrians with serious consequences. Tram de-wirements increased as a result of the many temporary junctions and crossings with trolleybus overhead wiring, and additional retrieval poles were hung from convenient traction poles at locations potentially at risk.

Clough Smith then directed their attention to the Copnor route, all additional poling work in New Road and Lake Road being completed by mid-May 1936. On 10 May 1936 the necessary addition wiring and frogs at Bradford Junction, already used by services 3A, 4, was inserted. Gantries were constructed in Victoria Road North between Fratton Bridge and Bradford Junction and by now the hangers were in place on the bracket arms in Cambridge Road and Victoria Road North.

By the end of May 1936 trolley wires were hung along Pier Road from the Royal Pier Hotel to Clarence Pier and along Victoria Road North from Bradford Junction to Fratton Bridge. In the first few days of June 1936, the tramway trolley wires were removed from Victoria Road North, between Bradford Junction and Fratton Bridge, as the trams were now using the trolleybus conductor wires which, by now, had been extended into Goldsmith Avenue. At this time more junctions were inserted in the overhead at Fratton Bridge and a curve from the northbound Victoria Road North line into the southbound

Leyland TBD2 7 is seen at Bradford Junction leaving Bradford Road and turning into Victoria Road North sometime between November 1935 and November 1936 as evidenced by the absence of trolleybus overhead wiring continuing north towards Fratton Bridge. (Omnibus Society [photographer Norr])

A gentleman helps his wife alight from AEC661T/English Electric H26/24R No. 23 at the Victoria Grove stop in Victoria Road South. The advertisements of the H & G Simonds of Reading brewery with the well-known hop leaf trade mark were often seen in Portsmouth and elsewhere in Southern England, not least as Simonds had developed a reputation of supplying the Forces with beer, indeed they had branches in Gibraltar and Malta. (David Beilby collection [English Electric])

Shortly after leaving Cosham Railway Station, trolleybus 31 pulls away from the bus stop outside Highbury Buildings at the junction of Chatsworth Avenue with Portsmouth Road, on 6 September 1936. Street's Dairies were founded in 1855. Based in Duncan Road, Southsea, they had a number of branches in the city. In 1939 they merged with Taylor and Sons Dairies, and Hoar and Dumbrill to form Portsmouth Dairies. (D.A.P. Janes [photographer G.A. Tucker])

Fawcett Road line was inserted to enable short workings from Southsea South Parade Pier to turn back. These were rare, and the frogs and wiring were removed soon after the war. By 21 June 1936 the Copnor Bridge turning circle was aloft. In the week thereafter a turning circle was completed at Clarence Pier and all the wiring was now in position from there to the Guildhall, although the junctions with the other wiring at this point had not yet been made.

At the end of July 1936 approval was given for alterations to the crossing, presumably the sprung frog of the erstwhile reversing triangle, at the entrance to North End Depot at an estimated £65. The work was carried out during August 1936.

The first eight trolleybuses of the 76 AEC661Ts ordered in September 1935, numbers 25–32, entered service on 1 August 1936 and supplemented the 25 trolleybuses already operating on services 3, 3A, 4, 4A. Deliveries continued at the rate of 4–5 per week.

On 3 August 1936 the overhead wiring in Kingston Crescent, in place since September 1935, was brought into use for service vehicles and an undesignated service was introduced:

— Cosham Railway Station – Hilsea – North End – Kingston Crescent – Guildhall – Bradford Junction – Festing Hotel – Southsea *South Parade Pier*

Trolleybuses displayed no service number. It is assumed that only the latest deliveries, equipped with traction batteries, were used as a turning circle at Southsea South Parade Pier accessible from St Helens Parade was only installed in 1953. It is believed that this was a summer season service and that it was withdrawn early in September 1936.

The route along Northern Road from Portsbridge to Cosham 'Red Lion' was complete by 8 August 1936 and on 20 August 1936 trolleybuses 33–39 entered service. During September 1936 wiring work continued around the Eastney circle, along New Road and Lake Road, and under the Gunwharf Railway Bridge to The Hard. During the last few days of September 1936 the trolley wires were strung between Milton 'White House' and Eastney Depot, and between Cambridge Junction and the Guildhall, and the tram wires cut down. Trolley wires were in place in a northbound direction along High Street, Old Portsmouth but no connection had been made at Cambridge Junction.

In September 1936, a suggestion that Twyford Avenue should be made a one-way street northbound with southbound traffic following Stamshaw Road was rejected due to the expense of altering the trolleybus overhead equipment which was only some 10 months old.

By now there was over six route miles of new but unused trolleybus overhead wiring aloft along the new routes. Rather than leave this investment wasted the new wiring north of Portsbridge along Northern Road, London Road and Spur Road to Cosham 'Red Lion', and that between Guildhall Square and Clarence Pier along Commercial Road, Hampshire Terrace, Landport Terrace, Kings Terrace, Jubilee Terrace, Bellevue Terrace and Pier Road, was deemed ready for service. Work was underway at Eastney Depot filling in the tram pits. Thus on 1 October 1936 two more trolleybus services were introduced, replacing temporary motorbus services P and Q which had operated between Cosham Railway Station and Clarence Pier since the withdrawal of tram services 1 and 2 on 1 October 1934.

1 Cosham *Red Lion* – Hilsea – North End *Junction* – Kingston Crescent – Guildhall – Royal Pier Hotel – Clarence Pier *Unidirectional southbound service*

2 Clarence Pier – Guildhall – Kingston Crescent – North End *Junction* – Hilsea – Cosham *Red Lion*
Unidirectional northbound service

Mr Hall suggested that the original fleet of 24 trolleybuses should be equipped with traction manoeuvring batteries as fitted to the 76 AEC661Ts on order and he was authorised to invite quotations, however, the work was never carried out.

The training of tram drivers on the new vehicles was underway and trolleybuses on training duties were to be seen on those sections of overhead wiring that were now complete. In October 1936 the remaining gaps in the overhead wiring were progressively closed and frogs inserted at junctions. The junctions of Lake Road with Kingston Road, and New Road with Kingston Road were completed on 24 October 1936, as was the reversing triangle at Floating Bridge. The trams were immediately cut-back to the end of the double track at East Street.

By mid-October 1936 there were a total of 63 trolleybuses in stock, including 39 of the new AEC661T/Cravens vehicles. As it was decided to reduce the Sunday frequency from 10 minutes to 12 minutes for the winter it was calculated that by the end of the month there would be sufficient trolley vehicles available to operate the winter services and that the remaining trams could be withdrawn at any time thereafter.

The official MoT inspection of the new trolleybus overhead installations between the Guildhall and Copnor Bridge, the Dockyard, and Floating Bridge, Old Portsmouth, was carried out on 29 October 1936. The work was considered satisfaction although the majority of new traction poles along these routes remained unpainted. Trams ran on services 11, 12, 15, 16 for the last time on Saturday 31 October 1936. The following morning four new trolleybus services following the same route as their predecessors began to operate:

11 Copnor Bridge – Guildhall – Dockyard *Main Gate*
Unidirectional southbound service worked in conjunction with service 12

12 Dockyard *Main Gate* – Guildhall – Copnor Bridge
Unidirectional northbound service worked in conjunction with service 11

15 Copnor Bridge – Guildhall – Old Portsmouth – Floating Bridge
Unidirectional southbound service worked in conjunction with service 16

16 Floating Bridge – Old Portsmouth – Guildhall – Copnor Bridge
Unidirectional northbound service worked in conjunction with service 15

Portsmouth's Last Tram, No. 106, driven by Alderman Sir John Timpson, makes its way east along Greetham Street on the morning of 10 November 1936 at the start of its final journey to Eastney Depot. In the background is Portsmouth's dignified Guildhall and on the right Portsmouth & Southsea Station. (Transport World)

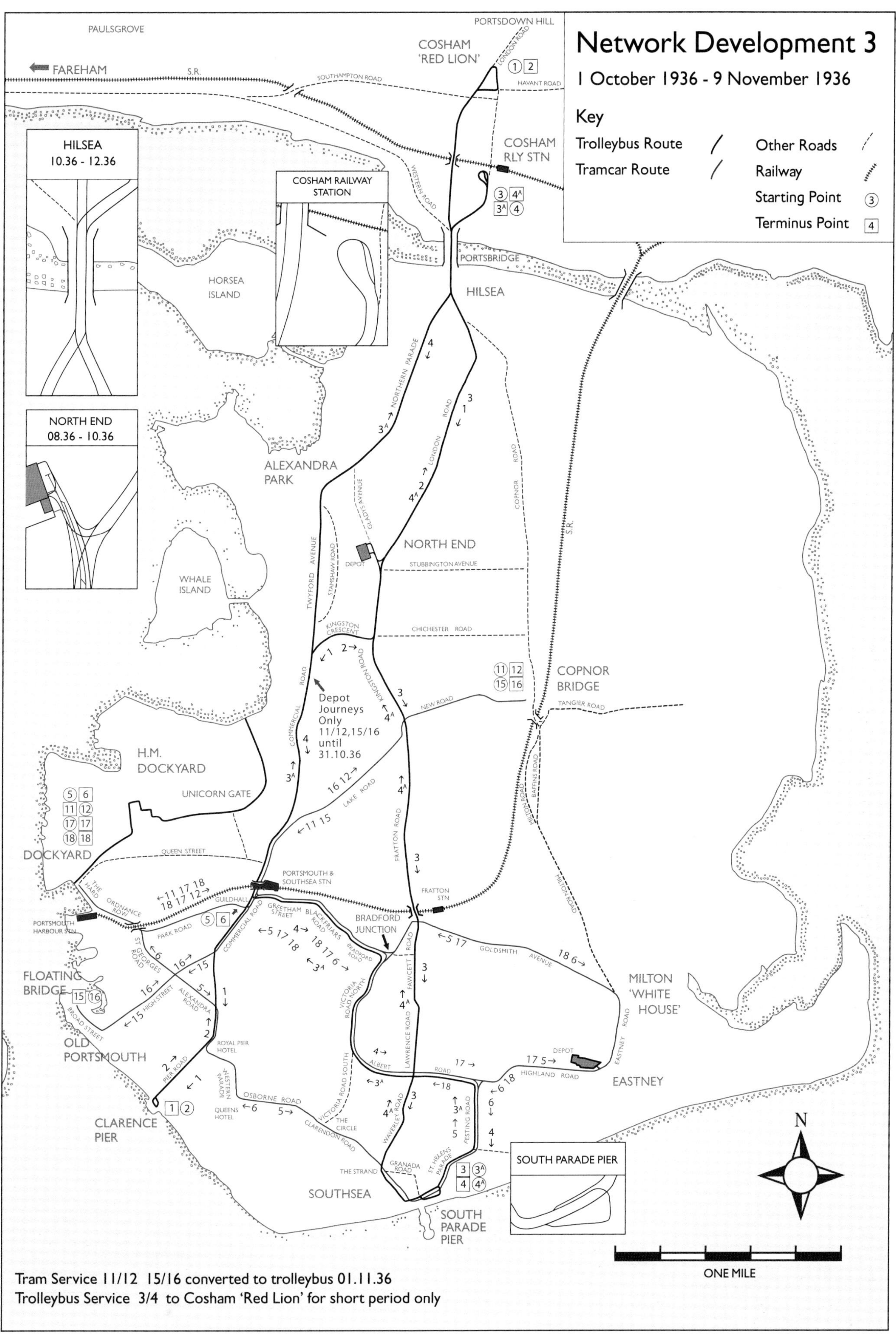
Network Development 3
1 October 1936 - 9 November 1936
Key
Trolleybus Route
Tramcar Route
Other Roads
Railway
Starting Point
Terminus Point
HILSEA
10.36 - 12.36
NORTH END
08.36 - 10.36
COSHAM RAILWAY STATION
PAULSGROVE
FAREHAM
PORTSDOWN HILL
COSHAM 'RED LION'
COSHAM RLY STN
PORTSBRIDGE
HILSEA
HORSEA ISLAND
ALEXANDRA PARK
WHALE ISLAND
NORTH END
COPNOR BRIDGE
H.M. DOCKYARD
UNICORN GATE
DOCKYARD
Depot Journeys Only 11/12,15/16 until 31.10.36
PORTSMOUTH & SOUTHSEA STN
BRADFORD JUNCTION
FLOATING BRIDGE
OLD PORTSMOUTH
CLARENCE PIER
MILTON 'WHITE HOUSE'
EASTNEY
SOUTHSEA
SOUTH PARADE PIER
ONE MILE
N
Tram Service 11/12 15/16 converted to trolleybus 01.11.36
Trolleybus Service 3/4 to Cosham 'Red Lion' for short period only

A total of 49 trolleybuses were now required for peak-hour services.

The only tram services now remaining were 5 and 6 Dockyard – Osborne Road – Southsea South Parade Pier – Eastney – Milton 'White House' – Bradford Junction – Guildhall and 17 and 18 Dockyard – Guildhall – Bradford Junction – Albert Road – Eastney – Milton 'White House' – Fratton Bridge – Guildhall – Dockyard.

An unconfirmed report suggests that on 3 November 1936 the 3, 3A, 4, 4A group of trolleybus services was revised to also serve the Hilsea – Cosham 'Red Lion' extension, although journeys continued to originate and terminate at Cosham Railway Station. No corroborative evidence has been found and if such extension took place it was short-lived.

The tramway conductor wires providing access to Eastney Depot were replaced by trolleybus overhead and on 4 November 1936 tram wires were removed from Guildhall Square.

On Tuesday 10 November 1936 the ceremonial last trams left the Guildhall for Eastney at 11.45 a.m., four of the 1920 English Electric totally enclosed top-covered cars being specially decorated for the occasion. Alderman Sir John Timpson, Chairman of the Passenger Transport Committee, drove car 106 from the Guildhall and through Victoria Road, its front destination indicator displaying 'Journey's End' and that at the rear 'Speed with Comfort,' whilst the service number boxes showed '1901–1936'. He then passed the controls to Councillor F. J. Spickernell, Lord Mayor of Portsmouth for 1936–37. It was recorded that in their lifetime the Corporation's electric trams had travelled some 89,402,686 miles and carried 1,054,046,665 passengers.

Trolleybuses were immediately substituted on the following services:

5 Dockyard *Main Gate* – Royal Pier Hotel – Southsea *South Parade Pier* – Festing Hotel – Eastney – Milton *White House* – Fratton Bridge – Bradford Junction – Guildhall
Unidirectional service (anti-clockwise) worked in conjunction with service 6

6 Guildhall – Bradford Junction – Fratton Bridge – Milton *White House* – Eastney – Festing Hotel – Southsea *South Parade Pier* – Royal Pier Hotel – Dockyard *Main Gate*
Unidirectional service (clockwise) worked in conjunction with service 5

17 Dockyard *Main Gate* – Guildhall – Bradford Junction – Festing Hotel – Eastney – Milton *White House* – Bradford Junction – Guildhall – Dockyard *Main Gate*
Unidirectional circular service (anti-clockwise) worked in conjunction with service 18

18 Dockyard *Main Gate* – Guildhall – Bradford Junction – Milton *White House* – Eastney –Festing Hotel – Bradford Junction – Guildhall – Dockyard *Main Gate*
Unidirectional circular service (clockwise) worked in conjunction with service 17

Once again these were direct replacements of tram services that had followed the same route and displayed the same service numbers. Trolleybuses terminating at the Guildhall used their traction batteries to turn in the width of Park Road.

AEC661T/English Electric 18 at St Marys Church, Fratton Road, heading south on service 3 to Southsea South Parade Pier. (D.A.P. Janes collection [photographer's name not recorded])

CHAPTER 4

CONSOLIDATION

With the abandonment of tramway operation on 10 November 1936 the Portsmouth trolleybus system as then foreseen was complete and by the end of the year there were 88 trolleybuses licensed and available for service in the city operating the following services:

1 Cosham *Red Lion* – Hilsea – North End *Junction* – Kingston Crescent – Guildhall – Royal Pier Hotel – Clarence Pier
Unidirectional southbound service

2 Clarence Pier – Guildhall – Kingston Crescent – North End *Junction* – Hilsea – Cosham *Red Lion*
Unidirectional northbound service

3 Cosham Railway Station – Hilsea – North End *Junction* – Fratton Bridge – Southsea *South Parade Pier*
Unidirectional southbound service

3A Southsea *South Parade Pier* – Bradford Junction – Guildhall – Alexandra Park – Hilsea – Cosham Railway Station
Unidirectional northbound service
Circular route working with service 3 commenced.

4 Cosham Railway Station – Hilsea – Alexandra Park – Guildhall – Bradford Junction – Southsea *South Parade Pier*
Unidirectional southbound service

4A Southsea *South Parade Pier* – Fratton Bridge – North End *Junction* – Hilsea – Cosham Railway Station
Unidirectional northbound service

5 Dockyard *Main Gate* – Royal Pier Hotel – Southsea *South Parade Pier* – Festing Hotel – Eastney – Milton *White House* – Fratton Bridge – Bradford Junction – Guildhall
Unidirectional service (anti-clockwise) worked in conjunction with service 6

6 Guildhall – Bradford Junction – Fratton Bridge – Milton *White House* – Eastney – Festing Hotel – Southsea *South Parade Pier* – Royal Pier Hotel – Dockyard *Main Gate*
Unidirectional service (clockwise) worked in conjunction with service 5

11 Copnor Bridge – Guildhall – Dockyard *Main Gate*
Unidirectional southbound service worked in conjunction with service 12

12 Dockyard *Main Gate* – Guildhall – Copnor Bridge
Unidirectional northbound service worked in conjunction with service 11

15 Copnor Bridge – Guildhall – Old Portsmouth – Floating Bridge
Unidirectional southbound service worked in conjunction with service 16

16 Floating Bridge – Old Portsmouth – Guildhall – Copnor Bridge
Unidirectional northbound service worked in conjunction with service 15

17 Dockyard *Main Gate* – Guildhall – Bradford Junction – Festing Hotel – Eastney – Milton *White House* – Bradford Junction – Guildhall – Dockyard *Main Gate*
Unidirectional circular service (anti-clockwise) worked in conjunction with service 18

18 Dockyard *Main Gate* – Guildhall – Bradford Junction – Milton *White House* – Eastney –Festing Hotel – Bradford Junction – Guildhall – Dockyard *Main Gate*
Unidirectional circular service (clockwise) worked in conjunction with service 17

AEC661T 78 with Cravens all-metal bodywork brings up the rear of a column of three identical trolleybuses waiting at the kerbside on The Hard outside HM Dockyard Main Gate. The masts and rigging of Admiral Lord Nelson's Flagship, HMS Victory, can be espied behind the trailing frog. The Police Licence plate, No. 878, can be seen beneath the seating capacity information, whilst beneath the rear panels the two tubes for carrying the bamboo trolley retrieval poles are evident. Corporation motorbuses wait in the centre of the road. (David Beilby collection [English Electric])

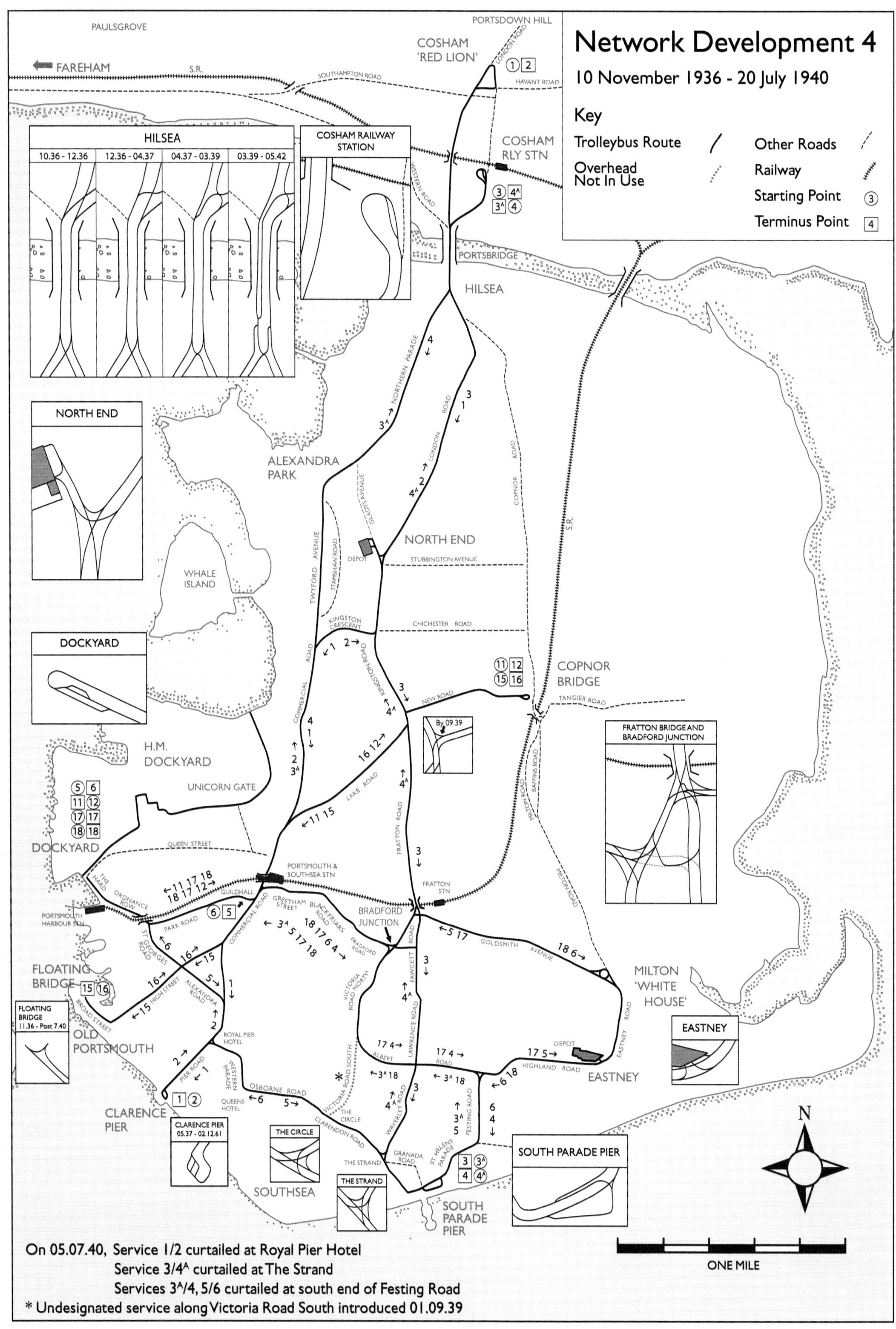
Network Development 4
10 November 1936 - 20 July 1940
Key
Trolleybus Route
Overhead Not In Use
Other Roads
Railway
Starting Point
Terminus Point
PAULSGROVE
FAREHAM
S.R.
PORTSDOWN HILL
COSHAM 'RED LION'
LONDON ROAD
HAVANT ROAD
SOUTHAMPTON ROAD
HILSEA
10.36 - 12.36
12.36 - 04.37
04.37 - 03.39
03.39 - 05.42
COSHAM RAILWAY STATION
COSHAM RLY STN
WESTERN ROAD
PORTSBRIDGE
NORTH END
NORTHERN PARADE
LONDON ROAD
ALEXANDRA PARK
COPNOR ROAD
GLADYS AVENUE
TWYFORD AVENUE
STAMSHAW ROAD
DEPOT
STUBBINGTON AVENUE
WHALE ISLAND
CHICHESTER ROAD
KINGSTON CRESCENT
DOCKYARD
COMMERCIAL ROAD
KINGSTON ROAD
NEW ROAD
COPNOR BRIDGE
TANGIER ROAD
H.M. DOCKYARD
UNICORN GATE
By 09.39
LAKE ROAD
FRATTON ROAD
MILTON ROAD
BAFFINS ROAD
FRATTON BRIDGE AND BRADFORD JUNCTION
QUEEN STREET
PORTSMOUTH & SOUTHSEA STN
THE HARD
ORDNANCE ROW
GUILDHALL
FRATTON STN
PORTSMOUTH HARBOUR STN
PARK ROAD
GREETHAM STREET
BLACKFRIARS ROAD
BRADFORD JUNCTION
BRADFORD ROAD
GOLDSMITH AVENUE
FLOATING BRIDGE
ST GEORGES ROAD
HIGH STREET
ALEXANDRA ROAD
VICTORIA ROAD NORTH
FAWCETT ROAD
MILTON 'WHITE HOUSE'
FLOATING BRIDGE 11.36 - Post 7.40
BROAD STREET
OLD PORTSMOUTH
ROYAL PIER HOTEL
LAWRENCE ROAD
EASTNEY ROAD
EASTNEY
ALBERT ROAD
HIGHLAND ROAD
PIER ROAD
WESTERN PARADE
OSBORNE ROAD
VICTORIA ROAD SOUTH
WAVERLEY ROAD
FESTING ROAD
CLARENCE PIER
QUEENS HOTEL
THE CIRCLE
CLARENDON ROAD
CLARENCE PIER 05.37 - 02.12.61
GRANADA ROAD
ST HELENS PARADE
THE STRAND
SOUTH PARADE PIER
SOUTHSEA
N
ONE MILE
On 05.07.40, Service 1/2 curtailed at Royal Pier Hotel
Service 3/4^A curtailed at The Strand
Services 3^A/4, 5/6 curtailed at south end of Festing Road
* Undesignated service along Victoria Road South introduced 01.09.39

Clough Smith's tower wagons and pole carrying lorries could still be seen in the City making final adjustments. On 14 November 1936 they planted stronger traction poles at the junctions of Lake Road and New Road with Kingston Road and during the next few weeks they removed redundant tramway traction poles at various points.

Two sections of trolleybus overhead wiring were not yet in regular use, namely that along Victoria Road South between the junction with Albert Road and Clarendon Road (The Circle), and Rugby Road between Victoria Road North (Bradford Junction) and Fawcett Road. Trolleybuses only began to use Victoria Road South regularly on 1 September 1939 when an undesignated service began to operate between Cosham Railway Station and North End via Hilsea, North End, Fratton Bridge, Victoria Road, Osborne Road, the Guildhall, Royal Pier Hotel and Kingston Crescent. This was possibly integrated into services 1 and 2 from 21 July 1940. In respect of Rugby Road, although overhead equipment was in place to permit a Waverley Road – Guildhall service as foreseen in November 1930, the complex layout in Rugby Road was used solely by short workings of services 3, 4 from the north turning back to Fratton Bridge and beyond.

The cost of filling in the tram lines and road resurfacing, amounting to £13,792, was paid from the Tramways Renewals Fund. It was hoped to sell enclosed trams 105–116, which were still in good condition, to another operator for further service; however, no expressions of interest were received. They were broken up for scrap by the Department at Eastney Depot. Some of the older tram bodies passed to the Juvenile Employment Committee for use as shelters for those attending gardening courses at Battenburg Avenue and another went to Alexandra Park as a pavilion. The other tramcars were all scrapped with the exception of 84, rebuilt for electric traction in 1903 from a North Metropolitan Tramways Co. Ltd. (London) horse tram and which was retained for museum purposes, and Ben Hall's 1930 experimental domed-roof car 1 which was sold in April 1936 to Sunderland Corporation Tramways and& Motors Department for £90. It proved impossible to sell some 700–800 single and double tramcar seats and these were offered to the Parks and Open Spaces Committee in January 1937.

Until now the Department had been using traditional geographical and later numbered fare stage colour-coded tickets and cancelling punches for ticket issuing purposes on all their vehicles. However, the ticket punches were now considered life-expired and Mr Hall was eager to experiment with ticket issuing machines (TIM). Having compared TIM and Verometer machines, in December 1936 it was decided to obtain 240 TIM machines. The machines were acquired free of charge by committing to purchase blank paper rolls upon which the tickets were printed for a period of years at the rate of 260,000 tickets per machine p.a. at the price of 7½d per thousand. In July 1937 the Department's ticket contractors, Punch and Ticket Co., London, agreed to accept £51 10s to close their present contract. More TIM machines were bought for £14 each in September 1937 followed by a further

Three Cravens bodied AEC661T trolleybuses with No. 30 on a football special bringing up the rear, unload fans, several in Royal Navy uniform, at the Rushkin Road stop in Goldsmith Avenue prior to a match at the Fratton Park Ground. The crowd is making its way up Frogmore Road. (David Beilby collection [English Electric])

14 machines in September 1938. The changeover to TIMs was completed on 10 April 1938. Some 600 Bell Punch machines remained in stock but it proved possible to dispose of 400 of them to other transport operators in June 1939.

In an effort to cope better with increasing traffic across Portsbridge, the sole road access to Portsea Island at this time, experimental traffic islands were placed at the junction of Western Road and Northern Road, Cosham, and at the junction of Northern Parade and London Road, Hilsea, in May 1936. These were deemed successful and permanent islands were installed at the junction of Western Road and Northern Road with Portsmouth Road on the mainland, and a roundabout at the junction of Northern Parade with London Road at Hilsea. The road and overhead wiring works were paid for by the Roads Works and Drainage Department. Starting on the Cosham side, Clough Smith realigned the existing trolleybus overhead wiring to suit the new road layout between 21 November and 1 December 1936. Work then moved to Hilsea, the overhead at this point being realigned between 2 and 10 December 1936.

The realignment of the overhead wiring led to Cosham-bound trolleybuses hugging the left hand side of the road at Portsbridge and then crossing in front of traffic proceeding north along Northern Road when they had to make the right hand turn into Portsmouth Road. A newspaper criticised:

'They hug the left-hand side of the roundabout although they have to turn right. The result is that they foul a line of traffic. The trolleybus driver however has to be careful not to "unship" his pole while negotiating this bend, and he has to decide whether he will risk the chance of a breakdown by travelling on the inside curve or impede traffic by taking the outside course. It would appear that after all the trolleybus wires have not been placed in the best position.'

Here it should be remembered that a trolleybus driver will always endeavour to steer a wider radius around a corner than that of the overhead wiring.

A letter to the local press on 2 December 1936 complained that the destination screen display 'Cosham Red Lion' or 'Red Lion Cosham' was misleading as the alighting point was not at the hostelry but at the foot of Portsdown Hill, by the entrance to Queen Alexandra Hospital. As far as can be ascertained, passengers were never carried beyond this point southwards along London Road, Cosham and into Spur Road, although the Passenger Transport Committee approved proposals to make Cosham 'Red Lion' an unloading stage on 15 November 1938. Indeed the crews took this as an opportunity to use the public conveniences at the junction of Northern Road and London Road.

In general the press had responded favourably to the introduction of trolleybuses or 'trollybuses' as they insisted on naming them, although the *Evening News* commented that it required Herculean strength to make any impression on the half-drop window openers on some of the Cravens-bodied trolleybuses.

By 9 December 1936 there were 100 trolleybuses in stock, the largest number working on any one day during December 1936 being 87, and it was announced that the final deliveries of the Cravens-bodied AEC661Ts, 91–100, would not enter service until summer 1937. In November 1936 trolleybuses ran 166,686 miles over a network of 19.285 route miles, compared to 56,182 in November 1935 when only services 3, 3A, 4, 4A covering 9.4 route miles were trolleybus operated. As a result of having equipped AEC661Ts 25–100 with a 60 volt battery it had been necessary to change the voltage of the lamps, signal arm equipment and windscreen wipers at a cost of £1 2s 9d per vehicle, adding an additional £86 9s to the contract price.

In December 1936 the Chief Constable complained about the obstruction of the exit to the Fire Station by trolleybuses turning around (using their traction batteries) in the width of Park Road at the side of the Guildhall. Mr Hall suggested that trolleybuses could reverse into Nelson Square, which ran south from Park Road opposite the College of Science and Technology. The estimated cost of a reversing triangle and a long siding was £169 but the matter was not taken any further. After investigating a better solution for parking buses at The Hard, the General Manager suggested that the existing taxi rank be moved to the centre of the road and that buses use the vacated space. This was approved and he was instructed to liaise with the Chief Constable about moving the rank nearer to Harbour Station Approach.

Mr Hall first recommended the use of electrically-operated 'auto frogs' at important junctions in October 1936 and it is likely that these were installed immediately in conjunction with final tram-to-trolleybus conversions; however, formal approval to purchase 16 sets of Forest City equipment at a cost of £20 each plus installation was only given on 8 December 1936. These were installed at the following locations (there is some uncertainty about those marked with an asterisk):

Bellevue Terrace southbound, Southsea Terrace/Pier Road junction (Royal Pier Hotel)*
Bradford Road eastbound, Bradford Junction, Victoria Road North/Rugby Road junction*
Clarendon Road/Waverley Road junction (The Strand) westbound
Commercial Road northbound, Lake Road junction
Commercial Road northbound, Kingston Crescent ('Air Balloon') junction
Greetham Street westbound, Commercial Road junction (Guildhall Square)*
Guildhall Square, Commercial Road southbound, Commercial Road/Greetham Street junction
Guildhall Square, Commercial Road northbound, Commercial Road/Greetham Street junction
Guildhall Square, Commercial Road southbound, Commercial Road/Park Road junction
Highland Road/Festing Road junction ('Festing Hotel') westbound
Kings Terrace northbound, Alexandra Road/Landport Terrace junction*
Kingston Cross, London Road southbound, Kingston Road/Kingston Crescent junction
Kingston Road/New Road junction northbound
Kingston Road/Lake Road junction southbound
London Road/Northern Parade junction (Hilsea) southbound
Ordnance Row eastbound, Park Road/St. Georges Road junction

During December 1936, a curve from London Road into Gladys Avenue was installed enabling southbound trolleybuses to turn into North End Depot without having to de-pole at the junction. It remains unclear how those vehicles without traction batteries had managed to carry out this manoeuvre for the preceding two years!

On Christmas Day 1936 a 15-minute service operated from 10 a.m. to 4 p.m. It has proved impossible to establish if this skeleton service was operated by trolleybuses or indeed if they ever ran on Christmas Day services.

The road surface on the east side of Commercial Road beneath Portsmouth and Southsea Station railway bridge had to be lowered and the trolley wires were slewed towards the kerbside to provide sufficient clearance for the trolleybuses as evidenced by this view of AEC661T/Cravens 275. (Omnibus Society)

Mr F. H. Peacock, Assistant Engineer, who had only joined the Department in March 1936, resigned effective 16 January 1937 having obtained the appointment of General Manager and Engineer at Cleethorpes where the conversion from tram to trolleybus operation was underway. The Portsmouth Passenger Transport Committee was concerned that the salary he had been receiving may have been insufficient and the then salary of £350 rising by two annual increments of £25 to £400 p.a. was increased to £400 rising by four annual increments of £25 to a maximum of £500 p.a., and the vacant position advertised as Chief Assistant Engineer. Some 23 applications were received and having interviewed three candidates Mr J. E. Ash of Halifax Corporation Tramways was selected on 2 July 1937 subject to a medical examination. Unfortunately, he failed this examination and the post was advertised again in October 1937, resulting in the selection and appointment of Mr Chaceley T. Humpidge, Engineering Assistant, Liverpool Corporation Passenger Transport. He joined the undertaking in January 1938 taking on operational responsibility for the overhead line maintenance and traction power supply in addition to the motorbus and trolleybus fleet. Mr Humpidge was later to make his name in electric traction; however, Portsmouth only benefited from his services until July 1939 when he resigned to take up an appointment with Nottingham City Transport as Rolling Stock Superintendent.

At the beginning of 1937 it was proposed to divert trolleybus services 1 and 2 heading south along Northern Road along the existing private road into Cosham Compound to provide better facilities for passengers. The estimated cost for overhead equipment was £181 2s 7d but in fact the work was not carried out until 1942.

Clough Smith were still busy about the City during the early part of 1937, painting the many new traction poles and gantries. Their local presence probably led to the company being awarded the contract to change the overhead wiring layout at Clarence Pier, which, due to delays in altering the road layout there, had been strung as a simple turning circle above the tramway turning loop a few yards north of the intended terminus. The new roundabout and passenger loading bays were now complete, and work commenced with the planting of additional traction poles on 1 February 1937. While work was underway a temporary turning circle in Pier Road was used. The new terminal layout came into service on 9 May 1937.

In March 1937 two trolleybuses collided in Clarendon Road. The first vehicle had suffered a de-wirement and the second ran into the back of the first, damaging both.

When Mr Hall reported to the Passenger Transport Committee in February 1937 on the rising price of petrol and suggested that the trolleybus system should be extended. He was asked to investigate and report.

A constitutional crisis, culminating in the abdication of King Edward VIII before he was crowned, had been going on throughout 1936. National preparations for the coronation, scheduled for Wednesday 12 May 1937, were well underway and when he was succeeded by his younger brother it was decided not to further strain public opinion by changing the date. The Passenger Transport Committee resolved to put an amount of up to £400 aside for decorating the fleet to celebrate the Coronation of HM King George VI and Queen Elizabeth. It was decided to illuminate a trolleybus in the tradition of the electric trams at an estimated £200, AEC661T 4 being selected. The rest of the fleet were also to be decorated at a cost of about £160 whilst an illuminated model battleship

Trolleybus 4 especially decorated and illuminated for the Coronation of King George VI inside Eastney Depot. (City of Portsmouth Archives)

AEC661T trolleybus 4 decorated and illuminated for George VI's Coronation. (City of Portsmouth Archives)

An unidentified Cravens bodied trolleybus unloads at the steps of the Guildhall. Immediately to the rear HMS Coronation, an illuminated model battleship built around the Guildhall Square passenger waiting shelter to celebrate the Coronation of HM King George VI and Queen Elizabeth in May 1937, can be seen. (D.A.P. Janes collection)

Queen Victoria looks down on HMS Coronation dressed overall with a Cravens bodied trolleybus in the foreground. (Stephen Lockwood collection)

was to be placed on the roof of the Guildhall Square passenger waiting shelter. This latter materialised as HMS *Coronation* which encased the entire shelter. The Cosham Businessmen's Association was granted permission to attach decorations to the traction poles in Cosham subject to this not interfering with trolleybus operations.

This was a particularly busy period for the Department. Coronation Day was declared a Bank Holiday whilst on Thursday 20 May 1937, HM King George VI reviewed the fleet at Spithead, there being 160 ships present including five Royal Navy aircraft carriers and Germany's new pocket battleship *Graf Spee*. A number of temporary one-way streets for all traffic except buses were introduced for the Coronation period and in view of the large number of visitors to the City the police asked that two breakdown gangs be available to deal with any traffic obstructions. Trolleybuses 1–14 were noted parked in Blackfriars Road with their booms down that evening.

The daily trolleybus run-out published in April 1937 shows:

Winter Schedules

Weekday, off-peak service:	46 trolleybuses with 16 specials.
Saturday, off-peak service:	66 trolleybuses with 29 football specials.

Summer Schedules

Weekday, off-peak service:	63 trolleybuses with 16 specials.
Saturday:	82 trolleybuses required.
Bank Holidays and Navy Days:	99 trolleybuses required.

It is understood that unnumbered extras operated between the Dockyard and Clarence Pier during the summer holiday periods 1937–39.

Trolleybus services for year ending 31 March 1937

	1936–37	1935–36
Net total income	£96,097	£37,026
Working expenses	£77,488	£25,173
Gross surplus	£18,609	£11,854
Interest on bank balance	£518	£290
Capital charges, etc.	£18,266	£6,909
(incl. revenue charges and income tax)		
Net Profit	£861	£5,235
Mileage	1,543,874	567,685
Passengers	15,603,291	6,196,798

Numbers and percentage of the total of passengers at the several fares stages

778,903	at ½d fare cash	5%	£1,622 14s 4d
6,573,810	at 1d	42.13%	£27,390 17s 6d
3,583,101	at 1½d	22.97%	£22,394 7s 7½d
2,204,727	at 2d	14.13%	£18,372 14s 6d
783,258	at 2½d	5.02%	£8,158 18s 9d
995,230	at 3d	6.38%	£12,440 7s 6d
37,763	at 3½d	0.24%	£550 14s 2½d
117,461	at 1d Exchange	0.75%)	£723 19s 4½d (sic)*
55,279	at 1½d	0.35%)	
138	at 2d	0.00%)	(*actually £836 1s 3½d)
221,800	Workmen's returns	2.84%	£2,592 19s 2½d
30,021	Vouchers, Special Buses	0.19%	£63 1s 1d
	School and season tickets		£542 2s 10d
15,603,291			£94,852 16s 11d

Average stage lengths and corresponding fare charge:

Services	1d	1½ d	2d	2½d	3d	3½d Miles
1 & 2	0.91	1.34	1.78	2.20	3.64	4.23
3 & 4	0.94	1.40	1.92	2.14	3.38	
5 & 6	0.90	1.40	1.86	2.37	3.06	
11 & 12	0.91	1.27	1.79	2.12	2.56	
15 & 16	0.94	1.29	1.85	2.28	2.81	
17 & 18	0.91	1.38	1.89	2.41	2.94	
Average	0.92	1.35	1.85	2.25	3.06	4.23

Average fare per mile on all routes 0.98d

1,116 regular staff

Officers and staff	49
Motorbus and trolleybus drivers	361
Conductors	350
Inspectors and timekeepers	31
Other traffic employees	19
Trolleybus shed employees	146
Motorbus shed employees	139
Overhead	21

Fleet:
132 motorbuses
100 trolley vehicles
5 Sea front runabouts
1 Daimler car
2 motor tower wagons
1 horse tower wagon
4 vans and lorries

In June 1937 it was agreed to award members of the National Federation of Vehicle Workers a retrospective increase of ½d per hour from the first pay week in April and a further ½d per hour from June. However, a request for increased wages from Inspector Warren, as he was the Certifying Officer for Trolley Vehicle Drivers, was not granted. These were soon followed by torrent of applications for increased salaries from different groups of workers and officials. The NJIC for the Road Passenger Transport Industry awarded 2s per week for adult employees and 1s for those under 21 years of age effective from first full pay period in December 1937. This was estimated to increase the Department's costs by £4,098 16s p.a. with an additional sum of £90 during the season, making £5,000 p.a. overall. An application for an increase of wages of ¾d per hour effective 1 December 1937 was received from the NJIC for the Electricity Supply Industry effecting 33 employees including 17 overhead linesmen and two electrical fitters. As the result of a survey of other towns, the salary of Mr Hall, General Manager and Engineer, was also increased, from £1,200 to £1,350, by three annual increments of £50.

During the morning of the 24 July 1937, following a collision with a coach and a cyclist, an unidentified trolleybus ran into a traction pole at the junction of Park Road and St. Michael's Road. A further accident involving a trolleybus occurred on 5 August 1937 when a trolley boom broke free and fell on a boy in Commercial Road.

In September 1937, the General Manager stated that, as a result of the trolleybuses' success, it had been seriously suggested that the petrol buses should be replaced by trolleybuses. He was evaluating the matter. In May 1938 he was elected to a Special Committee of the Electrical Development Association on Trolleybus Research. However, the overhead wiring which Estler Bros. had installed in 1935 between Southsea South Parade Pier and London Road, Hilsea via Bradford Junction, the Guildhall and Alexandra Park, had proved unsatisfactory with 18 breaks in the trolley wires. On 11 October 1937 it was decided to renew these wires at a cost of £2,000. Estler Bros. were now in liquidation. The renewal costs were comparatively low as sub-contractors had shown flexibility with a fee of £750 plus £500 for the cost of the wire. Nonetheless, by the end of the year, Mr Hall reported that a total of £1,506 more than expected had been spent on the conversion of the overhead equipment and it was decided to apply for a supplementary loan sanction rather than charge this to the Revenue Account.

Following a serious illness Alderman Sir John Timpson, who had been Chairman of the Passenger Transport Committee and a close political ally of the Department since 1917, died on 19 October 1937. He was succeeded by Alderman W. S. R. Pugsley who remained in office until his death in 1942.

There were a number of incidents involving trolleybuses in the summer and autumn of 1937. Olive McNally, a 15-year-old cyclist, collided with trolleybus 86 in London Road on 15 June 1937 and died as a result of her injuries. This accident was followed by two suicides: on 24 July 1937 William France threw himself in front of trolleybus 7 in Fratton Road at Fitzroy Street, and on 23 September 1937 D. Harrigan did the same in front of no. 33 in Albert Road. On 2 October 1937 part of a house fell on to the back of a trolleybus in Broad Street, Old Portsmouth, whilst on 13 November 1937 a trolleybus caught fire in Spur Road, Cosham.

Removal of the tram track in the narrow New Road necessitated its closure on 17 November 1937. Motorbuses running along a variety of parallel streets replaced trolleybuses on services 11, 12, 15, 16 for the duration of the work. Trolleybuses returned to the Copnor Bridge services on 31 May 1938, although tram track lifting in Lake Road still delayed some journeys. It was decided that in future tram track removal and associated road works would be carried out on one side of the road at a time thereby allowing trolleybus services to continue without interruption. Ominously it was decided to retain the lengths of tram rail removed and place them in store for use in the construction of air raid shelters.

As the trolleybuses were still operating in accordance with the Tramway Byelaws, the Town Clerk suggested that new Trolley Vehicle Byelaws should be prepared and he was asked to submit a suitable draft. No progress was made for 12 months and then the matter was placed in abeyance for a year.

Following a review of the Department's organisation (the number of vehicles owned and required in relation to revenue and capital expenditure) by a special committee in February 1938, they recommended reductions in motorbus services and some trolleybus timetable revisions. The Council were asked to lay down a definite policy as to whether the undertaking was to:

1. Run at a reasonable profit for the general good of the City.
2. Be commercially self-supporting
3. Run for the convenience of the public, special classes of workers, football crowds, visitors, etc., any loss being borne by the rates.

Loan charges would fall considerably (all amounts in £s):

	1938–39	1939–40	1940–41	1941–42	1942–43
Abandoned tram track	15,333	14,778	4,621	3,639	2,331
Motorbuses	17,343	16,729	12,507	7,618	–
Depots	6,228	6,090	5,952	5,814	5,676
Trolleybus	32,360	31,306	30,252	29,199	25,828
Overhead	4,316	4,199	4,082	3,965	3,848
Total loan	75,580	73,102	57,414	50,235	37,683

It was rumoured that there had been a number of incidents in which trolleybuses had attempted to overtake other trolley vehicles, the driver mistaking them for motorbuses, with disastrous results. Whether this was the reason or the change was made for administrative convenience cannot be confirmed, however, during the period 5 to 8 April 1938, the entire trolleybus fleet was renumbered 201–300. It was hoped that this would make trolleybuses more easily identifiable to other CPPTD drivers. An additional figure or figures were transferred before the existing fleet number on the front and rear panels, resulting in the new fleet numbers being offset until the vehicles were repainted. The fleet numbers were also carried internally on a white oval plastic disc, screwed to the front bulkhead in the lower saloon and between the front windows on the top deck. These discs were unscrewed and reversed, the new fleet numbers being painted on, as before, in black.

On Saturday evening 14 May 1938, six-year-old David Grant ran into the road and was knocked down by a trolleybus in Greetham Street. He died in the ambulance on the way to the Royal Hospital as a result of his injuries.

Mr Hall was elected in May 1938 to serve on the Special Committee of the Electrical Development Association on Trolleybus Research.

In May 1938 the Milton and Southsea Ratepayer's Association complained that loading and unloading of buses on the Esplanade adjacent to Southsea South Parade Pier was dangerous. They suggested that to avoid accidents loading bays should be constructed or the steps continued east of the pier entrance. The Association also recommended that all vehicles coming from Festing Road should unload in the turning circle at the west end of the Canoe Lake. The Passenger Transport Committee considered such changes impossible.

On 17 May 1938 the newspapers published an article on the undertaking's financial position:

'The outstanding point is that the undertaking is struggling with the burden of the loan on the old tramways. The trams have been abolished, the lines are in the process of being removed at considerable expense, but the money borrowed to pay for the vehicles and track has not been entirely repaid and this is a severe drag which will continue for another three years. It is unfortunate that the charges on the trolley buses should be at their heaviest at this time, but the fact is that the changeover from trams to buses was made earlier than it should have been, from a financial point of view. After 1941 the position will be easier and the prospect of prosperity is encouraging.'

It continued:

'As the disturbances caused by road construction declines, and the loan charges lessen, both the "dead" portion for tramways and the "live" part for trolleybuses, the Passenger

The 1938 trolleybus fleet renumbering saw an additional figure transferred in advance of the original fleet number causing the number to be offset as can be seen on 240 photographed in Guildhall Square on an unscheduled journey to Eastney. The whole-side, hand-painted advertisement for Street's Dairies appeared on many of Portsmouth's trolleybuses. (D.A.P. Janes collection [photographer's name not recorded])

Recently renumbered AEC661T/ Cravens 279 at Canoe Lake terminus, Southsea South Parade Pier, prior to departure to Cosham Railway Station on a service 4A working. (D.A.P. Janes collection [photographer's name not recorded])

Transport Undertaking may be expected to show again the old profit which in the past did the City such good service.'

At about 10 p.m. during the evening of 29 May 1938 gale force winds caused the northbound positive conductor wire to break and fall into the road on Portsbridge disrupting services for a short time. Newspaper reports referred to the difficulties affecting the earlier trolleybuses not equipped with traction batteries: these vehicles had to be parked on the south side of Portsbridge and their passengers transferred to vehicles equipped with traction batteries to continue their journeys.

No doubt prompted by a series of complaints in the newspapers about the black smelly exhaust fumes forthcoming from Portsmouth motorbuses, in June 1938 the Chairman of the Transport Committee stated that 'oil buses have come to an end'. Nonetheless as an economy the Passenger Transport Committee recommended that service intervals on the main routes should be reduced from 10 to 12 minutes for the winter timetable period 1938–39.

A fire broke out on the roof of a trolleybus heading to Twyford Avenue, possibly due to a fuse, in Commercial Road during the afternoon of 2 July 1938. The driver had dealt with the matter by the time that the fire brigade arrived on the scene.

Plans to improve the overhead line layout at Portsbridge at an estimated cost of £172 were first discussed in July 1938 and carried out in March 1939. The northbound right-hand auto frog installed in March 1937 at Western Road was replaced by a 25° 'Y' auto frog on the south side of Portsbridge Creek opposite Southdown's Hilsea Garage. Parallel wiring was installed across the bridge enabling trolleybuses to position themselves in the appropriate traffic lane, left for Cosham 'Red Lion' and right for Cosham Railway Station. The southbound right-hand auto frog at Hilsea roundabout was set back some distance to the north enabling trolleybuses turning into Northern Parade to use the correct traffic lane.

Despite having a contract to supply timetables until 1940, Messrs Pearl, Dean and Pearl gave 3 months notice to cease publication after 30 September 1938. The Portsmouth firm of Charpentier & Co. were prepared to supply 10,000 copies p.a. subject to the Corporation guaranteeing six full pages of ...ments at £6 10s per page. This offer was accepted ...tober 1938 and in due course extended until ...40.

Portsmouth Trades Council asked in September 1938 that pensioners should be given free travel on the Corporation's vehicles. Mr Hall reported that similar requests were receiving consideration at a national level by the Municipal Tramways and Transport Association (MTTA) and that an area meeting addressing the topic would be held shortly. This meeting indicated that no municipal transport undertakings were in favour of introducing cheap or free travelling facilities. On 20 December 1938 the Transport Committee reviewed the MTTA report and its recommendations that, as the number of concessions already granted had seriously affected transport undertaking revenues, any further fare concessions should be charged to local authority funds, or in the case of disabled ex-servicemen, national pension funds.

In October 1938 plans to make Stamshaw Road (southbound) and Twyford Avenue (northbound) one-way streets were announced. Changes to the overhead equipment were estimated to cost ca. £1,000, all costs being borne by the Roads, Works and Drainage Committee. The Town Clerk was asked to take the necessary steps to obtain a Provisional Order for the operation of trolley vehicles through Stamshaw Road. Soon afterwards Cosham 'Red Lion' was made both a loading and unloading stage for trolley vehicles.

From the mid-1930s it became increasingly evident that Germany's expansionist aims would, sooner or later, make armed conflict inevitable. The British government was outwardly following a policy of appeasement; the horrors of the First World War and the aerial bombardments of the Spanish Civil War still being very real in the minds of much of the population. From early 1935 defence spending increased markedly after years of under-investment and the expansion of reservist forces slowly began. However, at the time of the September 1938 Munich Crisis, Britain was in no fit state to defend itself.

Some 38 reservists in the undertaking were called up for service during September 1938. An air raid exercise took place on 30 November 1938 involving imaginary damage in Edmund Road, Southsea. The Overhead Lines Department was involved: scaffolding represented a fallen traction pole and 30ft of rope some fallen overhead equipment. That night there were 12 different exercises involving 200 people. The city's Passive Air Defence Committee advised that, in their evacuation scheme, they had included the CPPTD motorbus fleet. By the end of

Recently renumbered AEC661T 285 turns off Southsea South Parade into Clarendon Road on a service 4A journey to Cosham Railway Station. The impressive South Parade Pier is evident behind the trolleybus. (Malcolm Pearce [photographer G.O.P. Pearce])

April 1939, 134 employees had enlisted in the Reserve Forces. Aware of the strategic necessity of a road bridge across Ports Creek an emergency bridge was constructed to the east of Portsbridge which remained in use until 1967–68.

At the junction of Gladys Avenue with Northern Parade, the Corporation owned a plot of land used as allotments but intended for use as a bus terminus. Portsmouth United Breweries, who intended to build a public house on the site, had owned the plot, but permission had been refused as there were other public houses nearby. In February 1939 the Passive Air Defence Committee's request to dig air raid trenches there was refused as construction work for the terminus was due to commence at the beginning of the next financial year. Site clearance began on 21 April 1939 and the work was completed on 25 May 1939 although the terminus was used solely for motorbus services until September 1942 or shortly thereafter.

Tram track removal in Blackfriars Road and Eastney Road, between Bransbury Park (about ¼ mile south of Milton 'White House') and Eastney Depot, necessitated single line traffic over these sections in February 1939. Bracket arms and the southbound overhead wiring in London Road, Hilsea were brought down when a tree being felled by Corporation workmen toppled into the road on 21 February 1939.

On 18 April 1939 it was decided to give Hants Relay Ltd. one year's notice to terminate the agreement for their use of traction poles to suspend their broadcast relay system but to offer them a new contract at the rate of 1s per pole.

Elderly Walter Furness died in hospital after being hit by a southbound trolleybus as he crossed the road near the Rex Cinema in Fratton Road during the evening of 21 April 1939.

In June 1939 the charge per unit for traction current, based on the basic fee plus the amount representing the rise in the cost of coal clause, increased from 0.635d to 0.830d and annual consumption rose from 5,656,508 to 6,105,319 units. This increased trolleybus operating costs per mile from 1.469d to 1.677d.

As hurried preparations for war continued the civilian population endeavoured to enjoy the rather poor summer weather and the trolleybus timetable was somewhat enhanced:

1 Cosham *Red Lion* – Clarence Pier
2 Clarence Pier – Cosham *Red Lion*
Together these services required six vehicles providing a 10-minute frequency.
3 Cosham Railway Station – Southsea *South Parade Pier*
3A Southsea *South Parade Pier* – Cosham Railway Station
Circular route working with service 3 commenced.
4 Cosham Railway Station – Southsea *South Parade Pier*
4A Southsea *South Parade Pier* – Cosham Railway Station
Together these services required nine vehicles providing a 10-minute frequency.
5 Dockyard *Main Gate* – Royal Pier Hotel – Southsea *South Parade Pier* – Festing Hotel – Eastney – Milton *White House* – Fratton Bridge – Bradford Junction – Guildhall
6 Guildhall – Bradford Junction – Fratton Bridge – Milton *White House* – Eastney – Festing Hotel – Southsea *South Parade Pier* – Royal Pier Hotel – Dockyard *Main Gate*
Together these services required eight vehicles providing a 10-minute frequency.
11 Copnor Bridge – Dockyard *Main Gate*
12 Dockyard *Main Gate* – Copnor Bridge
Together these services required four vehicles providing a 10-minute frequency.
15 Copnor Bridge – Floating Bridge
16 Floating Bridge – Copnor Bridge
Together these services required four vehicles providing a 10-minute frequency.
17 Dockyard *Main Gate* – Eastney – Milton *White House* – Dockyard *Main Gate*
18 Dockyard *Main Gate* – Milton *White House* – Eastney – Dockyard *Main Gate*
Together these services required nine vehicles providing a 10-minute frequency.

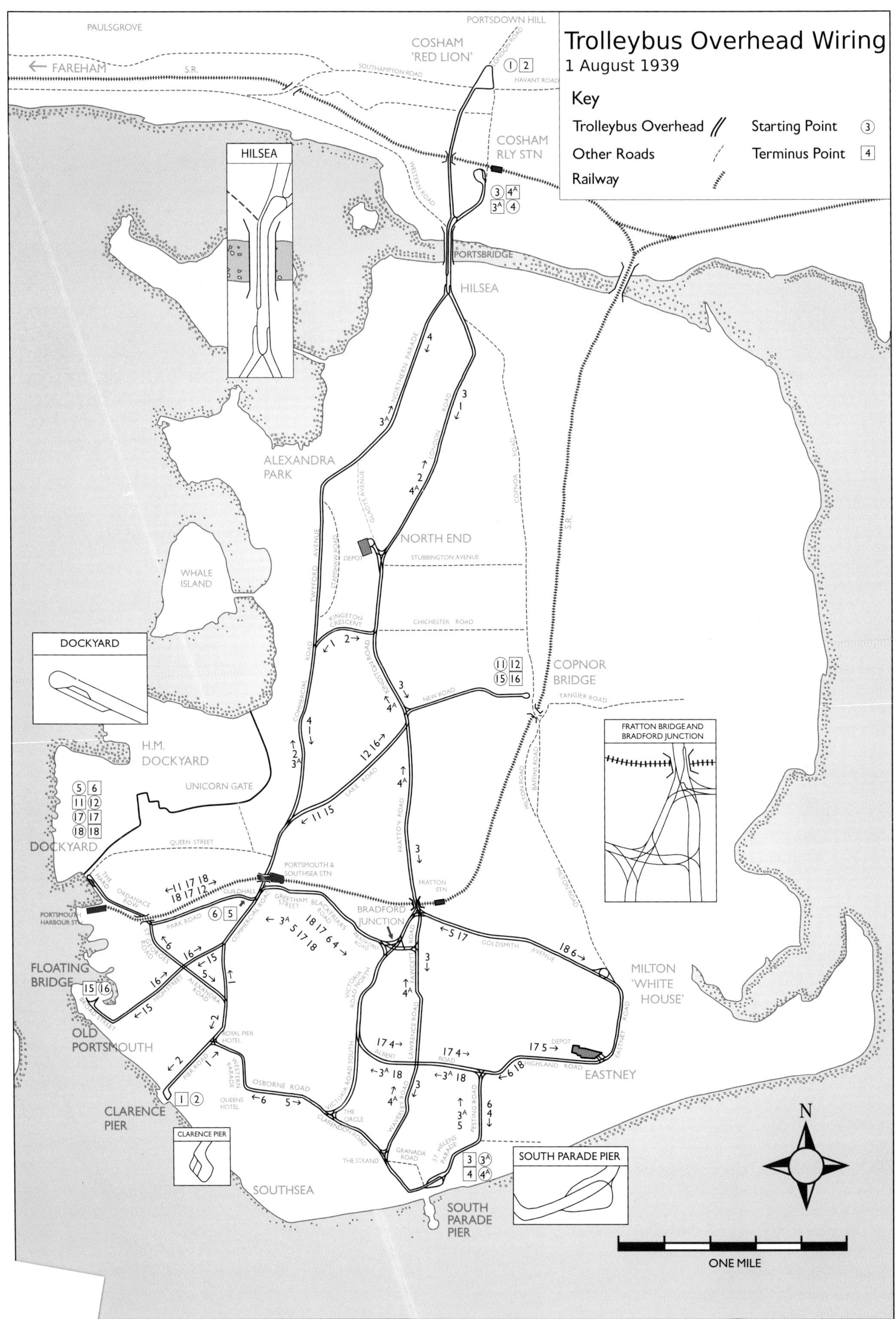

Trolleybus Overhead Wiring
1 August 1939
Key
Trolleybus Overhead
Other Roads
Railway
Starting Point
Terminus Point
PAULSGROVE
PORTSDOWN HILL
COSHAM 'RED LION'
FAREHAM
S.R.
SOUTHAMPTON ROAD
LONDON ROAD
HAVANT ROAD
COSHAM RLY STN
WESTERN ROAD
PORTSBRIDGE
HILSEA
NORTHERN PARADE
ALEXANDRA PARK
WHALE ISLAND
NORTH END
GLADYS AVENUE
DEPOT
STUBBINGTON AVENUE
COPNOR ROAD
STAMSHAW ROAD
TWYFORD AVENUE
KINGSTON CRESCENT
CHICHESTER ROAD
KINGSTON ROAD
NEW ROAD
COPNOR BRIDGE
TANGIER ROAD
COMMERCIAL ROAD
LAKE ROAD
FRATTON ROAD
BAFFINS ROAD
MILTON ROAD
DOCKYARD
H.M. DOCKYARD
UNICORN GATE
QUEEN STREET
THE HARD
PORTSMOUTH & SOUTHSEA STN
FRATTON STN
GUILDHALL
ORDNANCE ROW
PORTSMOUTH HARBOUR STN
PARK ROAD
GREETHAM STREET
BLACKFRIARS ROAD
BRADFORD JUNCTION
BRADFORD ROAD
GOLDSMITH AVENUE
FLOATING BRIDGE
ST. GEORGES ROAD
HIGH STREET
ALEXANDRA ROAD
BROAD STREET
OLD PORTSMOUTH
ROYAL PIER HOTEL
PIER ROAD
WESTERN PARADE
VICTORIA ROAD NORTH
FAWCETT ROAD
MILTON 'WHITE HOUSE'
EASTNEY ROAD
ALBERT ROAD
LAWRENCE ROAD
HIGHLAND ROAD
EASTNEY
OSBORNE ROAD
VICTORIA ROAD SOUTH
WAVERLEY ROAD
FESTING ROAD
CLARENCE PIER
QUEENS HOTEL
THE CIRCLE
CLARENDON ROAD
THE STRAND
GRANADA ROAD
ST. HELENS PARADE
SOUTHSEA
SOUTH PARADE PIER
HILSEA
DOCKYARD
FRATTON BRIDGE AND BRADFORD JUNCTION
CLARENCE PIER
SOUTH PARADE PIER
N
ONE MILE

CHAPTER 5

ON THE FRONT LINE

During the Second World War, Portsmouth was bombed extensively, indeed between July 1940 and July 1944 the city was attacked 67 times destroying many houses and the Guildhall. In addition to the many deaths and injuries in HM Dockyard and the naval establishments, 930 civilians were killed and nearly 3,000 others were injured. As the war progressed, the population dropped by one third, although the military presence expanded considerably with Nissen-hutted camps springing up in the surrounding areas.

In July 1939 the government published its Evacuation Scheme whereby infants and children living in potentially vulnerable industrial and strategic towns could be registered for evacuation to safer areas. Portsmouth was Britain's most important naval base and the Royal Navy had the largest fleet in the world. Situated just over 80 miles from the French coast the city was an obvious enemy target. The city's plans were based on the Southern Railway (SR) conveying 27,544 children from Portsmouth and Southsea Station over a 2-day period with a further 36,970 embarking at Clarence Pier on SR steamers for the Isle of Wight over three days. CPPTD and SMS motorbuses would carry the evacuees to the station or Clarence Pier.

A number of rehearsals involving individual schools took place in late July and early August 1939. The political situation deteriorated so much that the plans were put into effect on 1 September 1939 with 12,246 of Portsmouth's schoolchildren being sent to reception areas in Hampshire, Wiltshire and the Isle of Wight. Fewer children than expected were evacuated; nonetheless, almost half of all schoolchildren left in the first 4 days. This major logistical effort involved some 2,000 helpers, 80 motorbuses, 20 trains and three ferries.

As a large proportion of the CPPTD motorbus fleet was committed to the evacuation, three additional trolleybus services commenced on 1 September 1939 to partially replace motorbus services. The services were undesignated:

i. Copnor Bridge – Fratton Bridge – Fawcett Road – Osborne Road – Clarence Pier.
Partly replacing motorbus services K and L
ii. Cosham *Red Lion* – North End – Kingston Crescent – Guildhall – Royal Pier Hotel – Osborne Road – Southsea *South Parade Pier.*
Partly replacing motorbus services A and B
iii. Cosham Railway Station – Hilsea – North End – Fratton Bridge – Victoria Road – Osborne Road – Guildhall – Royal Pier Hotel – Kingston Crescent – North End.
Partly replacing motorbus services I and J

The official notice of these service alterations only appeared on 6 September 1939.

Both services i and ii ceased on 24 September 1939. Service iii was the first scheduled trolleybus service to run along Victoria Road South: it continued to operate and may possibly have continued to become the basis of the circular services 1 and 2 in July 1940.

An absolute 'black-out' was introduced on 1 September 1939. All external lighting whatsoever, whether from street lamps, shop fronts, private homes, torches or cigarettes, was prohibited and traffic groped along on side lights during the hours of darkness. In addition to the difficulties and inconvenience, there was a dramatic increase in the number of road accidents. A trolleybus hit young Miss Fagot of North End, on 16 September 1939 injuring her and damaging her bicycle. In February 1940 an *ex gratia* payment of £5 was sent to her father. Progressively 'black-out' hoods were fitted to vehicle headlamps and traffic lights, white lines were painted along the centre of the road and kerbs, and a 20 m.p.h. night time speed limit was introduced. At an early date in the war, possibly by October 1939, last departures from the city centre were brought forward from around 11.30 p.m. to about 10.30 p.m. A fire engine was stationed in North End depot and air raid shelters were built outside whilst in December 1939 the Eastney offices were sandbagged and shuttered.

Commencing in October 1939 vehicles were dispersed at night in an effort to minimise losses should bombs fall on a depot. A number of trolleybuses in regular use were dispersed to Northern Parade: each night a vehicle and a driver from the immediate vicinity were on hand to tow the trolleybuses away in the event of fire. As trolleybuses 201–224 were not equipped with traction batteries, something that could prove embarrassing in the case of damage to the overhead equipment, they were placed in open storage on an area of concrete specially laid on waste ground to the east of Northern Parade (the location of today's Conan Road, Doyle Avenue and Wyllie Road) after the 1940 summer season. The prototype trolleybuses 201–215 had been little used once the main AEC661T fleet arrived. Nos 201–211 were licensed for 6 months in summer 1939 and for 5 months in summer 1940 before being de-licensed at the end of September 1940. Three-axle 212–215 were de-licensed for much of 1939–40. Turning to the English Electric bodied AEC661Ts, 216–219 were licensed for 6 months in summer 1939 and for 5 months in summer 1940, before being de-licensed at the end of September 1940. No. 220 was used continually from its initial entry into service, except for 2 months in 1939, until de-licensed in November 1940; and 221–224 were mainly continually in service until de-licensed in September 1940. A pattern of summer season usage only for these vehicles had become evident and as the population began to fall CPPTD could accommodate the reduced number of trolleybuses available for service.

Operations were scaled back to allow for the reduced traffic resulting from the evacuation, less pronounced peak hours caused by the introduction of irregular working hours, the 'black-out' and fuel rationing. Although 130 employees had been called-up for the forces and all seasonal workers dismissed there remained a surplus of 52 traffic and over 20 depot staff, and thus a meeting with the TGWU was arranged. It was suggested that all employees lose one day a month or that they work a 45½ hour week and be paid accordingly. The TGWU rejected these alternatives and insisted on the department respecting the NJIC agreement guaranteeing the working week. No action was taken in the belief that after allowing for the gradual absorption of further employees into the forces it was likely that the situation would soon resolve itself. By the end of October 1939 the number of traffic staff had indeed fallen to the required level however there were still 13 surplus workshop employees and it was decided to terminate their employment in January 1940. By then that figure had fallen to just four and they were retained to redecorate the administrative offices. In view of the reduction in services the vacancy for Assistant Chief Engineer was not filled.

In October 1939 the southern end of Twyford Avenue was widened on the east side and some new traction poles erected. In November 1939 an application was made for a Provisional Order under Section 32 of the Portsmouth Corporation Act 1930 authorising the use of trolley vehicles on the proposed Twyford Avenue and Stamshaw Road one way traffic scheme. However the MoT responded that they would not be issuing any one way street orders during the prevailing 'emergency' and on 20 February 1940 plans for the scheme were abandoned for the duration of the war.

Efforts were made to make the vehicles less conspicuous from the air. In September 1939 the roof tops of the motorbus and trolleybus fleets were hurriedly painted matt grey although the upper-deck window surrounds, waistband and rear dome on each side of the emergency exit door remained white. To comply with lighting regulations the saloon windows were lacquered and 'black-out' hoods were fitted to trolleybus headlamps in November 1939 whilst to increase visibility the top of the front mudguards, the lifeguards beneath the body, the cab door steps and the beading at the bottom of the body at the rear, were painted white. During January 1940, the grey painted area was extended down to the upper deck waistband at the rear thereby including the dome and emergency exit door, and the lower three treads of the staircase were painted white. Later on in the war, on 15 March 1942 number 289 appeared with the upper deck front and side pillars also painted grey but this was the sole trolleybus to be so treated.

Interior lighting was reduced by applying blue lacquer to the light bulbs, but these proved unsatisfactory and during the early part of 1940 dulled light bulbs were adopted instead. During September 1941 a sheet of white paper, about 18in. by 12in., was pasted on the ceiling in both saloons, above those lamp sockets which retained a bulb. The paper was a better reflector of light than the dull ceilings.

There were fears that electric arcing from trolleybuses would be visible to enemy aircraft and during the course of 1939 carbon insert slider heads progressively replaced trolley wheels thereby reducing the risk of flashing and reducing wear on the overhead equipment. Mr Hall designed shields which were fitted above breakers, crossings and frogs in the wiring where flashing could be anticipated. Later in the war, tests carried out by the Ministry of War Transport (MoWT) in the Nottingham area recorded that an hour's observation from an altitude of 2,500ft showed only half a dozen weak and occasional flashes which were visible at up to 3 miles distance. In comparison to those produced by the SR 3-rail electric trains, the flashing produced by Portsmouth's trolleybuses was thus insignificant.

Wartime inflation had already started and the Passenger Transport Committee found itself handling wage demands that continued at regular intervals throughout the hostilities and which they could hardly refuse. The NJIC for the Road Passenger Transport Industry recommended a war wage of 4s per week to all adult employees with commensurate increases to juveniles effective from 7 December 1939. Although estimated to increase expenditure by £7,800 p.a., it was accepted for the duration of the war. Similar increases for electricians and vehicle builders soon followed. In view of the increases the Council decided on 9 January 1940 that the Passenger Transport Committee should consider revising services and fares to meet the additional costs. It was proposed that application be made to abolish Workmen's Fares until the war was over. At the end of March 1940 the MoWT and the RTC informed the Committee that they were not prepared to make an Order relaxing the obligation placed upon the Corporation by Section 31 of the Portsmouth Corporation Act 1930 to offer workmen's fares. The Passenger Transport Committee decided to review the situation again in June 1940 at the earliest and appointed a Special Subcommittee to consider all existing services, fares and fare stages. One of the first recommendations was to consider alternative fuels and to make maximum use of trolley vehicles using cheaper and home-produced energy.

By April 1940 there was a shortage of male traffic staff and permission was granted to recruit women conductors. It was soon decided that there should be no age limits or distinction between single, married or widow applicants, whilst there was no objection to employing employees' wives. Councillor Mrs Childs agreed to assist the CPPTD in selecting a suitable female uniform. Understandably by June 1940 it was felt that there should be a female supervisor for the conductresses and on 23 July 1940, having considered three candidates, Mrs M. A. Hyde was appointed at a rate of pay 10s above conductresses' pay. The conductresses received a waterproofed tunic with leather cuffs, skirt and cap. Due to the shortage of men, it was decided to employ female vehicle cleaners although they were not issued with protective clothing. By December 1941 it had been decided to offer part-time employment to married women as peak hour conductresses. Within a month 24 women were in training, a uniform overcoat and cap being provided. It is important to note how, in those less egalitarian times, the women responded excellently to the trying and often dangerous circumstances.

The MoWT encouraged undertakings to train women to drive single-deck motorbuses and the General Manager was authorised to train women with driving experience. The first woman to qualify on a trolleybus was Mrs K. E. Devine in October 1941. By 20 June 1942 there were ten female trolleybus drivers and the total eventually reached 20, seven of whom were licensed to drive both motorbuses and trolleybuses. General Manager Ben Hall wrote in the June 1944 *Bus and Coach* that he thought women 'possessed that light touch which makes for good manipulation of the power controls and rheostatic braking'. By 1945 there were almost 500 female drivers and conductors and in 1947 seven women drivers were still at work.

Plans to widen the private road from Northern Road to Cosham Railway Station at an estimated cost of £200 plus £233 for overhead line alterations were approved on 21 May 1940.

Due to a series of wage increases expected to cost almost £6,000 p.a., on 30 July 1940 the Passenger Transport Committee adopted their Subcommittee's recommendation to abolish all 1d fares (½d children) and introduce a 1½d minimum fare (1d children) for the duration of the war. The new minimum fare was introduced on 9 October 1940.

Interestingly the April–May 1940 timetable shows that portions of motorbus services I and J, namely between North End and Palmerston Road via Fratton and via the Guildhall on weekdays and on Sundays between Cosham

One of Portsmouth's wartime female trolleybus crews. (National Tramway Museum [Transport World magazine])

and Southsea South Parade Pier via Fratton Road, were operated by trolleybus. On weekdays this service duplicated services 1 and 2 between Royal Pier Hotel and Cosham. The trolleybus-operated portions of service I and J were merged with trolleybus services 1 and 2 either on 5 July 1940 when the seafront was closed or on 21 July 1940. The service designation was not shown on the number blinds.

I North End *Junction* – Fratton Bridge – Victoria Road – Southsea *The Circle* – Palmerston Road – Royal Pier Hotel – Guildhall – Kingston Crescent – North End *Junction*
Unidirectional circular service (anticlockwise), weekdays only

J North End *Junction* – Kingston Crescent – Guildhall – Royal Pier Hotel – Palmerston Road – Southsea *The Circle* – Victoria Road – Fratton Bridge – North End *Junction*
Unidirectional circular service (clockwise), weekdays only

I North End *Junction* – Fratton Bridge – Victoria Road – Southsea *The Circle* – Southsea *The Strand* – Southsea *South Parade Pier*
Unidirectional southbound service, Sunday only. Extended to originate at Cosham Railway Station Sunday afternoons (from 1.39 pm) only

J Southsea *South Parade Pier* – Southsea *The Strand* – Southsea *The Circle* – Victoria Road – Fratton Bridge – North End *Junction* – North End *Junction*
Unidirectional northbound service, Sunday only. Extended to terminate at Cosham Railway Station Sunday afternoons (from 1.11 pm) only

During the summer of 1940 'City of Portsmouth' was painted out from the legal lettering at the base of the nearside panels and 'Portsmouth Corporation' was no longer displayed in the lower indicator box at front and rear of trolleybuses 216–300 for security reasons.

The following public notice appeared in the local press in June 1940 relating to destination displays:

> Users of the Corporation trolley vehicles and motor omnibuses are hereby notified that by order of the Ministry of Transport and in the interests of Home Security, destination indicators on vehicles must not show a terminus at which a Government establishment, camp or aerodrome is situated.
>
> This instruction means that for the time being, destination on the C/D, 5/6, 11/12 and 17/18 routes will not show 'Dockyard' and C/D route vehicles will not show 'City Airport'.
>
> This prohibition will affect both special and workman's services.
> Signed
> E. J. Sparkes
> Town Clerk

This was achieved by masking the top of the large rectangular indicator boxes with black tape so that the final destination on the blind was no longer visible.

Due to the impending risk of invasion, on 5 July 1940 the seafront was closed to the public and trolleybus services were withdrawn from Southsea South Parade between The Strand and the south end of Festing Road, and from Pier Road between the Royal Pier Hotel and Clarence Pier. Services 4 and 6 travelling south along Festing Road reversed at the junction with St. Helens Parade and Eastern Parade; services 3 and 5 travelling south along Waverley Road and Clarendon Road respectively terminated at The Strand; and services 1 and 2 which served Clarence Pier are believed to have reversed at the junction with Southsea Terrace. In all cases the reversing manoeuvre was carried out using the vehicle's traction batteries although the overhead wiring junction at each point could have provided a makeshift reversing triangle by the expedient of changing the frog springing thereby avoiding the risk of flashes in the 'black-out'. Plans survive for a reversing triangle at either Kenilworth Road, which runs parallel to Waverley Road to the west of The Strand junction, or at St Helens Park Crescent, Clarendon Road, to the east of the junction with a reverse into Eastern Villas Road. In May 1942 the Kenilworth Road location, which would have offered reversing facilities for vehicles in Clarendon Road arriving from both east and west, was selected as the preferred option but as the seafront re-opened to trolleybuses in June 1942 nothing was constructed.

In view of these complicated turning arrangements on 21 July 1940 services 1 and 2 (Cosham 'Red Lion' – Royal Pier Hotel) were extended from the Royal Pier Hotel back to North End via Osborne Road, The Circle, Bradford Junction and Fratton Road; services 3 and 4A (Cosham Railway Gates – The Strand) were extended to operate to and from the Dockyard; and services 3A and 4 (Cosham Railway Station – Festing Road) were extended from Festing Road junction to the Guildhall via Eastney and Milton 'White House' and Blackfriars Road. Services 5 and 6 were withdrawn entirely. This reorganisation

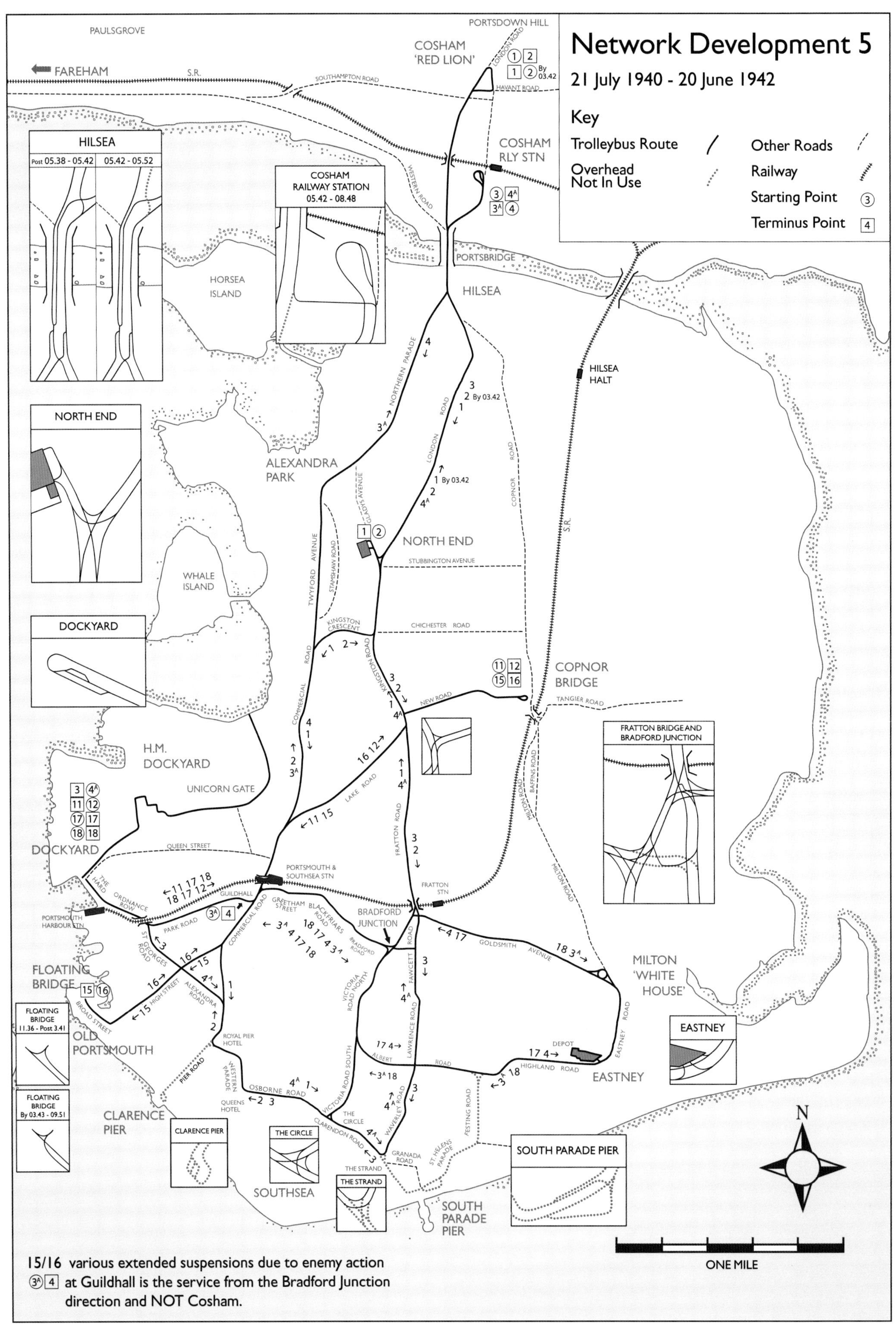

15/16 various extended suspensions due to enemy action
③ᴬ 4 at Guildhall is the service from the Bradford Junction direction and NOT Cosham.

reduced the daily vehicle requirement by three trolleybuses, ended the difficult turning arrangements and saw the end of service trolleybuses along Festing Road until the seafront re-opened.

1 Cosham *Red Lion* – Hilsea – North End *Junction* – Kingston Crescent – Guildhall – Royal Pier Hotel – Southsea *The Circle* – Bradford Junction – Fratton Bridge – North End
Unidirectional service (anti-clockwise) worked in conjunction with service 2

2 North End – Fratton Bridge – Bradford Junction – Southsea *The Circle* – Royal Pier Hotel – Guildhall – Kingston Crescent – North End *Junction* – Hilsea – Cosham *Red Lion*
Unidirectional service (clockwise) worked in conjunction with service 1

3 Cosham Railway Station – Hilsea – North End *Junction* – Fratton Bridge – Southsea *The Strand* – Royal Pier Hotel – Dockyard
Unidirectional southbound service worked in conjunction with service 4A

4A Dockyard – Royal Pier Hotel – Southsea *The Strand* – Fratton Bridge – North End *Junction* – Hilsea – Cosham Railway Station
Unidirectional northbound service worked in conjunction with service 3

3A Guildhall – Bradford Junction – Fratton Bridge – Milton *White House* – Eastney – Festing Hotel – Bradford Junction – Guildhall – Alexandra Park – Hilsea – Cosham Railway Station
Unidirectional service (clockwise) worked in conjunction with service 4

4 Cosham Railway Station – Hilsea – Alexandra Park – Guildhall – Bradford Junction – Festing Hotel – Eastney – Milton *White House* – Fratton Bridge – Bradford Junction – Guildhall
Unidirectional service (anti-clockwise) worked in conjunction with service 3A

An air raid on 11 July 1940 caused damage in Old Portsmouth and interrupted service 15 and 16 for a short period. The Overhead Line Department's wartime incident diary, prepared with foresight by Mr Humpidge during his short stay with CPPTD, records that overhead wiring was brought down, and traction poles and a section pillar destroyed at Kingston Cross. Although CPPTD vehicles had stopped during air raid warnings other operators had continued to run. The Emergency Committee was asked to instruct the police that all buses operating within the City should cease running for the period of an air raid warning and the passengers directed to the nearest public shelter. Tickets issued on CPPTD vehicles would remain valid for 30 minutes after the 'All Clear' signal had been given. By September 1940 it was evident that a national order was pending with the MoT.

The Broad Street area of Old Portsmouth was damaged in another air raid, on 12 August 1940 and services 15 and 16 were again interrupted. On 24 August 1940 a further raid led to services 11, 12, 15 and 16 being disrupted, due to overhead wiring being brought down in Park Road and outside the Prince's Theatre in Lake Road which suffered a direct hit. Overhead repairs were also necessary in Goldsmith Avenue near Fratton Station. The undertaking decided to build two additional surface shelters at Eastney and North End Depots

The reduction in the number of passengers carried in the late evening, not least due to the earlier closing of cinemas and theatres, led to the last journeys on all services being brought forward by 30 minutes from 6 October 1940. The April–May 1940 timetable shows that last trolleybuses on most services left the city centre at about 10.30 p.m. and thus henceforth last journeys departed at around 10 p.m. Where more than one pair of services operated along a route, e.g., Copnor Bridge, one pair, e.g., 11 and 12, ceased to run at about 8 p.m. Mr Hall was asked to investigate why the last trolleybus from Alexandra Park to Eastney returned empty to North End Depot upon completion of its journey.

As a result of heavy bombing and the evacuation of much of the civilian population CPPTD had a considerable surplus of motorbuses and trolleybuses. It will be recalled that the 24 trolleybuses without traction batteries were out of use in open air storage on waste ground in Northern Parade. No doubt due to 'insider' information provided by Mr Humpidge, who had moved from Portsmouth to Nottingham City Transport in July 1939, Nottingham offered to purchase the four 3-axle trolley vehicles 212–215. Nottingham's Transport Committee approved their purchase for £3,885 in November 1940; however, Portsmouth decided that the trolleybuses should be retained for possible future emergency use. Nottingham then offered to hire them and in December 1940 the Passenger Transport Committee approved the hire in principle. The Chairman, Vice-Chairman and Councillor Lay were delegated to reach mutually agreeable terms and the full Council approved the transaction on 11 February 1941; however, possibly due to the fear of further vehicle losses as occurred at Eastney Depot on 10–11 March 1941, the hire did not proceed and nothing further was recorded.

On 10 December 1941 the General Manager asked the Vehicle Subcommittee if they would now consider hiring out the 3-axle trolley vehicles but the matter was deferred for 3 months. Following further requests from Nottingham and now from Pontypridd, he again raised the question but was instructed not to bring up the subject again before December 1942. Presumably the Subcommittee wished to insure the undertaking against all eventualities. Interestingly, AEC 661Ts 219 and 220 were re-licensed in March 1942 and October 1942 respectively and moved from open storage at Northern Parade to North End Depot.

Pontypridd UDC operated a single trolleybus route serving innumerable collieries of great importance to the war effort. Their primarily single-deck trolleybus fleet had been reinforced by 4 Leyland TB4 double-deck vehicles on loan from Hull but these were now required by that city. The hire had been due to end on 30 April 1942 however in view of the special circumstances they were still in Pontypridd in June 1942. As they were unable to obtain replacement trolleybuses either on hire or to purchase, the Pontypridd management had no alternative but to ask their RTC for additional petrol to run motorbuses instead. No doubt the local RTC approached the Portsmouth Passenger Transport Committee and when a further application from Pontypridd was discussed on 21 July 1942 approval was immediately forthcoming, indeed Mr Hall was asked to handle the matter urgently.

It is assumed that Pontypridd UDC preferred to hire 3-axle vehicles due to their greater carrying capacity, the terms being £25 per vehicle per month. They agreed to return the trolleybuses within 72 hours should they be urgently needed in Portsmouth. The first two Portsmouth trolleybuses, 212 and 215, reached Pontypridd on 8 August 1942 and once they were ready for service the London motorbuses were taken off

A wartime view of Portsmouth AEC663T 215 at the John Street, Treforest terminus of the Pontypridd UDC trolleybus undertaking. Note the headlamp masks and white front mudguards required by wartime 'blackout' restrictions. The complete history of Pontypridd Trolleybuses is also available from Adam Gordon Books. (BTS Library [photographer W. Haynes])

the trolleybus route. The other two trolleybuses, 213 and 214, arrived on 14 August 1942. The hired vehicles were towed to Pontypridd via Newbury, Oxford, Gloucester (then the lowest bridging point on the River Severn), Abergavenny, Brecon and Merthyr Tydfil, presumably to avoid low bridges. Although plaques were subsequently mounted in the Portsmouth motorbuses loaned to LPTB 'London 1940–41', the trolleybuses hired to Pontypridd were never similarly treated.

Volunteer fire spotters were introduced at CPPTD depots and workshops. They were recompensed for their efforts with 10s per week and from early 1941 granted free travel to and from their fire watching duty. Due to the growing shortage of labour, employees who had reached 65 years of age and wished to continue working were offered employment for a further 12 months. Mild steel helmets were issued to traffic employees following union representations; however, it was to be another 18 months before drivers were equipped with civilian duty respirators and even then only 100 were acquired. Driver O. C. Moase was injured on 5 December 1940 moving a trolleybus away from an incendiary bomb. As his action was in the Department's interest it was decided that he should receive full wages for the three weeks that he was off duty due to his injuries.

The night of Friday 10 January 1941 witnessed the heaviest bombing raid on Portsmouth of the war when, over a 7-hour period, some 300 aircraft dropped 25,000 incendiaries and high explosives. This was the 31st raid on the city and it left

All four of Portsmouth's three axle trolleybuses were loaned to the hard-pressed Pontypridd UDC undertaking during the Second World War. Here, AEC663T 212 with English Electric composite body leaves John Street, Treforest during its wartime sojourn in South Wales. As evidenced by the offset fleet number on the front panel, 212 had not been repainted since the 1938 renumbering. Service numbers were not used by Pontypridd UDC and the '17' displayed has no meaning whatsoever. (BTS Library [photographer W. Haynes])

Another view of Portsmouth AEC663T 212 with English Electric composite body at John Street terminus, Treforest on the Pontypridd UDC system. It should be remembered that photographic film for private use was difficult to find during the Second World War and often of dubious quality in addition to the prohibition of photography in Restricted Areas such as Portsmouth. (BTS Library [photographer W. Haynes])

172 dead and 430 injured. There was extensive damage: the Guildhall, Clarence Pier, several churches, a hospital and the Commercial Road shopping centre were destroyed, Old Portsmouth suffered severe damage, and the Kings Road and Palmerston Road areas of Southsea were also badly hit. The trolley wires in Hampshire Terrace and Victoria Road North were brought down. Early in the raid the electricity power station at St Mary Street, Old Portsmouth, suffered a direct hit which brought the entire trolleybus system to a halt and left trolley vehicles marooned all over the city. All public electricity and gas supplies were cut-off and electricity was only restored at midday on 13 January 1941. However, HM Dockyard's own power station was able to supply essential needs to the city, in particular to the Burgoyne Road pumping station and traction current for the trolleybuses, through an emergency cable installed in 1938, until repairs could be made.

It is believed that severely restricted trolleybus services were already running on the morning of 11 January 1941; however, physical damage to the overhead equipment and road surface, as well as rubble in the street prevented any services reaching the Dockyard or Old Portsmouth. As far as can be established the following part services were operating:

1 Cosham *Red Lion* – Hilsea – North End *Junction* – All Saints Church
(All Saints Church is located some 300 yds north of Lake Road; trolleybuses turned at Church Street using their traction batteries.)
Guildhall – Osborne Road
Unidirectional southbound service

2 All Saints Church – North End *Junction* – Hilsea – Cosham *Red Lion*
Osborne Road – Guildhall
Unidirectional northbound service

3 Cosham Railway Station – Hilsea – North End *Junction* – Fratton Bridge – Osborne Road
Unidirectional southbound service

3A All Saints Church – Alexandra Park – Hilsea – Cosham Railway Station
Unidirectional northbound service

4 Cosham Railway Station – Hilsea – Alexandra Park – All Saints Church
Unidirectional southbound service

4A Osborne Road – Fratton Bridge – North End *Junction* – Hilsea – Cosham Railway Station
Unidirectional northbound service

11 Copnor Bridge – Lake Road
(Trolleybuses turned by reversing into a side road near Commercial Road.)
Unidirectional southbound service worked in conjunction with service 12

12 Lake Road near Commercial Road – Copnor Bridge
Unidirectional northbound service worked in conjunction with service 11

15 Copnor Bridge – Lake Road
(Trolleybuses turned by reversing into a side road near Commercial Road.)
Unidirectional southbound service worked in conjunction with service 16

16 Lake Road near Commercial Road – Copnor Bridge
Unidirectional northbound service worked in conjunction with service 15
17 Guildhall – Bradford Junction – Festing Hotel – Eastney – Milton *White House* – Bradford Junction – Guildhall
Unidirectional circular service (anti-clockwise) worked in conjunction with service 18
18 Guildhall – Bradford Junction – Milton *White House* – Eastney – Festing Hotel – Bradford Junction – Guildhall
Unidirectional circular service (clockwise) worked in conjunction with service 17

Newspapers of 24 January 1941 announced that 'trolleybuses will be running through Commercial Road, Lake Road and Park Road tomorrow morning'. Services 11, 12, 17, 18 were extended along their customary route to The Hard on Saturday 25 January 1941, whilst trolleybus services also ran between Cosham *Red Lion* and the Dockyard via Twyford Avenue and the Guildhall or via North End and the Guildhall. A further 12,000 people had been evacuated and passenger figures for 1 to 28 January 1941 were 1,425,322 down on the year preceding.

Portsbridge was closed to all traffic for a week due to an unexploded bomb following an air raid on Hilsea and Horsea Island on 4 March 1941. All trolleybuses turned short at the roundabout at the junction of London Road with Northern Parade using their traction batteries and other traffic was diverted over the emergency bridge across Ports Creek.

During the night of 10–11 March 1941 another air raid caused considerable damage in the Commercial Road, Lake Road, High Street and The Strand areas. The Overhead Line Department's Incident Diary records that the trolley wires were down in Alexandra Road, at the Dockyard, The Hard and at the Royal Pier Hotel junction. Eastney Depot suffered blast damage to the garage, machine shop, stores and body shop, whilst 11 motorbuses were destroyed by fire. The AFS and the Department's volunteer fire fighters fought the blaze whilst prompt action from an employee saved the paint shop from fire and possibly a worse conflagration. Royal Marines from Eastney Barracks helped clear the debris. Traction power was cut off and no trolleybuses ran on the morning of 11 March 1941. Subsequently services 1, 2, 3A, 4 were again curtailed to All Saints Church, and the 11, 12 to the junction of Commercial Road with Lake Road. During the period that Commercial Road was closed, it is believed that the south-eastern parts of services 3A/4 originated/terminated at Milton 'White House' (instead of the Guildhall) and that a shuttle service was operated over the Eastney section.

Commercial Road re-opened to traffic on 3 April 1941; however, trolleybus services 1, 2, 3A, 4, 11, 12 only resumed normal operations along Commercial Road on Monday 7 April 1941. A. J. Main and Co. Ltd., builders, was asked to report on the condition of Eastney Depot and submit an estimate for repairs. Stewarts and Lloyds Ltd. supplied 18 traction poles to replace those lost by enemy action at a cost of £280 10s.

Trolley wires were brought down in High Street on the night of 1 April 1941 and in Southsea Terrace at the junction with Castle Road on 11 April 1941. Another raid on Sunday 27 April 1941 caused further damage in Commercial Road and High Street, Old Portsmouth, and once again led to services 1, 2, 3A, 4 being cut-back to All Saints Church from the north, and services 11, 12, 15, 16 turning at the junction of Commercial Road with Lake Road.

From Monday 14 April 1941 SMS tickets were accepted on Portsmouth buses augmenting the SMS country services in the Portsmouth area. Return tickets issued on these routes by either undertaking continued to be available for return on the buses of the other undertaking without extra charge. These arrangements did not apply to CPPTD's normal City services.

Old Portsmouth had been without public transport since 27 April 1941 but on 19 May 1941 single-deck motorbuses began running every 20 minutes between Guildhall and Floating Bridge. On Sunday 6 July 1941 trolleybus services along High Street and through Old Portsmouth to/from Floating Bridge resumed and the temporary motorbus service withdrawn.

15 Copnor Bridge – Guildhall – Old Portsmouth – Floating Bridge via New Road, Kingston Road, Lake Road, Commercial Road, Guildhall Square, Commercial Road, Cambridge Road, High Street and Broad Street.
Unidirectional southbound service worked in conjunction with service 16
16 Floating Bridge – Old Portsmouth – Guildhall – Copnor Bridge via Broad Street, High Street, Cambridge Road, Commercial Road, Guildhall Square, Commercial Road, Lake Road, Kingston Road and New Road
Unidirectional northbound service worked in conjunction with service 15

The services ran every 20 minutes whereas pre-war there had been a 10-minute service.

Service 15	Weekdays first trolleybus 7.45 a.m., last 8.46 p.m.
	Sundays first trolleybus 9.06 a.m., last 8.46 p.m.
Service 16	Weekdays first trolleybus 8.05 a.m., last 9.05 p.m.
	Sundays first trolleybus 9.05 a.m., last 9.05 p.m.

In addition to the daily risk of death or injury at work and at home, employees worked under extreme conditions. From 2 March 1941 members of the Depot Home Guard Units on military duties from 8.30 p.m. to 5.30 a.m. had to proceed direct to their normal transport work. This meant that platform staff often worked in Home Guard uniform until there was an opportunity to change their apparel. Two accidents sustained by a long-service driver, resulting in repairs estimated to cost £250, were attributed by the Corporation's medical referee to the man being run-down and overworked as a result of air raids involving extra duty.

Good Friday 11 April 1941 was deemed a normal working day necessitating overtime rates. On Saturday 12 April and Sunday 13 April 1941, trolleybus services ran as normal with the usual early morning workmen's services; however, on Easter Monday 14 April 1941 there was a reduced service starting at about 6 a.m. with normal weekday operations starting at 8 a.m.

Up to 14 May 1941 the estimated cost of damage to the department's property by enemy action had reached £31,810 3s 9d. A. and J. Main and Co. Ltd. quoted £9,063 to restore Eastney Depot to its original state plus £132 for repairs to the main office block and employees' canteen. The work would take 3 months. An application to the MoWT was made for their approval of the reconstruction. Shortly afterwards, on the night of 13/14 June 1941, damage was done to a length of the depot screening and some vehicles were struck by splinters. In September 1941 representatives of the MoWT and Ministry of Works and Buildings inspected the damage and on 30 October 1941 gave authority for the necessary materials and authorised the Corporation to proceed with the reinstatement of the garage and workshops.

At the end of May 1941 Mr Hall was instructed to apply for scheduling of the undertaking under the Revised Schedule of Reserved Occupations and Essential Work (General Provisions) Order 1941 made by the Ministry of Labour and National Service as by providing transport services in an industrial area and to military establishments, CPPTD was engaged in essential work. This meant that employees were not able to freely leave the undertaking without permission but on the other hand the Corporation could not discharge an employee except for serious misconduct. The application was granted in September 1941 for the drivers of trolley vehicles, motorbuses, heavy lorries and overhead tower wagons, as well as all garage and workshop employees except labourers and cleaners.

After a raid on 26 June 1941 parachute mines were left hanging from the overhead wiring in Northern Road and the power was switched off until they could be safely removed.

On 2 July 1941 the newspaper carried the following announcement:

> City of Portsmouth Passenger Transport Department
>
> NOTICE TO DOCKYARD WORKERS
>
> In order to conserve motor fuel by making greater use of trolley vehicles, on and after Monday 7th July 1941 workmen's traffic between the Northern Districts and the Dockyard Main Gate will be carried by trolley vehicles instead of motorbuses. Passengers between the Northern Districts and the Unicorn Gate will be conveyed by motorbuses.
>
> The trolley vehicles on this service will be identified by destination indicators showing number '1' up to 8.10 a.m. from Red Lion Cosham; thereafter such vehicles will display Palmerston Road, Southsea.
>
> The trolley vehicles from Alexandra Park showing 'GUILDHALL' on the destination screens will all travel through to the MAIN GATE DOCKYARD, up to 7.40 a.m. from Alexandra Park.
>
> The timetable for the revised services is:
>
> TROLLEY VEHICLES TO MAIN GATE VIA NORTH END AND GUILDHALL
>
> From Red Lion Cosham — 5.16 a.m., 5.56 a.m. and then every 10 minutes until 7.46 a.m. then every 12 minutes until 8.10 a.m.
>
> From Alexandra Park — 5.50 a.m. and then every 10 minutes until 7.40 a.m. then every 12 minutes until 8.10 a.m.

In order to reduce the need for imported fuel, with effect from Monday 7 July 1941, workmen's services between the northern suburbs and the Dockyard Main Gate operated by motorbus were converted to trolleybus operation. This resulted in two additional services:

Cosham *Red Lion* – Hilsea – North End – Kingston Crescent – Guildhall – Dockyard *Main Gate*
Alexandra Park – Twyford Avenue – Guildhall – Dockyard *Main Gate*

The Cosham 'Red Lion' – Dockyard service was effectively a short-working of the 1 and 2. After 8.10 a.m. journeys were extended to Palmerston Road via Royal Pier Hotel as services 1 and 2, continuing thence to and from North End. The main services 1 and 2, which had been operating Cosham 'Red Lion' – North End – Guildhall – Royal Pier Hotel – Clarendon Road – Southsea *The Circle* – Fratton Bridge – North End, were extended that same day beyond North End to and from Cosham 'Red Lion' creating two circular services.

Trolleybuses on the Alexandra Park – Dockyard service displayed a white blank in the large indicator box normally used for the service number and list of intermediate points, and 'Guildhall' as the final destination in the narrower indicator box beneath as it will be recalled that it was not permissible to show Dockyard as the destination for security reasons. This was the first occasion that trolleybus services had started and/or terminated at the Alexandra Park, Gladys Avenue terminus on CPPTD property; however, there was no overhead wiring in place for this manoeuvre and battery power was used for turning purposes.

Also in July 1941 motorbus services K and L were curtailed to operate as a shuttle service to and from Eastern Road Estate connecting with trolleybuses at Copnor Bridge.

On 26 October 1941 the trolley wires were brought down and the mains damaged at the junction of North End Avenue with London Road. Demolition of bomb damaged buildings made it necessary to introduce single line trolleybus working in Commercial Road between Stanhope Road and Edinburgh Road from 6 February until 15 March 1942.

In February 1942 the NJIC for the Passenger Transport Industry granted a further wage award to traffic staff of 4s on the war wage of 11s already being paid and estimated to cost the undertaking an additional £7,000–£8,000 p.a. There was no alternative but to seek a fare increase to match the soaring costs and a renewed application was made to the MoWT and RTC on 19 May 1942 for a ½d increase on all ordinary fares (except the pre-war 1d fares which has already been increased to 1½d). No progress was made and the Passenger Transport Committee resolved on 15 December 1942 to leave the matter in abeyance for another 6 months. Traction power was not excluded from wartime inflation and by May 1942 the undertaking was paying rates 60% higher than pre-war basic charge.

The City Engineer was asked to give priority to widening the private road connecting Northern Road with Cosham Compound in February 1942. The work, including resurfacing with granite chippings by the Limmer and Trinidad Lake Asphalt Co. Ltd. at a cost of £65, was expected to take 5 to 6 weeks. Work on the overhead equipment began on 20 April 1942 and was completed on 26 April 1942. MoWT approval of the equipment was received on 21 April 1942 and permission was granted to use the new wiring from Northern Road to Portsmouth Road prior to an official inspection subject to compliance with certain requirements. All trolleybuses heading south from Cosham 'Red Lion' (at this time services 1 and 2) were diverted along the private road on Sunday 3 May 1942, and the southbound wiring along Northern Road from the Private Road to the Western Road roundabout fell into disuse. It was felt that this would provide improved interchange facilities with other services and offer a better service for the Highbury Estate; however, northbound passengers still needed to alight in Northern Road on journeys to Cosham 'Red Lion'.

The position of Chief Assistant Engineer had been vacant since the departure of Mr C. T. Humpidge in July 1939, now, following, a series of interviews the position was offered to Mr D. P. Martin, Assistant Engineer at Nottingham City Transport. In early April 1942 it was learned that the Nottingham Transport Committee would not permit Mr Martin to resign his present position and move to Portsmouth, and that they had referred the matter to the National Service Officer. Subsequently Mr Martin was offered the position of Chief Engineer at Nottingham and decided to remain there. The appointment was offered to Mr H. C. Simmons, Works Superintendent, Cleethorpes Corporation Transport, who started work in Portsmouth in June 1942.

On 26 May 1942 a barrage balloon broke loose and its cables trailed progressively across the trolleybus overhead wiring in Station Street, Commercial Road and High Street, Old Portsmouth disrupting services. There was a similar incident involving a drifting barrage balloon on 5 December 1942 in Northern Road.

Looking ahead to post-war reconstruction, Mr Hall was instructed to liaise with the City Architect and reserve spaces for trolleybus turning circles at Unicorn Road and the Dockyard Main Gate, as well as a piece of land abutting onto the existing Cosham Railway Station terminus. At the same meeting Ben Hall asked that consideration be given to re-opening St. Helen's Parade from Cumberland House to the Strand via Clarendon Road for CPPTD services. Following an approach by the Lord Mayor in early June 1942 authority was given to re-open the South Parade Pier area to the department's vehicles at specified times.

Prompted by this development and in a further effort to reduce the use of imported fuel, commencing Sunday 21 June 1942 the Commercial Road portion of motorbus services A and B operating between Cosham 'Red Lion' and Southsea South Parade Pier via London Road, North End, Kingston Crescent, Commercial Road, Guildhall, King's Road, Grove Road South and Palmerston Road were replaced by trolleybuses. Beyond the junction of King's Road with Alexandra Road the trolleybuses could only follow the nearest parallel roads with overhead wiring: they accordingly used the Terraces, Western Parade and Osborne Road as far as Palmerston Road. The areas left unserved had been devastated and offered few passengers. The new trolleybus services were designated 1A running south to Southsea and 2A when travelling towards Cosham. The remaining portion of services A and B between Queen's Hotel, Osborne Road and Cosham 'Red Lion' via Festing Road, Winter Road, Milton Road and Copnor continued to be motorbus operated. Services 1A and 2A continued from Southsea South Parade Pier to Eastney via Festing Road between 8.30 a.m. and about 7 p.m. Monday to Saturday and from 10 a.m. to about 7 p.m. on Sundays. This was the first trolleybus service to run between the Strand and Festing Road since this section was closed to traffic during July 1940. The other services which had operated along these streets pre-war were not reinstated at this time. It will be noted that a turning circle at Eastney was only installed in 1953 at the time of the Milton Road, Copnor Road extension, and it is not known how or where the trolleybuses turned at Eastney. This could have involved a turn using traction batteries into the depot entrance. In June or July 1942 services 1A and 2A were extended to Milton White House, presumably primarily for turning purposes.

1A Cosham *Red Lion* – Cosham Railway Station – Hilsea – North End *Junction* – Kingston Crescent – Commercial Road – Guildhall – Royal Pier Hotel – Southsea *The Circle* – Southsea *South Parade Pier* – Eastney – Milton *White House*
Unidirectional southbound service worked in conjunction with service 2A

2A Milton *White House* – Eastney – Southsea *South Parade Pier* – Southsea *The Circle* – Royal Pier Hotel – Guildhall – Commercial Road – Kingston Crescent – North End *Junction* – Hilsea – Cosham *Red Lion*
Unidirectional northbound service worked in conjunction with service 1A

Starting on Sunday 19 July 1942 trolleybus services 1 and 2, which had reverted to operating a circular route between Cosham 'Red Lion' and Southsea, The Circle on 7 July 1941, were divided on Sundays only at Southsea The Circle into two separate portions, one of which was extended to Southsea South Parade Pier.

1 Cosham *Red Lion* – Cosham Railway Station – Hilsea – Kingston Crescent – Guildhall – Royal Pier Hotel – Southsea *The Circle* – Southsea *South Parade Pier*
Southsea *The Circle* – Bradford Junction – Fratton Bridge – North End *Junction* – Hilsea – Cosham *Red Lion*
Unidirectional service worked in conjunction with service 2

2 Cosham *Red Lion* – Cosham Railway Station – Hilsea – North End *Junction* – Fratton Bridge – Bradford Junction – Southsea *The Circle* reversing at the junction with Clarendon Road
Southsea *South Parade Pier* – Southsea *The Circle* – Royal Pier Hotel – Guildhall – Kingston Crescent – North End *Junction* – Hilsea – Cosham *Red Lion*
Unidirectional service worked in conjunction with service 1
On weekdays they remained unaltered as circular services.

Trolleybus services 1A and 2A ceased to run between Southsea South Parade Pier and Milton 'White House' on Sunday 18 October 1942 for the winter period. There is no evidence that it was ever re-extended. On the same date the frequency of all Sunday trolleybus services was reduced and services 3A and 4 were curtailed to run between Cosham Railway Station and the Guildhall only via Twyford Avenue and Commercial Road, i.e., omitting the circular section via Eastney and Milton.

From 28 June 1942 the following request stops, served by both trolleybuses and motorbuses, were abolished in an effort to conserve electrical energy and extend tyre life:

Buckingham Place (Lake Road)
Cemetery Gates, junction of Whitworth Road and New Road
Clovelly Road (Goldsmith Avenue)
Commercial Road, junction with Surrey Street
Cosham High Street, junction with Northern Road and London Road
Ernest Road (New Road)
Fawcett Road at Fratton Bridge, travelling south towards the Strand
Festing Grove (Festing Road)
Gold Street (King's Terrace)
Hilsea Post Office
Kimberley Road (Highland Road)
Kingston Crescent, mid-way along
Lynn Road (New Road)
Middlesex Road (Eastney Road)
Oriel Road (London Road)
Spur Road, west end travelling south
Telegraph Street (Greetham Street)
Victoria Road South, junction with Hereford Road
Waverley Road southbound, south of Lawrence Road junction

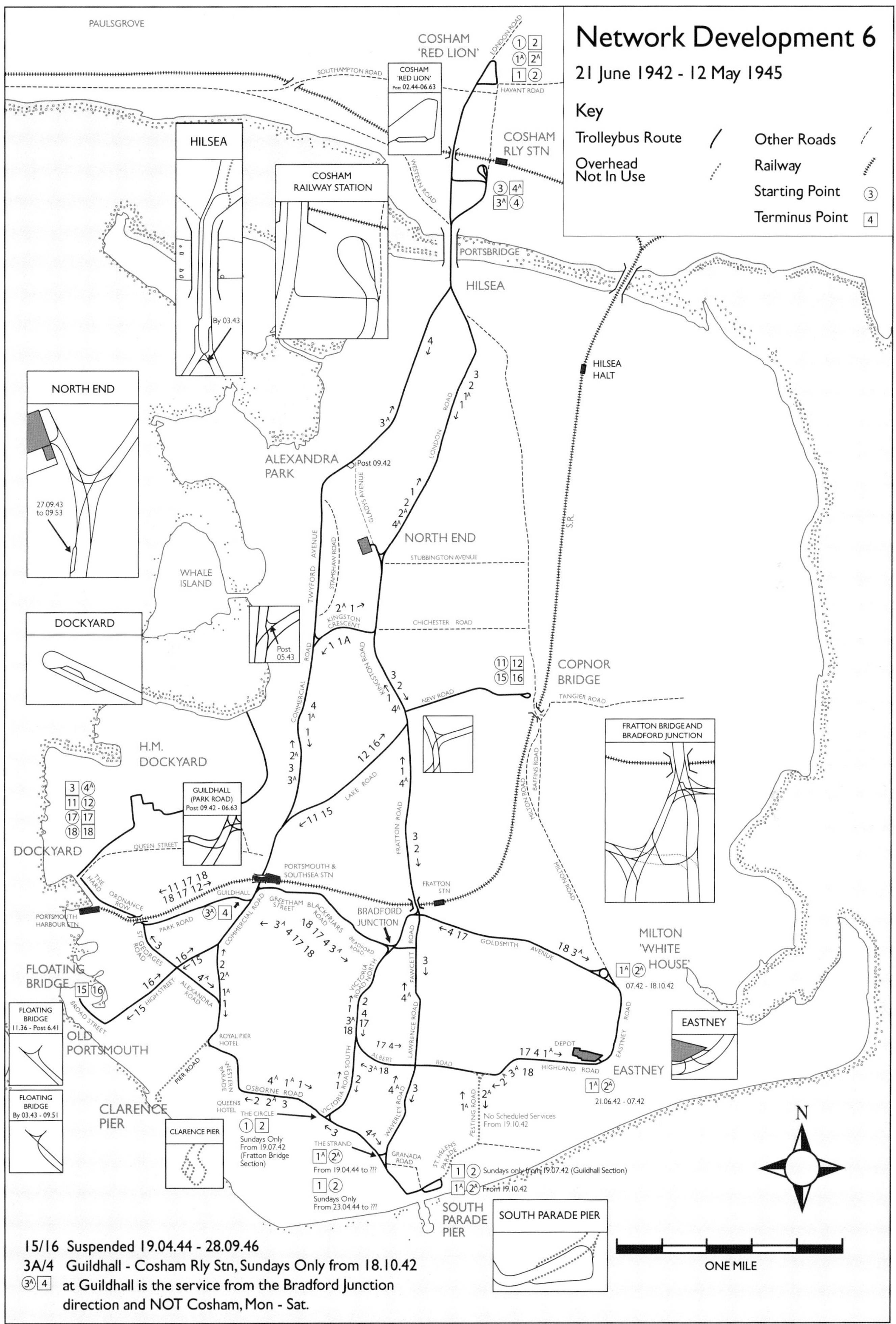
Network Development 6
21 June 1942 - 12 May 1945
Key
Trolleybus Route
Overhead Not In Use
Other Roads
Railway
Starting Point
Terminus Point
PAULSGROVE
COSHAM 'RED LION'
SOUTHAMPTON ROAD
LONDON ROAD
HAVANT ROAD
COSHAM 'RED LION' Post 02.44-06.63
HILSEA
COSHAM RAILWAY STATION
COSHAM RLY STN
WESTERN ROAD
PORTSBRIDGE
HILSEA
By 03.43
NORTH END
27.09.43 to 09.53
HILSEA HALT
ALEXANDRA PARK
Post 09.42
GLADYS AVENUE
NORTH END
STUBBINGTON AVENUE
TWYFORD AVENUE
STAMSHAW ROAD
S.R.
WHALE ISLAND
DOCKYARD
KINGSTON CRESCENT
CHICHESTER ROAD
Post 05.43
COMMERCIAL ROAD
KINGSTON ROAD
COPNOR BRIDGE
TANGIER ROAD
NEW ROAD
H.M. DOCKYARD
LAKE ROAD
FRATTON ROAD
BAFFINS ROAD
MILTON ROAD
FRATTON BRIDGE AND BRADFORD JUNCTION
GUILDHALL (PARK ROAD) Post 09.42 - 06.63
DOCKYARD
QUEEN STREET
PORTSMOUTH & SOUTHSEA STN
FRATTON STN
THE HARD
ORDNANCE ROW
GUILDHALL
PORTSMOUTH HARBOUR STN
PARK ROAD
GREETHAM STREET
BLACKFRIARS ROAD
BRADFORD JUNCTION
BRADFORD ROAD
FAWCETT ROAD
GOLDSMITH AVENUE
MILTON 'WHITE HOUSE'
07.42 - 18.10.42
ST. GEORGES ROAD
HIGH STREET
ALEXANDRA ROAD
VICTORIA ROAD NORTH
LAWRENCE ROAD
EASTNEY ROAD
FLOATING BRIDGE
BROAD STREET
FLOATING BRIDGE 11.36 - Post 6.41
OLD PORTSMOUTH
ROYAL PIER HOTEL
ALBERT ROAD
DEPOT
HIGHLAND ROAD
EASTNEY
EASTNEY
21.06.42 - 07.42
FLOATING BRIDGE By 03.43 - 09.51
PIER ROAD
WESTERN PARADE
OSBORNE ROAD
VICTORIA ROAD SOUTH
WAVERLEY ROAD
FESTING ROAD
No Scheduled Services From 19.10.42
CLARENCE PIER
QUEENS HOTEL
THE CIRCLE
Sundays Only From 19.07.42 (Fratton Bridge Section)
CLARENCE PIER
THE STRAND
GRANADA ROAD
ST. HELENS PARADE
From 19.04.44 to ???
Sundays only from 19.07.42 (Guildhall Section)
From 19.10.42
Sundays Only From 23.04.44 to ???
SOUTH PARADE PIER
SOUTH PARADE PIER
N
ONE MILE
15/16 Suspended 19.04.44 - 28.09.46
3A/4 Guildhall - Cosham Rly Stn, Sundays Only from 18.10.42
3A 4 at Guildhall is the service from the Bradford Junction direction and NOT Cosham, Mon - Sat.

Queue barriers were installed at Charlotte Street, Edinburgh Road and the Guildhall. The stop in Albert Road at Fawcett Road was moved closer to Francis Avenue and there was an experimental change to the loading points at North End Junction whereby SMS stopped south of Stubbington Avenue immediately past the Clarence Hotel enabling the Corporation to introduce queue barriers at their existing North End stop. At the same time a new style of sign was approved for use at stops served by both CPPTD and SMS services.

The absence of a turning circle at the Guildhall (Park Road), although services 3A and 4, as well as peak-hour journeys of the 17 and 18, terminated there, had been an acknowledged problem since the outbreak of war, not least due to flashes in the 'black-out' as conductors attempted to find the trolley wires after turning. In September 1942 construction of trolleybus turning circles in Park Road and at Alexandra Park (Gladys Avenue) was agreed, immediate approval being forthcoming from the MoWT. The cost was met from revenue,

In line with an RTC Instruction, shift workers and part time workers whose journeys did not fall within the hours of application for reduced rate workmen's fares were also granted these discounts from October 1942.

At the peak of the evening rush hour on 20 October 1942 a trolley wire fell free from its hanger near Hilsea Lido on London Road at Portsbridge causing a short circuit. All traffic to the north of Kingston Crescent, Twyford Avenue Junction and North End Junction, i.e. fed from Northern Parade substation, was held up for an hour. The traction power was cut off between Cosham and North End although some trolleybuses were able to reach live overhead using their traction batteries and a limited number of motorbuses were substituted.

Four trolleybuses were provided on 5/6 November 1942 to transport the crew of the light cruiser HMS *Penelope* to entertainment in the City. The ship had arrived after extensive repairs following a severe mauling in Malta. Several functions in Portsmouth had been arranged by Blackpool Council, the town having adopted the ship. The Passenger Transport Committee decided that no charge would be made for the trolleybuses. More generally there were several letters of thanks from HM Dockyard in respect of the excellent services and good humour of CPPTD employees.

At an operator's conference on 10 November 1942, the RTC instructed that both motorbus and trolleybuses services must be further reduced and requested that all services should cease at 9 p.m. daily. Effective Sunday 3 January 1943, the last departures of all CPPTD and SMS services were brought forward to 9 p.m. or shortly afterwards. On Sundays no motorbus services were operated between 9.30 a.m. and 2 p.m. except for a 30 minute service on services A and B although trolleybuses ran every 30 minutes on 'a limited number of main routes'. Normal Sunday services commenced after 2 p.m. This provoked a flurry of protests. It was suggested that SMS was providing a more frequent service between some points in the City than CPPTD whilst in Brighton services were reportedly still running until 9.30 p.m. The RTC granted a concession whereby by the end of January 1943 the last trolleybus left the Guildhall for Cosham 'Red Lion' at 9.25 p.m. and then returned to North End Depot.

The shortage of labour was compounded at the beginning of December 1942 when 10 conductresses and a timekeeper received call-up notices, and an Order was received to transfer a number of conductresses to City of Oxford Motor Services. The General Manager took up the matter with the National Service Officer; however, it was July 1944 before the last two conductresses were released, one of whom preferred to remain in Oxford.

A trolleybus parked on the highway was slightly damaged by fire at the beginning of December 1942. A 78-year-old widow was knocked down and killed by a trolleybus in London Road, North End, on Saturday afternoon 19 December 1942.

By this stage of the war metals were at a premium and every opportunity was being taken nationally to recycle items from which armaments could be manufactured. The Ministry of Works and Planning was paying £8 per ton for steel and there remained 2,600 tons of tram rails in Portsmouth's streets awaiting removal, a possible £20,800 windfall. The City Engineer, City Treasurer and Vice-Chairman of the Roads, Works and Drainage Committee proposed that the Transport Department be asked to contribute 7s 6d per square yard for the removal of tram track instead of 5s to meet increased costs. This was accepted, subject to any variation in the price from £8 per ton, increasing costs to the undertaking by £11,064 making a total cost of £33,192.

Further request stops were deleted in February 1943 to reduce wear and tear, as well as power consumption.

The RTC granted permission for trolley vehicles carrying allied forces stationed in the port to and from entertainment at South Parade Pier to run late on the evening of Friday 9 April 1943. It was noted that the account for the additional costs should be sent to the Lord Mayor indicating another example of the City's generosity to the forces.

Looking ahead to post-war reconstruction, a new road running along the northeast shore of Portsmouth Harbour – today's Western Road – was proposed. Although there is nothing to suggest that a trolleybus route along Western Road was ever discussed (the planned Paulsgrove extension would have run along Southampton Road and Allaway Avenue), the Admiralty stipulated that no overhead wiring or telegraph poles were to be erected along the proposed road in the vicinity of Horsea Island, where radio mast were located.

The annual reports of transport undertakings were not made public during the war; however, the trading profit for the year ending 31 March 1943 increased from £46,296 to £72,796 (and to £95,808 in the year ending 31 March 1944). Ben Hall noted that conversion of part of motorbus services A and B to trolleybus operation in June 1942 and the withdrawal of other motorbus services duplicating trolleybuses had reduced fuel needs by 40,000 gallons p.a. Nonetheless, he was disturbed that the cost of traction power was, as at 14 July 1942, 64% higher than the pre-war basic charge whereas imported fuel oil had only gone up by 40%, thereby removing one of the perceived advantages of trolleybuses in case of war. An application to increase fares had now been in abeyance for 6 months and on 15 June 1943 the Passenger Transport Committee, having reviewed the situation, resolved to take no action for a further period of 6 months.

On 25 May and again on 31 May 1943 a number of barrage balloons broke loose and their hawsers fell across overhead equipment in London Road and Cambridge Road causing damage to the extent of £43 11s 11d.

The heaviest air raid for 2 years took place during the night of 15/16 August 1943 when 91 bombers visited the skies above Portsmouth. The cost of repairs to the department's property amounted to £1,100 1s.

During September 1943 the left-hand junction frog in the northbound wiring at North End providing access into Gladys Avenue was replaced by a right-hand frog somewhat south of the road junction and a length of parallel wiring and a crossing inserted, enabling depot-bound vehicles to pass those loading at the bus stop prior to continuing along London Road.

Councillor Thorrowgood introduced a scheme to the Passenger Transport Committee for auxiliaries who assisted conductors in the loading and unloading of vehicles, as used in Edinburgh. The General Manager was instructed to prepare a similar trial and upon review on 21 December 1943 he was authorised to engage auxiliary conductors.

On 9 November 1943 a cyclist, Mr W.E. Parkes, was fatally injured when in collision with trolleybus 297.

There were no services on Christmas Day 1943 except for essential needs. A normal Sunday service operated on Sunday 26 December 1943 and on Monday 27 December, the latter augmented with some additional morning journeys.

The road passenger transport industry generally was having difficulties to attract additional employees; not least because wages were traditionally not paid to new entrants under training. The NJIC discussed the payment of wages in such cases with the Ministry of Labour and MoWT. It was decided that these should be 75% of the adult commencing rate.

Newspapers had been distributed to newsagents around the city since the tramway era, however, the publishers of the *Portsmouth Evening News* reported that the number of parcels sent had been falling since the beginning of 1941 and that it was now never more than four parcels per day. The charge reduced to 3d per parcel carried with a review at the end of the war. Generally, CPPTD did not offer a parcel service.

In preparation for the invasion on 25 February 1944 the Military Authorities requested that the traction poles at the junction of Gordon Road (100 yards south west of the Royal Pier Hotel, now Duisburg Way) and Pier Road to the Clarence Pier terminus be removed at their expense. Work started on 20 March 1944. New 'Specified Areas' were introduced on 19 April 1944 resulting in trolleybus services 15 and 16 being suspended from that date until further notice (it is assumed that services 11 and 12 were enhanced between Copnor Bridge and Guildhall) and services 1A and 2A, together with the Sundays only extension of services 1 and 2 ('Guildhall' section), were cut back to The Strand. Also in March 1944 the Passenger Transport Committee agreed to install a passing loop at Cosham 'Red Lion' at a cost of £179, which was met from revenue, in order to overcome congestion at the terminus.

More damage due to enemy action on 22, 27, 28 March 1944 increased the total cost of damage to the undertaking to £43,466 14s 7d. The department's stock of spare traction poles was now nearing exhaustion due to war damage replacements and the construction of additional terminal facilities. On 20 June 1944 Stewarts and Lloyds' quotation for six heavy poles at £31 18s 6d each, six medium at £21 6s 0d and 12 medium at £15 17s 0d each, totalling £509 11s 0d, was accepted with payment from revenue.

In early May 1944 it was learned that there had been a further application to the NJIC for an increased War Wage and that it was likely they would recommend an additional 5s on top of the then 19s 6d. The award was given from 18 May 1944 and was estimated to cost the undertaking an additional £8,500 p.a. This provoked a round of similar increases from various trades. Employees accredited to the Vehicle Building and Electricity Supply Industries received 1d per hour, affecting 38 employees with increased costs of £440 p.a. and 40 employees with increases costs of £460 p.a. respectively.

Portsmouth held its 'Salute the Soldier Week', a nationwide fund raising scheme for the war effort, 10–17 June 1944 and free advertising was offered on the department's vehicles.

The allied invasion of continental Europe, code-named Operation Overlord, began on 6 June 1944 (D-Day) with beach landings in Normandy. Portsmouth Harbour and Southsea beach were important military embarkation points. It proved possible to extend services 1A and 2A, which had been cut-back temporarily to The Strand on 19 April 1944, along Clarendon Road to South Parade Pier on 15 June 1944.

In July 1944 LPTB asked if Portsmouth would be prepared to loan trolley vehicles to relieve their own war-damaged stock. There were still 18 surplus trolley vehicles available albeit without traction batteries and it was agreed that they could be loaned; however, when LPTB examined the vehicles they found them too small for their requirements.

Sunday 3 September 1944 was designated a National Day of Prayer and for that day only a 15 minute frequency ran on trolleybus services 1A, 2A, 3, 4A, 3A, 4, 11, 12, 17 and 18, as well as some motorbus routes, commencing between 9 a.m. and 10 a.m.

By September 1944 trolleybus services on a Sunday were as follows:

1A Cosham *Red Lion* – Cosham Railway Station – Hilsea – North End *Junction* – Kingston Crescent – Commercial Road – Guildhall – Royal Pier Hotel – Southsea *The Circle* – Southsea *South Parade Pier*
Unidirectional southbound service worked in conjunction with service 2A

2A Southsea *South Parade Pier* – Southsea *The Circle* – Royal Pier Hotel – Guildhall – Commercial Road – Kingston Crescent – North End *Junction* – Hilsea – Cosham *Red Lion*
Unidirectional northbound service worked in conjunction with service 1A

3 Cosham Railway Station – Hilsea – North End *Junction* – Fratton Bridge – Fawcett Road – Southsea *The Strand*
Unidirectional southbound service worked in conjunction with service 4A

4A Southsea *The Strand* – Fawcett Road – Fratton Bridge – North End *Junction* – Hilsea – Cosham Railway Station
Unidirectional northbound service worked in conjunction with service 3

3A Guildhall – Commercial Road – Twyford Avenue – Alexandra Park – Hilsea – Cosham Railway Station
Unidirectional northbound service worked in conjunction with service 4

4 Cosham Railway Station – Hilsea – Alexandra Park – Twyford Avenue – Commercial Road – Guildhall
Unidirectional southbound service worked in conjunction with service 3A

11 Copnor Bridge – Lake Road – Guildhall – Dockyard *Main Gate*
Unidirectional southbound service worked in conjunction with service 12

12 Dockyard *Main Gate* – Guildhall – Lake Road – Copnor Bridge
Unidirectional northbound service worked in conjunction with service 11

17 Dockyard *Main Gate* – Guildhall – Bradford Junction – Festing Hotel – Eastney – Milton *White House* – Bradford Junction – Guildhall – Dockyard *Main Gate*
Unidirectional circular service (anti-clockwise) worked in conjunction with service 18
18 Dockyard *Main Gate* – Guildhall – Bradford Junction – Milton *White House* – Eastney – Festing Hotel – Bradford Junction – Guildhall – Dockyard *Main Gate*
Unidirectional circular service (clockwise) worked in conjunction with service 17

The government considered that by now there was little risk of further German aerial bombardment and on 17 September 1944 'black-out' restrictions were reduced and 'dim-out' became applicable in London and South East England. The Council applied to introduce reduced street lighting. When the RTC enquired in October 1944 what were the city's most urgent needs should it be possible to ease travel restrictions, the undertaking requested that they be permitted to restore Sunday morning trolleybus services, extend evening trolleybus services to 9.30 p.m. and extend some motorbus services too. On 19 November 1944 motorbus and trolleybus services were extended by 30 minutes to approximately 9.30 p.m.

There is no evidence that suspended services 15 and 16 had been reintroduced in the meantime and it is believed that a motorbus shuttle had been operating between the Guildhall and Floating Bridge since June 1944. On 21 November 1944 the Passenger Transport Committee approved Mr Hall's suggestion that services 11 and 12 Copnor Bridge – Dockyard justified a more frequent service and that as few passengers were travelling to/from severely damaged Old Portsmouth there was no necessity to operate a through service between Copnor Bridge and Floating Bridge. Suspended services 15 and 16 were considered as being withdrawn on 31 December 1944 and a shuttle service running every 20 minutes operated by single-deck motorbus was introduced between Floating Bridge and Cosham Street. The latter thoroughfare, which disappeared with the city's redevelopment, ran parallel and to the north of the western end of Lake Road.

By now there were over 22,000 workers in the Dockyard building, repairing and replenishing Royal Navy and allied ships in as short a time as possible. There were letters of complaint in the newspaper that there were no through services between Cosham and the Dockyard after 8.30 a.m., although many workers were travelling at different hours of the day. This meant that two fares totalling 5½d each way had to be paid whereas there was supposed to be a 3½d maximum fare within the city. It was suggested that transfer fares should be introduced.

On 15 December 1944 Mrs A. Monkcom was injured whilst attempting to board trolleybus in London Road, North End near Laburnum Grove. Her solicitors made a claim for £80 plus £5 5s legal costs and the Town Clerk was authorised to negotiate a settlement.

In March 1945 SMS informed the Passenger Transport Committee that they wished to increase their services within the city. The Cosham Rate Payers Association suggested that application be made to the RTC to run Corporation services to the city boundaries between Portsmouth and Farlington via the main Havant Road. Mr Hall responded that the MoWT did not encourage applications for new services or improvements to existing ones whilst the RTC were loath to vary conditions unless there was a definite need. At the subsequent meeting the Corporation agreed not to raise any objections subject to SMS reducing their total mileage operated, including duplicate journeys within the city and surrounding districts, to equate to that of their pre-war schedules.

Organised hostilities in Europe came to an end at the beginning of May 1945. The British government announced that this would be celebrated with 3 days of public holidays commencing on 8 May 1945 with VE (Victory in Europe) Day. On the recommendation of the MPTA it was decided that on VE Day transport services should continue to run, however, all employees would receive double pay.

CHAPTER 6

POST-WAR RECONSTRUCTION

The end of hostilities in Europe found the City of Portsmouth in a battered state: the principal shopping centre had been obliterated and the Guildhall burnt out whilst other public buildings destroyed included 30 churches or mission halls, four cinemas, one music hall and a hospital. Almost 70,000 properties existed in 1939 yet air raid damage was reported to over 80,000 properties clearly showing that some had been damaged two, three or even four times. Gradually the damaged housing was cleared and in the years to come there was an exodus to better quality properties in new developments such as Leigh Park and Paulsgrove.

Following a joint application by CPPTD and SMS authority was received to reintroduce pre-war schedules and extend evening operations until approximately 10 p.m. from the city centre and all termini effective from Sunday 13 May 1945.

Reviewing the 1944–45 financial results, the General Manager & Engineer, Mr Ben Hall, commented: 'Trolleybus operations had been entirely satisfactory. No less gratifying is the fact that both Vehicles and Overhead Line equipment have demonstrated their availability to cope with loads far in excess of any previously experienced with maximum reliability.'

By February 1945 war damage to the Transport Department's vehicles amounted to ten motorbuses destroyed and hardly any vehicle escaped damage of some kind, although no trolleybuses were lost. Maximum use continued to be made of trolleybuses on their 21 miles of route due to the need to economise on oil. The Overhead Lines Department was praised for their speedy repairs to trolleybus wires damaged by air raids. In most cases, the overhead equipment was repaired as quickly as the roads were cleared. In short he considered that 'trolleybuses are best'.

Efforts to secure lower traction current charges were successful from 1 April 1945. The Electricity Department reduced their rates to:

First 20,000 units p.a. 1.25d per unit.
20,000 to 40,000 units p.a. 0.95d per unit.
Over 40,000 units 0.8d per unit.

The previous agreement had been 0.8d per unit with an adjustment of 0.015d per 1s per ton rise or fall in the price of coal. It was estimated that power costs would fall by £7,000 during 1945–46 making trolleybus operation even more attractive. Indeed, the intensive use of trolleybuses saw the costs per mile start to fall. It was decided to set £14,000 aside for repairs and renewals deferred by the war and carry forward the balance of £24,253 4s 5d to the Renewals Fund.

The undertaking staged a series of VE celebration dinners on 21, 23 and 28 May 1945 in order that services could be maintained and yet all employees participate. Ben Hall welcomed staff back after war service whilst there was a reunion of wartime conductresses. He noted with sadness that nine employees had been killed.

On 13 May 1945, with the end of seafront access restrictions, daily trolleybus services 3 and 4A were withdrawn from the Southsea *The Strand* – Dockyard portion of their route and reverted to serve Southsea South Parade Pier resulting in the following changes:

3 Cosham Railway Station – Hilsea – North End *Junction* – Fratton Bridge – Southsea *South Parade Pier*
Unidirectional southbound service worked in conjunction with service 4A

4A Southsea *South Parade Pier* – Fratton Bridge – North End *Junction* – Hilsea – Cosham Railway Station
Unidirectional northbound service worked in conjunction with service 3

5 Dockyard *Main Gate* – Royal Pier Hotel – Southsea *South Parade Pier* – Festing Hotel – Eastney – Milton *White House*
Unidirectional service worked in conjunction with service 6

6 Milton *White House* – Eastney – Festing Hotel – Southsea *South Parade Pier* – Royal Pier Hotel – Dockyard *Main Gate*
Unidirectional service worked in conjunction with service 5

It will be noted that services 5 and 6 were reintroduced but only between the Dockyard and Milton 'White House'. Although motorbus services A and B were re-introduced on the same date between Cosham and Palmerston Road via North End and the Guildhall, thereby reverting to their pre-war form, trolleybus services 1A and 2A introduced on 21 June 1942 to replace these motorbus services continued to operate.

The RTC suggested in May 1945 that the CPPTD and SMS should consider a co-ordination scheme for the City and surrounding areas. Mr Hall was instructed to look into similar schemes in other towns and cities. Having considered different options, on 1 August 1945 a subcommittee recommended basing such a scheme on that in place in Plymouth with 'agreed shares' of mileage and receipts, namely 57% to the Corporation and 43% to Southdown. Until the CPPTD was in a position to fulfil this mileage obligation, the lacking mileage would be operated by SMS at the rate of 1s 7d per mile. The proposal was adopted by the Passenger Transport Committee on 15 September 1945.

The *Evening News* letter columns began to fill with comments, dependent on one's individual experiences or favourite, as to the Corporation Transport Department or Southdown's success or otherwise in coping with traffic during the hostilities and in the post-war environment. On 15 May 1945 a Drayton resident wrote: 'The population of Drayton and Farlington pay a large sum of money to the City of Portsmouth annually in the way of rates. Why then are we refused adequate public transport facilities as are other districts? I am told it is because we are served by Southdown. I would point out that the Southdowns run through the district, but those that are Portsmouth bound are invariably full before reaching Farlington. Give us service or reduce our rates.'

A few days later another correspondent wrote: 'It is high time the Corporation stood up for the citizens they represent. Why do they not insist on running their own buses to all the City Boundaries'?

Illuminated trolleybus 204 reappeared on the streets at the Lord Mayor's behest for the Royal and Merchant Navies Week 19–26 May 1945 and continued to operate periodically until the fund closed. During May 1945, a new livery application

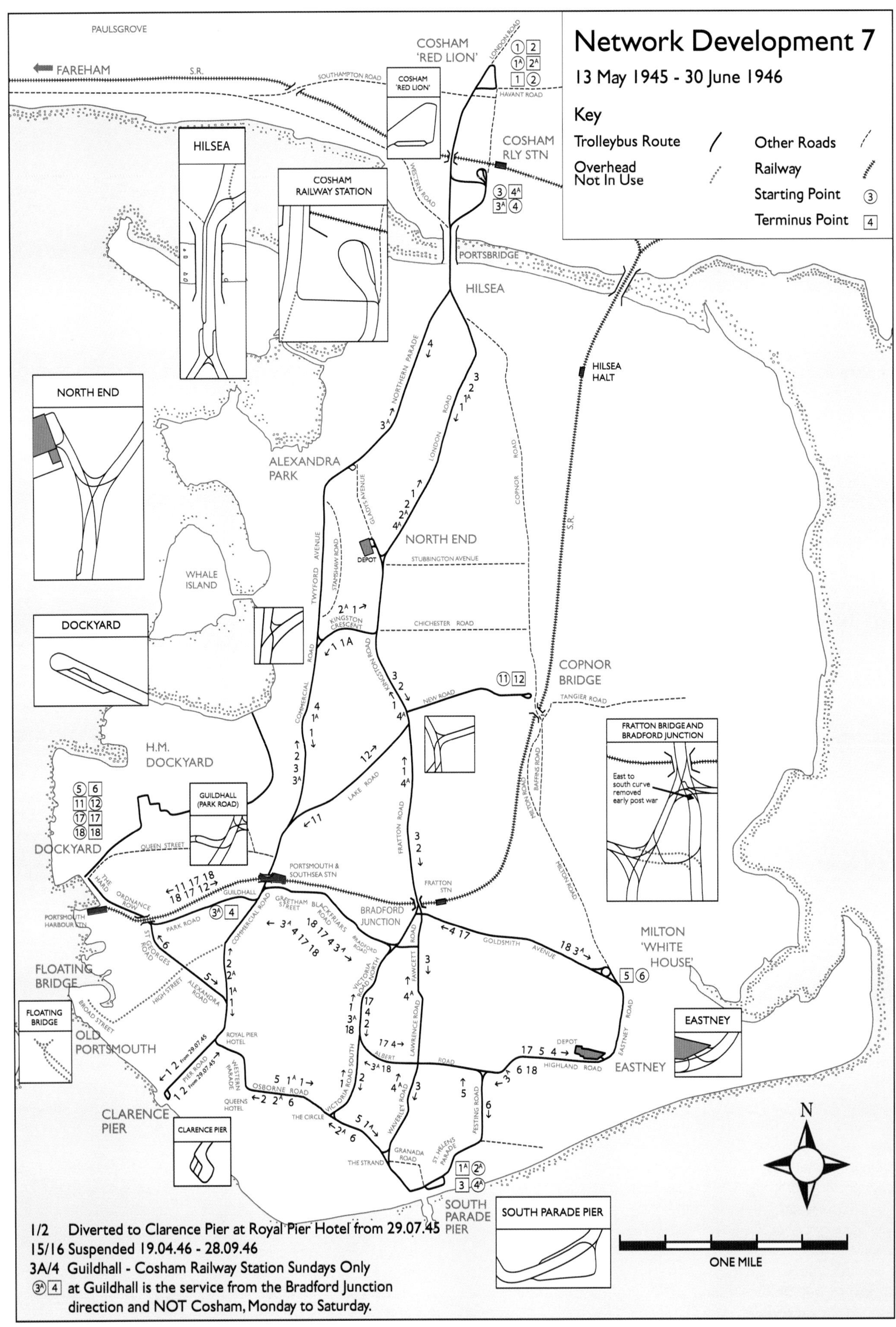

Network Development 7
13 May 1945 - 30 June 1946
Key
Trolleybus Route
Overhead Not In Use
Other Roads
Railway
Starting Point
Terminus Point
PAULSGROVE
FAREHAM
S.R.
SOUTHAMPTON ROAD
COSHAM 'RED LION'
LONDON ROAD
HAVANT ROAD
COSHAM RLY STN
WESTERN ROAD
HILSEA
COSHAM RAILWAY STATION
PORTSBRIDGE
NORTH END
NORTHERN PARADE
LONDON ROAD
COPNOR ROAD
HILSEA HALT
ALEXANDRA PARK
GLADYS AVENUE
DEPOT
STUBBINGTON AVENUE
TWYFORD AVENUE
STAMSHAW ROAD
WHALE ISLAND
DOCKYARD
KINGSTON CRESCENT
CHICHESTER ROAD
KINGSTON ROAD
COMMERCIAL ROAD
NEW ROAD
COPNOR BRIDGE
TANGIER ROAD
H.M. DOCKYARD
LAKE ROAD
FRATTON ROAD
BAFFINS ROAD
MILTON ROAD
FRATTON BRIDGE AND BRADFORD JUNCTION
East to south curve removed early post war
GUILDHALL (PARK ROAD)
QUEEN STREET
PORTSMOUTH & SOUTHSEA STN
FRATTON STN
THE HARD
ORDNANCE ROW
GUILDHALL
PORTSMOUTH HARBOUR STN
PARK ROAD
GREETHAM STREET
BLACKFRIARS ROAD
BRADFORD JUNCTION
BRADFORD ROAD
GOLDSMITH AVENUE
MILTON 'WHITE HOUSE'
ST GEORGES ROAD
FLOATING BRIDGE
HIGH STREET
ALEXANDRA ROAD
VICTORIA ROAD NORTH
FAWCETT ROAD
BROAD STREET
OLD PORTSMOUTH
ROYAL PIER HOTEL
LAWRENCE ROAD
ALBERT ROAD
DEPOT
HIGHLAND ROAD
EASTNEY ROAD
EASTNEY
PIER ROAD
WESTERN PARADE
OSBORNE ROAD
VICTORIA ROAD SOUTH
WAVERLEY ROAD
FESTING ROAD
QUEENS HOTEL
THE CIRCLE
CLARENCE PIER
GRANADA ROAD
ST. HELENS PARADE
THE STRAND
SOUTH PARADE PIER
N
ONE MILE
1/2 Diverted to Clarence Pier at Royal Pier Hotel from 29.07.45
15/16 Suspended 19.04.46 - 28.09.46
3A/4 Guildhall - Cosham Railway Station Sundays Only
3A 4 at Guildhall is the service from the Bradford Junction direction and NOT Cosham, Monday to Saturday.

appeared on trolleybuses. The matt grey paint applied from September 1939 to the roof, front and rear domes, the upper deck rear corner panels on either side of the rear emergency exit and the door itself was retained. The white paint applied to the top of the front mudguards, side life guard rails and base of the rear panels to aid visibility in the 'black-out' was discontinued, 295 being the first trolleybus noted without these aids. The beading was no longer picked out in black. AEC661T trolleybuses 225–300, which were equipped with two tubes beneath the chassis to carry a bamboo trolley retrieval pole or poles, had a plate fitted at the rear of the nearside tube to prevent the pole from sliding out in November 1945.

After protracted correspondence with the military authorities consent was given to re-open Pier Road and Clarence Pier for trolleybuses. It was announced that services would recommence on Sunday 22 July 1945, however, although the overhead equipment was available from that date, services were only restored 1 week later. Services 1 and 2, which had, in principle, operated circular routings between Cosham 'Red Lion' and Southsea *The Circle* since 7 July 1941, reverted to the routing followed until 4 July 1940 and the seafront by providing directional services between Cosham 'Red Lion' and Clarence Pier on Sunday 29 July 1945. Operationally the vehicles terminated at Clarence Pier and did not complete an entire circle:

1 Cosham *Red Lion* – Cosham Railway Station – Hilsea – North End *Junction* – Guildhall – Royal Pier Hotel – Clarence Pier
and
Clarence Pier – Royal Pier Hotel – Southsea *The Circle* – Bradford Junction – Fratton Bridge – North End *Junction* – Cosham *Red Lion*
Unidirectional circular service (anti-clockwise) worked in conjunction with service 2

2 Cosham *Red Lion* – Cosham Railway Station – Hilsea – North End *Junction* – Fratton Bridge – Bradford Junction – Southsea *The Circle* – Royal Pier Hotel – Clarence Pier
and
Clarence Pier – Royal Pier Hotel – Guildhall – North End *Junction* – Hilsea – Cosham *Red Lion*
Unidirectional circular service (clockwise) worked in conjunction with service 1

These services operated from approximately 9 a.m. on weekdays and 1.30 p.m. on Sundays. The 1A and 2A continued to run from Cosham 'Red Lion' to Southsea South Parade Pier in parallel with the 1 and 2 as far as the Royal Pier Hotel and thence via Southsea Terrace, Western Parade, Osborne Road and Clarendon Road to Southsea South Parade Pier. On the same date a new pair of trolleybus services was introduced between Copnor Bridge and Clarence Pier via Fratton Bridge and The Strand. Initially undesignated, these became services 7 and 8 on 1 July 1946.

Although the undertaking was doing its best to get services back to pre-war standards they were hampered by a shortage of crews whilst by July 1945 workmen were complaining at the heavy passenger loads due to holidaymakers returning to Southsea and the South Coast. One correspondent to the newspaper complained that during the early part of the evening trolleybuses were arriving at Fratton Bridge from Southsea full to capacity. 'One or two may alight, allowing a few to get on, but quite a lengthy queue is left behind, and the majority are workers who have already had a long train journey from work, and have probably had to stand in the corridor all the way.' He referred to the example of Bournemouth where there was a priority queuing system for workmen.

Just after midnight on 14/15 August 1945 it was officially announced that the Japanese had surrendered. Public holidays were declared on VJ (Victory in Japan) Day, Wednesday 15 August 1945, and 16 August 1945. Large bonfires were lit on Portsdown Hill, Southsea Common and on Eastern Road whilst community singing in Guildhall Square was led by a Royal Marines band. The crowds heading for the city centre led to traffic diversions resulting in motorbuses replacing trolleybuses on some services. On 16 August 1945 there was a Service of Thanksgiving in Guildhall Square and festivities continued for the rest of the week.

Following their landslide victory in the first post-war General Election, held on 26 July 1945, the new Labour Government introduced a series of Bills to bring key industries into public ownership. The country's municipal transport undertakings anticipated that this could lead to their nationalisation and although this did not happen, the Transport Bill, introduced into the House of Commons on 27 November 1946, and the Electricity Bill, which followed in early 1947, were to have far-reaching effects on trolleybus operators throughout the country.

Part IV (Passenger Road Transport) of the Transport Bill proposed that the foreseen British Transport Commission might 'for any area approved by the MoT, prepare and submit to the Minister a scheme as to the road passenger transport services serving the area, being a scheme devised for the purpose of promoting or facilitating the promotion of the co-ordination of the passenger transport services serving the area, whether by road or by rail, and the provision of adequate suitable and efficient passenger road transport services to meet the needs of the area'. Compensation to municipal undertakings was not included except for annual sums to cover the sinking fund and interest charges on their outstanding debts.

By now some 65 employees had returned to duty from HM Forces having been deemed fit to resume duties. In addition 103 traffic and 18 depot employees were engaged in the course of summer 1945 resulting in a net gain of 111 to the labour force.

Pontypridd UDC Transport Department wrote on 10 October 1945 that they were now able to release the two remaining trolley vehicles on hire, AEC663Ts 212 and 215, and that arrangements would be made for their return to Portsmouth. They arrived back at the end of April 1946, although 212 never re-entered service in the City. The first of the four trolleybuses loaned to Pontypridd to re-enter service in Portsmouth was Sunbeam MS3 214 during October 1947. Sunbeam MS3 213 still retained its pre-war double lining and AEC663T 215, which was rebuilt upon its return and featured single lining, reappeared in July 1949.

Dockyard Outmuster times, i.e. the end of the day shift, changed around the beginning of November 1945. Shortly afterwards the RTC enquired if, in view of the undertaking's financial position over the last 3 years, they were now considering restoring the penny fares withdrawn in October 1940. They were informed that this was not the case.

SMS informed the Subcommittee looking into a Joint Agreement in November 1945 that they sought a 21 year agreement whereas Portsmouth Corporation felt it should

Rear views of two AEC661T Cravens bodied trolleybuses, 252 and 248, on The Hard in front of the Dockyard Main Gates. The devastation caused by wartime bombing is very evident on the other side of the road. A conductor under training prior to uniform issuance is on rear platform. (Omnibus Society)

initially be limited to 5 years. Correspondence in the press was generally against the idea of a co-ordination agreement and a public meeting on 18 December 1945 at the Royal Beach Hotel resulted in 75 electors voting in favour but 107 against thereby refusing public consent for the promotion of the necessary Bill in Parliament.

On the evening of 17 January 1946 City Councillors gave their views on the proposed co-ordination agreement with Southdown to electors in ten wards. At the St. Simon Ward meeting Lieutenant-Colonel G. M. O'Rorke presiding said that the proposed Corporation Bill merely gave the Council powers to make an agreement. Southdown Motor Services would not benefit at the expense of the City as the division of receipts assured that the increased traffic on any particular route would be shared in an agreed proportion. In terms of profits from the transport undertaking being used to reduce the rates or deficiencies of the undertaking being supported by the rates there had been a net loss of £4,345 over the last

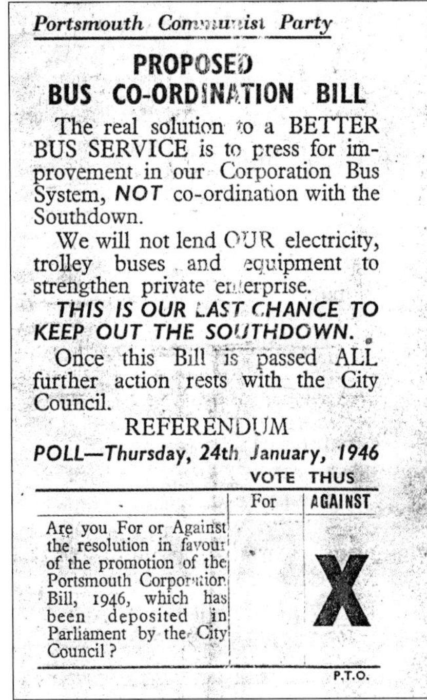

Portsmouth Communist Party

PROPOSED BUS CO-ORDINATION BILL

The real solution to a BETTER BUS SERVICE is to press for improvement in our Corporation Bus System, ***NOT*** co-ordination with the Southdown.

We will not lend OUR electricity, trolley buses and equipment to strengthen private enterprise.

THIS IS OUR LAST CHANCE TO KEEP OUT THE SOUTHDOWN.

Once this Bill is passed ALL further action rests with the City Council.

REFERENDUM

POLL—Thursday, 24th January, 1946

VOTE THUS

	For	AGAINST
Are you For or Against the resolution in favour of the promotion of the Portsmouth Corporation Bill, 1946, which has been deposited in Parliament by the City Council?		**X**

P.T.O.

DO YOU KNOW THAT—

This Enabling Bill will allow the City Council to negotiate with Southdown to share all receipts.

Trolley Bus Profits cannot be shared with Southdown without this Enabling Bill.

The Trolley Buses made £72,272 profit in seven months, from April 1st to Dec. 7th, prior to deduction of Income Tax. This was DOUBLE the profit made on the petrol buses.

The total profit after deduction of Income Tax, for the same period, was £48,523 for the whole transport service.

This is sufficient to give us back the PENNY FARE.

This Bill will strengthen the claim of Southdown to greater compensation when transport is NATIONALISED.

These are some of the Reasons why you should

VOTE AGAINST THE BILL

Published by the Portsmouth Communist Party, 288a, Fratton Road, Portsmouth, and Printed by London Caledonian Press Ltd. (T.U. all Depts.), 74 Swinton Street, W.C.1.—22289

thirty years. The transport undertaking was now in a much improved position. Based on the estimated earnings for the financial year ending on 31 March 1946 it was expected that the Corporation would take £540,000 and run 5,060,000 miles whereas SMS would take £530,000 and run 5,300,000 miles. The Corporation would thus run 48.5% of the mileage and take 50.49% of the receipts. However, the estimated figures were expected to grow to £746,000 and 7,500,000 miles against £555,000 and 5,500,000 miles in the financial year ending 31 March 1947. The Corporation would then run 57% of the mileage and receive 57% of the receipts.

Replying to a question Lieutenant-Colonel O'Rorke said that the Corporation would probably want to extend their trolleybus services and if in the future it was necessary to lease trolleybus equipment to the Company, terms which were fair to the Corporation would be negotiated.

SMS remained intransigent as to the duration of a co-ordination agreement and this proposal was finally recommended to Portsmouth Council by their Finance and General Purposes Committee. This provoked letters in the press complaining of how SMS had a history of 'hoodwinking' the citizens into a 'merger' of services! Nonetheless the agreement was signed on 24 May 1946 effective from 1 July 1946 for a period of 21 years and in 1946 SMS wrote to terminate the Wartime Operating Agreement from 30 June 1946.

The Portsmouth Corporation Act of 1946 authorised the Corporation and SMS to provide and work a co-ordinated passenger transport network in Portsmouth and surrounding area bounded by Fareham, Petersfield and Emsworth. Within this area the CPPTD were to operate 57% of the total mileage and SMS the other 43% with receipts pooled in the same proportions. Although there is no evidence whatsoever that any such move was ever considered, should SMS wish to operate trolley vehicles on any routes within the co-ordinated area, the provisions of the Portsmouth Corporation (Trolley Vehicles) Act and Orders of 1930 and 1935 would apply. If Southdown were to operate trolleybuses the Corporation were to allow the company to use Corporation overhead equipment and afford the company such facilities as might be necessary in or for the working of such service or services.

On 29 December 1945 a little girl D. L. Arrow was knocked down and killed by a trolleybus. The department was asked for financial assistance towards the funeral expenses and an *ex gratia* grant of £10 was made.

Another round of wage increases affected the undertaking. The Joint Wages Board of Employers for the Vehicle Building

In early post-war condition AEC661T/English Electric trolleybus 201 from the experimental fleet waits on the east side of the Clarence Pier terminal layout. The conductor displays his TIM ticket machine. (A.D. Packer)

The revised terminal layout at Cosham Railway Station featuring an anti-clockwise loop and siding came into use in September 1948. Trolleybus 201 is seen here on a warm 9 October 1948 whilst one of the 1935 AEC661T / English Electric vehicles, 216–224, possibly 223, is operating on services 19 and 20 (an unusual duty for this class) which used the outer loop. (Online Transport Archive [photographer V.C. Jones])

This and a number of other images were kindly provided by OnlineTransport Archive, a UK-registered charity dedicated to the preservation of transport-related films and images. For further information see www.onlinetransportarchive.org

Industry notified an increase in the war bonus from 7 July 1945 involving 44 employees and costing £670 p.a. The 40 employees governed by AEU agreements for the electricity supply industry benefited from an increased war bonus of 6½d per hour from November 1945 and 7d from 17 December 1945 all costing an additional £450 p.a. Then from 14 February 1946 the NJIC for the Road Passenger Transport Industry awarded an increase of 7s per week to traffic staff estimated to cost £17,865 p.a.

Mr H.C. Simmonds, the Assistant to the General Manager, was appointed Assistant Manager and Engineer in January 1946.

At the request of local residents the stop in Clarendon Road at the corner of Worthing Road (withdrawn as a fuel economy in the war) was reinstated in January 1946.

Two spare traction motor armatures were purchased from English Electric at £172 17s 6d each in April 1946 to avoid trolleybuses being kept off the road for long periods due to breakdowns.

Commencing on Saturday 11 May 1946 illuminated trolleybus 204 re-appeared on the streets for Portsmouth Safety Week making a 4-hour tour each evening. Leaving Eastney Depot at 6.30 p.m. on the first evening 204 travelled via Southsea South Parade Pier to the Guildhall (7.10 p.m.) from whence it followed a circular route to North End, Cosham 'Red Lion', North End, Fratton Bridge, Southsea South Parade Pier, where it turned before continuing to the Dockyard and back to the Guildhall (9.25 p.m.). It then made another circular trip via Bradford Junction and Southsea South Parade Pier back to the Guildhall before finally leaving at 10.15 pm for Milton and Eastney Depot. The following day, 12 May 1946, 204 left Milton at 6.35 p.m. and made for the Guildhall via Fratton Bridge. Three circular tours covering different routes in the city were operated from the Guildhall with departures at 6.50 p.m., 7.20 p.m. and 8.50 p.m. before the vehicle returned to Eastney Depot via Southsea South Parade Pier leaving the Guildhall at 10.00 pm. On Monday the tours started at Eastney and the rest of the week from Milton. It was noted that the illuminated vehicle would not operate in wet weather.

A week of victory celebrations began on 26 May 1946 when some trolleybuses appeared decorated with the GR cypher, separated by the Crown, mounted on a piece of cardboard about 5ft by 1ft, beneath the cab windscreen. Illuminated 204 was again in use but details are not known. These excursions led to a complaint in the local press in June 1946 concerning the waste of electricity in running an illuminated trolleybus, at a time when restrictions were being enforced in the use of street lighting.

Free transport was granted to children at the Lord Mayor's request for the children's Victory Celebrations on Southsea Common 27 May–1 June 1946. Some 4,000 children were expected daily, estimated to cost £247 10s, the amount being charged to the Lord Mayor's account. In addition, free travel was granted to all naval personnel of Dominion's ships visiting the port. Finally, as recommended by the NJIC, all CPPTD employees were given a holiday with pay on Saturday 8 June 1946 for the Victory Celebrations; those who had to work were paid double time and given time off in lieu.

The Piers, Beach and Publicity Department loaned their 1935 Ford V8 mobile canteen, registration CGN232, to CPPTD in spring 1946 subject to it being overhauled, repainted and maintained. The canteen was regularly located at Cosham Railway Station Compound and was bought for £100 in April 1949.

Seen shortly after Cosham Railway Station terminus was rebuilt for anti-clockwise operation in 1948 (traction poles used to support the earlier clockwise layout are evident in the background) Karrier E4 211 with MCCW and F all-metal body waits in the sunshine. The mobile canteen can be seen to the right of the trolleybus but 211's conductor prefers to inhale deeply on his Senior Service cigarette! (Online Transport Archive [photographer V.C. Jones])

The following comparisons for the periods 27 April–24 May in 1945 and 1946 respectively show the resurgence of passenger travel (trolleybuses only):

	1946	1945	Increase (+) or decrease (-)
Traffic receipts	£24,905	£22,760	+ £2,145
Miscellaneous receipts	£732	£513	+£219
Total receipts	£25,637	£23,273	+£2,364
Passenger carried	3,549,281	3,206,893	+342,388
Mileage run	250,748	194,470	+56,378
Average number of trolleybuses in service per day	69	62	+7
Maximum number of trolleybuses in service on any one day	74	70	+4
Receipts per mile (pence)	24.54	28.74	-4.20
Average fare per passenger	1.73	1.74	-0.1

Extracts from the 1945–46 Annual Report accompanied by Mr Hall's comments on trolleybus operation:

	1945–46	1944–45	1938–39
Net total income	£312,975	£277,034	£166,439
Working expenses	£205,776	£179,972	£131,645
Gross or trading profit	£107,199	£ 97,062	£ 34,594
Trading profit as percentage of working expenses	52.1%	53.9%	26.3%
Bank interest	£495	£921	£798
Loan charges	£16,660	£22,386	£39,563
Capital expenditure from revenue	–	£1,550	£712
Air raid precautions	£42	£1,152	–
Net profit	£90,992	£72,895	-£4,528 (loss)
Mileage	2,851,297	2,308,548	2,520,907
Passengers carried	43,270,359	37,957,528	27,821,366

It is not surprising, in view of earlier remarks, to find that the financial results of the Trolley Bus operations this year should have proved so entirely satisfactory. Not less gratifying is the fact that both vehicles and Overhead Line Equipment have demonstrated their ability to cope with loads far in excess of any previously experienced, with maximum reliability.

The gross profit, as shown above, amounts to 52.1% of expenses, and the net profit amounts to 29.07% of income. Receipts per mile are 26.19d as compared with 28.80d last year (15.85d). Operating expenses, on the other hand, have decreased less in proportion from 18.71d to 17.32d (12.552d).

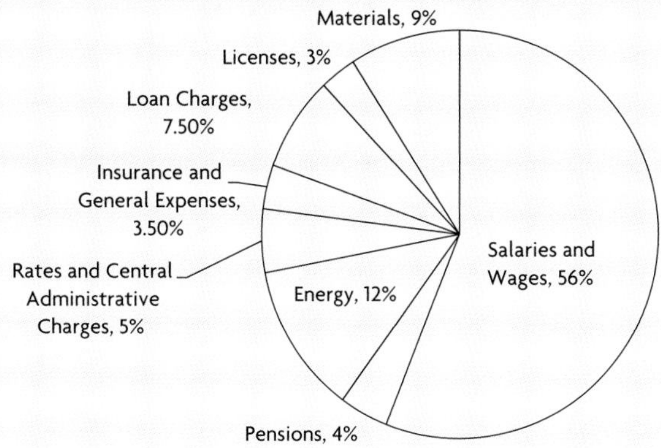

Total expenditure including Revenue Account Items for the 12 months ending 31 March 1946 – £222,478.

Mr Hall noted in respect of the financial results for the year ending 31 March 1946 that despite the substantially higher trolleybus mileage operated, the annual cost of traction power had fallen due to the lower power charges: 1944–45 £27,194; 1945–46 £25,836. During the course of the year a parking loop was installed in the westbound Albert Road line wiring immediately to the east of the Kings Theatre. As the Overhead Line Department began to catch up on its maintenance backlog, the cost of renewals and replacements rose from £4,544 in 1944–45 to £5,195 in 1945–46.

Vehicle advertising had been based on an informal arrangement with Griffiths and Millington since 1 January 1944 and it was decided to invite tenders on a percentage basis. The company had been granted an advertising contract for 5 years in 1931 for a fixed sum of £33 p.a. per tramcar and omnibus. When trolleybuses were introduced, a new agreement was made from 30 July 1934 granting the right to advertise on the trolley vehicles until such date as the conversion was complete and then for a further 7 years thereafter. Thus for 7 years from 1 January 1937 they would pay £25 per vehicle or 60% of receipts whichever was greater and £33 p.a. per motorbus. These conditions were suspended from 1 September 1939, the Company paying 60% of receipts. Messrs Griffiths and Millington suggested that the agreement should continue on these same terms for another 3 or 4 years and on 16 July 1946 their suggestion (60% of all receipts to be paid to the Corporation) was accepted for 3 years from 1 January 1946.

The Joint Services Co-ordination Agreement commenced on Monday 1 July 1946 together with the summer timetable which saw last departures of all services extended to 11 p.m. whilst some services were strengthened for the season. Additional trolleybus services introduced and Sunday morning journeys were revised from Sunday 7 July 1946. The undesignated services introduced on 29 July 1945 between Copnor Bridge and Clarence Pier were numbered as the 7 and 8 running every 12 minutes in the mornings and every 10 minutes in the afternoon and evening. Services 13 and 14 provided a new connection between Cosham Railway Station and Southsea South Parade Pier via Victoria Road. Services 3A and 4 were extended after midday from the Guildhall to Alexandra Park. Finally, the 'Fratton Road' portion, i.e. by way of Southsea The Circle, Bradford Junction, Fratton Bridge and North End Junction, of services 1 and 2 were subsumed into the new Monday–Saturday (only) circular services 9 and 10.

The trolleybus services from 1 July 1946 were therefore as follows:-

1 Cosham *Red Lion* – Hilsea – North End *Junction* – Guildhall – Royal Pier Hotel – Clarence Pier
Unidirectional southbound service worked in conjunction with service 2

2 Clarence Pier – Guildhall – North End *Junction* – Hilsea – Cosham *Red Lion*
Unidirectional northbound service worked in conjunction with service 1

1A Cosham *Red Lion* – Cosham Railway Station – Hilsea – North End *Junction* – Kingston Crescent – Commercial Road – Guildhall – Royal Pier Hotel – Southsea *The Circle* – Southsea *South Parade Pier*
Unidirectional southbound service worked in conjunction with service 2A

2A Southsea *South Parade Pier* – Southsea *The Circle* – Royal Pier Hotel – Guildhall – Commercial Road – Kingston Crescent – North End *Junction* – Hilsea – Cosham *Red Lion*
Unidirectional northbound service worked in conjunction with service 1A

3 Cosham Railway Station – Hilsea – North End *Junction* – Fratton Bridge – Southsea *South Parade Pier*
Unidirectional southbound service worked in conjunction with service 4A

4A Southsea *South Parade Pier* – Fratton Bridge – North End *Junction* – Hilsea – Cosham Railway Station
Unidirectional northbound service worked in conjunction with service 3

5 Dockyard *Main Gate* – Royal Pier Hotel – Southsea *South Parade Pier* – Festing Hotel – Eastney – Milton *White House*
Unidirectional service worked in conjunction with service 6

6 Milton *White House* – Eastney – Festing Hotel – Southsea *South Parade Pier* – Royal Pier Hotel – Dockyard *Main Gate*
Unidirectional service worked in conjunction with service 5

3A Alexandra Park – Guildhall – Bradford Junction – Fratton Bridge – Milton *White House* – Eastney – Festing Hotel – Bradford Junction – Guildhall – Alexandra Park – Hilsea – Cosham Railway Station
Monday – Saturday
Unidirectional northbound service worked in conjunction with service 4 involving the clockwise circumnavigation of the Bradford Junction – Fratton Bridge – Milton – Eastney Bradford Junction circle and operation between Guildhall Square and Bradford Junction in both directions.

3A Guildhall – Alexandra Park – Hilsea – Cosham Railway Station
Sundays only
Unidirectional northbound service worked in conjunction with Sunday service 4

4 Cosham Railway Station – Hilsea – Alexandra Park – Guildhall – Bradford Junction – Festing Hotel – Eastney – Milton *White House* – Fratton Bridge – Bradford Junction – Guildhall – Alexandra Park
Monday – Saturday
Unidirectional southbound service worked in conjunction with service 3A involving the all day anticlockwise circumnavigation of the Bradford Junction – Eastney – Milton – Fratton Bridge – Bradford Junction circle and operation between Guildhall Square and Bradford Junction in both directions

4 Cosham Railway Station – Hilsea – Alexandra Park – Guildhall
Sundays only
Unidirectional southbound service worked in conjunction with Sunday service 3A

7 Copnor Bridge – Fratton Bridge – Bradford Junction – Southsea *The Strand* – Royal Pier Hotel – Clarence Pier
Unidirectional southbound service worked in conjunction with service 8

8 Clarence Pier – Southsea *The Strand* – Bradford Junction – Fratton Bridge – Copnor Bridge
Unidirectional northbound service worked in conjunction with service 7

9 Cosham *Red Lion* – Cosham Railway Station – Hilsea – North End *Junction* – Guildhall – Royal Pier Hotel – Southsea *The Circle* – Bradford Junction – Fratton Bridge – North End *Junction* – Hilsea – Cosham *Red Lion*
Monday – Saturday
Unidirectional circular service (anti-clockwise) worked in conjunction with service 10.

10 Cosham *Red Lion* – Cosham Railway Station – Hilsea – North End *Junction* – Fratton Bridge – Bradford Junction – Southsea *The Circle* – Royal Pier Hotel – Guildhall – North End *Junction* – Hilsea – Cosham *Red Lion*
Monday – Saturday
Unidirectional circular service (clockwise) worked in conjunction with service 9

11 Copnor Bridge – Guildhall – Dockyard *Main Gate*
Unidirectional southbound service worked in conjunction with service 12

12 Dockyard *Main Gate* – Guildhall – Copnor Bridge
Unidirectional northbound service worked in conjunction with service 11.

13 Cosham Railway Station – Hilsea – North End *Junction* – Fratton Bridge – Bradford Junction – Southsea *The Circle* – Southsea *South Parade Pier*
Unidirectional southbound service worked in conjunction with service 14. Extended to Cosham Red Lion evenings and Sundays

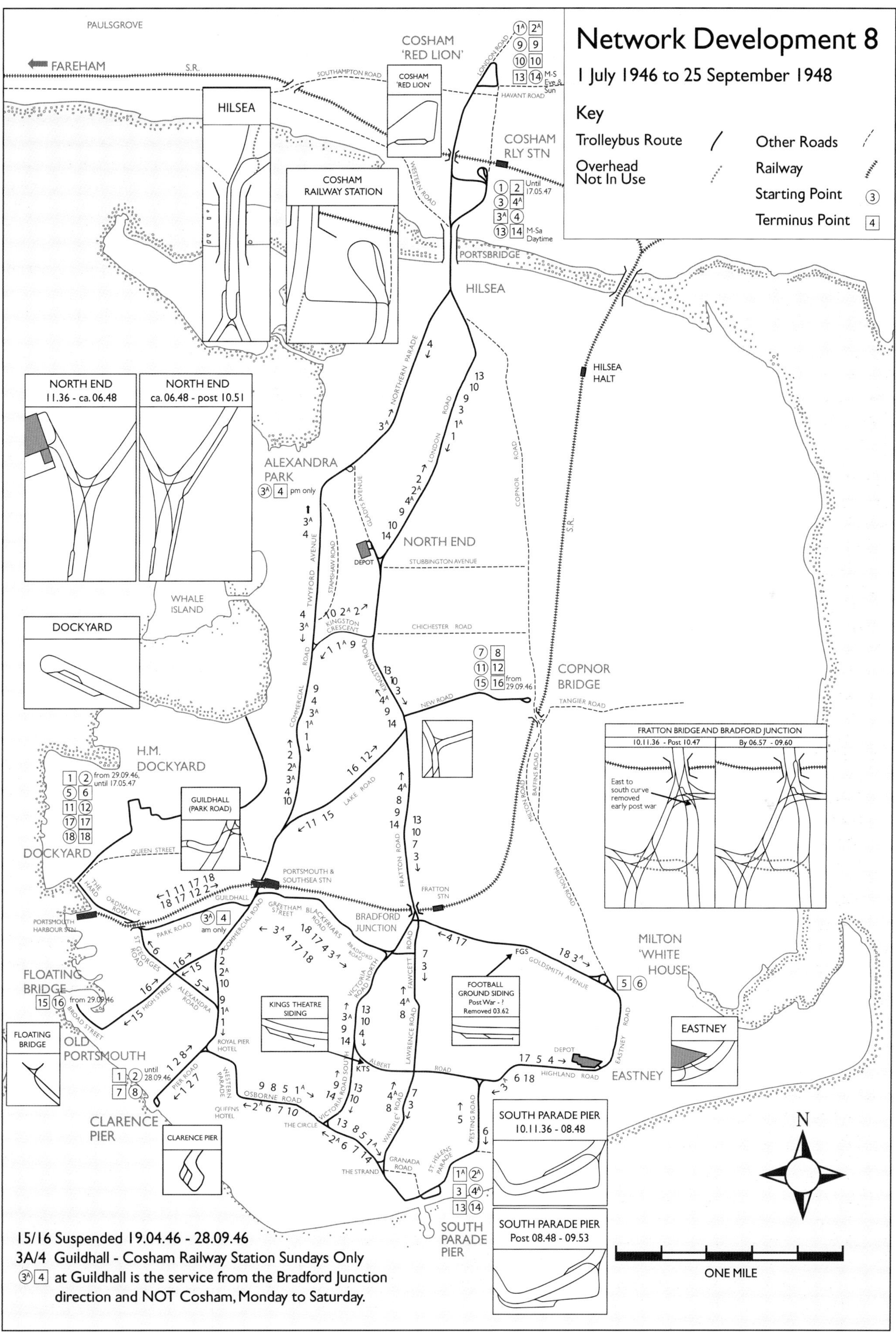

Network Development 8
1 July 1946 to 25 September 1948
Key
Trolleybus Route
Overhead Not In Use
Other Roads
Railway
Starting Point
Terminus Point
PAULSGROVE
FAREHAM
COSHAM 'RED LION'
COSHAM RLY STN
COSHAM RAILWAY STATION
HILSEA
PORTSBRIDGE
HILSEA HALT
NORTH END 11.36 - ca. 06.48
NORTH END ca. 06.48 - post 10.51
ALEXANDRA PARK
NORTH END
WHALE ISLAND
DOCKYARD
H.M. DOCKYARD
COPNOR BRIDGE
FRATTON BRIDGE AND BRADFORD JUNCTION
10.11.36 - Post 10.47
By 06.57 - 09.60
East to south curve removed early post war
GUILDHALL (PARK ROAD)
PORTSMOUTH & SOUTHSEA STN
FRATTON STN
BRADFORD JUNCTION
MILTON 'WHITE HOUSE'
FOOTBALL GROUND SIDING Post War - ? Removed 03.62
KINGS THEATRE SIDING
FLOATING BRIDGE
OLD PORTSMOUTH
CLARENCE PIER
EASTNEY
SOUTH PARADE PIER 10.11.36 - 08.48
SOUTH PARADE PIER Post 08.48 - 09.53
SOUTH PARADE PIER
ONE MILE
N
15/16 Suspended 19.04.46 - 28.09.46
3A/4 Guildhall - Cosham Railway Station Sundays Only
3A 4 at Guildhall is the service from the Bradford Junction direction and NOT Cosham, Monday to Saturday.

14 Southsea *South Parade Pier* – Southsea *The Circle* – Bradford Junction – Fratton Bridge – North End *Junction* – Hilsea – Cosham Railway Station
Unidirectional northbound service worked in conjunction with service 13. Extended to Cosham Red Lion evenings and Sundays

17 Dockyard *Main Gate* – Guildhall – Bradford Junction – Festing Hotel – Eastney – Milton *White House* – Bradford Junction – Guildhall – Dockyard *Main Gate*
Unidirectional circular service (anti-clockwise) worked in conjunction with service 18

18 Dockyard *Main Gate* – Guildhall – Bradford Junction – Milton *White House* – Eastney – Festing Hotel – Bradford Junction – Guildhall – Dockyard *Main Gate*
Unidirectional circular service (clockwise) worked in conjunction with service 17

The normal Monday–Saturday, off-peak frequencies were as follows and required 74 trolleybuses:

Service	Journeys per hour	Vehicles required
1 & 2	6	6
1A & 2A	6	6 (12 evenings)
3 & 4A	6	6 (12 evenings)
3A & 4	6	12
5 & 6	8	7
7 & 8	6	5
9 & 10	6	10
11 & 12	12	8
13 & 14	6	6
17 & 18	6	8

Services 9 and 10 ceased after the evening peak thus the 10 trolleybuses allocated to these services, changed over at Cosham 'Red Lion' to enhance the frequencies of the 1A, 2A, 3, 4A, 13 and 14 for the remainder of the evening. Trolleybuses 201–211 returned to service in 1946, with most from July 1946, after their wartime storage. These vehicles had not been used regularly after 1936, but they were now regularly employed on services 3, 4A, 9, 10, 13 and 14, most remaining continuously licensed until the end of the 1949 summer season.

On Wednesday evening 7 August 1946 a traction power failure in the Bradford Road-Albert Road area meant that trolleybus passengers heading for the King's Theatre in Albert Road missed the start of the performance. Motorbuses were substituted until power could be restored an hour later. There was another mishap on Saturday 7 September 1946 when one trolleybus tried to overtake another in Lawrence Road, Southsea. The de-wirement that followed led to a trolley head parting company with the trolley boom whereupon it crashed through the windows of one of the vehicles. Passenger Mrs Ena Grimes was fortunate to suffer only cuts to her face.

Although it had been decided in July 1946 to restore trolleybus services to Old Portsmouth as soon as possible, it was only with the introduction of the winter timetable on 29 September 1946 that services 15 and 16, running every 10 minutes, reappeared for the first time since 31 December 1944 (the Cosham Street – Floating Bridge motorbus shuttle service continuing in the meantime). Services 1 and 2 were rerouted to the Dockyard instead of Clarence Pier from the same date:

1 Cosham *Red Lion* – Cosham Railway Station – Hilsea – North End *Junction* – Guildhall – Dockyard *Main Gate*
Unidirectional southbound service worked in conjunction with service 2

2 Dockyard *Main Gate* – Guildhall – North End *Junction* – Hilsea – Cosham *Red Lion*
Unidirectional northbound service worked in conjunction with service 1

15 Copnor Bridge – Guildhall – Old Portsmouth – Floating Bridge
Unidirectional southbound service worked in conjunction with service 16

16 Floating Bridge – Old Portsmouth – Guildhall – Copnor Bridge
Unidirectional northbound service worked in conjunction with service 15

There was a collision between a service 8 trolleybus and a lorry near Clarendon Park, Southsea, on 5 November 1946 which led to four passengers and the lorry driver being taken to hospital. The trolleybus cab was damaged on the front nearside.

The County Borough of Bolton had owned four trolleybuses operated by South Lancashire Transport on their interurban trolleybus route to Leigh since 1936. However, abandonment of the town's remaining tram routes had been interrupted by the war. On 21 November 1946, a deputation from their Council visited Portsmouth to inspect the trolleybus system with a view to replacing their last trams with trolleybuses. The party visited Eastney and North End Depots, and watched rush hour departures from the Dockyard Main Gate. Bolton replaced its final tram route with motorbuses on 29 March 1947 whilst the interurban trolleybus route closed on 25 March 1956.

There were a number of requests for a direct trolleybus service between Eastney and North End via Goldsmith Avenue. A census of passengers transferring between services at Fratton Bridge suggested that the only solution would be to extend services 5 and 6 from Milton 'White House' to Fratton Bridge and then to North End. However, this did not appear to be justified as it would unnecessarily increase the frequency along Goldsmith Avenue, Fratton Road and Kingston Road. Despite agreeing in principle to a 3-month trial extension, on 18 February 1947 Mr Hall reported that this would be impossible as CPPTD's mileage stipulated in the co-ordination agreement had already been reached.

In an effort to improve passenger facilities a survey showed that 54 of the most frequented loading points had no passenger shelter provided and it was decided to rectify this situation.

Some of the worst winter weather on record, characterised by fog, ice and heavy snowfalls, was experienced in the first 3 months of 1947 making road and rail transport difficult. Coal was being exported in great quantities to help the nation's balance of payments difficulties and those coal stocks for domestic consumption froze solid; the result was coal shortages and widespread electricity cuts. Delivery of the coal that was available was subject to delays as the railways battled with the weather conditions and a shortage of fuel. The crisis deepened when dockers and lorry drivers went on strike, the forces taking over some of their work. By February 1947 heavy snow falls had made the fuel shortage worse and it was decided that, in an effort to conserve coal used in the generation of electricity, trolleybus services could be withdrawn from 10.30 p.m. or other suitable time as and when required.

There was also a spate of weather-related accidents. A car driven by Mr L. Crease collided with a trolley vehicle and the undertaking took legal action to cover the cost of the damage. Mr Wells the trolleybus driver died shortly afterwards, but it has proved impossible to clarify if this was as a result of the accident.

Agreement was reached to reconstruct the turning circle at Cosham Compound with a new overhead wiring layout at a net cost of £145, allowing for the value of the reclaimed materials. The additional traction poles necessary were planted in July 1947 and the new layout came into use in August 1948.

Vast crowds welcomed the Royal Family when they returned from South Africa onboard HMS *Vanguard* with a procession through the city on 12 May 1947 and a ceremony on the steps of the burnt-out Guildhall. No vehicles were permitted on the royal route between The Hard and Portsmouth and Southsea station, trolleybuses to and from the northern parts of the city turning at the junction of Commercial Road and Lake Road between 9 a.m. and 11 a.m.

At the first meeting of the Passenger Transport Committee in 1947 the General Manager was instructed to prepare a comprehensive report on future trolleybus route extensions. At their 18 February 1947 meeting it was resolved that the report be submitted to the Planning Committee and placed on the Joint Transport Committee Agenda with the addition of a route from Commercial Road through Unicorn Road to the Unicorn Gate of HM Dockyard. Neither the Planning and Reconstruction Committee or the Joint Transport Committee had objections to the plans or the additional proposal to extend trolleybuses from Cosham through the new Paulsgrove Housing Estate on the line of the proposed 'Link Road'.

On 20 May 1947 the Passenger Transport Committee resolved to apply to the MoT for a Provisional Order and recommended the following extensions to the City Council:

i. Cosham 'Red Lion' to Farlington Rectory Avenue via Havant Road (1.87 miles).
   Motorbus services M and N would thus be replaced by trolleybuses whilst the installations would simplify the proposal of an extension to Leigh Park.
ii. Milton 'White House' to Hilsea 'Coach and Horses' where there would be a junction with the London Road route via Milton Road and Copnor Road, returning via Copnor Road, Baffins Road and Milton Road (2.87 miles).
   This route had been covered by tramway extension powers. Either services 5 and 6 or a pair of the services then terminating at Copnor Bridge would be extended to Cosham.
iii. North End Junction to Northern Parade (Alexandra Park) via Gladys Road (0.46 miles).
   This link was seen primarily as a diversionary route and to avoid dead mileage of vehicles running to or from North End Depot.
iv. North End Junction to Copnor Road via Stubbington Avenue (0.66 miles).
   This link would permit the introduction of through services to and from Green Lane thereby improving public transport connections at the northern end of Copnor Road.
v. Copnor Bridge to Stanley Avenue via Tangier Road (0.66 miles).
   Stanley Avenue would be served by an extension of the services terminating at Copnor Bridge and a link to Palmerston Road and/or the Dockyard would be introduced.
vi. Commercial Road to HM Dockyard Unicorn Gate via Edinburgh Road and Unicorn Road (0.3 miles).
   An oft-requested improvement of public transport facilities for the Dockyard.
vii. London Road (junction with Spur Road), Cosham, to Portchester Cross Roads through the expanding Paulsgrove and Wymering Housing Estates (2.41 miles).
   Seen as an additional travel facility to and from the rapidly growing housing estates.

These extensions had an estimated cost of £36,920. The proposals did not require a major expansion of the trolleybus fleet (perhaps one or two vehicles for each service pair) and would eliminate the sometimes excessive terminal layover times. It was stated that single bracket arms would be used in Stubbington Avenue, Gladys Avenue, Baffins Road and Milton Road (between Milton roundabout and Hayling Avenue), with span wires being used elsewhere.

It will be noted that in May 1947 proposed extension (vii) to Portchester (cross roads of East Street, Castle Street, West Street and Station Road) was foreseen as being built along the proposed 'Link Road' as far as Tetbury Road, which has since been subsumed into Allaway Avenue and was immediately to the south of Washbrook Road, then via Allaway Avenue, Jubilee Avenue and Portsview Avenue, thereafter south along Hill Road and Station Road, and not along the length of Southampton Road as shown in pre-war plans. There was a low bridge beneath the railway at Portchester Station which would have necessitated the use of single deck trolleybuses! It is assumed that upon review it was decided that any extension through Paulsgrove and Wymering would have to terminate to the north of the railway line and it was then proposed to install a reversing triangle at the west end of Jubilee Avenue at its junction with Portsdown Road, Paulsgrove, i.e. the City Boundary (as shown by diagrams dated August 1947 that still exist).

It was also realised that proposed extension (ii) would need to be considered as two routes from a legislative perspective to accommodate the one way sections south of Copnor Bridge between Tangier Road and Priorsdean Avenue where Milton Road was followed northbound and Baffins Road was followed southbound. This led to proposal (ii) being renumbered as proposals (ii) and (iii), all further proposals being renumbered consecutively (the Wymering and Paulsgrove extension thus becoming proposal (viii)).

The Passenger Transport Committee recommended all the above, renumbered extensions to the City Council for their approval and application for a Provisional Order under Section 32 of the Portsmouth Corporation Act 1930. These were approved on 14 October 1947 by the City Council and application was made to the MoT for a Provisional Order. However, the formal announcement in the newspapers, dated 22 November 1947, makes no reference to proposal (viii) Cosham – Wymering – Paulsgrove, and it has proved impossible to ascertain at what stage in the process and by whom (the Passenger Transport Committee, the City Council or the MoT) this was deleted. Amongst the possible causes for its disappearance could be the post-war shortage of central government funds for a loan, the lack of progress with the dual carriageway 'Link Road' or the uncertain course of Allaway Avenue across the former Portsmouth racecourse.

Karrier E4/MCCW and F211 has just arrived at Cosham Railway Station terminus from Southsea South Parade Pier in summer 1947. The blinds are already set for its departure back to South Parade Pier on service 3. Portsmouth Road, Cosham, is to the rear. (David Harvey [photographer's name not recorded])

1934 Karrier E4 211 with MCCW and F body of the experimental fleet is seen on a service 3 journey in London Road just north of Kirby Road on 25 October 1947. In an early advertising coup Youngs have linked Nelson's HMS Victory, flagship of the Royal Navy and still open to visitors in HM Dockyard, and the recent wartime victory with one of their products. (D.A.P. Janes [photographer G.A. Tucker])

In September 1947 4 miles of trolley wire at a cost of £308 6s per ton were ordered from Johnson and Nephew.

On 22 November 1947 the newspapers carried an announcement concerning what the MoT would consider in their 1946–1947 session:

PORTSMOUTH CORPORATION ACT 1930

PORTSMOUTH CORPORATION (TROLLEY VEHICLES) PROVISIONAL ORDER

(Routes for trolley vehicles in the City of Portsmouth; Borrowing of money; Incorporation or amendment of Acts).

Notice is hereby given that pursuant to and in accordance with Section 32 of the Portsmouth Corporation Act 1930 the Lord Mayor Aldermen and Citizens of the City of Portsmouth (hereinafter referred to as 'the Corporation') intend to apply to the Minister of Transport on or before the 23rd day of December 1947 for a Provisional Order for all or some of the following amongst other purposes (that is to say):-

1. To authorise the Corporation to use trolley vehicles along the following routes in the City namely:

Route No. 1 (1 mile 7 furlongs 0.45 chains or thereabouts in length) commencing at the junction of Havant Road London Road and High Street (Cosham) proceeding along Havant Road to and terminating at a point 2 chains east of its junction with Rectory Avenue.

Route No. 2 (2 miles 7 furlongs 9.31 chains or thereabouts in length) commencing at the junction of Milton Road, Eastney Road and Goldsmith Avenue proceeding along Milton Road to and over Copnor Bridge thence proceeding along Copnor Road to and terminating at its junction with London Road.

Route No. 3 (2 furlongs 2.27 chains or thereabouts in length) commencing by a junction with Route No. 2 at the southern junction of Baffins Road and Milton Road proceeding along Baffins Road to and terminating by a junction with Route No. 2 at the northern junction of Baffins Road and Milton Road.

Route No. 4 (3 furlongs or thereabouts in length) commencing in Gladys Avenue at the terminus of the existing trolley vehicle system proceeding along Gladys Avenue to and terminating at its junction with Northern Parade.

Route No. 5 (5 furlongs 2.4 chains or thereabouts in length) commencing at the junction of London Road and Stubbington Avenue proceeding along Stubbington Avenue to and terminating by a junction with Route No. 2 authorised by this Order in Copnor Road at a point therein opposite Burrfields Road.

Route No. 6 (5 furlongs 3.9 chains or thereabouts in length) commencing by a junction with Route No. 2 authorised by this Order in Milton Road at a point 3 chains south-east of the centre of Copnor Bridge proceeding along Milton Road and Tangier Road to and terminating at a point therein 4.54 chains east of its junction with Stanley Avenue

Route No. 7 (2 furlongs 3.77 chains or thereabouts in length) commencing at the junction of Commercial Road and Edinburgh Road proceeding along Edinburgh Road and Unicorn Road to and terminating at its junction with Flathouse Road.

The Royal Assent was given on 30 July 1948. It was decided that the Overhead Line Department should carry out the overhead line construction for the trolleybus route extensions rather than invite tenders for the work. The post of Overhead Line Superintendent had been vacant since 1941 but in November 1947 Mr Hall suggested that in view of the major expansion plans Mr C. Cole, Overhead Line Foreman for just over a year and who was already performing all the Superintendent's duties, should be promoted to this position. Mr Cole's re-grading was postponed until after the Royal Assent and he was only promoted in November 1948.

On 18 May 1947, new motorbus services M and N, Farlington, Rectory Avenue – Cosham – North End – Dockyard, were introduced and, despite the prevailing enthusiasm for electric traction, trolleybus services 1 and 2, which followed the same route between Cosham and the Dockyard, were withdrawn completely after having operated for only 8 months.

It was decided on 20 May 1947 to considerably increase the number of passenger waiting shelters in the City based on a style of metal shelters supplied by The Equipment & Engineering Co. Ltd. of London WC2. There were two standard designs, enclosed 15ft 10¾in. x 3ft 9in., and open cantilever which could be extended in length with additional sections. The majority of sites were on current or planned trolleybus routes, namely:

Devonshire Avenue, junction Eastney Road	2 open
Priory Crescent, Milton Road	1 open
St Mary's Hospital, Milton Road	1 open extended
Milton Road, Hayling Avenue	1 open
Rectory Avenue, Farlington	1 enclosed
Cosham 'Red Lion'	2 open
Hilsea 'Coach & Horses', London Road stop	1 open
North End Junction (northbound)	2 open
North End Junction (southbound)	2 open
Chichester Road, London Road	1 open
Kingston Cross, Kingston Crescent (southbound)	1 open
New Road, Kingston Road (north side)	1 open
Kingston Church, Fratton Road (east side)	1 open
Kingston Church, Fratton Road (west side), move existing shelter on east side and re-erect on west side.	Remove
Goldsmith Avenue, Fratton Bridge (north side)	1 open extended
Goldsmith Avenue, Winter Road	1 open
Festing Hotel Junction	2 open
Albert Road, Festing Road	1 open
Trolleybus Private Road, Southsea *South Parade Pier*	1 open extended
Beach Hotel	1 open
Palmerston Road, Osborne Road	1 open
Osborne Road, Handley's Corner	1 open
Pier Hotel (northbound stop)	1 open
Guildhall Square (east side)	2 open extended
Guildhall Square (west side)	2 open
Park Road, Guildhall Square	3 open
Commercial Road, Edinburgh Road	2 open
The Hard (east side)	2 open extended

In June 1948 Equipment and Engineering advised that they were unable to obtain the necessary steel allocation and offered aluminium shelters instead with delivery in 5 to 6 weeks. This increased the cost from £3,120 to £4,441 7s 6d plus erection, glazing and painting by CPPTD. Delivery began at the beginning of December 1948 and the first cantilever shelter was erected in February 1949 at the Festing Hotel stop in Albert Road. In the meantime some sections of the cast metal passenger waiting shelter, which had previously stood in Guildhall Square, had been re-erected at Cosham Railway Station adjacent to the Private Road, on the southern side of the turning circle.

Due to the increased cost of production, the Electricity Department notified a new traction power tariff in September 1947. This was based on a unit charge of 0.80d per kWh subject to an increase or a decrease of 0.0007d for each rise or fall respectively of 1d per ton in the cost of fuel, based on a standard cost of 38s a ton at a calorific value of 11,000 BTUs per lb. The increase represented an increase of about 5% on the basic charge or £1,650 p.a. and was introduced on 10 October 1947 with a review after 12 months. As if to emphasise the validity of the Department's arguments the NJIC for the Electricity Supply Industry announced a reduction in the working week from 47 to 44 hours at the end of October 1947. Within CPPTD this affected 47 men resulting in additional costs of approximately £1,100 p.a.

Both booms of a trolleybus de-wired on Fratton Bridge soon after 4 p.m. on Friday 17 October 1947 with the Dockyard outmuster underway. This caused one of the trolley wires to burn through resulting in a short circuit which cut-off traction power within the Fratton Bridge – Lake Road section supplied from Vivash Road substation. Power was restored by 5.20 p.m. In the meantime motorbuses ran a shuttle service between Fratton Bridge and Lake Road, and between Fratton Bridge and the Guildhall.

The fleets of most road transport operators had suffered from neglect or damage during the war and Portsmouth was no exception. However, the large number of motorbuses and trolleybuses equipped with Cravens bodies supplied in 1936–37 had fared particularly badly. Cravens bodies did not enjoy a high reputation for longevity or solidity. Having committed themselves to a policy of extending the trolleybus system, the undertaking commenced a comprehensive programme of reconstructing the Cravens bodied vehicles in the fleet in late 1947. The first trolleybus to reappear from the workshops was AEC661T 229 in May 1948 and three further trolleybuses, 260, 265, 290, went through the reconstruction process in the course of the year (see Appendix A for details). The vehicles concerned represented a considerable capital investment and it would have been unacceptable to replace virtually the entire fleet with new trolleybuses. Another option would have been to re-body the entire batch. However an in-house solution was no doubt deemed more politically and socially acceptable.

A swan flew into the upper deck windows of a trolleybus crossing Portsbridge on 21 November 1947. On hearing crashing glass from the upper deck Driver Gilham stopped and found a swan had struck the bus. No passengers were injured but the RSPCA had to destroy the swan.

A broken trolley wire in London Road to the north of North End Junction in the early afternoon of 6 January 1948 brought trolleybuses between North End and Cosham to a halt dislocating services throughout the city. Single line working was instigated within 20 minutes and motorbuses temporarily served other portions of the services concerned. All was back in working order in time for the peak hour.

As further evidence of his high reputation in the industry, Mr Ben Hall, the General Manager and Engineer, was appointed in January 1948 to represent the PTA and the MPTA on the MoT's Road Safety Committee.

In view of the impending nationalisation of the electricity industry in February 1948 Mr Hall recommended that the Transport Department should take over responsibility for the street lighting extension pieces fitted to traction poles. As at 1 April 1947 their estimated value was £1,266 and from that date the Passenger Transport Committee was credited with a rental allowance of 2s p.a. for each extension piece plus 1s 6d per pole annually for painting. More generally, later in the year the Parks and Open Spaces Committee were granted permission to hang flower baskets from traction poles.

Griffiths and Millington, the undertaking's advertising contractors, offered to pay 66.67% of the amounts received from advertisers instead of 60% for the rental of advertising space for the next 5 years when their contract expired on 31 December 1948. Alternatively, they offered to pay 70% for the second period of 5 years in the case of a 10 year contract. The offer for 10 years was accepted in March 1948.

By April 1948 the undertaking had 1266 employees of whom 798 were engaged in traffic operating duties.

Roof repairs to North End Depot were badly needed by spring 1948 and £3,000 had been included in the current estimates for the work. Wolverhampton Corrugated Iron Co. Ltd.'s quotation of £2,704 for the supply and fixing of Robertson Protected Metal Roofing, excluding the removal of the present roof which would be done by CPPTD staff, was accepted. The Depot Stores had been severely damaged by enemy action and replacement of the brickwork in the south west corner was also needed. The work was completed on 9 May 1949.

During June 1948 a revised trolleybus livery appeared. This was identical with that applied to motorbuses since August 1936, but for the retention of the grey roof introduced in 1939, and featured a ⅜in. wide yellow line painted below the lower deck windows and rectangular lining out around the advertisement panels. Some trolleybuses, however, continued to appear in the livery introduced in May 1945.

Overhead line alterations at Bradford Junction, presumably the removal of the east to south curve from Victoria Road North into Fawcett Road, were completed on 14 May 1948. On 26 June 1948, the southbound Fratton Road stop at North End Junction was moved from just north of Stubbington Avenue to a point about 50 yards south of the latter road in order to accommodate a cross-over and passing loop in the overhead wiring. Changes to the overhead layout at Southsea South Parade Pier were completed on 14 August 1948 and at Cosham Railway Station (Cosham Compound) on 26 August 1948.

English Electric supplied two sample sets of trolleybus equipment in August 1948. These proved satisfactory and when they were offered for sale in September 1950 at £330 each they were immediately purchased and charged to capital.

Long overdue, there was a spate of letters to the newspapers about the 'Great Portsmouth bus mystery' suggesting that a more understandable service numbering system should be introduced. One correspondent wrote: 'Services 3 and 3A, for instance, seem to have no connection at all; services A and B are shaped like the profile of a pear with stalk, so that at Hilsea either version of it may be going in either direction, if you get me (you don't, nor will any visitor!)'. There was also a plea for the same service number or letter to be displayed in both directions.

When the winter timetable was introduced on 26 September 1948 all service numbers with an A suffix were eliminated. The

Sunbeam MS3 214 with MCCW and F all metal body stands at the Southsea South Parade Pier stop outside the Royal Beach Hotel following its February 1948 repaint in pre-war livery (Livery 1) but with roof, front and rear domes, and upper deck rear corner panels retaining the matt grey introduced in 1939. It will be noticed that the lower and upper deck waistband beadings were picked out in black; this had not been normal practice in the pre-war livery originally applied to the Metro-Cammell bodied trolleybuses. (Online Transport Archive [photographer G.F. Ashwell])

1A and 2A were renumbered 1 and 2, the 3 and 4A became the 3 and 4, and the 3A and 4 became the 20 and 19 thereby solving, in part, the 'mystery'.

1 Cosham *Red Lion* – North End *Junction* – Kingston Crescent – Guildhall – Royal Pier Hotel – Southsea *South Parade Pier*
Unidirectional southbound service worked in conjunction with service 2

2 Southsea *South Parade Pier* – Royal Pier Hotel – Guildhall – Kingston Crescent – North End *Junction* – Hilsea – Cosham *Red Lion*
Unidirectional northbound service worked in conjunction with service 1

3 Cosham Railway Station – Hilsea – North End *Junction* – Fratton Bridge – Southsea *South Parade Pier*
Unidirectional southbound service worked in conjunction with service 4
Southsea *South Parade Pier* – Fratton Bridge – North End *Junction* – Hilsea – Cosham Railway Station
Unidirectional northbound service worked in conjunction with service 3

19 Cosham Railway Station – Alexandra Park – Guildhall – Bradford Junction – Festing Hotel – Eastney – Milton *White House* – Fratton Bridge – Bradford Junction – Guildhall – Alexandra Park
Unidirectional anticlockwise service worked in conjunction with service 20

20 Alexandra Park – Guildhall – Bradford Junction – Fratton Bridge – Milton *White House* – Eastney – Festing Hotel – Bradford Junction – Guildhall – Alexandra Park – Cosham Railway Station
Unidirectional clockwise service worked in conjunction with service 19

The Town Clerk pointed out in October 1948 that there were no up-to-date byelaws; those in use still related to tramcars and had last been printed in 1929. It was suggested that these should be repealed and replaced with new ones in the terms of Part III of the Public Service Vehicles (Conduct of Drivers, Conductors and Passengers) Regulations, 1936, also with application to shelters and waiting rooms. The estimated cost was £200 but no action was taken.

With the exception of essential workmen's services all normal services were suspended on Christmas Day 1948. Normal services never operated again on Christmas Day and at some stage workmen's services also ceased.

Mr Hall was asked to consider including fare tables in the timetables and increased publicity given to their sale, potentially at enquiry offices and from conductors.

On 24 November 1948 tenders were invited for 236 steel tubular traction poles BSS No. 8/1939 for the first trolleybus

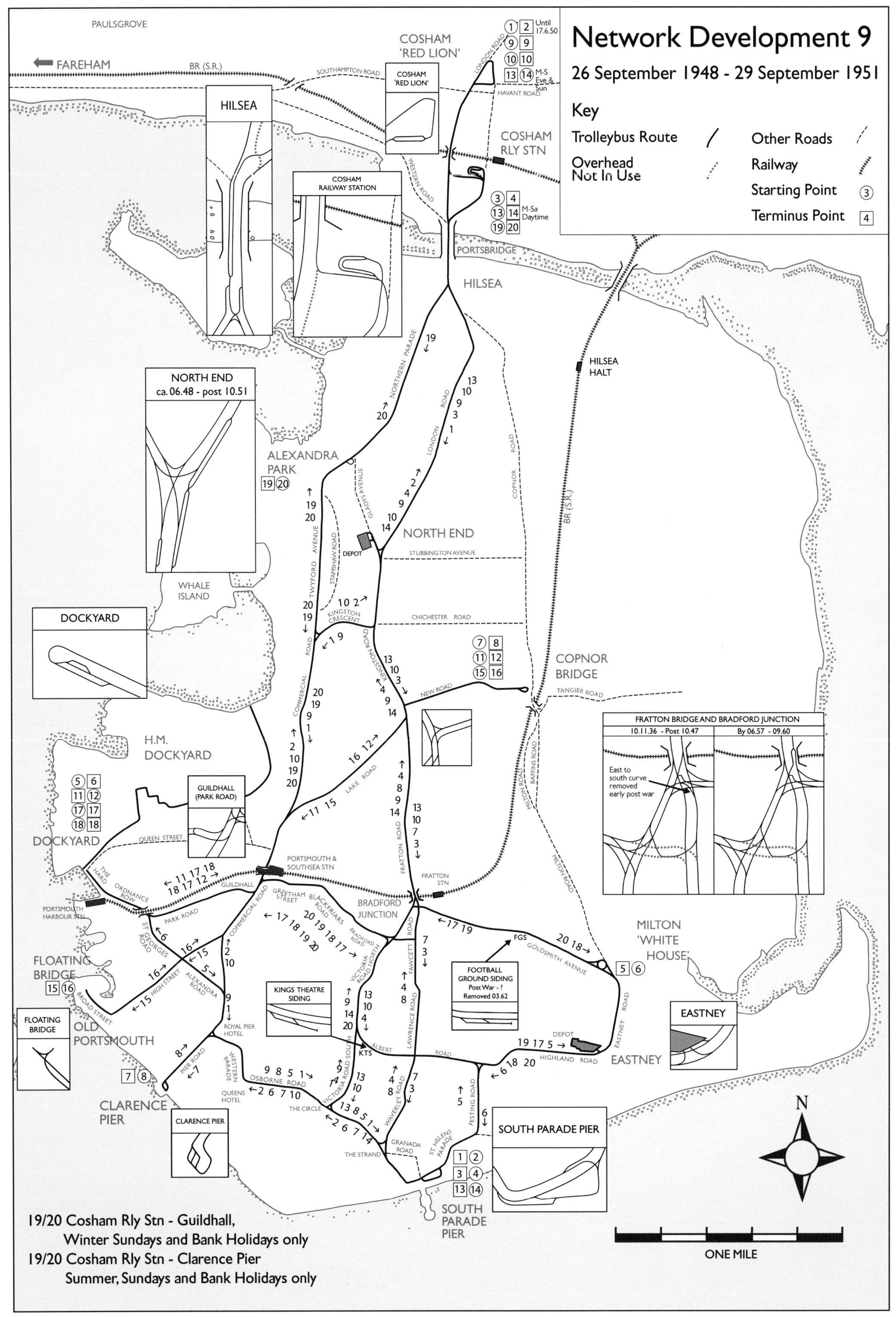
Network Development 9
26 September 1948 - 29 September 1951
Key
Trolleybus Route
Other Roads
Overhead Not In Use
Railway
Starting Point
Terminus Point
PAULSGROVE
FAREHAM
BR (S.R.)
SOUTHAMPTON ROAD
COSHAM 'RED LION'
HAVANT ROAD
LONDON ROAD
Until 17.6.50
M-S Eve & Sun
M-Sa Daytime
COSHAM RLY STN
HILSEA
COSHAM RAILWAY STATION
WESTERN ROAD
PORTSBRIDGE
HILSEA HALT
NORTH END ca. 06.48 - post 10.51
NORTHERN PARADE
ALEXANDRA PARK
GLADYS AVENUE
COPNOR ROAD
NORTH END
STUBBINGTON AVENUE
TWYFORD AVENUE
STAMSHAW ROAD
DEPOT
WHALE ISLAND
KINGSTON CRESCENT
CHICHESTER ROAD
DOCKYARD
COMMERCIAL ROAD
KINGSTON ROAD
NEW ROAD
COPNOR BRIDGE
TANGIER ROAD
H.M. DOCKYARD
LAKE ROAD
FRATTON BRIDGE AND BRADFORD JUNCTION
10.11.36 - Post 10.47
By 06.57 - 09.60
East to south curve removed early post war
GUILDHALL (PARK ROAD)
MILTON ROAD
BAFFINS ROAD
QUEEN STREET
FRATTON ROAD
PORTSMOUTH & SOUTHSEA STN
THE HARD
ORDNANCE ROW
GUILDHALL
FRATTON STN
PORTSMOUTH HARBOUR STN
GREETHAM STREET
BLACKFRIARS ROAD
BRADFORD JUNCTION
PARK ROAD
BRADFORD ROAD
FAWCETT ROAD
FGS
GOLDSMITH AVENUE
MILTON 'WHITE HOUSE'
ST GEORGES ROAD
FLOATING BRIDGE
HIGH STREET
ALEXANDRA ROAD
VICTORIA ROAD NORTH
KINGS THEATRE SIDING
FOOTBALL GROUND SIDING Post War - ? Removed 03.62
EASTNEY ROAD
EASTNEY
BROAD STREET
OLD PORTSMOUTH
ROYAL PIER HOTEL
LAWRENCE ROAD
DEPOT
ALBERT ROAD
KTS
HIGHLAND ROAD
PIER ROAD
WESTERN PARADE
OSBORNE ROAD
VICTORIA ROAD SOUTH
WAVERLEY ROAD
FESTING ROAD
QUEENS HOTEL
CLARENCE PIER
THE CIRCLE
SOUTH PARADE PIER
THE STRAND
GRANADA ROAD
ST HELENS PARADE
N
ONE MILE
19/20 Cosham Rly Stn - Guildhall, Winter Sundays and Bank Holidays only
19/20 Cosham Rly Stn - Clarence Pier Summer, Sundays and Bank Holidays only

1935 AEC661T 216 with English Electric all metal body waits at Cosham Railway Station bus terminal (Cosham Compound) beneath the 25° Y frog providing entry to the loop installed in August/September 1948 as part of the revised overhead wiring layout here. A cover has been fixed over the ventilators above each driver's windscreen to prevent water ingress and reduce draughts into the driver's cab. (Roy Marshall)

AEC661T/English Electric 203 heads a line of trolleybuses at Cosham Railway Station terminus. BTS Library (photographer's name not recorded)

route extensions totalling approximately 3 miles. Two tenders were received and the lowest, from Stewarts and Lloyds Ltd. at £5,287 17s 0d, was accepted on 10 January 1949.

Tenders were invited on 1 December 1948 for 20 2-axle trolleybus chassis complete with 50 or 52 seat double-deck Highbridge bodies, or alternatively for the supply and delivery of chassis only or bodies only. Responses were required by 13 January 1949 although two tenders were received late. Nonetheless they were added to the list. Subsequently Crossley Motors Ltd. wrote on 21 February 1949 that due to revised prices for certain items of electrical equipment, they could reduce the cost of their chassis with English Electric equipment by £43 per chassis. It was decided that their amended tender could not be considered. Restrictions on building developments at Leigh Park resulted in the Passenger Transport Committee reducing the number of vehicles required from 20 to 15. On 24 February 1949 they accepted the tender of British United Traction Ltd. for the supply of BUT9611T chassis with English Electric equipment at £2,371 13s per chassis, subject to Mr Hall's report why this tender, although not the lowest, was recommended. It is presumed that the BUT9611T was favoured due to the close similarities to the AEC661T. They also accepted the tender of H. V. Burlingham Ltd. for all metal 52-seat bodies at £2,820 each this being the lowest tender received for this type of body. Unfortunately it has proved impossible to establish what other tenders were received although it is known that the local company of Reading and Co. Ltd. tendered for the bodywork.

It was proposed to apply to the Public Works Loan Board for a loan to purchase the new trolley vehicles and overhead line equipment. The Corporation had powers to borrow £80,000 for vehicles and £37,000 for the provision of equipment along the routes authorised by the Order. In view of Britain's poor financial situation at this time, the application had to be considered first by the MoT before they made a recommendation to the Board and the Treasury that the expenditure was essential and that the borrowing was necessary.

It was discovered on 21 January 1949 that thieves had stolen 17 cwt 17 lb of trolley wire worth £80 from Eastney Depot over the preceding 6 weeks.

Hants Relay Ltd. had some 969 fixtures to traction poles supporting cables for distributed radio services for which they paid 1s each p.a. In March 1949 the Department gave 12 months notice to terminate the agreement with the intent of negotiating a higher payment. This proved successful and from 1 May 1950 the company paid 2s 6d p.a. per pole.

The MPTA held their annual congress in Portsmouth 14–17 June 1949 and free travel was provided for delegates with lunch being offered to the 21-member Executive Council.

After 23 years service to Portsmouth, Ben Hall was nearing retirement and it was decided to place him on the maximum salary £1,650 p.a., an increase of £50, effective from 1 January 1949. His experience was still sought after and in May 1949 the Road Transport Executive asked if the Corporation would agree to release him for 2 days a week for c. 12 months to assist in the valuation of the road haulage vehicle fleets which would be acquired under the Transport Act, 1947. This was agreed to, the Executive refunding his Corporation salary, superannuation and NI payments, and paying Mr Hall a £350 p.a. retaining fee plus expenses.

On 29 May 1949, summer schedules came into operation and services 19 and 20 were extended to Clarence Pier on Sundays, instead of turning at the Guildhall, exactly as the 3A and 4 had done in previous summers.

CPPTD was confronted by a further wage award from the NJIC Electricity Supply Industry in June 1949 of 1½d per hour effecting 53 of their employees in the Overhead Line Department, estimated to cost an additional £1,263 p.a.

A letter in the 4 September 1949 edition of the *Evening News* from a Mr F. E. J. Ward commented that a large number of trolleybuses had not turned a wheel in service throughout the summer. Only 208 and 210 of the original 15 trolleybuses were used in rush-hour services but ratepayers were being asked to foot the bill for 75 new motorbuses and trolley vehicles over the next three years. He went on 'the reintroduction of services 1 and 2 would relieve the motorbuses going beyond Cosham if, and only if, a protective fare was reintroduced on the latter in rush hours or if limited-stop buses were run. If this is impossible why not carry out the original intention of extending the overhead wires to Paulsgrove (temporarily along Southampton Road until the new road is built into the Estate) and thereby obviate the need for changing vehicles with such waste and delay of transport?'.

The City Treasurer reported on 20 September 1949 that as it was not proposed to proceed for the time being with the construction of Route No. 1 (Cosham 'Red Lion' to Farlington Rectory Avenue via Havant Road) authorised by the 1948

AEC661T/Cravens 236 stands on The Hard at the Dockyard terminus in the 1948 livery with simplified lining application. (Malcolm Pearce [photographer G.O.P. Pearce])

265 stands on The Hard at the Dockyard terminus. (Malcolm Pearce [photographer G.O.P. Pearce])

Order Confirmation Act, 1948 or for the proposed Route No. 8 (Cosham to Paulsgrove via Jubilee Avenue and Allaway Avenue), for which MoT approval had not yet been sought, the estimated cost had fallen to £21,080. It is understood that an initial loan application was made for £90,845 to cover the cost of equipping the routes and the 15 new trolley vehicles.

At the beginning of October 1949 the MoT responded that in view of the economic situation it was necessary to reduce capital expenditure to a minimum; only proposals that were vital to maintaining the efficiency of transport systems could be supported. They asked that the application be reviewed and the proposals reduced or postponed. The Passenger Transport Committee did not waiver from their view that there was full justification for an immediate loan. The object of purchasing trolleybuses was to economise and reduce the use of imported liquid fuels. Fuel oil continued to increase in price, costing the undertaking an additional £5,000 a year. The Council had a contract to buy 15 trolleybuses and it was suggested that if the Treasury approval was refused these vehicles would have to be purchased from revenue. Despite considering an amendment to defer construction of the extensions by 12 months it was decided to proceed with the application for a reduced loan of £69,765 in respect of the trolley vehicles and the equipment of Routes 2 (Milton 'White House' to Hilsea 'Coach and Horses' via Copnor Road) and 7 (Edinburgh Road (junction with Commercial Road) to Dockyard Unicorn Gate) as authorised by the Portsmouth Corporation (Trolley Vehicles) Order Confirmation Act, 1948. Treasury Consent for the reduced amount was given on 2 August 1950.

The British Electricity Authority, Southern Division, warned Mr Hall in September 1949 that a substantial increase in traction current charges could be expected. This materialised in June 1950 with notification from what had now become the Southern Electricity Board (SEB) of their intention to terminate the present agreement and introduce one based on maximum demand and units consumed. In the event of a national agreement for traction supplies being reached with the MPTA, the SEB would adopt its provisions. Mr Hall stated that the result would be an annual increase of £820 or 2½% based on the current equipment and consumption but an increase of £2,900 or almost 9% when all the extensions had been brought into service. These figures included the capital and service charges payable on the new substation equipment.

The frequency on services 15 and 16 was reduced from 15 minutes to 18 minutes on the 25 September 1949. This prompted the Port of Portsmouth Floating Bridge and Steam Launch Co. and the Portsmouth and Gosport Joint Board in February 1950 to ask for an improved trolleybus service to and from Point, i.e. Floating Bridge, as their ferry service was proving uneconomic. The Department responded that a more frequent service would be loss-making. The Floating Bridge vehicular ferry ceased to operate on 31 December 1959.

At lunchtime on 12 October 1949 a power cut brought trolleybuses between North End and Cosham to a halt for about 30 minutes. Also in October 1949 two Crompton Parkinson C.422 traction motors were purchased at £495 net each.

The Association of Municipal Corporations held a conference in London on 23 March 1949 to discuss the Road Transport Executive's preparation of area road transport schemes under Part IV of the Transport Act 1947. Around 400 delegates gathered from all over the country to discuss means of ensuring that local authorities would retain control of the Road Passenger Transport Undertakings in their area, in the event of the MoT creating area road transport schemes under the Act, and of retaining local authority ownership of the undertakings concerned. Portsmouth, together with many other municipalities, lodged their objection with the Executive

AEC663T 215 with MCCW and F all metal body was loaned to Pontypridd UDC from August 1942 until April 1946. It was completely rebuilt in May–June 1949 and repainted into the 1948 livery (Livery 4), returning to service in July 1949. It is seen in this condition outside Milanis store North End on clockwise circular service 10 to/from Cosham 'Red Lion'. (David Harvey collection [photographer's name not recorded])

AEC661T 283 turns out of Western Parade into Bellevue Terrace at the Royal Pier Hotel on the edge of Southsea Common on a service 2 (iii) journey. The overhead wiring branching off to the right of the photograph leads to Pier Road and Clarence Pier (John Carter [photographer C. Carter]) (David Harvey collection [photographer's name not recorded])

in October 1949 in respect of the proposed Northern Area Scheme. Ben Hall agreed to remain as General Manager and Engineer for a further year or until such time as the position of the undertaking might be decided under any future legislation after reaching his retirement age in January 1950.

A growing pile of traction poles at the Cosham Compound prompted an enquiry in March 1950 as to when the Copnor Road extensions were to be started. During the ensuing months it became clear that 168 poles would be planted in Milton Road and Copnor Road, and a further 32 in Stubbington Avenue. It was foreseen that the street lighting on these sections would be transferred to the traction poles. A further 254 traction poles for the proposed extensions were purchased: 100 second-hand from London Transport at £20 16s 8d, each and the remainder new from Stewarts and Lloyds at £38 each.

The City staged an Industrial and Civic Exhibition on Southsea Common from 17 June 1950 to 1 July 1950. AEC661T 204 was re-licensed for the month of June and appropriately decorated and illuminated for the occasion. It ran to a special timetable for the fortnight. A circular journey was operated from Eastney departing at 2 p.m. each afternoon taking 2½ hours, whilst each evening a more complex routing, varying each evening, was run starting from Eastney or Milton at about 6.30 p.m. and returning to Eastney Depot between 11.00 and 11.25 p.m. (dependent on the day of the week). Passengers could board or alight at any stop on the route; however, a 6d minimum fare applied and no half fares were available for children.

By June 1950 the Joint Transport Committee realised that higher fares were needed on both the trolleybuses and motorbuses. The City Council delegated to the Passenger Transport Committee power to apply to the MoT and Licensing Authority for the South Eastern Traffic Area as appropriate and an application for revised fares was made in February 1951.

There was a power failure in Southsea during the evening peak of 15 August 1950. Trolleybuses came to a halt in Albert Road, Fratton Road, Greetham Street and Victoria Road, normal service being resumed soon after 6.0 p.m. In the meantime, the few motorbuses not already in use operated an emergency service.

On 1 November 1950 the first four BUT9611Ts, 301–304, entered service from North End Depot. The remainder appeared during the next four months, the last, 315, entering service on 25 March 1951. The majority of the BUT9611Ts were based at North End for their first year or so and ran on all North End Deport services. The Burlingham bodies incorporated an offside destination screen, the last vehicles in the Portsmouth fleet to be delivered with this feature, and a pair of single seats amidships in the lower saloon, aimed at easing congestion caused by standing passengers. Due to increased material and labour costs the total cost of the 15 vehicles was £3,550 higher than when the order had been placed.

Sunbeam MF2 210 heading to Cosham 'Red Lion' approaching North End Junction opposite the Odeon cinema. The road on the nearside is Derby Road with St Marks Church on the corner. (A.D. Packer)

Karrier E4/MCCW and F 211 beneath the southbound Fawcett Road and Goldsmith Avenue wiring, crests Fratton Bridge over the railway on 5 October 1947. (A.D. Packer)

Seen pulling away from the Guildhall Square stop in Greetham Street on another anti-clockwise trip around the Eastney circle is AEC661T/Cravens 249. The burnt out remains of the Guildhall are evident in the background. (BTS Library [photographer C. Carter])

CHAPTER 7

INDIAN SUMMER

On 1st January 1951 the transport undertaking was 50 years old and that same month Mr Ben Hall, General Manager and Engineer of the Transport Department, retired after 25 years' service to the City of Portsmouth and 47 years in the passenger transport industry. During that period he had seen the fleet grow from 34 motorbuses and 116 trams to 115 motorbuses and 109 trolleybuses, a co-ordination agreement had been introduced and the city had suffered on the front line of the war. He was succeeded by his deputy, Mr H. C. Simmonds, and the vacancy so created was subsequently filled by Mr A. W. Fielder, Traffic Superintendent CPPTD.

At this time there were 100 trolleybuses in the fleet that were at least 12 years old and it was considered that at least the ten oldest would need replacement within the next 10 years. In view of the longer life expectancy of trolley vehicles, the Department felt that their motorbus fleet required earlier replacements as it included 31 vehicles over 15 years old and 49 between ten and 15 years of age. It was proposed that these motorbuses should be replaced within the next 5 years at a rate of 25 in 1951–52 and 25 in each of the following 2 years. This was criticised on the grounds that motorbus services M and N had replaced trolleybus services 1 and 2 in May 1947 increasing pressure on the motorbus fleet whilst trolley vehicles were redundant, some even de-licensed.

In January 1951 Independent Arbitration awarded platform staff 7s 6d per week, which would cost the undertaking an additional £20,500 p.a. Faced with a significant rise in costs, the Passenger Transport Committee debated applying for a fare increase. As far as fares on trolley vehicles were concerned the Council had power under the Portsmouth Corporation Act 1930 to amend fares as required, however, this power was overruled by the wartime Defence Regulation 56, which was still in force. This required an application for approval to the MoT. Motorbus fares were subject to approval by the appropriate Licensing Authority, this being the South-Eastern Traffic Area in the case of Portsmouth. Clearly fare increases uniformly applicable to both motorbus and trolley vehicles services were needed. The MoT responded on 16 June 1951 stating that the Minister was prepared to make an Order under Defence Regulation 56 authorising the fares proposed in the February 1951 application, subject to an assurance that no further transfers from the transport undertaking to the relief of local rates would be given without consulting the Minister. This assurance was given and the fare increases were introduced on 8 July 1951.

Plans to relocate the bus stop at Florence Road on Clarendon Road were approved on 17 April 1951. As the Planning Committee had decided that it was impractical to widen London Road at North End Junction it was decided to experimentally relocate the north and southbound stops. This move undoubtedly had a bearing on the recommendation to equip Chichester Road rather than Stubbington Avenue for trolleybus operation.

Mr Simmonds' report to the 19 June 1951 Passenger Transport Committee meeting recommended that only a limited number of the extensions approved in the 1948 Order Confirmation Act should be constructed and that the remainder abandoned. In his view approved Route 5 (Stubbington Avenue) could serve no meaningful purpose for a north–south trolleybus service. It seems that over a period of time the Committee had been persuaded that Chichester Road, running between Copnor Road and London Road at Kingston Cross, offered a more suitable east–west connection than the route authorised in 1948 along Stubbington Avenue 400 yards to the north. He suggested that the equipment of Chichester Road, for which no approval was to hand, was pivotal to the success of Routes 2 (Milton Road and Copnor Road), 3 (Baffins Road) and 4 (Gladys Avenue) as together this would permit the conversion of services E and F to electric traction. This would achieve optimum use of existing trolleybus infrastructure and permit the introduction of a summer extension to Southsea South Parade Pier. The portion of services R and S between Cosham 'Red Lion' and Southsea South Parade Pier could be converted to trolleybus operation running via Copnor Road, Milton Road, Highland Road and Festing Road (instead of Priory Crescent and Winter Road), and the other portion to/from Portchester retained as a motorbus operation running in conjunction with SMS service 45.

He made no mention of Route 1 (Cosham 'Red Lion' – Farlington) whatsoever. Route 6 (Tangier Road) was already adequately served by motorbus services C and D, whilst Route 7 Unicorn Gate was no longer economically justified as it would be primarily served by infrequent workmen's services. The current motorbus journeys were able to make their way directly to other parts of the City avoiding the busy centre whereas replacement trolleybuses would have to travel via Commercial Road.

In respect of Chichester Road, a month's public notice that a draft Provisional Order would be deposited with the MoT on or before 18 September 1951 was given in the 16 August 1951 newspapers. Application was approved by a City Council resolution on 11 September 1951 although one Councillor was concerned that this was an inappropriate moment in view of the prevailing electricity shortages and power cuts.

Two Leyland TD2 motorbuses, fleet numbers 17 and 18, were converted for use as tower wagons at an estimated total cost of £2,500. The extending towers were purchased from specialist sources but the conversion and fitting work was done by the Department. Tenders were received from S. Rawlinson and Co. Ltd. at £347 each and The Eagle Engineering Co. Ltd., Warwick, for £424 10s each, that from Rawlinson being accepted on 18 September 1951. These vehicles took over the fleet numbers and replaced the existing tower wagons, fleet numbers TW1 (registration number TP181) and TW2 (TP765) in the service fleet, based on Dennis single deck motorbus chassis dating from 1924 and 1925 respectively. The earlier vehicles were dismantled and disposed of in 1953 and June 1952 respectively.

A further 100 serviceable traction poles this time at £10 each were purchased from LPTB for the proposed extensions. This was £1,200 less than new poles.

The NJIC for the Road Passenger Transport Industry agreed on a further award effective 7 June 1951 on increased national rates of pay. The total additional cost to the undertaking including overtime was estimated as £25,000 p.a.

Having driven into East Street and then reversed into Broad Street AEC661T 231 is seen waiting at the kerbside at Floating Bridge terminus prior to the abandonment, after many prior suspensions, of the Old Portsmouth routes (services 15 and 16) on 29 September 1951. The tram tracks still remain today (2012). It will be noted that 231 is devoid of any semaphore arm illuminated traffic indicators. (Roy Marshall)

1935 AEC661T 216 with English Electric all metal body heads towards Southsea South Parade Pier along Victoria Road North just south of Bradford Junction. Sun hats and shorts were de rigueur for children that summer. (Roy Marshall)

AEC661T 229 beneath the 1948 overhead wiring layout on the north side of Cosham Railway Station bus terminus. The semaphore arm illuminated traffic indicators have been removed. Cosham's ex-LSWR signal box, which controlled the level crossing gates, and a tall Victorian telegraph pole are visible in the background. Portsmouth Dairies continued to use the Street's advertising slogan. (Roy Marshall)

Consecutively numbered vehicles, AEC661T 300 (100) of 1937 and BUT9611T 301 of 1950, stand at Cosham Railway Station bus terminus. The driver of 301 points out a feature of the frog providing access to the waiting loop. Both crew members have white summer season tops to their uniform caps whilst the driver sports a lightweight dust jacket. (Roy Marshall)

Brigadier Langley of the MoT inspected the Copnor Bridge–Green Lane trolleybus route, which terminated at a reversing triangle in Madeira Road (on the opposite side of Copnor Road to Green Lane) at its junction with Compton Road, in late November 1951 and certified the route fit for public service. Many traction poles in Copnor Road remained unpainted at this stage although they had been planted in the spring. He also visited Chichester Road, which he considered rather narrow for any kind of bus operation although he anticipated that these objections could be overcome.

There was a series of letters in the newspapers at the end of August 1951 about motorbuses to and from Paulsgrove and

'Last of the Few'

What does it feel like to be the driver of a seven ton trolleybus? To Mrs Ina Docherty of 70 Henderson Road, it is just another job. 'Of course', she said, 'I was nervous at first, and I lost weight. The men used to have bets whether we would finish our routes on time, and there was a standing joke in the sheds that they would have to come after us with a tower wagon.' Originally 20 women were trained as Portsmouth Corporation trolleybus drivers during the war when there was an acute shortage of drivers. The three who remain, Mrs Ina Docherty, Miss Mary E. Matthews and Mrs V. M Porter, all have medals and diplomas for safe driving. They have driven for ten years. Mrs Docherty and Miss Matthews are also qualified to drive other types of buses, but they prefer driving trolleybuses because they are lighter, and there are no fumes.

Evening News, 25 August 1951

Leigh Park being delayed by the frequent stops to pick up and drop off short stage passengers between Commercial Road and Hilsea. Suggestions to introduce a minimum fare were met with pleas to reintroduce a 6-minute frequency on trolleybus services 1 and 2. One writer added: 'Short distance passengers could use the trolleybuses which, with their high acceleration, are admirably suited to a service which entails many stops.'

As an economy measure, on 18 September 1951 the General Manager suggested that services 15 and 16 Copnor Bridge – Floating Bridge be withdrawn and the overhead equipment between Victoria Hall and Floating Bridge along Cambridge Road, High Street and Broad Street removed. It will be recalled that Old Portsmouth had been devastated during the war and as a result the services were poorly used. SMS were prepared to extend one of their services, then terminating at the Theatre Royal, to the Floating Bridge in place of the trolleybuses. The frequency of trolleybus services operating between Copnor Bridge and the Guildhall could be reduced by two journeys to eight per hour, which would adequately meet the need. The Passenger Transport Committee approved his suggestion which was quickly implemented, services 15 and 16 being withdrawn with the introduction of the winter timetable on 29 September 1951. The overhead wiring in Old Portsmouth was soon dismantled.

Until the advent of package holidays and cheap air travel, Southsea was a popular family holiday resort whilst Portsmouth was frequented by British and foreign sailors unfamiliar with the city, thus it was hardly surprising when, on 18 September 1951, the Piers, Beach and Publicity Committee asked that bus services should display the same service number or letter for both directions of travel rather than a directional number or letter.

Proposals were announced to enlarge the roundabout at the junction of Northern Road with Southampton Road (now Medina Road) requiring overhead wiring changes estimated to cost £1,000. The MoT rejected this amount in the City Engineer's application for loan sanction and it was suggested that the cost should be divided equally between the Roads, Works and Drainage Committee and the Passenger Transport Committee, as had been agreed for the widening of the southern part of Commercial Road between Arundel Street and Edinburgh Road which also required the relocation of traction poles and slewing of the overhead line. In respect of the widening of Commercial Road, in March 1952 it was learned that the MoT were prepared to meet 10% of the costs of moving traction poles, estimated to cost £650, to new positions as they also supported street lighting. The contribution explicitly excluded any alteration to the trolleybus overhead equipment.

Notwithstanding the pending increases applied for in February 1951 (which were granted and introduced on 8 July 1951), in June 1951 it was decided to apply for a further revision of fares and stages. This second application was made on 18 December 1951, as follows:

1 stage	1½d
2 stages	2d
3	2½d
4	3d
6	4d

and for each additional two stages an extra 1d.

This was expected to raise an average of 2d per mile on each service. The increases in workmen's fares remained linked to the increase of the ordinary single fares, however, the new minimum workmen's return fare would be 6d in place of the existing 4d. Commensurate increases for season tickets were also foreseen. These further increases to the trolleybus fares contained in the Portsmouth Corporation Trolley Vehicles (Increase of Charges) Order 1952 were approved by the MoT on 5 April 1952 for introduction on 11 April 1952.

On 6 January 1952 the 1.1 mile long extension along Copnor Road came into use when trolleybus services 7, 8, 11 and12 were extended from Copnor Bridge to Green Lane.

7 Green Lane – Copnor Bridge – Fratton Bridge – Bradford Junction – Southsea *The Strand* – Royal Pier Hotel – Clarence Pier
Unidirectional southbound service

8 Clarence Pier – Southsea *The Strand* – Bradford Junction – Fratton Bridge – Copnor Bridge – Green Lane
Unidirectional northbound service

11 Green Lane – Copnor Bridge – Guildhall – Dockyard *Main Gate*
Alternate journeys commenced at Copnor Bridge.
Unidirectional southbound service worked in conjunction with service 12

12 Dockyard *Main Gate* – Guildhall – Copnor Bridge – Green Lane
Alternate journeys terminated at Copnor Bridge.
Unidirectional northbound service worked in conjunction with service 11

Due to the abandonment of the Floating Bridge route there was a net gain of just 0.1 miles to the trolleybus network as a whole.

Griffiths and Millington the advertising agents enquired in March 1952 if the Corporation would permit football pool advertising on vehicles but the request was refused.

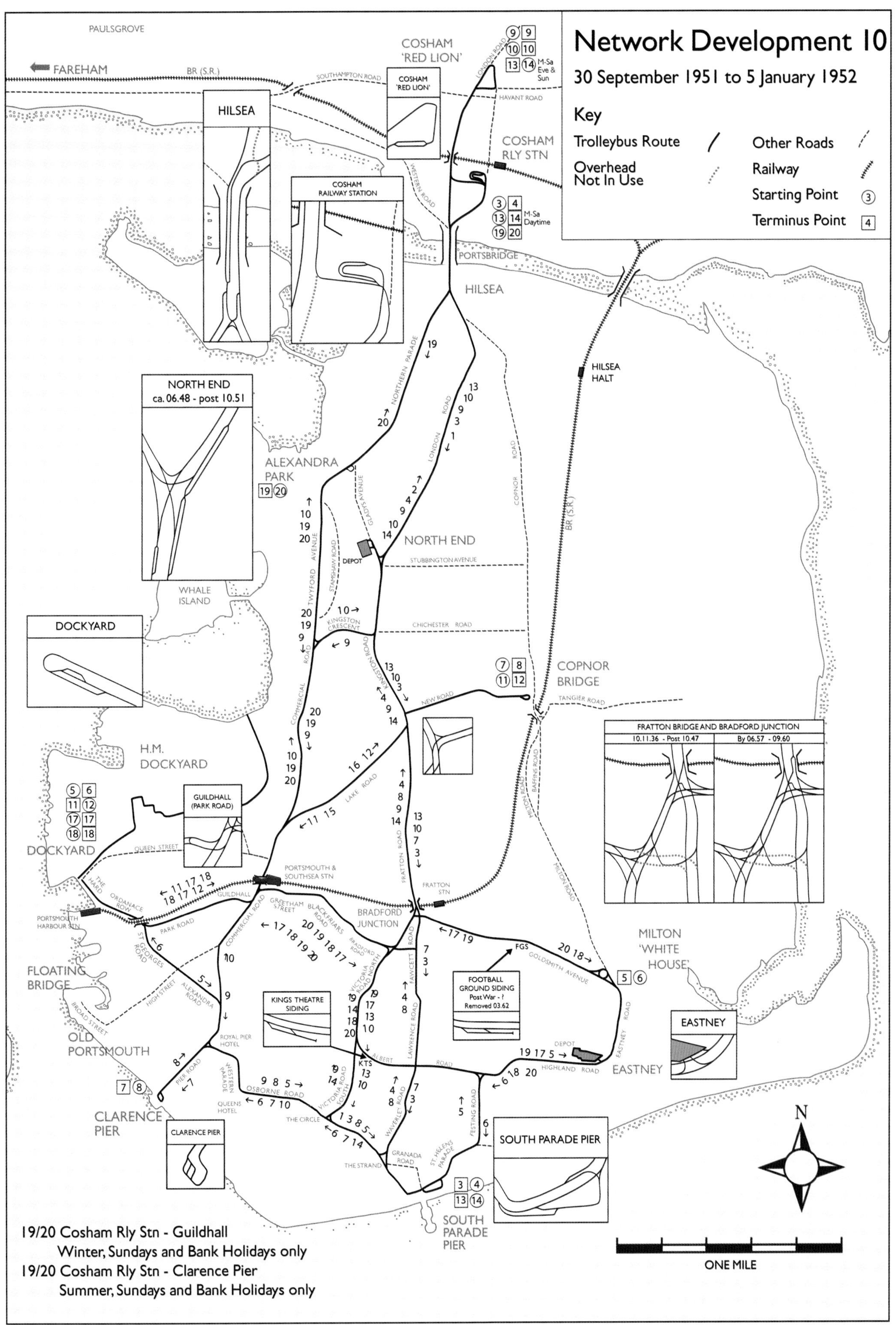

19/20 Cosham Rly Stn - Guildhall
Winter, Sundays and Bank Holidays only
19/20 Cosham Rly Stn - Clarence Pier
Summer, Sundays and Bank Holidays only

Two Cravens bodied AEC661Ts, 240 on service 5 followed by 290 on service 8, are seen in Clarendon Road heading east towards The Strand. The garage of Southsea Tours taken over by SMS in February 1925 can be seen behind 290. This same building passed to Wadhams Bros. who, in addition to being Austin and Morris agents, built bus and coach bodywork. (Roy Marshall)

Official notice was given in the newspapers of 17 April 1952 that the MoT, under the provisions of Section 32 of the Portsmouth Corporation Act 1930 as amended by Section 8 of the Portsmouth Corporation Act 1946, had issued a Provisional Order for the use of trolley vehicles along Chichester Road prior to the same being introduced into a Confirmation Bill. Its first reading in the House of Commons was on 15 May 1952.

Throughout the early part of the year the Department planted traction poles and strung overhead equipment along the northern part of Copnor Road from Green Lane to the junction with London Road, Hilsea. Second-hand traction poles purchased from the London Transport Executive, which had reportedly been used in Falcon Road and York Road, Battersea until 30 September 1950 when trolleybuses in that area were prematurely withdrawn in conjunction with the London tramway abandonment programme, were used for some of the work. These were somewhat shorter than the traction poles normally used by CPPTD and could not be used at those locations where a street lighting bracket was required. At these points poles from the Corporation's own stock were used.

On 22 May 1952 it was announced in the press that the wiring was complete and that services 5 and 6 would be extended from Milton 'White House' to Hilsea via Milton Road and Copnor Road, and thence along the existing route to and from Cosham 'Red Lion' on Sunday 25 May 1952, replacing motorbus services R and S on the route Guildhall – Copnor – Cosham 'Red Lion'.

5 Dockyard *Main Gate* – Royal Pier Hotel – Southsea *South Parade Pier* – Festing Hotel – Eastney – Milton *White House* – Copnor Bridge – Hilsea – Cosham *Red Lion*
Unidirectional northbound service worked in conjunction with service 6

6 Cosham *Red Lion* – Hilsea – Copnor Bridge – Milton *White House* – Eastney – Festing Hotel – Southsea *South Parade Pier* – Royal Pier Hotel – Dockyard *Main Gate*
Unidirectional service worked in conjunction with service 5

The MoT's official letter dated 23 May 1952 referring to Routes 2 and 3 of the Portsmouth Corporation (Trolley Vehicles) Order Confirmation Act 1948, noted that they had been equipped for trolley vehicle operation. They had no objections to them being brought into service on or after 25 May 1952 subject to the GPO being satisfied with any guarding arrangements. Just under ¾ mile of additional overhead route came into service. With this extension, North End Depot began to contribute two trolleybuses to the weekday allocation to services 5 and 6 both of which entered service from Cosham 'Red Lion'. In the evening, one vehicle ran out of service at Palmerston Road and returned to North End following the route of withdrawn service 1. The other operated as far as Copnor Bridge from Cosham and then ran into North End via New Road and Kingston Road. In principle all depot journeys were available to fare-paying passengers and most were shown in the timetables.

The *Evening News* commented that: 'The extension of the trolleybus service in the City comes at a time when petrol buses are expensive to run due to the increased petrol tax. The trolley vehicles are not only cheaper to operate but have a longer life by about five years than the petrol buses.'

The extension provoked some interesting reader's letters:

'It is a pleasure to comment upon the remarkably quick and neat work carried out by overhead linesmen in the erection of the overhead wires along Copnor Road as far as Milton. . . . Coming at a time when we are suffering from increased taxes on fuel, the new trolleybus services are a great asset and it is to be hoped that they may be further extended to Paulsgrove

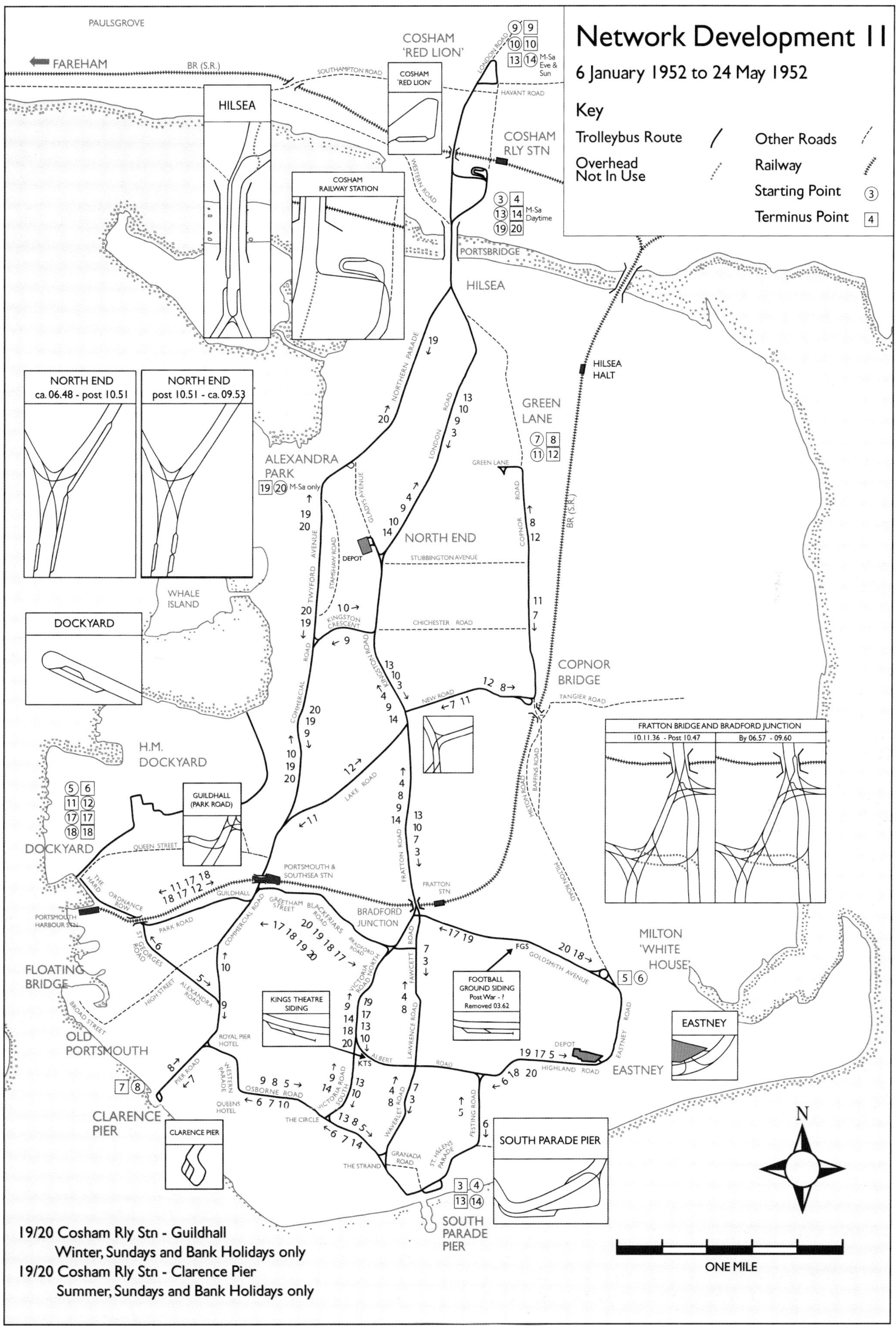

Network Development II
6 January 1952 to 24 May 1952
Key
Trolleybus Route
Overhead Not In Use
Other Roads
Railway
Starting Point
Terminus Point
PAULSGROVE
FAREHAM
BR (S.R.)
COSHAM 'RED LION'
HILSEA
COSHAM RAILWAY STATION
COSHAM RLY STN
PORTSBRIDGE
NORTH END ca. 06.48 - post 10.51
NORTH END post 10.51 - ca. 09.53
ALEXANDRA PARK
GREEN LANE
HILSEA HALT
NORTH END
WHALE ISLAND
DOCKYARD
COPNOR BRIDGE
H.M. DOCKYARD
GUILDHALL (PARK ROAD)
FRATTON BRIDGE AND BRADFORD JUNCTION
10.11.36 - Post 10.47
By 06.57 - 09.60
PORTSMOUTH & SOUTHSEA STN
FRATTON STN
BRADFORD JUNCTION
MILTON 'WHITE HOUSE'
FLOATING BRIDGE
OLD PORTSMOUTH
KINGS THEATRE SIDING
FOOTBALL GROUND SIDING Post War - ? Removed 03.62
EASTNEY
CLARENCE PIER
SOUTH PARADE PIER
ONE MILE
19/20 Cosham Rly Stn - Guildhall
Winter, Sundays and Bank Holidays only
19/20 Cosham Rly Stn - Clarence Pier
Summer, Sundays and Bank Holidays only

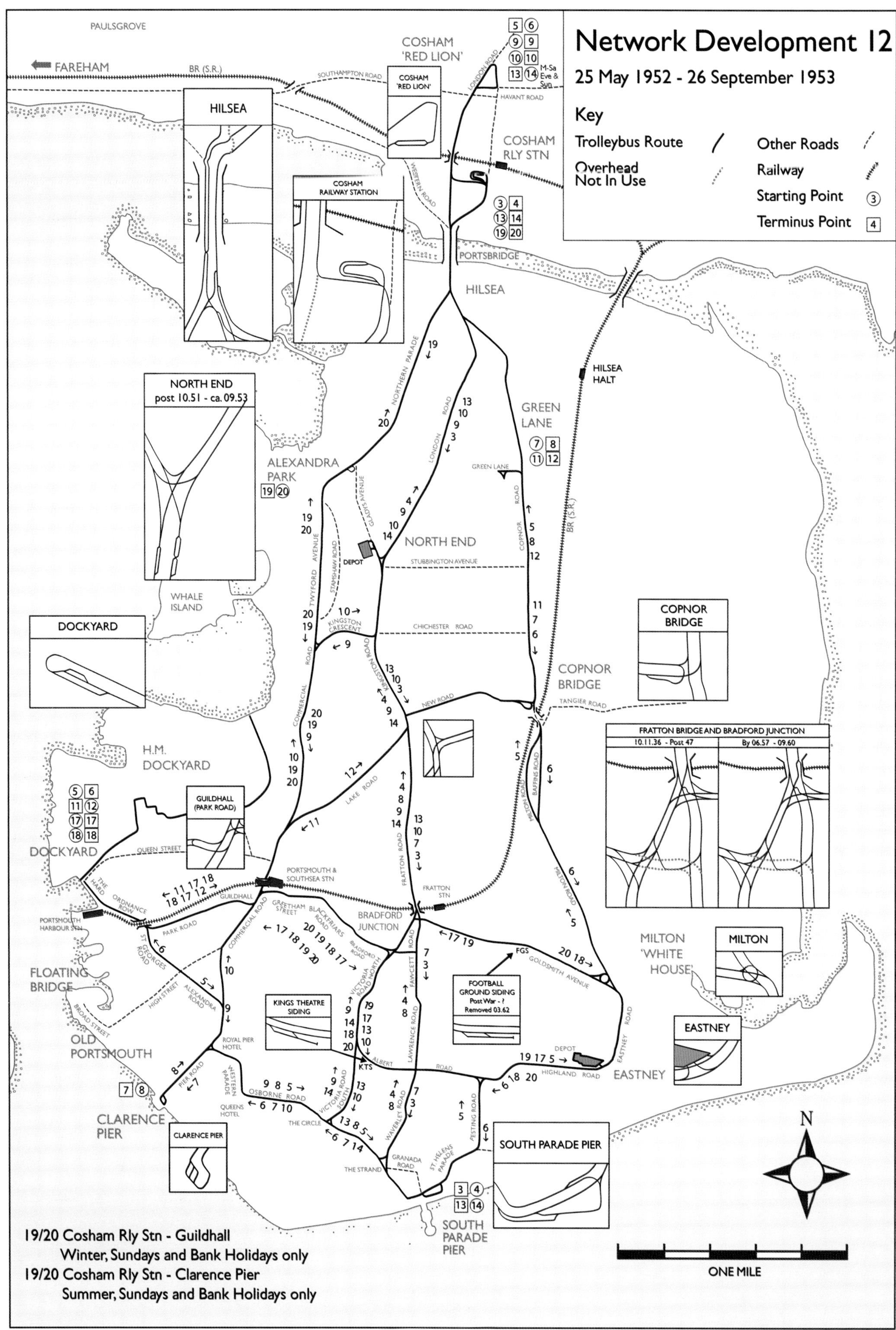
Network Development 12
25 May 1952 - 26 September 1953
Key
Trolleybus Route
Other Roads
Overhead Not In Use
Railway
Starting Point
Terminus Point
PAULSGROVE
FAREHAM
BR (S.R.)
SOUTHAMPTON ROAD
COSHAM 'RED LION'
LONDON ROAD
M-Sa Eve & Sun
HAVANT ROAD
HILSEA
COSHAM RAILWAY STATION
COSHAM RLY STN
WESTERN ROAD
PORTSBRIDGE
HILSEA HALT
NORTH END post 10.51 - ca. 09.53
NORTHERN PARADE
GREEN LANE
ALEXANDRA PARK
GLADYS AVENUE
NORTH END
STUBBINGTON AVENUE
DEPOT
COPNOR ROAD
TWYFORD AVENUE
STAMSHAW ROAD
WHALE ISLAND
DOCKYARD
KINGSTON CRESCENT
CHICHESTER ROAD
COPNOR BRIDGE
TANGIER ROAD
KINGSTON ROAD
NEW ROAD
COMMERCIAL ROAD
H.M. DOCKYARD
FRATTON BRIDGE AND BRADFORD JUNCTION
10.11.36 - Post 47
By 06.57 - 09.60
LAKE ROAD
MILTON ROAD
BAFFINS ROAD
GUILDHALL (PARK ROAD)
QUEEN STREET
PORTSMOUTH & SOUTHSEA STN
FRATTON ROAD
FRATTON STN
THE HARD
ORDNANCE ROW
GUILDHALL
PORTSMOUTH HARBOUR STN
PARK ROAD
GREETHAM STREET
BLACKFRIARS ROAD
BRADFORD JUNCTION
BRADFORD ROAD
MILTON 'WHITE HOUSE'
MILTON
FGS
GOLDSMITH AVENUE
FOOTBALL GROUND SIDING Post War - ? Removed 03.62
FLOATING BRIDGE
ST GEORGES ROAD
HIGH STREET
ALEXANDRA ROAD
VICTORIA ROAD NORTH
FAWCETT ROAD
KINGS THEATRE SIDING
LAWRENCE ROAD
EASTNEY
EASTNEY ROAD
BROAD STREET
OLD PORTSMOUTH
ROYAL PIER HOTEL
KTS
ALBERT ROAD
DEPOT
HIGHLAND ROAD
EASTNEY
PIER ROAD
WESTERN PARADE
OSBORNE ROAD
QUEENS HOTEL
VICTORIA ROAD SOUTH
WAVERLEY ROAD
FESTING ROAD
CLARENCE PIER
THE CIRCLE
SOUTH PARADE PIER
THE STRAND
GRANADA ROAD
ST HELENS PARADE
SOUTH PARADE PIER
N
ONE MILE
19/20 Cosham Rly Stn - Guildhall
Winter, Sundays and Bank Holidays only
19/20 Cosham Rly Stn - Clarence Pier
Summer, Sundays and Bank Holidays only

AEC661Ts 241 and 299 wait on The Hard at Dockyard terminus. (Roy Marshall)

It must have been a warm day as every window including the driver's windscreen is open on 242 as it travels south along Victoria Road North opposite Elm Grove. This is another AEC661T that has had its semaphore arm illuminated traffic indicators removed. Rebuilt in January 1951, 242 demonstrates the fixed glass panes in the upper-deck front windows and curved lower corners to these windows that typified the post-July 1949 rebuilds. (Roy Marshall)

without delay.' The writer continued: 'In view of the tree-lined verges along Copnor Road can one put in a plea that the poles are painted green not the horrible silver so usually employed, so that at least a degree of camouflaging is achieved?'

Another reader on holiday from Bristol wrote on 17 June 1952 'the Corporation have done an excellent job in their recent trolleybus extensions. In Bristol, although we have no trolleybuses, the lamp standards are painted green and blend better with the trees and keep their colour better than your silver standards do.'

A 5-year programme of capital expenditure to commence in the financial year 1953–54, including £400,000 for motorbuses and trolleybuses, was debated on 17 June 1952. This was to be followed by a 15-year programme to run from 1 April 1958 which included £450,000 for the purchase of trolley vehicles at an average of six vehicles p.a., £600,000 for motorbuses at 10 p.a., and £50,000 for an extension of Eastney Depot. The programme was adopted for submission with the City Development Plan.

The Passenger Transport Committee discussed introducing short-workings of services 5 and 6 between Cosham and Southsea South Parade Pier at their July 1952 meeting, but gave up the idea as there was no turning circle at South Parade Pier for trolleybuses from the Eastney direction. Traction battery turns were discounted although none of the early deliveries (201–24) which lacked this equipment were used during the 1952 summer season.

The Portsmouth Accident Prevention Council asked for the use of an illuminated trolleybus in connection with the National Road Safety Week 2–9 August 1952. Once again 204 was selected and licensed for the month of August, this being the final occasion that the vehicle was licensed and thus permitted to carry passengers. Details of the journeys operated are not known.

On 24 September 1952, as he drove his trolleybus across Portsbridge, Driver L. D. Castle noticed a man in difficulties in the water of Portscreek. He stopped the vehicle, dived from the parapet of the bridge and with the help of a policeman rescued a man who was in danger of drowning. Some days later the rescued man wrote to Driver Castle enclosing £5. He divided the amount between himself and the police constable deducting from his share 30s to replace a watch which he had lost and donated the rest to the Royal Life Saving Society.

A number of national wage awards were made towards the end of summer 1952 further influencing CPPTD's spiralling costs. The JIC for the Electricity Supply Industry granted 2d per hour from 1 August 1952 costing the undertaking £305 p.a., the NJIC for Craftsmen also awarded 2d per hour from 11 September 1952 costing £1,841 p.a., and the NJIC for Passenger Transport Industry awarded 7s per week from 11 September 1952 costing £21,400 p.a. Then it was learned from the Federation of Municipal Passenger Transport Employers, that their National Joint Council had recommended that the Portsmouth undertaking, due to its size and population served, should be re-graded into Group 1, something that Mr Simmonds could not dispute. This was estimated to cost a further £800 p.a.

Torrential rain during the evening of 17 December 1952 short-circuited a 580 volt feeder cable in Commercial Road. Flames three foot high shot out of the top of the traction pole and molten metal ran down the pole and splashed onto the pavement. Trolleybus services were suspended for half an hour and a motorbus shuttle service was provided between North End and Sultan Road.

Work started in April 1953 planting traction poles and stringing overhead wiring along Gladys Avenue between North End Deport and Alexandra Park, Northern Parade. On 21 April 1953 it was announced that ten trolleybuses would be disposed of by tender, however, 297, 256, 281 and 244 (in that order) were repainted and overhauled. It was decided to hang flower baskets from traction poles at South Parade near the Pier, and later in North End and around the Guildhall.

The *Evening News* of Thursday 4 June 1953 contained a photograph of trolleybus 204 decorated for the Coronation of HM Queen Elizabeth II and the summer season. The illuminations were made up of 1375 electric bulbs. The centre pieces were two large crowns, while plastic ornaments – a thistle, rose, encircled Union jack – flags and bunting make up 'this exceedingly colourful spectacle'. Weather permitting, 204 toured the city each afternoon throughout the summer for more than an hour and each evening between 7 p.m. and 11 p.m. The trolleybus operated on trade plates and carried no passengers. It was the final occasion that 204 was used. Floodlights were placed on traction poles AH4 and 5 at the end of Park Road to illuminate the main gate of HMS *Vernon* for the Fleet Review on 15 June 1953.

On 16 June 1953 the Passenger Transport Committee discussed the proposed new 'Link Road' (today's Southampton Road) from Spur Road, Cosham to Wymering Railway Bridge. Although the Joint Transport Committee had considered a motorbus service to Wymering and Paulsgrove it was pointed out that it would be more economic to extend trolleybuses from Cosham as had been proposed pre-war and again in 1947. It was estimated that 240,000 miles p.a., costing £7,500 p.a., could be saved if trolley vehicles served Wymering and Paulsgrove via the new road. The local authority was urged to expedite construction of the new road which was also part of the City's Development Plan. In fact the 'Link Road' opened in two stages in the first quarter of 1958.

In an effort to combat ever-increasing costs, in July 1953 the Passenger Transport Committee proposed abolishing workmen's fares and season tickets, the withdrawal of circular trolleybus services 9 and 10 Cosham 'Red Lion' – Guildhall – Royal Pier Hotel – Southsea *The Circle* – Bradford Junction – Fratton Bridge – Cosham 'Red Lion' and reduced frequencies for many motorbus services. The Corporation issued some 2.09 million workmen's tickets annually: if the same number of passengers were carried at normal fares the undertaking would be £17,000 p.a. better off.

Proposals to withdraw trolleybus services 9 and 10 and to divert SMS 45A along Victoria Street provoked much correspondence in the newspapers.

'I am all against this continual withdrawal of trolleybus services in favour of through Southdown services. It must be remembered that the overhead network has to be maintained, in any case, no matter how infrequent the service.

'I believe in official circles, it has been worked out that at least a 6-minute service has to be maintained to justify the overhead equipment.

'Purely to ensure a profit, trolleybuses should be worked intensively over the trolleybus network, and all other buses, whether Southdown or Corporation, withdrawn, as far as possible, from these sections.

'In recent years, we have seen the 1 and 2 trolleybus service withdrawn in favour of through 45 Southdown buses and

BUT9611T 303 pauses at the last stop in Commercial Road before the Portsmouth and Southsea Station railway bridge heading south in front of 'The Albany' public house ('The Criterion' was next door but one) on an unnumbered short working to the Guildhall. SMS Leyland Titan PD2/1 no. 342 waits behind. (Roy Marshall)

recently by the diversion of 40 and 42 Southdown buses to the 1 and 2 trolleybus route. Now it is proposed to withdraw the 9 and 10 over the Commercial Road section. This leaves Kingston Crescent with no trolleybuses running through it in spite of the existence of the expensive overhead equipment for which rates have to be paid although there is no turnover.'

Amongst similar comments, on 17 July 1953 a Mr E. Derwent of Paulsgrove wrote:

'The proposed cuts involved: motorbuses 129,500 miles p.a., trolleybuses 350,000 miles p.a. In short the vehicles which last year made a profit are to be subjected to almost three times as great a reduction as the buses which ran at a loss.

'It should be noted that those motorbus services which duplicate the trolley routes are to remain, presumably in the hope that passengers who used the trolleybuses will now travel by motorbus, from which it follows that the profit on the former will be reduced.

'There is no suggestion for any reduction in the fantastically extravagant duplication of services into Paulsgrove from Cosham, involving as it does idling time, waste mileage and inconvenience to passengers, nor is an indication given as to when the trollies (sic) will be extended as has been long promised into Paulsgrove estate.

'Saddled as we are with motorbuses which do not pay, it is alarming to learn that the profitable trolleybus services are to be interfered with, and altogether the situation is so unsatisfactory that an independent inquiry into the administration of the Corporation transport services is a matter of urgency.'

Other correspondents suggested that Winter Road, which runs north–south between Highland Road and Goldsmith Avenue, should be wired for trolleybuses to make fullest use of the overhead equipment through Copnor Road and enable motorbus services A and B to be withdrawn from Copnor Road. It was also suggested that trolleybus services 9 and 10 should be re-routed via Northern Parade and Gladys Avenue instead of London Road thereby providing a through service to Palmerston Road from Alexandra Park via both Fratton and Commercial Roads, and removing competition from SMS through services.

On 24 July 1953 Mr A. W. Fielder, then Deputy General Manager and Traffic Superintendent, responded in a statement to the *Evening News* that during the preceding financial year motorbuses had proved to be a little under ½d per mile cheaper to operate than trolleybuses. He quoted working costs of 25.164d per mile for motorbuses and 25.582d per mile for trolleybuses:

'It follows therefore, that the difference in operating results (a net deficit of £31,920 for motorbuses, and a net surplus of £24,549 for trolley vehicles) must be traced to the revenue, which was 28.788d per mile for trolleybuses, against 25.065d for motorbuses.'

He gave a number of contributing factors to the difference in revenue of more than 3½d per mile including the tapered fare tables whereby the longer distance passengers paid less per mile than the predominantly short distance travellers in trolley vehicles. Motorbuses operated 465,806 miles on workmen's services, against 41,220 miles by trolley vehicles.

He cited the conversion in 1952–53 of the remunerative Copnor Road part of motorbus services R and S to trolleybus services 5 and 6. The revenue remained the same making it apparent that the deficit was not attributable to the type of vehicle used but to the nature of the service provided. He went on to point out that the introduction of trolleybuses would not lead to increased revenues on services 15 and 16. Trolleybus services 3, 4, 11, 12, 17, 18, 19 and 20 ran through both commercial areas and residential districts and therefore earned high receipts per mile whereas motorbus services operating through sparsely populated areas yielded low revenues.

Since 1949 the undertaking had purchased 56 new motorbuses, 35% of the fleet, which now had an average age of 9.3 years. In the same period 15 trolleybuses had been bought, 13% of the fleet, which now had an average age of 14.9 years. 'It may be reasonably supposed that with an ageing trolley fleet, some replacements must be contemplated in the foreseeable future, and the incidence of loan charges on trolley vehicles will then increase comparably with the motorbuses.'

In respect of the proposed withdrawal of trolleybus services 9 and 10, Mr Fielder explained that these were not 'through' services and that to withdraw a longer service in favour of the shorter trolleybus services would cause greater inconvenience among more people than the present proposal. The withdrawal of services 1 and 2 were another example of a service having been rendered redundant. 'The fact is,' he said, 'Cosham has long been out-dated as a terminal point due to the natural growth of the City. It is now rather an intermediate point'.

On 21 August 1953 it was reported that the trolleybus overhead wiring was now in place in Chichester Road and Gladys Avenue, North End, and that subject to MoT inspection, services would start on Sunday 27 September 1953 with the introduction of the winter timetable. Once again some second-hand London Transport traction poles were used.

On 7 September 1953 the *Evening News* published a letter enquiring if the powers to extend trolleybuses to Unicorn Gate could now be exercised to utilise some of the surplus vehicles. The use of motorbus duplicates along routes equipped for trolleybus operation was also questioned. Mr Fielder responded that a regular service was not warranted and would cause 'inconvenience' to the majority of the travelling public although he did not stipulate how. The cost of the overhead equipment would not be justified by the operation of Dockyard specials alone. He reiterated that no motorbuses ran as duplicates over trolleybus routes during the evening peak although occasional school special motorbuses followed up their journey by travelling empty to the Dockyard evening outmuster.

Changes to the existing overhead equipment included the installation of a turning circle around an island at the north end of Cromwell Road (junction with Eastney Road and Highland Road), Eastney, for southbound vehicles accessed by a hand-operated frog immediately opposite Eastney Depot and which served as the southern terminus for the new services. Junctions to/from the north and south were installed at the Copnor Road end of Chichester Road, and to/from the north at the London Road end. A 'Y'-frog was inserted into the North End Depot exit wiring enabling trolleybuses to turn left (north) into the new Gladys Avenue northbound wiring whilst at Alexandra Park a connection into Northern Parade and a new turning circle overlapping that from Twyford Avenue were erected. There was a link from the Twyford Avenue northbound wiring into Gladys Avenue southbound wiring through the turning circle. It was proposed that the new services should run through to the Dockyard but, although destination screens carried the necessary displays, no such extension materialised.

Circular trolleybus services 9 and 10 ran for the last time on 26 September 1953, and the connections at The Circle from Clarendon Road into Victoria Road South and vice versa fell into disuse. This section of overhead wiring was the only part of the route which was not used by other services or special journeys. The frequency of services 13 and 14 were reduced for the winter.

A youthful BUT9611T/Burlingham, No. 310, stands at the starting point of service 13, Spur Road just west of Cosham 'Red Lion' public house. (A.D. Packer)

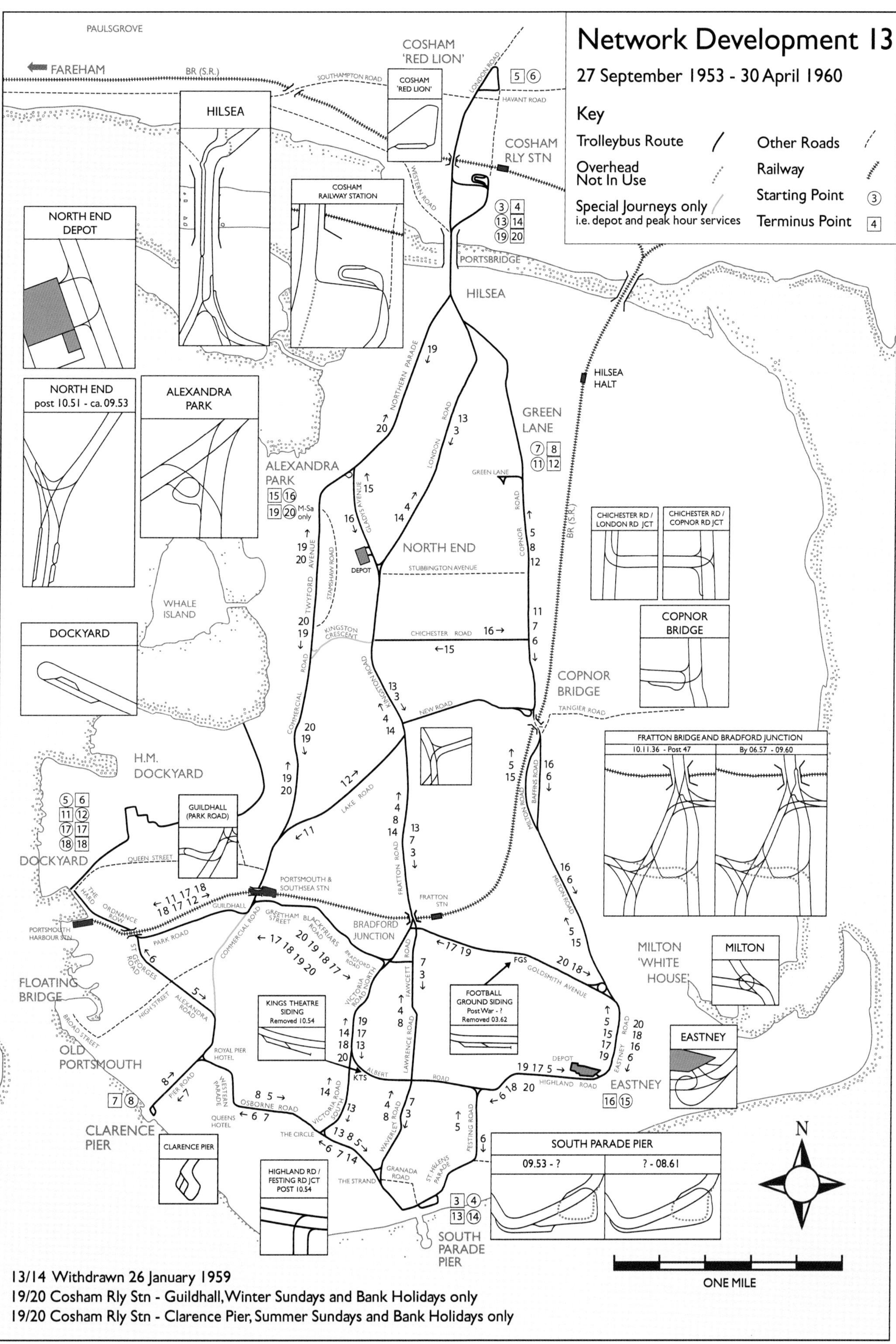

13/14 Withdrawn 26 January 1959

19/20 Cosham Rly Stn - Guildhall, Winter Sundays and Bank Holidays only

19/20 Cosham Rly Stn - Clarence Pier, Summer Sundays and Bank Holidays only

On 27 September 1953 services 15 and 16 were introduced replacing motorbus services E and F which had followed London Avenue affecting late evening journeys of other services. The 7, 8, 11 and 12 journeys terminating at Copnor Bridge and Green Lane now returned to North End Depot via Chichester Road instead of returning along New Road to the junction with Kingston Road where they would turn right using battery traction, no overhead wiring ever being available for this manoeuvre, before continuing along Kingston Road. The only late evening journey unaltered was a short working of service 6 running south to Copnor Bridge which continued to return to North End Depot along New Road and Kingston Road until 30 May 1954, when, with the introduction of summer schedules, this duty was routed to North End Depot via London Road.

The trolleybus network now appeared as:

3 Cosham Railway Station – North End *Junction* – Fratton Bridge – Southsea *South Parade Pier*
Unidirectional southbound service worked in conjunction with service 4

4 Southsea *South Parade Pier* – Fratton Bridge – North End *Junction* – Cosham Railway Station
Unidirectional northbound service worked in conjunction with service 3

5 Dockyard *Main Gate* – Southsea *South Parade Pier* – Eastney – Milton *White House* – Copnor Bridge – Cosham *Red Lion*
Unidirectional northbound service worked in conjunction with service 6

6 Cosham *Red Lion* – Copnor Bridge – Milton *White House* – Eastney – Southsea *South Parade Pier* – Dockyard *Main Gate*
Unidirectional southbound service worked in conjunction with service 5

7 Green Lane – Copnor Bridge – Fratton Bridge – Bradford Junction – Southsea *The Strand* – Royal Pier Hotel – Clarence Pier
Unidirectional southbound service worked in conjunction with service 8

8 Clarence Pier – Royal Pier Hotel – Southsea *The Strand* – Bradford Junction – Fratton Bridge – Copnor Bridge – Green Lane
Unidirectional northbound service worked in conjunction with service 7

11 Green Lane – Copnor Bridge – Guildhall – Dockyard *Main Gate*
Unidirectional southbound service worked in conjunction with service 12

12 Dockyard *Main Gate* – Guildhall – Copnor Bridge – Green Lane
Unidirectional northbound service worked in conjunction with service 11

13 Cosham Railway Station – Hilsea – North End *Junction* – Fratton Bridge – Bradford Junction – Southsea *The Circle* – Southsea *South Parade Pier*
Unidirectional southbound service worked in conjunction with service 14

14 Southsea *South Parade Pier* – Southsea *The Circle* – Bradford Junction – Fratton Bridge – North End *Junction* – Hilsea – Cosham Railway Station
Unidirectional northbound service worked in conjunction with service 13

15 Eastney – Milton *White House* – Copnor Bridge – North End *Junction* – Alexandra Park
Unidirectional northbound service worked in conjunction with service 16

16 Alexandra Park – North End *Junction* – Copnor Bridge – Milton *White House* – Eastney
Unidirectional southbound service worked in conjunction with service 15

17 Dockyard *Main Gate* – Guildhall – Bradford Junction – Festing Hotel – Eastney – Milton *White House* – Bradford Junction – Guildhall – Dockyard *Main Gate*
Unidirectional circular service (anti-clockwise) worked in conjunction with service 18

18 Dockyard *Main Gate* – Guildhall – Bradford Junction – Milton *White House* – Eastney –Festing Hotel – Bradford Junction – Guildhall – Dockyard *Main Gate*
Unidirectional circular service (clockwise) worked in conjunction with service 17

19 Cosham Railway Station – Alexandra Park – Guildhall – Bradford Junction – Festing Hotel – Eastney – Milton *White House* – Fratton Bridge – Bradford Junction – Guildhall – Alexandra Park
Unidirectional circular service (anti-clockwise) worked in conjunction with service 20

20 Alexandra Park – Guildhall – Bradford Junction – Fratton Bridge – Milton *White House* – Eastney – Festing Hotel – Bradford Junction – Guildhall – Alexandra Park – Cosham Railway Station
Unidirectional circular service (clockwise) worked in conjunction with service 19

The Portsmouth trolleybus system had now reached its maximum extent of 21.13 route miles.

Brigadier Langley of the MoT and Civil Aviation inspected Route No. 4 authorised by the Portsmouth Corporation (Trolley Vehicles) Order Confirmation Act 1948, i.e. Gladys Avenue, Route No. 1 authorised by the Portsmouth Corporation (Trolley Vehicles) Order Confirmation Act 1952, i.e. Chichester Road, and new turning circles at Eastney Depot and South Parade Pier on 30 October 1953. On 3 November 1953 the Ministry approved the routes for public service. Brigadier Langley commented that Chichester Road had a bumpy surface in places, perhaps due to the deterioration of the foundations. He felt that there should be a 20 m.p.h. speed restriction for trolleybuses until the road surface was improved. This prompted Mr Simmonds to approach the City's Civil Engineer who in January 1954 confirmed the Inspecting Officer's concerns. About 25% of the foundations remained sound and the cost of repairs to the road surface would be reasonable. The remaining foundations were poor and the road construction was inadequate for the heavy traffic which it was now carrying. One section of about 100 yards at the east end required urgent reconstruction. There were so many parked vehicles standing in the road and so many junctions with side roads that in his opinion it would be impossible for trolleybuses to run at a maximum of 30 m.p.h. with safety. He recommended partial road repairs over the next 2 or 3 years.

A visit to North End Depot in January 1954 found the following vehicles in store: AEC661T 201, 202, 203; Leyland TBD2 205, 206, 207; Sunbeam MF2 208, 210; Karrier E4 209, 211; Sunbeam MS3 213, 214; and AEC663T 215. The other two experimental vehicles 204 and 212 were in store at Eastney. Also there, from the Cravens bodied AEC661Ts were 229, 258,

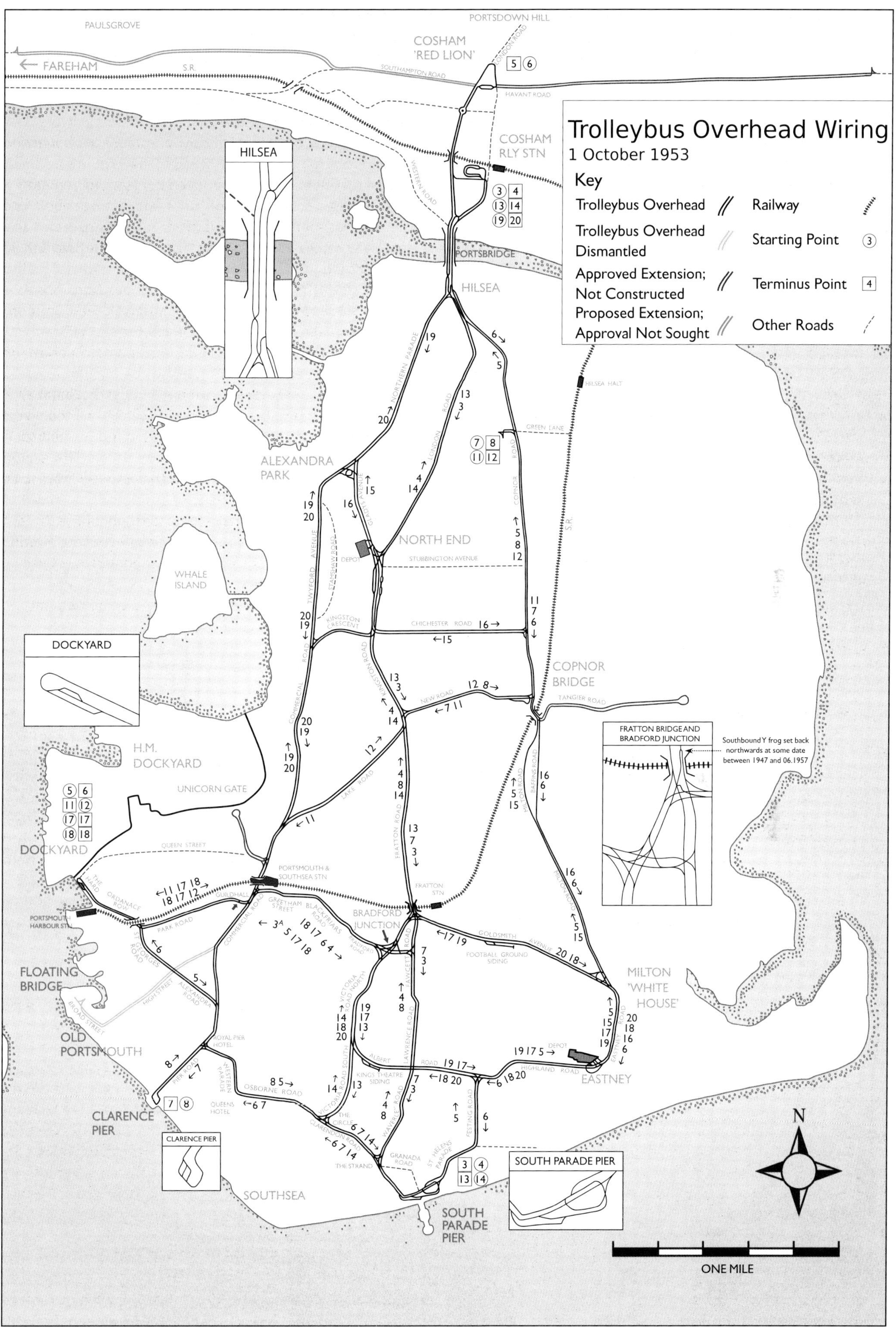
Trolleybus Overhead Wiring
1 October 1953
Key
Trolleybus Overhead
Trolleybus Overhead Dismantled
Approved Extension; Not Constructed
Proposed Extension; Approval Not Sought
Railway
Starting Point
Terminus Point
Other Roads
PAULSGROVE
PORTSDOWN HILL
FAREHAM
COSHAM 'RED LION'
COSHAM RLY STN
PORTSBRIDGE
HILSEA
ALEXANDRA PARK
WHALE ISLAND
NORTH END
COPNOR BRIDGE
H.M. DOCKYARD
UNICORN GATE
DOCKYARD
FLOATING BRIDGE
OLD PORTSMOUTH
CLARENCE PIER
SOUTHSEA
SOUTH PARADE PIER
EASTNEY
MILTON 'WHITE HOUSE'
BRADFORD JUNCTION
FRATTON BRIDGE AND BRADFORD JUNCTION
Southbound Y frog set back northwards at some date between 1947 and 06.1957
DOCKYARD
CLARENCE PIER
SOUTH PARADE PIER
N
ONE MILE

263, 264, 266, 272, 279, 280, 284, 285, 288, 289, 296. On 19 January 1954 the Passenger Transport Committee approved the offer of £500 for the purchase and removal of 10 redundant trolley vehicles, namely 205–214.

The Annual Estimates for 1954–55 were referred back by the Finance and General Purposes Committee as, allowing for recent wage awards by the NJICs for the road passenger transport industry, craftsmen and local authorities, they showed a deficit of £5,040. The estimated operating costs included £80,700 for motorbus fuel plus a further £1,450 for its distribution and £38,450 for traction power plus £10,700 for cables and feeders and £1,000 for overhead lines. The estimates provided insufficient for fleet replacement (£30,000) whilst for the year to close satisfactorily a surplus of at least £30,000 was needed. Another wage application for the road staff was pending which would increase costs by a further £8,000. As far as the 1953–54 financial year was concerned a small surplus of £500–£1,000 was expected, although a net amount of over £20,000 was the final result!

The Meredith and North End Ratepayers Association requested the City Council in February 1954 to make more use of its trolley vehicle system, to introduce a policy of replacement and renovation for trolleybuses and to extend their routes in the City. The Passenger Transport Committee observed that:

'The request to extend the trolley vehicle system is one which frequently emanates from members of the public where an undertaking operates trolley vehicles and motorbuses and the trolley vehicles make a profit and the motorbuses make a loss, leading to the assumption that the loss on the motorbuses would be eliminated by the substitution of trolley vehicles. This assumption is wrong. Trolley vehicles show a profit in Portsmouth because they operate in the densest traffic areas and consequently serve the most remunerative routes.

'In 1952–53 11.7 passengers were picked up per mile by trolley vehicles compared to 8.7 by motorbuses. From a traffic point of view, based on wide experience, the motorbus because of its flexibility is more advantageous, a view which is borne out by the policy in other undertakings. Darlington is now reported to be replacing all their trolley vehicles by motorbuses. This in general is the policy being adopted.

'One other question should be considered, namely – How can a fixed policy be adopted for trolley vehicles or motorbuses when the Chancellor of the Exchequer can completely transform the relative economic position of motor buses compared with trolley vehicles?

'The Department has carried out a policy of renovating trolley vehicles for some years.'

Nonetheless, in March 1954 the Ratepayers Association asked that interference with the established trolleybus routes should cease, as there were disturbing signs that the trolleybus system was going to be allowed to deteriorate.

The MoT continued to hinder construction of the 'Link Road' from Spur Road, Cosham to Southampton Road and thus plans to extend trolleybuses to Paulsgrove. This was adversely affecting the undertaking's finances. The extension of some of the trolleybus services terminating at Cosham to Paulsgrove would, it was estimated, economise 150,000 miles of duplicate motorbus services annually, and improve the Paulsgrove Estate travel facilities by providing direct services to more parts of the system. Replacement of motorbuses by trolleybuses, and a re-routing of services serving Paulsgrove, would also permit greater use of the existing overhead equipment resulting in further savings.

Mr Simmonds reported to the Passenger Transport Committee on 27 May 1954 on the fleet at his disposal and the vehicle replacement policy:

Trolleybuses

No.	Year	Age
5	1934	20
9	1935	19
76	1936–37	17.5
15	1950–51	2.5
105	average	15.7 years

Compared with an average of 10.7 years for double deck and 12.5 years for single deck motorbuses

In connection with the City Development Plan the following programme had been approved at the June 1952 Committee Meeting:

1954–55	purchase	25 motorbuses
1955–56	purchase	20 trolleybuses
1956–57	purchase	25 motorbuses
1957–58	purchase	20 trolleybuses
15 years from	purchase	10 motorbuses annually
1 April 1958		6 trolleybuses annually

He recommended some changes due to the recent mileage economies which appeared to be meeting traffic demand and in view of the trolleybus body overhaul programme. This foresaw giving priority to purchasing new motorbuses with an initial order for just 15 trolleybuses in the 1956–57 financial year to replace what would then be five 23-year-old trolley vehicles, nine 22-year-old and one 21-year-old.

If this programme was put into practice the position in 1957 would be:

76 trolleybuses	20.5 years old
15	6.5
15	new

This would leave a satisfactory position in the motorbus fleet but require major trolleybus fleet replacements in subsequent years.

The 1 June 1954 Passenger Transport Committee accepted its General Manager's programme which effectively meant placing an order for new trolleybuses during the 1956–57 financial year. They stated that ten trolleybuses had been sold in 1953–54 for £50 each, namely 212 (date given 4 July 1953) and 205–211, and 213–214 (all 23 January 1954).

By now, from the AEC 661T 216–224 batch only 216, 218, 220, 219 and 224 remained available for service. They were noted in use on services 3 and 4 Cosham Railway Station – Southsea South Parade Pier via Fawcett Road, and the 13 and 14 Cosham Railway Station – Southsea South Parade Pier via Victoria Road whilst a number of later vehicles were delicensed and stored:

North End Depot Yard	202, 203, 215, 217, 221, 222, 223
North End Depot inside	229, 258, 262, 263, 264, 266, 272, 276, 279, 280, 284, 285, 286, 287, 288, 289, 296
Eastney Depot inside	204, 230, 233, 242, 259 204 was still carrying its Coronation decorations

It was reported that 249 had returned to service after rebuilding with new seats.

BUT9611Ts 301–315 had moved from North End to Eastney Depot and tended to be seen most on services 5 and 6 Dockyard – Cosham; 15 and 16 Eastney – Alexandra Park; and 17 and 18 Dockyard – Eastney – Milton 'White House' – Dockyard.

During 1954, the following work is known to have taken place:

Rebuilding:	234, 241, 248, 249, 252, 259, 271, 291
Repaints:	225, 236, 253, 271 AEC663T
Repaints and overhauls:	307, 314, 315 BUT9611T

Application was made to the MoT in June 1954 for authority to abolish workmen's fares and increase adult season tickets charges on the trolleybus system to the nearest 6d in the case of monthly tickets and to the nearest shilling in the case of three-monthly tickets. A similar application was made to the Licensing Authority for the South Eastern Traffic Area was made in respect of motorbus services. As far as trolley vehicles were concerned the Council had power under the Portsmouth Corporation Act 1930, to make any fare alterations, but this power was over-ridden by Defence Regulation 56a, which was still in force and under which application had to be made for approval to the MoT. The Ministry replied on 15 September 1954 that they were prepared to make an Order under Defence Regulations 55ab and 56 in substitution of the Order made on 5 April 1952 authorising a schedule of the proposed fares and relieving the Corporation of their obligation to provide cheap fares for workmen on their trolley vehicle services. They asked for copies of the proposed fares together with the proposed date of their introduction.

Traction power failed at 1.30 p.m. on 13 July 1954 between Portsmouth and Southsea Station and Charlotte Street (just south of Lake Road) for about 10 minutes causing disruption to all traffic along Commercial Road.

In August 1954 the Milton and North End Ratepayers Association suggested that the redundant trolleybuses should be used between North End, The Guildhall and Clarence Pier and South Parade Pier during the holiday period, instead of the motorbuses. They also drew attention to the fact that services 1 and 2 between Cosham and Southsea South Parade Pier had not been reinstated for the summer holiday period as had once been proposed.

During October 1954 the frogs at the north end of Festing Road allowing northbound trolleybuses to turn west into Albert Road and eastbound vehicles in Albert Road to turn south into Festing Road, and associated wiring, were removed. This section had not been regularly used for many years. It is believed that the siding in the westbound wiring in Albert Road outside the Kings Theatre was also removed at this time.

A general agreement was reached between the GPO and representatives of operators and the Association of Municipal Corporations in October 1954 that where electrolytic damage to GPO cables was established, current and former tramway and trolleybus undertakings should meet 50% of the cost of the repair. In February 1957 CPPTD received such a claim and a payment of £150 11s 6d was made.

The *Evening News* of 27 December 1954 contained complaints that suggestions to extend trolleybuses at once to Paulsgrove by using Southampton Road (now Medina Road) as far as the railway bridge just past Bryson Road, as a temporary measure until such time as the new 'Link Road' was built, appeared to have been dismissed by officialdom as too expensive. Alderman Collins had stated on 12 July 1953 that the Paulsgrove trolleybus extension would save 240,000 miles p.a. representing a sum of £7,500. Comparison was made to Derby where Mr John E. Frith, General Manager and Engineer of the Omnibus Department there, had reportedly stated that he could construct a double line of trolleybus overhead equipment at a cost of £5,340 per mile including labour. If cheaper secondhand material were to be used on the temporary section, the cost would be even less. There would be immediate economies in operating costs and the trolleybuses, then stored out of service, could be used.

On 27 November 1954 the NJIC gave another award expected to cost the undertaking £26,000 p.a. By early 1955 further wage awards had increased labour costs by a total of £39,000 p.a. and to meet this the Joint Transport Committee decided that the Corporation and SMS should each make application to the Licensing Authority to increase fares. On 4 March 1955 it was resolved that the CPPTD would apply as follows: the 4d fare would be retained for journeys up to 2½ miles in length (previously up to 3 miles) and all higher fares would be increased by 1d. The minimum single fare upon which adult season ticket rates would be available being 4d.

The Passenger Transport Committee turned down a request to extend services 19 and 20 to Cosham 'Red Lion' to serve the Queen Alexandra Hospital, located adjacent to the Northern Road, London Road stop and effectively the terminal point for all services destined to Cosham 'Red Lion', in February 1955.

The reconstruction of London Road between Kingston Crescent and Connaught Road (just north of North End junction) led to this section being closed to traffic for six consecutive Sundays between December 1954 and February 1955. Trolleybus services 3, 4, 15 and 16 were temporarily operated by motorbuses, which followed diversions to avoid this section. These continuing road works reached the junction of Copnor Road with London Road, Hilsea, requiring northbound traffic to be diverted along Old London Road. Motorbuses replaced trolleybuses on services 5 and 6 on Saturday 16 and Sunday 17 July 1955. On 21 June 1955 authority was given to dismantle or dispose of trolleybuses 202, 203, 215, 217, 221–223 which were now considered to be in a derelict condition.

In the 12 months ending 30 June 1955 the following vehicles had their bodies rebuilt (in the sequence shown):

234, 248, 259, 242, 274, 230.

Over the same period, the following trolleybuses benefited from an overhaul and repaint including a complete reupholstering, where necessary, in order of overhaul:

313, 234, 253, 306, 248, 278, 259, 247, 242, 275, 298, 295, 309, 274, 246, 230, 283, 308, 292, 312, 201.

The British Electrical and Allied Manufacturers Association wrote to the Chairman of the Passenger Transport Committee in July 1955 to enquire if one of Walsall's new trolleybuses could operate on trial for the delegates and in normal service during the period of the MPTA Conference which was due to be held at Southsea South Parade Pier from 27 to 30 September 1955. The Association pointed out that the outstanding feature of the new trolleybus was its high seating capacity carried on just two axles. They added that it would give Committee members the opportunity to experience the use of such larger vehicles in the city. As there would be no costs for Portsmouth and as Walsall Corporation Transport were pleased to cooperate, it was resolved that the vehicle could operate in normal service

Walsall 864 stands on The Hard prior to departure on a normal passenger carrying service 5 journey. (M.P.M. Nimmo collection)

for the duration of the conference and for inspection by the Committee.

Walsall 864, a 1954 Sunbeam F4A trolleybus with 70-seat Willowbrook body, arrived on tow on 15 September 1955 and operated in normal passenger service from 23 to 28 September 1955 on at least services 5, 6, 19 and 20. The *Evening News* featured a photograph of the vehicle on service 6 at Cosham in its 16 and 28 September 1955 editions. The MPTA Conference attracted more than 200 delegates. After their 20 September 1955 meeting the Committee inspected the Walsall trolleybus although there is no indication that there was any interest in purchasing similar vehicles.

The Meredith and North End Ratepayers Association complained in the 20 September 1955 *Evening News* about the use of motorbuses over the full extent of trolleybus services 1 and 2. They also referred to motorbuses running short workings on services 5 and 6 between Dockyard and Milton 'White House' that could have been trolleybus operated. Furthermore they were concerned about another correspondent's reference to 18 'scrap' trolley vehicles, noting that there were 18 unserviceable trolleybuses at that time, and expressed concerns that the Passenger Transport Committee was following a secret abandonment policy.

Shopkeepers in Commercial Road asked for approval to attach illuminated Christmas Decorations to the traction poles and across the road above the trolleybus overhead wiring. The proposal was discussed with the MoT who had no objections subject to all wiring being fully insulated and supported so that it could not interfere with the trolleybus equipment, and permission was given.

Another round of wage increases began on 10 November 1955 when the NJIC for the Road Passenger Transport Industry awarded a rise expected to cost £29,400 p.a. and the NJ Council for Craftsmen awarded 3d per hour estimated to cost the undertaking £2,750 p.a. On 10 January 1956 the Joint Committee proposed increasing the current CPPTD 2½d, 3d and 4d single fares by ½d in order to cover the estimated deficit for the 1956–57 financial year. This prompt action was well-timed as in February 1956 the Joint Wages Board of Employers for the Vehicle Building Industry awarded an increase expected to cost £375 p.a. and the NJIC for the Electricity Supply Industry granted another rise expected to increase costs by £750 p.a.

Considering the 1956–57 estimates, Mr Simmonds noted that there was a continuing fall in passenger numbers, particularly on trolleybus services, no doubt due to the exodus of city dwellers to Leigh Park. The recent wage awards were expected to result in a £30,840 loss for the year ending 31 March 1957. He saw opportunities to reduce the mileage operated where trolleybuses and motorbuses ran side by side as the trolleybuses were ignored by passengers who wanted to travel beyond the trolleybus terminus. In other words a saving in vehicle mileage could be affected by replacing certain trolleybus routes and by re-organising motorbus services. This he acknowledged struck at the heart of the policy of operating both trolleybuses and motorbuses. The question of trolleybus fleet replacement would shortly need to be considered as 76 out of a fleet of 98 vehicles had been bought in 1936–37. This again impinged on the future of the trolleybus and the suggested trolleybus extension of routes along the new 'Link Road'. Ominously on 1 December 1955 AEC661T 217 was towed by lorry from North End Depot to Eastney Depot for scrapping after all electrical equipment had been removed for re-use in other vehicles.

Heading south, 290 leaves the south end of Twyford Avenue at the junction with Stamshaw Road. Although no longer a main road this location has little changed in more than half a century although 'The Beresford', once a Portsmouth United Breweries house, ceased business in 2010. (D.A.P. Janes [photographer G.A. Tucker])

AEC661T 285 waits at Clarence Pier bus station prior to departure on service 8 to Copnor Bridge. (Omnibus Society)

In January 1956 the Passenger Transport Committee considered renewed plans, held in abeyance since February 1940, to make Twyford Avenue a one-way street. The cost of construction of islands at both junctions with Stamshaw Road, road alterations, new traffic signs, alterations to the overhead equipment, and improved street lighting was estimated as £5,000. Trolleybus overhead equipment along Stamshaw Road was estimated to cost £2,360. Alderman H. E. Collins, Chairman of the Passenger Transport Committee, called a joint meeting involving the Passenger Transport, Watch and Roads, Works and Drainage Committees on 16 February 1956. He stated that his Committee was concerned about the cost of altering the overhead equipment in Twyford Avenue and erecting it in Stamshaw Road if a one-way scheme was adopted.

He felt that there was little evidence that the scheme was warranted. At the moment there were many reasons for and against trolleybus operation, although personally he felt that if one section of the overhead equipment was removed from Twyford Avenue, he would be reluctant to recommend that such equipment should be re-erected in Stamshaw Road. As far as Portsmouth was concerned, he considered trolleybus operation had become obsolescent.

The Watch Committee was in favour as Twyford Avenue carried the bulk of the north–south traffic although much of the congestion was caused by vehicles parked for loading or unloading. Mr Simmonds could foresee no difficulties if trolleybus operation through Twyford Avenue was abandoned and motorbuses substituted.

The meeting concluded that the one-way street scheme was necessary and recommended that the Passenger Transport Committee should not object to the overhead wiring alterations provided that they did not have to bear any cost. It was further recommended that trolleybus operation in Twyford Avenue should be discontinued and motorbuses substituted on the services involved. No action would be taken until the Passenger Transport Committee had reached a decision. On 20 March 1956 the abandonment of trolleybus operation along Twyford Avenue and the withdrawal of trolleybuses from services 19 and 20 were discussed. In view of the far-reaching consequences of any decision it was resolved to hold a special meeting to consider future policy in respect of trolleybuses.

By now rumours of gradual trolleybus abandonment, starting with services 13 and 14 and the recently introduced 15 and 16, had become rife in the Department. Alderman Collins stated that these were 'Rumours to which I pay no attention', although he personally considered trolleybuses were obsolete. He added that in respect of running costs there was little difference between motorbuses and trolleybuses, but as services were extended outwards it would be increasingly difficult to run trolleybuses economically.

On the 24 March 1956 the Cosham Ratepayers' Association said that Alderman Collins' statement conflicted with published figures that showed trolleybuses to be more economical to run than motorbuses whilst their working life was some five years longer than motorbuses. They said that in 1952 motorbus revenue were almost double that of the trolleybuses but the motorbus deficit was 250% of the trolleybuses' profit. It did not make sense to condemn trolleybuses.

There was much correspondence in the local press. One writer hoped that London's decision to abandon trolleybuses had not biased Alderman Collins and went on to suggest that his anti-trolleybus views were not in the least representative of public opinion. Another writer stated that no factual evidence had been given that trolleybuses were obsolete and that the estimated cost of the Twyford Avenue/Stamshaw Road one-way traffic scheme were too high as the total outlay for about a ½ mile would be little more than the cost of some 24 traction poles as the trolley wire could be moved from one road to the other. The costs of the Copnor Road and Chichester Road extensions had not been prohibitive so why should this trivial diversion put the Transport Department into insolvency?, he asked. In any case, Alderman Collins had repeatedly stated extending the trolleybuses to Paulsgrove would economise 240,000 miles p.a. and result in cash savings of £7,500.

The events that brought the Suez Crisis to its head occurred in spring 1956 and it is thus not surprising that on 11 April 1956 a further correspondent pointed out that with the worsening Middle East situation and the growing likelihood of the UK losing its oil supplies at any moment, any thought of trolleybus abandonment was short-sighted. He asked about the £250,000 spent on overhead equipment in recent years and why there was a sudden liking for motorbuses. The next day a letter was published in the newspapers in respect of rumours that trolleybuses would be withdrawn from several routes with the introduction of summer schedules. The writer wondered if the abandonment proposals had anything to do with the Co-ordination Agreement; if so, it was high time that it was cancelled.

In the meantime the undertaking's vehicle replacement programme had been discussed. It was decided to purchase 15 new motorbuses each year for the next 5 years and the General Manager was authorised to dismantle or dispose of nine obsolete motorbuses and 16 trolleybuses. There was no reference to new trolleybuses.

A special Passenger Transport Committee meeting was held on 24 April 1956. Alderman Collins stated that if it was decided to continue with trolleybus operation, a considerable outlay on the renewal of the fleet and of the underground cables which were now becoming old and worn would have to be faced. The General Manager had advised him that any extension of trolley vehicle routes would cost about £7,000–£8,000 per mile whilst any extension to the system would require additional traction power substations. The outstanding debt on trolley vehicles was £33,856 and this would be paid-off in 1962. The outstanding debt on overhead equipment was £23,760 and the normal repayment period would expire in 1967. Mr Simmonds added that the CPPTD had 96 trolley vehicles of which 65 were in daily service. The City's transport needs could be met with fewer vehicles if services were re-routed and motorbuses used. He referred to the age of the existing fleet and gave details of the programme for the renewal of trolleybus bodies where the chassis were in good condition. He also mentioned that a number of traction poles would soon need replacement due to corrosion at their base; however, the existing overhead equipment was in fairly good condition. It was decided to prepare a report incorporating the financial and technical aspects of a gradual abandonment of the trolleybus system and its replacement by motorbuses.

Trolleybuses on services 15 and 16 were replaced temporarily by motorbuses from 16 April to 26 May 1956 to permit repairs to Chichester Road, sections of which were completely closed to traffic. The replacement motorbuses were diverted along various side streets whilst late night journeys on services 7, 8, 11 and 12 reverted to using New Road instead of Chichester Road when returning to North End Depot.

In the period July 1955 to April 1956 the following trolleybuses, shown in order of their reappearance in service were rebuilt, including internal and external repaints:

300, 267, 233, 245, 286, 255, 250, 237, 231.

All had regenerative control except 265 and 274 which were converted to series dynamic control in 1951. BUT9611T 314 was repainted.

The financial and technical reports prepared by the City Treasurer and the General Manager, together with a summary of the replies received to a questionnaire sent to 92 local authorities, were considered by a special meeting on 30 July 1956. The summary showed that there were 2168 trolleybuses in municipal fleets at that time, compared with

15,728 motorbuses and 1979 trams. Portsmouth Ratepayers' Association, supported by both the Southsea and Cosham and District Ratepayers' Associations, wrote that they considered that the City Council would be very foolish to make such an important decision as the abandonment of trolleybuses without first holding a referendum among the ratepayers, whose money bought and built up the system. The Portsmouth Trades Council stated that the issue should be referred to a public enquiry and a ratepayer's referendum.

When speaking to the special committee on the Twyford Avenue one-way scheme in March 1956, Mr Simmonds had stated that CPPTD now operated over an area of 127 square miles as opposed to being confined to points south of Cosham and within an area of 10 square miles. Serious consideration should be given to the introduction of motorbuses instead of trolleybuses on the north and south routes. He explained that this policy had been followed to a limited extent by the withdrawal of services 1 and 2 and their replacement with motorbuses which permitted an extension to Portchester with the addition of two extra vehicles and the withdrawal of the 9 and 10 service and the re-routing of certain SMS services resulting in a saving of 450,000 miles p.a. Should the Passenger Transport Committee decide on the eventual abandonment of trolleybuses, the expenditure involved in re-routing them in Twyford Avenue could be avoided by introducing motorbuses. He recommended that services 3, 4, 19 and 20 should be extended through Cosham to Paulsgrove and served by motorbuses, relieving the Corporation of the heavy capital outlay involved in a trolleybus route extension. He added that if trolleybus operation was to continue a considerable outlay on the renewal of the fleet and underground cables would be required.

It was accordingly proposed that:

(1) The Committee's policy was not to extend the trolleybus system but to enable the General Manager and Engineer gradually to reduce it and in the interest of economy and efficiency of the undertaking, replace trolley vehicles by motorbuses.
(2) The appropriate officials were to prepare a further report showing the stages by which the changeover should be made and the financial implications of each step.

Alderman Birch and Councillor Evans suggested an amendment whereby the recommendation would simply be not to extend the trolleybus system but this was lost 3 to 14 and the original proposal was accepted 14 to 3 against.

The decision provoked uproar in the press as residents' and ratepayers' arguments had been conveniently disregarded. Amongst the comments writers pointed out that the trolleybus was essentially a short stage vehicle, and that motorbuses running onto Portsea Island from more distant points should not be permitted to pick up short distance passengers. Another writer wondered why thousands of pounds had been spent over the last 4 years on trolleybus route extensions along Gladys Avenue, Chichester Road and Copnor Road, when the decision-makers now considered trolleybuses 'obsolete'.

The *Evening News* leading article for 7 August 1956 stated that, in view of the troubles in the Middle East, it was an ill-chosen moment for the Transport Department to recommend trolleybus abandonment. There might be a case for not extending to Leigh Park or even to Paulsgrove, on the grounds of the cost of the equipment, but there should have been a better argument for withdrawing trolleybuses from the existing routes than had been presented. On 15 August 1956 it was suggested that the full report advocating abandonment should be made public knowledge and at the end of the month Portsmouth Trades Council held a special meeting to discuss the situation and passed a resolution that to abandon electrically operated transport was a retrograde step.

An 11-page report about Portsmouth's trolleybuses was drawn up in September 1956 by a committee representing the four local ratepayers' associations. This report favoured the trolleybus, due to its lack of dependence upon imported fuel and the absence of noxious fumes whilst in use. The proposal to scrap the trolleybus was considered as a serious threat to a valuable public asset. The Committee felt that no case had been submitted to the Passenger Transport Committee for retaining trolleybuses and that therefore councillors were unable to consider the scheme impartially. The suggestion that trolleybuses ran at a loss was considered untrue. It appeared that to suit the intended abandonment policy, costs and methods of trolleybus operation had been so arranged as to show a paper loss.

On 7 September 1956 the Portsmouth Labour Party passed the following resolution:

'That this Delegate Council views with alarm the proposals of the Portsmouth Transport Committee regarding the future of the trolleybus system in Portsmouth and demands that the City Council refers back their proposals to the Committee for consideration at a public enquiry.'

There was a complaint in the local press on 13 September 1956 concerning the use of motorbuses on services 5 and 6 as well as on special journey from Stubbington Avenue, Copnor Road to Southsea South Parade Pier, which ran immediately in front of the service 6 trolleybus running from Cosham past Stubbington Avenue! The correspondent wondered why services 15 and 16 could not be extended in the peak summer season beyond Eastney to Southsea South Parade Pier instead.

As a result the Passenger Transport Committee considered trolleybuses once again on 14 September 1956. They stated that abandonment would lead to savings in mileage, with no reduction in revenue, but a considerable reduction in capital expenditure. There was only 6 to 8 years of life left in much of the trolleybus fleet and equipment, and motorbuses were cheaper to operate. Duplication of both forms of transport was considered uneconomic and to cover the main routes the trolleybus infrastructure would have to be extended from its then 21.13 miles to 34.5 miles at a cost of £260,000 although it was not stated which extensions other than to Leigh Park, a 1670 acre site to the north of Havant bought by Portsmouth City Council in 1944 for use as a semi-rural post-war housing estate (some 5 miles), and Paulsgrove (2.125 miles) would contribute to make up this additional 13.37 route miles. The Provisional Order 1948 approved some 9 miles of which the Chichester Road, Copnor Road and Gladys Avenue routes had already been built and opened. It was also pointed out that it was sometimes more economical to use motorbuses for off-peak requirements on trolleybus routes due to the availability of vehicles at this particular time.

In the preceding financial year the trolleybuses had apparently made a loss of £4,774 whilst the motorbuses had returned a £22,193 profit, due in part to a £55,331 increase in revenue following a fares increase. It was suggested that this fares increase had come too late in the financial year to help the trolleybus fare stages, and that an extra ¼d per passenger during the period would have resulted in a profit on trolleybus operations of more than £28,000, despite artificially swollen maintenance charges.

The co-ordination agreement was also criticised as £11,000 of the Corporation's receipts had passed to SMS as the company had not achieved its 43% of total receipts. If this loss was to be maintained for 10 years, it would amount to the equivalent of having 21 trolleybuses reconditioned, the cost of the Paulsgrove and Rectory Avenue extensions, and also the Twyford Avenue alterations. The writer closed by asking whether the real truth was that the trolleys were in the way when fare increases were being sought because one party (to the agreement) did not run them.

The Ratepayers' Associations, in a letter to City Councillors who were meeting on 18 September 1956 to discuss the trolleybus issue, wrote that they were alarmed at an attempt to rush through a decision contrary to citizens' interests. They considered there was no need for haste and that nothing should be done before a public enquiry was held. Bearing in mind the trolleybus operations of the last 4 years, the City Council were asked whether in fact it had been given a fair deal. Were the reduction of services referred to in the General Manager's report in the Joint Committee's interests rather those of the users and owners of this valuable asset? It was observed that the only indication of any desire to do away with the trolleybuses had come from the Chairman of the Passenger Transport Committee or the CPPTD. The Associations noted that nobody had advocated 34½ miles of trolleybus route extensions: only the Paulsgrove extension was required and the Chairman himself had stated that this would save £7,500 and 240,000 miles p.a. by eliminating much uneconomical working where motorbuses and trolleybuses covered the same sections of routes.

They went on to comment on the fact that trolleybuses were reputedly now more expensive to operate than motorbuses, although they had been cheaper until 3 years ago and had only shown a loss once, in the year preceding. In a letter to the *Evening News* a Mr E. Derwent added that motorbus bodies had been treated as 'capital projects', whereas trolleybus bodies were being charged to 'repairs and maintenance' thereby increasing the operating costs. Although motorbuses ran indiscriminately along roads equipped with trolleybus overhead equipment, the rates which paid for this equipment were attributed solely to the trolleybuses and this had been increased in the previous year to 1.037d per mile whereas a comparison with other trolleybus operators showed an average of 0.6d per mile! He pointed out that although the 21 trolleybuses then stored out of use plus a number of further vehicles required reconditioning, this did not apply to the entire trolleybus fleet. Could a fleet of 20-year-old diesel buses be run as cheaply as Portsmouth's trolleybus fleet? To what extent trolleybus route abandonments were at the behest or suggestion of SMS was not known but the Portsmouth Ratepayers' Association felt that such information would be invaluable to enable Portmuthians to assess the true value of the Joint Working Agreement which was 'so acclaimed by its Chairman and so detested by the citizens'.

The City Council meeting on 18 September 1956 gave the Passenger Transport Committee Chairman the opportunity to reply to the Portsmouth Ratepayers' Association. The Chairman stated that trolleybus mileage was at that time more than 200,000 miles greater than that operated in 1939 but run by 18 fewer trolleybuses. The object of the agreement with SMS was to eliminate wasted mileage and thus trolleybus services surplus to requirements had been withdrawn. The withdrawal of services 9 and 10 had resulted in a saving of £40,000 p.a. The key point was that trolleybuses were more expensive to operate than motorbuses in comparable circumstances. Admittedly the repairs and maintenance of motorbuses had been greater than that of the trolleybuses, but this had been before the cost of overhead equipment maintenance was added. It was not the lack of mobility of the trolleybus on a road already provided with overhead equipment which was a disadvantage, but the inability of the infrastructure to be readily modified or extended to cater for changes in demand. The Paulsgrove extension would have cost £38,000 and that in Edinburgh Road and Unicorn Road would have cost £7,500 per mile. The majority of the trolleybuses were nearing the end of their economic life and more economic operation could be arranged with only one type of vehicle. It was the trolleybus routes which made a profit, not the trolleybuses themselves.

During the debate it was again suggested that any decision should be deferred due to the deteriorating situation in the Middle East (on 31 October 1956 the Suez Canal was blocked and Britain began its Egyptian campaign) and uncertain fuel oil supplies. It was also proposed that a bus station should be built at Cosham to serve as a transfer point from motorbuses to the trolleybuses serving Portsea Island. The meeting adjourned without decision.

On 9 October 1956 the City Council upheld the Passenger Transport Committee's recommendation to replace the trolleybuses with motorbuses by a majority of 30 to 25. The Portsmouth Ratepayers' Association deplored their decision stating that it would continue to fight to save the trolleybus to the bitter end. They hoped the Council would have the foresight to reverse the decision. A few days later, the General Manager of Bradford Corporation Transport, Chaceley Humpidge, addressing the Portsmouth & District Centre of the Institute of Traffic Administrators, said that 'anybody with brains can make a trolleybus run cheaper than a motorbus'.

An offer of £80 from the City and County of Bristol to buy a withdrawn trolleybus for conversion into a mobile public convenience was accepted on 16 October 1956; however, the purchase was not completed. A further enquiry was received in April 1957 and AEC 661T 258 less traction motor and control equipment was sold to Bristol for £80. It was decided that the other trolley vehicles then available for disposal would be put out to tender after serviceable parts required by the Department had been removed.

Road works commenced at the junction of Northern Road with Spur Road Cosham in the autumn requiring overhead wiring changes and the repositioning of some traction poles. The undertaking was not responsible for the estimated cost of £1,280. It was anticipated that the equipment would be required for a further 6 to 8 years under the contemplated replacement programme. Plans to construct refuges at the southern end of Northern Road, Cosham, meant that the southbound pair of trolley wires would have to be slewed where the road was widened. As this section of wiring, from the entrance to the private road leading to Cosham Compound, to the junction with Portsmouth Road had been redundant for 16 years, this portion of the overhead equipment was dismantled in 1956. The traction poles, equipped with single brackets arms, were also removed.

During the course of summer and autumn 1956 the following trolleybuses were rebuilt and freshly upholstered in upper and lower saloons: 269, 270, 251, 294, 246 (dealt with in the sequence shown). BUT 9611T 302 was repainted. The following vehicles were in store, de-licensed, inside North End Depot: 201, 219, 220, 229, 257, 262–264, 266, 272, 279, 280, 284, 285, 287–289, with 216 in the yard outside.

Councillor Dr Bresler moved a motion at the 20 November 1956 Passenger Transport Committee Meeting, that in view of changed circumstances since the trolleybus abandonment decision and the Minister of Fuel and Power's appeal that alternatives to diesel oil and petrol should be used wherever possible, the City Council be recommended to rescind their decision. When the motion was voted upon on 16 December 1956 it was defeated 7 to 9. It was said that if the decision was reversed, 15 trolleybuses costing £6,400 each would have to be ordered and £38,000 invested in equipment for the Paulsgrove extension. The Portsmouth Trades Council and Portsmouth Ratepayers' Associations remained unconvinced about the abandonment decision whilst the Fratton Labour Party called for all available trolleybuses to be put into service to reduce the use of imported fuel. SMS was forced to reduce services, especially in the evenings.

Despite the wish to start work on converting Twyford Avenue into a one-way street as soon as possible this could not begin until new motorbuses arrived. Mr Simmonds stated that these would only be delivered in 12 months' time whilst from an operational perspective he felt the conversion lay some 3 years ahead. Strangely, in summer 1957 traction poles throughout Twyford Avenue were repainted.

The Annual Delegate Conference of Portsea Island Society Cooperative Party passed a resolution in December 1956 that: 'This conference protests against any action being taken to reduce trolleybus services in the City. Furthermore the service should be extended, particularly to those areas controlled by the City Council and where petrol bus services are now being operated in rural (sic) areas.' On 18 December 1956 the Passenger Transport Committee considered a letter from the Portsmouth Trades Council requesting that all trolleybuses fit for service should be put back into operation. In this way it was stated a practical contribution could be made to the national effort to save oil fuel. The Trades Council felt that the oil crisis gave the Committee a further opportunity to reconsider their trolleybus abandonment policy. This was followed in January 1957 by a statement from a joint committee of the Ratepayers' Associations and the Trades Council sent to members of the City Council in which they claimed that 'the whole case for the abandonment of trolleybuses was rushed before Council'. It stressed the dependency of motorbuses on imported fuel and an inability to understand why operating both motorbuses and trolleybuses could be uneconomical as every other trolleybus operator also ran motorbuses.

Purchase tax on oil fuels increased by 1s per gallon and motorbus fuel rationing was imposed from 17 December 1956 whilst the price of oil by-products such as tyres, tubes, flaps and retreads rose by 10%. In order to meet this, temporary fare increases in the City area for the duration of the Suez Crisis also applicable to trolleybus services were introduced, apparently at one day's notice, from the same date: 1½d fares increased to 2d; 2d fares increased to 2½d. On 30 December 1956 motorbus service mileage was cut by 5%.

Public discontent was making the City Council increasingly uncomfortable and they debated the trolleybus issue once again on 8 January 1957 and by a majority of three instructed the Passenger Transport Committee to reconsider their plans to abandon electric traction. On 15 January 1957 the Committee's Chairman, Alderman Collins, stated that this decision must be interpreted as being a vote of no confidence in the recommendations of the Department officials, the majority of the Committee and himself as Chairman. He was strongly opposed to committing Portsmouth's citizens to further expenditure by extending the trolleybus system. As it was not in the Department's best interests to have this vexed question continually in the balance it left him with no alternative but to offer to resign. Vice Chairman Councillor Powell proposed that this offer of resignation be not accepted and the voting was carried with the abstention of Dr Bresler. Alderman Collins thanked the Committee for their vote of confidence and agreed to continue in the office of Chairman. As Alderman Collins headed a local firm of building contractors any personal interests can be ruled out. He went on to warn that trolleybus retention would require expenditure of £156,000 and the City would be committed to trolleybuses for about 20 years.

After discussion it was proposed and accepted that the Committee, while reaffirming its trolleybus abandonment recommendations, that every serviceable trolley vehicle should be used in order to reduce the use of motorbuses as much as possible. Mr Simmonds would address the Portsmouth Chamber of Commerce on 18 January 1957 on the trolleybus question. This led the Chamber to carry out its own investigation into the controversy. Having examined documentary evidence from both sides and questioned CPPTD officials as well as some of the principal critics, they concluded that it was a correct decision to abandon trolleybus operation. On 12 February 1957 Portsmouth City Council reaffirmed the Passenger Transport Committee's decision to abandon trolleybuses by a two-thirds majority.

It was decided on 19 February 1957 to equip some 275 bus stops with fare stage flags 13in. × 6½in. worded in 2in. high letters at a cost of £185. In the summer work began on experimentally painting 'Bus Stop' on the road surface at 12 stops in busy parts of the city.

Additional revenue was needed to meet increased costs since the last fare increase in March 1956 and in early February 1957 the Joint Committee decided that the 1½d and 2d fares within the City should be increased by ½d each. Inside the City area the temporary increases of ½d on 1½d and 2d fares implemented during the Suez Crisis under the Hydrocarbon Oil Duties (Temporary Increase) Act 1956 were combined with a proposal to also increase adult fares of 5d and over by ½d. The fare increases were approved on 15 March 1957. The Traffic Commissioner stated that operators were in a dilemma as costs continued to rise requiring them to either increase fares or reduce services. He thought it better to retain services rather than cut them. The RTC was conscious of the effect of fare increases on the inflationary spiral but their task was to see that services were kept running in the public interest.

The SEB notified the undertaking that effective 1 August 1957 their charges for traction current would be replaced by a Standard Industrial Tariff, thereby increasing power costs by around £2,500 p.a. based on the mileage then being operated. As in the past, the revised tariff was tied to the price of coal.

By now the long-discussed 'Link Road', known today as Southampton Road, was under construction requiring an additional roundabout on Northern Road, Cosham, at the junction with Spur Road, itself an extension of Havant Road, the main A27. The overhead wiring was slewed as necessary and a number of new traction poles planted during spring

1957 as the work progressed whilst throughout the summer southbound trolleybuses continued to follow, more or less, their original route as the other traffic followed a diversion. The new road, which effectively by-passed the western parts of Cosham, opened throughout on 3 March 1958.

The Joint Committee of Portsmouth Ratepayers' Associations enquired in May 1957 why trolleybuses were being sold at the low sum of £50 each, whilst others were quietly being scrapped at Eastney Depot, without being offered for tender. They were not satisfied that seven out of the 11 trolleybuses out of use could not be made roadworthy without major repairs. This provoked an invitation on 6 June 1957 to tender for seven trolleybuses, less certain components, reportedly 'the last of the "derelicts" which have been branded as unroadworthy'.

It was announced that no more trolleybuses would be rebuilt, completely overhauled or fitted with new upholstery and as a result a number of bodybuilders were given other tasks. Furthermore 14 stored trolleybuses, assumed to be the stored Craven-bodied AEC661Ts 229, 251, 262–264, 266, 272, 279, 280, 284, 285, 287–289, stated to be 'beyond reasonable repair' were to be sold for scrap once the electrical equipment had been removed.

1934 AEC661T 201 (1) with English Electric composite body is pictured at The Strand having just turned into Waverley Road on a short working to North End in c. 1957. The enlarged offside windscreen is the result of combining the small recessed window in the cream-painted central band or cantrail with the main windscreen in June 1955. The semaphore arm illuminated traffic indicators were removed when the windscreen was deepened. (Roy Marshall)

250, with a working nearside semaphore arm illuminated traffic indicator, is seen heading south in London Road, North End. Close observation shows that the driver sports a bow tie! In the background, behind the Humber car and the first traction pole, is the junction with Stubbington Avenue, once foreseen as a trolleybus route, with Whites furniture store on the nearest corner and Melanies, a more luxurious store in the Co-op group, on the other. (Colin W. Routh)

The August 1957 Bank Holiday and Navy Days weekend was warm and sunny. A number of additional trolleybus services operated over and above those normally expected possibly due to fears that an SMS strike over a wage claim (20–29 July 1957) would not be settled by then:

3 North End *Junction* – Fratton Bridge – Southsea *South Parade Pier* (short working)
4 Southsea *South Parade Pier* – Fratton Bridge – North End Junction (short working)
5 Dockyard *Main Gate* – Royal Pier Hotel – Southsea *South Parade Pier* – Festing Hotel – Eastney – Milton *White House* – Copnor Bridge – Green Lane (only)
5 Dockyard *Main Gate* – Royal Pier Hotel – Southsea *South Parade Pier* – Festing Hotel – Eastney – Milton *White House* (only)
5 Dockyard *Main Gate* – Royal Pier Hotel – Southsea *South Parade Pier* – Festing Hotel – Eastney (only)
5 Dockyard *Main Gate* – Royal Pier Hotel – Southsea *South Parade Pier* (only)
6 Green Lane – Copnor Bridge – Milton *White House* – Eastney – Festing Hotel – Southsea *South Parade Pier* – Royal Pier Hotel – Dockyard *Main Gate* (only)
6 Milton *White House* – Eastney – Festing Hotel – Southsea *South Parade Pier* – Royal Pier Hotel – Dockyard *Main Gate* (only)
6 Eastney – Festing Hotel – Southsea *South Parade Pier* – Royal Pier Hotel – Dockyard *Main Gate* (only)
6 Southsea *South Parade Pier* – Royal Pier Hotel – Dockyard *Main Gate* (only)
17 Dockyard *Main Gate* – Guildhall – Bradford Junction – Festing Hotel – Eastney – Milton *White House* – Bradford Junction – Guildhall – Dockyard *Main Gate* (double service)
18 Dockyard *Main Gate* – Guildhall – Bradford Junction – Milton *White House* – Eastney –Festing Hotel – Bradford Junction – Guildhall – Dockyard *Main Gate* (double service)
19 Alexandra Park – Guildhall – Clarence Pier (short working)
20 Clarence Pier – Guildhall – Alexandra Park (short working)

Some 70 trolleybuses were in use. Although trolleybuses operated the normal timetable on services 7 and 8, motorbuses ran short workings on services 7 and 8 between Clarence Pier and Copnor Bridge as all serviceable trolleybuses were in use.

Trolleybuses on services 17 and 18 were held up for 20 minutes in Albert Road on 3 September 1957 due to workmen piercing a porcelain pipe containing a traction feeder and puncturing the cable as they removed concrete tram track foundations with a pneumatic drill.

On 17 September 1957 it was decided to dispose of ten trolleybuses, namely 216, 219, 220, 280, 284, 285, 287–289, 296. Five of them, 285, 287–289, 296 were dismantled and their components retained for further use. The remainder were offered for tender at the best possible price, being subsequently sold in early 1958 to C. D. Jordan and Son Ltd. (Breaker), Locksway Road, Milton, Portsmouth.

The following repaints took place during the course of summer 1957:

May	315
June	253, 308
July	306, 307
August	241, 278

Traction poles were repainted in Clarendon Road and Osborne Road, Southsea, and in London Road between Kingston Cross and North End Junction.

The City Council enquired in November 1957 when they could expect a report on the financial implications of the trolleybus abandonment programme and were informed that the scheme had not yet reached the stage at which a report could be made.

The Cosham and District Ratepayer's Association informed the Passenger Transport Committee of their decision of 5 March 1958: 'That the trolleybus controversy in this City be brought before the full Council at the earliest and a fresh vote taken before any further reductions are made in the trolleybus strength.' Following their internal decision of 10 March 1958, the Portsmouth Ratepayer's Association called on 'the Passenger Transport Committee to publish the Financial Report on the implications of the changeover from Trollies (sic) to Diesel Buses. This Association calls for a public enquiry into the financial implications of the Co-ordination Agreement between the Corporation and Southdown Motor Services.'

The carefully orchestrated combined effort continued with a letter dated 10 March 1958 from the above two Associations and the Portsmouth Trades Council asking:

(a) To be informed when the Joint Report by the City Treasurer and Transport Manager (giving the full financial and other commitments involved in the changeover) will be submitted and to be furnished with a copy of such report.
(b) What is the purpose or motive in the continued reduction in the City's fleet of trolleybuses?
(c) Whether some of the oldest motorbuses are still in running and how many diesel buses have been scrapped as, or since, the last 15 new vehicles were put on the road? Can it be categorically stated that no further trolleybuses have been scrapped and the old motorbuses retained in service? They also asked for details of the registration of new vehicles and withdrawals, together with the year of manufacture of the latter.
(d) For an independent report to be prepared by a competent Electrical Engineer with operating experience in transport.
(e) It was considered that public opinion had already confirmed the wishes of the majority of the people of Portsmouth and the case so far presented by the Transport Committee had been biased in favour of diesel buses.

After much discussion, the Committee replied that:

(1) No trolley vehicle services have been reduced or replaced (apart from the normal reduced winter frequencies which also apply to motorbuses) but when it becomes necessary to reduce or replace any trolley vehicle service then before this is done the appropriate officers will submit a report as required by the City Council's 1956 decision.
(2) The information regarding the replacement of old motorbuses and trolleybuses by new diesel buses will be supplied by the General Manager.
(3) No useful purpose would be served by engaging the services of a competent Electrical Engineer with operating experience in transport.
(4) The policy of replacing the trolleybus services will come before the Council when the first financial report is presented.
(5) That the Portsmouth Ratepayer's Association be referred to their letter of 1 January 1957 placing on record their appreciation of the meeting which took place between traffic officers of the Corporation and the Southdown Company and the Association when the question of the Co-ordination Agreement was dealt with.

The Chairman of the Passenger Transport Committee stated that no reduction of the trolleybus fleet was contemplated until a decision had been reached on the Twyford Avenue one-way street scheme, although in due course a time would come when they had to consider the condition of vehicles. At the 8 April 1958 City Council meeting a motion stating that 'it was becoming increasingly evident that the trolleybus abandonment decision was an incorrect one' and calling on the Transport Department to 'prepare a scheme for increasing the use of the trolleybuses' was rejected.

The capital programme for the next 3 years including 45 motorbuses for 1959–62 was submitted on 17 June 1958. The financial year ending 31 March 1958 closed with a surplus of £5,156 which was carried forward to the Net Revenue Appropriation Account.

A collision took place in Highland Road on 15 September 1958 between BUT9611T 302 and a Kodak lorry. The trolleybus driver's health may have been a contributing factor and the Town Clerk was asked to settle on the most equitable terms without admitting liability but not exceeding two-thirds plus legal costs.

246 turns out of Spur Road, Cosham, and heads south along Northern Road at the roundabout built in 1957 at the east end of the Link Road (now Southampton Road). The proposed trolleybus route to Paulsgrove would have followed Link Road from this roundabout where a complex overhead wiring layout was foreseen. Portsdown Hill dominates the background. (Tony Belton)

Portsmouth's tram rails long survived the vehicles themselves, indeed some lengths survive today. Here BUT9611T 310 pauses to take on passengers at another of the undertaking's ornate passenger waiting shelters in Southsea Terrace. (Tony Belton)

CHAPTER 8

SWAN SONG

Mr Simmonds presented plans for the first stage of the trolleybus abandonment programme to the Passenger Transport Committee on 16 September 1958 proposing that trolleybuses on services 3, 4, 7, 8, 13 and 14 should be replaced by motorbuses in November 1958 and that the 3 and 4 should then be extended at peak hours to Farlington, Rectory Avenue. These services required 16 trolleybuses and there were now 14 trolleybuses in the fleet which were more than 21 years old and due for rebuilding. The conversion and extension were estimated to require five fewer vehicles and would economise 200,000 miles, reducing expenditure by £18,000. Councillor Dr Maxwell Bresler's proposal that no action be taken due to the inadequacy of the information given and that the report be submitted to the Finance and General Purposes Committee and the City Council for information was accepted. Portsmouth City Council considered the report on 14 October 1958 but did not know what to do with it! Councillor Bresler moved an amendment that the Council should ask for an independent enquiry into the transport department's finances. The Lord Mayor ruled that he was unable to accept this amendment and members advanced varying suggestions on what should or could be done about the report. The Council finally decided that 'this minute be not received', only one councillor voting against the proposal.

On 21 October 1958 the Passenger Transport Committee Chairman proposed a special meeting to consider a further report from the General Manager on the proposed conversion. He refused a vote on Councillor R.A. Bridger's suggestion that the City Council should rescind the abandonment decision and appoint an independent consultant to conduct an enquiry into the Corporation's passenger transport policy. The meeting was held on 30 October 1958 and considered a more detailed report from Mr Simmonds. After discussion Councillor Bridger again proposed that a firm of industrial consultants be appointed to make an independent enquiry into the undertaking in the following terms:

(1) Examine the present and future financial and economic aspects of the undertaking as a whole and of motor buses and trolleybuses individually.
(2) Make recommendations on any additions or withdrawals of motorbuses or trolleybuses (and equipment) that may be necessary to provide the most economical undertaking consistent with an adequate service to the public.
(3) Examine the operation of the joint agreement with SMS to determine the advantages or disadvantages to the Corporation and to make recommendations on any alterations in its operation (consistent with the agreement itself) which may be necessary to provide greater benefit to the Corporation.
(4) Recommend the most profitable line of action open to the Corporation when the existing agreement with SMS expires.
(5) Report or recommend on any matter which they feel may have a bearing on the future efficient operation of the Corporation Transport Undertaking.

This way forward was supported by eight members of the meeting (four voting against) who stressed that this course of action did not indicate any lack of faith in the Corporation's officials but more the changing economic and social circumstances and conflicting opinions within the Committee. A counter proposal to accept the General Manager's report and put into effect the first stage of the trolleybus abandonment programme was rejected. The City Council approved the recommendation that there should be an independent enquiry into the undertaking on 12 November 1958.

National pay rises in summer and autumn 1958, estimated to total £26,400 p.a., led to a decision on 19 November 1958 to reduce services with a minimum of inconvenience to the travelling public to meet this additional expenditure. This included a suggestion that services 13 and 14 should be withdrawn and the redundant trolley vehicles put into store until the consultant's report had been received. In the meantime the General Manager was authorised to dispose of 14 traction motors. The Joint Passenger Transport Committee considered Mr Simmonds' report on the effects of these increases on 16 December 1958 and agreed that further mileage economies over and above those already introduced were needed but that a fare increase could be avoided. It was decided that on services operating outside the city minor fare revisions, estimated to generate £10,000 more revenue in the Joint Area, would be sought. Further mileage reductions within the city would be achieved by withdrawing services 13 and 14, and reducing motorbus service 145. They pointed out that although the 13 and 14 were trolleybus operated this had not influenced their decision and that it was unrelated to any subsequent policy decision about trolleybuses that might be made by the Portsmouth City Council.

By 16 December 1958 some 21 applications had been received from consultants, of whom three were selected and invited to make a preliminary survey followed by a quotation: Associated Industrial Consultants Ltd., Harold Whitehead and Partners Ltd. and Mead Carney & Co. Ltd. It is unclear why the Passenger Transport Committee sought advice from firms far divorced from municipal transport operations. On 26 February 1959 they accepted the offer of Harold Whitehead and Partners, a specialist in what is today known as supply chain management, at £2,520 as this was the lowest price and offered the shortest time scale. Traditionally, operators seeking independent advice in such circumstances tended to approach former transport managers recently retired from other operators.

Trolleybus services 13 and 14 Cosham Railway Station – Southsea South Parade Pier were withdrawn on 26 January 1959 and the quarter of a mile of overhead wiring in Victoria Road South (Albert Road – The Circle) fell into disuse.

A pedestrian stepped out unexpectedly onto a pedestrian crossing in Northern Road, Cosham, causing a collision between AEC661T 239 and three other vehicles on 24 March 1959. Claims reached £533 4s 8d plus £162 11s 9d for repairs to 239.

The elderly driver of 293 jumps from his cab in Guildhall Square on a northbound service 20 journey to Cosham Railway Station. The wiring in Park Street can be seen in the background. (D.A.P. Janes)

The financial year ending 31 March 1959 resulted in a surplus of £34,666 which was carried forward to the Net Revenue Appropriation Account. It was decided that £100,000 of the accumulated surplus of £126,862 would be transferred to a Renewals and Reserve Fund.

The report of Harold Whitehead and Partners Ltd. was presented to the Passenger Transport Committee on the 1 September 1959 (see Appendix P). In brief, they considered that trolleybus abandonment over a 20-year period was a sound policy as this mode of transport was, in their view, inflexible and route-bound. The Portsmouth trolleybus system was complicated with a large number of corners, frogs and crossovers, which involved increased capital cost and slower running. The demand for services to outer suburbs and the surrounding area was increasing, whilst the demand for local passenger transport within the city was expected to decline. In the future, north–south services would no longer originate or terminate at Cosham, but would be extended beyond to newer suburbs and it would not be expedient to operate trolleybuses on these new services. They estimated that the total operating cost per mile for trolleybuses was higher than for motorbuses.

On 8 September 1959 the City Council discussed the consultant's report and on 15 September 1959 the Passenger Transport Committee accepted Mr Simmonds' recommendation that trolleybus services 19 and 20 should be immediately converted to motorbus operation and extended to Paulsgrove in peak hours. No additional motorbuses were required; however, 23 trolley vehicles now needed major repairs and it was decided that they should be withdrawn and sold. In the meantime the Ratepayers Association and the Portsmouth Trades Council had written to the Committee about the use of motorbuses on trolleybus services 5 and 6. Mr Simmonds was instructed to reply that this was handled in the consultant's report which was now with the Joint Committee.

The Portsmouth, Southsea, Cosham and District Ratepayers Association and the Portsmouth Trades Council Joint Committee enquired which municipal transport undertakings the consultants had visited and the name of the consultant expert in trolley vehicle development and operation. They were referred to the consultants, apparently with little success as in mid-November 1959 they wrote to the Lord Mayor with the same questions. The Joint Committee also suggested to the Lord Mayor that the City's oldest trolleybus (201) should be preserved by the undertaking. It was decided that there was no purpose in the undertaking retaining 201; however, if the Joint Committee wished to preserve the vehicle, it would be given to them without charge.

The City Treasurer and the City Engineer sought clarification as to who should absorb the cost of moving traction poles in the case of road improvements. The MoT Divisional Road Engineer stated that Parliament considered the cost of relocating poles and wires should be met by trolleybus operators. The cumulated cost of all such works since 6 August 1958 was £1,063 19s 7d. The Town Clerk recognised that there might be a good case for arguing that the cost of relocation should not be borne by CPPTD but it had to be considered whether or not it was better that the cost be borne by a trading undertaking or become a direct charge on the rates. On 17 November 1959 the Passenger Transport Committee resolved to bear the cost without prejudice to the question of future work.

On 15 December 1959 it was announced that the conversion of service 3 and 4 to motorbus operation, and their extension at peak hours to Drayton and Farlington, was likely in February 1960. Certain SMS services would be transferred during the

283 stands at Alexandra Park turning circle on 3 October 1959 prior to departure for, in the first instance, Eastney by way of Twyford Avenue and Commercial Road. (D.A.P. Janes)

evening from Commercial Road to Fratton Road thereby reducing service gaps and leading to a more even spacing of services along Fratton Road.

The Tramway Museum Society (TMS) wrote to the Lord Mayor in March 1960 asking whether the Corporation would consider loaning indefinitely or presenting prototype trolleybus 201, then in store in Eastney Depot Yard, to the Montagu Motor Museum at Beaulieu. The Passenger Transport Committee would only agree to sell it at its scrap value. Lord Montagu confirmed his interest in displaying the trolleybus and on 19 April 1960 it was decided to dispose of the vehicle to the TMS at a price which would be determined when offers were received for other vehicles which were being offered for sale, subject to the Society providing a plaque that identified the vehicle with the City when it was displayed in the Museum. However, 201 was bought by the Portsmouth Ratepayers Association that same month and following a repaint at Eastney, the trolleybus was presented to the Montagu Motor Museum.

In the trolleybus era Northern Road was part of the main London to Portsmouth road. Having crossed over the railway using the concrete bridge built in 1927, BUT9611T 305 turns into the private road leading to Cosham Railway Station bus terminus. The redundant southbound wiring along Northern Road from this point was removed in 1956. (Tony Belton)

Both the newsagents' and 307's rear are well covered with advertisements in this view taken at the junction of Festing Road with Albert Road and Highland Road. Despite the final destination display, 307 is heading east towards Eastney and beyond, past a branch of Smith and Vospers the bakers. (Tony Belton)

Beneath a length of gantries 310 passes the junction of Clegg Road with Highland Road on its way to Eastney, Milton and Cosham. The east end of Highland Road Cemetery is on the right. (Tony Belton)

A Ford Zephyr and a Morris Oxford wait in the taxi rank as BUT9611T 310 powers away from The Hard past the National Provincial Bank towards Southsea South Parade Pier. The layout of the bus stances on the west side of The Hard made it difficult for would-be passengers to know which bus to a destination served by more than one service would leave first and thus regular passengers tended to board at the stop on the east side of the road, where a clock was attached to a traction pole, served by all services. In the distance, beyond the piers of HM Dockyard Main Gate topped with golden ball-on-cushion finials, can be seen the masts of HMS Victory. (Tony Belton)

A further national pay increase in June 1960, estimated to cost the undertaking some £55,000 p.a., meant that the recent mileage economies would offset less than half of the increases and thus the Passenger Transport Committee decided on 26 May 1960 that in co-operation with SMS a fare increase was necessary. Proposals to increase the existing 3½d and 5½d fares within the city to 4d and 6d respectively, together with equivalent increases outside the city, were submitted to the Joint Transport Committee. Nonetheless there was a net surplus for the year ending 31 March 1960 of £51,522 which was forwarded to the Finance and General Purposes Committee and the Council; £50,000 of the accumulated surplus of £78,384 was transferred to a Renewals and Reserve Fund.

Mr Simmonds' recommendation that trolleybus services 15 and 16 Eastney – Alexandra Park, which followed the latest route extensions along Chichester Road and Gladys Avenue, should be converted to motorbus operation using one-man operated (OMO) standee-type single deck vehicles was approved by the Passenger Transport Committee on 30 March 1960. The frequency would be cut from 10 to 12 minutes and the timetable revised to encourage passengers boarding and alighting at points between Eastney and Chichester Road to use trolleybus services 5 and 6. He saw this solution as providing full utilisation of the motorbuses yet saving £5,530 p.a. without any reduction in service to the public. Services 15, 16, 19 and 20 were converted to motorbus operation on 30 April 1960 with the 19 and 20 extended to Paulsgrove during peak hours. The overhead equipment along Twyford Avenue between Kingston Crescent and Gladys Avenue, and the Alexandra Park turning circle accessed from Twyford Avenue now fell into disuse although it was not dismantled. Henceforth wiring along Chichester Road, Gladys Avenue and Northern Parade was only used for depot journeys whilst the turning circles at Eastney and at Alexandra Park accessed from Gladys Avenue ceased to be regularly used.

The Eastney turning circle at the junction of Cromwell Road, unused by regular services since the withdrawal of services 15 and 16 on 30 April 1960, is still aloft in this 6 April 1962 view of Cravens bodied AEC661T 283 (83) approaching the stop at the east end of Highland Road. On the opposite side of the road Crossley DD42/7T motorbus 32 loads outside the 'Highland Arms' public house. The maroon roofline of Eastney Depot is visible beyond the public house. (T.V. Runnacles)

BUT9611T 305 stands beneath the Eastney turning circle wiring (the through wiring is towards the centre of the road), terminus of service 16, at the junction of Highland Road with Eastney Road. Eastney Depot is to the right of the photograph together with a typical cast-iron passenger waiting shelter along the depot wall. Note the Eastney feeder pillar on the kerb in front of the trolleybus and the associated connection to the trolley wires immediately forward of the trailing frog. (Online Transport Archive [photographer A.P. Tatt])

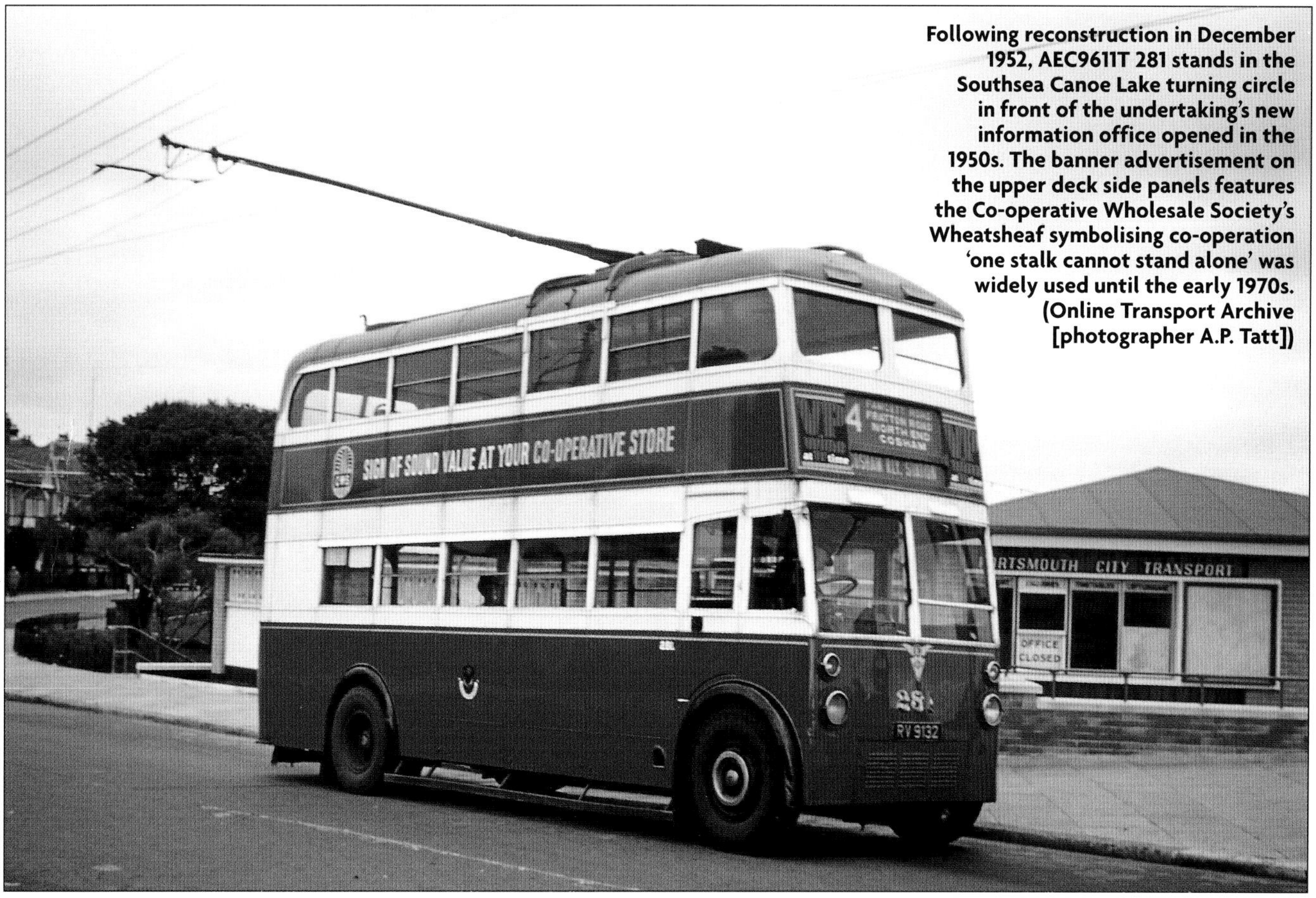

Following reconstruction in December 1952, AEC9611T 281 stands in the Southsea Canoe Lake turning circle in front of the undertaking's new information office opened in the 1950s. The banner advertisement on the upper deck side panels features the Co-operative Wholesale Society's Wheatsheaf symbolising co-operation 'one stalk cannot stand alone' was widely used until the early 1970s. (Online Transport Archive [photographer A.P. Tatt])

With a backdrop of Southsea Common, AEC661T 269 turns on to Clarence Esplanade just before the bus terminus and the main entrance to Clarence Pier. (Online Transport Archive [photographer A.P. Tatt])

The trolleybus system contracted to:

3 Cosham Railway Station – North End *Junction* – Fratton Bridge – Southsea *South Parade Pier*
Unidirectional southbound service worked in conjunction with service 4

4 Southsea *South Parade Pier* – Fratton Bridge – North End *Junction* – Cosham Railway Station
Unidirectional northbound service worked in conjunction with service 3

5 Dockyard *Main Gate* – Royal Pier Hotel – Southsea *South Parade Pier* – Festing Hotel – Eastney – Milton *White House* – Copnor Bridge – Hilsea – Cosham *Red Lion*
Unidirectional northbound service worked in conjunction with service 6

6 Cosham *Red Lion* – Hilsea – Copnor Bridge – Milton *White House* – Eastney – Festing Hotel – Southsea *South Parade Pier* – Royal Pier Hotel – Dockyard *Main Gate*
Unidirectional service worked in conjunction with service 5

7 Green Lane – Copnor Bridge – Fratton Bridge – Bradford Junction – Southsea *The Strand* – Royal Pier Hotel – Clarence Pier
Unidirectional southbound service

8 Clarence Pier – Southsea *The Strand* – Bradford Junction – Fratton Bridge – Copnor Bridge – Green Lane
Unidirectional northbound service

11 Green Lane – Copnor Bridge – Guildhall – Dockyard *Main Gate*
Unidirectional southbound service worked in conjunction with service 12

12 Dockyard *Main Gate* – Guildhall – Copnor Bridge – Green Lane
Unidirectional northbound service worked in conjunction with service 11

17 Dockyard *Main Gate* – Guildhall – Bradford Junction – Festing Hotel – Eastney – Milton *White House* – Bradford Junction – Guildhall – Dockyard *Main Gate*
Unidirectional circular service (anti-clockwise) worked in conjunction with service 18

18 Dockyard *Main Gate* – Guildhall – Bradford Junction – Milton *White House* – Eastney –Festing Hotel – Bradford Junction – Guildhall – Dockyard *Main Gate*
Unidirectional circular service (clockwise) worked in conjunction with service 17

Also in April 1960, the notorious blind corner at the junction of Somers Road and Blackfriars Road was eliminated by demolishing the offending off-licence and widening Blackfriars Road. Four gantries in the widened part of Blackfriars Road were replaced by span wires equipped with modern hangers, the traction poles used being taken from existing stocks and including at least one which had previously stood in Northern Road.

The Southern Counties Touring Society toured the trolleybus system with BUT9611T 304 on Sunday 3 July 1960 and was offered refreshments in the staff canteen.

Due to the deteriorating condition of many trolleybuses, it was decided on 19 July 1960 to convert services 3 and 4 Cosham Railway Station – Southsea South Parade Pier, the city's first trolleybus route, to motorbus operation. Mr Simmonds also suggested a reduced frequency of the 7 and 8 Green Lane – Clarence Pier due to falling passenger numbers. Revenue on these services had fallen to 4.89d per mile, below the average trolleybus revenue per mile and 2.02d below the average cost per mile. In the longer term he envisaged converting services 7 and 8 to motorbus operation, the six trolleybuses required for these services being replaced by six OMO single-deck motorbuses. He was instructed to invite tenders for 12 such vehicles so that motorbus services G and H could be similarly converted.

Trolleybuses ran on services 3 and 4 for the last time on Saturday 17 September 1960 and the replacement motorbuses were extended to Paulsgrove, not to Farlington as previously proposed, over the route of motorbus service 21. The new 3 and 4 ran every 15 minutes, compared with the trolleybuses' 12-minute frequency. Six double-deck motorbuses replaced five trolleybuses and two OMO single-deck motorbuses, economising 56,000 miles and £5,000 p.a.

The Cosham Railway Station turning circle, all overhead wiring along London Road between Hilsea and North End, Rugby Road, and the junction from Waverley Road into Clarendon Road and vice versa at The Strand fell into disuse. The auto-frog at the junction with Waverley Road in the westbound Clarendon Road line was transferred to the eastbound line, replacing the hand-operated pull frog used by service 8 for the left turn into Waverley Road. The overhead wiring along Northern Parade between Hilsea and North End Depot, unused by service trolleybuses since the abandonment of the 19 and 20, had been used by special and late night workings of services 3 and 4. In total, trolleybus route mileage was reduced by 4.28 miles and nine more trolley vehicles, 226, 228, 232, 234, 235, 239, 241, 243, 297, were offered for disposal.

From the same date extras on trolleybus services 11 and 12 ceased using Kingston Crescent and the northern part of Commercial Road on their journeys from North End to the Dockyard and used Lake Road instead. The late night duty on service 6, which until 17 September 1960 had traversed the Terraces and Commercial Road south of Guildhall Square, continued henceforth along the normal route to the Dockyard. Here it became an 18 for its depot journey, the duty being transferred to Eastney Depot. Thus the overhead wiring in the northern and southern parts of Commercial Road, in Kingston Crescent and along the Terraces ceased to be regularly used.

Until now no redundant overhead equipment had been removed but in October 1960 work began cutting down the wiring in Victoria Road South between Albert Road and The Circle. The frogs were removed and the through wiring reconnected at each end. On 4 December 1960 wiring removal between the junction of Commercial Road with Kingston Crescent and Alexandra Park commenced, the final part of this section being cut down on 15 January 1961. Work then ceased until March 1961 but thereafter dismantling work went on steadily until the final section of running wire was removed on 27 February 1964. Where overhead was cut, a short length of wire was inserted or retained to maintain the required tension. This took the form of clamps attached to the end of the running wires known as a back anchor. Where exact dates of dismantling are quoted they are for the morning following the night's work.

In October 1960 it was decided to dispose of the stock of spare traction poles stored at Cosham Compound whilst discussions began with the City Engineer about the retention of some 1,200 poles for street lighting purposes.

The Portsmouth Trades Council had discussed the planned introduction of OMO single-deck motorbuses on services 7 and 8 to replace trolleybuses and on 17 January 1961 stated that their members considered this an erroneous decision

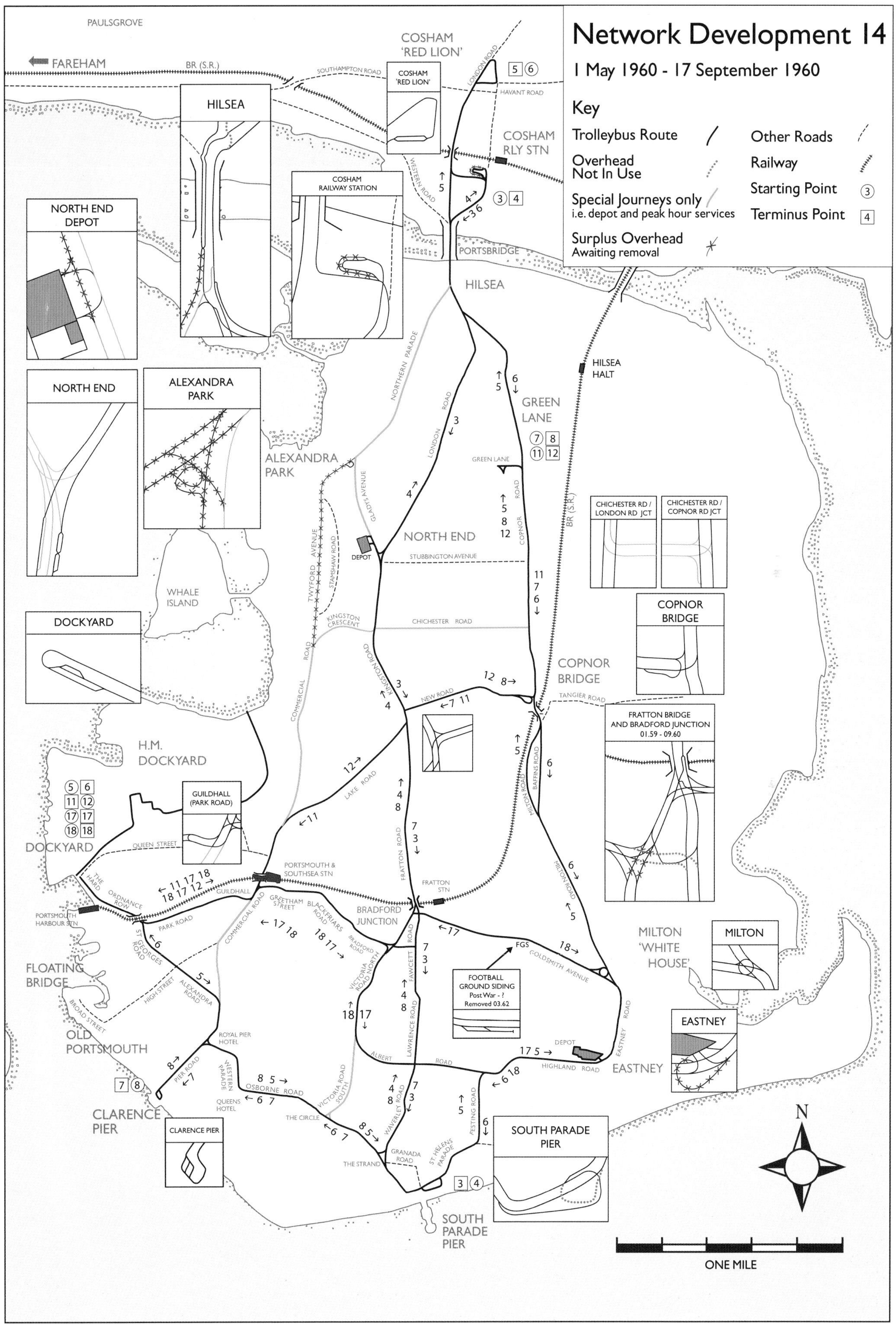

Network Development 14
1 May 1960 - 17 September 1960
Key
Trolleybus Route
Overhead Not In Use
Special Journeys only
i.e. depot and peak hour services
Surplus Overhead
Awaiting removal
Other Roads
Railway
Starting Point
Terminus Point
PAULSGROVE
FAREHAM
BR (S.R.)
SOUTHAMPTON ROAD
COSHAM 'RED LION'
HAVANT ROAD
LONDON ROAD
COSHAM RLY STN
WESTERN ROAD
PORTSBRIDGE
HILSEA
HILSEA HALT
GREEN LANE
NORTHERN PARADE
ALEXANDRA PARK
NORTH END
STUBBINGTON AVENUE
DEPOT
GLADYS AVENUE
TWYFORD AVENUE
STAMSHAW ROAD
WHALE ISLAND
KINGSTON CRESCENT
CHICHESTER ROAD
COPNOR ROAD
COPNOR BRIDGE
TANGIER ROAD
NEW ROAD
KINGSTON ROAD
COMMERCIAL ROAD
H.M. DOCKYARD
DOCKYARD
QUEEN STREET
LAKE ROAD
FRATTON ROAD
BAFFINS ROAD
MILTON ROAD
PORTSMOUTH & SOUTHSEA STN
FRATTON STN
GUILDHALL
THE HARD
ORDNANCE ROW
PORTSMOUTH HARBOUR STN
PARK ROAD
GREETHAM STREET
BLACKFRIARS ROAD
BRADFORD JUNCTION
BRADFORD ROAD
VICTORIA ROAD NORTH
FAWCETT ROAD
GOLDSMITH AVENUE
FGS
MILTON 'WHITE HOUSE'
ST GEORGES ROAD
FLOATING BRIDGE
HIGH STREET
ALEXANDRA ROAD
BROAD STREET
OLD PORTSMOUTH
ROYAL PIER HOTEL
LAWRENCE ROAD
ALBERT ROAD
DEPOT
HIGHLAND ROAD
EASTNEY ROAD
EASTNEY
PIER ROAD
WESTERN PARADE
OSBORNE ROAD
QUEENS HOTEL
CLARENCE PIER
THE CIRCLE
VICTORIA ROAD SOUTH
WAVERLEY ROAD
FESTING ROAD
THE STRAND
GRANADA ROAD
ST HELENS PARADE
SOUTH PARADE PIER
NORTH END DEPOT
HILSEA
COSHAM RAILWAY STATION
NORTH END
ALEXANDRA PARK
DOCKYARD
GUILDHALL (PARK ROAD)
CHICHESTER RD / LONDON RD JCT
CHICHESTER RD / COPNOR RD JCT
COPNOR BRIDGE
FRATTON BRIDGE AND BRADFORD JUNCTION 01.59 - 09.60
FOOTBALL GROUND SIDING Post War - ? Removed 03.62
MILTON
EASTNEY
N
ONE MILE

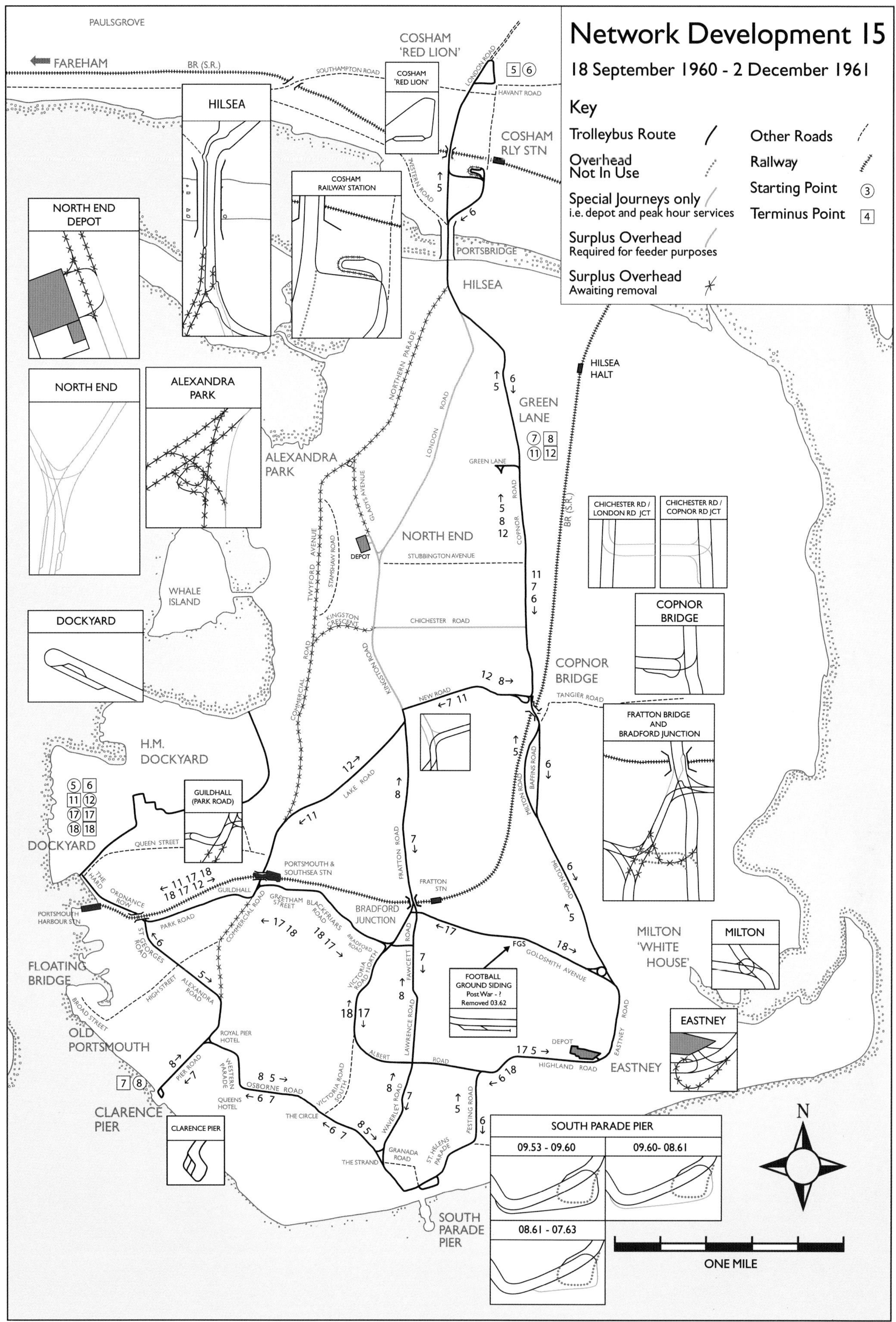
Network Development 15
18 September 1960 - 2 December 1961
Key
Trolleybus Route
Other Roads
Overhead Not In Use
Railway
Special Journeys only i.e. depot and peak hour services
Starting Point
Surplus Overhead Required for feeder purposes
Terminus Point
Surplus Overhead Awaiting removal
PAULSGROVE
FAREHAM
BR (S.R.)
COSHAM 'RED LION'
COSHAM RLY STN
HILSEA
NORTH END DEPOT
NORTH END
ALEXANDRA PARK
COSHAM RAILWAY STATION
PORTSBRIDGE
GREEN LANE
HILSEA HALT
WHALE ISLAND
DOCKYARD
H.M. DOCKYARD
GUILDHALL (PARK ROAD)
CHICHESTER RD / LONDON RD JCT
CHICHESTER RD / COPNOR RD JCT
COPNOR BRIDGE
FRATTON BRIDGE AND BRADFORD JUNCTION
PORTSMOUTH & SOUTHSEA STN
FRATTON STN
BRADFORD JUNCTION
PORTSMOUTH HARBOUR STN
FLOATING BRIDGE
OLD PORTSMOUTH
MILTON 'WHITE HOUSE'
MILTON
EASTNEY
FOOTBALL GROUND SIDING Post War - ? Removed 03.62
CLARENCE PIER
SOUTH PARADE PIER
09.53 - 09.60
09.60- 08.61
08.61 - 07.63
ONE MILE
N

246 leaves Bradford Junction and heads south into Victoria Road North on its anti-clockwise journey around the Eastney circle. (Tony Belton)

in view of the heavy traffic in the roads along the route, especially Fratton Road and New Road. They felt that the much slower loading and longer vehicles would slow down traffic and create traffic dangers, and went on to ask the Passenger Transport Committee's future policy regarding the operation of such buses over long routes with dense traffic. The General Manager stated that he expected services 7 and 8 to be as successful as the introduction of OMO had proved on services 15 and 16. Longer vehicles did not impair traffic flow. Unless there was a considerable fall in traffic higher capacity double-deck vehicles would be purchased for use on longer routes when replacement vehicles were needed. The Trades Council replied that they could not support the introduction of OMO on services 7 and 8, and requested that the matter be reconsidered.

Effective 1 April 1961 the SEB increased their charges for traction power, estimated to increase the department's costs by £1,500 p.a. based on the then level of trolleybus operation. It was felt that a part of this increase could be offset by reducing the number of SEB supply points and terminating the contracts for Northern Parade and Western Parade.

As part of the on-going programme of overhead removal, the feeder mid-way along Northern Parade, adjacent to Kipling Road, was disconnected on 7 March 1961 and the running wires progressively dismantled as far as Alexandra Park by 25 March 1961. The wiring from Kipling Road to Hilsea was cut down by early May 1961.

Whilst running on service 6 during the evening of 11 April 1961 Driver C. Peachmann swerved BUT9611T 303 and collided with a traction pole in Milton Road. Eight passengers were injured, one, Mr M. R. Wilson, who had been sitting on the front upper-saloon seat, being catapulted through the front window to land in the road below. The vehicle's nearside and front was extensively damaged. As repairs to make it roadworthy were estimated at £1,572 it was written off as a total loss. In October 1961 a claim for damages amounting to £1,200 plus costs was received from Mr Wilson.

The official fleet list of 17 May 1961 shows that 29 Cravens bodied AEC661Ts remained in service:

230, 231, 233, 237, 244, 246, 248–252, 254–256, 259, 269, 270, 273, 274, 282, 283, 286, 291, 293, 294, 295, 298–300
as well as 14 of the 15 BUT9611Ts.

An Arbitration Court award at the end of June 1961 increasing costs by some £38,000 p.a., made another fare increase unavoidable. Effective Sunday 17 September 1961 fares within the city for a 2-mile stage rose from 4d to 5d, and the 6d stage for a 3½ mile stage to 7d.

The southbound auto-frog immediately in front of the SMS Hilsea Garage providing access to Northern Parade was removed on 2 August 1961 but the overhead wiring beyond remained intact. By 26 August 1961 all remaining overhead wiring in Commercial Road between the junction with Lake Road and the junction with Kingston Crescent was cut down.

Having selected the nearside line at the auto frog some 50 yards behind, AEC661T 273 climbs over Fratton Bridge on its way to Clarence Pier. Another example of catenary overhead suspension is evident. (Tony Belton)

The trolley heads are not more than a foot before the Albert Road Police Station feeder as a somewhat care-worn 246 (which survived to be the last AEC661T/Cravens in use in Portsmouth on 22 June 1963) edges forward at the junction of Albert Road with Victoria Road South. (Roger Funnell)

During the week ending 2 September 1961, the junction frog connecting the Southsea South Parade Pier turning circle with the westbound through wiring was moved some 50 yards east from Clarendon Road into South Parade.

By mid-October 1961 a further 19 trolley vehicles were considered to be unroadworthy and it was decided to offer them for disposal to the highest bidder. In fact only 11 were sold in November/December 1961 comprising a mixture of vehicles held in store, accident victims and failures, namely 230, 231, 237, 251, 256, 282, 291, 293, 295, 299, 303.

The new OMO single-deck motorbuses intended to replace trolleybuses on services 7 and 8 Green Lane – Clarence Pier were now expected in early November. The poor condition of many surviving members of the trolley vehicle fleet warranted their urgent withdrawal and on 17 October 1961 the Passenger Transport Committee agreed to the conversion of trolleybus service 11 and 12 Green Lane – Dockyard to motorbus operation on the same date as services 7 and 8. Double-deck motorbuses, released from services G and H, which would be converted to OMO single-deck operation, would be used and alternate journeys, which until the conversion terminated at Green Lane, were to be extended to Devon Road about ¼ mile east of Copnor Road, instead of Madeira Road, and those terminating at Copnor Bridge would be extended to the junction of Hayling Avenue and Ebery Grove on weekdays until 6.30 p.m.

The last trolleybuses ran on these services on Saturday 2 December 1961 and trolleybuses disappeared from Portsmouth's premier shopping street. On the same date North End Depot ceased to operate electric traction after 60 years. Five more miles of overhead wiring was made redundant, namely in New Road, Lake Road, Chichester Road, Commercial Road, Fratton Road, Kingston Road, London Road, at North End Junction and in Waverley Road, Fawcett Road and Pier Road and also at Clarence Pier. The Green Lane reversing triangle in Madeira

AEC661T 259 backs into Compton Road on the Green Lane reverser. The majority of the Madeira Stores window display seems to be hidden behind transparencies and other advertisements. (Tony Belton)

Having used the Green Lane reversing triangle, AEC661T 259 has turned out into Copnor Road and is seen just south of Madeira Road. (Tony Belton)

BUT9611T 304 turns out of Northern Road into the private road leading to Cosham Railway Station (Cosham Compound). (Roger Funnell)

The semaphore arm illuminated traffic indicators would hardly be suitable for today's traffic conditions as can be seen from this view of 311 turning into Portsmouth Road from Cosham Railway Station bus terminal. Much of the ornate cast iron passenger waiting shelter in the background was incorporated into the Gunwharf retail centre some 40 years later. (Roger Funnell)

Road ceased to be used by normal services but a service 5 short working continued to turn here at 6.0 p.m. on Fridays only until the withdrawal of services 17 and 18.

Tenders were immediately invited for the disposal of nine more trolleybuses made up of previously withdrawn vehicles, namely 244, 249, 254, 259, and those made available as a result of the conversion of services 7, 8, 11, 12, nos. 252, 255, 270, 273, 298.

The Portsmouth trolleybus system thus contracted to just two pairs of services, the 5 and 6 Dockyard – Cosham 'Red Lion' and the 17 and 18 Dockyard – Eastney circular. These

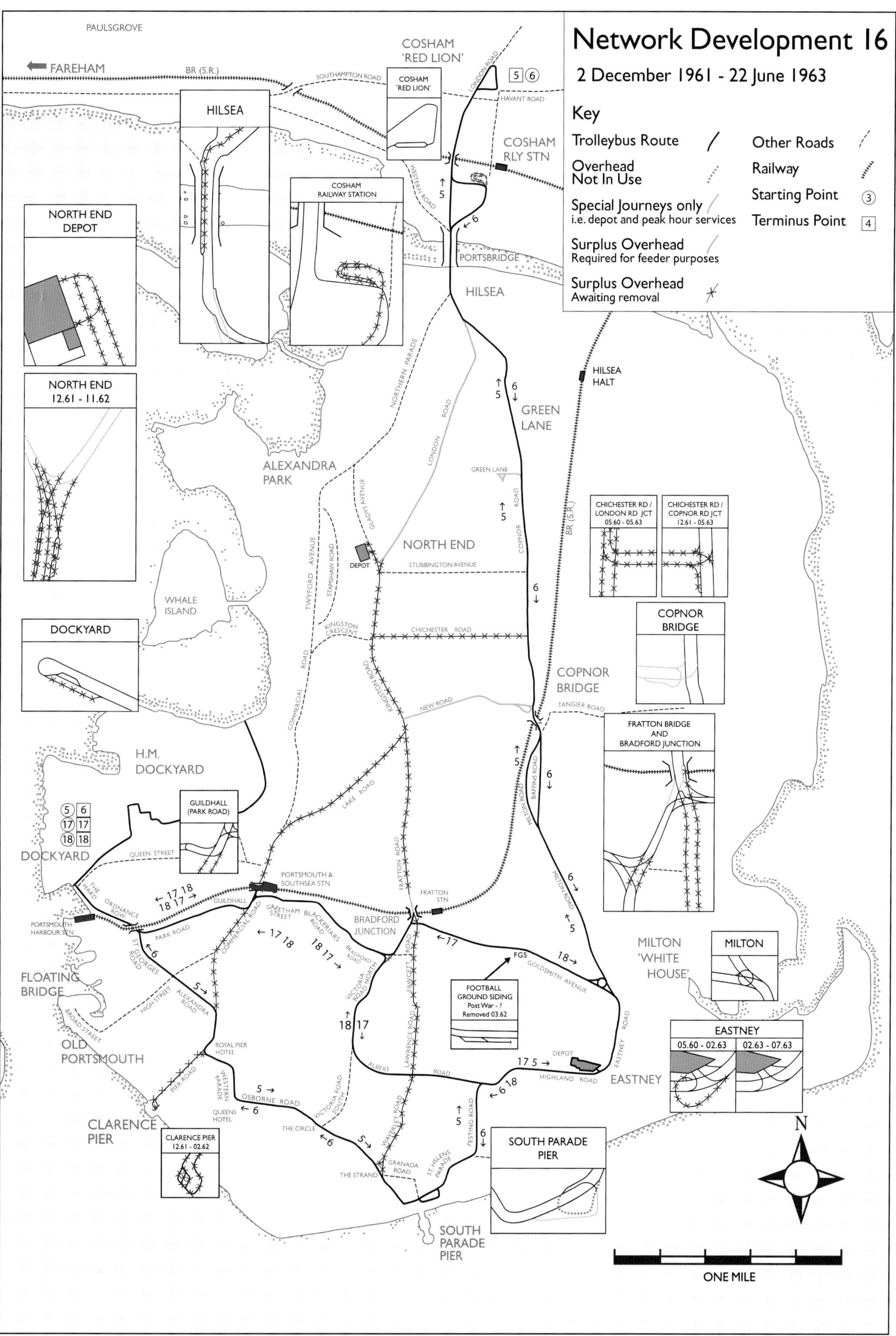

Network Development 16
2 December 1961 - 22 June 1963
Key
Trolleybus Route
Overhead Not In Use
Special Journeys only i.e. depot and peak hour services
Surplus Overhead Required for feeder purposes
Surplus Overhead Awaiting removal
Other Roads
Railway
Starting Point
Terminus Point
PAULSGROVE
FAREHAM
BR (S.R.)
COSHAM 'RED LION'
HILSEA
COSHAM RAILWAY STATION
NORTH END DEPOT
NORTH END 12.61 - 11.62
DOCKYARD
GUILDHALL (PARK ROAD)
CLARENCE PIER 12.61 - 02.62
CHICHESTER RD / LONDON RD JCT 05.60 - 05.63
CHICHESTER RD / COPNOR RD JCT 12.61 - 05.63
COPNOR BRIDGE
FRATTON BRIDGE AND BRADFORD JUNCTION
MILTON
EASTNEY 05.60 - 02.63 02.63 - 07.63
FOOTBALL GROUND SIDING Post War - ? Removed 03.62
SOUTH PARADE PIER
COSHAM RLY STN
PORTSBRIDGE
HILSEA HALT
GREEN LANE
ALEXANDRA PARK
NORTH END
WHALE ISLAND
H.M. DOCKYARD
COPNOR BRIDGE
PORTSMOUTH & SOUTHSEA STN
FRATTON STN
BRADFORD JUNCTION
PORTSMOUTH HARBOUR STN
FLOATING BRIDGE
OLD PORTSMOUTH
CLARENCE PIER
MILTON 'WHITE HOUSE'
EASTNEY
SOUTH PARADE PIER
ONE MILE
N

Shortly after arriving at Madeira Road, 307 reverses into Compton Road on the Green Lane reversing triangle. The Green Lane reverser ceased to be used by normal services on 2 December 1961 but a service 5 short working continued to turn here at 6 p.m. on Fridays only until the withdrawal of services 17 and 18. (Roger Funnell)

services, including extras, required 20 trolleybuses; however, of the 24 vehicles remaining in stock, 10, in Mr Simmond's opinion, would be life-expired within the next 12 months and at least one pair would have to be converted to motorbus operation. He considered this a wasteful solution. Complete abandonment would avoid continuing feeder cable and overhead line maintenance which he estimated cost £12,000 p.a. An additional £4,000 p.a. would be saved by inter-working services A and B with the 5 and 6 if the latter was operated by motorbus. The Passenger Transport Committee decided on 17 October 1961 to invite tenders for 22 high capacity double-deck motorbuses likely to cost about £146,500 and convert the remaining trolleybus services upon their delivery.

The Passenger Transport Committee accepted Leyland Motors' tender for 25 Atlantean PDR 1/1 chassis at £2,805 4s each and 25 Metro-Cammell-Weymann 77/78 seat bodies at £3,760 each on 16 January 1962. The City Treasurer later pointed out that it had been previously decided that these vehicles as well as seven Leyland Leopard chassis equipped with MCW single-deck bodies valued at £34,519 12s 6d were to be bought from the Renewals and Reserve Fund and that no loan was required.

A Civil Defence exercise which assumed that an aircraft had crashed in Kingston Crescent and involving a withdrawn motorbus and accident-damaged trolleybus 303 was held on Sunday morning 22 October 1961. BUT9611T 303 was fitted with a temporary front axle and towed to the mock incident from Eastney Depot. It was then overturned causing additional damage to the nearside and as part of the exercise the CPPTD 1931 Crossley Condor breakdown tender, formerly double-deck motorbus 74 (RV 720), righted the trolleybus which was then towed to North End Depot.

By 8 November 1961, the remaining overhead wiring was removed from Kingston Crescent together with double and single bracket arms. During the week ending 8 December 1961, Rugby Road was completely cleared of wire and gantries, and all connections with the Bradford Junction area were removed. No further removal work was carried out in December 1961 or January 1962.

At the beginning of February 1962 the overhead wiring running through the Clarence Pier terminal stance previously used by services 7 and 8 was removed whilst the outer turning circle wiring that had been used by services 19 and 20 remained intact until at least 10 February 1962. By 13 February 1962 all southbound wiring from the Royal Pier Hotel to Clarence Pier was removed and by the 18 February 1962 all overhead wiring above Pier Road in both directions was cut down.

During the week ending 10 March 1962, the siding in the westbound Goldsmith Avenue wiring used by extras serving the football ground in Fratton Park, which had not been used for many years, was removed. The trolley wires were used to replace the parallel main line wires which were worn out. In the following week the northbound trolley wires were cut down in Commercial Road, between the railway bridge at Portsmouth and Southsea Station and Arundel Street. The frogs at the junction of Lake Road with Fratton Road were removed and the through wires in Fratton Road reconnected although they were no longer in use.

On 1 April 1962 the curve from Commercial Road (southbound) into Greetham Street was removed, and by 8 April 1962 the remaining overhead from the railway bridge in Commercial Road to the junction at Lake Road had been dismantled. The following week overhead was removed in Lake Road, which was cleared by 23 April 1962. All unwanted

BUT9611T 311 turns the corner out of Blackfriars Road into Greetham Street. On the left is the footbridge over the railway approaching Portsmouth and Southsea Station whilst to the right is Brickwood's 'Morning Star' public house, site of a trolleybus accident on 7 November 1935. A blue police telephone box is on the corner itself. (Tony Belton)

sections of overhead in Guildhall Square were then removed and, on 22 May 1962, southbound wiring along the southern part of Commercial Road and the Terraces from Guildhall Square to the junction with Alexandra Road (now known as Museum Road) was removed. This was followed by the removal of the northbound line and the bracket arms and cross spans in this section were dismantled.

There were a number of wage awards in the first half of 1962 increasing financial pressure on the undertaking by £22,800 p.a. The estimates for 1962–63 had anticipated a net surplus of £37,175; however, the proportion of these wage increases to be met in 1962–63 would reduce the surplus to below £20,000. Having spent £198,650 on new vehicles to be delivered later in the current year and transferred £29,805 from revenue, the balance in the Renewals and Reserves Fund at the end of 1962–63 was now expected to fall to about £67,800 and in view of the accelerated vehicle replacement programme this was seen as insufficient.

The Joint Committee recommended a fare increase for journeys of more than 2½ miles within the city of ½d or 1d, none of the affected fares having been increased in the 17 September 1961 revisions. Although the Passenger Transport Committee was not in favour of the proposals, which would increase the Corporation's revenues by £22,000 p.a., on 11 July 1962 the Joint Committee decided to implement them and on 17 July 1962 the City Council also supported the move, and an application was made to the RTC.

On 18 September 1962 the tender for ten more Leyland Atlantean PDR 1/1 chassis at £2,805 14s to be equipped with Metro-Cammell-Weymann 77/78 seat bodies at £3,840, totalling £66,457, to replace trolleybuses, was accepted. The General Manager was authorised on 18 June 1963 to offer the remaining trolley vehicles for disposal by tender upon their withdrawal from service.

Overhead removal work ceased for some 4 months during the summer and resumed during September 1962 with all wiring from Fratton Bridge along Fawcett Road and Lawrence Road as far as the crossing at Albert Road being removed by the end of the month. Dismantling of the complex North End wiring began on 17 November 1962 when the trolley wires from the exit of North End Depot along Gladys Avenue to the junction with London Road was removed. During the week ending 24 November 1962 disused overhead wiring at Fratton Bridge was cut down leaving only the Goldsmith Avenue and Fratton Road wiring into and out of Victoria Road North. The remaining 100 yards of wiring at the south end of Fratton Road had to be retained as the feeder from Vivash Road Fratton Substation at Fratton Grove still served Victoria Road North.

Talks began in late November 1962 about the replacement of North End Depot as part of the City Development Plan. The Department considered it the ideal location from an operational perspective but if this site would no longer be available the best alternative would be on Norway Road in the Hilsea Industrial Estate. A 3-acre site on the estate was reserved.

Particularly cold weather and snow falls in late December and throughout January 1963 stopped overhead removal and hampered snow clearance at bus stops. Some 53,000 additional passengers were carried in the week ending 4 January 1963. As at 1 January 1963 the trolleybus fleet was just 11 Cravens bodied AEC661Ts 233, 246, 248, 250, 255, 269, 274,

On 17 March 1963 BUT9611T 307 turns out of London Road into Spur Road, Cosham. The pseudo-Tudor half-timbered 'Red Lion' public house is on the corner whilst to the right of the photograph, beyond the workmen, Spur Road makes an end-on junction with Havant Road. Authority was received to extend trolleybuses from this point for almost 2 miles due east along Havant Road as far as Rectory Avenue, Farlington, in 1948, yet despite detailed planning of the overhead wiring layout and power supply, construction did not follow. (T.V. Runnacles)

283, 286, 294, 300 (all of which, except 250, 255, 274 survived until 21 or 22 June 1963) and 14 BUT9611Ts 301–302, 304–315 (all of which survived to 25–27 July 1963).

Overhead dismantling began again in February 1963 with the removal of the remnants of Eastney turning circle and work then moved to Lake Road Junction and continued progressively north along Kingston Road. A few yards of overhead as far as Fratton No. 7 feeder at the west end of New Road were also removed but the remaining equipment along New Road was retained so that the feeder could supply current to the Copnor Road route at Copnor Bridge if required. By May 1963 there was little disused overhead left in the city.

On 6 June 1963 the Cosham 'Red Lion' passing loop in Spur Road was removed. Work then started at Cosham Railway Station: the outside loop and its frogs were removed on 13 June 1963 and on 5 July 1963 the remaining single line turning circle and the trailing frog into the private road wiring were cut down, although the crossing of the northbound wiring leading into the turning circle with the southbound wiring turning into Portsmouth Road remained. This crossover was removed 1 week later and the trolley wires were cut back as far as the pole-mounted traction power feeder close by in Portsmouth Road.

All trolleybus operations ceased for 2 hours during the evening of Saturday 8 June 1963 to allow a carnival procession which crossed both routes to proceed. Services were maintained by motorbuses.

The last normal service trolleybuses on the Eastney circular services 17 and 18 ran on Saturday 22 June 1963 resulting in the withdrawal of the remaining pre-war AEC661T Craven bodied

286 passes beneath the junction of Highland Road and Albert Road with Festing Road on 7 May 1963. A Ford Anglia noses out of Festing Road to the right. Careful observation of the wiring from the frog (24 on the plan of Facing (Turnout) Frogs in Appendix H) leading into Festing Road reveals the restoring contact skate immediately after the insulated crossover of the positive wire. The transfer or setter skate is one span before the frog. (T.V. Runnacles)

The last trolleybus to use the Green Lane reverser was AEC661T 233, then the oldest trolleybus in the fleet, on Friday 21 June 1963. Here, 233 is seen reversing out of Madeira Road into Compton Road beneath the reverser on that last occasion. 233's return trip from Green Lane to Eastney Depot was its last passenger journey. (T.V. Runnacles)

trolleybuses, the oldest of which had been in the city for over 26½ years. Number 246 was the sole member of this class of vehicles used on 22 June 1963 and was consequently the last in normal service. Despite the service abandonment the majority of the route remained in use for trolleybuses entering or leaving service from Eastney Depot on the remaining services 5 and 6. One early morning duty on the 17 westbound along Goldsmith Avenue, Greetham Street and Park Road to the Dockyard, and two late evening journeys to Eastney Depot, one on service 17 eastbound along Park Road, Greetham Street, Victoria Road North and Albert Road, and the other on the 18 eastbound along Goldsmith Avenue, continued to run. The westbound overhead along Albert Road and Victoria Road North between Festing Road and Bradford Junction fell into disuse.

The remaining once-weekly trolleybus short-working on services 5 and 6 to Green Lane was converted to motorbus operation from the same date and the reversing triangle fell into disuse. The last trolleybus vehicle to use the reverser was AEC661T 233, then the oldest trolleybus in the fleet, on Friday 21 June 1963. Its return trip from Green Lane to Eastney Depot was its last passenger journey.

Sufficient replacement motorbuses were now in stock, the first Leyland Atlanteans having arrived on 21 May 1963, and thus on 16 July 1963 the Passenger Transport Committee decided that the final day of trolleybus operation in the city would be Saturday 27 July 1963. The *Evening News* reported:

'With no flags or ceremony, coloured lights or "Journey's End Notices" Portsmouth's last trolleybus will make its final trip on July 27.

'Thus, unsung and without thanks, the era of the trolleybus will come to an end – unlike the scene was 27 years ago, when the last tram, gaily lit, made its exit from the Portsmouth vista.

Having used the Green Lane reverser for the final time, 233 stands in Madeira Road prior to turning out into Copnor Road. (T.V. Runnacles)

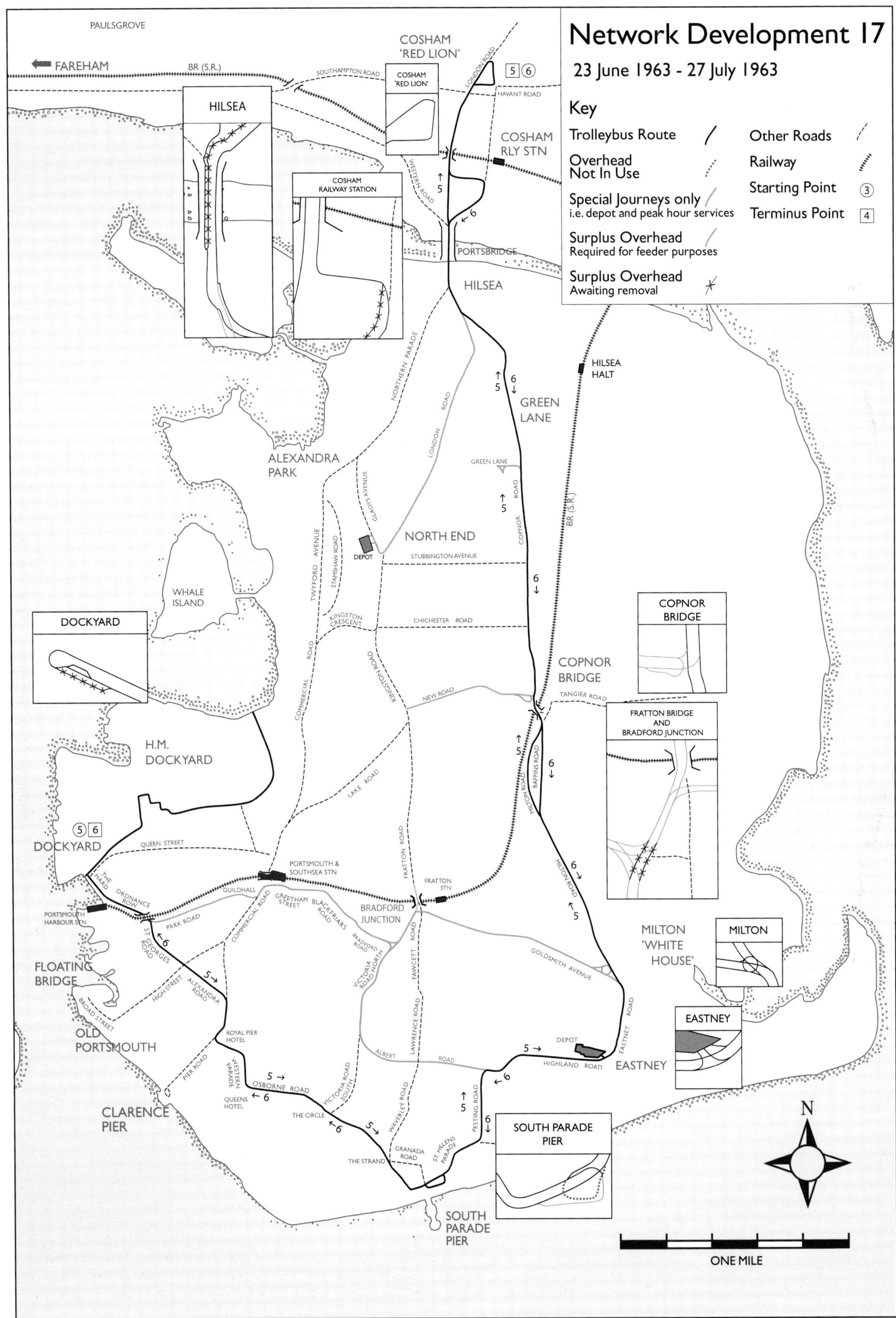
Network Development 17
23 June 1963 - 27 July 1963
Key
Trolleybus Route
Overhead Not In Use
Special Journeys only
i.e. depot and peak hour services
Surplus Overhead
Required for feeder purposes
Surplus Overhead
Awaiting removal
Other Roads
Railway
Starting Point
Terminus Point
PAULSGROVE
FAREHAM
BR (S.R.)
SOUTHAMPTON ROAD
COSHAM 'RED LION'
HAVANT ROAD
LONDON ROAD
COSHAM RLY STN
HILSEA
COSHAM RAILWAY STATION
WESTERN ROAD
PORTSBRIDGE
HILSEA HALT
NORTHERN PARADE
GREEN LANE
ALEXANDRA PARK
COPNOR ROAD
NORTH END
DEPOT
STUBBINGTON AVENUE
GLADYS AVENUE
TWYFORD AVENUE
STAMSHAW ROAD
WHALE ISLAND
KINGSTON CRESCENT
CHICHESTER ROAD
DOCKYARD
COPNOR BRIDGE
KINGSTON ROAD
NEW ROAD
TANGIER ROAD
FRATTON BRIDGE AND BRADFORD JUNCTION
COMMERCIAL ROAD
H.M. DOCKYARD
LAKE ROAD
BAFFINS ROAD
MILTON ROAD
FRATTON ROAD
QUEEN STREET
PORTSMOUTH & SOUTHSEA STN
THE HARD
ORDNANCE ROW
GUILDHALL
FRATTON STN
PORTSMOUTH HARBOUR STN
GREETHAM STREET
BLACKFRIARS ROAD
BRADFORD JUNCTION
PARK ROAD
ST GEORGES ROAD
BRADFORD ROAD
VICTORIA ROAD NORTH
FAWCETT ROAD
MILTON 'WHITE HOUSE'
MILTON
GOLDSMITH AVENUE
FLOATING BRIDGE
HIGH STREET
ALEXANDRA ROAD
BROAD STREET
OLD PORTSMOUTH
LAWRENCE ROAD
EASTNEY ROAD
EASTNEY
ROYAL PIER HOTEL
ALBERT ROAD
DEPOT
HIGHLAND ROAD
PIER ROAD
WESTERN PARADE
OSBORNE ROAD
VICTORIA ROAD SOUTH
QUEENS HOTEL
CLARENCE PIER
THE CIRCLE
WAVERLEY ROAD
PESTING ROAD
SOUTH PARADE PIER
THE STRAND
GRANADA ROAD
ST. HELENS PARADE
SOUTH PARADE PIER
N
ONE MILE

233 turns out of Madeira Road into Copnor Road on its way back to Eastney Depot. (T.V. Runnacles)

'The date for the final abolition of the trolleybuses was announced at today's meeting of the Passenger Transport Committee, when the Chairman (Alderman H. E. Collins) asked members, "Do you want to make a ceremony out of it?"

'Councillor C.W. Stevens said, "No, let them die a natural death and be finished with it. After all, they have been long enough about it."'

Four young local enthusiasts, Rodney Epps, Roger Funnell, David Janes and Tim Runnacles, watched the first trolleybus, BUT9611T 313, leave Eastney Depot early in the morning of 27 July 1963 and make its way along Goldsmith Avenue, across Guildhall Square, and along Park Road to the Dockyard terminus on The Hard. Here it entered service on the 5. Over the next 2 hours trolleybuses 301, 302, 305, 307, 312, 314 and 315 ran into service and maintained the timetable throughout the day. The normal heavy Saturday loadings were swollen by some 150 visitors who had come to pay their last respects.

Vehicle rostering on services 5 and 6 meant that the first trolleybus out of Eastney Depot in the morning was destined to be the last to return to the Depot in the evening and thus 313 was also the final trolleybus. It left the Dockyard Main Gate on its last through journey to Cosham 'Red Lion' well-laden with persons who wanted to be on the very last trolleybus journey in Portsmouth and there was little room for ordinary passengers. Once 313 had passed Eastney Depot trolleybus 304 was driven out to act as a relief and followed the service vehicle to Cosham. By use of its traction batteries, 304 overtook 313 at Spur Road, Cosham, whence the two trolleybuses made their way to the Dockyard in convoy. The final service journey to Cosham, operated by 302, was passed, just north of Green Lane. This trolleybus returned in service to Eastney Depot which it was due to reach at 11.38 p.m. Trolleybuses 304 and 313 reached the Dockyard at 11.27 p.m. and both vehicles immediately turned to return to Eastney Depot via Park Road, Guildhall Square and Goldsmith Avenue.

In those calmer days, a point duty policeman could stand safely in the road directing the traffic without fear of being driven into or asphyxiated with exhaust fumes! BUT9611T 312 absorbs a crowd of passengers at Handley's Corner on Osborne Road (Palmerston Road stop), Southsea on 24 July 1963. The circle painted on the road indicates precisely where the policeman should stand. (T.V. Runnacles)

Having just pulled out of Eastney Depot on the final day of trolleybus operation in Portsmouth, 27 July 1963, BUT9611T 307 heads west into Highland Road on its way to the Dockyard. The island between the trolleybus and Cromwell Road, to the left of Starmer's shop (advertising Campions Bread), was the location of Eastney turning circle until removed in two stages in December 1962 and February 1963. Campions had many branches in Portsmouth particularly in the inter-war years. In 1973 they became part of Manor Bakeries. (T.V. Runnacles)

CITY OF PORTSMOUTH PASSENGER TRANSPORT DEPARTMENT

The last Service journeys on Saturday, 27th July, 1963, to be operated by Trolley Buses will be, of course, over the 5-6 Service route as set out below:-

Service 5	p.m.	p.m.	p.m.	p.m.
Dockyard, Main Gate	10.35	10.47	10.59	11.11
Palmerston Road	10.44	10.56	11.08	11.20
Southsea, South Parade Pier	10.48	11.00	11.12	11.24
Eastney	10.54	11.06	11.18	11.30
Milton, White House	10.56	11.08	11.20	11.32
Copnor Bridge	11.01	-	-	-
Cosham Railway Bridge	11.13	-	-	-
Cosham, Red Lion	11.16	-	-	-

Service 6	p.m.	p.m.	p.m.	p.m.
Cosham, Red Lion	10.46	10.52	11.04	11.16
Cosham Railway Gates	10.49	10.55	11.07	11.19
Copnor Bridge	11.01	11.07	11.19	11.31
Milton, White House	11.06	11.12	11.24	11.36
Eastney	11.08	11.14	11.26	11.38
Southsea, South Parade Pier	11.14	-	-	-
Palmerston Road	11.18	-	-	-
Dockyard, Main Gate	11.27	-	-	-

Additional journeys will also operate over the 17-18 Service route as set out below:-

Service 17	p.m.
Dockyard, Main Gate	11.22
Guildhall	11.27
Bradford Junction	11.31
Festing Hotel	11.37
Eastney	11.41
Milton, White House	-
Bradford Junction	-
Guildhall	-
Dockyard, Main Gate	-

Service 18	p.m.
Dockyard, Main Gate	11.28
Guildhall	11.33
Bradford Junction	11.37
Milton, White House	11.43
Eastney	11.45
Festing Hotel	-
Bradford Junction	-
Guildhall	-
Dockyard, Main Gate	-

Amended Time Tables will be available shortly and may be obtained from all Corporation Passenger Transport and Southdown Motor Services Offices.

Eastney.
17th July, 1963.

H. C. SIMMONDS
General Manager and Engineer

Supervised by an inspector, once 304 had left the Dockyard with a good load of passengers, the last Portsmouth trolleybus of all, 313, departed with a full load. The Department had made no special preparations but a group of enthusiasts had produced souvenir 'Last Trolleybus' tickets which were distributed to the passengers on board, normal fares being paid and TIM tickets being issued by the conductor. Unfortunately the names of the crew seem not to have been recorded. A would-be passenger, prevented from boarding at Fratton Bridge because the trolleybus was so full, let fly a torrent of abuse which was greeted with a loud cheer from inside.

A large crowd, swollen by passengers from 304 who had alighted opposite the depot, awaited the arrival of 313, without a single light bulb left in the upper saloon, at Eastney. The Deputy General Manager, Mr A. W. Fielder placed a floral wreath over the driver's offside mirror, then amid much popping of flashbulbs and cheers Portsmouth's last trolleybus ran into the depot. Many members of the public streamed

Portsmouth's last trolleybus, BUT9611T 313, complete with floral wreath, stands in Eastney Road opposite the Depot. (Fred Ivey)

Portsmouth's last trolleybus, BUT9611T 313 turns into Eastney Depot. The hand-written poster in the nearside upper-deck window reads 'This is the last Portsmouth Trolley-Bus' (sic). (Fred Ivey)

into the depot building and were unofficially permitted to make their last farewells to the vehicles that had silently and efficiently served the City for almost 29 years. It was recorded that the trolleybuses had run a total of 72,128,974 miles and carried 811,782,627 passengers during this period.

On Sunday morning 28 July 1963 the trolleybuses remaining in stock were towed to North End Depot for storage pending sale. Messrs A. G. Figgins Ltd., Waterlooville, were contracted to remove the remaining 800-odd traction poles paying the Corporation 30s per pole for the privilege. Although the poles would have raised 39s each as scrap metal they would have had to be removed by the Department and the use of a contractor for this work was expected to save some £1300. Having found no other trolleybus operator wishing to buy the remaining BUT911Ts and stores, valued at £7,078 9s 4d, on 17 September 1963 it was decided to offer them for disposal.

Seemingly following Council policy there was only a brief report of the trolleybuses' demise in the newspaper: reports on swarms of flies in Southsea and the price of strawberries all seemed more important.

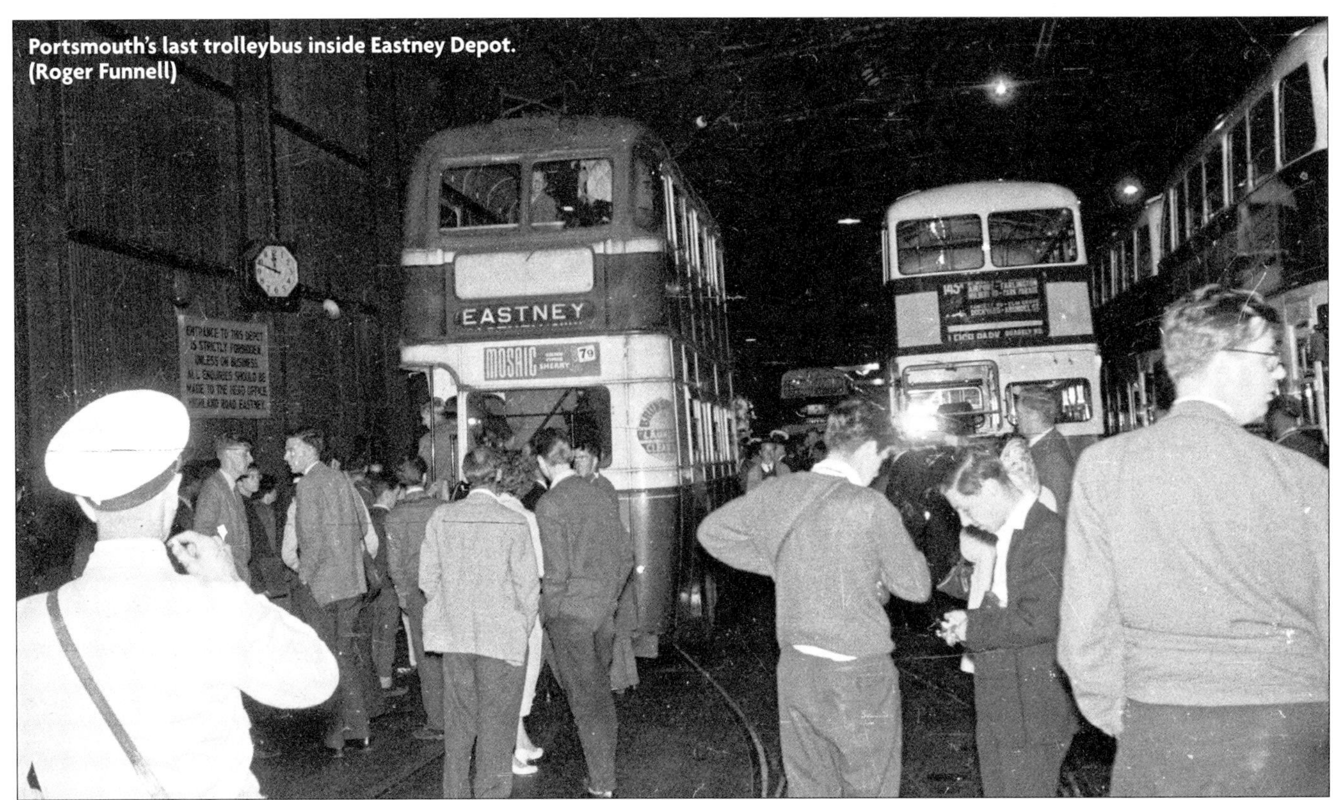

Portsmouth's last trolleybus inside Eastney Depot. (Roger Funnell)

1956 Leyland Titan PD2/12 / MCW motorbus 90 on trolleybus replacement service 6 passes Leyland TD2 tower wagon TW1 removing hangers, etc., from gantries in Festing Road. (Roger Funnell)

PHOTOGRAPHIC SUPPLEMENT TO THE FINAL YEARS (1960–63)

BUT9611T 308 with Burlingham body leaves Canoe Lake private road turning circle Southsea South Parade on a short working to Dockyard. (Roger Funnell)

Seen turning out of St Helens Parade into Canoe Lake turning circle Southsea South Parade is BUT9611T 313 on a short working to Dockyard. The amusements at Clarence Pier were operated by Butlins until about 1958 when Billy Manning took over. They began to advertise on the trolleybuses in 1959. (Roger Funnell)

Numerically the last AEC661T but not the last to enter service, 300 was photographed in Highland Road at the Eastney Depot stop just past 'The Mayflower' public house. (Roger Funnell)

On its clockwise journey around the Eastney circle AEC661T 246, by now devoid of its AEC chassis and English Electric equipment maker's badge, is seen beneath the eastbound Goldsmith Avenue wiring at Prince Albert Road just past the hand-operated frog (17) providing access to Milton 'White House' turning circle. (Roger Funnell)

Closely followed by a learner driver in a Morris 1000, BUT9611T 301, by now devoid of its maker's symbol, heads south along Eastney Road just north of the depot. (Roger Funnell)

304 seen travelling east along Highland Road. (Roger Funnell)

BUT9611T/Burlingham 307 turning out of Southsea Terrace into Western Parade travelling east on a service 5 short-working. (Roger Funnell)

AEC661T 233 turns out of Goldsmith Avenue into Victoria Road North at Fratton Bridge on a 17 journey to HM Dockyard. (Tony Belton)

Viewed from Cumberland House BUT9611T 314 leaves the south end of Festing Road, prior to turning into St Helens Parade, en route to HM Dockyard. (Roger Funnell)

Heading towards Palmerston Road, Southsea, and beyond 301 is seen in Copnor Road as it climbs up the northern ramp to Copnor Bridge over the railway. (Roger Funnell)

The heart of Southsea's shopping district was the junction of Osborne Road at Palmerston Road, well-known in the trolleybus era as Handleys Corner. Handleys now trade as Debenhams. A decidedly weary point duty policeman in white coat stands on the kerb outside the store. On a warm summer's day BUT9611T 312 passes Knight and Lee's store at the west end of Clarendon Road. (Roger Funnell)

Only the southbound wiring between Hayling Avenue and Priorsdean Avenue followed the residential Baffins Road, although other traffic used it in both directions. Today this is a one-way street southbound with much of the nearside lane in this view blocked with parked cars at 90° to the kerb. Northbound traffic now follows Milton Road, as did the trolleybuses. BUT9611T 308 heads for Palmerston Road and beyond. (Roger Funnell)

Passing Kingston Prison in the one-way section of Milton Road BUT9611T 301 heads north to Cosham 'Red Lion' on a service 5 journey in the final weeks of the system. (Roger Funnell)

BUT9611T/Burlingham 308 pulls out of Copnor Road and crosses beneath the southbound London Road at the 'Coach and Horses' junction, Hilsea, heading north to Cosham 'Red Lion'. (Roger Funnell)

Heading south along Commercial Road just past Guildhall Square AEC661T 247 passes the impressive Theatre Royal on its way to Clarence Pier. (Online Transport Archive [photographer M. Eavis])

Having allowed 286 to overtake, the driver of 274 rewires his charge in Park Road at the side of the Guildhall. The building with the corner tower in the background was originally Portsmouth Municipal College, known by 1963 as the College of Technology, and known since 2013 as the Park Building of the University of Portsmouth. (Online Transport Archive [photographer D. Norman])

APPENDIX A

TROLLEYBUS FLEET DETAILS

Portsmouth pursued a trolleybus acquisition policy not found with any other British trolleybus operator.

It was common practice in the 1930s for the general managers of municipal transport undertakings to both seek the optimum solution for their operational needs and also display a certain individuality. This was normally achieved by a review of the vehicles used by similarly sized municipalities faced with comparable topography followed by a call for tenders for a small initial fleet of vehicles having the characteristics that the general manager considered appropriate. Any local manufacturer would often prove able to submit the most competitive offer.

In a next stage trolleybus chassis manufacturers tended to continually approach operators with their latest products, offering an extended trial, in the hope of benefiting from a major order, such as the fleet needed to convert an entire tramway system to trolleybus operation.

Portsmouth's General Manager, Ben Hall, subscribed to neither of these norms. It was decided to purchase an experimental fleet of 15 vehicles with varying equipment and bodywork from which to determine the optimum combination for the undertaking's needs. The most suitable chassis proved to be the 2-axle AEC661T with English Electric Co. Ltd. electrical equipment and traction motor whilst the preferred body was the all-metal design from English Electric. Thus the major tramway conversion order was based on this solution although subsequently Cravens Railway Carriage and Wagon Co. secured the bodywork order as their tender specifications entirely satisfied the undertaking's requirements, but was cheaper than that submitted by English Electric.

Nonetheless, despite the outward appearance of standardisation, by the 1950s the Portsmouth trolleybus fleet had developed into one with several standards and exceptions thereto!

Portsmouth was unique amongst municipal trolleybus operators in that for years it had a high percentage of vehicles that were surplus to requirements throughout the year. This surplus arose as soon as all the AEC661Ts had entered service in 1937. It seems that during the 1930s the entire fleet was licensed although 201–215 were rarely used. In September 1940 there were only five trolleybuses de-licensed, the four 3-axle vehicles and 235. Then in October 1940, 201–219 and 221–224 were de-licensed for the duration of the war (220 was de-licensed in December 1940). As far as is known this 24% reduction in the fleet did not present any operational difficulties.

Post-war the de-licensing situation for January (mid-winter) and August (mid-summer) in successive years was as follows:

	January (number of vehicles)	August (number of vehicles)
1946	4	11
1947	15	11
1948	9	5
1949	9	8
1950	23	20
1951	27	30
1952	35	30
1953	39	31
1954	47	32
1955	36	35
1956	32	25

After the golden years for passenger travel (1946–1949) the number of de-licensed vehicles rose sharply exacerbated by the arrival of the 15 BUT9611Ts but the undertaking was in no rush to dispose of older vehicles.

The de-licensed trolleybuses fell into three categories:

(1) Vehicles held against a possible increase in service demand.
In April 1950, 15 trolleybuses fell into this category.

(2) Vehicles scheduled for a complete overhaul or reconstruction.
In April 1950, five trolleybuses fell into this category including 212, definitely still de-licensed but not withdrawn.

(3) Short-term de-licensing of operational vehicles for repairs, repaints, etc.
In April 1950, three trolleybuses fell into this category.

The hoped-for increase in service demand never occurred but some of the vehicles in this category did see significant periods of further service, e.g. 219, in category (1) in April 1950, was licensed in August 1950 for 3 months, in August 1952 for 4 months, and again in May 1954 for 2 years.

Others remained de-licensed for years, some in the open and these deteriorated to such an extent that on withdrawal, the record was annotated as "derelict". 221 is a good example: category (1) in April 1950, it was licensed for one more period August–November 1950 inclusive and then de-licensed until withdrawal in June 1954. Even then it was only sold in March 1956.

1934 AEC661T/English Electric H26/24R

Fleet No.	1938 No.	Reg. No.	Chassis	Chassis No.	Body	Body No.	Into Service	Last licensed	Withdrawn	Sold
1	201	RV4649	AEC661T	028	Eng. Electric		11.08.1934	08.1958	10.1958	25.10.1960
2	202	RV4650	AEC661T	029	Eng. Electric		27.08.1934	05.1950	21.06.1955	16.01.1956
3	203	RV4651	AEC661T	030	Eng. Electric		12.08.1934	01.1950	21.06.1955	16.01.1956
4	204	RV4652	AEC661T	031	Eng. Electric		18.08.1934	09.1949	03.1955	14.03.1956

Last licensed = the final month in which the vehicle was licensed to operate.

Chassis: Two axle type AEC 661T manufactured by the Associated Equipment Company Ltd. at the AEC works, Windmill Lane, Southall, Middlesex.
Motor: English Electric Co. Ltd., Phoenix Works, Bradford, Yorkshire.
1–2 Type EE 405/9 (80 h.p. at 550 volts) compound-wound, regenerative.
3–4 Type EE 405/9 (80 h.p. at 550 volts) series-wound, augmented field.

The vehicles equipped with augmented field had eight notches including two weak field.

Electrical equipment: English Electric solenoid operated contactor Type 35 Form A controllers.
Dewirement indicator: single neon line-light.
Brakes: G.D. Peters compressed air and hand brakes. 1–2 regenerative.
Body: English Electric Co. Ltd., Dick, Kerr Works, Preston, Lancashire, composite H26/24R. Drawing PB33/1225 dated 12th December 1934.

Length: 25ft 11in.
Width: 7ft 4in. over pillars.
Height laden: 14ft 1in.
Wheelbase: 16ft 3in. giving a turning circle of 57ft 8in.

Unladen weight: 1, 3 — 7 tons 0 cwt 2 qtr
2 — 6 tons 13 cwt 1 qtr
4 — 6 tons 18 cwt 2 qtr

Chassis weight: 3 tons 5 cwt.

The contract price was £1,854. The final price upon completion was £1,811 8s 4d.

Tyres: Low pressure 20in. by 10in. tyres on front and 20in. by 9in. tyres on the rear.

Chassis: based on the AEC Regent 661 motorbus chassis and axles. The chassis cost £1,069 each.

Track: Front 6ft 3¹⁄₁₆in.; rear 5ft 10³⁄₁₆in.
Road clearance under rear axle: 7½in.

AEC661T 4 equipped with English Electric composite body, probably photographed at the English Electric Preston works (official view). (Tramway & Railway World)

The side members were pressed out of 5⁄16in. steel with a maximum depth of 11in. and 3in. wide flanges swept over the front and rear axles to permit the mounting of a low floor level body. The frame was held rigid by tubular cross-members; however, there were no dumb irons, the ends of the frame channels being left open and protruding a few inches in front of the foremost cross-member. Channel section cross-members amidships forward and to the rear of the traction motor.

The axles were made from 100 ton steel 3in. in diameter and mounted on adjustable taper roller bearings. A chrome vanadium spring steel torque blade was used permitting freedom of motion of each axle. The socket attachments of this cross-member formed a rigid assembly with the front end of the front axle spring anchorages and, on the offside, the steering box. The rear ends of the 50in. long front axle spring were shackled by a similar arrangement to the second chassis cross-member. The 62in. long cantilever springs of the rear axle were centrally pivoted upon needle-roller trunnion bearings carried by cast-steel brackets mounted beneath the wheel arches, to which they were riveted and joined by a large cross-tube. The ends of the springs had solid eyes and were anchored to brackets under the axle tubes.

A fully floating worm drive F156 rear axle with 8in. worm centres and a ratio of 9.33 to 1 was used. The rear axle casing was a one-piece nickel steel forging carrying the worm gearing in a separate casing. The 8½in. worm gear was offset to the nearside to avoid any obstruction of the gangway, and the worm and traction motor were skewed at an angle of 3° to maintain a straight drive line.

AEC L139 front axle equipped with AEC Marles M134 worm and nut steering. Forged alloy steel hubs.

Electrics: All electrical equipment, including the contactor panel, was mounted in an insulated unit on the nearside chassis frame member. The jointless, unbreakable and non-rusting resistance grid was carried on chassis cross-members to the rear of the front axle and in front of the traction motor. There were four main cable runs carried within the frame channel sheathed in rubber ply tubing. An English Electric, Dick Kerr system Type D automatic circuit breaker was fixed to the driver's cab ceiling. The controller was mounted to the nearside of driver's seat. An English Electric motor generator set coupled to a CAV dynamo mounted on the nearside of the driver's cab floor provided power for supplying exterior and emergency lighting, and auxiliary equipment.

A power consumption (kWh) meter was attached to the driver's cab bulkhead above the wide central pillar.

The upper-deck body pillars were slotted into the wooden rail of the framework above the upper saloon windows, i.e. the cantrail. There were curved steel brackets bolted to the metal roof (inside the roof there was a steel strengthening plate on each side) and each end of the three transverse pressed steel girders, between bays 1 and 2, bays 2 and 3, and bays 3 and 4, supporting the exposed trolley gantry, which was not in direct contact with the roof, rested on these brackets.

The main power cable made its way forward from the trolley gantry along the centre line of the roof before entering the front dome about 1ft 6in. to the rear of the upper-deck cantrail. The vehicles were equipped with Brecknell Willis lightweight trolley equipment and trolley bases. Radio interference suppressors were mounted towards the centre of the roof in bay 2 but to the nearside and offside of the trolley gantry. The access catwalk on the roof had a single step above the rear dome beneath the trolley boom retaining hooks which were, unusually, anchored to the roof by a single central arm. Traction batteries for manoeuvring purposes were not fitted.

Both the compound-wound and the series-wound, box frame, self-ventilated, flood-proof and roller-bearing-equipped EE405 traction motor was mounted amidships on Floatex rubber suspension on a rigid channel section sub-frame and cross members and offset to the nearside between the chassis frame members.

Brakes: G. D. Peters' compressed air brakes, incorporating AEC patents, used a compressor unit with 5 cubic feet capacity attached to the chassis with Silentbloc bushings to eliminate vibration and provide secondary insulation. The patented arrangement of combined reservoir unit and check-valve, silencer and governor, reduced piping and facilitated maintenance. The compressor unit was located behind the offside inspection hatch.

Nos 1 and 2 from this batch were equipped with regenerative brakes. Nos 3 and 4 from this batch were equipped with augmented field control and rheostatic brakes. The handbrake lever was to the offside of the driver's steering column. The hand brake was applied to the rear wheel brake camshafts only by means of mechanical linkage. The single brake shoe to each rear wheel was 6in. wide and could be operated by pedal or hand lever or simultaneously by both.

Each of the front wheels was provided with shoes 3in. wide connected to the foot brake. All shoe linings, front and rear, were half an inch thick, whilst the drum brakes, 17in. in diameter, were of cast iron alloy.

The staircase had four steps from the platform to the landing and then a further four steps to the upper deck, each riser having aluminium kicking panels.

Bodywork: Highbridge double-deck composite six bay construction with conventional, enclosed forwards-ascending half-turn (90°) staircase with semi-vestibuled open platform entrance and exit at the rear, built by English Electric Co. Ltd. at Preston. The bodies cost £785 each.

There was a slight 'tumble-under' to the lower deck side and rear panels with a shallow roof. The front elevation rose in a convex rake to the upper-deck waistline. Above the upper-deck waistline the front panel adopted a shallow 'vee' on plan which was retained for the slightly raked upper saloon front windows. There was a pronounced overhang, incorporating a ventilator above each pane, to the front dome. A double fold at the base of the upper-deck side panels, bays 1–5, provided a gutter. There were four roof-mounted torpedo vents, one above bay 1 the other above bay 5, two each side. The trolley poles were fitted on an exposed roof-mounted gantry above bays 2 and 3.

Metal louvres were fitted above the upper and lower saloon side windows. Half-drop openers equipped with a single 'pinch fastener' centrally at the top of each pane were fitted to the top rail of the side windows in bays 1, 3, 5 on both sides of the upper deck, and bays 2, 3, 4 on both sides of the lower deck. The upper saloon front windows were fixed. The upper pane dropped outside the fixed lower pane. Additional ventilation to the upper saloon was provided by two ventilators in the roof overhang above the front windows and somewhat closer to the corner pillars than to the central pillar, and four roof-mounted ventilators (with circular chromed covers inside) positioned midway along bays 1 and 5 on each side. Top hinged access doors were fitted at the base of the lower-deck off-side panel bay 1, 2, 3 and part of 4 providing access to the air brake compressor unit mounted on the outside of the off-side chassis member and on the nearside in bay 3 providing access to the contactors in an insulated unit mounted on the outside of the nearside chassis member.

The top outer corners of the two panes in the rear upper deck emergency exit window were radiused, the gutter around the edge of the roof curving down the upper deck rear corner panel to end beneath the emergency exit door. The gutter on the nearside reached the beading at the base of the upper deck waistband whilst that on the offside reached the beading above the waistband. There was a rail across the panes at half depth. The rear upper deck emergency exit door consisted of two oblong windows and had four hinges at its base. Small rubber bumpers on the nearside and offside of the emergency exit door aligned with similar bumpers in the upper outer corners of the protruding rear indicator boxes. When opened to its fullest extent the emergency exit door hung down and rested at a downwards angle on these bumpers. A separate platform, normally stowed behind the upper saloon rear nearside seat, fitted vertically into two metal retaining brackets in the door sill inside the upper saloon in front of the emergency exit door and tipped outwards into a horizontal position when the door was opened to provide access to the roof catwalk and thence the trolley gantry. The platform was retained securely in place by two chains which fitted into loops at the end of the metal strengtheners beneath the platform at one end of each chain and metal brackets inside the rear dome at the other.

The emergency door could be opened by an external handle mounted on the rear dome immediately above the rain strip and centrally above the door, or from inside by a comparable handle attached to a horizontal locking bar mounted on the cantrail immediately above the door. The horizontal bar was equipped with three prongs that engaged with brackets on the top of the door, centrally and in the two upper corners. Handrails were covered in black Doverite.

Bell pushes were mounted in the lower saloon on the nearside in the cove panels at the top of the pillar between bay 2 and bay 3; in the upper saloon on the nearside in the top rail of the window frames at the top of the pillar between bay 1 and bay 2, and on the offside at the top of the pillar between bay 5 and bay 6; plus on the rear platform above the bulkhead window.

The driver's cab was equipped with a single opening windscreen on the off-side, divided into two panes of equal depth, equipped with a central top-mounted windscreen wiper and painted frame, plus a single nearside fixed windscreen. There was a front hinged (three hinges) cab door on the offside only, with a square top. Two rubber bumpers at waist rail height, one on the door and the other on the side panel forward of the door, prevented body damage by a swinging door. The window of the offside cab door was divided horizontally into two panes, the upper portion being slightly deeper than the lower and an inset opening handle. The lower pane was equipped with a sliding 'signalling' window, the rear portion sliding forwards behind the front portion. There was a large fixed side window between the cab door and the front offside corner pillar and a matching panel and two fixed windows on the nearside. A pronounced, square vent was positioned on both sides of the cab beneath the foremost windows on each side. The driver's cab side windows were the same depth as, and aligned with, the lower saloon side windows, although this was not immediately evident due to the encroachment of the louvres above the saloon windows.

The base of the cab door was curved over the wheel arch to a position about 4in. from the rear of the door, thereafter the base, beneath the cab door handle, was horizontal, parallel to the cream-painted waistband and about 1ft 6in. below it.

A rectangular step was let into the upper part of the bay 1 side panel access door, but without any form of protection to the bodywork, immediately behind the front axle, on the offside. Both front wheels were fitted with chromed hub bosses and wheel nut guard rings. Individual mud flaps hung behind each wheel with a further mud flap extending the width of the vehicle at an angle beneath the rear platform.

There were two glazed panels in the bulkhead behind the driver with a wide central pillar. The panel behind the driver had two panes of glass, one pane sliding to allow the driver to communicate with the conductor. A small rectangular driver's rear view mirror was mounted externally towards the top of the offside front cab pillar. There was no maker's badge.

A removable panel, without any form of ventilation, extended across the base of the front panel between the headlamps; the top of the panel was aligned with the top of the chrome rims of the headlamps. The front registration number plate was mounted centrally on the front panel immediately above the removable portion. The rear registration number plate was mounted on the rear vent panel above the rear platform window and aligned with its offside pillar. The platform entrance was 4ft wide.

A single tubular lifeguard, held by protruding attachments or outriggers beneath the body panels, ran beneath the 'tumble-under' of the lower-deck side panels between the front and rear axles. A bamboo trolley retrieval pole was carried within the lower saloon nearside body panels at vent panel height (behind the cove panels) with a tube access above the nearside bulkhead window from the rear platform vestibule.

Lighting: External lighting was two chrome-rimmed headlights on wooden plinths at the base of the front panel with two front chrome-rimmed side lights also on wooden plinths at the top of the crimson-painted portion of the front panel aligned with the outer edges of the headlights. An orange-lensed Lucas 24-volt 36-watt spotlight was mounted beneath the front panel, almost aligned with, but slightly inboard of, the nearside headlamp.

Semaphore arm, illuminated traffic indicators accommodated in a black moulding were fitted in a vertical position in the lower half of the front face of the driver's cab corner pillars on both nearside and offside. The base of the indicator was aligned with the upper beading beneath the cab windscreen. At the rear, an inset panel mounted centrally beneath the lower beading to the white waist band below the rear platform window illuminated to show STOP with 2in. high letters when the brakes were applied.

There was a small single Allmet rear light, built into the triangular red reflector on the registration number plate which was located in the vent panel immediately above the offside upper corner of the rear platform window.

Interior lighting was provided by an installation of 24-volt, 12-watt traction type pearl bulbs in rectangular 'Floodlight' type diffused light fittings with chrome plated hinged rims: six lights were mounted in the ceiling cove panels on each side of the lower and upper saloons, centrally placed above

Manufacturer's view of the upper saloon of one of the four AEC661Ts equipped with English Electric composite bodies in the experimental fleet. Interestingly the poster in the bay 2 nearside window refers to 'Dick, Kerr Coachworks' although the company had been a part of English Electric since 1919. (David Beilby collection [English Electric])

the windows and one above the rear upper deck emergency window. There was also a light above the rear open platform, making 26 in all. They were wired in two series of six and two series of seven, the nearside bulbs being wired with the upper saloon rear dome and the platform light respectively. Lighting was supplied from the motor generator.

Internal emergency lighting was provided by means of separate low voltage battery-fed lights on each deck. One was mounted in the offside ceiling towards the rear and thus above the staircase and another was located above the last forward-facing offside double seat in the lower saloon. There was one daylight bulb in each service number indicator box and two in each route indicator box.

Seating: The sprung squabs were fitted to cast metal frames with black moulded grab handles curving gently upwards on the top of the seat and adjacent to the aisle. The grab handle equipped seat frames alternated with those having stanchions. A moquette seat covering was used with a heavy floral pattern motif of black, dark blue and possibly dark green with leather edges.

The lower saloon had a two-person inwards-facing bench seat on each side over the rear axle and five rows of forward-facing double seats. The upper saloon had six rows of double seats on the off-side at 2ft 8½in. pitch and seven rows on the nearside at 3ft pitch; the bench seat at the rear of the upper saloon above the open platform also accommodated two passengers. Vertical handrails rose up behind the first and fourth seat on the nearside and the second and fifth seat on the offside of the lower saloon and the second, fourth and sixth offside seats of the upper saloon.

Destination equipment: Large rectangular indicator boxes 36in. by 14in. capable of displaying up to three lines of information (final destination and two lines of intermediate points), aligned with a square indicator box 14in. by 14in. on the offside for displaying the service number, were mounted centrally at the front and rear in the lower three-quarters of the upper-deck panels. At the front the destination and intermediate points indicator box was on the nearside above the driver's cab windscreen (but encroaching a quarter of the way above the offside windscreen) and at the rear on the offside above the rear platform window. At the front the service number indicator box was on the offside and at the rear on the nearside.

There was a narrow indicator box 24in. by 6in. capable of displaying the final destination or the final destination and an intermediate point (two lines) located inside the lower saloon at the top of the rearmost lower saloon window (bay 6) on both sides.

Semaphore arm illuminated traffic indicators accommodated in a brown moulding were fitted at the base of the driver's cab corner pillars. At the rear, an inset panel mounted centrally beneath the rear platform window showed an illuminated STOP when the brakes were applied.

Internal livery: The interior panels and rear corner panels were lined with scratchproof brown Rexine with window mouldings and finishings in French-polished walnut. Cove panels edged in darker trim, ceilings cream, cab brown with cream ceiling.

External livery: Entered service in Livery 1 (see Appendix C). Trolleybuses 201 and 258 were the first two vehicles to appear with grey roof and white ARP markings.

Notes

Trolleybuses 1 and 3 arrived in Portsmouth on 9 August 1934, 4 arrived on 15 August 1934 and 2 arrived on 18 August 1934.

Trolleybus 1 carried Police Licence 801, a small rectangular white enamelled plate with black lettering, displayed at the nearside base of the rear panel adjacent to the platform. All other pre-war trolleybus deliveries carried such plates numbered consecutively.

Trolleybus 1 was issued with a Certificate of Ownership under the Road Traffic Act 1930 issued 9 August 1934, certificate number 305. The other numbers are not known.

Trolleybuses 1 and 3 were partially decorated for King George V's Silver Jubilee, 3 May–12 May 1935, with '1910 G M 1935' on the upper-deck side panels.

Trolleybus 4 was decorated and illuminated in varying styles on a number of occasions, including the Coronation of King George VI in 1937, then as 204 for the Coronation of Queen Elizabeth II in 1953.

In 1938, 1–4 were renumbered in sequence as 201–204.

201–204 were withdrawn from service and placed in open storage on waste ground to the east of Northern Parade in September 1940.

204 reappeared, carrying illuminations but no passengers, in May 1945 for the King George's Fund for Sailors during the Royal and Merchant Navies Week. It was licensed again for Thanksgiving Week 6 to 13 October 1945 carrying an advertisement for National Savings.

204 was relicensed for May–November 1946 thus embracing the May 1946 Portsmouth Safety Week, Portsmouth Victory Day on 31 May 1946 and related celebrations in late May and early June 1946, during which it again ran carrying illuminations but without passengers. It is likely that it ran in normal service but with the illuminations removed until the end of November 1946.

204 operated in normal passenger service, without illuminations, September 1947 to September 1949.

204 was re-licensed for one month only in June 1950 for the Industrial and Civic Exhibition. It ran carrying illuminations to a special timetable for the fortnight of the exhibition.

201–203 were reinstated into service in July 1946.

Subsequent alterations

The chassis and equipment maker's badge, AEC in an inverted triangle surmounted by the winged EE symbol, was fitted centrally beneath the driver's windscreen on the waistband and immediately above the fleet number in September 1934.

A small rectangular driver's rear view mirror was mounted externally towards the top of the nearside front cab pillar. In April 1935 an oblong conductor's mirror was fixed in the upper deck rear offside dome at the head of the stairs.

The shallow windscreen provided the driver with a restricted view of the overhead line above. A small recessed

AEC661T 202 seen at Cosham Railway Station after its January 1950 rebuild in which the small recessed window that had been added by summer 1935 above the offside driver's windscreen to improve the view of the overhead line above was removed and the entire windscreen deepened (the nearside windscreen retained its original shallow depth). (Online Transport Archive [photographer G.F. Ashwell])

window in the cream-painted central band or cantrail was added to improve the line of vision by summer 1935.

The small recessed window above the offside driver's windscreen was removed and the entire windscreen deepened on 201 (June 1955) and 202 (January 1950). The nearside windscreen retained its original shallow depth throughout. No such alterations were made to 203 and 204.

The semaphore arm illuminated traffic indicators were removed from 201 and 202 when their windscreens were deepened.

The half-drop openers on the lower deck offside were rearranged as bays 1, 3, 4.

By the late 1940s the rear registration number plate, on 204 at least, had been repositioned from the rear vent panel above the rear platform window to the offside top of the rear platform window and later to the base of the rear platform panel on the offside, beneath the advertisement position and fleet number. A circular red lens in a small painted red triangle aligned with the registration letters and above the final digit of the registration number served as a rear light.

At an unknown date, the diffused glass covers to the interior light fittings were removed leaving solely the rectangular bases and exposed tungsten bulbs. New style indicator blinds were fitted in 1947 whilst around 1948–49 the side indicator boxes inside the lower saloon fell into disuse (see Appendix E).

Disposal

201 Last licensed August 1958. Withdrawn in October 1958 and stored at North End Depot (October 1958–January 1960) being moved in August 1959 to the pits at the south end of the depot with 224, the only other survivor of the prototype fleet. It was then moved to Eastney Depot Yard (January 1960–September 1960) initially towards the front but from July 1960 at the rear. Purchased by Portsmouth Ratepayers Association on 1 April 1960 and following a repaint at Eastney, completed on 24 September 1960, 201 was presented to the Montague Motor Museum, Beaulieu, Hampshire, being towed there on 25 October 1960. The trolleybus was displayed in the open until 1967 when it was moved from the museum area to the rally park. On 22 May 1972, in connection with its acquisition by Portsmouth City Museums Department in June 1972, it was towed to Eastney Depot by a Central Transport lorry and placed in outdoor storage at the rear of the Depot Yard. In July 1976 the vehicle entered the Eastney body shop for some refurbishments and a repaint by CPPTD with a white painted roof and an inauthentic simplified 1948 livery. 201 then went into undercover storage in the depot building. It was towed on 3 May 1986 to the City Museum for an open day of transport related items and displayed.

Loaned to City of Portsmouth Preserved Transport Depot, Broad Street, Old Portsmouth, from March 1983 and towed to their premises, the trolley booms being removed and tyres partially deflated in order to squeeze 201 into the building.

April 1993	One of the lower deck front pillars collapsed whilst being moved.
June 1995–March 1999	The lower front end was replaced and the windscreen returned to its original form (work undertaken by Broad Street volunteers).
June 1995	Woodworm discovered in upper saloon wooden seat frames.
December 1995	Interior professionally sprayed to eradicate woodworm.
March 2000	Prepared for repaint.
June 2000	Agreed with City Museum that repaint should be as fleet number 1. Talk of 1934 livery but in the event repaint was in 1948 simplified livery but with white roof.
June 2000	Upper saloon seats removed by City Museum in order to handle woodworm again.
March 2003	Broad Street closes. The City Museum removes 201 to the Museum of Hampshire Life, latterly Milestones Museum, Basingstoke, where it was placed on display in a street scene.
1 June 2009	Moved from Milestones Museum to the City of Portsmouth Preserved Transport Depot at Wicor, Portchester. It remains the property of the City of Portsmouth Museums and Records Service.

202 Last licensed May 1950; subsequently taken out of passenger service and stored at North End Depot until sold in January 1956 to J. Strudwick, Horndean, Hampshire, and broken up in Eastney Depot Yard in March 1956.

203 Last licensed January 1950; subsequently taken out of passenger service and stored at North End Depot until sold in January 1956 to J. Strudwick, Horndean, Hampshire, and broken up in Eastney Depot Yard in March 1956.

204 Last licensed in August 1952 for the National Road Safety Week 2–9 August 1952. Last used in passenger service September 1949. Stored at North End Depot until spring 1953; decorated and used in June 1953 on non-passenger carrying duties for the Coronation of HM Queen Elizabeth II running on trade plates 170BK. Its last day of use was 7 June 1953; returned to store, still with decorations and illuminations, inside Eastney Depot. It remained there de-licensed and officially withdrawn from March 1955 until early in 1956 when it was stripped of its decorations and moved into Eastney Depot Yard where it was broken up by J. Strudwick, Horndean, Hampshire, in March 1956.

1934 Leyland TBD2/English Electric H26/24R

Fleet No.	1938 No.	Reg. No.	Chassis	Chassis No.	Body	Body No.	Into Service	Last licensed	Withdrawn	Sold
5	205	RV4653	Leyland TBD2	4546	Eng. Electric		31.07.1934	09.1949	21.04.1953	23.01.1954
6	206	RV4654	Leyland TBD2	4547	Eng. Electric		01.08.1934	09.1949	21.04.1953	23.01.1954
7	207	RV4655	Leyland TBD2	4548	Eng. Electric		01.08.1934	09.1949	21.04.1953	23.01.1954

Last licensed = the final month in which the vehicle was licensed to operate.

Chassis: Two-axle type Leyland TBD2 manufactured by Leyland Motors Ltd., Leyland, Lancashire.
Motor: General Electric Co. Ltd., Witton, Birmingham, Type GEC WT 254C (80 hp at 525 volts) order 114916.
Series wound: Seven notches, the first four of which were resistance steps, the three running notches including two weak-field.
Electrical equipment: General Electric Co. Ltd., Witton, Birmingham. Master Controller type M05. Regulated field control.
De-wirement indicator: Two neon line-lights.
Brakes: Westinghouse compressed air and hand brakes.
Body: English Electric Co. Ltd., Dick, Kerr Works, Preston, Lancashire, composite H26/24R.
Length: 26ft
Width: 7ft 6in.
Wheelbase: 16ft ⅛in.
Unladen weight: 7 tons 4 cwt 3 qtr
Tyres: 36in. by 8in. on all wheels.

The TBD2 was one of a new range of Leyland-GEC trolleybuses introduced in mid-1932 designed specifically for electric traction; all earlier Leyland trolleybuses having been based on a contemporary Leyland Titan motorbus chassis supplied to a traction equipment manufacturer.

The contract price was £1,832 10s. The final price upon completion was £1,786 8s 6d.

Chassis: Nickel-steel channel deep section frame upswept over the front and rear axles with tubular cross-member bracing having flanged ends bolted to the side members. "**I**" section nickel-steel front axle and Marles patent cam and roller steering.

All stressed parts of the axles were strengthened to cope with the higher starting torque experienced in a trolleybus compared to a motorbus, e.g. 8in. worm centres in the rear axle. The lubricating oil capacity was also commensurately increased to 2½ gallons. Both axles were equipped with shock absorbers.

A fully floating worm-driven rear axle was fitted in which the load was carried by the casing and the drive transmitted by stars forged on the ends of the nickel-steel axle shafts. One piece forged casing. The worm gear was carried on taper-roller races in adjustable sleeves in a light rigid casing.

The chassis, including electrical equipment, cost £1,047 10s.

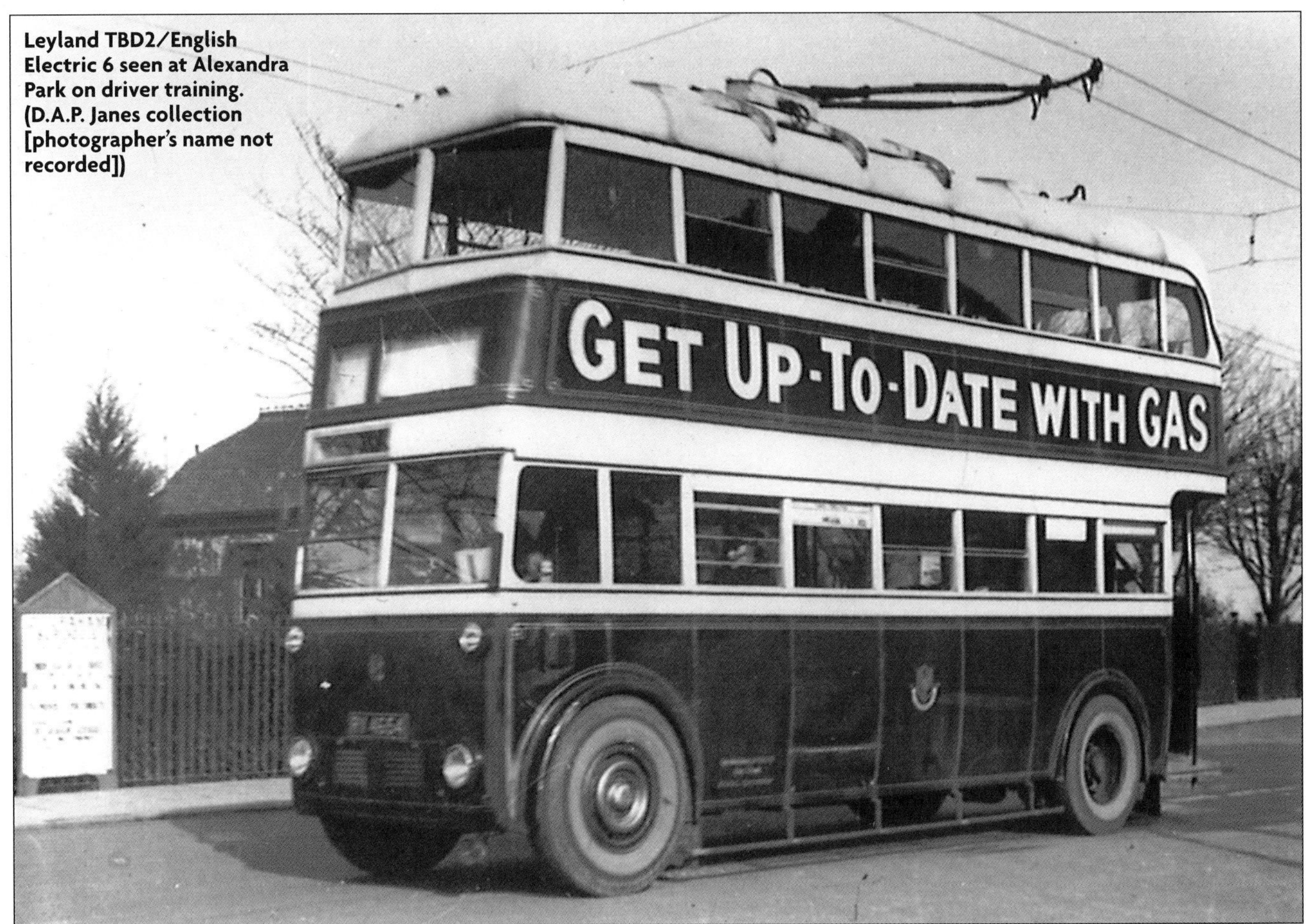

Leyland TBD2/English Electric 6 seen at Alexandra Park on driver training. (D.A.P. Janes collection [photographer's name not recorded])

Leyland TBD2 chassis.
(View from Leyland catalogue)

Leyland TBD2/English Electric 7 leaves the north end of Fawcett Road at Fratton Bridge heading north on a service 4 journey to Cosham. (Omnibus Society [photographer Norr])

Electrics: Compact box frame GEC traction motor constructed from high permeability steel mounted towards the centre of the chassis. Four adjustable brush-holders were provided with access through large detachable covers at the top and bottom of the motor. The series wound traction motor was considered to be particularly economical in operation.

The foot-operated master controller actuated a bank of electro-magnetic contactors which controlled the connections of the traction motor. When the foot pedal was operated, the appropriate contactors first cut out the resistances step by step until the motor was connected across the full line voltage, and finally weakened the series field by shunting it with suitable resistances until full speed was reached. The master controller drum was provided with adjustable spring fingers having renewable contacts, carried on ball bearings in the upper part of the controller, the reverse drum being mounted below. The two drums were mechanically interlocked so that the foot pedal had to be in the "off" position before the reversing switch could be operated. All contacts were closed by vertically mounted solenoids and were opened by gravity supplemented by suitable springs. The arc chutes were fitted with strong blowouts. The contactors were mounted on a Bakelite panel and enclosed in a wooden case fixed to the floor of the driver's cab.

Unbreakable, jointless and rustless main resistances were mounted towards the front of the chassis. Double insulation was used throughout.

Two automatic overload circuit breakers equipped with contactor-type mechanism and magnetic blowouts, each circuit being double-fuse protected, the auxiliary circuits being provided with main fuses and separate fuses for each circuit. Cartridge type fuses.

The lightweight Brecknell Willis trolley bases were equipped with Timkin taper roller bearings and Tecalemit lubricators; plus tapered steel trolley booms, taped and insulated, and equipped with trolley wheels.

The upper-deck body pillars slotted into the wooden rail of the framework above the upper saloon windows, i.e. the cantrail. There were curved steel brackets bolted to the metal roof (inside the roof there was a steel strengthening plate on each side) and each end of the three transverse pressed steel girders, between bays 1 and 2, bays 2 and 3, and bays 3 and 4, supporting the exposed trolley gantry, which was not in direct contact with the roof, rested on these brackets.

The main power cable made its way forward from the trolley gantry along the centre line of the roof before entered the front dome about 1ft 6in. to the rear of the upper-deck cantrail. Twin wireless anti-interference coil Type SE1 connected in the trolley lead circuits. The access catwalk on the roof had a single step above the rear dome beneath the trolley boom retaining hooks which were unusually anchored to the roof by a single central arm.

Traction batteries for manoeuvring purposes were not fitted.

Brakes: The Westinghouse compressed air brake system comprised a motor-driven compressor controlled by an automatic governor and a storage tank mounted on the offside of the chassis frame. Separate operating cylinders actuated the brake shoes on all wheels of the vehicle. The control valve, coupled to the driver's brake pedal, was mounted amidships in the chassis to ensure equalisation of movement of all the operating pistons.

Single 6in. wide shoes, lined with ½in. thick liners and operating in 17in. drums enclosed by pressed-steel shields were used on the rear wheels.

The handbrake operated the shoes in the rear wheels by use of a swinging link. The handbrake lever was to the offside of the driver's steering column.

Bodywork: The bodywork was basically identical to that fitted to 1934 AEC661T 1–4 and cost £785. The detail differences were:

Top hinged access doors were fitted at the base of the lower-deck off-side panel bay 2 and on the nearside in bay 2 providing access to the units mounted on the chassis members.

A large removable panel with two columns of six louvred ventilation vanes extended across the base of the front panel between the headlamps, the top of the panel aligned with the top of the headlamps and the base being curved backwards to match the convex front panel. The front registration number plate was centred immediately above. The rear registration number plate, encompassing a single red rear light to the offside of the upper row of letters, was affixed to the white-painted panel immediately above the rear platform window on the offside.

A small rectangular driver's rear view mirror was mounted externally on an outrigger aligned to the top of the lower fixed pane of the windscreen, immediately above the semaphore arm traffic indicator, on the offside front cab pillar.

There is no evidence that a chassis and/or equipment maker's badge was ever fitted.

A bamboo trolley retrieval pole was carried within the lower saloon nearside body panels at vent panel height (behind the cove panels) with a tube access above the nearside bulkhead window from the rear platform vestibule.

Lighting: See 1–4.
Lighting from motor generator (GEC Drawing 3C/515).

Seating: See 1–4.

Destination equipment: See 1–4.

Internal Livery: See 1–4.

External Livery: Entered service in Livery 1 (see Appendix C).

Notes

No. 7 arrived in Portsmouth on 28 July 1934 and was used for driver training purposes from 31 July 1934; 5 and 6 arriving on 30 July 1934 and were used for driver training purposes from 1 August 1934.

No. 6 was partially decorated for King George V's Silver Jubilee 3 May–12 May 1935 with "1910 G M 1935" on the upper-deck side panels.

In 1938, 5–7 were re-numbered in sequence as 205–207.

Nos. 205–207 were withdrawn from service and placed in open storage on waste ground in Northern Parade store in September 1940. They were reinstated into service as follows: 205 – 1 July 1946; 206 – 1 October 1946; 207 – 1 September 1946.

Subsequent alterations

In April 1935 a circular conductor's mirror was fixed in the upper deck rear offside dome at the head of the stairs.

The shallow windscreen provided the driver with a restricted view of the overhead line above. A small recessed window in the cream-painted central band or cantrail was added to improve the line of vision in summer 1935.

There is no evidence that the small recessed window above the offside driver's windscreen was subsequently removed and the entire windscreen deepened as with 1–4.

At an early date but after the windscreen alterations an orange-lensed Lucas 24-volt 36-watt fog spotlight was mounted beneath the front panel, slightly outboard of the nearside headlamp.

A small rectangular driver's rear view mirror was mounted externally towards the top of the nearside front cab pillar.

Post-war the semaphore arm illuminated traffic indicators were removed from two of the three vehicles.

In 206, 207 the half-drop openers on the lower deck offside were rearranged as bays 1, 3, 4.

New style indicator blinds were fitted in 1947 whilst around 1948–49 the side indicator boxes inside the lower saloon fell into disuse.

Disposal

205 Last licensed September 1949; subsequently taken out of passenger service and stored at North End Depot

until sold (23 January 1954) to Kingsway Coachworks, Emsworth, Hampshire, and broken up.

206 Last licensed September 1949; subsequently taken out of passenger service and stored at North End Depot until sold (23 January 1954) to Kingsway Coachworks, Emsworth, Hampshire, and broken up.

207 Last licensed September 1949; subsequently taken out of passenger service and stored at North End Depot until sold (23 January 1954) to Kingsway Coachworks, Emsworth, Hampshire, and broken up.

1934 Sunbeam MF2/English Electric H26/24R

Fleet No.	1938 No.	Reg. No.	Chassis	Chassis No.	Body	Body No.	Into Service	Last licensed	Withdrawn	Sold
8	208	RV4656	Sunbeam MF2	13004S	Eng. Electric		16.08.1934	04.1952	21.04.1953	23.01.1954

Last licensed = the final month in which the vehicle was licensed to operate.

Chassis: Two-axle type Sunbeam MF2 manufactured by Sunbeam Commercial Vehicles Ltd. (part of the Rootes Group), Moorfield Road, Wolverhampton.
Motor: British Thomson-Houston Co. Ltd., Rugby, Warwickshire. Type BTH 201 Form DX (80hp at 550 volts) with overwound series field for regulated field control.
Electrical equipment: British Thomson-Houston Co. Ltd., Rugby, Warwickshire.
Dewirement indicator: Single neon line-light.
Brakes: Lockheed hydraulic, rheostatic and hand brakes.
Body: English Electric Co. Ltd., Dick, Kerr Works, Preston, Lancashire, composite H26/24R.
Length: 26ft.
Width 7ft 6 in.
Wheelbase: 16ft giving a turning circle of 53ft.
Wheel track: Front 6ft 6in., rear 5ft 9½in.
Unladen weight: 7 tons 2 cwt 0 qtr.
Tyres: low pressure 20in. by 10.50in. tyres on front and 20in. b 9in. tyres on the rear.

Understood to be the fourth Sunbeam MF2 to be built.

Chassis: The frame had deep side members braced with tubular and pressed steel cross members for rigidity. The frame was upswept over both front and rear axles and the tail portion dropped to provide a single step entrance.

Front axle of high tensile steel drop forging with "**I**" section beam strengthened with deep webs extending from the spring seats to the swivel pin bosses. Taper roller bearings took the weight imposed on the swivel pins.

The traction motor was centrally mounted amidships, i.e. about halfway along the chassis between the axles and chassis frame, offset to the centre line of the frame nearside matching the differential, which was offset to the nearside of the rear axle. There was a short propeller shaft having a needle roller bearing universal joint at each end which transmitted the power to the under-slung worm-drive rear axle, the main axle casing being a nickel steel one-piece drop forging. The axle casing was similarly offset to provide a "straight" drive. The differential gearing comprised four planet wheel and two sun wheels, all of the bevel gear type, contained in a steel cage on which the worm wheel was mounted. The worms were made of 3% nickel steel hardened and ground, and meshing with phosphor bronze wheels. The worm shaft was of case-hardened steel with a phosphor bronze worm wheel.

Semi-elliptical springs manufactured from silico-manganese steel. The front springs were 44in. between the eyes, which were solid forged and not of the turned over type, and 3½in. wide. The rear springs were of the divided back plate type measuring 59¾in. and 3½in. respectively. Frame height from ground 2ft. Frame height of rear platform from ground 1ft.

The chassis including electrical equipment cost £1,065.

Electrics: The traction motor was centrally mounted amidships, carried in a sub-frame mounted on rubber bushes providing a

Especially decorated for the Silver Jubilee of King George V, 1934 Sunbeam MF2/English Electric 8 is seen at Kingston Cross on a warm 11 May 1935 heading south. A small recessed window in the cream-painted central band or cantrail has already been added to improve the driver's view of the overhead line above. (D.A.P. Janes [photographer G.A. Tucker])

floating suspension and easy removal for overhaul purposes (being retained by just four bolts).

The resistances were placed amidships mounted on the outside of the nearside chassis frame with a steel shield and stone guard beneath to protect the grids. The starting and braking resistances were of the rustless grid type, consisting of a continuous strip bent into grid form and supported on insulated rods thereby reducing the number of joints to a minimum. The shunt field resistances consisted of vitreous enamel tubes mounted in a frame with a louvred protecting cover. The full field speed was kept at a low figure to reduce rheostatic losses on starting. The BTH master controller was located beneath the driver's seat and operated by an organ type pedal controlled by the driver's right foot. The master controller and the contactor gear were carried on two aluminium dashes fitted to the chassis on the nearside of the driver's cab.

The controller is believed to have had five accelerating resistance points, one full field running point (providing up to 35mph) and five field weakening points.

There was a rotary exhauster at the forward end of the traction motor and a dynamo at the commutator end.

Brecknell Willis lightweight trolley bases were used.

A Sunbeam motor generator set powered by a generator belt driven from the rear end of the traction motor was mounted on the offside of the chassis frame to provide low voltage (24 volt) power for lighting and auxiliary equipment. The battery was only used to supply the small demands of the side and rear lights and regularly-used accessories such as the screen wiper, horn, bells, etc. The main current load was supplied direct from the motor generator. When the saloon lights were switched on the motor generator started and then supplied all lights and accessories whilst the battery was charged.

Traction batteries for manoeuvring purposes were not fitted.

Brakes: Standard Lockheed hydraulic brakes operating on all wheels, as used on all Sunbeam-BTH chassis of the period, were fitted. A patented multiple master cylinder provided compensation between the braking effort on each wheel and ensured against complete loss of braking in the event of a fractured pipe line. If a fracture did occur, the fractured pipe line was promptly sealed so that the brakes on only one axle were affected with full braking remaining on the other. This compensation also ensured smooth and progressive brake application and reputedly reduced wear on the shoe liners, this being a considerable maintenance cost where unbalanced braking took place.

The foot pressure required for brake application was amplified, reducing the driver's physical effort, by means of a Dewandre vacuum server interposed between the brake pedal and the master cylinders. A rotary exhauster was driven direct from the forward end of the traction motor to obtain the necessary vacuum for the servo, the vacuum tanks being carried on the offside of the main chassis frame.

A pull-on handbrake linked mechanically by rods acted on the rear wheels. The handbrake lever was located to the offside of the driver's steering column.

Brake drums 17in. in diameter with 3in. wide shoes. The hubs were mounted on taper roller bearings.

Bodywork: The bodywork was basically identical to that fitted to 1934 AEC661T 1–4 and cost £785. The detail differences were:

Top hinged access doors were fitted at the base of the lower-deck off-side panel bays 2 and 3, providing access to the vacuum cylinder, and on the nearside in bays 1 and 4 providing access to the resistances in an insulated unit mounted on the nearside chassis member.

The triangular Sunbeam chassis maker's badge was fitted centrally beneath the driver's windscreen with its base on the waistband lower beading separating the red and white coloured paint application, and immediately above the fleet number.

A small rectangular driver's rear view mirror was mounted externally on an outrigger aligned to the top of the lower fixed pane of the windscreen, immediately above the trafficator, on the offside front cab pillar.

Lighting: See 1–4.

Seating: See 1–4.

Destination equipment: See 1–4.

Internal Livery: See 1–4.

External Livery: Delivered in Livery 1 (see Appendix C).

Subsequent alterations

In April 1935 a circular conductor's mirror was fixed in the upper deck rear offside dome at the head of the stairs.

The shallow windscreen provided the driver with a restricted view of the overhead line above. A small recessed window in the cream-painted central band or cantrail was added to improve the line of vision by spring 1935.

There is no evidence that the small recessed window above the offside driver's windscreen was subsequently removed and the entire windscreen deepened as with 1–4.

Upper life guard removed from the protruding attachments or outriggers beneath the lower-deck body panels on both sides.

A small rectangular driver's rear view mirror was mounted externally towards the top of the nearside front cab pillar.

Notes

No. 8 arrived in Portsmouth on 15 August 1934.

No. 8 was partially decorated for King George V's Silver Jubilee 3 May – 12 May 1935 with an illuminated "1910 G M 1935" on the upper-deck side panels.

In 1938, No. 8 was renumbered as 208.

No. 208 was withdrawn from service and placed in open storage on waste ground to the east of Northern Parade in September 1940. The trolleybus was reinstated into service in November 1946.

Disposal

208 Last licensed April 1952; subsequently taken out of passenger service and stored at North End Depot until sold on 23 January 1954 to Kingsway Coachworks, Emsworth, Hampshire, and broken up.

1934 Karrier E4/English Electric H26/24R

Fleet No.	1938 No.	Reg. No.	Chassis	Chassis No.	Body	Body No.	Into Service	Last licensed	Withdrawn	Sold
9	209	RV4657	Karrier E4	55004	Eng. Electric		19.08.1934	09.1949	21.04.1953	23.01.1954

Last licensed = the final month in which the vehicle was licensed to operate.

Chassis: Two axle type E4 manufactured by Karrier Motors Ltd., Huddersfield, Yorkshire.
Motor: English Electric Co. Ltd., Phoenix Works, Bradford, Yorkshire. Type EE 405/5B (80 h.p.) series wound.
Electrical equipment: English Electric regulated field controller.
Brakes: Compressed air, rheostatic and hand brakes.
Body: English Electric Co. Ltd., Dick, Kerr Works, Preston, Lancashire, composite H26/24R.
Length: 26ft.
Width: 7ft 6in.
Wheelbase: 16ft, giving a turning circle of 58ft.
Wheel track: Front 6ft 6in.; rear 5ft 8in.
Unladen weight: 7 tons 4 cwt 3 qtr
Tyres: Low pressure 10.50 by 20 all round.

In June 1934, presumably shortly after the chassis had been passed to the body builders, Karrier Motors Ltd. went into receivership although by this time trolleybus manufacture was arguably the most successful side of the business. Karrier was sold to Rootes Securities Ltd. which in July 1935 also acquired Sunbeam Commercial Vehicles Ltd., the trolleybus producing arm of the erstwhile Sunbeam Motor Car Ltd. Subsequently production of Karrier trolleybuses was transferred to the Sunbeam factory in Wolverhampton and the Huddersfield premises closed.

The Karrier E4 chassis was similar to that of the Karrier 'Monitor' motor bus in its final form and more closely related to the three-axle E6A than the E6, having Kirkstall axles and Marles cam and roller steering. The E4 model was suitable for both single and double-decker bodywork. During 1935–36 the E4 wheelbase was quoted as 15ft 6in. for both, but in 1937 the single-decker was 16ft 10in. and the double-decker 16ft (54 and 56ft turning circle respectively).

The contract price was £1,858. The final price upon completion was £1,811 9s 11d.

Chassis: Conventional cranked high tensile pressed steel chassis side frame of deep section, braced by large diameter tubular cross members. The side members were upswept at front and rear. All spring and brake brackets were bolted on with fitted bolts in reamed holes. There were towing loops front and rear. A Tecalemit grouped-nipple chassis lubrication system was used.

Chassis length: 25ft 8¾in.
Chassis frame width: Front 3ft 3⅝in., rear 3ft 8in.
Overall width (over tyres): 7ft 4⅜in.
Frame height from ground between axles loaded: 1ft 11½in.
Frame height of rear platform from ground loaded: 11in.

A high tensile steel, drop forged front axle equipped with enclosed cam and roller steering was used, the weight on the steering pivots taken by taper roller bearings. The hubs were mounted on taper roller bearings and Karrier rear axles were used.

Both front and rear springs were of the semi-elliptical type made from silico-manganese steel with solid eyes incorporated

Karrier E4/English Electric 9 is seen heading south along London Road, Hilsea, outside the 'Coach & Horses' public house on 23 September 1934. (D.A.P. Janes [photographer G.A. Tucker])

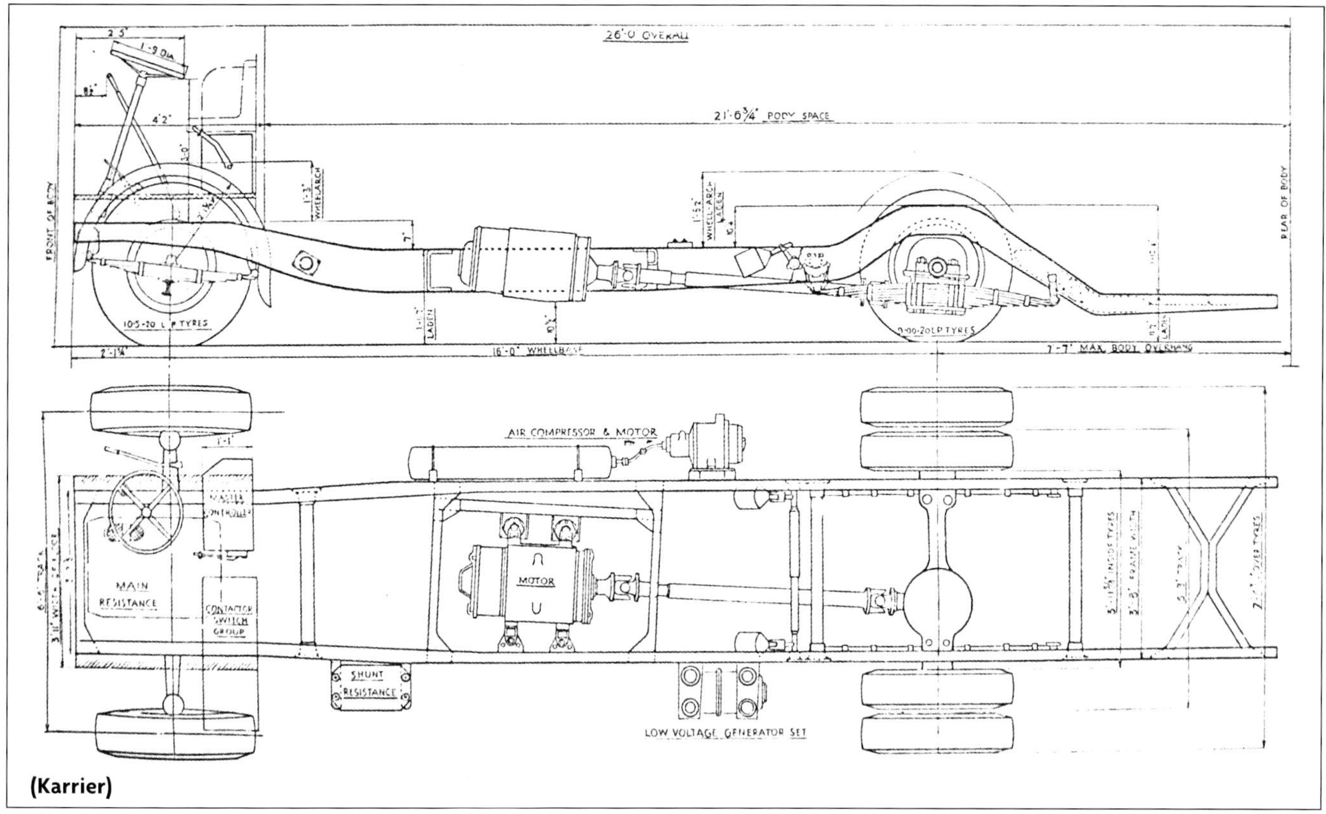

(Karrier)

at the anchored end. Shackles were adjustable for side wear. Rubber buffers limited the spring deflection. Front springs 44in. by 3½in., rear 59⅞in. by 3½in.

Inverted worm driven rear axle with fully floating hubs mounted on roller bearings. The axle casings were one piece nickel steel drop forgings with the differential casing offset to the nearside. A large diameter transmission shaft with needle roller type universal joints was used.

The chassis including electrical equipment cost £1,073.

Electrics: All electrical equipment was mounted in and around the driver's cab area or the nearside chassis frame member. The jointless, unbreakable and non-rusting main resistance grid was carried on chassis cross-members beneath the driver's cab and above the front axle whilst the shunt resistance was mounted on the outside face of the nearside chassis frame member. The contactor switch group was mounted to the nearside on the rear wall of the cab and the master controller was mounted underneath the driver's seat.

The series-wound, box frame, self-ventilated, flood-proof and roller bearing equipped EE405 traction motor was centrally mounted, i.e. about halfway along the chassis, amidships within the chassis frame on Floatex rubber suspension on a rigid channel section sub-frame and cross members, slightly offset to the nearside. The motor was skewed at an angle towards the rear nearside and tilting downwards towards the rear to ensure a straight drive line between the motor shaft, the propeller shaft and the rear differential which was offset to the nearside to avoid any obstruction of the gangway. The laden ground clearance of the traction motor was 10½in.

The upper-deck body pillars were slotted into the wooden rail of the framework above the upper saloon windows, i.e. the cantrail. There were curved steel brackets bolted to the metal roof (inside the roof there was a steel strengthening plate on each side) and each end of the three transverse pressed steel girders, between bays 1 and 2, bays 2 and 3, and bays 3 and 4, supporting the exposed trolley gantry, which was not in direct contact with the roof, rested on these brackets.

The main power cable made its way forward from the trolley gantry along the centre line of the roof before entered the front dome about 1ft 6in. to the rear of the upper-deck cantrail. The access catwalk on the roof had a single step above the rear dome beneath the trolley boom retaining hooks which were unusually anchored to the roof by a single central arm.

Traction batteries for manoeuvring purposes were not fitted.

Brakes: Westinghouse or Peters air brakes operating on all four wheels. Shoes were of the internal expanding type housed in 17in. diameter iron alloy drums. Brake air-pressure cylinders were mounted on the front axle swivels (operated through push rods passing through the kingpins) and on the main frame side members for the rear axle shoes. Total area of brake linings was 536 square inches.

The motor compressor unit was mounted on an insulated base on the offside of the main frame. An electric governor controlled the compressor motor. The air reservoir was fitted with a drain cock and safety valve, and an anti-freezing device was mounted on the chassis frame.

Bodywork: The bodywork was basically identical to that fitted to 1934 AEC661T 1–4 and cost £785. The detail differences were:

Top hinged access doors were fitted at the base of the lower-deck off-side panel bays 2 and 3 providing access to the air brake compressor unit and motor mounted on the outside of the off-side chassis member, and on the nearside in bay 2 providing access to the shunt resistance and low voltage generator set mounted on the outside of the nearside chassis member.

Offside front wheel fitted with large wheel nut guard ring.

There is no evidence that a chassis and/or equipment maker's badge was ever fitted.

Lighting: See trolleybuses 1–4.

Seating: See trolleybuses 1–4.

Destination equipment: See trolleybuses 1–4.

Internal livery: See trolleybuses 1–4.

External livery: Delivered in Livery 1 (see Appendix C).

Subsequent alterations

In April 1935 a circular conductor's mirror was fixed in the upper deck rear offside dome at the head of the stairs.

The shallow windscreen provided the driver with a restricted view of the overhead line above. A small recessed window in the cream-painted central band or cantrail was added to improve the line of vision in summer 1935.

There is no evidence that the small recessed window above the offside driver's windscreen was subsequently removed and the entire windscreen deepened as with 1–4.

At an early date, but after the windscreen alterations, an orange-lensed Lucas 24-volt 36-watt fog spotlight was mounted beneath the front panel, slightly outboard of the nearside headlamp.

A small rectangular driver's rear view mirror was mounted externally towards the top of the nearside front cab pillar.

In 1938, 9 was re-numbered as 209.

Notes

9 arrived in Portsmouth on 11 August 1934. 209 was withdrawn from service and placed in open storage on waste ground in Northern Parade store in September 1940. The trolleybus was reinstated into service in July 1946.

Disposal

209 Last licensed September 1949; subsequently taken out of passenger service and stored at North End (1951) until sold (January 1954) to Kingsway Coachworks, Emsworth, Hampshire, and broken up.

1934 Sunbeam MF2/Metro-Cammell H26/24R

Fleet No.	1938 No.	Reg. No.	Chassis	Chassis No.	Body	Body No.	Into Service	Last licensed	Withdrawn	Sold
10	210	RV4660	Sunbeam MF2	13003S	MCCW		25.07.1934	04.1952	21.04.1953	23.01.1954

Last licensed = the final month in which the vehicle was licensed to operate.

Chassis: Two axle type Sunbeam MF2 manufactured by Sunbeam Commercial Vehicles Ltd. (part of the Rootes Group), Moorfield Road, Wolverhampton.
Motor: British Thomson-Houston Co. Ltd., Rugby, Warwickshire. Type BTH 201 Form DX (80hp at 550 volts) with overwound series field for regulated field control.
Electrical equipment: British Thomson-Houston Co. Ltd., Rugby, Warwickshire.
Brakes: Lockheed hydraulic, rheostatic and hand brakes.
Body: Metropolitan-Cammell Weymann Motor Bodies Ltd., Midland Works, Saltley, Birmingham, all metal H26/24R. MCCW Contract No. 51 (which is known to have consisted of a pair of two-axle trolleybuses each with H26/24R bodies, the other vehicle so-equipped being Karrier E4 11).
Length: 26ft
Width: 7ft 6in.
Unladen weight: 8 tons 3 cwts 0 qrtrs

The contract price was £1,898. The final price upon completion was £1,829 15s 1d.

Chassis: The traction motor was centrally mounted i.e. about halfway along the chassis between the axles and chassis frame, offset to the centre line of the frame nearside matching the differential which was offset to the nearside of the rear axle. There was a short propeller shaft having a needle roller bearing universal joint at each end which transmitted the power to the underslung worm-drive rear axle, the axle casing being similarly offset to provide a "straight" drive. The differential was of the four-pinion type and the worm shaft was of case-hardened steel with a phosphor bronze worm wheel.

Divided back plate springs. The front springs were 44in. between the eyes, which were solid and not of the turned over type, and 3½in. wide. The rear springs measured 59¾in. and 3½in. respectively.

The chassis was equipped with special insulation points for all-metal bodies.

The chassis, including electrical equipment, cost £1,065.

Electrics: The traction motor was carried in a sub-frame mounted on rubber bushes providing a floating suspension and easy removal for overhaul purposes (being retained by just four bolts).

The resistances were placed amidships mounted on the nearside of the chassis frame with a steel shield and stone guard beneath to protect the grids. The contactor panels were in the driver's cab. The starting and braking resistances were of the grid type, consisting of a continuous strip bent into grid form and supported on insulated rods thereby reducing the number of joints to a minimum. The shunt field resistances

Sunbeam MF2 no. 10 equipped with MCCW all metal H26/24R body (official view). (D.A.P. Janes collection)

Sunbeam MF2/MCCW 10 on trial on another trolleybus system, potentially Wolverhampton, prior to its delivery to Portsmouth. (David Harvey collection)

Another manufacturer's view of Sunbeam MF2 10 not taken in Portsmouth. (Stephen Lockwood collection)

consisted of vitreous enamel tubes mounted in a frame with a louvred protecting cover. The full field speed was kept at a low figure to reduce rheostatic losses on starting. The BTH master controller was operated by an organ type pedal beneath the driver's right foot.

At the rear of the catwalk substantial cross-braced trolley boom retaining hooks were fitted as an integral part of a metal frame including an access step from the emergency door.

Brecknell Willis lightweight trolley bases were used.

There was a rotary exhauster at the forward end of the traction motor.

A Sunbeam motor generator set provided low voltage (24 volt) power for lighting and auxiliary equipment. The battery was only used to supply the small demands of the side and rear lights, and regularly-used accessories such as the screen wiper, horn, bells, etc. The main current load was supplied direct from the motor generator. When the saloon lights were switched on the motor generator started and then supplied all lights and accessories whilst the battery was charged.

Traction batteries for manoeuvring purposes were not fitted.

Brakes: Standard Lockheed hydraulic brakes, as fitted to all Sunbeam-BTH chassis of the period, were fitted. A patented multiple master cylinder provided compensation between the braking effort on each wheel and ensured against complete loss of braking in the event of a fractured pipe line. If a fracture did occur, the fractured pipe line was promptly sealed so that the brakes on only one axle were affected with full braking remaining on the other. This compensation also ensured smooth and progressive brake application and reputedly reduced wear on the shoe liners, this being a considerable maintenance cost where unbalanced braking took place.

The foot pressure required for brake application was amplified, reducing the driver's physical effort, by means of a Dewandre vacuum server interposed between the brake pedal and the master cylinders. A rotary exhauster was driven direct from the forward end of the traction motor to obtain the necessary vacuum for the servo, the vacuum tanks being carried on the offside of the main chassis frame.

A pull-on handbrake linked mechanically by rods acted on the rear wheels. The handbrake lever was located to the offside of the driver's steering column.

Bodywork: All metal (patented) six-bay Highbridge double-deck construction, forward-ascending half-turn (90°) staircase with conventional semi-vestibuled open platform entrance and exit at the rear, marketed by Metropolitan-Cammell Weymann Motor Bodies Ltd., and built by The Metropolitan-Cammell Carriage, Wagon & Finance Company Ltd., Midland Works, Saltley, Birmingham. The design was based on that of contemporary Birmingham Tramway & Omnibus Department (trading as Birmingham City Transport) motorbus and trolleybuses but together with Karrier E4 11 the final MCCW bodies built to this "interim" Birmingham design.

In profile, the front of the body featured a "swept-back" styling between the bulbous nose surmounting the less raked front panel of the driver's cab and the upper deck roof, the front line of the roof being in line with the front axle. The front of the upper-deck curved gently beneath the "V" shaped fixed front windows; the shallow driver's cab windscreen had a more pronounced "V-shaped" cross-section set-back beneath the upper deck front panels and with a bulbous top to the front panel beneath. There was an upright rear profile, the base of the rear panel curving gently in to match the concave side panels. The trolley poles were fitted on an exposed roof-mounted gantry above bay 2. Platform handrails and stanchions were covered with black Doverite.

Brackets were bolted to the roof rail immediately above the upper-deck body pillars between bays 1 and 2, and bays 2 and 3, to support the two girders of the exposed trolley gantry which was mounted above bay 2, and not in direct contact with the roof.

Metal louvres were fitted above the upper and lower deck saloon side windows. Chromium plated half-drop openers with a clip-operated gripper at the top on each side of the upper pane were fitted to the side windows in bays 1, 3 and 4 of both sides of the upper deck, bays 1, 3 and 4 of the lower-deck nearside and bays 1, 2 and 3 of the lower-deck offside. The upper pane dropped outside the fixed lower pane. Immediately above the lower deck side windows in bays 1 and 3 nine-vane ventilation vents slanting rearwards somewhat from the vertical at the top were fitted. The rearmost offside panel behind the staircase was also glazed. The rearmost upper saloon side windows had a pronounced "D" shape at the rear. There were six roof ventilators, one on each side midway above bays 1, 3 and 5.

At the rear of the upper-saloon there was an emergency exit door having three hinges at its base and two oblong fixed window panes having slightly rounded upper and lower outer corners and a horizontal rail across both panes at half depth. The emergency exit door could be opened by an external handle mounted on the rear dome immediately above the rain strip and centrally above the door, or from inside by a comparable handle attached to a horizontal locking bar mounted on the cantrail immediately above the door. A second external bracket handle was fixed above the central window pillar. There were two protective rubber bumpers at half depth on the outer frame of the emergency door matching two further bumpers above the rear indicator boxes. When opened to its fullest extent the emergency exit door hung down and rested facing downwards on these bumpers. A separate platform, normally stowed behind the upper saloon rear nearside seat, fitted into retaining slits in the door sill and was retained securely in place by two detachable rods which fitted into this platform at one end and brackets inside the rear dome at the other to provide access to the roof catwalk and thence the trolley gantry.

The driver's steering wheel was noticeably raked back. The top two thirds of the offside driver's windscreen was chromium plated and opened outwards. It carried a top-mounted windscreen wiper. There were two glazed panels in the bulkhead behind the driver. There was a front-hinged door on the offside provided with a square sliding "signalling" window in lower one-third of the pane and an inset, opening handle. There was a matching panel and window on the nearside, the window being vertically divided (on a slant to match the front pillar) and enabling the rear pane to slide forwards outside the fixed front pane or vice versa. There was a large fixed quarter light between the offside cab door and the cab front pillars. The base of the cab door was curved over the wheel arch to a position about 5in. from the rear of the door thereafter the base, beneath the cab door handle, was horizontal. Two large hooded inlet ducts were installed on each side above the driver's cab door and side windows; one rose gently upwards from the cab front pillar and one fell gently downwards towards the cab rear bulkhead.

The staircase had four steps from the platform to the half-landing and then four steps to the upper deck. There were two lifeguard rails on each side extending between the flared rear of the front wheel mudguard to the rear mudguard.

A chromed wheel nut guard ring and hub bosses was fitted to all wheels. The front offside wheel was equipped with a step ring to aid access to the driver's cab.

A flap mudguard hung at an angle beneath the rear platform.

Top hinged access doors were fitted at the base of the lower-deck off-side panel bays 1 to 4 providing access to the vacuum cylinder and on the nearside in bays 1 to 4 providing access to the resistances in an insulated unit mounted on the nearside chassis member.

The flat front panel incorporated a single fluted column of three louvred vanes placed centrally aligned vertically with the centre of the headlamps with the fleet number transferred immediately above. There was no removable front panel for towing purposes. The registration number plate was affixed at the base of the front panel.

The triangular Sunbeam chassis maker's badge was fitted centrally beneath the driver's windscreen with its base on the waistband beading separating the red and white coloured paint application, and immediately above the fleet number.

A small rectangular driver's rear view mirror was mounted externally at the top of the offside front cab pillar.

Lighting: External lighting consisted of two headlights mounted half-way up the front panel and noticeably inboard and two circular front side lights exactly on the beading between the red lower panels and the white window area. A single red rear light was incorporated into the rear registration number plate, immediately above the rear platform window on the offside.

At the rear, an inset panel somewhat to the offside of the centre line of the rear panels and aligned with the lower beading of the white-painted waistband beneath the rear platform window illuminated to show STOP when the brakes were applied.

Semaphore arm illuminated traffic indicators accommodated in a black moulding were fitted in the lower half of the driver's cab corner pillars on both sides. Although photographs show the trolleybus on trial in Wolverhampton prior to delivery without indicators, these are evident on photographs taken on the first day of public services in Portsmouth.

There were square diffused light fittings in the ceiling cove panels in the lower saloon and in the upper saloon towards the sides of the ceiling itself in bays 1 to 5 on each side and one in the offside of the rear dome above the staircase. There was a single exposed light on the platform.

Seating: The lower saloon had a two-person inward-facing bench seat on each side over the rear axles and five rows of forward-facing double seats. The upper saloon had six rows of double seats on the offside and seven rows on the nearside, i.e. the bench seat at the rear of the upper saloon above the open platform also accommodated two passengers. Vertical handrails rose up behind the first and fourth seat on the offside and the second and fifth seat on the nearside of the lower saloon and the first, fourth and sixth seat on the offside and the second and fifth seat nearside seats of the upper saloon.

Destination equipment: A large rectangular indicator box 36in. by 14in. capable of displaying up to three lines of information (final destination and two lines of intermediate points) with a square service number indicator box 14in. by 14in. alongside, were mounted centrally at the front and rear in the lower half of the upper-deck panels. At the front the destination and intermediate points indicator box was on the nearside above the driver's cab windscreen (but encroaching a quarter of the way above the offside windscreen) and at the rear on the offside above the rear platform window. At the front the service number indicator box was on the offside and at the rear on the nearside.

There was a narrow box 24in. by 6in. capable of displaying the final destination or the final destination and an intermediate point (two lines) built into the white-painted vent panel above the rearmost lower saloon window (bay 5) on both sides.

Internal livery: Ceilings and coves were covered with white enamelled panels with varnished/polished wood frames. The ceiling of the driver's cab and the upper portions of the bulkheads were painted cream. The window surrounds and saloon front bulkhead above the windows were varnished wood. The floors were brown. Handrails were covered in black Doverite.

External livery: Delivered in Livery 1 (see Appendix C).

Subsequent alterations

In April 1935 a circular conductor's mirror was fixed in the upper deck rear offside dome at the head of the stairs.

It is not known if 10 and potentially the other MCCW-bodied trolleybuses were delivered with a square metal fleet number plate, as 14, or with Bakelite discs displaying the fleet number inside the upper and lower saloons. Thus it is not known how the 1938 re-numbering affected this vehicle.

A spotlight was fitted beneath the flat front panel aligned with the nearside headlight. Post-war the front wheels were fitted with chromed wheel nut guard rings. A rear view mirror was mounted externally to the front nearside cab pillar.

The rear registration number plate was moved to the lower offside of the rear platform panel.

By July 1946 the semaphore arm traffic indicators had been removed.

Notes

No. 10 arrived in Portsmouth on 28 July 1934.

In 1938, No. 10 was re-numbered as 210.

No. 210 was withdrawn from service and placed in open storage on waste ground to the east of Northern Parade in September 1940. The trolleybus was reinstated into service in September 1946.

Disposal

210 Last licensed April 1952; subsequently taken out of passenger service and stored at North End Depot until sold in January 1954 to Kingsway Coachworks, Emsworth, Hampshire and broken up.

1934 Karrier E4/Metro-Cammell H26/24R

Fleet No.	1938 No.	Reg. No.	Chassis	Chassis No.	Body	Body No.	Into Service	Last licensed	Withdrawn	Sold
11	211	RV4661	Karrier E4	55005	MCCW		25.07.1934	09.1949	21.04.1953	23.01.1954

Last licensed = the final month in which the vehicle was licensed to operate.

Chassis: Two-axle type Karrier E4 manufactured by Karrier Motors, Huddersfield, Yorkshire.
Motor: British Thomson-Houston Co. Ltd., Rugby, Warwickshire. Type BTH 201 Form DX (80 h.p. at 550 volts) series wound for regulated field control.
Electrical equipment: British Thomson-Houston Co. Ltd., Rugby, Warwickshire.
Brakes: believed to have had G. D. Peters compressed air, as well as rheostatic and hand brakes.
Body: Metropolitan-Cammell Weymann Motor Bodies Ltd., Midland Works, Saltley, Birmingham, all metal H26/24R. MCCW Contract No. 51 (which is known to have consisted of a pair of two-axle trolleybuses each with H26/24R bodies, the other vehicle so-equipped being Sunbeam MF2 10).
Length: 26ft.
Width: 7ft 6in.
Wheelbase: 16ft.
Wheel track: Front 6ft 6in.; rear 5ft 8in.
Unladen weight: 7 tons 4 cwt 3 qtr.
Tyres: Low pressure 10.50 by 20 all round.

In June 1934, presumably shortly after the chassis had been passed to the body builders, Karrier Motors Ltd. went into receivership although by this time trolleybus manufacture was arguably the most successful side of the business. Karrier was sold to Rootes Securities Ltd. which in July 1935 also acquired Sunbeam Commercial Vehicles Ltd., the trolleybus producing arm of the erstwhile Sunbeam Motor Car Ltd. Subsequently production of Karrier trolleybuses was transferred to the Sunbeam factory in Wolverhampton and the Huddersfield premises closed.

The Karrier E4 chassis was similar to that of the Karrier 'Monitor' motor bus in its final form and more closely related to the three-axle E6A than the E6, having Kirkstall axles and Marles cam and roller steering. The E4 model was suitable for both single and double-deck bodywork. During 1935–36 the E4 wheelbase was quoted as 15ft 6in. for both but in 1937 the single-decker was 16ft 10in. and double-decker 16ft (54 and 56ft turning circle respectively).

The contract price was £1,906. The final price upon completion was £1,859 10s 9d.

Chassis: Conventional cranked high tensile pressed steel chassis side frame of deep section, braced by large diameter tubular cross members. The side members were upswept at front and rear. All spring and brake brackets were bolted on

1934 Karrier E4 211 (11) with MCCW all metal body waits at Cosham Railway Station terminus on 18 April 1949. Traffic stands at Cosham Railway Station level crossing gates, in the background behind 211, until a train passes. Many late-1940s views of Portsmouth trolleybuses feature advertisements for Tyne Brand products. The company originated from North Shields on the River Tyne as fish canners in 1901 and gradually expanding their range to include meat products, military rations and soups. Since acquisition by Spillers in 1967 the brand name has had various owners and still appears on tinned foods today. (Online Transport Archive [photographer V.C. Jones])

with fitted bolts in reamed holes. There were towing loops front and rear. A Tecalemit grouped-nipple chassis lubrication system was used.

Chassis length: 25ft 8¾in.
Chassis frame width: Front 3ft 3⅜in.; rear 3ft 8in.
Overall width (over tyres): 7ft 4⅜in.
Frame height from ground between axles loaded: 1ft 11½in.
Frame height of rear platform from ground loaded: 11in.

A high tensile steel, drop forged front axle equipped with enclosed cam and roller steering was used, the weight on the steering pivots taken by taper roller bearings. The hubs were mounted on taper roller bearings and Karrier rear axles were used.

Both front and rear springs were of the semi-elliptical type made from silico-manganese steel with solid eyes incorporated at the anchored end. Shackles were adjustable for side wear. Rubber buffers limited the spring deflection. Front springs were 44in. by 3½in. and the rear 59⅞in. by 3½in.

An inverted worm-driven rear axle, with fully floating hubs mounted on roller bearings, was used. The axle casings were one piece nickel steel drop forgings with the differential casing offset to the nearside. A large diameter transmission shaft with needle roller type universal joints was fitted.

The chassis including electrical equipment cost £1073.

Electrics: The BTH201 traction motor was mounted amidships carried in a sub-frame within the chassis frame, slightly offset to the nearside, and mounted on rubber bushes providing a floating suspension and easy removal for overhaul purposes (being retained by just four bolts). The motor was skewed at an angle towards the rear nearside and tilting downwards towards the rear to ensure a straight drive line between the motor shaft, the propeller shaft and the rear differential which was offset to the nearside to avoid any obstruction of the gangway.

The resistances were placed amidships mounted on the outside of the nearside chassis frame with a steel shield and stone guard beneath to protect the grids. The starting and braking resistances were of the rustless grid type, consisting of a continuous strip bent into grid form and supported on insulated rods thereby reducing the number of joints to a minimum. The shunt field resistances consisted of vitreous enamel tubes mounted in a frame with a louvred protecting cover. The full field speed was kept at a low figure to reduce rheostatic losses on starting. The BTH master controller was located beneath the driver's seat and operated by an organ type pedal controlled by the driver's right foot. The master controller and the contactor gear were carried on two aluminium dashes fitted to the chassis on the nearside of the driver's cab.

At the rear of the catwalk substantial cross-braced trolleyboom retaining hooks were fitted as an integral part of a metal frame including an access step from the emergency door.

Traction batteries for manoeuvring purposes were not fitted.

Brakes: This trolleybus was believed to have been equipped with G. D. Peters compressed air brakes, as well as rheostatic and hand brakes.

Shoes were of the internal expanding type housed in a 17in. diameter iron alloy drum. Brake air-pressure cylinders were mounted on the front axle swivels (operated through push rods passing through the kingpins) and on the main frame side members for the rear axle shoes. Total area of the brake linings was 536 square inches.

The motor compressor unit was mounted on an insulated base on the offside of the main frame.

The handbrake lever was to the offside of the driver's steering column.

Bodywork: The bodywork was basically identical to that fitted to 1934 Sunbeam MF2 10 and thus one of the final MCCW bodies built to this 'interim' Birmingham design. It cost £833. The detail differences were:

Top hinged access doors were fitted at the base of the lower-deck off-side panel bays 2 and 3 providing access to the air brake compressor unit and motor mounted on the outside of the off-side chassis member, and on the nearside in bay 2 providing access to the shunt resistance and low voltage generator set mounted on the outside of the nearside chassis member.

There is no evidence that a chassis and/or equipment maker's badge was ever fitted.

A wheel nut cover, which was used as a step into the driver's cab, was fitted to both front wheels.

Lighting: See trolleybus 10.

Seating: See trolleybus 10.

Destination equipment: See trolleybus 10.

Internal Livery: See trolleybus 10.

External Livery: Delivered in Livery 1 (see Appendix C).

Subsequent alterations

In April 1935 a circular conductor's mirror was fixed in the upper deck rear offside dome at the head of the stairs.

A spot light was fitted beneath the flat front panel aligned with the nearside headlight.

A small rectangular driver's rear view mirror was mounted externally towards the top of the nearside front cab pillar.

In 1938, 11 was renumbered as 211. It is not known if 11 and potentially the other MCCW-bodied trolleybuses were delivered with a square metal fleet number plate, as 14, or with Bakelite discs displaying the fleet number inside the upper and lower saloons. Thus it is not known how the 1938 renumbering affected this vehicle.

211 retained its semaphore arm traffic indicators throughout.

Notes:

11 was the third trolleybus to arrive in Portsmouth on 24 July 1934.

211 was withdrawn from service and placed in open storage on waste ground to the east of Northern Parade in September 1940. The trolleybus was reinstated into service in July 1946.

Disposal

211 Last licensed September 1949; subsequently taken out of passenger service and stored at North End (1951) until sold (January 1954) to Kingsway Coachworks, Emsworth, Hampshire, and broken up.

1934 AEC 663T/English Electric H32/28R

Fleet No.	1938 No.	Reg. No.	Chassis	Chassis No.	Body	Body No.	Into Service	Last licensed	Withdrawn	Sold
12	212	RV4658	AEC663T	074	Eng. Electric		14.08.1934	09.1939	1946	23.01.1954

Last licensed = the final month in which the vehicle was licensed to operate.

Chassis: Three axle type AEC 663T manufactured by the Associated Equipment Company Ltd. at the AEC works, Windmill Lane, Southall, Middlesex.
Motor: English Electric Co. Ltd., Phoenix Works, Bradford, Yorkshire, Type EE 405 (80 h.p. at 550 volts) compound-wound, regenerative.
Electrical equipment: English Electric Co. Ltd., regenerative control.
Dewirement indicator: neon line-light.
Brakes: Westinghouse compressed air, English Electric electric rheostatic and hand brakes.
Body: English Electric Co. Ltd., Dick, Kerr Works, Preston, Lancashire, composite H32/28R.
Drawing PB33/1226 dated 2 October 1933.
Length: 27ft 5½in.; width 7ft 4in. over pillars.
Height laden: 14ft 1in.
Wheelbase: 16ft 6in.
Bogie wheelbase: 4ft
Wheel track: Front 6ft 5⅜in.; rear 6ft 2¾in.
Unladen weight: 8 tons 6 cwt 2 qtr
Tyres: 36in. by 8in. high-pressure pneumatic singles on all wheels
Frame overall length: 26ft 9in.
Height of frame laden: 22½in.
Turning circle diameter: 59ft
Chassis weight: 4 tons 4 cwt.

The contract price was £2,068. The final price upon completion was £2,021 13s 6d.

Chassis: Conventional cranked chassis frame over rear bogie based on the AEC Regent 663 motorbus chassis and axles.

The side members were pressed out of 5⁄16in. steel with a maximum depth of 11⅛in. and 3in. wide flanges swept over the front and rear axles to permit the mounting of a low floor level body. The arches over the rear bogie were reinforced by inserted channels of the same thickness. The frame was held rigid by tubular cross-members; however, there were no dumb irons, the ends of the frame channels being left open and protruding about 10in. in front of the foremost cross-member.

The axles were made from 100 ton steel 3in. in diameter and mounted on adjustable taper roller bearings. A chrome vanadium spring steel torque blade was used permitting freedom of motion of each axle. The socket attachments of this cross-member formed a rigid assembly with the front end of the front axle spring anchorages and, on the offside, the steering box. The rear ends of the 50in. long front axle spring are shackled by a similar arrangement to the second chassis cross-member. The 57in. long cantilever springs of the rear axles were centrally pivoted upon needle-roller trunnion bearings carried by cast-steel brackets mounted beneath the wheel arches, to which they were riveted and joined by a large cross-tube. The ends of the springs had solid eyes and were anchored to brackets under the axle tubes.

The rear axles were one-piece nickel steel forgings with fully floating shafts, the drive being from underslung worms with 7in. centres (ratio 10.3 to 1). The hubs are forged alloy steel.

AEC663T/English Electric 12 in London Road, Hilsea, outside the 'Coach & Horses' public house on 16 September 1934. (D.A.P. Janes [photographer G.A. Tucker])

There was a short tubular propeller shaft, fitted with a Hardy-Spicer needle-roller self-aligning bearing universal joint at each end, connecting the traction motor with the foremost rear axle where there was a third differential to ensure an even distribution of the driving torque between the two rear axles. Steering was by AEC Marles worm and nut.

The chassis, including electrical equipment, cost £1,230.

Electrics: The series-wound box frame self-ventilated inter-polar traction motor was mounted amidships and offset to the nearside between the chassis frame members. There was a single armature mounted in roller bearings. Carbon brushes were carried in four holders provided with radial adjustment, and inspection of the commutator and brush gear was facilitated by two large removable covers. The armature bearings were packed with grease, requiring replenishment by grease gun every 3 months. The armature could be easily removed. The ventilator fan was fitted at the rear end of the armature shaft. Maximum temperature rise was 35°C under service conditions, well below the maximum of BESA requirements. At the rear end of the armature shaft there was a speedometer drive.

All electrical equipment, including the contactor panel, was mounted in an insulated unit on the nearside chassis frame member. There were two groups of cables carried under the frame channel sheathed in rubber ply tubing.

The upper-deck body pillars slotted into the wooden rail of the framework above the upper saloon windows, i.e. the cantrail. There were curved steel brackets bolted to the metal roof (inside the roof there was a steel strengthening plate on each side) and each end of the three transverse pressed steel girders, between bays 1 and 2, bays 2 and 3, and bays 3 and 4, supporting the exposed trolley gantry, which was not in direct contact with the roof, rested on these brackets, each foot being secured by four metal bolts.

The main power cable made its way forward from the trolley gantry along the centre line of the roof before entered the front dome about 1ft 6in. to the rear of the metal louvres above the front upper-deck windows. The vehicle was equipped with Brecknell, Willis and Co. Ltd., Bristol, lightweight trolley equipment and trolley bases. The booms were 18ft 6in. long, equipped with de-wirement buffers; these allowed for up to 13ft deviation from the centre line of the overhead. Radio interference suppressors were mounted towards the centre of the roof in bay 2 but to the nearside and offside of the trolley gantry. The access catwalk on the roof had two steps above the rear dome beneath the trolley boom retaining hooks.

Traction batteries for manoeuvring purposes were not fitted.

Brakes: A Westinghouse two-cylinder reciprocating compressor, with 5 cubic feet capacity and driven by an EEC 500-volt motor, was carried on the offside of the chassis frame, from which it was electrically and mechanically insulated. The compressor was equipped with an anti-freezer, the intake to which was connected by a short rubber tube (for insulation) to one of the chassis cross members, which was utilised as an intake silencer, the air being admitted at the farther end through a filter. The air reservoir and governor were attached forward of the compressor on insulated mountings with a buffer chamber on the compressor side of the valve. The governor was set to maintain a reservoir pressure of 85 lb per square inch and the control valve was operated by an organ type pedal mounted on the bracket carrying both the valve and power pedal. Reservoir and brake cylinder pressures were shown on gauges on the dashboard attached to the driver's steering column.

The front brake drums were 17in. diameter castings with 3in. wide facings ¾in. thick. The track rods were adjustable by means of screwed and clipped ends. All four wheels of the rear bogie were fitted with 17in. diameter brake drums having 6in. wide facings ¾in. thick. The total effective brake area was 825 square inches.

Apart from a single flexible pipe connection, all air piping was solid drawn steel. Air cylinders were mounted on the cross tube in front of the rear bogie, whence rod connections were taken to double-armed levers on a cross-shaft carried behind the central bogie cross-member. The lower arms of the levers were coupled by pull rods to the cam levers on the leading axle any by tubular push-rods to the rear axle levers. The same mechanism was used by the handbrake. The front wheel brake cylinders were mounted on top of the king pins, the piston rods passing through the borings in the latter and operating directly on the camshaft.

Regenerative braking was obtained by the driver relieving pressure on the master controller (power) pedal so that the controller returned towards the full field position. Braking was increased as the pedal rose and strengthened the shunt field in stages. In the first notch position rheostatic braking was obtained. Regeneration was effective down to a speed of c. 12 m.p.h. and rheostatic braking down to c. 4 m.p.h.

Pull-on handbrakes linked by a cross-shaft, and pull and push rods to the camshaft levers and expanding in the bogie wheel brake drums to operate on the same pairs of shoes as those operated by the air brake system. The handbrake lever was to the offside of the driver's steering column.

Bodywork: Highbridge double-deck composite six bay construction with conventional, enclosed forward-ascending half-turn (90°) staircase with semi-vestibuled open platform entrance and exit at the rear, and roof ribbing. The body cost £838.

There was a slight 'tumble-under' to the lower deck side and rear panels with a shallow roof. The front elevation rose in a convex rake to the upper-deck waistline. Above the upper-deck waistline the front panel adopted a shallow 'vee' on plan which was retained for the slightly raked upper saloon front windows. There was a pronounced overhang, incorporating a ventilator above each pane, to the front dome. A double fold at the base of the upper-deck side panels around the vehicle provided a gutter. The trolley poles were fitted on an exposed roof-mounted gantry above bays 2 and 3.

Metal louvres were fitted above the upper and lower saloon side windows. Half-drop openers equipped with a single 'pinch fastener' centrally at the top of each pane were fitted to the top rail of the side windows in bays 1, 3, 5 on both sides of the upper deck, and bays 2, 3, 4 on both sides of the lower deck. The upper saloon front windows were fixed. The upper pane dropped outside the fixed lower pane. Additional ventilation to the upper saloon was provided by two ventilators in the roof overhang above the front windows and somewhat closer to the corner pillars than to the central pillar, and four roof-mounted ventilators (with circular chromed covers inside) positioned midway along bays 1 and 5 on each side. Top hinged access doors were fitted at the base of the lower-deck off-side panel bay 1, 2, 3 and part of 4 providing access to the air brake compressor unit and on the nearside from approximately midway across bay 2 to midway across bay 3 providing access to the contactors in an insulated unit mounted on the nearside chassis member.

A bamboo trolley retrieval pole was carried within the lower saloon nearside body panels at vent panel height (behind the cove panels) with a tube access above the nearside bulkhead window from the rear platform vestibule.

The top corners of the rear platform window and the top outer corners of the windows of the upper deck emergency exit were radiused, the gutter around the edge of the roof curving down the upper deck rear corner panel to end beneath the emergency exit windows (that on the nearside reaching the beading at the base of the upper deck waistband). There was a rail across the panes at two thirds depth. The rear upper deck emergency door was attached by four hinges at its base and had a central opening handle at the top; it could be retained open by leather-covered chains on each side to provide access to the trolley gantry.

The emergency door could be opened by an external handle mounted on the rear dome immediately above the rain strip and centrally above the door, or from inside by a comparable handle attached to a horizontal locking bar mounted on the cantrail immediately above the door. The horizontal bar was equipped with three prongs that engaged with brackets on the top of the door.

Small rubber bumpers on the nearside and offside of the emergency exit door aligned with similar bumpers on the nearside and offside top corners of the rear indicator boxes. Handrails were covered in black Doverite.

The staircase had three steps from the platform to the landing and then a further three steps to the upper deck, each riser having aluminium kicking panels. The platform entrance was 4ft wide.

Bell pushes were mounted in the lower saloon on the nearside in the cove panels at the top of the pillar between bay 2 and bay 3; in the upper saloon on the nearside in the top rail of the window frames at the top of the pillar between bay 1 and bay 2, and on the offside at the top of the pillar between bay 6 and bay 7; and on the rear platform above the bulkhead window.

The fleet number was displayed inside the vehicle by a small white Bakelite oval disc screwed at cantrail height above the central front pillar in the upper saloon and on the front bulkhead in the lower saloon upon which the numbers were painted in black.

The driver's cab was equipped with a single opening windscreen on the off-side, the upper pane being approximately double the depth of the lower pane, equipped with a central top-mounted windscreen wiper and painted frame. There was a single nearside fixed windscreen and a front hinged (three hinges) cab door on the offside only, with a square top. Two rubber bumpers at waist rail height, one on the door and the other on the side panel forward of the door, prevented body damage by a swinging door. The window of the offside cab door was divided horizontally into two panes, the upper portion being slightly deeper than the lower and an inset opening handle. The lower pane was equipped with a sliding 'signalling' window, the rear portion sliding forwards behind the front portion. There was a large fixed side window between the cab door and the front offside corner pillar. There was a matching panel and two windows on the nearside, the rear of the two windows being vertically divided and enabling the rear pane to slide forwards outside the fixed front pane. A pronounced, square vent was positioned on both sides of the cab beneath the foremost windows on each side. The driver's cab side windows were the same depth as, and aligned with, the lower saloon side windows although this was not immediately evident due to the encroachment of the louvres above the saloon windows.

The base of the cab door was curved over the wheel arch to a position about 4in. from the rear of the door thereafter the base was horizontal, parallel to the white-painted waistband and about 2ft below it. A rectangular step was let into the upper part of the bay 1 side panel access door, but without any form of protection to the bodywork, immediately behind the front axle, on the offside. Both front wheels were fitted with chromed hub bosses and wheel nut guard rings. Individual mud flaps hung behind each wheel with a further mud flap extending the width of the vehicle diagonally beneath the rear platform.

There were two glazed panels in the bulkhead behind the driver, separated by a wide central pillar. A small rectangular driver's rear view mirror was mounted externally on an outrigger aligned to the top of the lower fixed pane of the windscreen, immediately above the trafficator, on the offside front cab pillar.

The vehicle was delivered without a chassis and equipment maker's badge.

A large removable panel with three columns of eight louvred ventilation vanes extended across the base of the front panel between the two low-mounted headlights (the top of the panel aligned with the top of the headlight rim) with the front registration number plate centred immediately above.

The rear registration number plate, encompassing a single red rear light to the offside of the upper row of letters, was affixed to the white-painted panel immediately above the rear platform window on the offside.

A small rectangular white enamelled Police Licence plate with black lettering was displayed at the nearside base of the rear panel adjacent to the platform.

A single tubular lifeguard, held by attachments beneath the body panels, ran beneath the side panels between the front and rear axles.

Lighting: External lighting was by two chrome-rimmed headlights on wooden plinths mounted at the base of the front panel with two front chrome-rimmed side lights also on wooden plinths immediately above mounted slightly more towards the extremity of the panel and aligned with the outer edges of the headlights. A spotlight was mounted beneath the nearside end of the nearside column of ventilation louvres in the removable front panel. A single red rear light was incorporated into the rear registration number plate, immediately above the rear platform window on the offside.

Semaphore arm, illuminated traffic indicators accommodated in a black moulding were fitted in the lower half of the driver's cab corner pillars on both sides. At the rear, an inset panel mounted centrally beneath the rear platform window illuminated to show STOP when the brakes were applied.

There were square diffused light fittings in the ceiling cove panels in the lower saloon mounted centrally in bays 1 to 6 each side (12); and in the upper saloon in bays 1 to 6 on each side (12), the position in bay 1 being immediately to the rear of the body pillar but then progressively a little further towards the rear in each bay so that by bay 6 the fitting was in the centre of the bay, and one in the offside of the rear dome above the staircase. There was a further fitting in the rear dome above the staircase and above the rear platform.

Seating: The lower saloon had a four-person inwards-facing bench seat with 5ft 6in. cushion on each side over the rear axle and five rows of forward-facing double seats at 2ft 5½in. pitch. The upper saloon had seven rows of double seats at 2ft 7in. pitch on the off-side and nine rows at 2ft 6in. on the nearside (the bench seat at the rear of the upper saloon above the open platform also accommodated two passengers). The seat cushions were covered in moquette. Vertical handrails rose up behind the third and fifth seat on the nearside and the second and fourth seat on the offside of the lower saloon and the third and fifth seat on the nearside and second and fourth seat on the offside of the upper saloon. There were black Doverite coated ceiling mounted handrails equipped with short leather straps above the lower saloon gangway parallel with the longitudinal seats. The driver's seat was in brown leather.

Destination equipment: A large rectangular indicator box 36in. by 14in. displayed three lines of information (final destination and two lines of intermediate points), with a square service number indicator box 14in. by 14in. alongside, were mounted centrally at the front and rear in the lower two-thirds of the upper-deck panels. At the front the destination and intermediate points indicator box was on the nearside above the driver's cab windscreen (but encroaching a quarter of the way above the offside windscreen) and at the rear on the offside above the rear platform window. At the front the service number indicator box was on the offside and at the rear on the nearside.

There was a narrow box 24in. by 6in. capable of displaying the final destination or the final destination and an intermediate point (two lines) located inside the lower saloon at the top of the bay 6 window both sides.

Internal livery: The interior panels and rear corner panels were lined with scratchproof brown Rexine with window mouldings and finishings in French-polished walnut. The cove panels were edged in darker trim and the ceilings were cream. The cab was brown with a cream ceiling.

External livery: 12 entered service in Livery 1 (see Appendix C). There is nothing to indicate that this vehicle ever received a repaint and it never carried the white fleet numerals applied from June 1938 onwards immediately beneath the lower deck waist rail and lining on both sides to the rear of the driver's cab rear bulkhead.

Notes

12 arrived in Portsmouth on 12 August 1934. It was de-licensed on 17 November 1937 and although re-licensed in July 1939 as 212 this was only for a 3-month period during which it only ran on 3 days: 7 July 1939 (40 miles), 12 July 1939 (168) and 20 July 1939 (60).

212 was withdrawn from service and placed in open storage on waste ground in Northern Parade in late 1940. In August 1942 it was prepared for loan to Pontypridd UDC and towed to South Wales reaching Pontypridd on 8 August 1942.

At 9.20 p.m. on 25 April 1944 whilst operating in service in Pontypridd, trolleybus 212 ran away down Corn Stores Hill due to a braking defect and only due to the driver's skill and reactions was it finally eventually brought to a stop half way across Victoria Bridge thereby preventing a serious accident.

The trolleybus was returned to Portsmouth in late April 1946, towed by George Park and Co., hauliers of Portsmouth, and stored in Eastney Depot Yard. It was never reinstated into service although official records state that in April 1950 it was 'scheduled for complete overhaul'.

Subsequent alterations

A chassis and equipment maker's badge, AEC in an inverted triangle surmounted by the winged EE symbol, was fitted centrally beneath the driver's windscreen below the waistband in September 1934.

An oblong conductor's mirror was fitted in April 1935 in the upper saloon rear dome above the stairs.

The shallow windscreen provided the driver with a restricted view of the overhead line above. A small recessed window in the white-painted central band or cantrail, above but not as wide as the offside windscreen, was added to improve the line of vision by summer 1935.

External advertising began to be displayed on the offside lower deck panels by August 1935.

The original small offside driver's rear view mirror mounted on an outrigger was replaced by a somewhat larger rectangular mirror mounted towards the top of the offside front cab pillar

In 1938, 12 was re-numbered 212. On the front and rear panels an additional '2' prefixed the original fleet number resulting in an off-centre appearance. The Bakelite discs displaying the fleet number inside the upper and lower saloons were reversed and the new number painted thereon when renumbering took place.

Photographic evidence shows that during its time on loan to Pontypridd UDC there was only one semaphore arm illuminated traffic indicator on the offside.

When 212 returned from Pontypridd it was equipped with three supporting hooks in the nearside ventilator panel fixed centrally above the pillars between bays 1 and 2, 3 and 4, and 5 and 6 for carrying the bamboo trolley retrieval pole. It is not known when this was fitted.

Disposal

212 Withdrawn on 21 April 1953. Sold July 1953 to Kingsway Coachworks (dealer), Emsworth, Hampshire, for £40, but considered unsafe to be moved and broken up in situ January 1954 in Eastney Depot Yard.

1934 Sunbeam MS3/English Electric H32/28R

Fleet No.	1938 No.	Reg. No.	Chassis	Chassis No.	Body	Body No.	Into Service	Last licensed	Withdrawn	Sold
13	213	RV4659	Sunbeam MS3	12042S	Eng. Electric		06.08.1934	08.1949	21.04.1953	23.01.1954

Last licensed = the final month in which the vehicle was licensed to operate.

Chassis: Three-axle type Sunbeam MS3 manufactured by Sunbeam Motor Car Ltd., Moorfield Road, Wolverhampton.
Motor: British Thomson-Houston Co. Ltd., Rugby, Warwickshire, Type 201BXY (80hp at 550 volts) with overwound series field for regulated field control.
Electrical equipment: British Thomson-Houston Co. Ltd., Rugby, Warwickshire, Regulated Field Control (No. 201 Form DK).
De-wirement indicator: Assumed to have been fitted with line-lights.
Brakes: Lockheed vacuum assisted hydraulic, BTH electric rheostatic and hand brakes.
Body: English Electric Co. Ltd., Dick, Kerr Works, Preston, Lancashire, composite H32/28R. Drawing PB33/1226 dated 2 October 1933.
Length: 27ft 5½in.
Width: 7ft 4in. over pillars.
Height laden 14ft 1 in.
Wheelbase: 16ft 8in. from front axle to centre of bogie, giving a turning circle of less than 60ft.
Bogie wheelbase: 3ft 11¼in.
Unladen weight: 8 tons 13 cwt 2 qtr
Tyres: 10.5in. by 20in. low-pressure singles on all wheels
Track: Front axle 6ft 6⅜in., rear axle 6ft 6in.

Only in November 1934 did Sunbeam separate its trolleybus activities from its private car business renaming as Sunbeam Commercial Vehicles Ltd., which from July 1935 became part of the Rootes Group.

The Sunbeam MS3 chassis was designed to take a low-loading double-deck body, the low-loading line being achieved by offsetting the motor and transmission.

All but three of the Sunbeam MS3 chassis built were bought by Wolverhampton Corporation Transport, the exceptions beings Portsmouth 13 and 14, and Huddersfield 4.

The contract price was £2,025. The final price upon completion was £1,947 13s 6d.

Chassis: The main frame was constructed from high tensile steel with a depth of 11in. in the most heavily loaded portions and 3in. wide flanges.

Marles cam and roller type steering, requiring 4¼ turns of the wheel from lock to lock. The side steering connection was made from weldless steel tube, the ball sockets being formed solid with the tube.

The front axle was of the reversed Elliott type with an "I" section beam 4in. deep and 3in. wide. The thrust on the king pin was taken on a taper roller bearing. Underslung worm type rear axles were used, the main axle casing being made from

On its way south to Southsea South Parade Pier Sunbeam MS3/English Electric 13 is seen in Kingston Road at New Road on 17 August 1935. The driving position of this trolleybus and other of the experimental vehicles was rather high and a small recessed window has already been added to improve the driver's view of the overhead line above. Note the two broad red bands on the traction pole to the nearside of the trolleybus indicating a compulsory stop. A Southdown Motor Services Tilling Stevens Express motorbus (UF7364) brings up the rear. (D.A.P. Janes [photographer G.A. Tucker])

a steel drop forging. The differential was made up of four planet wheels and two sun wheels, contained in a steel cage to which was also mounted the worm and wheel (ratio 9.33 to 1). The worms were of hardened and ground steel meshing with a phosphor bronze wheel, mounted on ball bearings. A short propeller shaft, fitted with a universal joint at each end, connected the traction motor with the foremost rear axle where there was a third differential to ensure an even distribution of the driving torque between the two rear axles.

All wheels were fitted with cast steel hubs mounted on taper roller bearings. The front brake drums were 16¾in. diameter alloy castings with 3⅜in. wide shoes. The track rods were adjustable by means of screwed and clipped ends. All four wheels of the rear bogie were fitted with brake drums of 19¾in. diameter with 4in. wide shoes. The brake shoes on all six drums were suitable for ⅜in. linings.

Chassis length: 27ft 5½ in.
Frame height (laden): 2ft.
Frame height at platform end (laden): 1ft 11in.
The chassis, including electrical equipment, cost £1,187.

Electrics: The traction motor was mounted on a separate sub-frame amidships but on the offside of the vehicle within the chassis frame. It was attached to the main chassis frame at four points and insulated from the main frame and the transmission to permit the use of all-metal bodies by shock-absorbing and noise-reducing Silentbloc rubber bushes on the steel fixing bolts. The motor protruded a few inches above the top of the frame but as it was located beneath the lower saloon seats it did not encroach on the gangway floor space.

The resistances were also placed amidships mounted on the nearside within the chassis frame with a steel shield and stone guard beneath to protect the grids. The contactor panels were in the driver's cab. The contactors which short-circuited sections of the shunt field resistance were mounted on a panel secured to the dashboard in front of the driver, while those which made and broke the line circuit and short-circuit the starting resistance section were secured to the dashboard and the cab bulkhead. The full field speed was kept at a low figure to reduce rheostatic losses on starting. The master controller was operated by an organ type pedal beneath the driver's right foot.

Choke capacity filters were provided in the contactor circuits and radio interference coils were mounted centrally on the roof in front of the trolley gantry in an effort to eliminate radio interference. The main cable runs carried within the frame channel were encased in flexible metallic tubing.

The upper-deck body pillars slotted into the wooden rail of the framework above the upper saloon windows, i.e. the cantrail. There were curved steel brackets bolted to the metal roof (inside the roof there was a steel strengthening plate on each side) and each end of the three transverse pressed steel girders, between bays 1 and 2, bays 2 and 3 and bays 3 and 4, supporting the exposed trolley gantry, which was not in direct contact with the roof, rested on these brackets, each foot being secured by four metal bolts.

The main power cable made its way forward from the trolley gantry along the centre line of the roof before entered the front dome about 1ft 6in. to the rear of the metal louvres above the front upper-deck windows. The vehicle was equipped with Brecknell, Willis & Co. Ltd., Bristol, lightweight trolley equipment and trolley bases. These permitted a reduced spring pressure of less than 30lb. The booms were 18ft long and equipped with de-wirement buffers. The access catwalk on the roof had two steps above the rear dome beneath the utilitarian trolley boom retaining hooks.

A Sunbeam motor generator set provided low voltage (24 volt) power for lighting and auxiliary equipment. The battery was only used to supply the small demands of the side and rear lights, and regularly-used accessories such as the screen wiper, horn, bells, etc. The main current load was supplied direct from the motor generator. When the saloon lights were switched on the motor generator started and then supplied all lights and accessories whilst the battery was charged.

Traction batteries for manoeuvring purposes were not fitted.

Brakes: Lockheed vacuum assisted hydraulic brakes were fitted, activated by the brake pedal and operating on all wheels. Movement of the brake pedal was transmitted by push-rod to the master cylinder bolted to the chassis frame. Three 1½in. diameter master cylinders in a single casting were operated by a single pivoted lever formed with three ball-ended arms. Each cylinder operated the brakes on an axle; the outer casing of the master cylinder unit formed a reservoir to maintain the system full of fluid. A compensating and sealing unit was secured to a machined face on the front of the main casting housing three rubber cups and needle valves. When the brake pedal was depressed, pressure was created in the master cylinders making the rubber cups lift and unseating the needle valves thereby compensating for any discrepancies between the cylinders and ensuring equal braking effort on all axles. In the case of any leakage in one of three braking systems, the rubber cup of the affected system did not lift but the other two systems were unaffected.

All brake shoes were expanded hydraulically by 2in.-diameter application cylinders operating short push-rods and connected to the master cylinders by copper tubing and flexible hoses. A 4in. wide pair of brake shoes was applied within each drum and expanded independently by the hydraulic system or the handbrake lever.

A pull-on handbrake linked mechanically by rods acted on all the rear wheels and operated on the same pairs of shoes as those operated by the hydraulic system. The handbrake lever was to the offside of the driver's steering column.

Bodywork: The bodywork was basically identical to that fitted to 1934 AEC663T 12 and cost £838.

Lighting: See 12.

Seating: See 12.

Destination equipment: See 12.

Internal livery: See 12.

External livery: Delivered in Livery 1 (see Appendix C).

By August 1935 advertisements were displayed on the offside rearmost panels at window height and on the lower deck body panels behind the staircase.

There is nothing to indicate that this vehicle ever received a repaint and it never carried the white fleet numerals applied from June 1938 onwards immediately beneath the lower deck waist rail and lining on both sides to the rear of the driver's cab rear bulkhead.

Notes

No. 13 arrived in Portsmouth on 5 August 1934. It was de-licensed on 13 November 1937 and only infrequently used in 1938 and 1939. In 1938, it was renumbered as 213.

No. 213 was withdrawn from service and placed in open storage on waste ground in Northern Parade in late 1940. In August 1942 it was prepared for loan to Pontypridd UDC and towed to South Wales reaching Pontypridd on 14 August 1942.

The trolleybus was returned to Portsmouth on 3 November 1945, towed by George Park & Co., hauliers of Portsmouth, and stored in Eastney Depot before being reinstated to service in February 1949 still in full pre-war livery (Livery 1) but with a matt grey roof. It was licensed until 31 August 1949 and then saw no further service. It was stored at North End Depot from 1951.

Subsequent alterations

In April 1935 an oblong conductor's mirror was fixed in the upper deck rear offside dome at the head of the stairs.

The original small offside driver's rear view mirror mounted on an outrigger was replaced by a somewhat larger rectangular mirror mounted towards the top of the offside front cab pillar. However, there is photographic evidence showing 13 circulating with both the small and large rear view mirrors in August 1935.

The shallow windscreen provided the driver with a restricted view of the overhead line above. A small recessed window in the white-painted central band or cantrail above but not as wide as the offside windscreen was added to improve the line of vision by August 1935. At some date between November 1945 and March 1949 both near and offside windscreens were increased in depth incorporating the small recessed window. The nearside windscreen retained a single fixed pane.

External advertising began to be displayed on the offside lower deck panels by August 1935.

It is believed that the semaphore arm illuminated traffic indicators had been removed by the time of the vehicle's loan to Pontypridd UDC.

Disposal

213 Withdrawn on 21 April 1953, it remained at North End until sold 23 January 1954 for £40 to Kingsway Coachworks, Emsworth, Hampshire and broken up.

1934 Sunbeam MS3/Metro-Cammell H32/28R

Fleet No.	1938 No.	Reg. No.	Chassis	Chassis No.	Body	Body No.	Into Service	Last licensed	Withdrawn	Sold
14	214	RV4662	Sunbeam MS3	12026S	MCCW		11.07.1934	09.1949	21.04.1953	23.01.1954

Last licensed = the final month in which the vehicle was licensed to operate.

Chassis: Three-axle type Sunbeam MS3 manufactured by Sunbeam Motor Car Ltd., Moorfield Road, Wolverhampton.
Motor: British Thomson-Houston Co. Ltd., Rugby, Warwickshire, Type 202BXY (80hp at 550 volts) compound-wound main field for regenerative control.
Electrical equipment: British Thomson-Houston Co. Ltd., Rugby, Warwickshire, Regenerative Control (No. 201 Form DK).
Brakes: Lockheed vacuum assisted hydraulic brakes, BTH regenerative electric, BTH electric rheostatic and hand brakes.
Body: Metropolitan-Cammell Weymann Motor Bodies Ltd., Midland Works, Saltley, Birmingham, all metal H32/28R.
Length: Not known, recommended body length in 1933–34 was 27ft 1¾in.
Width 7ft 6 in.
Wheelbase: 16ft 8in. from front axle to centre of bogie
Bogie wheelbase: 3ft 11¼in.
Track: Front axle 6ft 6⅜in., rear axle 6ft 6in.
Height: Not known.
Unladen weight: 8 tons 13 cwt 2 qtr.
Tyres: Single, 36in. by 8 in. high pressure all round.

Only in November 1934 did Sunbeam separate its trolleybus activities from its private car business renaming as Sunbeam Commercial Vehicles Ltd., which from July 1935 became part of the Rootes Group.

The Sunbeam MS3 chassis was designed to take a low-loading double-deck body, the low-loading line being achieved by offsetting the motor and transmission.

All but three of the Sunbeam MS3 chassis built were bought by Wolverhampton Corporation Transport, the exceptions beings Portsmouth 13 and 14, and Huddersfield 4.

The contract price was £2,095. The final price upon completion was £2,017 13s 6d.

Chassis: Conventional cranked chassis frame over rear bogie with special insulation points for all-metal bodies.

The chassis, including electrical equipment, cost £1,208.

All other details – see No. 13.

Electrics: The exposed trolley gantry was constructed of pressed steel Welsh hat and channel sections framed together and mounted on the upper deck cantrail structure. The Brecknell Willis lightweight trolley base was mounted as follows: a steel plate, to both sides of which insulating rubber was moulded through holes in the plate and mounted between the channel members of the gantry. The moulded rubber and plate were of similar construction to that then used for railway carriage buffers and draw-gear springs by Messrs Spencer Moulton. The bolts securing the trolley base passed entirely through the rubber and could not come into contact with any portion of the steel structure providing a resilient mounting, insulated electrically from the vehicles' body, and reducing the transmission of trolley noises to the interior. A rubber covered plate with its front and rear edges bent upwards to ensure that rain water ran off at the sides, provided dry-spot insulation between the trolley base and its rubber mounting.

Sunbeam MS3 14 equipped with MCCW all-metal body (official view). (David Beilby collection [BTH])

The full field speed was kept at a low figure to reduce rheostatic losses on starting and to ensure that regeneration was obtained over the widest possible range of speeds.

All other details – see No. 13.

Brakes: See No. 13.

Regenerative braking was obtained by the driver relieving pressure on the master controller (power) pedal so that the controller returned towards the full field position. Braking was increased as the pedal rose and strengthened the shunt field. The starting resistance was held out of circuit until the controller reached the "off" position, providing full regeneration down to a speed of c. 10mph. A relay was mounted on the shunt field resistance contactor panel to insert resistance in the lamp circuit should a dangerous rise in voltage occur; for example, due to an interruption of the main circuit during generation, which would otherwise burn out the lamps. Rheostatic braking came into operation when the braking effort due to regeneration fell to a low value.

Bodywork: All metal (patented) six-bay Highbridge double-deck construction, forward-ascending half-turn (90°) staircase with conventional semi-vestibuled open platform entrance and exit at the rear, marketed by Metropolitan-Cammell Weymann Motor Bodies Ltd. and built by The Metropolitan-Cammell Carriage, Wagon and Finance Company Company Ltd., Midland Works, Saltley, Birmingham. The design was based on that of contemporary Birmingham Tramway and Omnibus Department (trading as Birmingham City Transport) motorbus and trolleybuses. The body cost £887.

In profile, the front of the body featured a "swept-back" styling between the bulbous nose surmounting the less raked front panel of the driver's cab and the upper deck roof, the front line of the roof being in line with the front axle. The front of the upper-deck curved gently beneath the "V" shaped fixed front windows; the shallow driver's cab windscreen had a more pronounced "V-shaped" cross-section set back beneath the upper deck front panels and with a bulbous top to the front panel beneath. There was an upright rear profile, the base of the rear panel curving gently in to match the concave side panels. The trolley poles were fitted on an exposed roof-mounted gantry above bay 2. Platform handrails and stanchions were covered with black Doverite.

Brackets were bolted to the roof rail immediately above the upper-deck body pillars between bays 1 and 2, and bays 2 and 3, to support the two girders of the exposed trolley gantry which was mounted above bay 2 and not in direct contact with the roof.

Metal louvres were fitted above the upper and lower deck saloon side windows. Chromium plated half-drop openers with a clip-operated gripper at the top on each side of the upper pane were fitted to the side windows in bays 1, 3 and 5 of both sides of the upper deck, bays 1, 3 and 4 of the lower-deck nearside and bays 1, 2 and 3 of the lower-deck offside. The upper pane dropped outside the fixed lower pane. Immediately above the lower deck side windows in bays 1, 3 and 5, nine-vane ventilation vents slanting rearwards somewhat from the vertical at the top were fitted. There were six roof ventilators, one on each side above and towards the front of bays 1, 4 and 6. At the rear of the upper-saloon there was an emergency door having three hinges at its base and two oblong fixed window panes having slightly rounded upper and lower outer corners and a horizontal rail across both panes. There was an upright opening handle mounted centrally immediately above the gutter in the rear dome above the emergency door and two protective rubber bumpers on the outer frame matching two further bumpers above the indicator screens. The rearmost offside panel behind the staircase was also glazed.

The driver's steering wheel was noticeably raked back. The top two thirds of the offside driver's windscreen was chromium plated and opened outwards. It carried a top-mounted windscreen wiper. There was a front-hinged door on the offside provided with a square sliding "signalling" window in the lower one-third of the pane and an inset, opening handle. There was a large fixed quarter light window between the offside cab door and the cab front corner pillar. On the nearside there was a matching panel and a single window, the window being divided vertically to enable the rear pane to slide forwards outside the fixed front pane. The base of the cab door was curved over the wheel arch to a position about 5in. from the rear of the door, thereafter the base, beneath the cab door handle, was horizontal. Two large hooded inlet ducts were installed on each side above the driver's cab door and side windows; one rose gently upwards from the cab front pillar and one fell gently downwards towards the cab rear bulkhead.

A small "reverse L-shape" protruding step was let into the base of the offside side panel towards the rear of the mudguard, but without any form of protection to the bodywork, immediately behind the front axle, slightly above the height of the wheel hub to aid access to the driver's cab.

There were two glazed panels in the bulkhead behind the driver with two bevel-edged mirrors shaped to match the curve of the ceiling immediately above. The fleet number was displayed inside the vehicle by a small white Bakelite oval disc screwed at cantrail height above the central front pillar in the upper saloon and centrally on the front bulkhead in the lower saloon above the glazed panels upon which the numbers were painted in black. Early manufacturers' photographs show a dark rectangular plate displaying the fleet number in white on the lower saloon bulkhead but it is likely that this was a temporary solution replaced at an early date.

A rectangular driver's rear view mirror was mounted externally towards the top of the offside front cab pillar.

Bell pushes were mounted in the top of the nearside window mouldings in the lower saloon towards the front of bays 2 and 5 and on the rear platform. None are evident in photographs of the upper saloon suggesting that one may have been placed at the top of the staircase.

There was a step up into the lower saloon. The staircase had three steps from the platform to the half-landing and then three steps to the upper deck. There was a single lifeguard rail on each side extending between the flared rear of the front wheel mudguard to the leading rear axle.

There were separate mudguards to the rear wheels and a mud flap hung between the second and third axle.

There were top-hinged valance panels on both the nearside and offside in bays 1, 2, 3 and 4 (part) to access contactor equipment, resistances and other equipment.

The flat front panel incorporated a single fluted column of three horizontal louvred vanes placed centrally and aligned vertically with the centre of the headlamps with the fleet number transferred immediately above. The triangular Sunbeam chassis maker's badge was fitted centrally beneath the driver's windscreen with its base on the beading separating the red and white coloured paint application. There was no removable front panel for towing purposes. The registration number plate was affixed at the base of the front panel. The rear registration number plate, encompassing a single red rear light to the offside of the upper row of letters, was affixed to the white-painted panel immediately above the rear platform window on the offside. The registration number plate was affixed at the base of the front panel. A bamboo trolley retrieval pole was carried within the lower-saloon nearside body panels at waist rail height with a tube access from the rear platform vestibule.

Lighting: External lighting consisted of two headlights mounted half-way up the front panel and noticeably inboard, two circular front side lights exactly on the beading between the red lower panels and the white window area. A single red rear light was incorporated into the rear registration number plate, immediately above the rear platform window on the offside.

At the rear, an inset panel somewhat to the offside of the centre line of the rear panels and aligned with the lower beading of the white-painted waistband beneath the rear platform window illuminated to show STOP when the brakes were applied.

Semaphore arm illuminated traffic indicators accommodated in a black moulding were fitted in the lower half of the driver's cab corner pillars on both sides.

Interior lighting was provided by an installation of 30-volt, 40-watt traction type pearl bulbs.

There were rectangular diffused light fittings in the ceiling cove panels in the lower saloon mounted centrally in bays 1 to 6 on each side (12), and in the upper saloon towards the front of bays 1 to 6 on each side (12), the position in bay 1 being immediately to the rear of the body pillar but then progressively a little further towards the rear in each bay so that by bay 6 the fitting was in the centre of the bay, and one in the offside of the rear dome above the staircase. There was an exposed lamp above the rear platform.

Seating: The sprung squabs were fitted to cast metal frames with black moulded grab handles curving gently upwards on the top of the seat and adjacent to the aisle. The seat frames equipped with grab handles alternated with those having stanchions. There were cigarette stubbers mounted centrally behind the double seats in the upper saloon.

A moquette seat covering was used with a heavy floral pattern motif of black, dark blue and possibly dark green with leather edges.

The lower saloon had a six-person inward-facing bench seat on each side over the rear axles and four rows of forward-facing double seats. The upper saloon had seven rows of double seats on the offside and nine rows on the nearside.

There were upright stanchions covered in black Doverite in both saloons attached to the ceiling, back of the seat and floor:

Lower saloon: Behind seat 2, 4 nearside; seats 1, 3 offside.
Upper saloon: Behind seat 3 nearside; seats 1, 5 offside.

Lower saloon interior view of Sunbeam MS3 14 equipped with MCCW all metal H32/28R body. (Paul Knight collection)

Upper saloon interior view of Sunbeam MS3 14 equipped with MCCW all metal H32/28R body. (Paul Knight collection)

The driver's seat was quilted leather.

Destination equipment: A large rectangular indicator box 36in. by 14in. capable of displaying up to three lines of information (final destination and two lines of intermediate points) with a square service number indicator box 14in. by 14in. alongside were mounted centrally at the front and rear in the lower half of the upper-deck panels. At the front the destination and intermediate points indicator box was on the nearside above the driver's cab windscreen (but encroaching a quarter of the way above the offside windscreen) and at the rear on the offside above the rear platform window. At the front the service number indicator box was on the offside and at the rear on the nearside.

There was a narrow box 24in. by 6in. capable of displaying the final destination or the final destination and an intermediate point (two lines) built into the white-painted vent panel above the rearmost lower saloon window (bay 6) on both sides.

Internal livery: The interior panels and rear corner panels were lined with scratchproof brown Rexine with window mouldings, cove panel edgings and finished in varnished wood. Ceilings and coves were white.

Driver's cab brown with ceiling and upper part of bulkhead white.

The floors were covered in brown linoleum and grey waterproof paint was applied to the rear platform.

External livery: Delivered in Livery 1 (see Appendix C).

The beadings were not picked out in black in the livery originally applied to the Metro-Cammell bodied trolleybuses.

Subsequent alterations: An oblong conductor's mirror was fitted in April 1935 in the upper saloon rear dome above the stairs.

In 1938, 14 was re-numbered 214. On the front and rear panels an additional "2" prefixed the original fleet number resulting in an off-centre appearance. No. 14 and potentially the other MCCW-bodied trolleybuses were delivered with a square metal fleet number plate. It is not known how the 1938 renumbering affected these vehicles.

External advertising began to be displayed on the offside lower deck panels beneath the staircase window by August 1935.

A spotlight was fitted beneath the flat front panel, its nearside frame aligned with the nearside frame of the nearside headlight.

All wheels were fitted with chromed wheel nut guard rings at an early date.

Prior to the wartime loan to Pontypridd the chromed hub bosses and wheel nut guard rings were removed. Post-war a plain wheel nut guard ring was fitted to the front offside wheel.

A rear view mirror was mounted externally to the front nearside cab pillar

At the rear end of the roof-mounted catwalk and immediately in front of the trolley retaining hooks brackets

1934 Sunbeam MS3 214 with MCCW all metal body is seen at Cosham Railway Station during its short period of post-war operation (but after its February 1948 repaint). Part of the ornate cast iron passenger waiting shelter surrounded by trolleybuses in this view is now in the Gunwharf Quays residential and shopping complex. (Online Transport Archive [photographer H. Luff])

secured a transverse rod with down-swept ends which extended across much of the width of the vehicle to avoid roof damage when pulling down the trolley booms and stowing them beneath the retaining hooks.

In February 1948 214 was repainted in full pre-war livery (Livery 1) with roof, front and rear domes, and upper deck rear corner panels retained in matt grey. The lower and upper deck waistband beadings were additionally picked out in black as were the cantrail beadings. This had not been normal practice in the pre-war livery originally applied to the Metro-Cammell bodied trolleybuses.

Post-war by October 1948 214 displayed non-standard final destination and intermediate points indicator blinds; however, by April 1949 it had been equipped with the then standard version employing reduced size lettering and enabling up to four lines of information to be displayed.

Notes

No. 14 was the first trolleybus to arrive in Portsmouth on 10 July 1934, the first to be used for driver training (from 11 July 1934) and the first to enter public service.

214 was withdrawn from service and placed in open storage on waste ground to the east of Northern Parade in late 1940. In August 1942 it was prepared for loan to Pontypridd UDC and towed to South Wales reaching Pontypridd on 14 August 1942. The trolleybus arrived back in Portsmouth on 11 November 1945, towed by George Park & Co., hauliers of Portsmouth, and was subsequently reinstated to service.

Disposal

214 Withdrawn on 21 April 1953 and stored at North End Depot until sold in January 1954 to Kingsway Coachworks, Emsworth, Hampshire, for £50 and broken up.

1934 AEC663T/Metro-Cammell H32/28R

Fleet No.	1938 No.	Reg. No.	Chassis	Chassis No.	Body	Body No.	Into Service	Last licensed	Withdrawn	Sold
15	215	RV4663	AEC663T	075	MCCW		17.07.1934	09.1950	21.06.1955	14.03.1956

Last licensed = the final month in which the vehicle was licensed to operate.

Chassis: Three axle type AEC 663T manufactured by the Associated Equipment Company Ltd. at the AEC works, Windmill Lane, Southall, Middlesex.
Motor: English Electric EE405 (80 h.p. at 550 volts) series-wound, augmented field, manufactured by English Electric Co. Ltd. at the Phoenix Works, Bradford, Yorkshire.
Electrical equipment: English Electric Regulated Field Control.
De-wirement indicator: Neon line-light.
Brakes: Westinghouse compressed air and hand brakes.
Body: Metropolitan-Cammell Weymann Motor Bodies Ltd., Midland Works, Saltley, Birmingham, all metal H32/28R.
Length: Not known, recommended body length in 1933–34 was 26ft.
Width: 7ft 6in.
Height: Not known.
Wheelbase: 16ft 6in..
Bogie wheelbase: 4ft.
Wheel track: Front 6ft 5⅜in.; rear 6ft 2¾in.
Unladen weight: 8 tons 3 cwts 0 qrtrs
Tyres: 36in. by 8in. high-pressure pneumatic singles on all wheels.
Frame overall length: 26ft 9in..
Height of frame laden: 22½in.
Turning circle diameter: 59ft.
Chassis weight: 4 tons 4 cwt.

The contract price was £2,117. The final price upon completion was £2,070 13s 7d.

Chassis: Conventional cranked chassis frame over rear bogie based on the AEC Regent 663 motorbus chassis and axles with special insulation points for all-metal bodies. The chassis, including electrical equipment, cost £1,230.

All other details, see trolleybus 12.

Electrics: See trolleybus 12.

Brakes: A Westinghouse two-cylinder reciprocating compressor with 5 cubic feet capacity and driven by an EEC 500-volt motor was carried on the offside of the chassis frame, from which it was electrically and mechanically insulated. The compressor was equipped with an anti-freezer, the intake to which was connected by a short rubber tube (for insulation) to one of the chassis cross members, which was utilised as an intake silencer, the air being admitted at the farther end through a filter. The air reservoir and governor were attached forward of the compressor on insulated mountings with a buffer chamber on the compressor side of the valve. The governor was set to maintain a reservoir pressure of 85 lb per square inch and the control valve was operated by an organ type pedal mounted on the bracket carrying both the valve and power pedal. Reservoir and brake cylinder pressures were shown on gauges on the dashboard attached to the driver's steering column.

AEC663T / English Electric 15 at the southbound stop outside 'The Clarence Gardens' public house in London Road, North End on 9 September 1934. The public house was reconstructed in 1937 and has a totally different appearance today. Long's Brewery was acquired by Brickwoods in 1933. (D.A.P. Janes [photographer G.A. Tucker])

The front brake drums were 17-inch-diameter castings with 3-inch-wide facings ¾in. thick. The track rods were adjustable by means of screwed and clipped ends. All four wheels of the rear bogie were fitted with 17-inch-diameter brake drums having 6in. wide facings ¾in. thick. The total effective brake area was 825 square inches.

Apart from a single flexible pipe connection, all air piping was solid drawn steel. Air cylinders were mounted on the cross tube in front of the rear bogie, whence rod connections were taken to double-armed levers on a cross-shaft carried behind the central bogie cross-member. The lower arms of the levers were coupled by pull rods to the cam levers on the leading axle and by tubular push-rods to the rear axle levers. The same mechanism was used by the handbrake. The front wheel brake cylinders were mounted on top of the king pins, the piston rods passing through the borings in the latter and operating directly on the camshaft.

Pull-on handbrakes linked by a cross-shaft, and pull and push rods to the camshaft levers and expanding in the bogie wheel brake drums to operate on the same pairs of shoes as those operated by the air brake system. The handbrake lever was to the offside of the driver's steering column.

Bodywork: The bodywork was basically identical to that fitted to the 1934 Sunbeam MS3 14 and also cost £838. The detail differences were:

The flat front panel incorporated a single fluted column of three louvred vanes placed centrally aligned vertically with the centre of the headlamps with the fleet number transferred immediately above. Beneath that was a removable front panel for towing purposes incorporating the front registration number plate in its lower half.

The vehicle was delivered without a chassis and equipment maker's badge.

Lighting: See trolleybus 14.

Seating: See trolleybus 14.

Destination equipment: See trolleybus 14.

Internal livery: See trolleybus 14.

External livery: Delivered in Livery 1 (see Appendix C).

Subsequent alterations: A chassis and equipment maker's badge, AEC in an inverted triangle surmounted by the winged EE symbol, was fitted centrally beneath the driver's windscreen below the waistband in September 1934.

Also by September 1934 a spot light was fitted beneath the flat front panel, its nearside frame aligned with the nearside frame of the nearside headlight (this was retained in the 1949 reconstruction); all wheels were fitted with chromed wheel nut guard rings.

An oblong conductor's mirror was fitted in April 1935 in the upper saloon rear dome above the stairs.

External advertising began to be displayed on the offside lower deck panels beneath the staircase window by August 1935.

In 1938, 15 was re-numbered 215. On the front and rear panels an additional '2' prefixed the original fleet number resulting in an off-centre appearance. It is not known if 15 and potentially the other MCCW-bodied trolleybuses were delivered with a square metal fleet number plate, as 14, or with Bakelite discs displaying the fleet number inside the upper and lower saloons. Thus it is not known how the 1938 renumbering affected this vehicle.

Post war a rear view mirror was mounted externally to the front nearside cab pillar.

At the rear end of the roof-mounted catwalk, and immediately in front of the trolley retaining hooks, brackets secured a transverse rod with down-swept ends which extended across much of the width of the vehicle to avoid roof damage when pulling down the trolley booms and stowing them beneath the retaining hooks.

215 was completely rebuilt in May–June 1949, returning to service in July 1949. The offside glazed panel behind the staircase and the offside indicator box built into the white-painted vent panel above the rearmost lower saloon window (bay 6) were panelled over (that on the nearside was retained but not used). Although the semaphore arm illuminated traffic indicators had been retained on both sides pre-war and during the vehicles loan to Pontypridd, they were removed during the rebuilding. The lettering used on the final destination and intermediate points blinds was reduced in size enabling up to four lines of information to be displayed.

Trolleybus 215 was repainted in the revised 1948 livery (Livery 4) in June 1949.

AEC663T 215 with MCCW all metal body in North End Depot after its 1949 rebuilding and repainting. The circular, domed top radio interference suppressors are clearly seen in front of the trolley gantry. (Online Transport Archive [photographer J. Joyce])

Notes

15 was the second trolleybus to arrive in Portsmouth on 16 July 1934 and was licensed on 17 July 1934.

Trolleybus 215 was withdrawn from service and placed in open storage on waste ground to the east of Northern Parade in late 1940. In August 1942 it was prepared for loan to Pontypridd UDC and towed to South Wales reaching Pontypridd on 8 August 1942. The trolleybus was returned to Portsmouth at the end of April 1946, towed by George Park and Co., hauliers of Portsmouth, and subsequently reinstated to service.

Disposal

215 Withdrawn 21 June 1955 and stored at North End Depot until sold to J. Strudwick (dealer), Horndean, 14 March 1956 for £40 and believed broken up at Eastney Depot in May 1956.

1935 AEC661T/English Electric H26/24R

Fleet No.	1938 No.	Reg. No.	Chassis	Chassis No.	Body	Body No.	Into Service	Last licensed	Withdrawn	Sold
16	216	RV6374	AEC661T	069	Eng. Electric		27.10.1935	04.1956	05.1957	11.04.1958
17	217	RV6375	AEC661T	070	Eng. Electric		03.11.1935	01.1951	02.1951	14.03.1956
18	218	RV6376	AEC661T	071	Eng. Electric		03.11.1935	07.1955	08.1955	14.03.1956
19	219	RV6377	AEC661T	072	Eng. Electric		10.11.1935	04.1956	05.1957	11.04.1958
20	220	RV6378	AEC661T	073	Eng. Electric		03.11.1935	04.1956	05.1957	22.03.1958
21	221	RV6379	AEC661T	074	Eng. Electric		03.11.1935	11.1950	06.1954	01.03.1956
22	222	RV6380	AEC661T	075	Eng. Electric		03.11.1935	04.1950	03.1956	03.1956
23	223	RV6381	AEC661T	076	Eng. Electric		03.11.1935	01.1951	02.1951	03.1956
24	224	RV6382	AEC661T	077	Eng. Electric		09.04.1936	08.1958	10.1958	22.02.1960

Last licensed = the final month in which the vehicle was licensed to operate.

Chassis: Two-axle type AEC 661T manufactured by the Associated Equipment Co. Ltd. at the AEC works, Windmill Lane, Southall, Middlesex.
Motor: English Electric Co. Ltd., Phoenix Works, Bradford, Yorkshire, Type EE405 (80hp at 550 volts) compound-wound, regenerative.
Electrical equipment: English Electric Co. Ltd., Phoenix Works, Bradford, Yorkshire.
De-wirement indicator: Single line-light and buzzer.
Brakes: G.D. Peters compressed air, regenerative rheostatic and hand brakes.
Body: English Electric Co. Ltd., Dick, Kerr Works, Preston, Lancashire, all-metal H26/24R.
Length: 26ft.
Width 7ft 6in.
Wheelbase: 16ft 3in.
Unladen weight: 7 tons 8 cwt 3 qtr.
Tyres: 36in. by 8in. on all wheels.

These nine vehicles were ordered in January 1935 for the Southsea South Parade Pier – Hilsea via Festing Road, Albert Road, Bradford Junction, Guildhall, Twyford Avenue and Northern Parade conversion. The design was similar to London Transport's sole 2-axle prototype trolleybus, fleet number 63.

The contract price was £1,908 8s. The final price upon completion was £1,923 8s.

Manufacturer's view of AEC661T 24 with English Electric all-metal body probably photographed at the English Electric Preston Works. (David Beilby collection [English Electric])

Manufacturer's view of AEC661T 21 with English Electric all-metal body probably photographed at the English Electric Preston Works. (David Beilby collection [English Electric])

Chassis: based on the AEC Regent 661 motorbus chassis and axles.

Nickel steel frame, the maximum section was 11in. deep with cross-bracing to prevent distortion. The frame rose up over the front and rear axles. Frame level under load was 1ft 10½in.

The propeller shaft from the traction motor was equipped with Spicer needle roller couplings. The laden ground clearance of the traction motor was 10½in.

The rear axle was fitted with a 9.7 to 1 spiral-bevel and double-helical, double-reduction final drive in place of the standard 9.33 to 1 worm gear which had been shown to be insufficiently strong to cope with the stress reversals created by regenerative braking. The double-reduction axle proved reliable but produced more noise than the worm gear. The worm gear and road wheel were all mounted on large roller bearings with bellows gland type oil seals. The brake drums could be removed without disturbing the wheel hubs.

A nickel steel forged front axle was used equipped with Marles steering, ratio 4¾ to 1. The steering king-pins were provided with a roller thrust race and large bronze journal bearings.

The springs were made from silico-manganese steel equipped with solid eyes.

Electrics: The compound-wound, box-frame, self-ventilated, flood-proof and roller-bearing-equipped EE405 traction motor was mounted amidships on Floatex rubber suspension on a rigid channel section sub-frame and cross members and offset to the nearside between the chassis frame members. The propeller shaft from the traction motor was equipped with Spicer needle roller couplings at each end.

A motor generator set was mounted on insulated rubber suspension on the external face of the offside chassis side frame forward of the rear axle. A CAV control box was used. Operated in parallel with the battery this provided low tension power for the interior and exterior lighting, and auxiliary equipment. Emergency lighting was provided from the 48-volt battery in the event of a failure of the power supply.

"Regenostatic" electrical equipment providing regenerative rheostatic braking. The "Regenostatic" control system was advertised as providing differential braking practically throughout retardation, thereby virtually permitting the driver to control the vehicle by use of a single pedal (the air brake pedal remaining untouched).

The contactor panel, complete with main starting field-shunting contactors, relays and field shunt resistance, and the circuit breakers were mounted on insulated panels in an asbestos-lined case, in the driver's cab.

Each end of the two substantial transverse pressed steel girders, between bays 1 and 2, and bays 2 and 3, supporting the exposed trolley gantry continued down the two body pillars to about one third of the depth of the upper saloon side windows. The trolley gantry, which was not in direct contact with the roof, was secured by three metal bolts to the upper portion of each body pillar. The front girder was perforated with two holes each side of the trolley bases and the rear girder by three each side for weight reduction purposes.

The main power cable made its way forward from the trolley gantry along the centre line of the roof before it entered the front dome about 6in. above and to the rear of the central pillar between the front upper-deck windows. The vehicles were equipped with Brecknell Willis lightweight trolley equipment and trolley bases. A radio interference suppressor was mounted centrally in front of the trolley gantry. There was a single step combined with the utilitarian trolley boom retaining hooks anchored by a single central bracket to the rear of the access catwalk on the roof above the rear dome.

Traction batteries for manoeuvring purposes were not fitted.

Brakes: The G.D. Peters compressed air brakes used a motor driven air compressor controlled by an automatic governor. The compressor unit driven by a ¾hp English Electric compressor motor and 5 cubic feet capacity air reservoir were attached to the offside of the chassis frame and accessible behind a valence panel. The internal expanding air brake operated on all four wheels. The front air cylinders were mounted directly over the hollow king pins through which the piston rods operated the front camshaft levers. The rear wheel brakes were operated by two cylinders mounted forward of the rear axle.

The hand brake was applied to the rear wheel brake camshafts only by means of a mechanical linkage. The single brake shoe to each rear wheel was 6in. wide and could be operated by pedal or hand lever or simultaneously by both.

Each of the front wheels was provided with shoes 3in. wide connected to the foot brake. All shoe linings, front and rear, were ½in. thick, whilst the drum brakes, 17in. in diameter, were of cast iron alloy.

Bodywork: This was of Highbridge double-deck all metal five bay construction with a conventional, enclosed forward-ascending half-turn (90°) staircase with semi-vestibuled open platform entrance and exit at the rear and roof ribbing built by English Electric Co. Ltd. at Preston.

In profile, the front elevation of the body curved gently backwards from the lower-deck waist rail height to the upper-deck roof whereas the rear was rather upright. The upper saloon was equipped with four Colt roof-mounted extractor ventilators (two on each side) located towards the rear of bay 1 and the rear of bay 5 on each side. A double fold at the base of the upper-deck side panels provided a gutter. The trolley equipment was fitted to an overbearing, massive, exposed roof-mounted gantry above bay 2. No. 24 was equipped with heavy-looking longitudinal "spats" between the trolley gantry girders.

Metal louvres were fitted above the upper and lower saloon side windows. Half-drop windows were fitted to the side windows in bays 1, 3 and 4 on both sides of the lower and upper deck and to the front upper-deck windows. In the front dome there were two-vane louvred ventilators, matching those above the driver's windscreen, above each front upper-deck window. Three top hinged access doors were fitted at the base of the lower-deck off-side panel running the entire available length of bays 1 to 4 between the two axles, providing access to the air brake compressor unit, air reservoir and motor generator set.

The top outer corners of the two panes in the rear upper deck emergency exit window were radiused, the gutter around the edge of the roof curving down the upper deck rear corner panel to end beneath the emergency exit door. The rear upper deck emergency exit door consisted of two oblong windows and had four hinges at its base. Despite the protruding rear destination box, small rubber bumpers on the nearside and offside of the emergency exit door aligned with similar bumpers on the panel beneath, to the nearside and offside of the rear indicator box. When opened to its fullest extent the emergency exit door hung down and rested on these bumpers. A separate platform, normally stowed behind the upper saloon rear nearside seat, fitted vertically into two metal retaining brackets in the door sill inside the upper saloon in front of the emergency exit door and tipped outwards into a horizontal position when the door was opened to provide access to the roof catwalk and thence the trolley gantry. The platform was retained securely in place by two chains which fitted into loops at the end of the metal strengtheners beneath the platform at one end of each chain and metal brackets inside the rear dome at the other.

The emergency door could be opened by an external handle mounted on the rear dome immediately above the rain strip and centrally above the door, or from inside by a comparable handle attached to a horizontal locking bar mounted on the cantrail immediately above the door. The horizontal bar was equipped with three prongs that engaged with brackets on the top of the door.

Handrails were covered in black Doverite.

There was a deep step up from the platform to the lower saloon and a commode handle rail on the nearside rear platform bulkhead. The staircase had four steps from the platform to the landing and then four steps to the upper deck, each riser having aluminium kicking panels.

The driver's cab windscreens were both chromium plated but only that on the offside opened and was equipped with a top-mounted windscreen wiper. The frame of both panes had gently radiused corners. Above each windscreen, two-vane louvred ventilators were mounted centrally on the white-painted cantrail. There was a front-hinged cab door on the offside only provided with a square sliding "signalling" window in the lower third of the pane and an inset opening handle, with a fixed quarter light between the door and the cab front pillar. On the nearside there was a matching panel and a single window that increased in height towards the front of the vehicle to align itself with the top of the windscreen. The base of the cab door was curved over the wheel arch to a position about 4in. from the rear of the door, thereafter the base, beneath the cab door handle, was horizontal, parallel to the waist rail and about 1ft 6in. below it.

A step was inset into the offside bay 1 side panel access door, but without any form of protection to the bodywork, immediately behind the front axle. The front wheels were equipped wheel trims. Individual mud flaps hung behind each front wheel with a further mud flap angled from the nearside to the offside extending the width of the vehicle beneath the rear platform.

There were two shallow glazed panels in the bulkhead behind the driver with a central pillar. The panel behind the driver had two panes of glass, one pane sliding to allow the driver to communicate with the conductor. A raked steering wheel was used. There was a small rectangular driver's rear view mirror mounted externally towards the top of the front offside cab pillar. The chassis and equipment maker's badge, AEC in an inverted triangle surmounted by the winged EE symbol, was fitted centrally beneath the driver's windscreen below the waistband and immediately above the fleet number. Although not evident in the manufacturer's photographs these were fitted upon delivery.

A large removable panel with three columns of eight louvred ventilation vanes extended across the base of the front panel with the front registration number plate centred immediately above. The vertical extremities of the panel were aligned with the innermost part of the headlight rims and the top edge was about 4in. below the base of the headlight rims. The rear registration number plate was mounted on the rear cantrail above the rear platform window and aligned with its offside pillar.

A small rectangular white enamelled Police Licence plate with black lettering was displayed at the nearside base of the rear panel adjacent to the platform.

A single lifeguard, in the form of a round-section steel tube, ran beneath the side panels between the front and rear axles. A bamboo trolley retrieval pole was carried in a tube mounted towards the nearside under the chassis.

Lighting: External lighting was two chrome-rimmed headlights on wooden plinths just over half-way up the front panel with two front chrome-rimmed side lights, also on wooden plinths immediately above, mounted slightly more towards the extremity of the panel and aligned with the outer edges of the headlights. An orange-lensed Lucas 24-volt 36-watt spotlight was mounted beneath the nearside end of the nearside column of ventilation louvres in the removable front panel.

There was a single red rear light incorporated into the rear registration plate, the lens positioned above the final digit of the registration number.

Semaphore arm illuminated traffic indicators accommodated in a black moulding were fitted in a vertical position in the lower half of the driver's cab corner pillars. The base of the indicator was aligned with the base of the upper pane in the offside windscreen. At the rear, an inset panel mounted at the nearside beneath the rear platform window comprised illuminated left-turn arrow, STOP and right-turn arrow sections.

Interior lighting was provided by installation of 24-volt, 12-watt traction type pearl bulbs in rectangular "Floodlight" type fittings with chrome plated hinged rims: six lights were mounted in the ceiling cove panels on each side of the lower and upper saloons, centrally placed above the windows, and one above the rear upper deck emergency window. There was also a light above rear open platform, making 26 in all. They were wired in two series of six and two series of seven, the nearside bulbs being wired with the upper saloon rear dome and the platform light respectively.

Interior lighting was supplied from a low tension 24-volt generator lighting set driven by an English Electric motor, the armature of which is mounted on the same shaft as the 24-volt generator armature, the motor and generator being coupled together to form a single unit. Internal emergency lighting was provided by means of separate low voltage battery-fed lights on each deck. One was mounted in the offside ceiling towards the rear and thus above the staircase and another was located above the last forward-facing offside double seat in the lower saloon. Emergency lighting for side and rear lights was also provided in case of the failure of the power supply.

Seating: The sprung squabs were fitted to cast metal frames with black moulded grab handles curving gently upwards on the top of the seat and adjacent to the aisle. The grab handle equipped seat frames alternated with those having stanchions.

There was a moquette seat covering with a heavy floral pattern motif of black, dark blue and possibly dark green with leather edges.

The lower saloon had a two-person inward-facing bench seat on each side over the rear axle and five rows of forward-facing double seats. The upper saloon had 6 rows of double seats on the off-side and seven rows on the nearside, i.e. the bench seat at the rear of the upper saloon above the open platform also accommodated two passengers. There were upright stanchions in both saloons attached to the ceiling, back of the seat and floor behind the first and fourth seat on the offside and the second and fifth seat on the nearside of the lower saloon and the second, fourth and sixth offside seats of the upper saloon.

Destination equipment: Large rectangular indicator boxes 43in. by 14in. capable of displaying a service number and up to four lines of information (final destination and three lines of intermediate points), with a second rectangular indicator box 43in. by 6in. for a single line of supplementary information immediately beneath, were mounted centrally at the front on the upper-deck front panel above the driver's cab windscreen and at the rear above the rear platform window. The rear indicator boxes were housed in a single unit that protruded some inches beyond the upper-deck rear body panels. The indicator blinds were printed with the service number to the left of the information, the number being in a broader style as deep as three lines of information. The single line indicator box displayed "Portsmouth Corporation" when on normal service and the final destination when operating short-workings or special journeys.

A further rectangular indicator box 31½in. by 14in. (somewhat smaller than the larger ones at front and rear) displaying up to four lines of information (final destination and three lines of intermediate points) was fitted immediately above the rear open platform entrance encroaching somewhat into bay 5.

All box apertures had square corners.

An additional single line indicator box displaying the final destination was located inside the lower saloon at the top of the offside bay 5 window.

Internal livery: Not known. The interior panels were lined with scratchproof colour Rexine with window mouldings and other finishes in French-polished walnut.

External livery: Entered service in Livery 1 (see Appendix C).

Notes

No. 20 was loaned to Brighton Corporation 11–17 December 1935 as part of that transport undertaking's evaluation of trolleybuses for tramway replacement purposes. It operated beneath temporary overhead wiring around The Level, a triangular park surrounded by tram routes along Ditchling Road, Union Road and Lewes Road (Waterloo Place), the first trip being made on 11 December 1935.

No. 24 was displayed at the 1935 Commercial Motor Show at Olympia London, 7–16 November 1935. It had a somewhat different trolley gantry to the other vehicles in this batch, incorporating "spats" between the transverse gantry girders and omitting the three protruding retaining bolts at the top of the body pillars.

In 1938, Nos. 16 to 24 were re-numbered in sequence as 216 to 224.

Nos. 216 to 224 were withdrawn from service and placed in open storage on waste ground to the east of Northern Parade in September 1940. 219 was re-licensed in March 1942 and 220 on 14 October 1942; 221, 224 followed in August 1944; 216, 217, 222 in March 1946; 218 in April 1946 and finally 223 in May 1946.

A post-war view of AEC661T 224. (Peter Carter [photographer C. Carter])

Subsequent alterations

No. 224 was experimentally equipped with a strip bell in the lower saloon at an unknown date.

It is assumed that all vehicles retained their semaphore arm illuminated traffic indicators until at least September 1939; however, by the post-war period several trolleybuses from this batch had lost their traffic indicators: namely 216, 219, 220 and 224.

There are no proven explanations to this policy. During war-time the illuminated traffic indicators could not be practically adapted for the "black-out" whilst it is possible that any failure of the operating mechanisms could not be repaired due to an absence of spare parts and a shortage of labour. The latter situation may have prevailed post-war too.

At some stage, assumed to be post-war and in connection with similar alterations carried out on Cravens-bodied 225–300, a cover was fixed over the two-vane louvred ventilators above each driver's windscreen on 216 and 220 to prevent water ingress, not least in the vicinity of the main power cable, and reduce draughts into the driver's cab. These were of the same styles as used on 225–300: the "standard" version in the form of a hood of triangular cross-section was fitted to 220 and the slightly larger but less protruding "flanged" version identifiable by four rivets across the top was fitted to 216. The "standard" version was also fitted to the louvred ventilators in the front dome above each front upper-deck window on 220. No changes were made to the other vehicles in this batch.

The single line indicator box displaying the final destination inside the lower saloon at the top of the offside bay 5 window was removed early post-war.

Disposal

216 Last licensed in April 1956. Withdrawn in May 1957 and stored at North End Depot until sold in April 1958 to C.D. Jordan & Son Ltd. (Breaker), Locksway Road, Portsmouth, for £74 10s, and broken up in April 1958.

217 Last licensed in January 1951. Withdrawn in 1951 and stored at North End Depot until sold in March 1956 to J. Strudwick, Horndean, Hampshire, for £40, and broken up in Eastney Depot Yard in March 1956.

218 Last licensed in July 1955. Withdrawn in July 1956 and stored at Eastney Depot until sold in March 1956 to J. Strudwick, Horndean, Hampshire, for £40, and broken up in Eastney Depot Yard in March 1956.

219 Last licensed in April 1956. Withdrawn in May 1957 and stored at North End Depot until sold in April 1958 to C.D. Jordan & Son Ltd. (Breaker), Locksway Road, Portsmouth, for £74 10s; used as a store until December 1959 then broken up.

220 Last licensed in April 1956. Withdrawn in May 1957 and stored at North End Depot until sold in March 1958 to C.D. Jordan & Son Ltd. (Breaker), Locksway Road, Portsmouth, for £74 10s and broken up in May 1958.

221 Last licensed in November 1950 and stored at North End Depot until sold in March 1956 to J. Strudwick, Horndean, Hampshire, for £40, and broken up in Eastney Depot Yard possibly as early as November 1955.

222 Last licensed in April 1950. Withdrawn in 1951 and stored at North End Depot until sold in February 1956 to J. Strudwick, Horndean, Hampshire, for £40, and broken up in Eastney Depot Yard in March 1956.

223 Last licensed in January 1951. Withdrawn in 1951 and stored at North End Depot until sold in February 1956 to J. Strudwick, Horndean, Hampshire, for £40, and broken up in Eastney Depot Yard in March 1956.

224 Last licensed in August 1958. Withdrawn in October 1958 and stored at North End Depot (October 1958–January 1960); transferred to Eastney Depot in January 1960 and stored there until sold in April 1960 to George Cohen, Southampton, for £90 10s (being removed by Hill, Botley), and broken up by their subsidiary Pollock & Brown at Northam Ironworks, Southampton, in July 1960.

1936 AEC661T/Cravens H26/26R

Fleet No.	1938 No.	Reg. No.	Chassis	Chassis No.	Body	Body No.	Into Service	Last licensed	Withdrawn	Sold
25	225	RV8307	AEC661T	090	Cravens		01.08.1936	05.1959	06.1959	22.02.1960
26	226	RV8308	AEC661T	109	Cravens		01.08.1936	08.1960	09.1960	03.11.1960
27	227	RV8309	AEC661T	105	Cravens		01.08.1936	04.1960	04.1960	11.07.1960
28	228	RV8310	AEC661T	104	Cravens		01.08.1936	08.1960	09.1960	03.11.1960
29	229	RV8311	AEC661T	097	Cravens		01.08.1936	06.1953	06.1953	CPPTD
30	230	RV8312	AEC661T	099	Cravens		02.08.1936	09.1961	30.09.1961	02.1962
31	231	RV8313	AEC661T	091	Cravens		01.08.1936	06.1961	07.1961	12.196
32	232	RV8314	AEC661T	093	Cravens		03.08.1936	09.1960	09.1960	10.1960
33	233	RV8315	AEC661T	102	Cravens		19.08.1936	06.1963	21.06.1963	09.1963
34	234	RV8316	AEC661T	095	Cravens		19.08.1936	08.1960	09.1960	03.11.1960
35	235	RV8317	AEC661T	100	Cravens		20.08.1936	09.1960	09.1960	03.11.1960
36	236	RV8318	AEC661T	103	Cravens		22.08.1936	04.1960	04.1960	11.07.1960
37	237	RV8319	AEC661T	094	Cravens		22.08.1936	10.1961	10.1961	12.196
38	238	RV8320	AEC661T	101	Cravens		22.08.1936	04.1960	30.04.1960	11.07.1960
39	239	RV8321	AEC661T	096	Cravens		22.08.1936	09.1960	09.1960	03.11.1960
40	240	RV8322	AEC661T	117	Cravens		03.10.1936	06.1956	1958	CPPTD
41	241	RV8323	AEC661T	118	Cravens		06.10.1936	08.1960	09.1960	03.11.1960
42	242	RV8324	AEC661T	123	Cravens		05.10.1936	04.1960	30.04.1960	11.07.1960
43	243	RV8325	AEC661T	129	Cravens		03.10.1936	09.1960	09.1960	03.11.1960
44	244	RV8326	AEC661T	126	Cravens		06.10.1936	11.1961	11.1961	03.1962
45	245	RV8327	AEC661T	130	Cravens		03.10.1936	02.1960	04.1960	22.02.1960
46	246	RV8328	AEC661T	134	Cravens		08.10.1936	06.1963	22.06.1963	09.1963
47	247	RV8329	AEC661T	124	Cravens		10.6.1936	04.1960	30.04.1960	11.07.1960
48	248	RV8330	AEC661T	119	Cravens		10.10.1936	06.1963	22.06.1963	09.1963
49	249	RV8331	AEC661T	132	Cravens		09.10.1936	10.1960	10.12.1961	03.1962
50	250	RV8332	AEC661T	133	Cravens		06.11.1936	01.1963	02.1963	09.1963
51	251	RV8333	AEC661T	125	Cravens		04.11.1936	10.1961	11.1961	12.1961
52	252	RV8334	AEC661T	121	Cravens		04.11.1936	12.1961	03.12.1961	03.1962
53	253	RV8335	AEC661T	120	Cravens		08.11.1936	04.1960	30.04.1960	11.07.1960
54	254	RV8336	AEC661T	122	Cravens		05.11.1936	12.1961	12.1961	03.1962
55	255	RV9106	AEC661T	127	Cravens		04.11.1936	11.1961	03.12.1961	03.1962
56	256	RV9107	AEC661T	128	Cravens		07.11.1936	07.1961	23.08.1961	12.1961
57	257	RV9108	AEC661T	092	Cravens		07.11.1936	10.1954	10.1954	08.1957
58	258	RV9109	AEC661T	098	Cravens		05.11.1936	09.1952	10.1952	04.1957
59	259	RV9110	AEC661T	106	Cravens		09.11.1936	12.1961	12.1961	03.1962
60	260	RV9111	AEC661T	107	Cravens		09.11.1936	12.1956	12.1956	CPPTD
61	261	RV9112	AEC661T	108	Cravens		10.11.1936	04.1960	30.04.1960	11.07.1960
62	262	RV9113	AEC661T	110	Cravens		09.11.1936	04.1954	04.1954	08.1957
63	263	RV9114	AEC661T	111	Cravens		10.11.1936	09.1953	09.1953	08.1957
64	264	RV9115	AEC661T	113	Cravens		09.11.1936	09.1953	09.1953	08.1957
65	265	RV9116	AEC661T	114	Cravens		10.11.1936	06.1958	07.1958	22.02.1960
66	266	RV9117	AEC661T	115	Cravens		10.11.1936	02.1951	03.1951	08.1957
67	267	RV9118	AEC661T	116	Cravens		10.11.1936	04.1960	30.04.1960	11.07.1960
68	268	RV9119	AEC661T	138	Cravens		10.11.1936	04.1960	30.04.1960	11.07.1960
69	269	RV9120	AEC661T	112	Cravens		10.11.1936	06.1963	22.06.1963	09.1963
70	270	RV9121	AEC661T	135	Cravens		10.11.1936	12.1961	03.12.1961	03.1962
71	271	RV9122	AEC661T	131	Cravens		11.11.1936	04.1960	30.04.1960	11.07.1960
72	272	RV9123	AEC661T	136	Cravens		11.11.1936	07.1953	07.1953	08.1957
73	273	RV9124	AEC661T	137	Cravens		14.11.1936	12.1961	03.12.1961	03.1962
74	274	RV9125	AEC661T	139	Cravens		12.11.1936	04.1963	16.05.1963	09.1963
75	275	RV9126	AEC661T	143	Cravens		14.11.1936	09.1956	1957	CPPTD
76	276	RV9127	AEC661T	146	Cravens		14.11.1936	02.1954	02.1954	08.1957
77	277	RV9128	AEC661T	140	Cravens		14.11.1936	06.1956	07.1956	CPPTD
78	278	RV9129	AEC661T	141	Cravens		18.11.1936	09.1959	10.1959	22.02.1960
79	279	RV9130	AEC661T	142	Cravens		17.11.1936	08.1951	09.1951	CPPTD
80	280	RV9131	AEC661T	144	Cravens		12.12.1936	09.1953	1957	1958
81	281	RV9132	AEC661T	145	Cravens		12.12.1936	04.1960	30.04.1960	11.07.1960

Fleet No.	1938 No.	Reg. No.	Chassis	Chassis No.	Body	Body No.	Into Service	Last licensed	Withdrawn	Sold
82	282	RV9133	AEC661T	147	Cravens		12.12.1936	09.1961	30.09.1961	12.1961
83	283	RV9134	AEC661T	148	Cravens		12.12.1936	06.1963	22.06.1963	09.1963
84	284	RV9135	AEC661T	149	Cravens		12.12.1936	09.1953	1957	1958
85	285	RV9136	AEC661T	150	Cravens		12.12.1936	12.1950	1956	CPPTD
86	286	RV9137	AEC661T	151	Cravens		12.12.1936	06.1963	21.06.1963	09.1963
87	287	RV9138	AEC661T	152	Cravens		12.12.1936	04.1954	1956	CPPTD
88	288	RV9139	AEC661T	153	Cravens		19.12.1936	03.1951	1956	CPPTD
89	289	RV9140	AEC661T	154	Cravens		12.12.1936	09.1951	1957	CPPTD
90	290	RV9141	AEC661T	155	Cravens		19.12.1936	09.1958	10.1958	22.02.1960
91	291	RV9142	AEC661T	156	Cravens		12.05.1937	09.1961	30.09.1961	12.196
92	292	RV9143	AEC661T	160	Cravens		03.06.1937	04.1960	30.04.1960	11.07.1960
93	293	RV9144	AEC661T	157	Cravens		29.07.1937	10.1960	12.1960	12.196
94	294	RV9145	AEC661T	158	Cravens		26.06.1937	06.1963	21.06.1963	09.1963
95	295	RV9149	AEC661T	159	Cravens		03.06.1937	12.1960	30.11.1961	12.196
96	296	RV9150	AEC661T	163	Cravens		12.05.1937	09.1953	1956	CPPTD
97	297	RV9151	AEC661T	165	Cravens		17.05.1937	05.1960	07.1960	01.1961
98	298	RV9152	AEC661T	161	Cravens		12.05.1937	12.1961	31.12.1961	03.1962
99	299	RV9153	AEC661T	162	Cravens		12.05.1937	08.1961	08.1961	12.196
100	300	RV9154	AEC661T	164	Cravens		12.05.1937	04.1963	21.06.1963	09.1963

225–239, 241–254, 255–256, 259–261, 265, 267–271, 273–275, 277–278, 281–283, 286, 290, 291–295, 297–300 rebuilt by Portsmouth Corporation using Metal Components fabrications between 1949 and 1956.
Last licensed = the final month in which the vehicle was licensed to operate.

Chassis: Two-axle type AEC 661T manufactured by the Associated Equipment Company Ltd. at the AEC works, Windmill Lane, Southall, Middlesex.
Motor: English Electric Co. Ltd., Phoenix Works, Bradford, Yorkshire, Type EE406/1C1 (80hp at 500 volts, compound-wound, regenerative.
Electrical equipment: English Electric Co. Ltd., Phoenix Works, Bradford, Yorkshire.
EE Drawing RWS-92D-1O8F dated 27 August 1936.
Dewirement indicator: Single line-light and buzzer operated from a 4½ volt dry cell battery.
Brakes: Westinghouse compressed air, rheostatic and hand brakes. Regenerative electric braking.

Body: Cravens Railway Carriage and Wagon Co., Darnall, Sheffield, all-metal H26/26R.
Order 7700. Drawing R.V. 1167 dated 31 May 1935.
Length: 26ft.
Width: 7ft 6 in.
Height: 14ft 4½in. unladen to the top of trolleyplank.
Wheelbase: 16ft 3in. giving a turning circle of 56ft 6in.
Wheel track: front 6ft 5¾ins, rear 5ft 10in.
Unladen weight: 7 tons 4 cwt 6 qtr
Tyres: low pressure 20 in. by 10.50 in. tyres on front and 20in. by 9in. tyres on the rear.
The Cravens bodywork on these trolleybuses was of identical design to that carried by 30 Leyland Titan TD4 motorbuses but

AEC661T 25 with Cravens all-metal body photographed at the Cravens Railway Carriage & Wagon Co. Ltd. works in Darnall, Sheffield (official view). (Paul Fox collection [Cravens])

34 at AEC Works Southall with the GWR mainline behind (official view). (D.A.P. Janes collection)

Portsmouth AEC661T chassis at AEC works Southall (official view). (Roger Funnell collection [AEC-EE])

for the driver's cab layout. Cravens had never previously built double-deck trolleybus bodies although they had supplied Rotherham Corporation with single-deck trolleybus bodies from 1931.

The contract price was £1,838 11s. The final price upon completion was £1,832 2s 9d.

Chassis: This was based on the AEC Regent 661 motorbus chassis and axles. The chassis cost £1,058 11s each.

Nickel steel frame, the maximum section was 11in. deep with cross-bracing to prevent distortion. The frame rose up over the front and rear axles. Frame level under load was 1ft 10½in.

Fully floating worm drive rear axle with 8in. worm centres and a ratio of 9.7 to 1. The rear axle casing was a one-piece nickel steel forging carrying the worm gearing in a separate casing. The 8½in. worm gear was offset to the nearside to avoid any obstruction of the gangway, and the worm and traction motor were skewed at an angle of 3° to maintain a straight drive line. The worm gear and road wheel were all mounted on large roller bearings with bellows gland type oil seals. The brake drums could be removed without disturbing the wheel hubs.

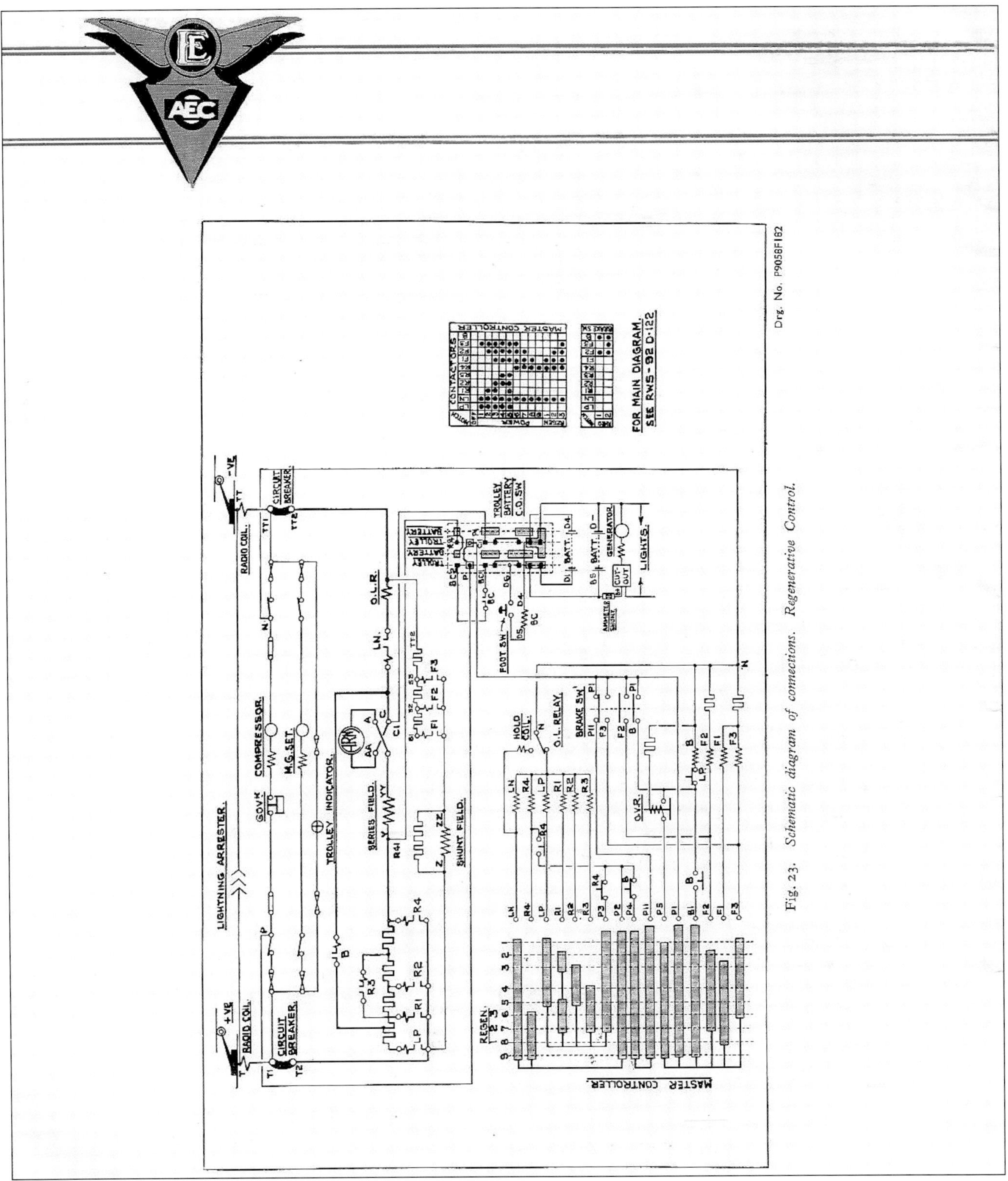

AEC-EE regenerative control diagram. (Geoff Burrows collection [AEC-EE])

Nickel steel forged front axle equipped with Marles steering, ratio 4¾ to 1. The steering king-pins were provided with a roller thrust race and large bronze journal bearings.

The springs were made from silico-manganese steel equipped with solid eyes.

Electrics: The compound-wound, box frame, self-ventilated by a fan at the commutator end, flood-proof and roller bearing equipped EE406 traction motor was mounted amidships on Floatex rubber suspension on a rigid channel section sub-frame and cross members, and offset to the nearside between the chassis frame members. The armature had a single turn winding and both the armature and field coils were wound with Class B insulation, whilst the field pole and interpole bodies were laminated. The large diameter propeller shaft from the traction motor was equipped with Spicer needle roller couplings at each end. The laden ground clearance of the traction motor was 10½in.

A motor generator set was mounted on insulated rubber suspension on the external face of the offside chassis side frame forward of the rear axle. CAV control box. Operated in parallel with the battery this provided low tension power

AEC6613T/Cravens 25 undergoing the compulsory tilt test (official view). (Paul Fox collection [Cravens])

for the interior and exterior lighting, and auxiliary equipment. Emergency lighting was provided from the 60-volt battery in the event of a failure of the power supply.

The shunt field resistances were installed in the driver's cab with the main resistance mounted between the chassis frames at the front end, protected from wheel splash by side plates, and having secondary cooling by the discharge from the compressed-air brake system.

The KM505A master controller was mounted beneath the driver's seat, readily accessible from the driver's cab, and other control equipment was mounted on the driver's cab nearside bulkhead or on nearside chassis frame member.

Regeneration was available on both pedals:

- The motoring or power pedal, if brought back slowly from any position, applied regeneration. Under normal driving conditions, the power pedal was released smartly allowing the vehicle to either coast or be retarded by depressing the brake pedal.
- The brake pedal, if progressively depressed, applied regeneration first, decelerating the vehicle down to about 14mph, then rheostatic braking which brought speed down to about 2mph, and then finally the air brakes which brought the vehicle to a standstill.

There was an amber de-wirement indicator light mounted in a round black Bakelite case above the other dashboard dials.

The upper-deck body pillars slotted into the framework above the upper saloon windows, i.e. the cantrail. There were curved steel brackets bolted to the metal roof (inside the roof there was a steel strengthening plate on each side) and each end of the two transverse pressed steel girders, between bays 1 and 2 and bays 2 and 3, supporting the exposed trolley gantry, which was not in direct contact with the roof, rested on these brackets, each foot being secured by four metal bolts. External steel channels continued down the body pillars to about one third of the depth of the upper saloon side windows with a strengthening bar running between the pillars above the window louvres on each side.

The main power cable made its way forward from the trolley gantry along the centre line of the roof before entering the front dome about 1ft 6in. to the rear of the metal louvres above the front upper-deck windows. The vehicles were equipped with Brecknell Willis lightweight trolley equipment and trolley bases. Trolley wheels were fitted. Radio interference coils were mounted centrally on the roof in front of the trolley gantry. Auxiliary choke coil PD-6A and radio choke coil PD-7A

These AEC 661Ts had battery manoeuvring equipment and ironclad traction batteries (60 volt) although the location of the batteries is not known. This same set of batteries supplied power under a split and balanced load, at 30 volts, for lighting purposes.

Brakes: The Westinghouse compressed air brakes used a motor driven air compressor controlled by an automatic governor. The compressor unit and air reservoir were attached to the offside of the chassis frame and accessible behind a valence panel. The internal expanding air brake operated on all four wheels. The front air cylinders were mounted directly over the hollow king pins through which the piston rods operated the front camshaft levers. The rear wheel brakes were operated by two cylinders mounted forward of the rear axle.

The hand brake operated the four foot brake shoes in the rear drums by means of mechanical linkage. The rear liners were 6in. wide and ¾in. thick. Total brake liner area was 504sq. in.

The brake drums were made of ribbed cast iron alloy. The hand brake lever was to the offside of the driver's steering column.

Bodywork: Highbridge double-deck all metal five bay construction with conventional, enclosed forward-ascending half-turn (90°) staircase with semi-vestibuled open platform entrance and exit at the rear. Roof ribbing built by Cravens Railway Carriage and Wagon Co., Sheffield. The bodies cost £780 each.

The front elevation rose in a convex curve to the upper-deck floor and then sloped gently rearwards to the roofline. A double fold at the base of the upper-deck panels provided a gutter. The trolley poles were fitted on an exposed roof-mounted gantry above bay 2.

Metal louvres were fitted above the upper and lower saloon side windows, and above the upper saloon front windows. Half-drop openers equipped with two "pinch fasteners" at the top of each pane were fitted to the side windows in bays 1, 3 and 4 on both sides of the lower and upper deck and to the front upper-deck windows. The upper pane dropped outside the fixed lower pane. Additional ventilation to the upper saloon was provided by two ventilators with shallow louvres immediately above the roofline, somewhat closer to the central pillar than to the outer pillars, and four roof-mounted ventilators (with circular chromed covers inside) positioned midway along bays 1 and 5 on each side. Top hinged valence panels were fitted at the base of the lower-deck off-side panel bays 1, 2 and 3 providing access to the air brake compressor unit, air reservoir and motor generator set, and on the nearside in bay 1 providing access to the contactors in an insulated unit mounted on the nearside chassis member.

The top corners of the rear platform window and the top outer corners of the windows of the upper deck emergency exit were radiused, the gutter around the edge of the roof curving down the upper deck rear corner panel to end beneath the emergency exit door. The rear upper deck emergency exit door consisted of two windows and had four hinges at its base. Despite the slightly protruding rear destination box, small rubber bumpers on the nearside and offside of the emergency exit door aligned with similar bumpers on the lower beading to the white-painted upper-deck waistband beneath, to the nearside and offside of the rear indicator box. When opened to its fullest extent the emergency exit door hung down and rested on these bumpers. A separate platform, normally stowed behind the upper saloon rear nearside seat, fitted into retaining slits in the door sill and was retained securely in place by two detachable rods which fitted into this platform at one end and brackets inside the rear dome at the other to provide access to the roof catwalk and thence the trolley gantry. There was a single cantilevered step on the rear dome beneath the trolley boom retaining hooks to provide access from the open emergency door to the roof catwalk.

The emergency door could be opened by an external handle mounted on the rear dome immediately above the rain strip and centrally above the door, or from inside by a comparable handle attached to a horizontal locking bar mounted on the cantrail immediately above the door. The horizontal bar was equipped with three prongs that engaged with brackets on the top of the door.

The handrails were covered in black Doverite.

The staircase had three steps from the platform to the landing and then four steps to the upper deck, each riser having aluminium kicking panels. There was an oblong conductor's mirror above the stairs.

Bell pushes were mounted in the lower saloon on the nearside towards the front of bay 2 and midway along bay 4, in the upper saloon on the nearside on the body pillar between bay 1 and 2, and on offside midway along bay 5 above the staircase. In all cases the pushes were mounted at the base of the ceiling cove panels on the cantrail. There was a further bell push on the nearside rear platform bulkhead above the window towards the saloon entrance

The fleet number was displayed inside the vehicle by a small white Bakelite oval disc screwed at cantrail height above the central front pillar in the upper saloon and on the front bulkhead in the lower saloon upon which the numbers were painted in black.

The driver's cab was equipped with a single opening windscreen on the off-side equipped with a central top-mounted windscreen wiper and painted frame. The frame of the opening pane had radiused upper corners and the glass increased in depth progressively towards the centre of the pane. There was a single nearside fixed windscreen. There were two ventilators with shallow louvres (to prevent draughts or water ingress) at the base of the white-painted central band immediately above the windscreen, somewhat closer to the central pillar than to the outer pillars and aligned with those immediately above the roofline. There was a front hinged (three hinges) cab door on the offside only, with a square top and the base curving over the wheel arch and then continuing horizontally some 4in. towards the rear. The cab door was equipped with a "signalling" window, the lower half of the pane sliding upwards behind the fixed upper pane, and a black-painted opening handle mounted in an almost square black-painted concave insert. There was a fixed side window between the cab door and the front offside corner pillar.

There was a matching panel and a single large window on the nearside. The driver's cab side windows were aligned at the base with the lower saloon side windows but rose towards the front of the vehicle to align with the top of the deeper windscreens. The base of the cab door was curved over the wheel arch to a position about 4in. from the rear of the door, thereafter the base, beneath the cab door handle, was horizontal, parallel to the white-painted waistband and about 1ft 3in. below it.

A step was let into the base of the bay 1 side panel access door, the insert having a rounded top but without any form of protection to the bodywork, immediately behind the front axle, on the offside. Both front wheels were fitted with chromed hub bosses and wheel nut guard rings. Individual mud flaps hung behind each wheel with a further mud flap extending the width of the vehicle at an angle beneath the rear platform.

There were two glazed panels in the bulkhead behind the driver, separated by a wide central pillar, with two bevel-edged mirrors shaped to match the curve of the ceiling immediately above.

Attached to the bulkhead above each glazed panel inside the lower saloon, but beneath the respective mirror, was a fold down blind to prevent reflections from the lower saloon on to the driver's windscreen during the hours of darkness. There was a protective rail across the glazed panels at half depth in the lower saloon. Small rectangular driver's rear view mirrors were mounted externally towards the top of the front cab pillars.

Lower saloon view of AEC661T 73 equipped with a Cravens all-metal body. (D.A.P. Janes collection)

Upper saloon view of AEC661T 73 equipped with a Cravens all-metal body. (D.A.P. Janes collection)

Except for the early deliveries, the chassis and equipment maker's badge, AEC in an inverted triangle surmounted by the winged EE symbol, was fitted centrally beneath the driver's windscreen below the waistband. The badge was added to the early deliveries at a later date. The driver's windscreen was of Triplex toughened safety glass.

A large removable panel with three columns of eight louvred ventilation vanes extended across the base of the front panel with the front registration number plate centred immediately above. The vertical extremities of the panel were about 4in. inboard of the innermost part of the headlight rims and the top edge was about 4in. below the base of the headlight rims. The panel was removable for access and towing purposes.

The rear registration number plate was at the base of the rear platform panel on the offside, beneath the advertisement position and fleet number.

A small rectangular white enamelled Police Licence plate with black lettering and numbers 825–900 in sequence with the fleet number was displayed at the nearside base of the rear panel adjacent to the platform.

A single wooden lifeguard, held by attachments beneath each body pillar, ran beneath the side panels between the front and rear axles. Two tubes were mounted under the chassis, somewhat off-centre to the nearside, to carry a bamboo trolley retrieval pole(s).

Lighting: External lighting was two chrome-rimmed headlights on wooden plinths just over half-way up the front panel with two front chrome-rimmed side lights also on wooden plinths immediately above, mounted slightly more towards the extremity of the panel and aligned with the outer edges of the headlights. An orange-lensed spotlight was mounted beneath the nearside end of the nearside column of ventilation louvres in the removable front panel (some vehicles appear to have been delivered without such spotlight but these were added at an early date).

There was a single red rear light incorporated into the rear registration plate, the lens aligned with the registration letters and positioned above the final digit of the registration number within a small painted red triangle.

Semaphore arm illuminated traffic indicators accommodated in a black moulding were fitted in a vertical position in the lower half of the driver's cab corner pillars on both nearside and offside (see Figure A below). The base of the indicator was aligned with the upper beading beneath the cab side windows. At the rear, an inset panel mounted centrally beneath the rear platform window comprised illuminated left-turn arrow, STOP and right-turn arrow sections.

Interior lighting was provided by an installation of 30-volt traction type tungsten bulbs in rectangular "Floodlight" type diffused light fittings with chrome plated hinged rims in the ceiling cove panels in the lower saloon towards the front of bays 1, 2 and 3 each side, and towards the rear of bays 3, 4 and 5 each side (12), i.e. there were four fittings in bay 3; and in the upper saloon forward of each body pillar on each side (12) and one in the rear dome centrally above the rear upper deck emergency window. The rearmost offside light in each saloon was designated an emergency lamp and wired separately.

Seating: The sprung squabs were fitted to cast metal frames with black moulded grab handles curving gently upwards on the top of the seat and adjacent to the aisle. The seat frames equipped with grab handles alternated with those having stanchions.

A moquette seat covering was used with a heavy floral pattern motif of black, dark blue and possibly dark green with leather edges. The driver's seat was also covered in moquette.

The lower saloon had a three-person inward-facing bench seat on each side over the rear axle and five rows of forward-facing double seats. The upper saloon had six rows of double seats on the off-side and seven rows on the nearside, i.e. the bench seat at the rear of the upper saloon above the open platform also accommodated two passengers. There were upright stanchions in both saloons attached to the ceiling, back of the seat and floor:

Lower saloon: Behind seats 3, 5 nearside; seats 2, 4 offside.
Upper saloon: Behind seats 3, 5 nearside; seats 2, 4, and stair head offside.

A glass-fronted panel at the rear of the longitudinal offside seat in the lower saloon was used to display fare table information.

There were black Doverite coated ceiling mounted handrails equipped with short leather straps above the lower saloon gangway parallel with the longitudinal seats. Single internal grab rails were fixed behind the front upper-deck windows at half the depth of the lower fixed pane and behind the rear emergency exit windows.

Destination equipment: Large rectangular indicator boxes 43in. by 14in. capable of displaying a service number and up to four lines of information (final destination and three lines of intermediate points), with a second rectangular indicator box 43in. by 6in. immediately beneath for a single line of supplementary information, were mounted centrally at the front on the upper-deck front panel above the driver's cab windscreen and at the rear above the rear platform window. The rear indicator boxes were housed in a single unit that protruded some inches beyond the upper-deck rear body panels. The indicator blinds were printed with the service number to the left of the information, the number being in a broader style as deep as three lines of information. The single line indicator box displayed 'Portsmouth Corporation' when on normal service and the final destination when operating short-workings or special journeys.

A further rectangular indicator box, somewhat smaller than the larger ones at front and rear displaying the final destination and up to four lines of en route point information, was fitted immediately above the rear open platform entrance encroaching somewhat into bay 5.

Additional single line indicator boxes displaying the final destination was located inside the lower saloon at the top of the bay 5 window on both sides. The nearside box measured 24in. by 14in. and that on the offside 24in. by 6in.

All box apertures had square corners.

Internal livery: The interior panels and rear corner panels were lined with scratchproof brown Rexine coverings with window mouldings and finishes in French-polished walnut. The ceilings were cream and the platform floor a light brown-grey. The cab area was painted brown.

External livery: Entered service in Livery 1 (see Appendix C). Nos. 258 and 201 were the first two vehicles to appear with a grey roof and white ARP markings.

Subsequent alterations

Soon after delivery, approximately 1937–38, a second internal grab rail was fixed behind the front upper-deck windows at the height of the lower edge of the upper pane of the half-drop opener with the existing one a few inches below. When the half-drop openers were replaced by a single fixed pane the original lower grab rail sufficed.

In April 1938, 25 to 100 were re-numbered in sequence as 225 to 300.

The additional digit in the fleet number resulted in many vehicles circulating without the transfers properly centred on the respective panel until the next repaint. The small white Bakelite oval discs upon which the fleet number was displayed internally were reversed and the new number painted on.

In 1939, 232 was experimentally fitted with sliding-head trolley collector gear with renewable carbon inserts. The entire fleet was subsequently so equipped.

At an unknown date, the diffused glass covers to the interior light fittings were removed leaving solely the rectangular bases and exposed tungsten bulbs.

At an unknown date, probably post-war, 20in. by 10in., 14-ply tyres were fitted to the front wheels when the 20in. by 10.50in. tyres required replacement.

By the end of the war, the nearside single fixed pane windscreen was divided into two panes with a horizontal wooden separation but the upper pane was fixed, matching the offside two-piece opening windscreen. There is no photographic evidence of opening nearside windscreens pre-war and none of nearside fixed single panes post-war, suggesting that all 76 vehicles were converted 1939–46.

The removable front panels having three columns of eight louvred ventilation vanes on some vehicles were replaced post-war by different versions having three columns of six or seven vanes presumably to replace damaged originals. Photographs have identified that the following vehicles were so equipped:

Six vane:
Before rebuilding: 274, 280, 283.
After rebuilding: 227, 230, 231, 237, 251, 255, 260, 263, 283, 286, 292, 294.

Seven vane:
Before rebuilding:
After rebuilding: 241, 248, 259, 271, 273, 277.

No. 231 ran with a removable front panel having three columns of four louvred ventilation vanes of non-standard appearance early post-war and the maker's badge removed. Later, probably after rebuilding in 1956, it was equipped with a three-column, six-vane removable panel and the chassis and equipment maker's badge was reinstated. Nos. 238 (post-1951 until rebuilding), 268 and 295 (both prior rebuilding) were equipped with a three-column, five-vane panel.

Some vehicles operated for various periods without one or both semaphore arm illuminated traffic indicators. There seems to have been no obvious pattern in these changes and there are cases where vehicles from which trafficators had been removed receiving them again at a later date.

Post-war the half-drop openers to the upper saloon front windows were progressively replaced with a single fixed pane on each side on most vehicles (but not all) including some which were not subsequently involved in the rebuilding programme, including 257, 259, 262, 263, 280, 284, 287. Those vehicles which had not gained a single pane prior to rebuilding had this modification made as part of the rebuilding package.

A plate was fitted in November 1945 at the rear of the offside retaining tube beneath the body to stop the bamboo trolley retrieval pole from sliding out.

The single line indicator box displaying the final destination inside the lower saloon at the top of the offside bay 5 window was removed early post-war.

Commencing in 1947 a cover was fixed over the ventilators immediately above the roofline at the front of the upper-deck and above the driver's cab windscreen in the form of a hood of triangular cross-section intended to prevent water ingress, not least in the vicinity of the main power cable, and reduce draughts into the upper saloon and driver's cab. The covers appear to have been to three styles: a "standard" version in the form of a hood of triangular cross-section; a slightly larger but less protruding "flanged" version identifiable by four rivets across the top, e.g. 234, 238, 240, 250, 259, 279; and a half-cylindrical or tube version. Some vehicles, e.g. 251, 252, 255, 259, 281, 289, 296 ran with solely the cab louvres covered. All vehicles involved in the post-war rebuilding programme emerged with hoods over both the roof and cab louvres to the "standard" design.

It is assumed that all vehicles retained their semaphore arm illuminated traffic indicators until at least September 1939; however, post-war, but prior to rebuilding, the majority of the class were in service without traffic indicators. In so far as it is known the situation was:

Indicators retained: 232, 234, 240*, 247, 251, 254, 257, 262, 287.
Indicators removed: 231, 237, 240*, 241, 244, 246, 252, 255, 258, 259, 260, 263, 265, 266, 270, 271, 272, 274, 276, 279, 280, 281, 284, 285, 286, 291, 292, 295, 296, 298, 299, 300.
(*240 lost its indicators at a later date, post-war.)

Those vehicle involved in the rebuilding programme reappeared with semaphore arm illuminated traffic indicators fitted on, and parallel to, the driver's cab corner pillars on both nearside and offside, but mounted a few inches higher than had been pre-war practice. However, 226, 229, 260, 261 did not benefit from traffic indicators after rebuilding, whilst 227, 237, 239, 267, 268, 269, which were refitted with traffic indicators, subsequently lost them again.

Photographic evidence of the thoroughness of the rebuilding. (City of Portsmouth Archives)

There are no proven explanations to this policy. During war-time the illuminated traffic indicators could not be practically adapted for the "black-out" whilst it is possible that any failure of the operating mechanisms could not be repaired due to an absence of spare parts and a shortage of labour. The latter situation may have prevailed post-war too.

No. 267 ran without a front fleet number for a period around October 1958.

The undertaking commenced a comprehensive rebuilding programme in 1948, including the Cravens-bodied motorbuses. This continued until 1956 when it was abruptly terminated as it became clear that the trolleybus system was going to be abandoned. The programme consolidated the earlier modifications to individual members of the batch, which had led to many variations amongst the 76 vehicles, and a standard version appeared after rebuild although changes were made during the course of the programme and the rebuilt vehicles did not have a common appearance. The trolleybuses rebuilt were:

225–239, 241–254, 255–256, 259–261, 265, 267–271, 273–275, 277–278, 281–283, 286, 290, 291–295, 297–300

REBUILDING DETAILS CRAVENS BODIED AEC661Ts 225–300

Fleet No.	Reg. No.	Date rebuilt	Condition date	Roof vents	Cab vents	Upper-saloon front windows	Front panel	Rear upper windows	Rear lower windows	Front upper rainshield
		C	D	E	F	G	H	I	J	K
225	RV8307	09.1949	RB	C	C	F				
226	RV8308	04.1952	RB	C	C	F				
227	RV8309	03.1950	RB	C	C	F				Yes
228	RV8310	07.1952	Not known							
229	RV8311	1948	RB	C	C	F				No
230	RV8312	04.1955	RB	C	C	F				
231	RV8313	-	URB	F	F	O				No
		-	URB by 1952	C	C	O				No
		03.1956	RB	C	C	F				Yes
232	RV8314	03.1953	URB	F	F	F				No
		08.1953	RB	C	C	F				
233	RV8315		URB	F	F	O				No
		10.1953	RB	C	C	F		Mk 2	Mk 2	
234	RV8316	-	URB	C	C	O				No
		08.1954	RB	C	C	F				
235	RV8317	11.1953	URB	C	C	O			Mk 2	No
236	RV8318	08.1951	RB	C	C	F		Mk 1	Mk 1	
237	RV8319	1956	URB	C	C	O				No
			RB	C	C	F				
238	RV8320	07.1955	RB	C	C	F		Mk 2	Mk 2	
239	RV8321	07.1950	RB	C	C	F				
240	RV8322	-	URB	C	C	O				No
241	RV8323	06.1954	RB	C	C	F				
242	RV8324	01.1955	RB	C	C	F				
243	RV8325	-	URB	C	C	F				No
		07.1952	RB	C	C	F				
244	RV8326	-	URB	F	C	O				No
		01.1953	RB	C	C	F				
245	RV8327	01.1952	RB	C	C	F				
246	RV8328	11.1956	RB	C	C	F		Mk 2	Mk 2	
247	RV8329	04.1949	RB	C	C	F				No
248	RV8330	-	URB	C		F		Mk 1	Mk1	
		10.1954	RB	C	C	F				Yes
249	RV8331	05.1954	RB	C	C	F			Mk1	
250	RV8332	06.1953	RB	C	C	F				
251	RV8333		pre-1952 URB	F	C	O				No
			by mid 1950s URB	F	C	F				No
		07.1956	RB	C	C	F				Yes
252	RV8334	-	URB	F	C	O		Mk 1	Mk 1	
		02.1952	RB	C	C	F				
253	RV8335	01.1950	RB	C	C	F				
254	RV8336	09.1953	URB	F	F	O				No
			RB	C	C	F				
255	RV9106	-	URB	F	C					No
		-	URB	C	C					
		12.1955	RB	C	C	F				
256	RV9107	12.1952	RB	C	C	F				
257	RV9108	-	URB	C	C	F				No
258	RV9109	-	URB	C	C	F				Yes
259	RV9110	-	URB	F	C	O				No
		12.1954	RB	C	C	F		Mk 2	Mk2	Yes
260	RV9111	-	URB	C	C	F				Yes
		06.1948	RB	C	C	F				Yes
261	RV9112	03.1952	RB	C	C	F				
262	RV9113	-	URB	C	C	F				No
263	RV9114	-	URB	C	C	F		Mk 1		No

Fleet No.	Reg. No.	Date rebuilt C	Condition date D	Roof vents E	Cab vents F	Upper-saloon front windows G	Front panel H	Rear upper windows I	Rear lower windows J	Front upper rainshield K
264	RV9115	-	URB	C	C	O				No
265	RV9116	06.1948	RB	C	C	F				No
266	RV9117	-	Not known							
267	RV9118	1949	RB	C	C	F		Mk 1	Mk 1	
268	RV9119	02.1951	RB	C	C	F		Mk 1	Mk 1	
269	RV9120	-	URB	F	F	O				No
		04.1956	RB	C	C	F				
270	RV9121	-	URB	C	C	O		Mk 1	Mk 1	No
		06.1956	RB	C	C	F				
271	RV9122	03.1954	RB	C	C	F				
272	RV9123	-	URB	F	F	O				No
273	RV9124	10.1955	RB	C	C	F				
274	RV9125	-	URB	C	C	F				No
		03.1955	RB	C	C	F				
275	RV9126	03.1949	RB	C	C	F				No
276	RV9127	-	Not known							
277	RV9128	12.1948	RB	C	C	F		Mk 1	Mk 1	No
278	RV9129	-	URB	C	C	O				No
		07.1949	RB	C	C	F				
279	RV9130	-	URB	C	C	O				
280	RV9131	-	URB	C	C	F		Mk 1	Mk 1	No
281	RV9132	-	URB	F	C	O				No
		12.1952	RB	C	C	F				
282	RV9133	06.1952	RB	C	C	F				
283	RV9134	08.1949	RB	C	C	F				
284	RV9135	-	URB	C	C	F				No
285	RV9136	-	URB	C	C	O				No
286	RV9137	-	URB	F	C	O				No
		11.1955	RB	C	C	F				
287	RV9138		URB	C	C	F				No
288	RV9139		Not known							
289	RV9140		URB	F	C	O				
290	RV9141	10.1948	RB	C	C	F				
291	RV9142	-	URB							
		12.1953	RB	C	C	F				No
292	RV9143	00.1949	RB	C	C	F				No
293	RV9144	03.1953	RB	C	C	F				
294	RV9145	07.1956	RB	C	C	F				
295	RV9149	12.1951	RB	C	C	F				
296	RV9150	-	URB	F	C	O				
297	RV9151	08.1952	RB	C	C	F				
298	RV9152	-	URB	C	C	O				No
		-	URB	C	C	F				No
		11.1956	RB							
299	RV9153	-	URB	C	C	F				No
		05.1953	RB	C	C	F				
300	RV9154	-	URB	C	C	F				No
		06.1955	RB	C	C	F		Mk 2	Mk 2	

Column

D = date or period in condition indicated in columns E-J

E = Shallow louvred ventilators above roofline (as delivered) indicated by F
= Louvred ventilators above roofline covered with hood indicated by C

F = Shallow louvred ventilators above driver's cab windscreen (as delivered) indicated by F
= Louvred ventilators above driver's cab windscreen covered with hood indicated by C

G = Opening half-drop upper saloon front windows (as delivered) indicated by O
= Fixed single pane upper saloon front windows indicated by F

H = Number of rows of ventilation vanes and number of columns in front panel

Loading outside Hilsea SMS Garage, 275 has covers over the ventilators immediately above the roofline at the front of the upper-deck and above the driver's cab windscreen. Rebuilt in March 1949, the trolleybus has single panes of glass in the front upper saloon windows but the lower corners of the front upper-saloon windows remain square. An SMS utility-bodied Guy follows behind whilst the frog (8, see the Facing (Turnout) Frogs map in Appendix H) providing access to the southbound Northern Parade line can be seen immediately above the trolleybus. (Roy Marshall)

The first vehicle to be rebuilt was 229 in May 1948 (de-licensed: 1 October 1947), and by the time that the final vehicle emerged in November 1956, 54 trolleybuses and 21 buses had been rebuilt.

It took 1–3 months to rebuild each vehicle, depending on the quantity of other work in the body shop. It comprised replacing the front upper-deck wooden window pillars, which by then were usually rotten, and fitting pre-fabricated Metal Components top hat sections to the steel side body pillars which were suffering from corrosion and decay of the wooden inserts, and similar strengthening to other parts of the bodywork Other work as deemed necessary was undertaken. The completed rebuild produced a body that was subtly different in appearance to the original style.

The changes in appearance were:

(1) Those vehicles which still possessed the upper-deck front half-drop openers had them replaced with fixed glass and one internal grab rail. The lower corners of the windows remained square until July 1949 when 278 emerged with curved lower corners which remained standard thereafter for all rebuilds. A similar change was made to the lower corners of the rear platform window (and those in the upper deck emergency exit door) but this seems to have occurred in 1953, possibly with 233 in November 1953. Early rebuilds ("Mk 1") retained the same style of gently radiused curved top corners to the rear platform window and the top outer corners to the windows of the upper deck emergency exit with which they were originally supplied, even after radiused windows had started to appear in the front windows of the upper saloon. About 1953 the upper radiused curve to the windows became more acute and the right angle of the lower corners was replaced by a sharper very acute curve ("Mk 2"), which can be difficult to detect on photographs. As examples, 236 rebuilt in August 1951 retained "Mk 1" but 271 rebuilt in March 1954 carried "Mk 2".

(2) Those vehicles which on rebuild still had the front roof and cab vents as delivered and those which had gained the "flanged" cover referred to above had them covered or replaced with the "standard" version upon rebuild, e.g. 234.

(3) In about 1949, possibly initially with 278, metal louvres were fitted above the front upper-deck windows matching those above the upper and lower saloon side windows.

From mid-1950 the lower saloon half-drop openers in bay 1 were replaced by single fixed panes and a half-drop opener fitted to bay 2 instead. The position of the upper saloon openers remained unchanged.

There is no evident policy in the selection of vehicles for reconstruction and it is believed that the decision was taken by the workshop foreman although it is not clear which criteria was used.

The programme started in 1948 with 229, which was one of the first vehicles in service and seems an obvious selection, followed by 260 which had suffered accident damage. The other two 1948 rebuilds were 265 and 290 which were not such obvious candidates. For 1949 Nos. 225, 247, 267, 277, 278, 283 were rebuilt which gives a reasonable spread throughout the class and not a concentration amongst the earlier vehicles which might have been expected.

By the beginning of 1950 there were 24 surplus trolleybuses, seven of which were from this batch (226, 227, 236, 239, 261, 268, 297). Six of these vehicles were rebuilt prior to returning to service but whilst No. 227 was rebuilt in March 1950, 226 had to wait de-licensed for nearly two and a half years before rebuilding in April 1952. No. 297 was returned to service un-rebuilt for a period prior to rebuilding in August 1952. Perhaps being the newest of the seven determined this selection. 1951 saw an average surplus of 30 trolleybuses, excluding two withdrawals, in 1952 a surplus of 34 and this surplus continued at around the 30 mark until the disposal programme began in earnest in 1958.

As a consequence of this persistent surplus, a group of long term de-licensed trolleybuses from this batch were stored at North End depot. They were used as a source of spares and with one exception (229) they were neither rebuilt vehicles nor subsequently selected for rebuilding. These vehicles were latterly stored in the first three rows of the depot nearest the entrance/exit. A start was made with removing these vehicles to Eastney for disposal in late 1956/early 1957 and by May 1957, 229 (last in service June 1953), 258 (April 1952), 276 (February 1954) and 279 (August 1951) had been moved.

On 8 May 1957 the following vehicles remained:

257	last ran Oct. 1954	266	last ran Feb. 1951	287	last ran April 1954
262	April 1954	272	July 1953	288	Mar. 1951
263	Sept. 1953	280	April 1958	289	Sept. 1951
264	Sept. 1953	284	Sept. 1953	290	Jan. 1952
285	Dec. 1950	296	Sept. 1953		

The removal of these stored vehicles from North End was not effected in the obvious manner of the front vehicles first. Some of the vehicles in the middle of the block were extricated early on in the removal process with, it would seem, some difficulty, whilst others near the front remained unmoved. Clearly there were some specific selection criteria which are not known. The un-rebuilt vehicles contained a preponderance of the later vehicles in the 260–290 range which is surprising and the reason for this is not known. There seems to be no pattern to the selection for rebuilding. Thus 230 (de-licensed October 1953) was rebuilt in April 1955 whereas 263, 264, 280, 284, which were de-licensed at the same time, were never rebuilt and saw no further service. Some vehicles were de-licensed for short periods prior to rebuilding, e.g. 252 de-licensed in October 1953 and rebuilt in May 1954, whereas others waited a year or more de-licensed before reconstruction, e.g. 270 de-licensed October 1954 for a 1956 rebuild. The last rebuild was 246 in November 1956, after continuous service since at least 1 January 1950. It might be thought that vehicles out of service since 1951–53, e.g. 263, 288, 289, would have been structurally a better choice but presumably cannibalisation over the years precluded this.

No. 283 (rebuilt in 1949) is quoted as having been rebuilt a second time in 1956. It was de-licensed November 1955–March 1956, but whether it was rebuilt again at this time or merely had heavier routine body maintenance, is not known.

De-licensed vehicles

These trolleybuses can be broadly grouped into two categories:

(1) Those which spent long periods de-licensed (years in many cases) prior to disposal. These existed in the years prior to 1957 and thus before any abandonment decision. They were seen as a resource for the future and classified as de-licensed by CPPTD. Some returned to service with or without rebuilding but some 15 were never reinstated to service. It is impossible to determine exactly what caused a vehicle in this group to be classified as withdrawn although in some cases it may simply reflect a decision to dispose of the vehicle.

(2) Those de-licensed as a consequence of the conversion programme and for which disposal swiftly followed.

Storage prior to disposal

Nos. 231, 238

Direct to Eastney Depot Yard immediately on withdrawal from service.

Nos. 216, 219, 220, 229, 257, 258, 262, 263, 264, 266, 275, 276, 279, 284, 285, 287, 288, 289, 296

Long-term under cover storage at North End Depot, tightly parked in three/four rows immediately inside the entrance/exit. Except for 216, 219, 220, 229, all the stored vehicles from this batch had not been rebuilt. Removal commenced with 229 and 258, the latter for Bristol, in April 1957.

Disposal

225 Last licensed May 1959. Withdrawn following accident damage in June 1959; stored in Eastney Depot Yard from August 1959 until sold in February 1960 to G. Cohen, Southampton, and broken up by their subsidiary Pollock & Brown at Northam Ironworks, Southampton, in July 1960.

226 Last licensed August 1960; sold to Southern Counties Demolitions Ltd., Bedhampton Chalk Pit, in November 1960 and broken up February 1961.

227 Last licensed 30 April 1960; sold to Southern Counties Demolitions Ltd., Bedhampton Chalk Pit, in July 1960 and broken up April–October 1961.

228 Last licensed August 1960; sold to Southern Counties Demolitions Ltd., Bedhampton Chalk Pit, in November 1960 and broken up February 1961.

229 Last licensed June 1953; stored in Eastney Depot Yard until broken up by CPPTD in August 1957.

230 Last licensed 30 September 1961; stored at North End Depot until sold in December 1961 to J. & J. Maybank (Southern) Ltd., Portsmouth, a waste paper merchant. Collected on 12 February 1962, moved to Maybank's Gosport depot adjacent to the gasworks where it was broken up in April 1962.

231 Last licensed in June 1961; stored at Eastney Depot Yard until sold in December 1961 to Hants and Sussex Aviation, Portsmouth Airport. Broken up March 1963.

232 Last licensed September 1960; stored at Eastney Depot Yard until sold in November 1960 to Southern Counties Demolitions Ltd., Bedhampton Chalk Pit, and broken up July–September 1961.

233 Last licensed 21 June 1963; stored at Eastney Depot Yard until sold in September 1963 to C.D. Jordan & Son Ltd. (Breaker), Dundas Spur, and broken up by 12 September 1963.

234 Last licensed August 1960; stored at Eastney Depot Yard until sold in November 1960 to Southern Counties Demolitions Ltd., Bedhampton Chalk Pit, and broken up April–July 1961.

235 Last licensed September 1960; stored at Eastney Depot Yard until sold in November 1960 to Southern Counties Demolitions Ltd., Bedhampton Chalk Pit, and broken up February–July 1961.

236 Last licensed April 1960; stored at Eastney Depot Yard until sold in July 1960 to Southern Counties Demolitions Ltd., Bedhampton Chalk Pit, and broken up April–September 1961.

237 Last licensed October 1961; stored at Eastney Depot Yard until sold in December 1961 to C.D. Jordan & Son Ltd. (Breaker), Locksway Road, Portsmouth, where it was used as a store, being moved to Jordan's new yard at Dundas Spur, Copnor, near Portsmouth Airport, in May 1963. By 5 September 1965, 237 was the sole vehicle still at this scrap yard where it continued to be used as a store until c. 1977 after which it became increasingly inaccessible due to the surrounding heaps of scrap metal. It was still extant in an increasingly collapsed and dilapidated state throughout the 1990s but no trace now remains.

238 Last licensed 30 April 1960; stored at Eastney Depot Yard until sold in July 1960 to Southern Counties Demolitions Ltd., Bedhampton Chalk Pit, and broken up April–September 1961.

239 Last licensed September 1960; stored at Eastney Depot Yard until sold November 1960 to Southern Counties Demolitions Ltd., Bedhampton Chalk Pit, and broken up in July 1961.

240 Last licensed June 1956; stored at Eastney Depot Yard until broken up in March 1958 by CPPTD.

241 Last licensed August 1960; stored at Eastney Depot Yard until sold in November 1960 to Southern Counties Demolitions Ltd., Bedhampton Chalk Pit, and broken up February–September 1961.

242 Last licensed 30 April 1960; stored at Eastney Depot Yard until sold July 1960 to Southern Counties Demolitions Ltd., Bedhampton Chalk Pit, and broken up May–July 1961.

243 Last licensed September 1960; stored at Eastney Depot Yard until sold in November 1960 to Southern Counties Demolitions Ltd., Bedhampton Chalk Pit, and broken up April–August 1961.

244 Last licensed November 1961; stored at Eastney Depot Yard until sold in March 1962 to Southern Counties Demolitions Ltd., Bedhampton Chalk Pit, and broken up in March 1962.

245 Last licensed February 1960; stored at Eastney Depot Yard until sold in February 1960 to G. Cohen, Southampton, and broken up by their subsidiary Pollock & Brown at Northam Ironworks, Southampton, in July 1960.

246 Last licensed 22 June 1963; towed from Eastney Depot to North End Depot on 23 June 1963 and stored at North End Depot. Sold in September 1963 to C.D. Jordan & Son Ltd. (Breaker), Dundas Spur, Copnor and broken up 1–9 October 1963.

247 Last licensed 30 April 1960; stored at Eastney Depot Yard until sold in July 1960 to Southern Counties Demolitions Ltd., Bedhampton Chalk Pit, and broken up March–September 1961.

248 Last licensed 22 June 1963; transferred from Eastney Depot to North End Depot on 23 June 1963 (under own power to Stubbington Avenue). Sold to C.D. Jordan & Son Ltd. (Breaker), Dundas Spur, Copnor, in September 1963 and broken up 2–9 October 1963.

249 Last licensed October 1961; stored at Eastney Depot Yard until sold in March 1962 to Southern Counties Demolitions Ltd., Bedhampton Chalk Pit, and broken up in April 1962.

250 Last licensed January 1963: stored at Eastney Depot 23 February 1963–April 1963 following a failure in service, moved into Eastney Depot Yard in April 1963 until sold in September 1963 to C.D. Jordan & Son Ltd. (Breaker), Dundas Spur, Copnor, and broken up 12–18 September 1963.

251 Last licensed October 1961; stored at Eastney Depot Yard until sold in December 1961 to Hants and Sussex Aviation, Portsmouth Airport, and broken up (by August 1962).

252 Last licensed 3 December 1961; stored at Eastney Depot Yard until sold in March 1962 to Southern Counties Demolitions Ltd., Bedhampton Chalk Pit, and broken up by 8 April 1962.

253 Last licensed 30 April 1960; stored at Eastney Depot Yard until sold in July 1960 to Southern Counties Demolitions Ltd., Bedhampton Chalk Pit, and broken up April–October 1961.

254 Last licensed December 1961; stored at Eastney Depot Yard until sold in March 1962 to Southern Counties Demolitions Ltd., Bedhampton Chalk Pit, and broken up March 1962.

255 Last licensed November 1961; stored at Eastney Depot Yard until sold in March 1962 to Southern Counties Demolitions Ltd., Bedhampton Chalk Pit, and broken up March 1962.

256 Last licensed July 1961. Withdrawn 23 August 1961 following a collision; stored at Eastney Depot Yard from October 1961 until sold in December 1961 to Hants and Sussex Aviation, Portsmouth Airport, and broken up April 1962.

257 Last licensed October 1954; stored at North End Depot until sold in August 1957 to G. Bunney (Breaker), Southampton, and broken up.

258 Last licensed September 1952; stored at North End Depot until sold in April 1957 to City of Bristol Transport & Cleansing Department and converted to a mobile Ladies Convenience in May 1957. Sold to an unknown Bristol dealer for scrap in April 1973.

259 Last licensed December 1961; stored at Eastney Depot Yard until sold in March 1962 to Southern Counties Demolitions Ltd., Bedhampton Chalk Pit, and broken up April 1962.

260 Last licensed December 1956; stored at Eastney Depot Yard until July 1957 when broken up *in situ* by CPPTD.

261 Last licensed 30 April 1960; stored initially at North End Depot but moved to Eastney Depot Yard later in May 1960, remaining until sold July 1960 to Southern Counties Demolitions Ltd., Bedhampton Chalk Pit, and broken up January 1961.

262 Last licensed April 1954; stored at North End Depot until August 1957 when sold to G. Bunney (Breaker), Southampton and broken up.

263 Last licensed September 1953; stored at North End Depot until sold in August 1957 to G. Bunney (Breaker), Southampton, and broken up.

264 Last licensed September 1953; stored at North End Depot until sold in August 1957 to G. Bunney (Breaker), Southampton, and broken up.

265 Last licensed June 1958; stored at Eastney Depot until December 1958 when transferred to storage at North End Depot. Removed to storage at Eastney Depot Yard in January 1960 until sold February 1960 to G. Cohen,

Southampton, and broken up by Pollock & Brown at Northam Ironworks, Southampton, in July 1960.

266 Last licensed February 1951; stored at North End Depot until sold in August 1957 to G. Bunney (Breaker), Southampton, and broken up.

267 Last licensed 30 April 1960; stored at Eastney Depot Yard until sold in July 1960 to Southern Counties Demolitions Ltd., Bedhampton Chalk Pit, and broken up May–July 1961.

268 Last licensed 30 April 1960; stored at North End Depot (May 1960) and transferred to store at Eastney Depot Yard in May 1960 until sold July 1960 to Southern Counties Demolitions Ltd., Bedhampton Chalk Pit, and broken up January 1961.

269 Last licensed 22 June 1963; transferred on 23 June 1963 from Eastney Depot to North End Depot (under own power as far as Stubbington Avenue); stored until September 1963 when sold to C.D. Jordan & Son Ltd. (Breaker), Dundas Spur, Copnor, and broken up 9–12 October 1963.

270 Last licensed 3 December 1961; stored at Eastney Depot Yard until sold in March 1962 to Southern Counties Demolitions Ltd., Bedhampton Chalk Pit, and broken up by 8 April 1962.

271 Last licensed 30 April 1960; stored initially at North End Depot then removed to store at Eastney Depot Yard in May 1960 remaining until sold July 1960 to Southern Counties Demolitions Ltd., Bedhampton Chalk Pit, and broken up April–October 1961.

272 Last licensed July 1953; stored at North End Depot until sold August 1957 to G. Bunney (Breaker), Southampton, and broken up.

273 Last licensed 3 December 1961; stored at Eastney Depot Yard until sold in March 1962 to Southern Counties Demolitions Ltd., Bedhampton Chalk Pit, and broken up March 1962.

274 Last licensed 15 May 1963; stored at Eastney Depot Yard (May 1963) until sold in September 1963 to C.D. Jordan & Son Ltd. (Breaker), Dundas Spur, Copnor, and broken up 18–28 September 1963.

275 Last licensed September 1957; stored at North End Depot and broken up by CPPTD.

276 Last licensed February 1954; stored at North End Depot until sold August 1957 to G. Bunney (Breaker), Southampton, and broken up.

277 Last licensed June 1956; stored at Eastney Depot Yard until August 1957 when broken up by CPPTD.

278 Last licensed September 1959; stored in Eastney Depot until February 1960 when removed and stored in Eastney Depot Yard; sold February 1960 to G. Cohen, Southampton, and broken up by Pollock & Brown at Northam Ironworks, Southampton, in July 1960.

279 Last licensed August 1951; stored at North End Depot until broken up in August 1957 in Eastney Depot Yard by CPPTD.

280 Last licensed September 1953; stored at North End Depot until sold in early 1958 to C.D. Jordan & Son Ltd. (Breaker), Locksway Road, Milton, Portsmouth, and broken up.

281 Last licensed 30 April 1960; stored at Eastney Depot Yard until sold July 1960 to Southern Counties Demolitions Ltd., Bedhampton Chalk Pit, and broken up May–June 1961.

282 Last licensed 30 September 1961; stored at North End Depot until sold December 1961 to Hants and Sussex Aviation, Portsmouth Airport. Broken up March 1965.

283 Last licensed 22 June 1963; transferred 23.June 1963 from Eastney Depot to North End Depot (under own power as far as Stubbington Avenue) and stored until September 1963 when sold to C.D. Jordan & Son Ltd. (Breaker), Dundas Spur, Copnor, and broken up 12–16 October 1963.

284 Last licensed September 1953; stored at North End Depot until sold in early 1958 to C.D. Jordan & Son Ltd. (Breaker), Locksway Road, Milton, Portsmouth, and broken up June 1958.

285 Last licensed December 1950; stored North End Depot until February 1958 when broken up at Eastney Depot Yard by CPPTD.

286 Last licensed 21 June 1963; stored at Eastney Depot Yard until sold in September 1963 to C.D. Jordan & Son Ltd. (Breaker), Dundas Spur, Copnor, and broken up 12–16 October 1963.

287 Last licensed April 1954; stored North End Depot until January 1958 when broken up at Eastney Depot Yard by CPPTD.

288 Last licensed March 1951; stored North End Depot until March 1958 when broken up at Eastney Depot Yard by CPPTD.

289 Last licensed September 1951; stored North End Depot until March 1958 when broken up at Eastney Depot Yard by CPPTD.

290 Last licensed September 1958; stored at Eastney Depot until December 1958 when transferred to store at North End Depot. Removed to store at Eastney Depot Yard January 1960 and sold in February 1960 to G. Cohen, Southampton, and broken up by Pollock & Brown at Northam Ironworks, Southampton, in July 1960.

291 Last licensed 30 September 1961; stored at North End Depot until sold in December 1961 to Hants and Sussex Aviation, Portsmouth Airport and broken up April 1962.

292 Last licensed 30 April 1960; stored at Eastney Depot Yard until sold in July 1960 to Southern Counties Demolitions Ltd., Bedhampton Chalk Pit and broken up between April 1961 and October 1961.

293 Last licensed October 1960; stored at North End Depot and transferred to Eastney Depot later in December 1960. Removed to Eastney Depot Yard July 1961; sold December 1961 to Hants and Sussex Aviation and broken up by August 1962.

294 Last licensed 21 June 1963; stored at Eastney Depot Yard until sold in September 1963 to C.D. Jordan & Son Ltd. (Breaker), Dundas Spur, Copnor and broken up 18–28 September 1963.

295 Last licensed December 1960; stored at North End Depot until sold in December 1961 to Hants and Sussex Aviation, Portsmouth Airport. Broken up by July 1966.

296 Last licensed in September 1953; stored at North End Depot until October 1957 when broken up at Eastney Depot Yard by CPPTD.

297 Last licensed May 1960; stored at Eastney Depot being transferred to store at Eastney Depot Yard in September 1960; sold to J. Wells, Buckland, Portsmouth, and parked on a bomb site at Merry Row, Landport, Portsmouth, in January 1961. The vehicle was moved into a cramped yard on 30 January 1961 but no evidence remained by 27 October 1961.

298 Last licensed 3 December 1961; stored at Eastney Depot Yard until sold in March 1962 to Southern Counties

Demolitions Ltd., Bedhampton Chalk Pit and broken up April 1962.

299 Last licensed August 1961; stored at Eastney Depot until sold in December 1961 to Hants and Sussex Aviation, Portsmouth Airport. Broken up by May 1963.

300 Last licensed 21 June 1963; stored at Eastney Yard until sold in September 1965 to C.D. Jordan & Son Ltd. (Breaker), Dundas Spur, Copnor and broken up 18–19 September 1965.

AEC 661T 258 was sold in April 1957 to the City of Bristol Transport & Cleansing Department who immediately converted it into a mobile Ladies Convenience. It continued in use for this purpose until the early 1970s. (photographer's name not recorded)

In December 1935 Portsmouth AEC661T 20 was loaned to Brighton Corporation Tramways as a part of their evaluation of trolleybuses as successors to their tramways. This view shows the vehicle standing beneath temporary trolleybus overhead wiring making an anticlockwise loop round The Level in Brighton. (M.P.M. Nimmo collection)

DISPOSAL OF AEC 661T / CRAVENS 225-300

Batch	For sale date Note 1	Sold date	Sale price	Vehicles	Purchaser	Note
A		04.1957	£80	258	City of Bristol Transport & Cleansing Department	
B	06.06.1957	08.1957	£50	257, 262–264, 266, 272, 276	G. Bunney (Breaker), Southampton	
C	29.01.1958	1958	£74 10s	280, 284 *also 216, 219, 220*	C.D. Jordan (Breaker), Locksway Road, Milton, Portsmouth	
D	14.03.1960	22.02.1960	£90 10s	225, 245, 265, 278, 290 *also 224*	G. Cohen, Southampton	2
E	17.05.1960	11.07.1960	£85 5s	227, 236, 238, 242, 247, 253, 261, 267, 268, 271, 281, 292	Southern Counties Demolitions Ltd., Bedhampton Chalk Pit, Havant	3
F		03.11.1960	£77 10s	226, 228, 232, 234, 235, 239, 241, 243	Southern Counties Demolitions Ltd., Bedhampton Chalk Pit, Havant	4
G	13.01.1961		£78 10s 6d	297	J. Wells, Merry Row, Landport, Portsmouth	
H	13.11.1961	12.1961	£87 2s 10d	231, 251, 256, 282, 291, 293, 295, 299 *also 303*	Hants and Sussex Aviation, Portsmouth Airport	5
I	13.11.1961	12.1961	£87 2s 10d	237	C.D. Jordan (Breaker), Locksway Road, Milton, Portsmouth	5
J	29.12.1961	02.1962	£91	230	J. & J. Maybank (Southern) Ltd., Gosport	
K	1/12/1962		£92 10s	244, 249, 252, 254, 255, 259, 270, 273, 298	Southern Counties Demolitions Ltd., Bedhampton Chalk Pit, Havant	6
L	15.07.1963	09.1963	£86 10s	233, 246, 248, 250, 269, 274, 283, 286, 294, 300	C.D. Jordan (Breaker), Dundas Spur, Copnor	

Notes

1 These dates are from CPPTD records and pre-date the appearance of the Invitation to Tender in the local press. Thus, this may be the date that the decision to sell was taken.
2 Broken up by Pollock & Brown Co. Ltd. at Northam Ironworks, Southampton, in July 1960.
3 These vehicles had already been moved to Bedhampton Chalk Pit between 9-18 June 1960 prior to the official "Sold Date"
4 These vehicles had already been moved to Bedhampton Chalk Pit by 20 October 1960 prior to the official "Sold Date"
5 The Invitation to Tender was for nine trolleybuses which it is assumed were the AEC 661T batches H and I, however solely 237 went to C.D. Jordan (as a store).It is unclear if 303 was added to batch H to make up to 9 vehicles. Interestingly, it was Jordan's tow truck, registration TPX562, which collected some if not all the AEC661Ts and 303 for Hants and Sussex Aviation, in addition to 237. C.D. Jordan moved from Locksway Road, Milton, to a larger site at Dundas Spur.
6 These vehicles were all moved to Bedhampton Chalk Pit by 1 March 1962.

1950–51 BUT9611T/Burlingham H28/24R

Fleet No.	Reg. No.	Chassis	Chassis No.	Body	Body No.	Into Service	Last licensed	Withdrawn	Sold
301	ERV926	BUT9611T	135	Burlingham	4081	01.11.1950	07.1963	27.07.1963	12.1963
302	ERV927	BUT9611T	136	Burlingham	4082	01.11.1950	07.1963	27.07.1963	12.1963
303	ERV928	BUT9611T	137	Burlingham	4083	01.11.1950	04.1961	11.04.1961	12.1961
304	ERV929	BUT9611T	138	Burlingham	4084	01.11.1950	07.1963	27.07.1963	12.1963
305	ERV930	BUT9611T	139	Burlingham	4085	01.12.1950	07.1963	27.07.1963	12.1963
306	ERV931	BUT9611T	140	Burlingham	4086	01.01.1951	07.1963	25.07.1963	12.1963
307	ERV932	BUT9611T	141	Burlingham	4087	01.01.1951	07.1963	27.07.1963	12.1963
308	ERV933	BUT9611T	142	Burlingham	4088	01.01.1951	07.1963	27.07.1963	12.1963
309	ERV934	BUT9611T	143	Burlingham	4089	01.01.1951	07.1963	25.07.1963	12.1963
310	ERV935	BUT9611T	144	Burlingham	4090	01.02.1951	07.1963	25.07.1963	12.1963
311	ERV936	BUT9611T	145	Burlingham	4091	01.03.1951	07.1963	25.07.1963	12.1963
312	ERV937	BUT9611T	146	Burlingham	4092	01.03.1951	07.1963	27.07.1963	12.1963
313	ERV938	BUT9611T	147	Burlingham	4093	01.03.1951	07.1963	27.07.1963	12.1963
314	ERV939	BUT9611T	148	Burlingham	4094	01.03.1951	07.1963	27.07.1963	12.1963
315	ERV940	BUT9611T	149	Burlingham	4095	25.03.1951	07.1963	27.07.1963	12.1963

Last licensed = the final month in which the vehicle was licensed to operate.

Chassis: Two-axle type BUT 9611T manufactured by the British United Traction Ltd., Hanover House, 14 Hanover Square, London W1 at the AEC works, Windmill Lane, Southall, Middlesex.
Motor: English Electric Ltd., Phoenix Works, Bradford, Yorkshire Type EE 410/4B (120nhp at 550 volts), compound-wound, non-regenerative.
Electrical equipment: English Electric Ltd., Phoenix Works, Bradford, Yorkshire, Series Dynamic.
De-wirement indicator: BTH line-light and buzzer.
Brakes: Westinghouse compressed air, hand and rheostatic brakes.
Body: H.V. Burlingham Ltd., Preston New Road, Marton, Blackpool, Lancashire, all metal H28/24R.
Length: 26ft.
Width: 7ft 6in.
Wheelbase: 16ft 4in. giving a turning circle on either lock of 59ft.
Wheel track: front 6ft 5$\frac{1}{2}$in., rear 5ft 9$\frac{3}{16}$in.
Unladen weight: 8 tons 4 cwt 2 qtr.

BUT9611T 312 with Burlingham body waits at Cosham Railway Station bus terminal (Cosham Compound) beneath the 25° Y frog providing entry to the loop installed in August/September 1948 as part of the revised overhead wiring layout here. A CPPTD utility-bodied Daimler motorbus on service J crosses Cosham Railway Station level crossing in the background. (Roy Marshall)

Tyres: Single front and twin rear wheels 11.00in. by 20in. low pressure.

In late 1946 AEC and Leyland Motors combined their trolleybus activities with the formation of British United Traction Ltd. (BUT), manufacture being initially based at the Leyland factory at Ham just north of Kingston upon Thames, Surrey. Falling demand for new trolleybuses following the nationalisation of the power supply industry led to the construction of chassis for double-deck trolleybuses being transferred to the AEC factory at Southall, Middlesex from 1948.

The BUT9611T chassis was similar to that of the pre-war AEC661T and was available in two widths to accommodate either a 7ft 6in. or an 8ft wide body, the latter giving a 2in. increase to the width of each double seat and 2in. to the gangway.

The contract price was £5,191 13s. The final price upon completion was:

301–305	£4,923 16s 8d
306–311	£4,924 10s 3d
312–315	£4,929 14s 8d

Chassis: The BUT9611T chassis was based on AEC Regent III motorbus chassis and was thus a development of the pre-war AEC663T. The chassis also incorporated most of the modifications introduced with the 3-axle BUT9641T. The chassis cost £2,371 13s each.

Chassis length: 26ft.
Chassis frame width: Front 3ft 3⅞in., rear 3ft 9¹¹⁄₃₂.
Overall width (over tyres): 7ft 5⅝in.

When compared with the pre-war AEC661T the chassis featured a re-designed rear axle with underslung worm drive, improved shaft and worm-wheel bearings. The propeller shaft, equipped with Layrub bushes, improved commutation by preventing transmission vibrations from reaching the traction motor.

A channel section shallow steel frame was used, braced by tubular cross members. The front axle beam was an alloy steel stamping with taper fit swivel pins and taper roller thrust bearings to take vertical loads.

Fully floating axles, both axles being equipped with stabiliser bars. Newton telescopic shock absorbers were fitted on the front axles only. The front axle and steering gear were common components with the AEC Regent III.

On the rear axle renewable strip-type thrust bearings were fitted behind the differential pinions and the axle shaft bevel wheels. Involute splines were used on the axle shafts with detachable cast inserts carrying the oil seals at the splined ends of the shafts.

Tecalemit slide-on individual nipples were used for lubrication.

Electrics: The compound-wound series traction motor was equipped with English Electric Series Dynamic control with a heavy series field and a comparatively light shunt field. During motoring only the series field was used and to attain normal speed field reduction was employed. During electric braking, which was rheostatic in character with all the generated energy being absorbed in the vehicle's starting resistances, only the motor shunt field was used.

The flood-proof motor was mounted between the chassis frames offset to the nearside, just ahead of the rear axle. The resistances, believed to have been manufactured by the Rheostatic Brake Co., were placed between the chassis frame in front of the traction motor with the shunt field resistance located under the cab. English Electric KM16-A10 master controller was underneath the driver's seat. The contactor cabinet was mounted on the rear wall of the cab to the nearside of the driver's seat. EE Contract 6X0692.

An overhung generator charged the Oldham lead-acid batteries, located beneath the first and second seats on each side towards the front of the lower saloon, which were

BUT9611T 310 loads outside Hilsea SMS Garage. An SMS Leyland TD5 (CCD947) re-bodied post-war by Northern Counties follows behind whilst the frog (8) providing access to the southbound Northern Parade line can be seen immediately above the trolleybus. (Roy Marshall)

used for manoeuvring and lighting purposes. Series-parallel switching was used for battery manoeuvring. The changeover switch for battery manoeuvring was located on the driver's cab floor.

There was a CAV dynamo on the commutator end of the traction motor.

A radio interference suppressor was mounted centrally immediately in front of the trolley gantry. The main power cables from the trolley gear made their way forward from the trolley gantry along the centre line of the roof before entered the front dome at the front of bay 1 immediately in front of the radio interference suppressor. The cables continued forwards in a conduit inside the front upper deck window pillar into the driver's cab.

Switches for low tension head, side, tail and auxiliary lights were arranged on the front dash, together with a speedometer and air pressure gauge. There was a round green de-wirement indicator light mounted in a square case above the other dashboard dials.

Brecknell Willis lightweight trolley bases.

Brakes: Westinghouse air brakes, hand and rheostatic brakes. The rheostatic brake was used down to 2–3mph; further pressure on the brake pedal at this speed bringing the compressed air brake into use and bringing the vehicle to rest. Both rheostatic and air brakes were operated by a single pedal on the right side of the power pedal. Slight depression of the pedal brought the first rheostatic brake notch, further depression the second rheotatic notch and still further depression brought in the air brake with an intensity proportional to the amount depressed. The air brakes acted on all wheels, with the control equipment providing two stages of rheostatic braking.

The compressor and air reservoir were bolted directly to the offside external face of the chassis frame and accessible behind a valence panel. Brake actuation was by air pressure cylinders mounted directly on the stub axles for the front brakes and also on the rear axle for the rear brakes.

The handbrake lever was to the offside of the driver's steering column.

Bodywork: Metal-framed, all-metal, five-bay Highbridge double-deck construction, enclosed forward-ascending half-turn (90°) staircase with conventional semi-vestibuled open platform entrance and exit at the rear built by H.V. Burlingham, Blackpool, Lancashire. The design was typified by its deeply domed roof accentuated by the livery application and ribbing. These were the first trolleybus bodies to be constructed by Burlingham who went on to secure orders from Glasgow, Manchester and Reading over the next 11 years. The bodies cost £2,820 each.

Forward-mounted integral trolley gantry above bay 1. Access to the trolley gear was by means of a removable platform stored behind the rear nearside seat which could be fitted to the rear window of the upper saloon, thence to the walking plank on the roof. There was cross-bracing between the trolley boom retention hooks.

Metal louvres were fitted above the upper and lower saloon side windows, and above the upper saloon front windows. Simplastic windows in steel pans were fitted throughout. Young's constant-balance half-drop openers in chromium-plated frames equipped with "continuous bar fasteners" at the top of each pane were fitted to the side windows in bays 1, 3 and 5 (both sides) of the upper and lower-deck. The upper pane dropped outside the fixed lower pane. The front upper-deck windows were fixed.

Ventilation was provided to the front end of the lower saloon and in the driver's cab through two vanes with pronounced louvres or covers, one above each of the driver's cab windscreens, somewhat to the nearside respectively offside of the windscreen. There were four roof-mounted Ashanco extractors (with two rectangular grills inside), one above bay 2 (towards the rear) and the other above bay 5 (towards the front) on each side.

Top hinged access doors were fitted at the base of the lower-deck offside panels in bay 1, behind the step giving access to the driver's cab, and 2, giving access to the compressor and air tank.

The mudguards above all four wheels deepened progressively towards the rear those towards the rear of the rear axle being particularly deep.

The rear upper deck emergency exit door had three hinges at its base and two oblong windows which were unusually more deep than broad, the additional depth being accommodated by reducing the width of the upper deck waist moulding (white-painted band) from behind each rear side window beneath the corner panels and door. There was an opening handle in the rear dome immediately above the emergency door to the offside of the grab handle and step providing access to the roof catwalk. The emergency exit door could be retained open in the horizontal position by leather-covered chains on each side. A separate platform, normally stowed behind the upper saloon rear nearside seat, fitted into retaining slits in the door sill to provide access to the roof catwalk and thence the trolley gantry. Small rubber bumpers half way up the frame on the nearside and offside of the emergency exit door aligned with similar bumpers on the panel beneath to the nearside and offside of the rear indicator boxes.

All windows had gently radiused, almost square, corners. The rear registration number plate was recessed, increasingly towards the top, immediately beneath the rear light which was about halfway up the offside of the rear lower panel. A circular conductor's mirror was fixed in the upper deck rear offside dome at the head of the stairs.

The staircase had three steps from the platform to a landing and then three steps to the upper deck, all equipped with aluminium kicking plates and rubber nosings on the treads. A step was also let into the platform side of the rear panels, on the nearside immediately beneath the rear platform window, to enable the conductor to reach the indicator blind handles. All platform, saloon and staircase handrails and stanchions were coated with black Doverite.

The base of the side and front glazing in the driver's cab area was some 2in. deeper than the base of the windows in the lower saloon and the cream-painted band beneath the windows became narrower at the position of the cab rear bulkhead to accommodate the deeper side windows and windscreen. The driver's cab had an offside front-hinged door (three hinges) equipped with a forwards sliding "signalling" window, and a black-painted opening handle mounted in a black-painted shield-shaped concave insert. The fixed upper window pane and the door deepened progressively towards the front of the vehicle to align with the foremost offside cab window. The nearside driver's cab windows were both fixed and deepened progressively towards the front of the vehicle to align with the deep windscreens.

There were two windows in the bulkhead behind the driver, separated by a wide central pillar, with two bevel-edged mirrors shaped to match the curve of the ceiling immediately above. Attached to the bulkhead above each window inside the driver's cab was a fold down blind to prevent reflections from the lower saloon on to the driver's windscreen during the hours of darkness. There was a protective rail across the glazed panes at half depth in the lower saloon. The nearside bulkhead window was fitted with a continuous or piano hinge at its base and opened to offer an emergency exit from the driver's cab. The upper portion of the wide central pillar between the two windows opened into the lower saloon to provide access to the control equipment wiring.

Both windscreens were chromium-plated and divided horizontally at approximately half depth into two panes, the upper pane on both sides opening outwards. The upper opening pane of the offside windscreen was equipped with a top-mounted wiper. There was a large black-painted metal contactor cabinet with plunger catches on the nearside of the driver's cab. The waist band beneath the driver's cab side windows and the windscreens was approximately half the depth of that beneath the lower saloon side windows, and the base of the side windows and windscreens were extended somewhat lower.

A step was let into the base of the off-side bay 1 side panel, but with no protective "kicking plate", immediately behind the front axle. Both front wheels were equipped with chromed wheel nut protector rings. "BUT" manufacturer's badges were on the hubs of all wheels.

Small rectangular driver's rear view mirrors were mounted externally towards the top of the front cab pillars on both sides.

A large removable panel which carried the registration plate and two columns of four ventilation vanes with gauze netting behind extended across the front of the cab from beneath the offside to beneath the nearside headlamp, the extremities of the vane aligned with the inside rim of the headlights. The "BUT" maker's symbol was fitted centrally beneath the driver's windscreen and between the headlamps.

The rear bulkhead featured a small window with radiused corners on the nearside with a used tickets box beneath and on the offside a glass fronted panel for official notices. There was a mirror above each window in the front lower saloon bulkhead. Diagonally-ribbed rubber rear platform floor covering.

A single tubular metal lifeguard ran beneath the side panels between the front and rear axles. A bamboo trolley retrieval pole was carried in a tube mounted centrally under the chassis and was accessible from the rear of the vehicle.

Lighting: External lighting was two relatively low-set chrome-rimmed headlights on the front panel, the top of the headlights being in line with the highest point of the front mudguards, with two front chrome-rimmed side lights in the limited space between the outer edge of the headlights and the extremity of the panel. A chrome-rimmed orange-lensed spotlight was fitted below the front panel in line with the nearside headlight. There was a single rear light, also chrome-rimmed, on the offside of the rear lower panel which also illuminated the inset rear registration number plate immediately beneath. At the rear, mounted centrally on the lower cream-painted band immediately beneath the rear platform window, an inset panel with red glass contained fretwork which could display an illuminated left-turn arrow, STOP warning and a right-turn arrow (the arrows did not flash).

To the offside of the rear registration number plate there was a circular red reflector with a second one on the nearside both at approximately the mid height of the registration number plate.

Semaphore arm illuminated traffic indicators accommodated in the panelling were fitted to the lower side panels beneath and immediately to the rear of the driver's cab corner pillars above the front mudguards, the top of the housing aligned with a gap in the gold horizontal lining around the top of lower body panels.

Internal lighting was provided by exposed tungsten bulbs with chrome surrounds, fed from the traction batteries. There were light fittings in the ceiling cove panels in the lower saloon positioned centrally in each bay on the nearside and bays 1 to 4 on the offside (total nine), the presence of an offside indicator box preventing a fitting in bay 5, and in the upper saloon centrally in bays 1 to 5 on each side (10). There was an additional lamp on the platform.

No internal emergency lighting was fitted.

Bell pushes were located in the ceiling cove panels in the upper saloon on the nearside in bay 3 slightly forward of the light fitting and on the offside towards the rear of bay 5, and in the lower saloon on the nearside in bay 1 somewhat to the rear of the light fitting and in bay 4 slightly forward of the light fitting, and on rear platform bulkhead

Seating: The seating was based on stove-enamelled brown painted tubular steel frames with chromium-plated top rails and integrated grab handles on the gangway side of the top rails. The rubber-filled squabs and hair-filled seat backs were upholstered in figured moquette, having a red, blue, green and brown pattern on a beige background, and brown leather with Rexine trimmings. The seat cushions measured 16in. by 16in. by 4in.

The lower saloon had a three-person inwards-facing bench seat on each side over the rear axle and five rows of forward-facing seats, the first two rows behind the front bulkhead being double seats, then a row of single seats (one on each side) intended to avoid congestion in the gangway, followed by two more rows of double seats. The upper saloon had six rows of double seats on the off-side and eight rows on the nearside, i.e. the bench seat at the rear of the upper saloon above the open platform also accommodated two passengers. There were upright stanchions covered in black Doverite in both saloons attached to the ceiling, back of the seat and floor:

Lower saloon: Behind seat 1 nearside; seats 2, 5 offside.

Upper saloon: Behind seats 4, 7 nearside; seats 2, 5 and stair head offside.

The driver's seat had a moquette-covered squab and a leather back.

Destination equipment: Single rectangular indicator boxes 43in. by 14in. capable of displaying a service number and up to four lines of intermediate point information, with a second rectangular indicator box 43in. by 6in. for a single line final destination immediately beneath, were mounted centrally at the front on the upper-deck front panel above the driver's cab windscreen and at the rear above the rear platform window. The rear indicator boxes were accommodated in a protruding panel which rose vertically from the level of the upper saloon floor line whilst the main body panels curved progressively to the rear dome. A further rectangular indicator box 24in. by 14in. displaying up to four lines of information (three lines

Lower saloon view of preserved and restored BUT9611T/Burlingham 313 at the East Anglia Transport Museum. (David Bowler)

Upper saloon view of preserved and restored BUT9611T/Burlingham 313 at the East Anglia Transport Museum. (David Bowler)

of intermediate points and the final destination) was fitted immediately above the rear open platform entrance. The front and rear indicator boxes almost entirely filled the depth between the upper-deck floor line and the waistrail. There was a narrow indicator box 30in. by 5in. built into the white-painted vent panel immediately above the offside rearmost lower saloon window (bay 5) and aligned with its rearmost edge capable of displaying a single line of information.

The boxes had radiused corners to match the design of the windows. The indicator blinds were printed with the service number to the left of the information, the number being in a broader style as deep as three lines of information.

Internal livery: White cellulosed ceiling and cove panels with polished walnut mouldings. The windows were surrounded by polished walnut wood frames with light brown Rexine covered panels below. El Dorado cork tile floor covering in both saloons. All handrails and stanchions were covered with black Doverite. Cab area painted brown.

External livery: Delivered in Livery 4 (see Appendix C).

Subsequent alterations

The spotlight was moved towards the centre line of the vehicle about one-third inboard beneath the removable front panel.

During the course of 1958 12-ply tyres were fitted to the front wheels when the previous tyres required replacement.

Notes

No. 313 was subsequently preserved and following a long period of restoration is now on display in an operating condition at the East Anglia Transport Museum near Lowestoft, Suffolk.

Disposal

Tenders for disposal were due by 29 November 1963: all vehicles being at Jordan by 7 December 1963 and with Hants and Sussex Aviation by 25 July 1964.

301 Withdrawn 27 July 1963; towed from Eastney Depot to North End Depot 28 July 1963 and stored there until sold in December 1963 to C.D. Jordan & Son Ltd. (Breaker), Dundas Spur, Copnor; re-sold to Hants and Sussex Aviation, Portsmouth Airport in July 1964 and partly broken up on 28 December 1964. The remains of the vehicle had gone by March 1965.

302 Withdrawn 27 July 1963; towed from Eastney Depot to North End Depot 28 July 1963 and stored there until sold in December 1963 to C.D. Jordan & Son Ltd. (Breaker), Dundas Spur, Copnor; re-sold to Hants and Sussex Aviation, Portsmouth Airport in July 1964 and broken up between January 1966 and July 1966.

303 Withdrawn on 11 April 1961 following an accident. In October 1961 a temporary front axle was fitted and the vehicle was towed to Civil Defence exercise at Kingston Crescent, Portsmouth on 22 October 1961 where it was overturned and re-righted by 1931 Crossley Condor breakdown wagon RV720. Towed to North End Depot and stored there until December 1961 when sold to Hants and Sussex Aviation, Portsmouth Airport and broken up by August 1962.

304, 305 Withdrawn on 27 July 1963; towed from Eastney Depot to North End Depot 28 July 1963 and stored until there until sold in December 1963 to C.D. Jordan & Son Ltd. (Breaker), Dundas Spur, Copnor; resold to Hants and Sussex Aviation, Portsmouth Airport in July 1964 and broken up between July 1966 and December 1966.

306, 311 Withdrawn 25 July 1963; towed from Eastney Depot to North End Depot 26 July 1963 and stored there until sold in December 1963 to C.D. Jordan & Son Ltd. (Breaker), Dundas Spur, Copnor; resold to Hants and Sussex Aviation, Portsmouth Airport in July 1964 and broken up between January 1966 and July 1966.

307, 308 Withdrawn 27 July 1963; towed from Eastney Depot to North End Depot 28 July 1963 and stored there until sold in December 1963 to C.D. Jordan & Son Ltd. (Breaker), Dundas Spur, Copnor; re-sold to Hants and Sussex Aviation, Portsmouth Airport in July 1964 and broken up between January 1966 and July 1966.

309 Withdrawn 25 July 1963; towed from Eastney Depot to North End Depot 26 July 1963 and stored there until sold in December 1963 to C.D. Jordan & Son Ltd. (Breaker), Dundas Spur, Copnor; resold to Hants and Sussex Aviation, Portsmouth Airport in July 1964 and broken up between July 1966 and December 1966.

310 Withdrawn 25 July 1963; towed from Eastney Depot to North End Depot 26 July 1963 and stored until sold in December 1963 to C.D. Jordan & Son Ltd. (Breaker), Dundas Spur, Copnor; re-sold to Hants and Sussex Aviation, Portsmouth Airport in July 1964 and broken up between March 1965 and March 1967.

312, 314 Withdrawn 27 July 1963; towed from Eastney Depot to North End Depot 28 July 1963 and stored there until sold in December 1963 to C.D. Jordan & Son Ltd. (Breaker), Dundas Spur, Copnor; resold to Hants and Sussex Aviation, Portsmouth Airport in July 1964 and broken up between January 1966 and July 1966.

313 Withdrawn 27 July 1963; towed from Eastney Depot to North End Depot 28 July 1963 and stored there until sold in December 1963 to C.D. Jordan & Son Ltd. (Breaker), Dundas Spur, Copnor; re-sold to Hants and Sussex Aviation, Portsmouth Airport in July 1964. Sold to Mr John Reeves as the vehicle in best condition, on 1 January 1965, and towed to Bognor Regis, Sussex, on 6 March 1965. Subsequently presented to the National Trolleybus Association in February 1966 and stored at Basingstoke. Following test runs in Bournemouth on 12 March 1967, 313 ran an enthusiasts tour of the Bournemouth system on 30 May 1967. The vehicle was collected from Basingstoke by Crossley Condor RV720 and towed to North End Depot on 16 August 1967 on long term loan to the City. It was stored there until February 1970 when it was moved to an unknown location. The loan is believed to have ended in April 1974 when 313 was sold to the Trolleybus Museum Co. and stored at an unknown location before being resold in March 1983, 313 was sold to the London Trolleybus Preservation Society and moved to Castle Point Transport Museum, Canvey Island, Essex, where some restoration took place. In September 1990, the vehicle was moved to the East Anglia Transport Museum, Carlton Colville near Lowestoft and following restoration re-entered passenger carrying service on 28 April 2007.

315 Withdrawn 27 July 1963: towed from Eastney Depot to North End Depot 28 July 1963 and stored there until sold in December 1963 to C.D. Jordan & Son Ltd. (Breaker), Dundas Spur, Copnor; resold to Hants and Sussex Aviation, Portsmouth Airport in July 1964 and broken up between July 1966 and December 1966.

TROLLEYBUS REPAINT DATES

1938 no.	Reg. no.	1st repaint	2nd repaint	3rd repaint	4th repaint	5th repaint	6th repaint	Final Livery	Notes
201	RV4649	btwn 01.-06.1946	06.1955	09.1960	-	-	-	1948	
202	RV4650	01.1947	01.1950	-	-	-	-	1948	
203	RV4651	01.1947	-	-	-	-	-	OL (B)	
204	RV4652	not known	-	-	-	-	-	OL (B)	
205	RV4653	02.1948	-	-	-	-	-	OL	
206	RV4654	not known	-	-	-	-	-	OL (B)	Repainted early post-war
207	RV4655	11.1946	-	-	-	-	-	OL (B)	
208	RV4656	not known	01.1950	-	-	-	-	not known	
209	RV4657	not known	-	-	-	-	-	not known	Assumed final livery OL (B)
210	RV4660	10.1949	-	-	-	-	-	OL	
211	RV4661	not known	-	-	-	-	-	OL	Repainted early post-war
212	RV4658	-	-	-	-	-	-	OL	Never repainted
213	RV4659	-	-	-	-	-	-	OL (B)	Never repainted
214	RV4662	not known	02.1948	-	-	-	-	OL (B)	
215	RV4663	06.1949	-	-	-	-	-	1948	
216	RV6374	not known	06.1948	-	-	-	-	OL	Pre-war repaint possible
217	RV6375	not known	01.1948	-	-	-	-	OL (B)	Pre-war repaint possible
218	RV6376	not known	1939	03.1950	-	-	-	1948	Pre-war repaint possible
219	RV6377	not known	by 07.1950	05.1953	-	-	-	1948	Pre-war repaint possible
220	RV6378	not known	07.1947	-	-	-	-	OL	Pre-war repaint possible
221	RV6379	not known	-	-	-	-	-	OL (B)	No dates known
222	RV6380	not known	03.-04.1946	-	-	-	-	OL (B)	Pre-war repaint possible
223	RV6381	not known	02.1948	-	-	-	-	1948	Pre-war repaint possible
224	RV6382	not known	04.1947	01.1954	-	-	-	1948	Pre-war repaint possible
225	RV8307	03.1945	01.1945	03.1949	05.1951	06.1954	02.1958	1948	
226	RV8308	not known	not known	not known	04.1951	06.1955	12.1957	1948	
227	RV8309	not known	not known	12.1949	05.1952	01.1955	01.1958	1948	
228	RV8310	not known	05.1946	09.1950	09.1952	12.1955	05.1958	1948	
229	RV8311	not known	05.1948	-	-	-	-	1948	
230	RV8312	not known	10.1945	05.1946	05.1955	06.1958	-	1948	

1938 no.	Reg. no.	1st repaint	2nd repaint	3rd repaint	4th repaint	5th repaint	6th repaint	Final Livery	Notes
231	RV8313	not known	11.1945	by 09.1951	03.1956	07.1959	-	1948	
232	RV8314	10.1943	by 08.1953	08.1953	09.1956	07.1959	-	1948	
233	RV8315	not known	not known	10.1955	09.1958	-	-	1948	
234	RV8316	02.1945	09.1954	10.1956	09.1957	-	-	1948	
235	RV8317	10.1939	12.1945	by 11.1953	11.1953	10.1956	05.1959	1948	
236	RV8318	not known	not known	08.1951	11.1954	10.1956	09.1957	1948	
237	RV8319	12.1944	09.1946	01.1950	01.1956	06.1959	-	1948	
238	RV8320	not known	05.1947	08.1953	02.1958	-	-	1948	
239	RV8321	10.1940	not known	07.1950	06.1956	08.1958	-	1948	
240	RV8322	not known	1948	not known	-	-	-	1948	
241	RV8323	09.1943	not known	07.1954	08.1957	-	-	1948	
242	RV8324	not known	not known	02.1955	03.1958	-	-	1948	
243	RV8325	not known	by 07.1952	07.1952	11.1955	09.1958	-	1948	
244	RV8326	1941	by 02.1953	02.1953	02.1956	01.1959	-	1948	
245	RV8327	02.1940	not known	01.1952	11.1955	03.1958	-	1948	
246	RV8328	not known	12.1948	04.1955	09.1956	01.1960	-	1948	
247	RV8329	not known	04.1949	02.1955	04.1958	-	-	1948	
248	RV8330	03.1940	not known	10.1954	01.1958	-	-	1948	
249	RV8331	not known	01.1949	05.1954	10.1957	-	-	1948	
250	RV8332	06.1945	06.1953	01.1956	02.1958	-	-	1948	
251	RV8333	09.1944	by 05.1952	05.1952	07.1956	-	-	1948	
252	RV8334	not known	by 02.1954	02.1954	11.196	-	-	1948	
253	RV8335	10.1946	11.1947	01.1950	10.1954	05.1957	-	1948	
254	RV8336	11.1944	not known	by 09.1953	09.1953	02.1957	06.1959	1948	
255	RV9106	not known	01.1948	02.1955	03.1959	-	-	1948	
256	RV9107	not known	12.1952	05.1956	11.1958	-	-	1948	
257	RV9108	05.1942	08.1947	by 1952	-	-	-	1948	
258	RV9109	02.1946	05.1949	-	-	-	-	1948	
259	RV9110	01.1942	02.1948	10.1952	12.1954	10.1956	06.1958	1948	
260	RV9111	not known	06.1948	not known	-	-	-	1948	
261	RV9112	02.1945	03.1952	12.1955	12.1955	03.1959	-	1948	
262	RV9113	11.1947	by 09.1953	-	-	-	-	1948	

1938 no.	Reg. no.	1st repaint	2nd repaint	3rd repaint	4th repaint	5th repaint	6th repaint	Final Livery	Notes
263	RV9114	1947	not known	-	-	-	-	1948	
264	RV9115	not known	not known	01.1952	-	-	-	1948	
265	RV9116	not known	07.1948	07.1953	11.1956	-	-	1948	
266	RV9117	not known	not known	-	-	-	-	1948	
267	RV9118	01.1943	11.1949	04.1952	07.1955	10.1958	-	1948	
268	RV9119	06.1942	'02.1951	12.1953	11.1956	-	-	1948	
269	RV9120	1946	09.1951	04.1956	11.1959	-	-	1948	
270	RV9121	06.1946	09.1951	10.1954	06.1956	12.1959	-	1948	
271	RV9122	05.1946	11.1949	04.1954	12.1957	-	-	1948	
272	RV9123	01.1945	02.1949	-	-	-	-	1948	
273	RV9124	not known	04.1948	11.1955	04.1959	-	-	1948	
274	RV9125	not known	not known	03.1955	05.1958	-	-	1948	
275	RV9126	05.1941	03.1949	09.1952	-	-		1948	
276	RV9127	1940	07.1946	08.1952	-	-	-	1948	
277	RV9128	06.1941	12.1948	01.1952	-	-	-	1948	
278	RV9129	not known	07.1949	not known	10.1954	8.196	-	1948	
279	RV9130	07.1945	-	-	-	-	-	OL (B)	
280	RV9131	06.1942	11.1946	by 09.1951	-	-	-	1948	
281	RV9132	not known	by 01.1953	01.1953	02.1957	-	-	1948	
282	RV9133	not known	10.1948	07.1949	06.1952	04.1956	07.1959	1948	
283	RV9134	01.1946	07.1949	04.1955	03.1956	10.1959	-	1948	
284	RV9135	06.1941	07.-10.1948	07.1953	-	-	-	1948	
285	RV9136	1945	by 12.1950	-	-	-	-	1948	
286	RV9137	1948	06.1951	11.1955	08.1959	-	-	1948	
287	RV9138	05.1947	by 04.1954	-	-	-	-	1948	
288	RV9139	not known	not known	-	-	-	-	OL / OL (B)	Possibly a single repaint
289	RV9140	not known	10.1950-02.1951	-	-	-	-	1948	
290	RV9141	not known	11.1948	04.1952	07.1955	-	-	1948	
291	RV9142	not known	06.1949	01.1954	12.1956	06.1959	-	1948	
292	RV9143	not known	02.1949	06.1955	08.1958	-	-	1948	
293	RV9144	06.1942	06.1949	03.1953	12.1955	04.1958	-	1948	
294	RV9145	06.1947	04.1950	07.1956	01.1960	-	-	1948	

1938 no.	Reg. no.	1st repaint	2nd repaint	3rd repaint	4th repaint	5th repaint	6th repaint	Final Livery	Notes
295	RV9149	not known	01.1952	03.1955	10.1957	-	-	1948	
296	RV9150	not known	06.1951	-	-	-	-	1948	
297	RV9151	07.1945	09.1952	08.1956	12.1958	-	-	1948	
298	RV9152	02.1946	04.1950	03.1955	11.1956	05.1957	01.1960	1948	
299	RV9153	10.1946	06.1953	05.1956	02.1958	-	-	1948	
300	RV9154	02.1949	06.1955	04.1957	09.1959	-	-	1948	
301	ERV926	04.1953	11.1956	02.1958	07.1959	-	-	1948	
302	ERV927	not known	05.1956	03.1957	09.1959	-	-	1948	
303	ERV928	not known	11.1954	01.1957	-	-	-	1948	
304	ERV929	not known	12.1956	01.1959	-	-	-	1948	
305	ERV930	not known	12.1954	01.1957	10.1959	-	-	1948	
306	ERV931	not known	06.1956	07.1957	09.1959	-	-	1948	
307	ERV932	not known	05.1956	07.1957	12.1959	-	-	1948	
308	ERV933	not known	05.1957	10.1958	01.1960	-	-	1948	
309	ERV934	not known	03.1957	05.1959	-	-	-	1948	
310	ERV935	not known	04.1957	11.1958	01.1960	-	-	1948	
311	ERV936	not known	12.1956	05.1959	-	-	-	1948	
312	ERV937	not known	03.1957	07.1959	02.1960	-	-	1948	
313	ERV938	not known	10.1956	02.1959	02.1960	-	-	1948	
314	ERV939	not known	02.1956	07.1958	09.1959	-	-	1948	
315	ERV940	not known	05.1956	05.1957	10.1959	-	-	1948	

KEY

- \- This repaint was not carried out on the vehicle
- OL (B) Original pre-war livery with beading painted black but with grey roof
- OL Original pre-war livery but with grey roof (no beading)
- 1948 Post-war simplified 1948 livery

NOTES

It is understood that CPPTD followed a programme of giving trolleybuses a full external repaint every 3-4 years however little information on pre-1945 repaints is known.

201-211 Due to their infrequent use pre-war after 1936 it is quite likely that the 1940s dates above are the first full repaints received by these vehicles.

212-215 Due to their infrequent use pre-war after 1936 none of these vehicles received a full repaint until after the war. 212 & 213 were never repainted.

216-224 These vehicles were used continuously until September 1939 and it is possible that 218 was the first one handled in a repainting programme interrupted by the war. The 1940s dates above are the first full repaints received by the other vehicles.

225-300 These vehicles would not have been scheduled to a full repaint pre-war. Many of these trolleybuses were delicensed for long periods and this must have been reflected in the repainting programme.

APPENDIX B
DEMONSTRATORS

During the 1930s it was common practice for trolleybus chassis manufacturers to offer operators their latest products, usually equipped with opulent bodywork, for a protracted trial. Operators were usually asked to pay just a small mileage rate for the period the vehicle was in service. In view of Portsmouth's decision to purchase an experimental fleet of 15 vehicles with varying equipment and bodywork from which to determine the optimum combination for the undertaking's needs, and follow this with a further 85 AEC661Ts to provide a total fleet well exceeding their operating needs, they were hardly a prospective purchaser of additional trolleybuses.

There is no indication in the surviving records that CPPTD was ever approached by a manufacturer in respect of a vehicle trial and accordingly not a single demonstrator appeared on the streets of Portsmouth until 1955. In July 1955 the British Electrical & Allied Manufacturers Association approached the Passenger Transport Committee to enquire if one of Walsall's new Sunbeam F4A trolleybus with Willowbrook body could operate on trial for the delegates to the 1955 MPTA Conference at Southsea, and in normal passenger service.

864 Sunbeam F4A

Chassis: Two axle type Sunbeam F4A manufactured by the Sunbeam Trolleybus Co. Ltd., at the Guy Motors factory in Park Lane, Fallings Park, Wolverhampton.
Motor: British Thomson-Houston Co. Ltd.
Motor Type: British Thomson Houston Type 209 (95hp).
Electrical equipment: Automatic acceleration.
De-wirement indicators: Two green line-lights and buzzer.
Brakes: Lockheed accumulator-type hydraulic, hand and rheostatic brakes.
Body: Lightweight composite double deck highbridge construction built by Willowbrook Ltd., Derby Road, Loughborough, Leicestershire.
Seating: H36/34RD.
Length: 30ft.
Width: 8ft.
Wheelbase: 18ft 6in.
Unladen weight: 7 tons 5 cwt 0 qtr
Tyres: Front 11.00in. by 20in.; rear 9.00in. by 20in. (twins).
Wheel track: 6ft 10½in. front; 6ft rear.

The Sunbeam Motor Car Co. Ltd. began manufacturing trolleybus chassis in 1931 to complement its range of quality motorcars, which was suffering from the global economic crisis of the time, and a limited selection of motorbuses. The trolleybus designs proved extremely successful; however, losses in the rest of their business led to the company being sold to the Rootes Group in 1935. Trolleybus production continued under the trade name of Sunbeam Commercial Vehicles. Rootes had recently acquired Karrier Motors Ltd.,

Walsall's first Sunbeam F4A/Willowbrook, 851, prepared for exhibition at the 1954 Commercial Motor Show. (Photographer's name not recorded [assumed to be official view])

Huddersfield, and their trolleybus manufacture was moved to the Sunbeam plant at Moorfield Road, Wolverhampton although the two companies' products continued to be marketed separately.

In July 1946 Sunbeam was sold to Brockhouse & Co. Ltd. who subsequently renamed the company the Sunbeam Trolleybus Co. Ltd. and re-sold it to Guy Motors Ltd. in October 1948. Guy Motors ceased to market its own range of trolleybus chassis and concentrated on developing an increased range of Sunbeam products, including the two-axle F4A. In 1953 Guy moved production to its own factory in Fallings Park, Wolverhampton.

Walsall 864 entered service in Walsall on 2 June 1955 prior to its demonstration at Portsmouth. It had Sunbeam F4A chassis number 9035.

Walsall 864 was towed to Portsmouth arriving on 15 September 1955. It operated in normal passenger service on services 5, 6, 15, 16, 19 and 20 for the duration of the Municipal Passenger Transport Association Conference, 27–30 September 1955, which was held at Southsea South Parade Pier.

Chassis: Based on the Guy Arab IV motorbus chassis and axles of the period, the Sunbeam F4A was introduced at the beginning of 1953, the first such vehicles being delivered to Glasgow Corporation Transport in March 1953.

Suspension was provided by four semi-elliptical leaf springs, 4in. wide and 4ft 2in. long at the front and 5ft at the rear. Anti-roll stabilisers were fitted to both front and rear axles. The chassis incorporated a short needle roller bearing transmission shaft and underslung worm drive rear axle with 8½in. centres. Rubber-bonded bushes requiring no lubrication were used at the spring mountings, the rotary oscillation between the eyes and the spring and shackle pins being wholly absorbed in the rubber bushes. Luvax-Girling hydraulic dampers controlled the spring action at front and rear.

The chassis frame was constructed of alloy steel side members of channel section, braced by channel section and tubular cross members. The frame was upswept over the axles with an overhang at the rear.

Cam and double roller steering gear.
Chassis length: 30ft.
Chassis frame width: 7ft 11½in.
Overall width (rear axle): 8ft.

Electrics: A BTH non-regenerative 95hp flood-proof traction motor was supplied with two stages of rheostatic braking and mounted offset to the nearside of the vehicle.

A belt from the front end of the traction motor drove a dynamo for 12 volt lighting.

BTH automatic acceleration was fitted. The reverser was alongside and to the nearside of the driver's seat. The front-opening contactor box was located on the nearside of the driver's cab rear bulkhead and the master switch above the large central window in the bulkhead.

The resistor grid was in a protective metal cage towards the front of the vehicle behind the front axle. Other control equipment, the battery manoeuvring gear and traction batteries, were carried on the offside of the chassis in bay 1.

The upper-deck body pillars slotted into the wooden rail of the framework above the upper saloon windows, i.e. the cantrail. There were curved steel brackets bolted to the metal roof (inside the roof there was a steel strengthening plate on each side) and each end of the two transverse pressed steel girders, between bays 2 and 3 and bays 3 and 4, supporting the exposed trolley gantry, which was not in direct contact with the roof, rested on these brackets.

A radio interference suppressor was mounted centrally immediately in front of the trolley gantry. The main power cables from the trolley gear made their way forward from the trolley gantry along the centre line of the roof before turning to the offside and entering the curved roof panels above and towards the front of the bay 2 upper saloon offside window. The upper deck side pillar between bays 1 and 2 was broadened to accommodate the cable trunking and the bay 2 window was commensurately narrower. The cables continued forwards in a conduit inside the offside lower deck vent panels to the circuit breakers on the ceiling of the driver's cab.

Brakes: Lockheed accumulator-type hydraulic, hand and rheostatic brakes were fitted.

The pull-on handbrake was on the offside of the driver's cab and operated on the rear wheels only through a mechanical linkage. The ratchet mechanism was completely enclosed and operated in an oil bath.

The brake drum diameters were 16 ½in. at the front and 16 ¼in. at the rear.

Brake lining area: Front 208 sq. in. Rear 364 sq. in.

Bodywork: The bodywork was of teak-framed, single-skin, composite five-bay highbridge double-deck lightweight construction, with a forward-ascending half-turn (90°) staircase with a semi-vestibuled platform entrance and exit equipped with four-leaf power-operated folding doors at the rear, built by Willowbrook Ltd., Derby Road, Loughborough, Leicestershire.

The unique design was typified by its rounded corners, rather bulky streamlined appearance and the low-cost utilitarian finish. Willowbrook were not well-known for constructing trolleybus bodies: excluding single bodies built for South Shields in 1937 and Walsall in 1953, the company only secured two orders, namely 20 double-deck bodies on Sunbeam F4 chassis for Derby Corporation in 1952–53 and these 22 bodies for Walsall Corporation supplied in two batches, Walsall fleet numbers 851–865 and 866–872, on Sunbeam F4A chassis.

The single-skin metal panels on a teak frame resulted in a robust lightweight vehicle well within the target weight limits and easily passed the obligatory tilt test.

There was an exposed trolley gantry above bay 3. Horizontally sliding half-width openers were fitted to the tops of the side windows in bays 1, 3 and 5 (both sides) of the upper saloon and bays 2 and 4 (both sides) of the lower saloon. The rear portion of the opener slid forwards. The front upper-deck windows were fixed. All windows had radiused corners.

Ventilation was provided to the front end of the lower saloon and in the driver's cab through two vanes with rectangular louvres or covers immediately above the driver's cab windscreen to left and right of the central pillar. Similar but broader covered vanes were placed immediately above the upper-deck front windows with a much larger hooded ventilator in the front dome above the ribbing surrounding the front windows and located above the central window pillar. At a later date, following 864's return to Walsall, the ventilator in the front dome was greatly increased in size whilst other similar vehicles received extended hoods over the vanes above the driver's cab windscreen.

The four-leaf, air operated folding Glider doors on the rear platform were half-glazed to match the saloon side windows.

The foremost two doors folded towards the front of the vehicle and the other two towards the rear. There was a single step up from the street to the rear platform, and then a second step up to the saloon.

Top hinged access doors were fitted at the base of the offside panel bay 1 towards its rear and provided access to the control equipment, the battery manoeuvring gear and traction batteries.

The staircase had eight steps from the platform to the upper deck, all equipped with aluminium nosings on the treads. There was no staircase landing as such. All platform, saloon and staircase handrails and stanchions were coated with white Doverite.

The rear upper deck emergency exit door was top hinged, opening upwards and outwards, and incorporated a single oblong window with an opening handle towards the bottom offside of the door. It provided no access to the roof and trolley gear. There was a small glazed rectangular hatch about 4in. by 6 in. located centrally in the rear dome above the rear upper deck emergency exit door and to the rear to the trolley boom retaining hooks.

The driver's cab was equipped with deep curved windows where the corner pillars would have been placed on more angular designs. These, in addition to the other substantial glazed area ensured that the driver had good all-round vision. The base of the side and front glazing in the driver's cab area was aligned with the base of the windows in the lower saloon but rose some 8in. or more above their upper edge being aligned with the upper deck floor line at the side of the vehicle. The curved corner windows were even an inch or two taller rising to touch the yellow-painted upper-deck floor level beading.

There was a single opening windscreen on the offside, both sections having a chromium-plated frame. The offside windscreen had a top-mounted wiper whilst that on the nearside was mounted at the base of the windscreen.

There was a narrow full-depth semi-triangular window between the curved corner window and the driver's cab door. The driver's cab had an offside front-hinged door (three hinges) equipped with a fixed upper square window pane and a lower smaller section incorporating a sliding "signalling" window, the rear portion sliding forwards behind the front portion. The base of the cab door over the wheel arch deepened in a straight line from beneath the lowest hinge to a position above the rear of the wheel hub and then continued at this depth horizontally to the rear of the door. There was a black-painted opening handle mounted in a black-painted shield-shaped concave insert. The equivalent single nearside window incorporated a top-hinged emergency exit with a black-painted shield-shaped concave inset opening handle towards the rear of the side panel beneath.

A step with rounded top was let into the offside panelling, but without any form of protection to the bodywork, immediately behind the front axle, on the offside. The offside front wheel was fitted with a wheel nut guard ring. Individual mud flaps hung behind each wheel.

There were three windows in the bulkhead behind the driver with an aluminium panel beneath. A wide central pane flanked by narrow panes to the nearside and offside, and a rectangular ventilator centrally above.

There was a black, four-spoke, steering wheel. Small, black-painted, rectangular driver's rear view mirrors were mounted externally towards the top of both front cab pillars.

There was a removable panel approximately as wide as the space between the two headlights, incorporating, centred at the bottom, the registration number plate, at the base of the front panel beneath the windscreen. A single wooden lifeguard ran beneath the side panels between the front and rear axle.

The rear lower deck panels were divided vertically into two equal sections, that on the nearside incorporating an emergency exit door with a rectangular window opening outwards and supported by three hinges towards the nearside of the vehicle, and that on the offside incorporating solely a matching rectangular window. The emergency exit door was progressively a little deeper towards the nearside and incorporated a downwards opening window pane surmounted with a louvre to reduce water ingress when the window was open. The rear registration number plate was recessed, increasingly towards the top, inboard of the rear offside light fitting and aligned with the top of it, in the bottom offside of the rear lower panel.

A bamboo trolley retrieval pole was carried in a metal tube mounted centrally under the chassis and was accessible from the rear of the vehicle.

Lighting: External lighting was provided by two headlights at the base of the front panel, two front sidelights in vertically mounted off-white plastic rectangular mouldings mounted outboard of the headlights towards the top of the curved corner panels, and combined rear light and flashing traffic indicator mouldings with chrome surrounds towards the base of the rear corner panels. A spotlight was recessed into the front panel immediately beneath the nearside headlight aligned with its nearside edge.

Flashing traffic indicators made of an orange plastic material with rounded top and bottom mouldings secured to a cast metal base were mounted immediately above the yellow-painted lower deck waistrail beading in the panel between the driver's cab emergency exit and the bay 1 side windows on the nearside, and between the driver's cab door and the bay 1 side window on the offside.

Internal lighting was provided by exposed 12-volt tungsten lamp bulbs in chromed shell fittings recessed into the lower deck cove panels and the upper deck ceiling, fed from a dynamo. There were light fittings in the ceiling cove panels in the lower saloon positioned centrally in bays 1 to 4 on the nearside, the presence of an offside indicator box preventing a fitting in bay 5, and bays 1 to 5 on the offside (total nine), and in the upper saloon towards the front in bay 1, centrally in bay 2, somewhat to the rear in bay 3, above the window pillar between bay 4 and bay 5, and above the rearmost "D" window (that on the offside being further to rear than that on the nearside due to the presence of an emergency light) on both sides (ten).

There was an additional lamp on the platform.

Internal emergency lights, employing smaller exposed tungsten lamp bulbs in chrome-edged circular fittings, were located in the lower saloon in the offside bay 2 and 4 cove panels and in the upper saloon in the offside bay 1 and 4 ceiling and above the top of the stairs immediately forward of the normal light fitting. There was a further recessed emergency lamp on the rear platform located on the nearside rear bulkhead beneath the cleaners switch.

A bell rope ran from inside the nearside longitudinal ceiling grab rail along the nearside ceiling to the driver's cab bulkhead. There were also ceiling mounted bell bushes in bays

2 and 4 offside, and bay 3 nearside, although it is not clear if both were installed when the vehicle was in Portsmouth. In the upper saloon there was a single bell push in the offside ceiling towards the rear of bay 5, immediately forward of the emergency light fitting at the top of the stairs. On the rear platform there were two bell pushes; one was located on the nearside rear bulkhead above the window and the other on the offside rear bulkhead at waist height.

Seating: The seats were based on stove-enamelled dark blue painted cast metal frames with chromium-plated top rails and integrated grab handles on the gangway side of the top rails. The squabs and seat backs were upholstered with blue quilted leathercloth.

The lower saloon had a three-person inward-facing bench seat on each side over the rear axle and seven rows of forward-facing double seats. The upper saloon had eight rows of double seats on the off-side and ten rows on the nearside; the bench seat at the rear of the upper saloon above the open platform also accommodated two passengers. There were upright stanchions covered in cream Doverite in the lower saloon attached to the ceiling, back of the seat and floor behind seat four nearside and seats two and six offside.

The driver's seat had a blue quilted leathercloth squab and back.

Destination equipment: A single indicator box, capable of displaying the final destination and a single line of intermediate point information, and a slightly deeper rectangular service number indicator box, were placed side by side in the lower one third of the upper-deck front panels, centred immediately above the driver's windscreen. The service number indicator was on the nearside.

There was a narrow indicator box capable of displaying the final destination and a single line of intermediate point information located in the lower saloon vent panel above the rearmost lower saloon window (bay 5) on the nearside.

There were no indicator boxes at the rear. All the apertures had rounded corners.

Internal livery: The window surrounds were painted cream and the ceilings off white with a pale blue separating line immediately above the window line. The lower body panels were painted light grey, except for the lower part of the driver's cab bulkhead in the lower saloon and the area beneath the front windows backing on to the indicator boxes, which were both covered with protective chequer-plate aluminium sheeting. The staircase and rear platform area were painted light grey, the platform floor having transverse wooden battens. All flooring was finished in red oxide and equipped with longitudinal non-slip metal strips.

A circular conductor's mirror was fixed in the upper deck rear offside dome at the head of the stairs.

The cab area was painted light blue.

External livery: Delivered in full Walsall Corporation Transport light blue livery of the period. The overall colour was Chelsea blue with yellow painted beadings beneath the upper and lower deck windows, and at upper deck floor level.

The County Borough of Walsall arms in a pale yellow "patch" were carried on the side panels centred in bay 3 with the title "WALSALL CORPORATION" in block yellow lettering immediately beneath. The Walsall arms, again in a pale yellow "patch", were also carried centrally on the front panels with the comment "TROLLEYBUS" in white block lettering beneath.

The undertaking's title and other legal lettering were transferred in pale yellow at the base of the side panels immediately behind the nearside front axle and in white to the rear of the rear axle.

Fleet numbers were applied with large yellow transfers centrally to the removable front panel immediately above the registration number plate, on the lower deck side panels immediately below the waistband beading towards the front of bay 1, and at the rear centrally in the lower half of the rear panel with "Trolleybus" in white block lettering beneath.

Mudguards, lifeguard rails and wheels were blue.

Notes

The idea of using two-axle 30ft long double-deck trolleybuses in the UK and the design of the bodywork emanated from the General Manager and Engineer of Walsall Corporation Transport, Ronald Edgley Cox, an enthusiastic transport manager and engineer convinced in the superiority of the trolleybus.

Appointed to Walsall from St Helens in 1952, Mr Edgley Cox soon developed plans to enlarge the trolleybus system and purchase new vehicles. An experimental three-axle passenger-flow Pay-as-you-Enter Sunbeam S7 with Willowbrook body proved unsuccessful and his thoughts then turned to seeking MoT permission to operate 30ft long two-axle trolleybuses, a maximum length of 27ft then being permissible.

A functional, lightweight and low-cost body was designed by Willowbrook in accordance with Mr Edgley Cox's requirements and construction of an initial batch of 15 bodies on Sunbeam F4A chassis, which were already available in 30ft length for the export market, began in 1954 before MoT approval had been given! The MoT was convinced by Mr Edgley Cox's arguments that such a vehicle could operate safely on Britain's roads whilst there would be economies in the initial purchase and maintenance costs as well as improved tyre and overall vehicle life. Accepting that such a move for motorbuses would follow (this occurred in 1956) and that approval for trolleybuses would provide a low-risk operating experience, the MoT, having carefully reviewed the design, relaxed the regulations with effect from late 1954 by which time the first such vehicle, 851, was already in service.

The trolleybuses, Walsall fleet numbers 851–865, registration TDH901–915, foreseen for use on the new Blakenall route which opened in June 1955 and to replace pre-war vehicles, entered service between November 1954 and June 1955. The first one, 851, was exhibited at the Commercial Motor Show in September 1954 prior to delivery to Walsall.

A second batch of seven similar trolleybuses, Walsall fleet numbers 866–872, registration XDH66–72, entered service between June and October 1956 for use on the new route to the Beechdale Estate which had opened in September 1955 and an extension of the Blakenall route to Bloxich, which had opened in October 1955, and to replace the remaining pre-war vehicles.

Although operationally successful, these vehicles were not universally popular due to their spartan finish whilst their unusual appearance resulted in them being commonly referred to as "goldfish bowls"! They were reportedly light and lively to drive.

Disposal

No. 864 remained in service at Walsall until the last day of trolleybus operation in the town, 3 October 1970.

It was purchased by the National Trolleybus Association from the West Midlands Passenger Transport Executive, successors to Walsall Corporation Transport, in December 1970, although it was only collected on 5 August 1972 and taken to a farm in Stanwick, Northamptonshire for storage. It was discovered in a Molesworth scrapyard some six months later minus its traction motor and differential. Subsequently it was moved on 5 May 1973 to Four Marks, near Alton; to an ill-fated museum project in Greenwich in 1978, to Fleet on 27 July 1979 and then to Amen Corner, near Reading, in February 1983. It is understood that 864 was stored outside throughout. It was sold to David Edlestone on 19 March 1983 and a year later it was acquired by Steve Collins for use as a source of seat bases for another preservation project. The vehicle was moved to The Trolleybus Museum at Sandtoft, near Doncaster where it remains outside, painted green and in use as a shed. Some parts have since been removed for use in the preservation of sister trolleybus 872.

The teak side pillars are now badly rotten and 864 is now on the verge of structural failure.

APPENDIX C

LIVERY

In Portsmouth 1929 the fully enclosed tramcars, the rebuilt open-top tramcars and motorbuses began to appear in a brighter livery of crimson and white in place of the "maroon and cream" (officially referred to as scarlet lake and Oxford ochre) colours which had been used by the undertaking's vehicles since the municipalisation and electrification of the tramways in 1901. Notwithstanding use of the term "crimson" the colour was generally considered as a lighter shade of maroon.

An even brighter "red", which will be referred to in this book as vermilion, was used as the main body colour on motorbuses in place of crimson with effect from 1931. The tramcars retained their maroon and cream or crimson and white livery until withdrawal. When trolleybuses appeared in 1934 they adopted the 1929 colours of crimson and white. This main body colour being retained until 1948 when the trolleybuses adopted the vermilion used on motorbuses since 1931 and the livery application was simplified.

Other than this, there were only minimal differences to the style of application relating primarily to the colour of the roof, lining and location of transferred lettering, etc., throughout the trolleybus era.

It is important to note that the vehicles circulating on the streets did not necessarily all appear in the then current livery application at the same time.

1. 1934–1939

Details follow of the livery applied to the following vehicles upon delivery:

1–4	AEC661T/English Electric
5–7	Leyland TBD2/English Electric
8	Sunbeam MF2/English Electric
9	Karrier E4/English Electric
10	Sunbeam MF2/Metro-Cammell
11	Karrier E4/Metro-Cammell
12	AEC 663T/English Electric
13	Sunbeam MS3/English Electric
14	Sunbeam MS3/Metro-Cammell
15	AEC663T/Metro-Cammell
16–24	AEC661T/English Electric
25–90	AEC661T/Cravens
91–100	AEC661T/Cravens

The lower deck and upper deck window surrounds, upper and lower-deck waistbands, vent panel area above the lower-deck windows, and the entire roof were white. The main upper and lower deck body panels were painted crimson. The lower and upper deck waistband beadings, vent panel and cantrail beadings were picked out in black.

The crimson panels were lined in tramcar-style double lining, comprising an outer yellow line ⅜in. broad and an inner white line ⅛in. broad, the yellow line having ornate Greek corner pattern inset square designs and the white line having matching indentations. The lining was applied to divide the crimson panels into separate front, side, rear corner, lower saloon platform bulkhead and rear portions. Mudguards and lifeguard rails were painted black, and wheels maroon.

Trolley gear and related equipment, and trolley boom restraining hooks were black. From August 1937 the roof catwalks on some trolleybuses were painted black instead of white.

The Portsmouth coat of arms was displayed on both sides of the lower deck side panels, centred beneath one of the side windows, the position varying, i.e. initially in bay 2 on 10, 11 (both having five-bay saloons) and 14 (six-bay saloon); and bay 3 on 1–9, 12, 13, 15 (six-bay saloon), and 16–100 (five-bay saloon). It will be noted that the position was not strictly in relation to the length of the body or number of bays.

Ownership details with the General Manager's name and title beneath were applied in small white script typeface at the base of the nearside lower deck panels, bay 1, immediately to the rear of the front axle, viz:

Corporation Tramway and Omnibus Dept.
Eastney, Portsmouth
BEN HALL Engineer and Manager

Following the June 1936 decision to change the title of the undertaking by the late 1930s this had been amended to reflect the new name whilst "*Dept.*" was now shown in full:

City of Portsmouth Passenger Transport Department
Eastney, Portsmouth
Ben Hall Engineer and Manager

The unladen weight was shown in upper case white typeface at the base of the offside lower deck panels immediately in front of the (leading) rear axle with the maximum permitted speed in white script typeface behind the rear axle.

The seating capacity was indicated in lower case left justified white typeface at the nearside base of the rear platform panel. There was a small rectangular white enamelled Police Licence plate carrying the City coat of arms and licence number, the vehicle's original fleet number plus 800, immediately beneath the seating capacity information on all pre-war deliveries. Upon repaint the seating capacity was moved higher up the panel to avoid being partially covered by the Police Licence plate.

Large gold numerals, shaded in two tones of blue and in white, were mounted on the front panel centrally beneath the driver's cab windscreen (their position varying according to the presence or otherwise of the maker's nameplate or ventilators and the position of the headlamps), and centrally on the lower deck rear platform panels. In May 1935 the position of the rear numerals on trolleybuses 1–15 was lowered to enable advertisements to be applied to the rear platform panels and all post-1934 deliveries had the rear numerals positioned somewhat lower on the rear panels.

In the period 5–8 April 1938 the trolleybus fleet was re-numbered as 201–300. An additional figure was transferred in advance of the existing fleet number on the front and rear panels, causing the number to be offset until the vehicles were repainted.

From June 1938 the fleet number was additionally displayed in 1½in. tall white numerals, followed by a full stop, immediately beneath the lower deck waistrail and lining on both sides to

Leyland TBD2 6 waits in the Canoe Lake turning circle in its original livery (Livery 1). The splendid, hand-painted advertisement praises the Portsea Island Mutual Co-operative Society (PIMCO), which was founded in 1873 by workers transferred to HM Dockyard Portsmouth upon the closure of the Woolwich naval dockyard. In 1998 PIMCO became a constituent of the Southern Co-operative. (Omnibus Society [photographer Norr])

the rear of the driver's cab rear bulkhead. Trolleybuses 270 and 271 were the first vehicles to be so treated.

Small upper-case black lettering appeared centrally above the two window panes of the upper-deck rear emergency exit, on the door itself, reading EMERGENCY DOOR. On at least 16–24 this information appeared centrally on the rear dome immediately above the rain guttering and the door opening handle, and was supplemented by TO OPEN accompanied by an arrow indicating how the handle should be turned, applied above the nearside window pane towards the central pillar, on the door itself.

External banner advertising was carried on the upper deck side panels. These were normally sign-written on to the panels and frequently extended the entire length of the vehicle, not only bays 1–5 (6). Circular advertisements began to appear on the white-painted rear corner panel of 1–15 by November 1934. In addition poster-style advertising was displayed on the offside lower deck panels beneath the staircase window or panel from c. 1935 and progressively on the lower deck rear platform panels beneath the rear platform window.

Detail differences by vehicle type

The English Electric- and Cravens-bodied trolleybuses also had the vent panels beading picked out in black.

No. 24 appeared at the 1935 Commercial Motor Show without the cantrail beading picked out in black and subsequently entered service thus.

2. 1939–1945

On the outbreak of war in September 1939 the livery application was altered as follows.

The lower deck and upper deck window surrounds, upper and lower-deck waistbands, and cantrail or vent panel area above the lower-deck windows were white. The main upper and lower deck body panels were painted crimson. Both the lower and upper deck waistband beadings were picked out in black.

The roof, and front and rear domes were repainted matt grey but initially this did not extend down beyond the cantrail. During the course of the war, perhaps commencing as early as January 1940, the grey area was extended down to the upper deck waist band at the rear embracing the upper deck rear corner panels, the emergency exit door and its surrounds. Wartime trolleybus views, particularly of the rear of vehicles, are rare, but the four trolleybuses loaned to Pontypridd UDC in August 1942 all exemplified this livery application. The matt grey rear application was considered as standard by May 1945 at the latest. No. 300, at least, retained the initial matt grey application into the post-war period. Trolley gear and related equipment, and trolley boom restraining hooks were black.

The base of the rear panels, the top of the front mudguards and the side life guard rails were painted white to fulfil wartime "blackout" restrictions. To further aid the driver, the outline of cab access step in the offside lower deck panels was also painted white. The first trolleybuses to appear in the wartime livery were 201 and 258 in September 1939.

The crimson panels were lined in tramcar-style double lining, comprising an outer yellow line ⅜in. broad and an inner white line ⅛in. broad, the yellow line having ornate Greek corner pattern inset square designs and the white line having matching indentations. The lining was applied to divide the crimson panels into separate front, side, rear corner, lower

1935 AEC663T 17 heads north along Victoria Road South past a branch of Smeed & Smeed the wine merchants on the corner of Outram Road, opposite Elm Grove. It again exemplifies Livery 1. In the background the overhead wiring can be seen turning off into Albert Road. The driver's white summer dustcoat, and the open offside windscreen and upper saloon front windows suggest it was a warm day. A Rover 12 saloon is in hot pursuit. (David Beilby collection [English Electric])

saloon platform bulkhead and rear portions. There is no evidence of the ornate lining being simplified during the war. The programme for the first external repaint of the AEC661Ts 225–300 was scheduled to commence when war broke out but little information has survived as to how far this continued unhindered. Complete re-paints appear to have been limited to about 25 vehicles apparently indiscriminately selected from amongst these trolleybuses perhaps reflecting accident and air-raid damage. Those parts of the mudguards which were not painted white remained black. The wheels were maroon.

The Portsmouth coat of arms was displayed on both sides of the lower deck side panels, centred beneath one of the side windows, the position varying, i.e. initially in bay 2 on 210, 211 (both having five-bay saloons) and 14 (six-bay saloon); and bay 3 on 201–209, 212, 213, 215 (six-bay saloon), and 216–300 (five-bay saloon). It will be noted that the position was not strictly in relation to the length of the body or number of bays.

Limited ownership details (the city name and head office address were removed or painted over as a security measure), were applied in small white script typeface at the base of the nearside lower deck panels, bay 1, immediately to the rear of the front axle, viz:

Passenger Transport Department

Ben Hall Engineer and Manager

(Note the space or painted-out wording at the beginning of the first line and the blank middle line.)

The maximum permitted speed in small white script typeface followed by the unladen weight in upper-case typeface were shown at the base of the nearside lower deck panels immediately in front of the (leading) rear axle. The seating capacity was indicated in upper case white typeface at the nearside base of the rear platform panel.

Large gold numerals, shaded in two tones of blue and in white, were mounted on the front panel centrally beneath the driver's cab windscreen (the height varying according to the presence or otherwise of the maker's nameplate or ventilators and the position of the headlamps), and centrally in the lower half of the rear panels beneath the advertisement space.

The fleet number was additionally displayed in 1½in. tall white numerals, followed by a full stop, immediately beneath the lower deck waistrail and lining on both sides to the rear of the driver's cab rear bulkhead.

Small upper-case white lettering appeared centrally above the two window panes of the upper-deck rear emergency exit, on the door itself, reading EMERGENCY DOOR.

External banner advertising was carried on the upper deck side panels. These were normally sign-written on to the panels and frequently extended the entire length of the vehicle, not only bays 1–5 (6). Advertisements were also displayed on the lower deck rear platform panels beneath the rear platform window and on the vent panel area above the rear platform window. Subject to the wartime availability of paper when contracts expired, painted advertisements on the upper deck side panels were increasingly replaced by paper poster advertisements.

Detail differences by vehicle type

The English Electric and Cravens bodied trolleybuses also had the vent panels beading picked out in black.

AEC661T 289 appeared with matt grey paint extending down the corner pillars and all the upper-deck window pillars on 15 March 1942.

AEC661T 295 was the first trolleybus to appear without white "blackout" aids in May 1945.

No. 202, one of the four AEC661T trolleybuses equipped with English Electric composite body, stands at the Cosham Railway Station terminus passenger waiting shelter on 10 September 1948 immediately prior to the change in the terminal layout. It exemplifies the 1939 livery application (Livery 2). (BTS Library [photographer V.C. Jones])

3. 1945–1948

During May 1945 the livery application was altered as follows.

The lower deck and upper deck window surrounds, upper and lower-deck waistbands, and vent panel area above the lower-deck windows were white. The main upper and lower deck body panels were painted crimson. Beadings were no longer picked out separately.

The roof, front and rear domes, and upper deck rear corner panels remained matt grey, this colour being extended at the rear to include the emergency exit door and its surrounds. Trolley gear and related equipment, and trolley boom restraining hooks were black.

The crimson panels continued to be fully lined in tramcar-style double lining, comprising an outer yellow line ⅜in. broad and an inner white line ⅛in. broad, the yellow line having ornate Greek corner pattern inset square designs and the white line having matching indentations. The lining was applied to divide the crimson panels into separate front, side, rear corner, lower saloon platform bulkhead and rear portions. Mudguards and lifeguard rails were painted black, and wheels maroon.

The Portsmouth coat of arms was displayed on both sides of the lower deck waist panels, centred in bay 3.

Full ownership details with the General Manager's name and title beneath were applied in small white script typeface at the base of the nearside lower deck panels, bay 1, immediately to the rear of the front axle, viz:

City of Portsmouth Passenger Transport Department
Eastney, Portsmouth
Ben Hall Engineer and Manager

The maximum permitted speed in small white script typeface followed by the unladen weight in upper-case typeface were shown at the base of the nearside lower deck panels immediately in front of the (leading) rear axle. The seating capacity was indicated in upper case white typeface at the nearside base of the rear platform panel.

Large gold numerals, shaded in two tones of blue and in white, were mounted on the front panel centrally beneath the driver's cab windscreen (the height varying according to the presence or otherwise of the maker's nameplate or ventilators and the position of the headlamps), and centrally in the lower half of the rear panels beneath the advertisement space.

The fleet number was additionally displayed in 1½in. tall white numerals, followed by a full stop, immediately beneath the lower deck waistrail and lining on both sides to the rear of the driver's cab rear bulkhead.

Small upper-case white lettering appeared centrally above the two window panes of the upper-deck rear emergency exit, on the door itself, reading EMERGENCY DOOR.

External banner advertising was carried on the upper deck side panel, bays 1–5 (6); on the lower deck rear platform panels beneath the rear platform window and on the vent panel area above the rear platform window. Sign written painted advertisements on the upper deck side panels were increasingly replaced by paper poster advertisements.

Detail differences by vehicle type

Nos 201–211 returned to service June 1946 with a very short-lived black patch painted onto the glass of the service number indicator box as it was known that the coordination scheme with SMS would involve the renumbering of services or the addition of an A-suffix to some numbers.

AEC661T no. 232 seen here at Cosham Railway Station ready for the first leg of the convoluted service 19 routing, demonstrates Livery 3 used in the immediate post-war years. (Online Transport Archive [photographer G.F. Ashwell])

4. 1948–1963

From June 1948 a further change was made to the livery, trolleybuses adopting that used on motorbuses. This was applied to the following vehicles upon delivery and earlier vehicles in the fleet upon repaint:

301–315 BUT9611T

The lower deck and upper deck window surrounds, upper and lower deck waistbands, and vent panel area above the lower deck windows were white. The main upper and lower deck body panels were painted vermilion, namely the brighter "red" which had been used as the main body colour on motorbuses with effect from 1931.

The upper edge of the lower deck vermilion panels featured a single yellow line ⅜in. broad beneath the waistband, ending with a very slight downwards curve at the extremities of the front and nearside panels. The offside line extended around the offside corner panel to the rear panels as a single continuous line. The upper deck vermilion panels also had a single yellow line ⅜in. broad applied to divide them into separate front and side portions (there was no lining at the rear). The lining on the front panels had vertical uprights whilst the horizontal lines were interrupted by the indicator boxes. When particularly large twin advertisements were applied on each side of the indicator box this could cover the lining. The lining on the upper deck sides continued along the length of the panels, although often not visible beneath paper advertisements, and surrounded the nearside indicator box above the platform. The "uprights" on the side panels matched the contours of the bodywork. Where advertisements had been painted onto the upper deck side panels, the lining was curtailed towards the front and to the rear of the advertisement and an upright applied.

Use of vermilion, but with the simplified lining application introduced in August 1936, reflected the livery of CPPTD motorbuses since 1931. The first trolleybus to appear in the simplified livery was 293 on 23 June 1948; however, it is known that some trolleybuses continued to receive crimson paintwork with ornate double lining, i.e. May 1945 livery, possibly to use up stocks of paint and transfers. AEC661T 278 was rebuilt in July 1949 but was still in pre-war livery in May 1952 if not later. By 1953 all of the licensed AEC661Ts with Craven bodywork were in the 1948 livery, 278 being the last vehicle to be so treated (implying that on rebuilding 278 appeared in the 1934 livery).

The roof, front and rear domes, and upper deck rear corner panels were retained in matt grey. Trolley gear and related equipment, and trolley boom restraining hooks were black.

Mudguards and lifeguard rails were black. Wheels were vermilion.

The Portsmouth coat of arms was displayed on both sides of the lower deck waist panels, centred in bay 3.

Ownership details with the General Manager's name and title beneath were applied in small white script typeface at the base of the nearside lower deck panels, bay 1, immediately to the rear of the front axle.

City of Portsmouth Passenger Transport Department
Eastney, Portsmouth.
Ben Hall Engineer and Manager.

On 9 October 1948, freshly out of the paint shop in the simplified 1948 livery (Livery 4), 1936 AEC661T/Cravens 284 leaves the Canoe Lake turning circle at Southsea South Parade Pier and pulls on to Southsea Esplanade still displaying blinds for service 1 upon which it presumably arrived. The private road now displays a sign "Corporation Buses Only" rather than the "Trolley Vehicles Only" originally used. (Online Transport Archive [photographer V.C. Jones])

The style was amended somewhat from 1951 with the change of General Manager, viz:

*City of Portsmouth Passenger Transport Dep*t*.,*
Eastney, Portsmouth.
H.C. Simmonds. A.M. INST *T.*
Manager and Engineer.

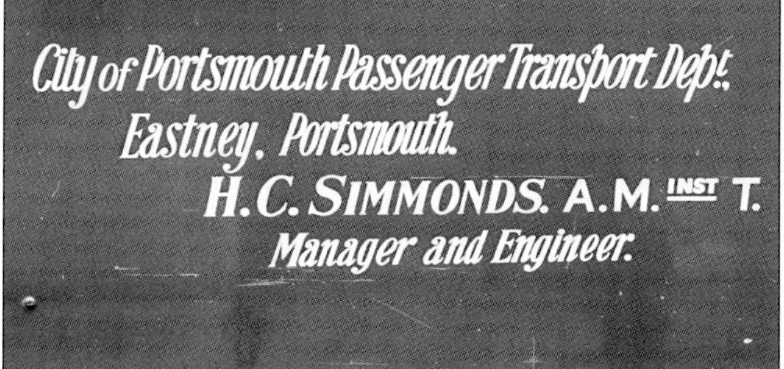

The maximum permitted speed in small white script typeface followed by the unladen weight in upper-case typeface were shown at the base of the nearside lower deck panels immediately in front of the (leading) rear axle. The seating capacity was indicated in upper case white typeface at the nearside base of the rear platform panel.

Large gold numerals, shaded blue and white, were mounted on the front panel centrally beneath the driver's cab windscreen, the height varying according to the continuing presence or otherwise of the maker's symbol, and centrally in the lower half of the rear panels beneath the advertisement space. The fleet number was additionally displayed in 1½in. tall white numerals, followed by a full stop, immediately beneath the lower deck waistrail and lining on both sides to the rear of the driver's cab rear bulkhead.

Small upper-case white lettering appeared centrally above the two window panes of the upper-deck rear emergency exit, on the door itself, reading EMERGENCY EXIT.

External paper poster or painted advertising was carried on the upper deck side panel bays ("banners") bays 1–5 (6); on the lower panels beneath the rear platform window, on the vent panel area above the rear platform window, on either side of the front destination box and on the offside rear platform panel (circular "spot"). Infrequently advertisements were also applied to the offside staircase panels to the rear of the lower saloon windows.

Seating capacity details on 225–300 were shown in white script typeface left justified. White 1in. tall capitals and normal type face began to appear upon repaint from an unknown date, possibly from January 1958, but not all trolleybuses received this style. Capitals were used on 233 (September 1958), 238 (February 1958), 248 (January 1958) 259 (June 1958), 267 (October 1958), 269 (November 1959), 274 (May 1958), 292 (last repaint August 1958), 298 (January 1960), 300 (September 1959), at least.

Detail differences by vehicle type

301–315 BUT9611T: There was no beading around the top of the upper deck vermilion painted panels; however, there was a painted black line all the way around the vehicle. The roof folding at cantrail height was painted grey until first repaint (thereafter white).

Upon delivery, the matt grey paint applied to the front dome continued a short distance down the front corner pillar in a "V" shape.

Only the upper horizontal line on the front upper deck panels was interrupted by the indicator boxes (both the upper and lower lines were interrupted on AEC661Ts 225–300).

Details of the lower rear panel of AEC661T/Cravens 298. Note the white enamelled Police Licence plate and covering plate over the offside retaining tube beneath the body to stop the bamboo trolley retrieval pole from sliding out. (Roger Funnell collection)

Internal livery, lettering and numerals

Throughout the trolleybus era lower and upper saloons were painted in varying applications of brown and cream or off-white, accompanied by varnished woodwork and brown scratchproof brown leather clothe (Rexine or similar) coverings to waistrail height. The ceiling panels on the English Electric bodied prototype vehicles 1–9, 12, 13, at least, and AEC661Ts 25–100 were lined out with a single brown or maroon line.

All seat fittings were painted black. The floors were normally finished in brown linoleum, grey waterproof paint being applied to the open rear platform area. Handrails were covered in black Doverite.

The platform area, excluding the nearside lower saloon rear bulkhead, and the staircase were finished in crimson, respectively vermilion.

The driver's cab (panels and ceiling) and equipment was brown. The date of the most recent external repaint was shown in white, e.g. 6/48, above the nearside cab windows.

AEC661Ts 225–300 had off-white Bakelite bell pushes with a brown central push button and PUSH ONCE in dark red lettering around the outside.

No. 201, at least, had circular chromed bell pushes with a chromed central push button (which often stuck and conductors, latterly, used penknives to extract them) and no lettering.

No. 224 was equipped with a single continuous rubber bell strip along the left hand side of the ceiling above the gangway in the lower saloon and possibly in the upper saloon too.

On all the trolleybuses there was a white strip with concave corners normally on the window surrounds below each bell push, but on the cove panels of certain prototype vehicles inside the saloons and next to other bell push locations reading TO STOP THE VEHICLE RING ONCE. Those on the BUT9611Ts, on the window surrounds and to the left of the platform bell push on the nearside bulkhead, read TO STOP THE VEHICLE PRESS ONCE in black lettering.

Paper advertisements, normally referring to local events or traffic notices, were applied to the lower saloon side windows and upper saloon stairhead window throughout the trolleybus era. Advertisements were also pasted on the lower saloon ceiling cove panels but there is no evidence that they were ever carried on the upper saloon ceiling cove panels.

The fleet number was displayed in black numbering on a white oval plastic disc screwed to the lower saloon front bulkhead centrally just beneath the ceiling on the pre-war vehicles and on the central panel between the two bulkhead windows on the BUT9611Ts, and above the central pillar of the upper saloon front windows. When the fleet was re-numbered in early April 1938 these discs were reversed and the new fleet numbers applied in the previous form. No. 14 and potentially the other MCCW-bodied trolleybuses were delivered with a square metal fleet number plate in the lower saloon. It is not known how the 1938 renumbering affected the plates on these vehicles.

Details of the internal notices and lettering on trolleybuses 1–24 (201–224) are incompletely known; however, the later deliveries displayed the following and it can be assumed that the earlier deliveries were not dissimilar:

Upper Saloon

The exhortation SPITTING STRICTLY PROHIBITED was transferred on the window frame mouldings above the nearside front window on 1–24; on the AEC661Ts 225–300 the transfers read SPITTING PROHIBITED with "spitting" being placed above the nearside and "prohibited" above the offside front window. The transfers used gold letters having cut-off corners and two-tone blue shading.

There was a long rectangular notice with light coloured background instructing passengers TO SAVE TIME AND TROUBLE PLEASE TENDER EXACT FARE AND STATE DESTINATION and SEASON TICKETS TO BE SHOWN in the front dome and at various locations along the ceiling cove panels, a rectangular red notice (having the same overall dimensions as the oval notice) believed to refer to a requirement that passengers retain and show their ticket upon request, and a small rectangular label (believed to be black on yellow) requesting passengers not to place their feet on the seat cushions.

AEC661Ts 225–300 had a small rectangular yellow notice centred on the dome above the fleet number disc requesting in black lettering passengers not to place their feet on the seat cushions.

There were no notices on the front dome of the BUT9611Ts.

Lower Saloon

The exhortation SPITTING STRICTLY PROHIBITED was transferred on the driver's cab rear bulkhead between the bevel-edged mirrors and the ceiling on the nearside and NO SMOKING ALLOWED on the offside on 1–24. On other vehicles the transfers read NO SMOKING ALLOWED on the nearside and SPITTING PROHIBITED on the offside. The transfers used gold letters having cut-off corners and two-tone blue shading.

An oval red notice, 7¾in. by 4¾in., with yellow lettering headed NOTICE TO PASSENGERS then NOT MORE THAN 5 STANDING PASSENGERS ARE ALLOWED IN THIS SALOON BY ORDER (in some cases with a sticker to amend that maximum number from 5 to 8) was applied to the ceiling cove panels.

There was a long rectangular notice with light coloured background instructing passengers to state their destination and tender correct fare, a rectangular red notice (having the same overall dimensions as the oval notice) believed to refer to a requirement that passengers retain and show their ticket upon request, and a small rectangular label (believed to be black on yellow) instructing passengers not to place their feet on the seat cushions.

The seating capacity was indicated in upper case black typeface at the top of the offside rear bulkhead above the glass-fronted time table case:

AEC661Ts 25–100 having script typeface for each saloon, viz:

SEATING CAPACITY 52
Upper Saloon 26
Lower Saloon 26

BUT9611Ts 301–315 having block typeface, viz:

SEATING CAPACITY 52
LOWER SALOON 24
UPPER SALOON 28

Beneath, aligned with the depth of the windows, was a glass-fronted case for a fare table sheet.

BUT9611Ts 301–315 had an undesignated single metal pouch on the nearside bulkhead above the window, possibly for storing the CPPTD Bye-laws or the conductor's way sheet, but and latterly always empty.

The lower saloon of AEC661T/Cravens 294 almost at the end of its operating life. Photographed on 12 June 1963, the trolleybus was withdrawn on 21 June 1963. (T.V. Runnacles)

Rear platform

There was a used ticket box in the nearside platform bulkhead of all trolleybuses, the precise wording varying between bodybuilders and period, e.g. PLEASE DEPOSIT USED TICKETS IN THIS BOX on 1–4, USED TICKETS on 25–100, USED TICKET BOX on 16–24, 301–315.

Beneath these words the following transfer appeared in white lettering on 25–100 and gold shaded blue on 301–305:

PASSENGERS
ENTERING OR LEAVING
THE BUS WHILST IN
MOTION DO SO AT
THEIR OWN RISK

The same exhortation also appeared above the platform rear window on 301–315 whilst 25–100 displayed:

SAFETY FIRST
WAIT UNTIL THE BUS STOPS

During January 1940, the lower three stair treads were painted white.

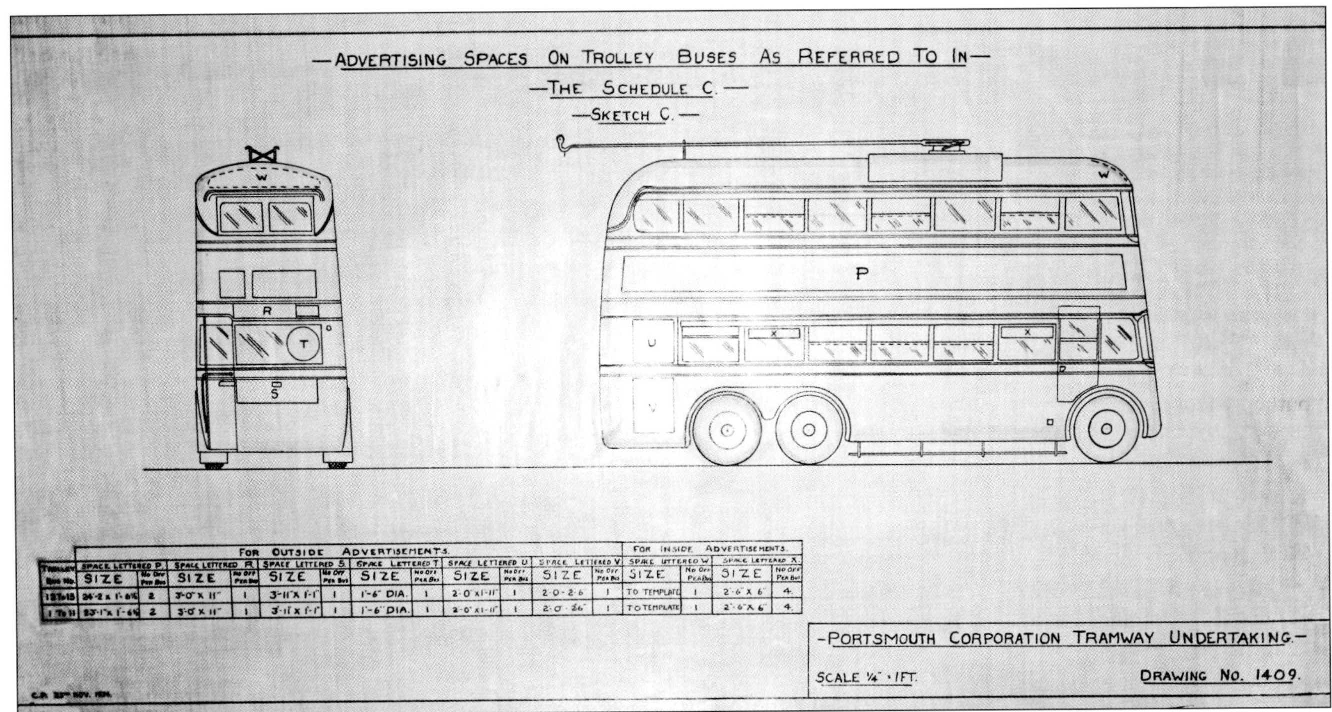

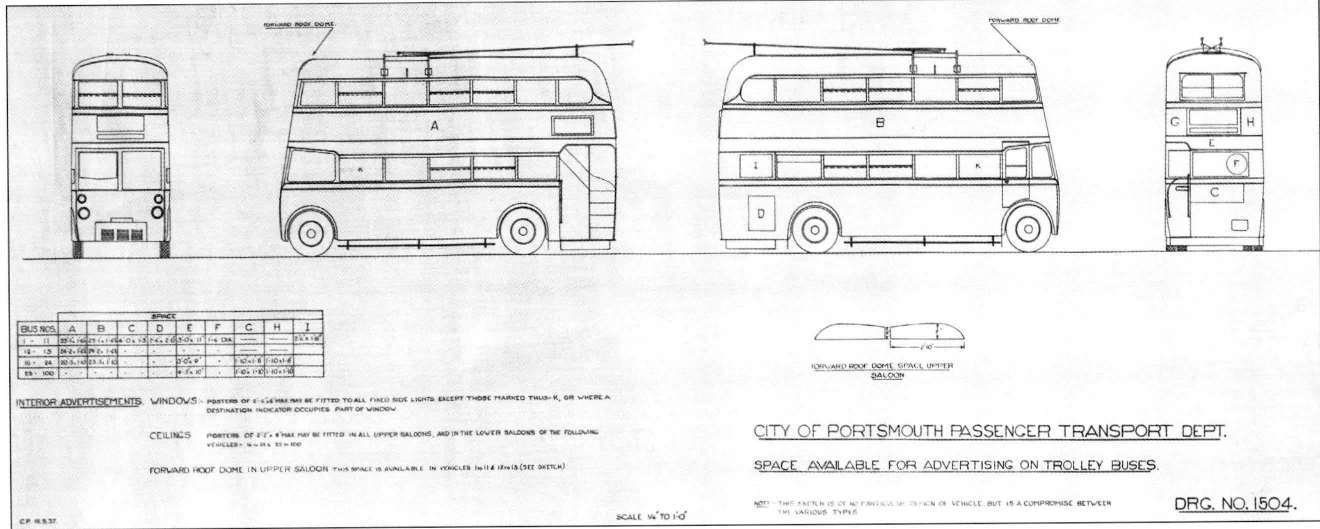

Advertising spaces on trolleybuses. (CPPTD Drawings)

APPENDIX D

SERVICES AND SERVICE ALTERATIONS

Portsmouth's trolleybus services were complex and potentially confusing. Trolleybus services were designated according to a practice introduced on the City's tramways in 1927 whereby service numbers were allocated in consecutive pairs, one for each direction of travel. Services running basically north–south had the uneven number allocated to southbound journeys whereas the uneven number signified the anti-clockwise direction for those services which were of a mainly circular nature. In accordance with this approach the first trolleybus route between Cosham Railway Station and Southsea South Parade Pier received service numbers 3 southbound and 4 northbound.

The decision to convert the tramways system to trolleybus operation and extend beyond the confines of the tramways to Cosham *Red Lion* resulted in the adoption of a policy whereby "short workings" to Cosham Railway Station but not from would carry an A suffix. Thus with this first extension of trolleybus services, producing a distorted "figure 8" from Cosham Railway Station, the existing services 3 and 4 were re-designated 3 and 4A as the northbound service terminated at Cosham Railway Station. Similarly the extension of service 3 from Southsea *South Parade Pier* back to Cosham Railway Station became the 3A. The southbound service was 4.

The situation was confused by prototype trolleybuses 1–15 not having service number blinds including numbers with suffixes and, of necessity, they displayed 3 and 4 when running on services 3A and 4A. This situation was compounded by pre-war and early post-war timetables which referred to all journeys as having service number 3 and 4 whilst official announcements and notices often excluded the A suffix too!

The A suffix policy was broken in 1942 with the introduction of services 1A and 2A which terminated at Cosham *Red Lion* and the southbound designation 2A to distinguish it from the 1 and 2 which was also terminating there at the time as a circular service.

A combination of public confusion and service rationalisation led to the A suffix policy being abandoned post-war although services continued to display even und uneven numbers according to the direction of travel until the end of trolleybus operation.

Service 1 (i)

01.10.36	Trolleybus service commenced Cosham *Red Lion* – Hilsea – North End *Junction* – Guildhall – Royal Pier Hotel – Clarence Pier via Spur Road, Northern Road, London Road, Kingston Road, Kingston Crescent, Commercial Road, Guildhall Square, Commercial Road, Hampshire Terrace, Landport Terrace, Kings Terrace, Jubilee Terrace, Bellevue Terrace and Pier Road. *Unidirectional southbound service worked in conjunction with service 2.*
05.07.40	Curtailed to terminate at Royal Pier Hotel (closure of seafront) reversing at junction with Southsea Terrace.
21.07.40	Extended from Royal Pier Hotel – Southsea *The Circle* – Bradford Junction – Fratton Bridge – North End, turning by running through North End Depot, via Southsea Terrace, Western Parade, Osborne Road, Clarendon Road, Victoria Road South, Victoria Road North, Fratton Road, Kingston Road and London Road.
07.07.41	Extended from North End to Cosham *Red Lion* thus operating Cosham *Red Lion* – Hilsea – North End *Junction* – Guildhall – Royal Pier Hotel – Southsea *The Circle* – Bradford Junction – Fratton Bridge – North End *Junction* – Hilsea – Cosham *Red Lion* via Spur Road, Northern Road, London Road, Kingston Crescent, Commercial Road, Guildhall Square, Commercial Road, Hampshire Terrace, Landport Terrace, Kings Terrace, Jubilee Terrace, Bellevue Terrace, Southsea Terrace, Western Parade, Osborne Road, Clarendon Road, Victoria Road South, Victoria Road North, Fratton Road, Kingston Road, London Road, Northern Road and London Road. *Unidirectional circular service (anti-clockwise) worked in conjunction with service 2.*
07.07.41	Early morning journeys prior to and including the 8.10 am from Cosham curtailed to operate Cosham *Red Lion* – Alexandra Park – Guildhall – Dockyard via Spur Road, Northern Road, Northern Parade, Twyford Avenue, Commercial Road, Guildhall Square, Park Road, Ordnance Row and The Hard. *Unidirectional southbound service worked in conjunction with service 2.*
03.05.42	Southbound journeys (only) diverted at Northern Road along private road to Cosham Railway Station thence via Portsmouth Road to rejoin the previous route at Portsbridge.
By 21.06.42	Early morning curtailment Cosham *Red Lion* – Alexandra Park – Guildhall – Dockyard ceased.
19.07.42	Sunday service divided into two separate portions: (i) Cosham *Red Lion* – Cosham Railway Station – Hilsea – Guildhall – Royal Pier Hotel – Southsea *The Circle* – Southsea *South Parade Pier* (ii) Southsea *The Circle* – Bradford Junction – Fratton Bridge – North End *Junction* – Hilsea – Cosham *Red Lion*
By 03.09.44	Sunday service withdrawn.
29.07.45	Service rerouted and divided into two separate portions operating daily: (i) Cosham *Red Lion* – Cosham Railway Station – Hilsea – North End *Junction* – Guildhall – Royal Pier Hotel – Clarence Pier via Spur Road, Northern Road, private road, Portsmouth Road,

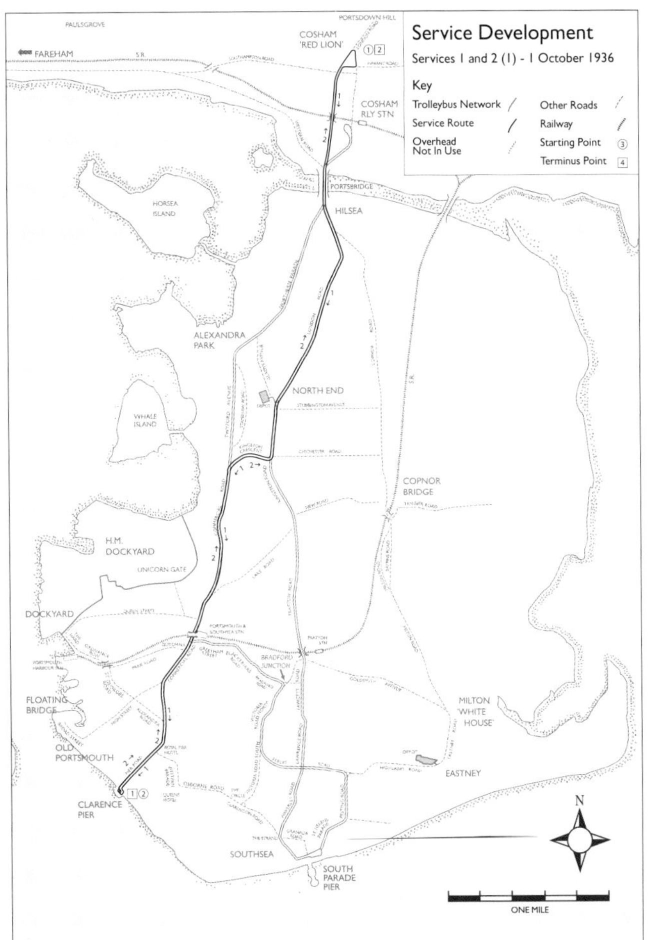
Service Development
Services 1 and 2 (1) - 1 October 1936
Key
Trolleybus Network
Service Route
Overhead Not In Use
Other Roads
Railway
Starting Point
Terminus Point
PORTSDOWN HILL
PAULSGROVE
FAREHAM
COSHAM 'RED LION'
COSHAM RLY STN
PORTSBRIDGE
HILSEA
HORSEA ISLAND
ALEXANDRA PARK
NORTH END
WHALE ISLAND
COPNOR BRIDGE
H.M. DOCKYARD
UNICORN GATE
DOCKYARD
FLOATING BRIDGE
OLD PORTSMOUTH
CLARENCE PIER
MILTON 'WHITE HOUSE'
EASTNEY
SOUTHSEA
SOUTH PARADE PIER
N
ONE MILE

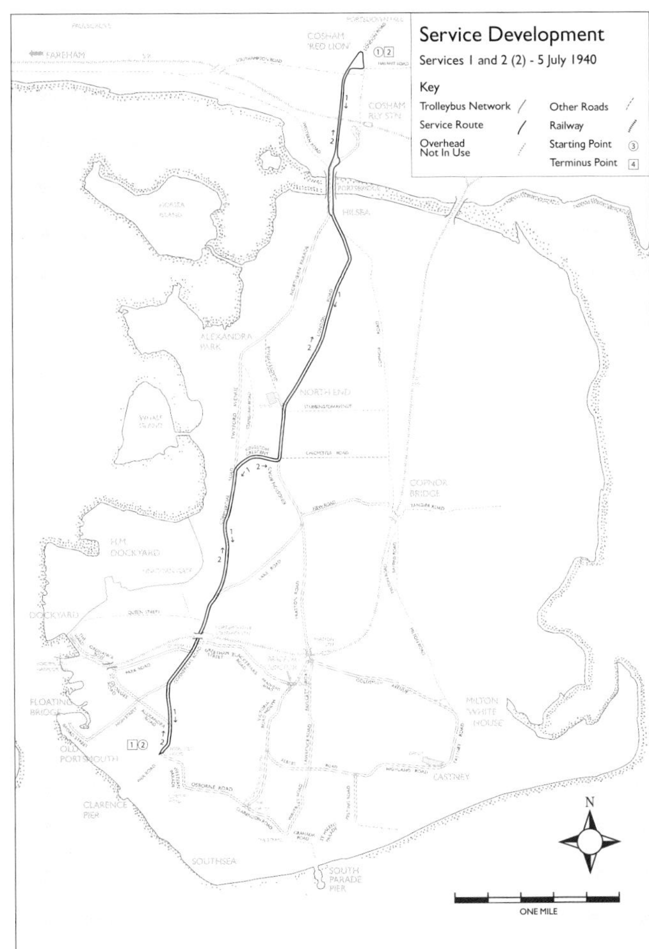
Service Development
Services 1 and 2 (2) - 5 July 1940
Key
Trolleybus Network
Service Route
Overhead Not In Use
Other Roads
Railway
Starting Point
Terminus Point
FAREHAM
COSHAM 'RED LION'
COSHAM RLY STN
HILSEA
ALEXANDRA PARK
NORTH END
COPNOR BRIDGE
H.M. DOCKYARD
DOCKYARD
FLOATING BRIDGE
OLD PORTSMOUTH
CLARENCE PIER
MILTON 'WHITE HOUSE'
EASTNEY
SOUTHSEA
SOUTH PARADE PIER
N
ONE MILE

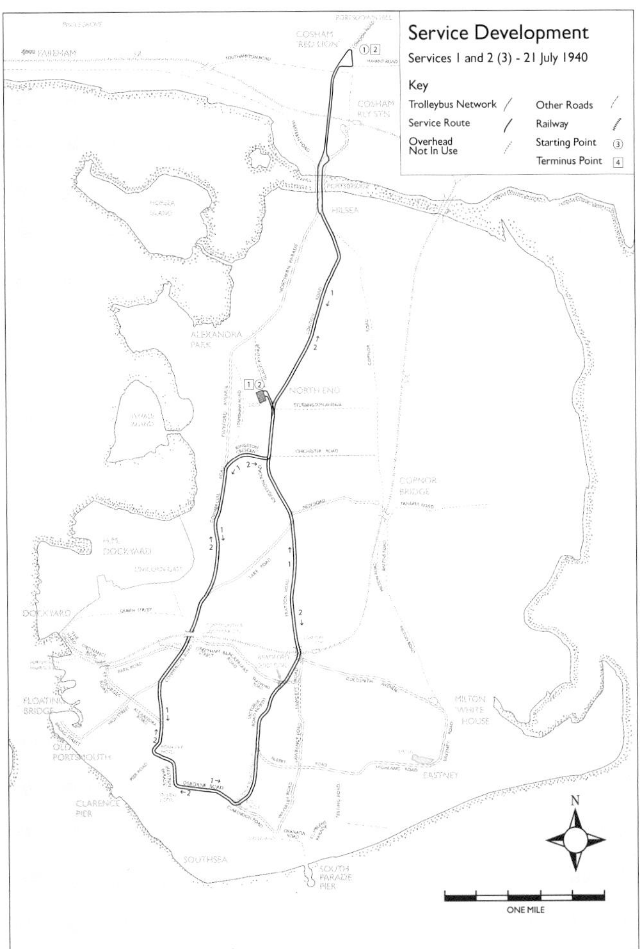
Service Development
Services 1 and 2 (3) - 21 July 1940
Key
Trolleybus Network
Service Route
Overhead Not In Use
Other Roads
Railway
Starting Point
Terminus Point
FAREHAM
COSHAM 'RED LION'
COSHAM RLY STN
HILSEA
ALEXANDRA PARK
NORTH END
COPNOR BRIDGE
H.M. DOCKYARD
UNICORN GATE
DOCKYARD
FLOATING BRIDGE
OLD PORTSMOUTH
CLARENCE PIER
MILTON WHITE HOUSE
EASTNEY
SOUTHSEA
SOUTH PARADE PIER
N
ONE MILE

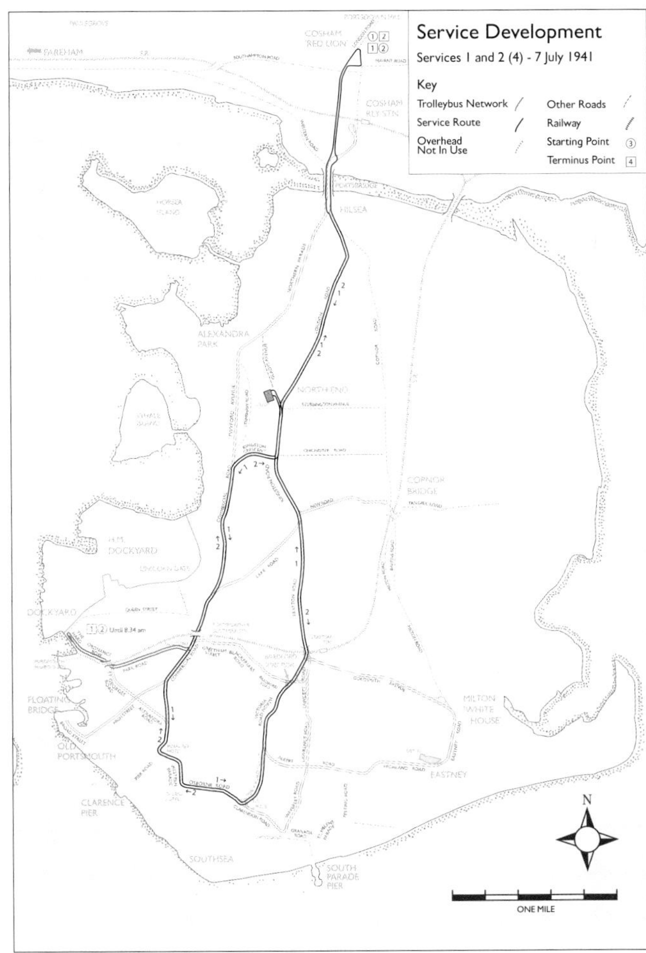
Service Development
Services 1 and 2 (4) - 7 July 1941
Key
Trolleybus Network
Service Route
Overhead Not In Use
Other Roads
Railway
Starting Point
Terminus Point
FAREHAM
COSHAM 'RED LION'
COSHAM RLY STN
PORTSBRIDGE
HILSEA
HORSEA ISLAND
ALEXANDRA PARK
NORTH END
COPNOR BRIDGE
H.M. DOCKYARD
UNICORN GATE
DOCKYARD
FLOATING BRIDGE
OLD PORTSMOUTH
CLARENCE PIER
MILTON WHITE HOUSE
EASTNEY
SOUTHSEA
SOUTH PARADE PIER
N
ONE MILE

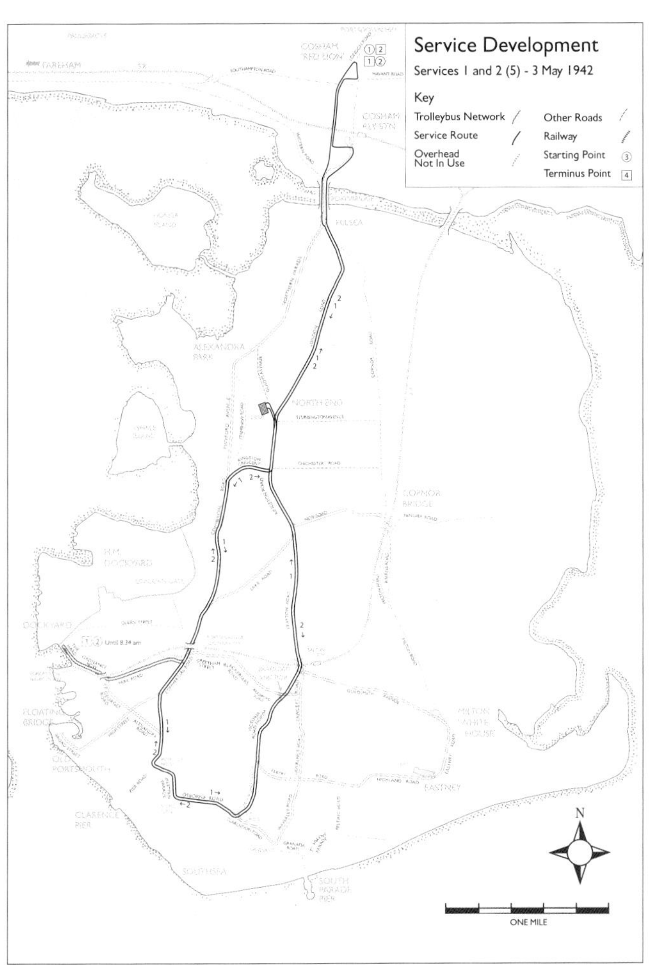
Service Development
Services 1 and 2 (5) - 3 May 1942
Key
Trolleybus Network
Service Route
Overhead Not In Use
Other Roads
Railway
Starting Point
Terminus Point
COSHAM RED LION
FAREHAM
COSHAM RLY STN
HILSEA
ALEXANDRA PARK
NORTH END
COPNOR BRIDGE
H.M. DOCKYARD
DOCKYARD
FLOATING BRIDGE
OLD PORTSMOUTH
CLARENCE PIER
MILTON WHITE HOUSE
EASTNEY
SOUTHSEA
SOUTH PARADE PIER
N
ONE MILE

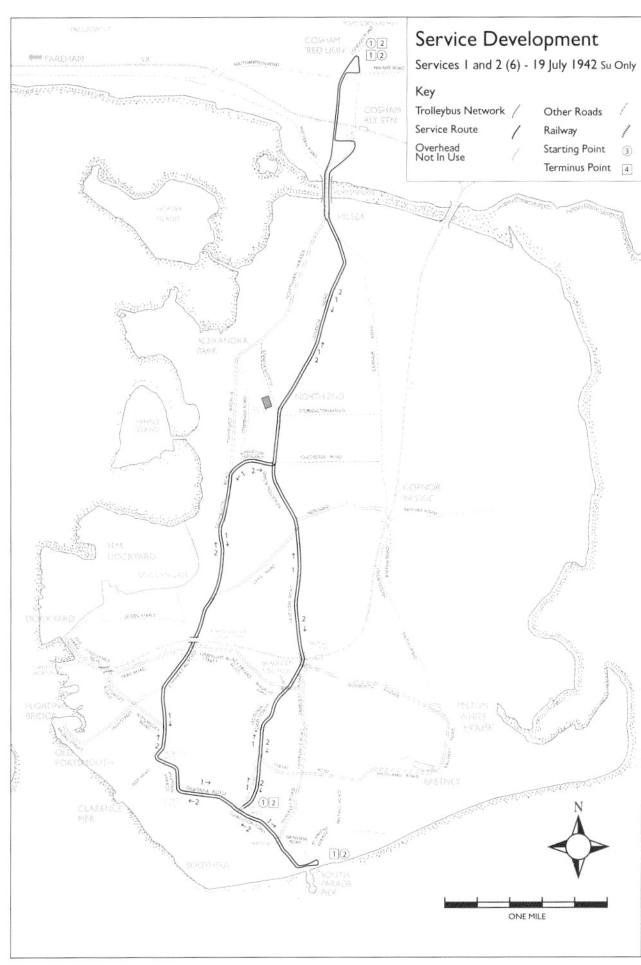
Service Development
Services 1 and 2 (6) - 19 July 1942 Su Only
Key
Trolleybus Network
Service Route
Overhead Not In Use
Other Roads
Railway
Starting Point
Terminus Point
COSHAM RED LION
FAREHAM
COSHAM RLY STN
HILSEA
ALEXANDRA PARK
NORTH END
COPNOR BRIDGE
H.M. DOCKYARD
DOCKYARD
FLOATING BRIDGE
OLD PORTSMOUTH
CLARENCE PIER
MILTON WHITE HOUSE
EASTNEY
SOUTHSEA
SOUTH PARADE PIER
N
ONE MILE

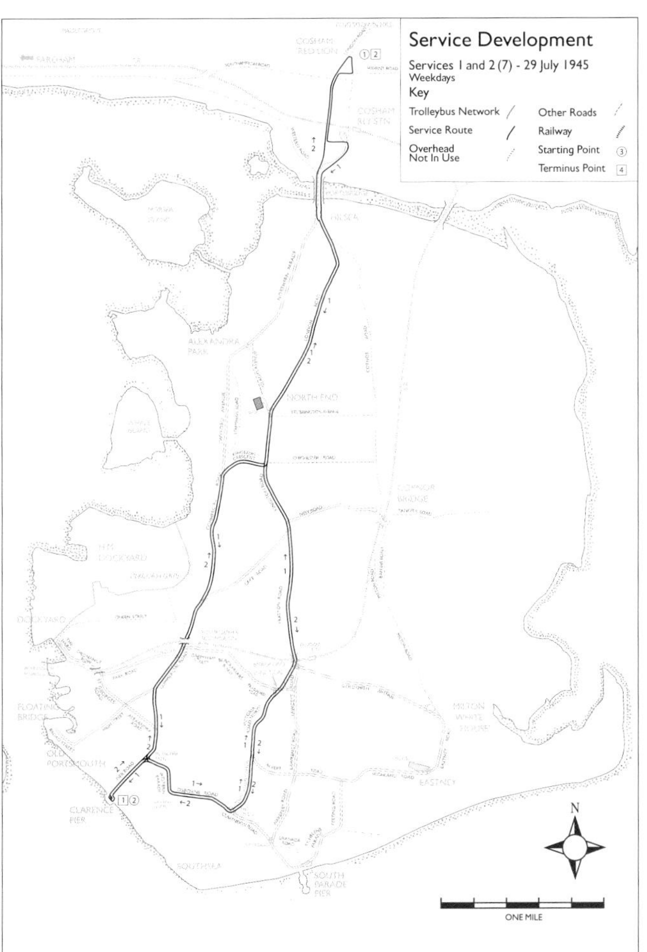
Service Development
Services 1 and 2 (7) - 29 July 1945 Weekdays
Key
Trolleybus Network
Service Route
Overhead Not In Use
Other Roads
Railway
Starting Point
Terminus Point
COSHAM RED LION
FAREHAM
COSHAM RLY STN
HILSEA
ALEXANDRA PARK
NORTH END
COPNOR BRIDGE
H.M. DOCKYARD
DOCKYARD
FLOATING BRIDGE
OLD PORTSMOUTH
CLARENCE PIER
MILTON WHITE HOUSE
EASTNEY
SOUTHSEA
SOUTH PARADE PIER
N
ONE MILE

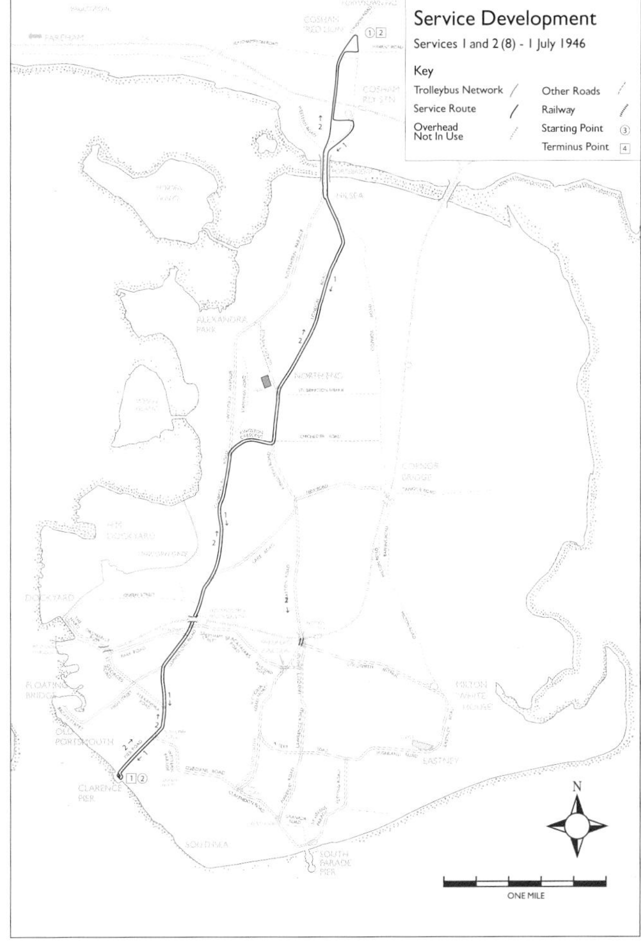
Service Development
Services 1 and 2 (8) - 1 July 1946
Key
Trolleybus Network
Service Route
Overhead Not In Use
Other Roads
Railway
Starting Point
Terminus Point
COSHAM RED LION
FAREHAM
COSHAM RLY STN
HILSEA
ALEXANDRA PARK
NORTH END
COPNOR BRIDGE
H.M. DOCKYARD
DOCKYARD
FLOATING BRIDGE
OLD PORTSMOUTH
CLARENCE PIER
MILTON WHITE HOUSE
EASTNEY
SOUTHSEA
SOUTH PARADE PIER
N
ONE MILE

London Road, Kingston Crescent, Commercial Road, Guildhall Square, Commercial Road, Hampshire Terrace, Landport Terrace, Kings Terrace, Jubilee Terrace, Bellevue Terrace and Pier Road.

(ii) Clarence Pier – Royal Pier Hotel – Southsea *The Circle* – Bradford Junction – Fratton Bridge – North End *Junction* – Cosham *Red Lion* via Pier Road, Southsea Terrace, Western Parade, Osborne Road, Clarendon Road, Victoria Road South, Victoria Road North, Fratton Road, Kingston Road, London Road, Northern Road and London Road.

Unidirectional circular service (anti-clockwise) worked in conjunction with service 2.

Sunday service reintroduced on or by 29.07.45.

30.06.46 Both portions of the circular service cease and (ii) above replaced by service 9.

Service 1 (ii)

01.07.46 Revised trolleybus service 1 commenced Cosham *Red Lion* – Cosham Railway Station – Hilsea – North End *Junction* – Guildhall – Royal Pier Hotel – Clarence Pier via Spur Road, Northern Road, private road, Portsmouth Road, London Road, Kingston Crescent, Commercial Road, Guildhall Square, Commercial Road, Hampshire Terrace, Landport Terrace, Kings Terrace, Jubilee Terrace, Bellevue Terrace and Pier Road.

Unidirectional southbound service worked in conjunction with service 2.

29.09.46 Diverted at Guildhall Square via Park Road, Ordnance Row and The Hard to terminate at Dockyard *Main Gate* (remainder of route unchanged).

18.05.47 Trolleybus service Cosham *Red Lion* – North End *Junction* – Guildhall – Dockyard withdrawn and replaced by motorbus service M.

Service 1 (iii)

26.09.48 Revised trolleybus service (formerly service 1A) commenced Cosham *Red Lion* – North End *Junction* – Guildhall – Royal Pier Hotel – Southsea *South Parade Pier* via Spur Road, Northern Road, private road, Portsmouth Road, London Road, Kingston Crescent, Commercial Road, Guildhall Square, Commercial Road, Hampshire Terrace, Landport Terrace, Kings Terrace, Jubilee Terrace, Bellevue Terrace, Southsea Terrace, Western Parade, Osborne Road and Clarendon Road.

Unidirectional southbound service worked in conjunction with service 2.

17.06.50 Last day of operation by trolleybus. Replaced by motorbus service R.

Service 1A

21.06.42 Trolleybus service commenced Cosham *Red Lion* – Cosham Railway Station – Hilsea – North End *Junction* – Guildhall – Royal Pier Hotel – Southsea *The Circle* – Southsea *South Parade Pier* – Eastney, turning by battery at Eastney Depot via Spur Road, Northern Road, private road, Portsmouth Road, London Road, Kingston Crescent, Commercial Road, Guildhall Square, Commercial Road, Hampshire Terrace, Landport Terrace, Kings Terrace, Jubilee Terrace, Bellevue Terrace, Southsea Terrace, Western Parade, Osborne Road, Clarendon Road, St Helens Parade, Festing Road, and Highland Road.

Unidirectional southbound service worked in conjunction with service 2A.

06. or 07.42 Extended to Milton *White House* via Eastney Road presumably to avoid difficult battery turn into Eastney Depot.

18.10.42 Curtailed to terminate at Southsea *South Parade Pier*.

19.04.44 Curtailed to terminate at Southsea *The Strand* reversing at the junction with Waverley Road.

15.06.44 Monday–Saturday service extended to Southsea *South Parade Pier.*

By 03.09.44 Sunday service extended to Southsea *South Parade Pier.*

25.09.48 Service Cosham *Red Lion* – Hilsea – North End *Junction* – Guildhall – Royal Pier Hotel – Southsea *The Strand* – Southsea *South Parade Pier* renumbered 1(iii).

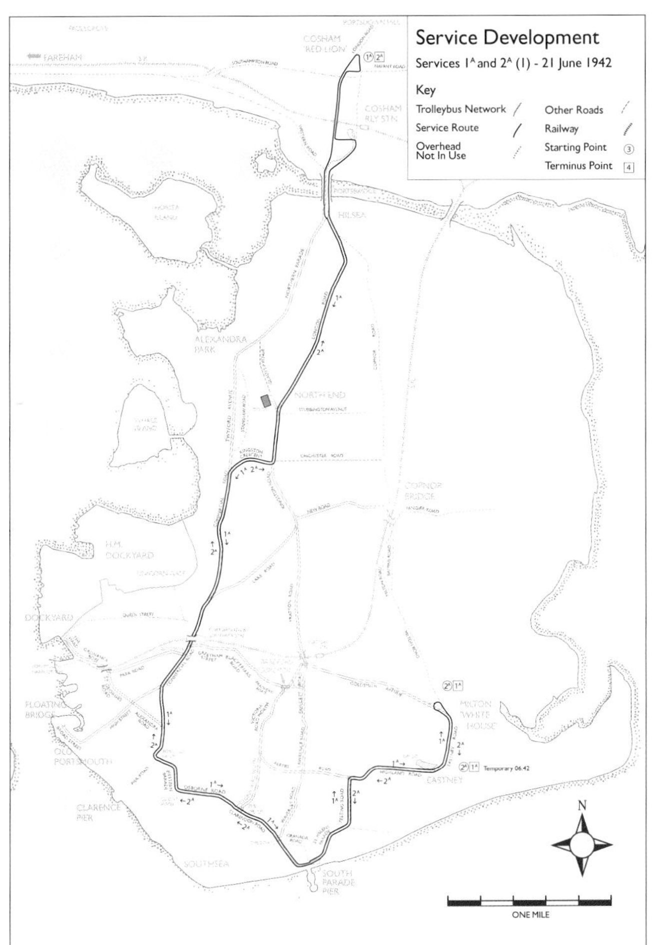
Service Development
Services 1A and 2A (1) - 21 June 1942
Key
Trolleybus Network
Service Route
Overhead Not In Use
Other Roads
Railway
Starting Point
Terminus Point
FAREHAM
COSHAM RED LION
COSHAM RLY STN
HILSEA
ALEXANDRA PARK
NORTH END
COPNOR BRIDGE
H.M. DOCKYARD
DOCKYARD
FLOATING BRIDGE
OLD PORTSMOUTH
CLARENCE PIER
SOUTHSEA
SOUTH PARADE PIER
MILTON WHITE HOUSE
EASTNEY
Temporary 06.42
N
ONE MILE

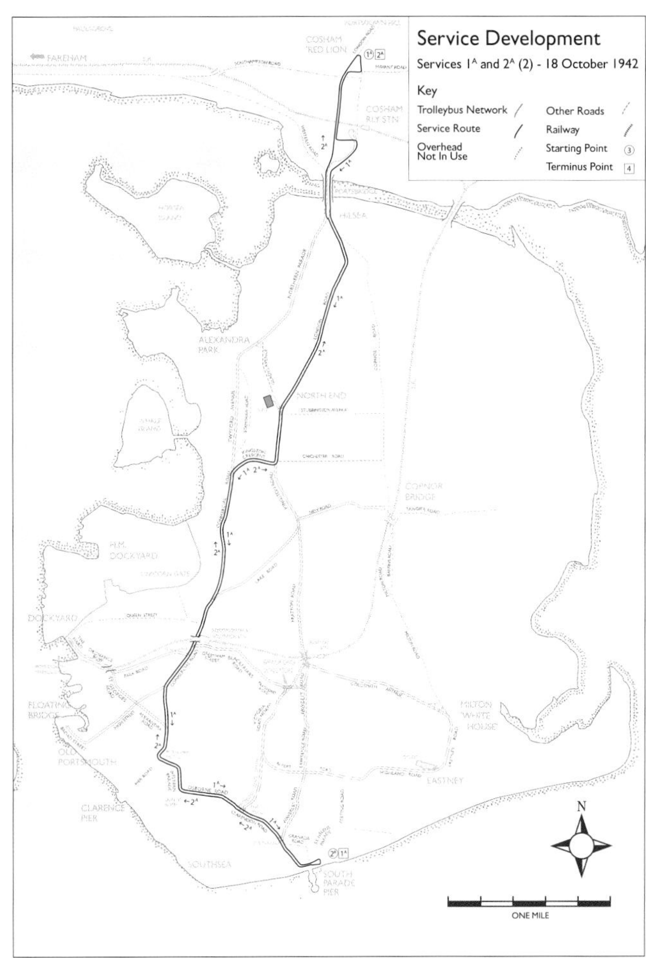
Service Development
Services 1A and 2A (2) - 18 October 1942
Key
Trolleybus Network
Service Route
Overhead Not In Use
Other Roads
Railway
Starting Point
Terminus Point
FAREHAM
COSHAM RED LION
COSHAM RLY STN
HILSEA
ALEXANDRA PARK
NORTH END
COPNOR BRIDGE
H.M. DOCKYARD
DOCKYARD
FLOATING BRIDGE
OLD PORTSMOUTH
CLARENCE PIER
SOUTHSEA
SOUTH PARADE PIER
MILTON WHITE HOUSE
EASTNEY
N
ONE MILE

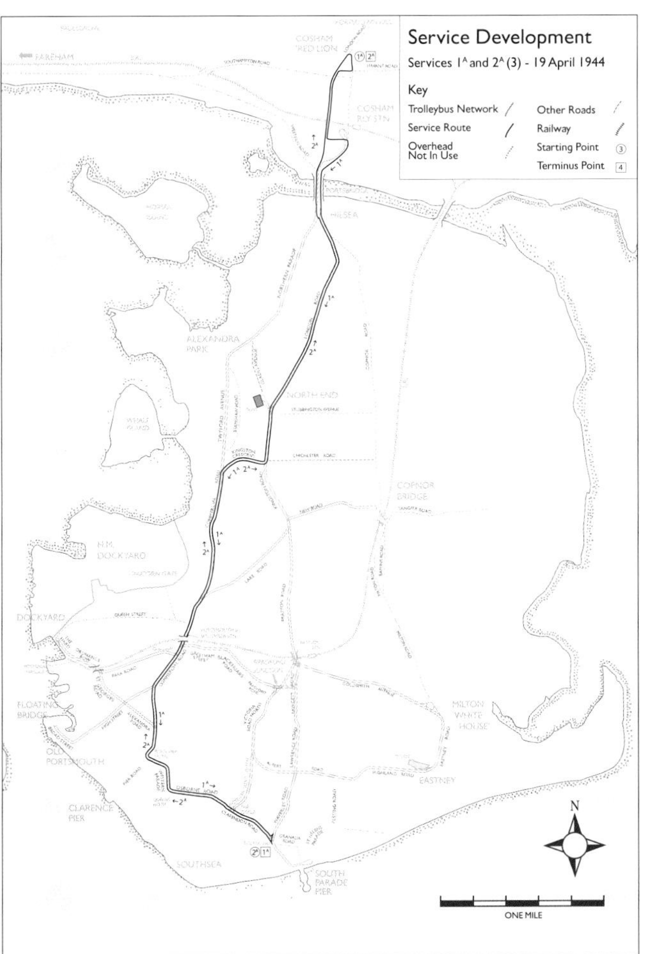
Service Development
Services 1A and 2A (3) - 19 April 1944
Key
Trolleybus Network
Service Route
Overhead Not In Use
Other Roads
Railway
Starting Point
Terminus Point
FAREHAM
COSHAM RED LION
COSHAM RLY STN
HILSEA
ALEXANDRA PARK
NORTH END
COPNOR BRIDGE
H.M. DOCKYARD
DOCKYARD
FLOATING BRIDGE
OLD PORTSMOUTH
CLARENCE PIER
SOUTHSEA
SOUTH PARADE PIER
MILTON WHITE HOUSE
EASTNEY
N
ONE MILE

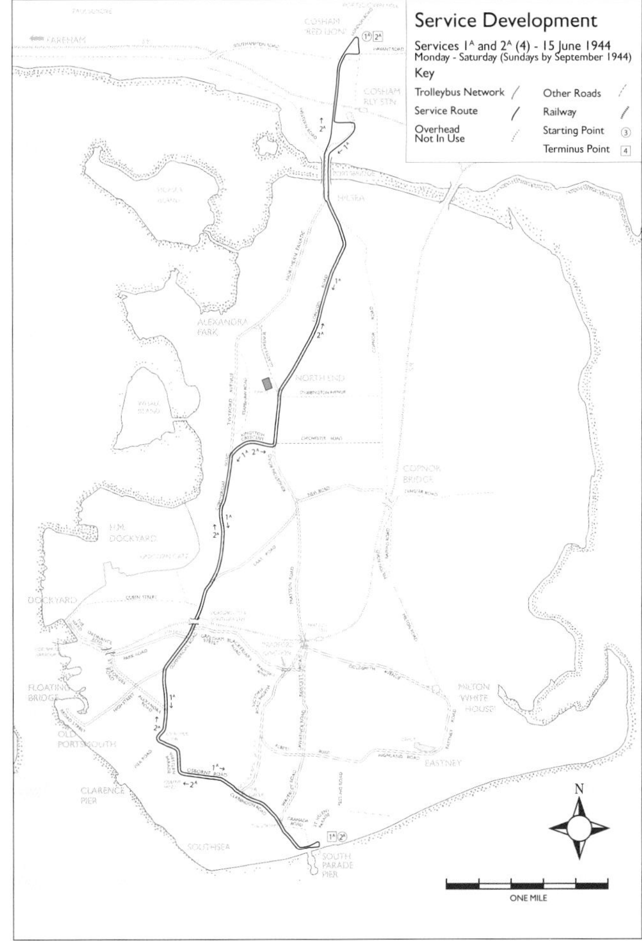
Service Development
Services 1A and 2A (4) - 15 June 1944
Monday - Saturday (Sundays by September 1944)
Key
Trolleybus Network
Service Route
Overhead Not In Use
Other Roads
Railway
Starting Point
Terminus Point
FAREHAM
COSHAM RED LION
COSHAM RLY STN
HILSEA
ALEXANDRA PARK
NORTH END
COPNOR BRIDGE
H.M. DOCKYARD
DOCKYARD
FLOATING BRIDGE
OLD PORTSMOUTH
CLARENCE PIER
SOUTHSEA
SOUTH PARADE PIER
MILTON WHITE HOUSE
EASTNEY
N
ONE MILE

Service 2 (i)

01.10.36 Trolleybus service commenced Clarence Pier – Guildhall – North End *Junction* – Hilsea – Cosham *Red Lion* via Pier Road, Bellevue Terrace, Jubilee Terrace, Kings Terrace, Landport Terrace, Hampshire Terrace, Commercial Road, Guildhall Square, Commercial Road, Kingston Crescent, London Road, Northern Road and London Road. *Unidirectional northbound service worked in conjunction with service 1.*

05.07.40 Curtailed to originate at Royal Pier Hotel (closure of seafront).

21.07.40 Extended to originate at North End via Kingston Road, Fratton Road, Victoria Road North, Victoria Road South, Clarendon Road, Osborne Road, Western Parade and Southsea Terrace to Royal Pier Hotel and thence by the previous route to Cosham *Red Lion*.

07.07.41 Service extended to originate at Cosham *Red Lion* thus operating Cosham *Red Lion* – Hilsea – North End *Junction* – Fratton Bridge – Bradford Junction – Southsea *The Circle* – Royal Pier Hotel – Guildhall – North End *Junction* – Cosham *Red Lion* via Spur Road, Northern Road, London Road, Kingston Road, Fratton Road, Victoria Road North, Victoria Road South, Clarendon Road, Osborne Road, Western Parade, Southsea Terrace, Bellevue Terrace, Jubilee Terrace, Kings Terrace, Landport Terrace, Hampshire Terrace, Commercial Road, Guildhall Square, Commercial Road, Kingston Crescent, London Road, Northern Road and London Road. *Unidirectional circular service (clockwise) worked in conjunction with service 1.*

07.07.41 Early morning journeys curtailed to originate at Dockyard and thence Guildhall – Alexandra Park – Cosham *Red Lion* via The Hard, Ordnance Row, Park Road, Guildhall Square, Commercial Road, Twyford Avenue, Northern Parade, Northern Road, and London Road. *Unidirectional northbound service worked in conjunction with service 1.*

03.05.42 Southbound journeys (only) diverted at Northern Road along private road to Cosham Railway Station thence via Portsmouth Road to rejoin the previous route at Portsbridge.

By 21.06.42 Early morning curtailment Dockyard – Guildhall – Alexandra Park – Cosham *Red Lion* ceased.

19.07.42 Sunday service divided into two separate portions:
(i) Cosham *Red Lion* – Cosham Railway Station – Hilsea – North End *Junction* – Fratton Bridge – Bradford Junction – Southsea *The Circle* reversing at the junction with Clarendon Road.
(ii) Southsea *South Parade Pier* – Southsea *The Circle* – Royal Pier Hotel – Guildhall – North End *Junction* – Hilsea – Cosham *Red Lion*.

By 03.09.44 Sunday service withdrawn.

29.07.45 Service re-routed and divided into two separate portions operating daily:
(i) Cosham *Red Lion* – Cosham Railway Station – Hilsea – North End *Junction* – Fratton Bridge – Bradford Junction – Southsea *The Circle* – Royal Pier Hotel – Clarence Pier via Spur Road, Northern Road, private road, Portsmouth Road, London Road, Kingston Road, Fratton Road, Victoria Road North, Victoria Road South, Clarendon Road, Osborne Road, Western Parade, Southsea Terrace and Pier Road
(ii) Clarence Pier – Royal Pier Hotel – Guildhall – North End *Junction* – Hilsea – Cosham *Red Lion* via Pier Road, Bellevue Terrace, Jubilee Terrace, Kings Terrace, Landport Terrace, Hampshire Terrace, Commercial Road, Guildhall Square, Commercial Road, Kingston Crescent, Kingston Road, London Road, Northern Road and London Road.
Unidirectional circular service (clockwise) worked in conjunction with service 1.

Sunday service reintroduced on or by 29.07.45.

30.06.46 Both portions of the circular service cease and (1) above replaced by service 10.

Service 2 (ii)

01.07.46 Revised trolleybus service 2 commenced Clarence Pier – Royal Pier Hotel – Guildhall – North End *Junction* – Hilsea – Cosham *Red Lion* via Pier Road, Bellevue Terrace, Jubilee Terrace, Kings Terrace, Landport Terrace, Hampshire Terrace, Commercial Road, Guildhall Square, Commercial Road, Kingston Crescent, Kingston Road, London Road, Northern Road and London Road. *Unidirectional northbound service worked in conjunction with service 1.*

29.09.46 Diverted to originate at Dockyard *Main Gate* via The Hard, Ordnance Row and Park Road to Guildhall Square (remainder of route unchanged).

18.05.47 Trolleybus service Dockyard – Guildhall – North End *Junction* – Cosham *Red Lion* withdrawn and replaced by motorbus service N.

Service 2 (iii)

26.09.48 Revised trolleybus service (formerly service 2A (ii)) commenced Southsea *South Parade Pier* – Southsea *The Circle* – Royal Pier Hotel – Guildhall – North End *Junction* – Hilsea – Cosham *Red Lion* via Clarendon Road, Osborne Road, Western Parade, Southsea Terrace, Bellevue Terrace, Jubilee Terrace, Kings Terrace, Landport Terrace, Hampshire Terrace, Commercial Road, Guildhall Square, Commercial Road, Kingston Crescent, London Road, Northern Road and London Road. *Unidirectional northbound service worked in conjunction with service 1.*

17.06.50 Last day of operation by trolleybus. Replaced by motorbus service S.

Service 2A

21.06.42 Trolleybus service commenced Eastney – Southsea *South Parade Pier* – Southsea *The Circle* – Royal Pier Hotel – Guildhall – North End *Junction* – Hilsea – Cosham *Red Lion* via Highland Road, Festing Road, St Helens Parade, Clarendon Road, Osborne Road, Western Parade, Southsea Terrace, Bellevue Terrace, Jubilee Terrace, Kings Terrace, Landport Terrace, Hampshire Terrace, Commercial Road, Guildhall Square, Commercial Road, Kingston Crescent, London Road, Northern Road and London Road.
Unidirectional northbound service worked in conjunction with service 1A.

06. or 07.42 Service extended to originate at Milton *White House* via Eastney Road presumably to avoid difficult battery turn into Eastney Depot.

18.10.42 Curtailed to originate at Southsea *South Parade Pier*.

19.04.44 Curtailed to originate at Southsea *The Strand*, junction with Waverley Road.

15.06.44 Monday – Saturday service extended to Southsea *South Parade Pier.*

By 03.09.44 Sunday service extended to Southsea *South Parade Pier.*

25.09.48 Service Southsea *South Parade Pier* – Southsea *The Circle* – Royal Pier Hotel – Guildhall – North End *Junction* – Hilsea – Cosham *Red Lion* renumbered 2 (iii).

Service 3

04.08.34 Trolleybus service commenced Cosham Railway Station – Hilsea – North End *Junction* – Fratton Bridge– Southsea *South Parade Pier* via Portsmouth Road, London Road, Kingston Road, Fratton Road, Fawcett Road, Lawrence Road, Waverley Road, Clarendon Road and South Parade.
Unidirectional southbound service worked in conjunction with service 4.

03.11.35 Circular route working with service 3A commenced.

Services 3 and 3A provided a unidirectional circular service (clockwise) Cosham Railway Station – Hilsea – North End *Junction* – Fratton Bridge – Southsea *South Parade Pier* – Bradford Junction – Guildhall – Alexandra Park – Hilsea – Cosham Railway Station via Portsmouth Road, Northern Road, London Road, Kingston Road, Fratton Road, Fawcett Road, Lawrence Road, Waverley Road, Clarendon Road, South Parade, St Helen's Parade, Festing Road, Albert Road, Victoria Road North, Bradford Road, Blackfriars Road, Greetham Street, Guildhall Square, Commercial Road, Twyford Avenue, Northern Parade, London Road and Portsmouth Road.
Unidirectional circular service (clockwise) worked in conjunction with service 3A. The anti-clockwise service was provided by services 4 and 4A.

05.07.40 Curtailed to terminate at Southsea *The Strand* (closure of seafront) reversing at the junction with Clarendon Road.
Unidirectional southbound service worked in conjunction with service 4A.
Unidirectional circular service originating and terminating at Cosham Railway Station, and inter-working with service 3A both cease.

21.07.40 Extended from Southsea *The Strand* to Dockyard *Main Gate* via Clarendon Road, Osborne Road, Western Parade, Southsea Terrace, Bellevue Terrace, Jubilee Terrace, Kings Terrace, Alexandra Road, St George's Road, Gun Wharf Road, Ordnance Row and the Hard.
Unidirectional southbound service worked in conjunction with service 4A.

13.05.45 Daily service reverts to operate Cosham Railway Station – Hilsea – North End *Junction* – Fratton Bridge – Southsea *South Parade Pier* via Portsmouth Road, London Road, Kingston Road, Fratton Road, Fawcett Road, Lawrence Road, Waverley Road, Clarendon Road and South Parade.
Unidirectional southbound service worked in conjunction with service 4A (service 4 from 26.09.48).

17.09.60 Last day of operation by trolleybus. Replaced by motorbus service 3.

Service 3A

03.11.35 Trolleybus service commenced Southsea *South Parade Pier* – Bradford Junction – Guildhall – Alexandra Park – Hilsea – Cosham Railway Station via St Helen's Parade, Festing Road, Albert Road, Victoria Road North, Bradford Road, Blackfriars Road, Greetham Street, Guildhall Square, Commercial Road, Twyford Avenue, Northern Parade, London Road and Portsmouth Road.

Circular route working with service 3 commenced.

Services 3 and 3A provided a unidirectional circular service (clockwise) Cosham Railway Station – Hilsea – North End *Junction* – Fratton Bridge – Southsea *South Parade Pier* – Bradford Junction – Guildhall – Alexandra Park – Hilsea – Cosham Railway Station (the anti-clockwise service was provided by services 4 and 4A).

05.07.40 Curtailed to originate at Festing Road south end (closure of seafront), trolleybuses are assumed to have turned at the junction with St Helens Parade/Eastern Parade by use of their traction batteries.
Unidirectional northbound service worked in conjunction with service 4.

Inter-working with service 3 from Cosham Railway Station ceased.

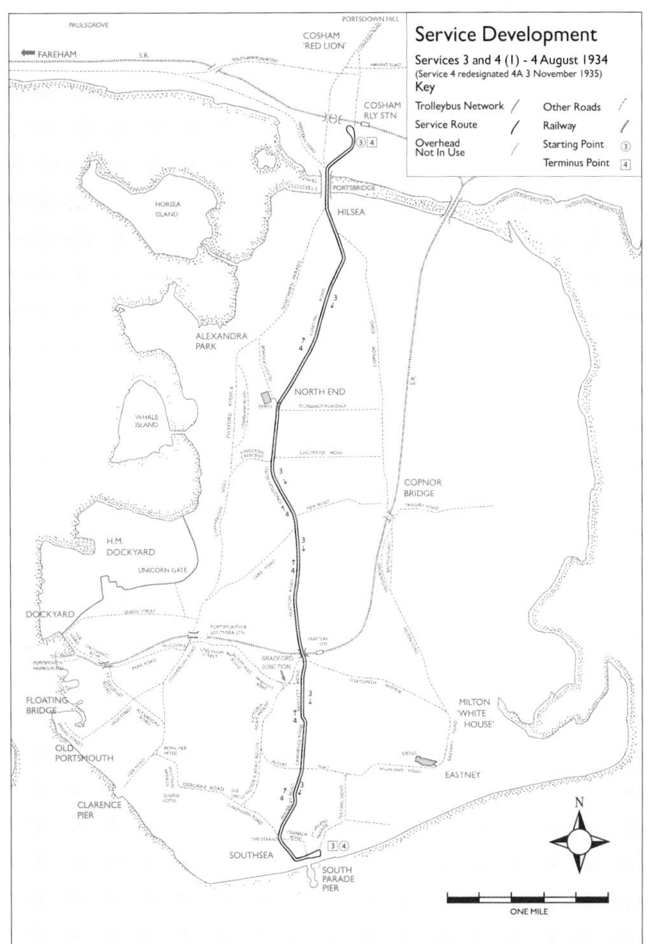
Service Development
Services 3 and 4 (1) - 4 August 1934
(Service 4 redesignated 4A 3 November 1935)
Key
Trolleybus Network
Service Route
Overhead Not In Use
Other Roads
Railway
Starting Point
Terminus Point
PORTSDOWN HILL
PAULSGROVE
FAREHAM
S.R.
COSHAM 'RED LION'
COSHAM RLY STN
PORTSBRIDGE
HILSEA
HORSEA ISLAND
ALEXANDRA PARK
NORTH END
WHALE ISLAND
COPNOR BRIDGE
H.M. DOCKYARD
UNICORN GATE
DOCKYARD
FLOATING BRIDGE
OLD PORTSMOUTH
CLARENCE PIER
MILTON 'WHITE HOUSE'
EASTNEY
SOUTHSEA
SOUTH PARADE PIER
N
ONE MILE

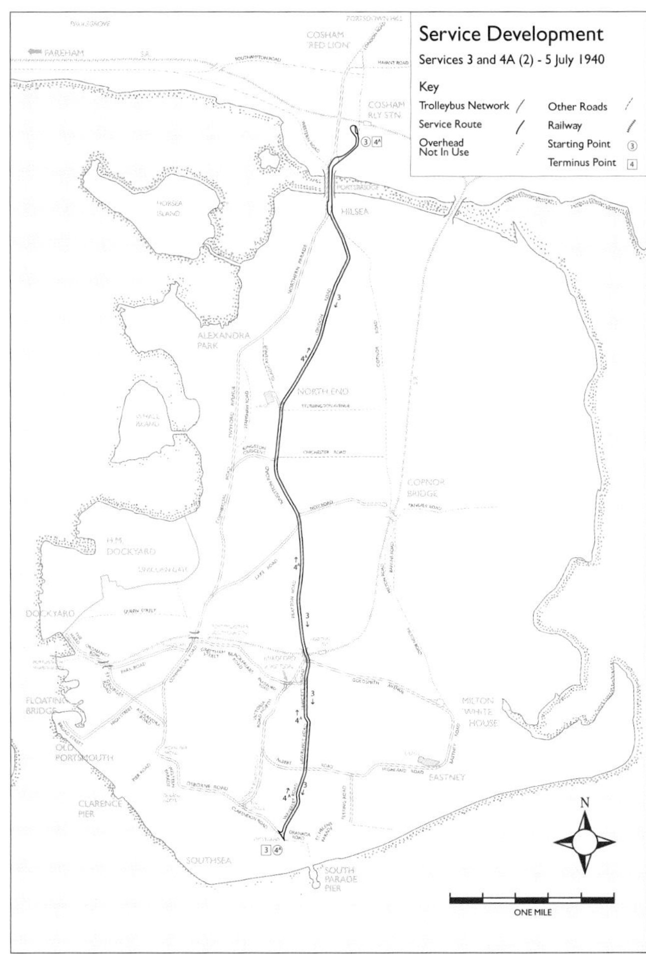
Service Development
Services 3 and 4A (2) - 5 July 1940
Key
Trolleybus Network
Service Route
Overhead Not In Use
Other Roads
Railway
Starting Point
Terminus Point
N
ONE MILE

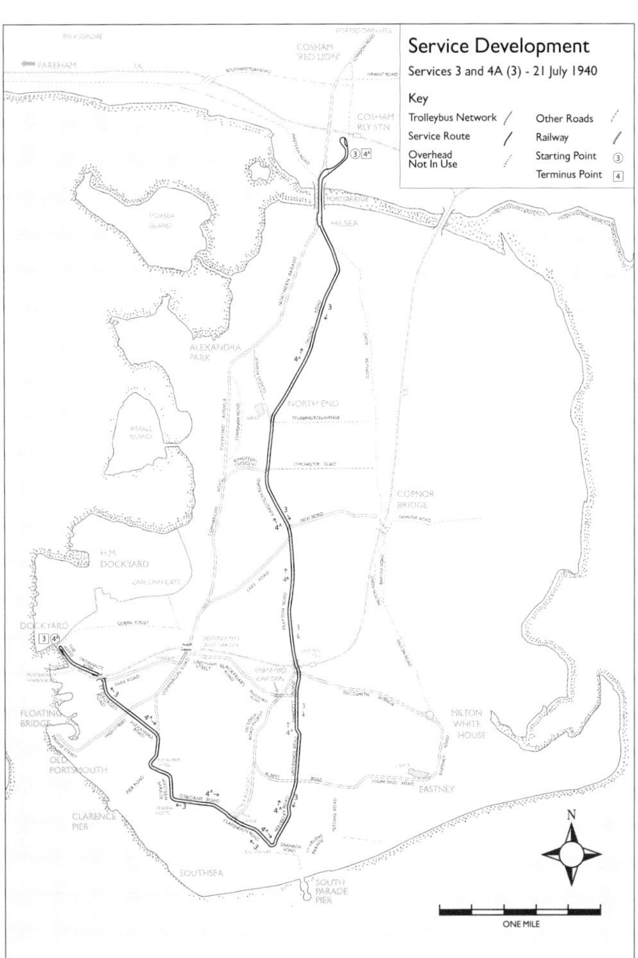
Service Development
Services 3 and 4A (3) - 21 July 1940
Key
Trolleybus Network
Service Route
Overhead Not In Use
Other Roads
Railway
Starting Point
Terminus Point
N
ONE MILE

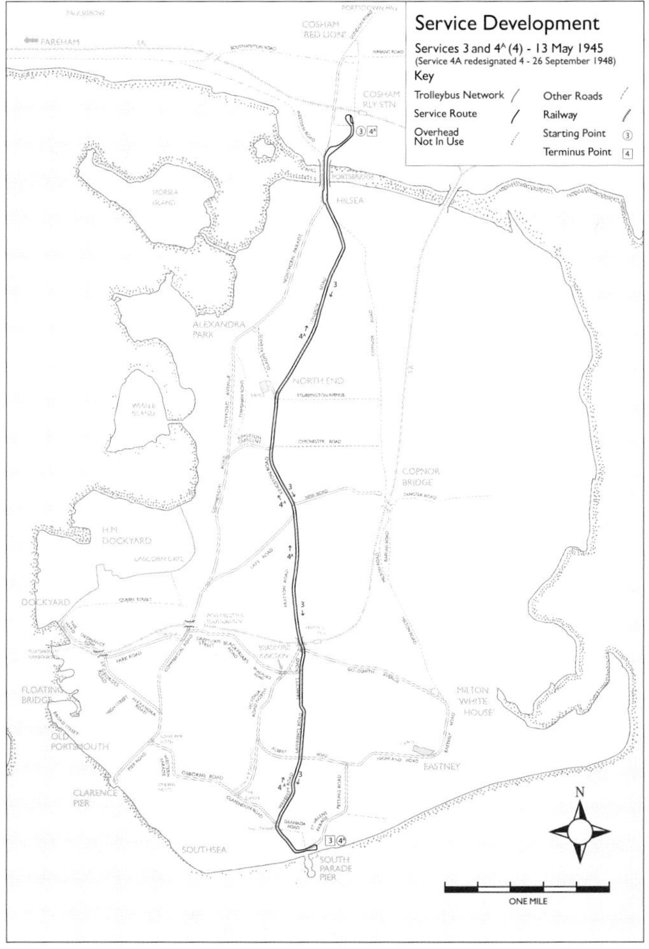
Service Development
Services 3 and 4^A (4) - 13 May 1945
(Service 4A redesignated 4 - 26 September 1948)
Key
Trolleybus Network
Service Route
Overhead Not In Use
Other Roads
Railway
Starting Point
Terminus Point
N
ONE MILE

21.07.40 Extended to originate at The Guildhall (instead of Festing Road south end) via Park Road, Guildhall Square, Greetham Street, Blackfriars Road, Bradford Road, Victoria Road North, Goldsmith Avenue, Eastney Road and Highland Road, rejoining the previous route at the junction with Festing Road.
Unidirectional northbound service involving the clockwise circumnavigation of the Bradford Junction – Fratton Bridge – Milton – Eastney – Bradford Junction circle and operation between Guildhall Square and Bradford Junction in both directions.

18.10.42 Sunday service curtailed to operate Guildhall – Alexandra Park – Hilsea – Cosham Railway Station only via Commercial Road, Twyford Avenue, Northern Parade, London Road and Portsmouth Road.

01.07.46 Daily service extended after midday to originate at Alexandra Park (first departure 12.21pm) via Northern Parade, Twyford Avenue and Commercial Road (earlier journeys continue to originate at Guildhall).

Unidirectional northbound service involving the all day clockwise circumnavigation of the Bradford Junction – Fratton Bridge – Milton – Eastney – Bradford Junction circle and operation between Guildhall Square and Bradford Junction in both directions.

25.09.48 Service Alexandra Park – Guildhall – Bradford Junction – Fratton Bridge – Milton *White House* – Eastney – Festing Hotel – Bradford Junction – Guildhall – Alexandra Park – Cosham Railway Station re-numbered trolleybus service 20.

Service 4 (i)

04.08.34 Trolleybus service commenced Southsea *South Parade Pier* – Fratton Bridge – North End *Junction* – Hilsea – Cosham Railway Station via South Parade, Clarendon Road, Waverley Road, Lawrence Road, Fawcett Road, Fratton Road, Kingston Road, London Road and Portsmouth Road.
Unidirectional northbound service worked in conjunction with service 3.

02.11.35 Service 4 redesignated 4A.

Service 4 (ii)

03.11.35 Trolleybus service commenced Cosham Railway Station – Hilsea – Alexandra Park – Guildhall – Bradford Junction – Festing Hotel – Southsea *South Parade Pier* via Portsmouth Road, Northern Parade, Twyford Avenue, Commercial Road, Guildhall Square, Greetham Street, Blackfriars Road, Bradford Road, Victoria Road North, Albert Road, Festing Road and St. Helen's Parade.
Unidirectional circular service (anti-clockwise) worked in conjunction with service 4A.

Services 4 and 4A provided a unidirectional circular service (anti-clockwise) Cosham Railway Station – Hilsea – Alexandra Park – Guildhall – Bradford Junction – Festing Hotel – Southsea *South Parade Pier* – Fratton Bridge – North End *Junction* – Hilsea – Cosham Railway Station via Portsmouth Road, London Road, Northern Road, Northern Parade, Twyford Avenue, Commercial Road, Guildhall Square, Greetham Street, Blackfriars Road, Bradford Road, Victoria Road North, Albert Road, Festing Road, St. Helen's Parade, South Parade, Clarendon Road, Waverley Road, Lawrence Road, Fawcett Road, Fratton Road, Kingston Road, London Road and Portsmouth Road.

The clockwise service was provided by services 3 and 3A.

05.07.40 Curtailed to terminate at Festing Road south end (closure of seafront); trolleybuses are assumed to have turned at the junction with St. Helens Parade/Eastern Parade by use of their traction batteries.

Unidirectional southbound service worked in conjunction with service 3A.
Unidirectional circular service originating and terminating at Cosham Railway Station, and inter-working with service 4A to Cosham Railway Station both cease.

21.07.40 Extended to terminate at The Guildhall (instead of Festing Road south end) via Highland Road, Eastney Road, Goldsmith Avenue, Victoria Road North, Bradford Road, Blackfriars Road, Greetham Street, Guildhall Square and Park Road.
Unidirectional southbound service involving the anticlockwise circumnavigation of the Bradford Junction – Eastney – Milton – Fratton Bridge – Bradford Junction circle and operation between Guildhall Square and Bradford Junction in both directions.

18.10.42 Sunday service curtailed to operate Cosham Railway Station – Hilsea – Alexandra Park – Guildhall only via Portsmouth Road, London Road, Northern Parade, Twyford Avenue and Commercial Road.

01.07.46 Daily service extended after midday from Guildhall to Alexandra Park via Commercial Road, Twyford Avenue and Northern Parade (earlier journeys continue to terminate at Guildhall).
Unidirectional southbound service involving the all day anticlockwise circumnavigation of the Bradford Junction – Eastney – Milton – Fratton Bridge – Bradford Junction circle and operation between Guildhall Square and Bradford Junction in both directions.

25.09.48 Service Cosham Railway Station – Hilsea – Alexandra Park – Guildhall – Bradford Junction – Festing Hotel – Eastney – Milton *White House* – Fratton Bridge – Bradford Junction – Guildhall – Alexandra Park re-numbered trolleybus service 19.

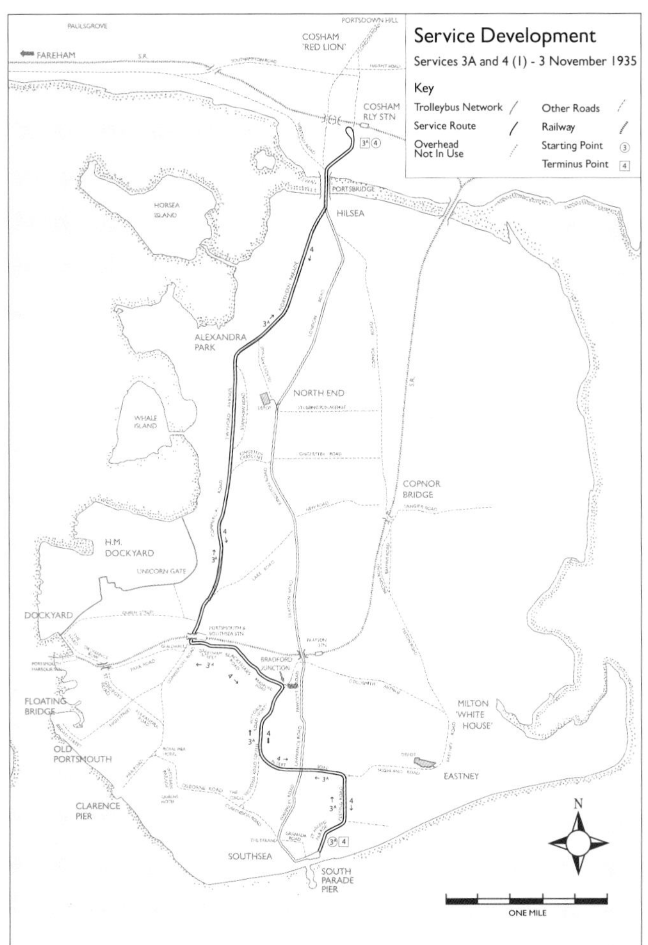
Service Development
Services 3A and 4 (1) - 3 November 1935
Key
Trolleybus Network
Other Roads
Service Route
Railway
Overhead Not In Use
Starting Point
Terminus Point
PORTSDOWN HILL
PAULSGROVE
FAREHAM
COSHAM 'RED LION'
COSHAM RLY STN
HORSEA ISLAND
HILSEA
ALEXANDRA PARK
NORTH END
WHALE ISLAND
COPNOR BRIDGE
H.M. DOCKYARD
UNICORN GATE
DOCKYARD
BRADFORD JUNCTION
FLOATING BRIDGE
MILTON 'WHITE HOUSE'
OLD PORTSMOUTH
EASTNEY
CLARENCE PIER
SOUTHSEA
SOUTH PARADE PIER
N
ONE MILE

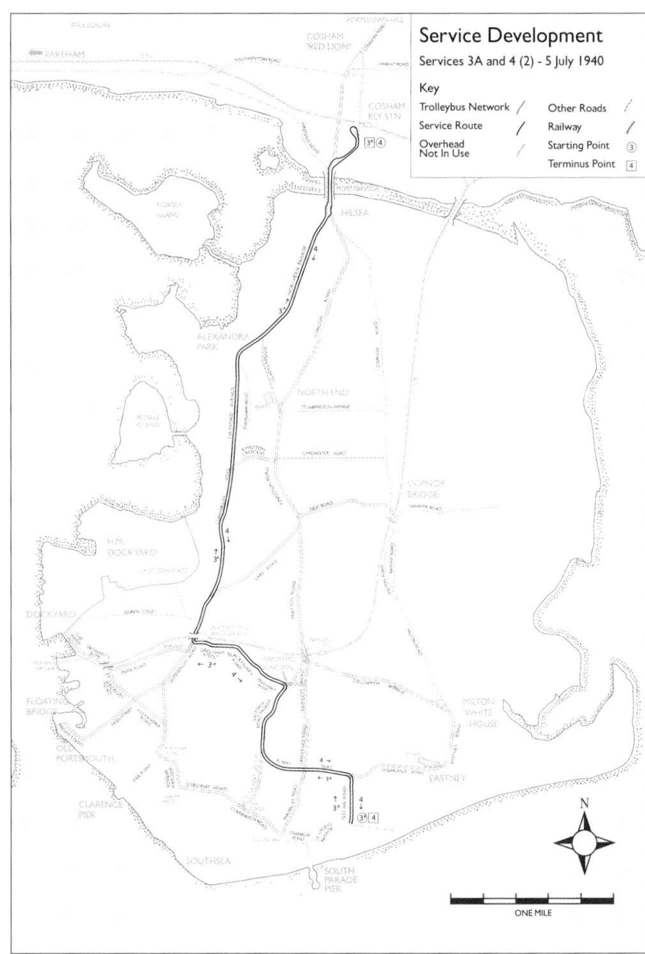
Service Development
Services 3A and 4 (2) - 5 July 1940
Key
Trolleybus Network
Other Roads
Service Route
Railway
Overhead Not In Use
Starting Point
Terminus Point
N
ONE MILE

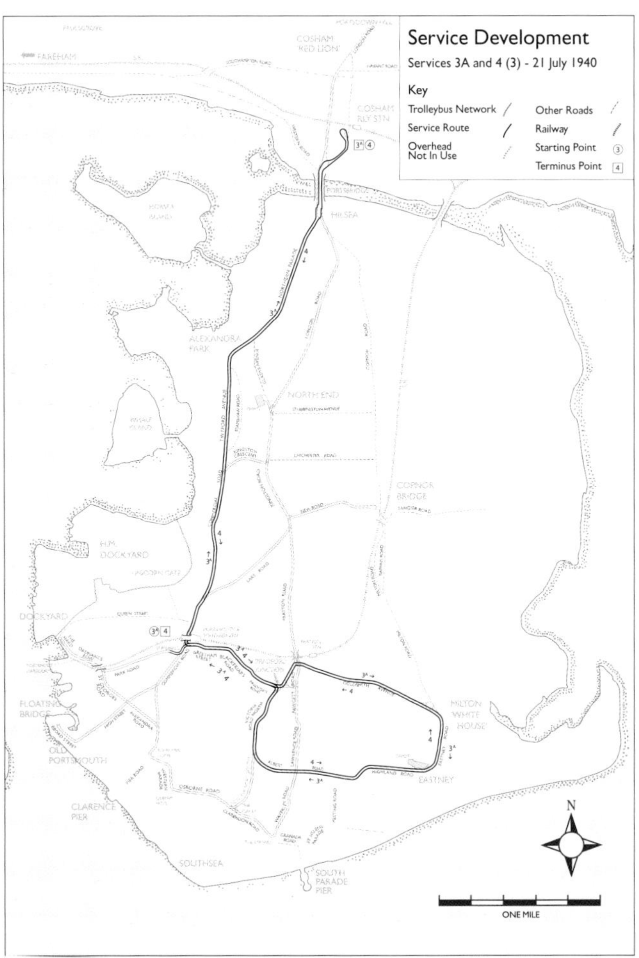
Service Development
Services 3A and 4 (3) - 21 July 1940
Key
Trolleybus Network
Other Roads
Service Route
Railway
Overhead Not In Use
Starting Point
Terminus Point
N
ONE MILE

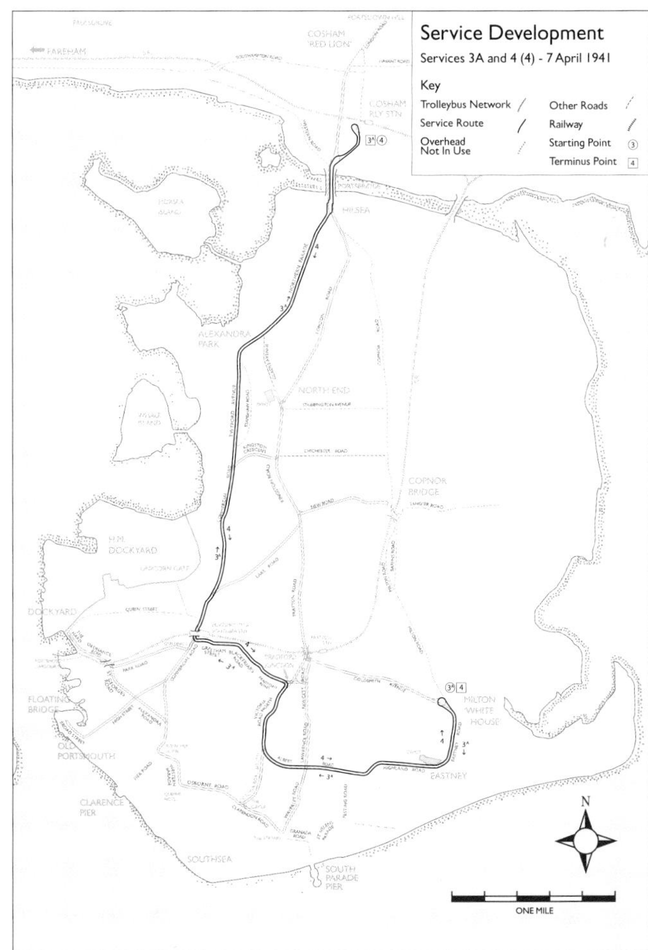
Service Development
Services 3A and 4 (4) - 7 April 1941
Key
Trolleybus Network
Other Roads
Service Route
Railway
Overhead Not In Use
Starting Point
Terminus Point
N
ONE MILE

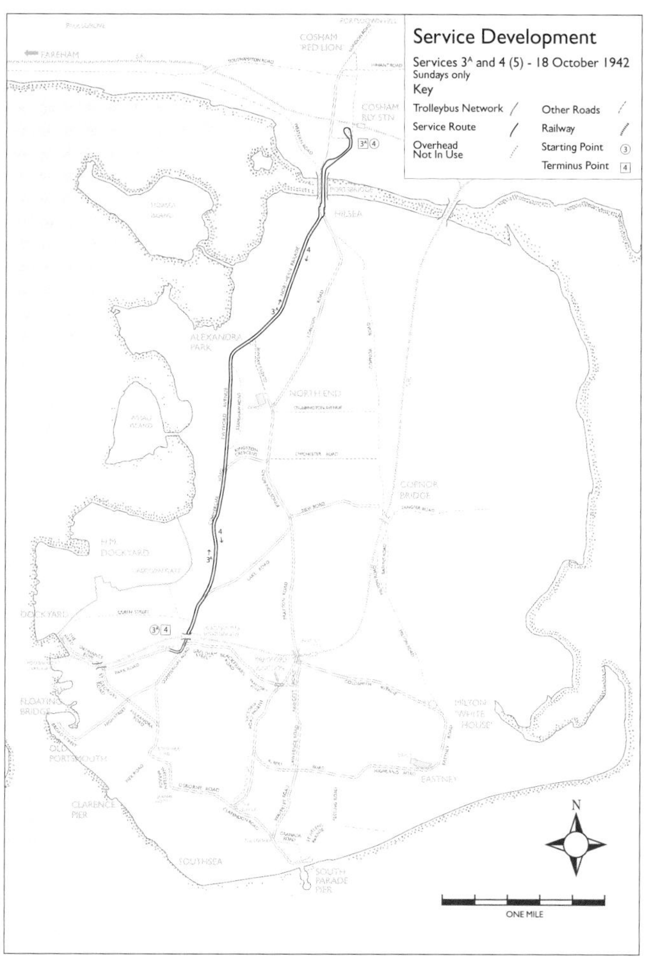

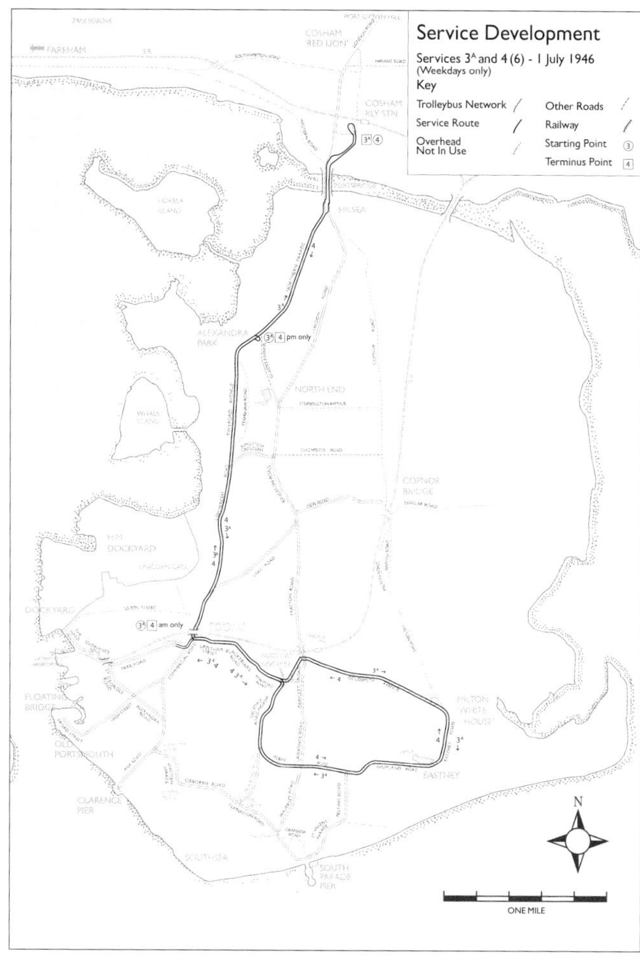

Service 4 (iii)

26.09.48 Redesignated trolleybus service (formerly service 4A) commenced Southsea *South Parade Pier* – Fratton Bridge – North End *Junction* – Hilsea – Cosham Railway Station via South Parade, Clarendon Road, Waverley Road, Lawrence Road, Fawcett Road, Fratton Road, Kingston Road, London Road, and Portsmouth Road.
Unidirectional northbound service worked in conjunction with service 3.

17.09.60 Last day of operation by trolleybus. Replaced by motorbus service 4.

Service 4A

03.11.35 Revised trolleybus service (formerly service 4) commenced Southsea *South Parade Pier* – Fratton Bridge – North End *Junction* – Hilsea – Cosham Railway Station via South Parade, Clarendon Road, Waverley Road, Lawrence Road, Fawcett Road, Fratton Road, Kingston Road, London Road and Portsmouth Road.

Circular route working with service 4 commenced.

Services 4 and 4A provided a unidirectional circular service (anti-clockwise) Cosham Railway Station – Hilsea – Alexandra Park – Guildhall – Bradford Junction – Festing Hotel – Southsea *South Parade Pier* – Fratton Bridge – North End *Junction* – Hilsea – Cosham Railway Station (the clockwise service was provided by services 3 and 3A).

05.07.40 Curtailed to originate at Southsea *The Strand* (closure of seafront); trolleybuses are assumed to have turned at the junction with Clarendon Road.
Unidirectional circular service and inter-working with service 4 from Cosham Railway Station both cease.

21.07.40 Extended to originate at Dockyard *Main Gate* (instead of Southsea *The Strand*) via the Hard, Ordnance Row, Gun Wharf Road, St. George's Road, Alexandra Road, Kings Terrace, Jubilee Terrace, Bellevue Terrace, Southsea Terrace, Western Parade, Osborne Road, Clarendon Road and thence via previous route to Cosham Railway Station.

09.44 Sunday service reverts to originate at Southsea *The Strand* but extended at its northern end to Cosham *Red Lion* via Northern Road, London Road and Spur Road.

13.05.45 Daily service reverts to operate Southsea *South Parade Pier* – Fratton Bridge – North End *Junction* – Hilsea – Cosham Railway Station via South Parade, Clarendon Road, Waverley Road, Lawrence Road, Fawcett Road, Fratton Road, Kingston Road, London Road and Portsmouth Road.
Unidirectional northbound service worked in conjunction with service 3.

25.09.48 Service Southsea *South Parade Pier* – Fratton Bridge – North End *Junction* – Hilsea – Cosham Railway Station renumbered trolleybus service 4 (iii).

Service 5 (i)

10.11.36 Trolleybus service commenced Dockyard *Main Gate* – Royal Pier Hotel – Southsea *South Parade Pier* – Festing Hotel – Eastney – Milton *White House* – Fratton Bridge – Bradford Junction – Guildhall – Dockyard *Main Gate* via The Hard, Ordnance Row, St George's Road, Alexandra Road, Kings Terrace, Jubilee Terrace, Bellevue Terrace, Southsea Terrace, Western Parade, Osborne Road, Clarendon Road, South Parade, St Helens Parade, Festing Road, Highland Road, Eastney Road, Goldsmith Avenue, Victoria Road North, Bradford Road, Blackfriars Road, Greetham Street, Commercial Road, Guildhall Square, Park Road, Ordnance Row and The Hard. *Unidirectional circular service (anti-clockwise) worked in conjunction with service 6.*

By 05.37 Service curtailed to operate Dockyard *Main Gate* – Royal Pier Hotel – Southsea *South Parade Pier* – Festing Hotel – Eastney – Milton *White House* – Fratton Bridge – Bradford Junction – Guildhall only.

05.07.40 Service split into two parts (closure of seafront) operating:

Dockyard *Main Gate* – Royal Pier Hotel – Southsea *The Strand* via The Hard, Ordnance Row, St. George's Road, Alexandra Road, Kings Terrace, Jubilee Terrace, Bellevue Terrace, Southsea Terrace, Western Parade, Osborne Road and Clarendon Road.

Festing Road (south end) – Festing Hotel – Eastney – Milton *White House* – Fratton Bridge – Bradford Junction – Guildhall via Festing Road, Highland Road, Eastney Road, Goldsmith Avenue, Victoria Road North, Bradford Road, Blackfriars Road, Greetham Street, Commercial Road, Guildhall Square and Park Road.

21.07.40 Service(s) withdrawn.

Service 5 (ii)

13.05.45 Revised trolleybus service reintroduced as Dockyard *Main Gate* – Royal Pier Hotel – Southsea *South Parade Pier* – Festing Hotel – Eastney – Milton *White House* via The Hard, Ordnance Row, St George's Road, Alexandra Road, Kings Terrace, Jubilee Terrace, Bellevue Terrace, Southsea Terrace, Western Parade, Osborne Road, Clarendon Road, South Parade, St Helens Parade, Festing Road, Highland Road and Eastney Road.
Unidirectional service worked in conjunction with service 6.

25.05.52 Extended from Milton *White House* – Copnor Bridge – Cosham *Red Lion* via Milton Road, Copnor Road, London Road, Northern Road and London Road (remainder of route unchanged). *Unidirectional northbound service worked in conjunction with service 6.*

27.07.63 Last day of operation by trolleybus. Replaced by motorbus service 5.

Service 6 (i)

10.11.36 Trolleybus service commenced Dockyard *Main Gate* – Guildhall – Bradford Junction – Fratton Bridge – Milton *White House* – Eastney – Festing Hotel – Southsea *South Parade Pier* – Royal Pier Hotel – Dockyard *Main Gate* via The Hard, Ordnance Row, Park Road, Guildhall Square, Commercial Road, Greetham Street, Blackfriars Road, Bradford Road, Victoria Road North, Goldsmith Avenue, Eastney Road, Highland Road, Festing Road, St Helens Parade, South Parade, Clarendon Road, Osborne Road, Western Parade, Southsea Terrace, Bellevue Terrace, Jubilee Terrace, Kings Terrace, Alexandra Road, St George's Road, Ordnance Row and The Hard. *Unidirectional circular service (clockwise) worked in conjunction with service 5.*

By 05.37 Service curtailed to operate Guildhall – Bradford Junction – Fratton Bridge – Milton *White House* – Eastney – Festing Hotel – Southsea *South Parade Pier* – Royal Pier Hotel – Dockyard *Main Gate* only.

05.07.40 Service split into two parts (closure of seafront) operating:

Guildhall – Bradford Junction – Fratton Bridge – Milton *White House* – Eastney – Festing Hotel – Festing Road (south end) via Park Road, Guildhall Square, Greetham Street, Blackfriars Road, Bradford Road, Victoria Road North, Goldsmith Avenue, Eastney Road, Highland Road and Festing Road,

Dockyard *Main Gate* – Royal Pier Hotel – Southsea *The Strand* via The Hard, Ordnance Row, St George's Road, Alexandra Road, Kings Terrace, Jubilee Terrace, Bellevue Terrace, Southsea Terrace, Western Parade, Osborne Road and Clarendon Road.

21.7.40 Service(s) withdrawn.

Service 6 (ii)

13.05.45 Revised trolleybus service reintroduced as Milton *White House* – Eastney – Festing Hotel – Southsea *South Parade Pier* – Royal Pier Hotel – Dockyard *Main Gate* via Eastney Road, Highland Road, Festing Road, St Helens Parade, South Parade, Clarendon Road, Osborne Road, Western Parade, Southsea Terrace, Bellevue Terrace, Jubilee Terrace, Kings Terrace, Alexandra Road, St George's Road, Ordnance Row and The Hard. *Unidirectional service worked in conjunction with service 5.*

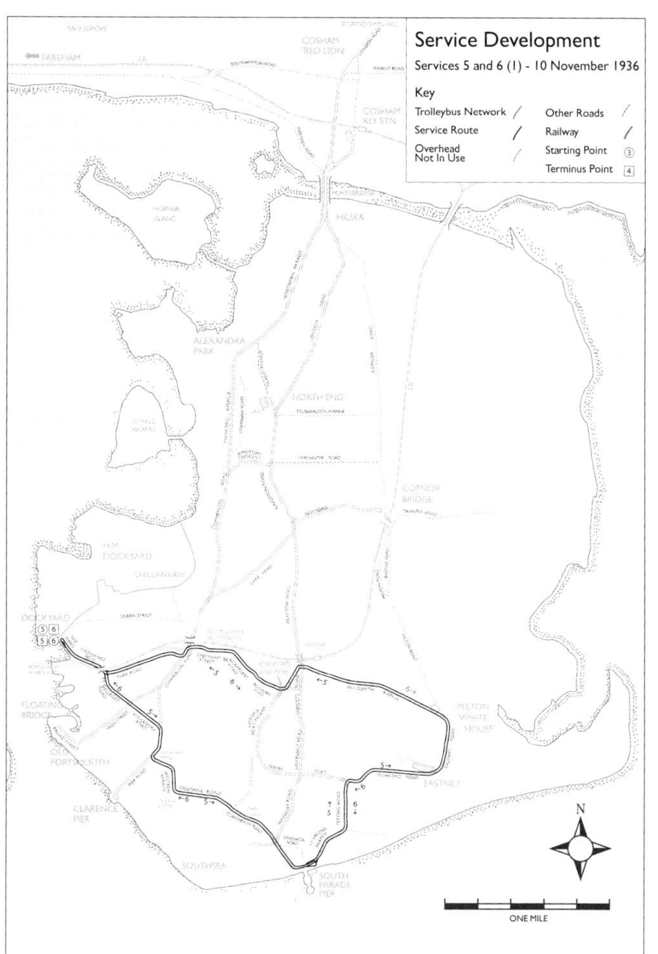
Service Development
Services 5 and 6 (1) - 10 November 1936
Key
Trolleybus Network
Service Route
Overhead Not In Use
Other Roads
Railway
Starting Point
Terminus Point
FAREHAM
COSHAM 'RED LION'
COSHAM RLY. STN
HILSEA
ALEXANDRA PARK
NORTH END
COPNOR BRIDGE
H.M. DOCKYARD
DOCKYARD
FLOATING BRIDGE
OLD PORTSMOUTH
CLARENCE PIER
SOUTHSEA
SOUTH PARADE PIER
EASTNEY
MILTON 'WHITE HOUSE'
N
ONE MILE

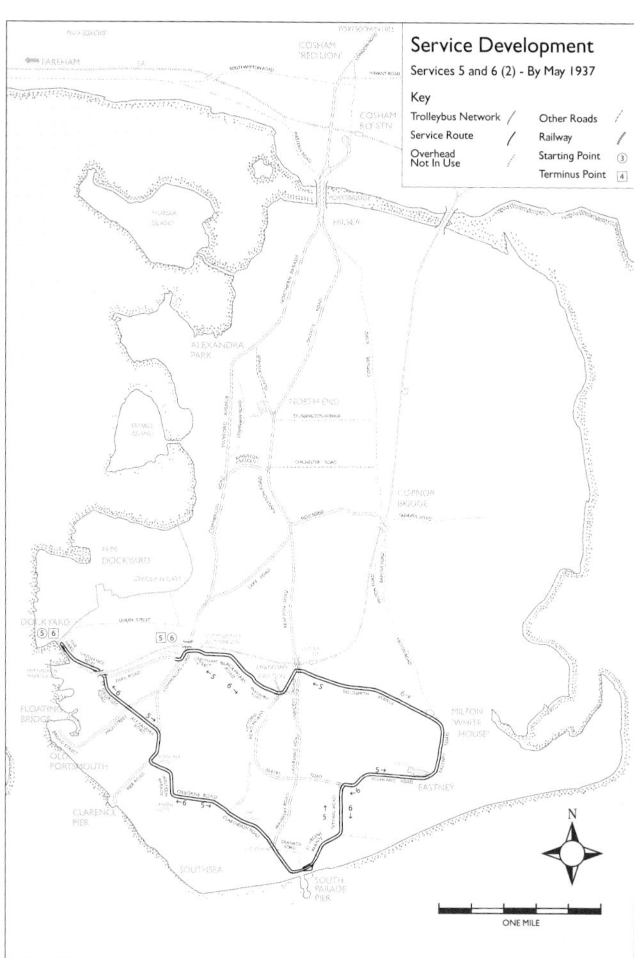
Service Development
Services 5 and 6 (2) - By May 1937
Key
Trolleybus Network
Service Route
Overhead Not In Use
Other Roads
Railway
Starting Point
Terminus Point
FAREHAM
COSHAM 'RED LION'
COSHAM RLY. STN
HILSEA
ALEXANDRA PARK
NORTH END
COPNOR BRIDGE
H.M. DOCKYARD
DOCKYARD
FLOATING BRIDGE
OLD PORTSMOUTH
CLARENCE PIER
SOUTHSEA
SOUTH PARADE PIER
EASTNEY
MILTON 'WHITE HOUSE'
N
ONE MILE

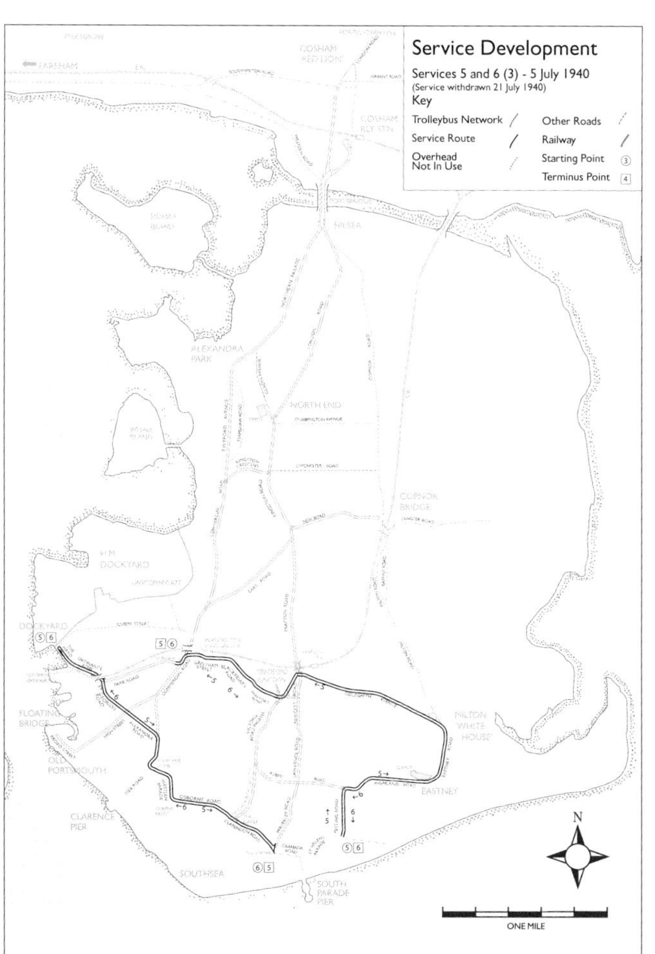
Service Development
Services 5 and 6 (3) - 5 July 1940
(Service withdrawn 21 July 1940)
Key
Trolleybus Network
Service Route
Overhead Not In Use
Other Roads
Railway
Starting Point
Terminus Point
FAREHAM
COSHAM 'RED LION'
COSHAM RLY. STN
HILSEA
ALEXANDRA PARK
NORTH END
COPNOR BRIDGE
H.M. DOCKYARD
DOCKYARD
FLOATING BRIDGE
OLD PORTSMOUTH
CLARENCE PIER
SOUTHSEA
SOUTH PARADE PIER
EASTNEY
MILTON 'WHITE HOUSE'
N
ONE MILE

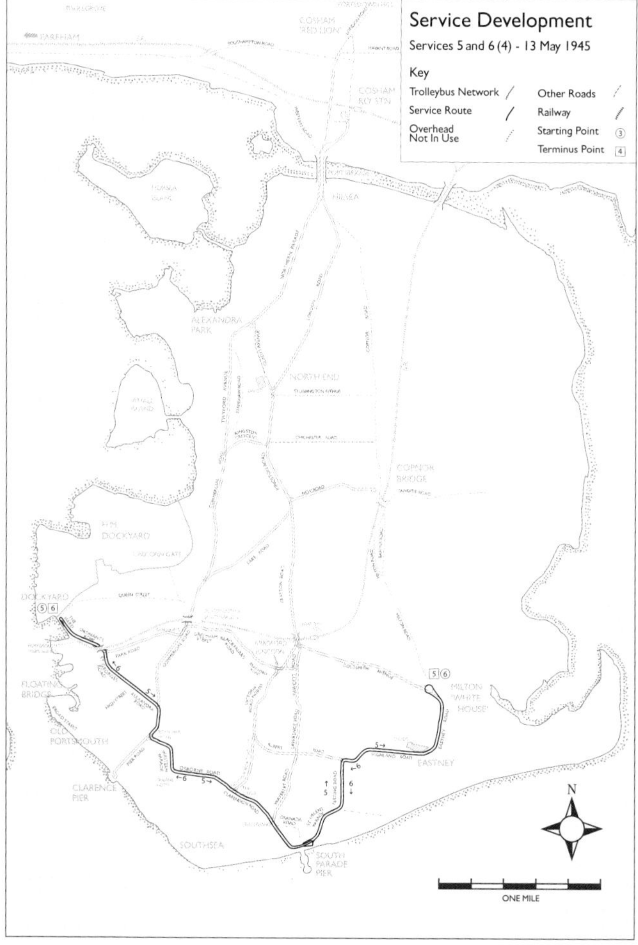
Service Development
Services 5 and 6 (4) - 13 May 1945
Key
Trolleybus Network
Service Route
Overhead Not In Use
Other Roads
Railway
Starting Point
Terminus Point
FAREHAM
COSHAM 'RED LION'
COSHAM RLY. STN
HILSEA
ALEXANDRA PARK
NORTH END
COPNOR BRIDGE
H.M. DOCKYARD
DOCKYARD
FLOATING BRIDGE
OLD PORTSMOUTH
CLARENCE PIER
SOUTHSEA
SOUTH PARADE PIER
EASTNEY
MILTON 'WHITE HOUSE'
N
ONE MILE

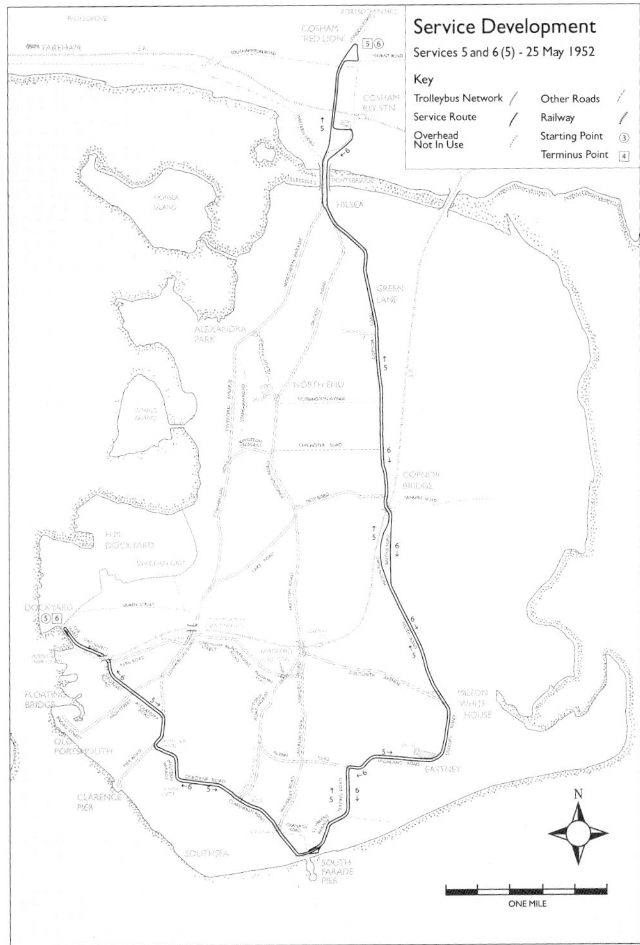

25.05.52 Extended to originate at Cosham *Red Lion* – Copnor Bridge – Milton *White House* via Spur Road, Northern Road, private road, Portsmouth Road, London Road, Copnor Road, Milton Road, Baffins Road and Milton Road, thence by previous route to Dockyard *Main Gate*.
Unidirectional southbound service worked in conjunction with service 5.

27.07.63 Last day of operation by trolleybus. Replaced by motorbus service 6.

Service 7

29.07.45 Unnumbered trolleybus service commenced Copnor Bridge – Fratton Bridge – Bradford Junction – Southsea *The Strand* – Royal Pier Hotel – Clarence Pier via New Road, Fratton Road, Fawcett Road, Lawrence Road, Waverley Road, Clarendon Road, Osborne Road, Western Parade, Southsea Terrace and Pier Road.
Unidirectional southbound service.

01.07.46 Unnumbered trolleybus service allocated service number 7.
Unidirectional southbound service worked in conjunction with service 8.

06.01.52 Extended to originate at Madeira Road (known as Green Lane terminus) – Copnor Bridge via Copnor Road thence by the prevailing route to Clarence Pier.

02.12.61 Last day of operation by trolleybus. Replaced by motorbus service 7.

Service 8

29.07.45 Unnumbered trolleybus service commenced Clarence Pier – Southsea *The Strand* – Bradford Junction – Fratton Bridge – Copnor Bridge via Pier Road, Southsea Terrace, Western Parade, Osborne Road, Clarendon Road, Waverley Road, Lawrence Road, Fawcett Road, Fratton Road and New Road.
Unidirectional northbound service.

01.07.46 Unnumbered trolleybus service allocated service number 8.
Unidirectional northbound service worked in conjunction with service 7.

06.01.52 Extended to operate from Copnor Bridge to Madeira Road (known as Green Lane terminus) via Copnor Road.

02.12.61 Last day of operation by trolleybus. Replaced by motorbus service 8.

Service 9

01.07.46 Redesignated trolleybus service (formerly service 1 (i)) commenced Cosham *Red Lion* – Cosham Railway Station – Hilsea – North End *Junction* – Guildhall – Royal Pier Hotel – Southsea *The Circle* – Bradford Junction – Fratton Bridge – North End *Junction* – Hilsea – Cosham *Red Lion* via Spur Road, Northern Road, private road, Portsmouth Road, London Road, Kingston Crescent, Commercial Road, Guildhall Square, Commercial Road, Hampshire Terrace, Landport Terrace, Kings Terrace, Jubilee Terrace, Bellevue Terrace, Southsea Terrace, Western Parade, Osborne Road, Clarendon Road, Victoria Road South, Victoria Road North, Fratton Road, Kingston Road, London Road, Northern Road and London Road.
Unidirectional circular service (anti-clockwise) worked in conjunction with service 10. No evening or Sunday service.

26.09.53 Service withdrawn.

Service 10

01.07.46 Redesignated trolleybus service (formerly service 2 (i)) commenced Cosham *Red Lion* – Cosham Railway Station – Hilsea – North End *Junction* – Fratton Bridge – Bradford Junction – Southsea *The Circle* – Royal Pier Hotel – Guildhall – North End *Junction* – Hilsea – Cosham *Red Lion* via Spur Road, Northern Road, private road, Portsmouth Road, London Road, Kingston Road, Fratton Road, Victoria Road North, Victoria Road South, Clarendon Road, Osborne Road, Western Parade, Southsea Terrace, Bellevue Terrace, Jubilee Terrace, Kings Terrace, Landport Terrace, Hampshire Terrace, Commercial Road, Guildhall Square, Commercial Road, Kingston Crescent, London Road, Northern Road and London Road.
Unidirectional circular service (clockwise) worked in conjunction with service 9. No evening or Sunday service.

26.09.53 Service withdrawn.

Service 11

01.11.36 Trolleybus service commenced Copnor Bridge – Guildhall – Dockyard *Main Gate* via New Road, Kingston Road, Lake Road, Commercial Road, Guildhall Square, Park Road, Ordnance Row and The Hard
Unidirectional southbound service worked in conjunction with service 12.

17.11.37 Trolleybuses temporarily replaced by motorbuses due to tramway track removal in New Road.

31.5.38 Trolleybuses re-introduced.

06.01.52 Alternate journeys except on Sunday mornings extended to operate from Madeira Road (known as Green Lane terminus) – Copnor Bridge via Copnor Road thence by the prevailing route to Dockyard *Main Gate*.

02.12.61 Last day of operation by trolleybus. Replaced by motorbus service 11.

Service 12

01.11.36 Trolleybus service commenced Dockyard *Main Gate* – Guildhall – Copnor Bridge via The Hard, Ordnance Row, Park Road, Guildhall Square, Commercial Road, Lake Road, Kingston Road and New Road.
Unidirectional northbound service worked in conjunction with service 11.

17.11.37 Trolleybuses temporarily replaced by motorbuses due to tramway track removal in New Road.

31.05.38 Trolleybuses re-introduced.

06.01.52 Alternate journeys except on Sunday mornings extended to terminate at Madeira Road (known as Green Lane terminus) instead of Copnor Bridge via Copnor Road.

02.12.61 Last day of operation by trolleybus. Replaced by motorbus service 12.

Service 13

01.07.46 Trolleybus service commenced Cosham Railway Station – Hilsea – North End *Junction* – Fratton Bridge – Bradford Junction – Southsea *The Circle* – Southsea *South Parade Pier* via Portsmouth Road, London Road, Kingston Road, Fratton Road, Victoria Road North, Victoria Road South, Clarendon Road and South Parade.

Service extended to originate at Cosham *Red Lion* via Spur Road, Northern Road and private road on weekday evenings and all day Sunday.
Unidirectional southbound service worked in conjunction with service 14.

27.09.53 All day service curtailed to originate at Cosham Railway Station operating weekdays only.

26.01.59 Last day of operation by trolleybus. No direct replacement.

Service 14

01.07.46 Trolleybus service commenced Southsea *South Parade Pier* – Southsea *The Circle* – Bradford Junction – Fratton Bridge – North End *Junction* – Hilsea – Cosham Railway Station via South Parade, Clarendon Road, Victoria Road South, Victoria Road North, Fratton Road, Kingston Road, London Road and Portsmouth Road.

Service extended to terminate at Cosham *Red Lion* via Northern Road and London Road on weekday evenings and all day Sunday.
Unidirectional northbound service worked in conjunction with service 13.

27.09.53 All day service curtailed to terminate at Cosham Railway Station operating weekdays only.

26.01.59 Last day of operation by trolleybus. No direct replacement.

Service 15 (i)

01.11.36 Trolleybus service commenced Copnor Bridge – Guildhall – Old Portsmouth – Floating Bridge via New Road, Kingston Road, Lake Road, Commercial Road, Guildhall Square, Commercial Road, Cambridge Road, High Street and Broad Street.
Unidirectional southbound service worked in conjunction with service 16.

17.11.37 Trolleybuses temporarily replaced by motorbuses due to tramway track removal in New Road.

31.05.38 Trolleybuses re-introduced.

11.7.40 Service suspended due to air raid damage.
(The following list of service suspensions and reintroductions may be incomplete as few records survive).

??.07.40 Service reintroduced.

12.08.40 Service suspended due to air raid damage.

??.08.40 Service reintroduced.

11.01.41 Service suspended due to air raid damage.

??.01.41 Service reintroduced.

10.03.41 Service suspended due to air raid damage.

??.03.41 Service reintroduced.

27.04.41 Service suspended due to air raid damage.

05.05.41 Service reintroduced.

19.05.41 Service suspended due to severe air raid damage in Old Portsmouth and replaced by a motorbus shuttle service Guildhall – Floating Bridge.

06.07.41 Trolleybus service re-introduced (Copnor Bridge – Floating Bridge).

19.04.44 Service suspended due to preparations for the allied invasion of Continental Europe and evacuation of most of the civilian population of Old Portsmouth.

31.12.44 Service withdrawn, having, it is assumed, not been reintroduced in the meantime, and replaced by a motorbus shuttle service Cosham Street – Floating Bridge.

29.09.46 Trolleybus service reintroduced Copnor Bridge – Guildhall – Old Portsmouth – Floating Bridge via New Road, Kingston Road, Lake Road, Commercial Road, Guildhall Square, Commercial Road, Cambridge Road, High Street and Broad Street.
Unidirectional southbound service worked in conjunction with service 16.

29.09.51 Service withdrawn. Replaced between Guildhall and Floating Bridge by SMS service 39 and from 05.52 by service R.

Service 15 (ii)

27.09.53 Trolleybus service commenced Eastney – Milton *White House* – Copnor Bridge – North End *Junction* – Alexandra Park via Eastney Road, Milton Road, Copnor Road, Chichester Road, London Road and Gladys Avenue.
Unidirectional northbound service worked in conjunction with service 16.

16.04.56 Trolleybuses temporarily replaced by motorbuses due to road works in Chichester Road.

26.05.56 Trolleybuses re-introduced.

30.04.60 Last day of operation by trolleybus. Replaced by motorbus service 15.

Service 16 (i)

01.11.36 Trolleybus service commenced Floating Bridge – Old Portsmouth – Guildhall – Copnor Bridge via Broad Street, High Street, Cambridge Road, Commercial Road, Guildhall Square, Commercial Road, Lake Road, Kingston Road and New Road.
Unidirectional northbound service worked in conjunction with service 15.

17.11.37 Trolleybuses temporarily replaced by motorbuses due to tramway track removal in New Road.

Trolleybuses re-introduced.

Service suspended due to air raid damage. (The following list of service suspensions and reintroductions may be incomplete as few records survive).

??.07.40 Service reintroduced.

12.08.40 Service suspended due to air raid damage.

??.08.40 Service reintroduced.

11.01.41 Service suspended due to air raid damage.

??.01.41 Service reintroduced.

10.03.41 Service suspended due to air raid damage.

??.03.41 Service reintroduced.

27.04.41 Service suspended due to air raid damage.

05.05.41 Service reintroduced.

19.05.41 Service suspended due to severe air raid damage in Old Portsmouth and replaced by a motorbus shuttle service Floating Bridge – Guildhall.

06.07.41 Trolleybus service reintroduced (Floating Bridge – Copnor Bridge).

19.04.44 Service suspended due to preparations for the allied invasion of Continental Europe and evacuation of most of the civilian population of Old Portsmouth.

31.12.44 Service withdrawn, having, it is assumed, not been reintroduced in the meantime, and replaced by a motorbus shuttle service Floating Bridge – Cosham Street.

29.09.46 Trolleybus service reintroduced Floating Bridge – Old Portsmouth – Guildhall – Copnor Bridge via Broad Street, High Street, Cambridge Road, Commercial Road, Guildhall Square, Commercial Road, Lake Road, Kingston Road and New Road.
Unidirectional northbound service worked in conjunction with service 15.

Service withdrawn. Replaced between Floating Bridge and the Guildhall by SMS service 39 and from 05.52 by service S.

Service 16 (ii)

27.09.53 Trolleybus service commenced Alexandra Park – North End *Junction* – Copnor Bridge – Milton White House – Eastney via Gladys Avenue, London Road, Chichester Road, Copnor Road, Milton Road, Baffins Road, Milton Road and Eastney Road.
Unidirectional southbound service worked in conjunction with service 15.

16.04.56 Trolleybuses temporarily replaced by motorbuses due to road works in Chichester Road.

26.05.56 Trolleybuses re-introduced.

30.04.60 Last day of operation by trolleybus. Replaced by motorbus service 16.

Service 17

10.11.36 Trolleybus service commenced Dockyard *Main Gate* – Guildhall – Bradford Junction – Festing Hotel – Eastney – Milton *White House* – Bradford Junction – Guildhall – Dockyard *Main Gate* via The Hard, Ordnance Row, Park Road, Commercial Road, Guildhall Square, Greetham Street, Blackfriars Road, Bradford Road, Victoria Road North, Albert Road, Highland Road, Eastney Road, Goldsmith Avenue, Victoria Road North, Bradford Road, Blackfriars Road, Greetham Street, Guildhall Square, Commercial Road, Park Road, Ordnance Row and The Hard.
Unidirectional circular service (anti-clockwise) worked in conjunction with service 18.

22.06.63 Last day of operation by trolleybus. Replaced by motorbus service 17.

Service 18

10.11.36 Trolleybus service commenced Dockyard *Main Gate* – Guildhall – Bradford Junction – Milton *White House* – Eastney –Festing Hotel – Bradford Junction – Guildhall – Dockyard *Main Gate* via The Hard, Ordnance Row, Park Road, Commercial Road, Guildhall Square, Greetham Street, Blackfriars Road, Bradford Road, Victoria Road North, Goldsmith Avenue, Eastney Road, Highland Road, Albert Road, Victoria Road North, Bradford Road, Blackfriars Road, Greetham Street, Guildhall Square, Commercial Road, Park Road, Ordnance Row and The Hard.
Unidirectional circular service (clockwise) worked in conjunction with service 17.

22.06.63 Last day of operation by trolleybus. Replaced by motorbus service 18.

Service 19

26.09.48 Redesignated trolleybus service (formerly trolleybus service 4 (ii)) commenced Cosham Railway Station – Alexandra Park – Guildhall – Bradford Junction – Festing Hotel – Eastney – Milton *White House* – Fratton Bridge – Bradford Junction – Guildhall – Alexandra Park via Portsmouth Road, London Road, Northern Parade, Twyford Avenue, Commercial Road, Guildhall Square, Greetham Street, Blackfriars Road, Bradford Road, Victoria Road North, Albert Road, Highland Road, Eastney Road, Goldsmith Avenue, Victoria Road North, Blackfriars Road, Greetham Street, Guildhall Square, Commercial Road, Twyford Avenue and Northern Parade.
Unidirectional anticlockwise service Monday – Saturday worked in conjunction with service 20.

Sunday service operated Cosham Railway Station – Alexandra Park – Guildhall only.

29.05.49 Sunday service operated Cosham Railway Station – Alexandra Park – Guildhall – Clarence Pier only for the summer season.

18.09.49 Sunday service reverted to Cosham Railway Station – Alexandra Park – Guildhall only for the winter season.

The summer season extension of the Sunday service to terminate at Clarence Pier was repeated each year until 1959, the date of commencement being a little later each year, viz. 06.07.58.

30.04.60 Last day of operation by trolleybus. Replaced by motorbus service 19.

Service 20

26.09.48 Redesignated trolleybus service (formerly trolleybus service 3A) commenced Alexandra Park – Guildhall – Bradford Junction – Fratton Bridge – Milton *White House* – Eastney – Festing Hotel – Bradford Junction – Guildhall – Alexandra Park – Cosham Railway Station via Northern Parade, Twyford Avenue, Commercial Road, Guildhall Square, Greetham Street, Blackfriars Road, Bradford Road, Victoria Road North, Goldsmith Avenue, Eastney Road, Highland Road, Albert Road, Victoria Road North, Bradford Road, Blackfriars Road, Greetham Street, Guildhall Square, Commercial Road, Twyford Avenue, Northern Parade and Portsmouth Road.
Unidirectional clockwise service Monday – Saturday worked in conjunction with service 19.

Sunday service operated Guildhall – Alexandra Park – Cosham Railway

Station only.

29.05.49 Sunday service operated Clarence Pier – Guildhall – Alexandra Park – Cosham Railway Station only for the summer season.

18.09.49 Sunday service reverted to Guildhall – Alexandra Park – Cosham Railway

Station only for the winter season.

The summer season extension of the Sunday service to originate at Clarence Pier was repeated each year until 1959, the date of commencement being a little later each year, viz. 06.07.58.

30.04.60 Last day of operation by trolleybus. Replaced by motorbus service 20.

Football Ground Extras
Pre-war trolleybuses operated from Cosham and North End via Fratton Bridge, and possibly from the Dockyard, to Goldsmith Avenue for Fratton Park football ground. There is no evidence that any of the various extras were operated by electric traction post-war.

APPENDIX E

DESTINATION DISPLAYS

The indicator box layout on Portsmouth's trolleybuses falls into two categories, that used on the prototype fleet and that used for all subsequent deliveries. The use of each box and the blind displays were more complex. Displays were stencilled in black onto white linen blinds up to 40ft long stretched between rollers at the top and base of the glass-fronted indicator boxes.

Prototype trolleybuses

The experimental fleet of trolleybuses, whichever body manufacturer, appeared with a style of indicator box layout and destination displays that was entirely new to the undertaking and which was also used on the 1935 Leyland TD4 Leyland bodied double-deck motorbus deliveries. However, this style was not perpetuated.

Rectangular indicator boxes 36in. by 14in. capable of displaying up to three lines of information (final destination and two lines of intermediate points) aligned with a square indicator box 14in. by 14in. for displaying the service number, were mounted centrally on the upper-deck panels at front and rear. At the front the destination and intermediate points indicator box was on the nearside with the service number indicator box on the offside. At the rear the destination and intermediate points indicator box was on the offside with the service number indicator box on the nearside.

There was a narrow indicator box 24in. by 6in. capable of displaying the final destination (one or two lines) or the final destination and an intermediate point (two lines) located inside the lower saloon at the top of the rearmost lower saloon window of the English Electric-bodied vehicles or in the vent panel immediately above (on 10, 11, 14, 15) on both sides.

Service number blinds

Pre-war blinds contained service number 1–20 without any A suffix. This meant that when service numbers with suffixes were introduced in November 1935 the prototype trolleybuses continued to display the equivalent number without suffix. The numbers were printed on the blinds in a large and rather old-fashioned style and completely filled the aperture.

New blinds were introduced in c. 1947 with smaller, plainer numbers better suited to size of the aperture. The range of numbers still ran 1–20 but with the addition of the A suffix services, it is assumed in the following sequence 1, 2, 1A, 2A, 3, 3A, 4, 4A, 5, 6, etc.

Destination blinds

The character style and layout was unique to these vehicles, each service screen having three lines of large print with **VIA** and **AND** in smaller print.

The blinds in the nearside and offside lower saloon indicator boxes displayed the final destination in large print in one line or in small print in two lines, e.g.

COSHAM
VIA RAILWAY S^TN

or the final destination and an intermediate point (two lines) with **VIA** and **AND** in smaller print, e.g.

COSHAM
VIA BRADFORD ROAD

Displays for the initially limited range of services between Cosham and Southsea *South Parade Pier* were stencilled on the blinds. There were few subsequent additions made to the blinds: it is likely that displays for services 1 and 2, as well as associated short-workings, were added but none thereafter in view of the prototype trolleybuses inability to operate on journeys requiring battery power for turning purposes and reduced use in the later 1930s.

In 1936 further displays were added in the same print style but with two changes to the layout: the destination moved from the top line to the bottom line thus eliminating the need for **VIA** and Cosham was qualified as either **'RED LION' COSHAM** or **COSHAM RAILWAY STN**. The original displays had simply shown Cosham and whether these were amended in October 1936 when journeys to Cosham "Red Lion" was introduced is not known.

New blinds were introduced c. 1947, each display having four lines of information in a plain style, the fourth line being the destination in slightly larger lettering. Some single line displays were used for special workings, e.g. Cosham 'Red Lion', Football Ground, North End, in larger capital letters. Such post-war blinds were fitted to 201–211, 213 and 215 (212 never returned to service in Portsmouth after its loan to Pontypridd and 214 was fitted with a unique blind(s) having a non-standard layout and lettering).

The indicator boxes to the nearside and offside of the lower saloon seem to have fallen into disuse on these vehicles by mid-1949.

Experimental fleet pre-war main indicator blinds (front & rear)

3 — SOUTH PARADE PIER
VIA NORTH END, FRATTON
AND FAWCETT ROADS

3 — SOUTH PARADE PIER
VIA FRATTON
AND FAWCETT ROADS

3 — COSHAM VIA ALBERT ROAD
GUILDHALL
TWYFORD AVENUE

4 — COSHAM VIA FRATTON
AND FAWCETT ROADS
AND NORTH END

All other trolleybuses

All subsequent deliveries had a revised screen layout in which the service number, intermediate points and destination were shown in the same main display at front and rear. Over the years there were many variations of blinds carried by AEC661Ts 16–24 and 25–100, and the BUT9611Ts 301–315, given that CPPTD freely amended blinds so as to meet operating requirements.

The AEC661Ts had rectangular indicator boxes 43in. by 14in., capable of displaying a service number and up to four lines of information (final destination and three lines of intermediate points), with a second rectangular indicator box 43in. by 6in. immediately beneath for a single line of supplementary information or final destination, mounted centrally on the upper-deck panels at front and rear. At the front the service number was on the offside of the destination and intermediate points information and at the rear on the nearside, the number being in a broader style as deep as three lines of information.

Pre-war the single line indicator box displayed **PORTSMOUTH CORPORATION** when on normal service and the final destination when operating short-workings or special journeys.

A further rectangular indicator box 31½in. by 14in., displaying the final destination and up to four lines of information (final

Pre-war main indicator blind (front & rear)

Service	Display
1	NORTH END GUILDHALL PALMERSTON RD
1	VICTORIA RD FRATTON RD NORTH END
2	BRADFORD JUNCTION VIA NORTH END FRATTON RD
1	CLARENCE PIER VIA NORTH END COMMERCIAL ROAD GUILDHALL
2	"RED LION" COSHAM VIA GUILDHALL COMMERCIAL ROAD NORTH END
2A	COSHAM RAILWAY STN VIA GUILDHALL COMMERCIAL ROAD NORTH END
13	NORTH END FRATTON RD VICTORIA RD CIRCLE
14	CIRCLE VICTORIA RD FRATTON RD NORTH END
3	SOUTH PARADE PIER VIA NORTH END FRATTON ROAD FAWCETT ROAD
3	"RED LION" COSHAM VIA ALBERT ROAD GUILDHALL TWYFORD AVENUE
3A	COSHAM RAILWAY STN VIA ALBERT ROAD GUILDHALL TWYFORD AVENUE
4	SOUTH PARADE PIER VIA TWYFORD AVENUE GUILDHALL ALBERT ROAD
4	"RED LION" COSHAM VIA FAWCETT ROAD FRATTON ROAD NORTH END

continued ⇗

Service	Display
4A	COSHAM RAILWAY STN VIA FAWCETT ROAD FRATTON ROAD NORTH END
5	EASTNEY VIA KING'S ROAD PALMERSTON ROAD SOUTH PARADE PIER
5	DOCKYARD VIA MILTON FRATTON BRIDGE GUILDHALL
5	GUILDHALL VIA MILTON FRATTON BRIDGE BRADFORD JUNCTION
6	EASTNEY VIA GUILDHALL FRATTON BRIDGE MILTON
6	DOCKYARD VIA SOUTH PARADE PIER PALMERSTON ROAD KING'S ROAD
7	FRATTON RD FAWCETT RD PALMERSTON ROAD STRAND
8	PALMERSTON RD FAWCETT RD FRATTON RD NEW ROAD
9	NORTH END COMMERCIAL RD GUILDHALL
9	VICTORIA RD FRATTON RD NORTH END
10	NORTH END FRATTON RD VICTORIA RD CIRCLE
10	GUILDHALL COMMERCIAL RD NORTH END
11	DOCKYARD VIA LAKE ROAD GUILDHALL

continued ⇗

Service	Display
12	COPNOR BRIDGE VIA GUILDHALL LAKE ROAD NEW ROAD
15	FLOATING BRIDGE VIA LAKE ROAD GUILDHALL HIGH STREET
16	COPNOR BRIDGE VIA GUILDHALL LAKE ROAD NEW ROAD
17	EASTNEY VIA GUILDHALL BRADFORD ROAD ALBERT ROAD
17	DOCKYARD VIA MILTON FRATTON BRIDGE BRADFORD JUNCTION
18	EASTNEY VIA GUILDHALL FRATTON BRIDGE MILTON
18	DOCKYARD VIA ALBERT ROAD ELM GROVE GUILDHALL
	ALEXANDRA PARK VIA ELM GROVE GUILDHALL
	GUILDHALL VIA TWYFORD AVENUE COMMERCIAL RD
	DOCKYARD VIA NORTH END GUILDHALL
	COSHAM RAILWAY STN VIA GUILDHALL NORTH END
	DOCKYARD VIA TWYFORD AVENUE GUILDHALL
	COSHAM RAILWAY STN VIA GUILDHALL TWYFORD AVENUE

The standard pre-war blind for AEC661Ts 16-100 with a number of additions:

- **Wartime extension of services 1 and 2**
- **Early post-war services 7–10, 13 and 14**

Another pre-war main indicator blind (front & rear)

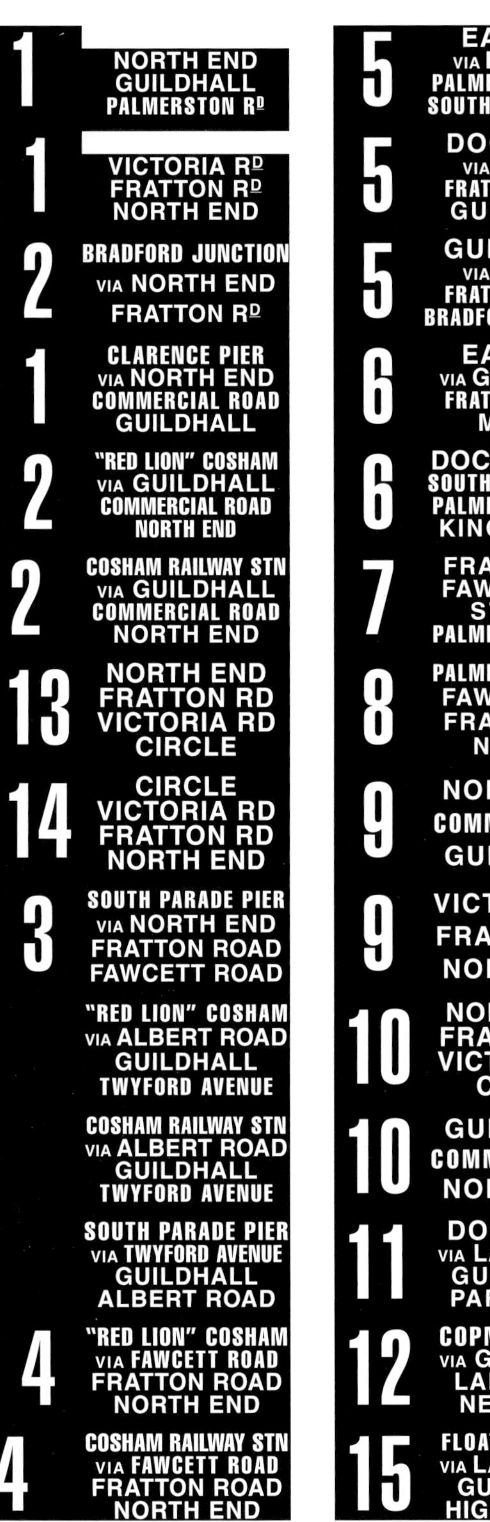

continued

5 EASTNEY
VIA KING'S ROAD
PALMERSTON ROAD
SOUTH PARADE PIER
5 DOCKYARD
VIA MILTON
FRATTON BRIDGE
GUILDHALL
5 GUILDHALL
VIA MILTON
FRATTON BRIDGE
BRADFORD JUNCTION
6 EASTNEY
VIA GUILDHALL
FRATTON BRIDGE
MILTON
6 DOCKYARD VIA
SOUTH PARADE PIER
PALMERSTON ROAD
KING'S ROAD
7 FRATTON RD
FAWCETT RD
STRAND
PALMERSTON ROAD
8 PALMERSTON ROAD
FAWCETT RD
FRATTON RD
NEW RD
9 NORTH END
COMMERCIAL RD
GUILDHALL
9 VICTORIA RD
FRATTON RD
NORTH END
10 NORTH END
FRATTON RD
VICTORIA RD
CIRCLE
10 GUILDHALL
COMMERCIAL RD
NORTH END
11 DOCKYARD
VIA LAKE ROAD
GUILDHALL
PARK ROAD
12 COPNOR BRIDGE
VIA GUILDHALL
LAKE ROAD
NEW ROAD
15 FLOATING BRIDGE
VIA LAKE ROAD
GUILDHALL
HIGH STREET

continued

16 COPNOR BRIDGE
VIA GUILDHALL
LAKE ROAD
NEW ROAD
17 EASTNEY
VIA GUILDHALL
BRADFORD ROAD
ALBERT ROAD
17 DOCKYARD
VIA MILTON
FRATTON BRIDGE
GUILDHALL
17 GUILDHALL
VIA MILTON
FRATTON BRIDGE
BRADFORD JUNCTION
18 EASTNEY
VIA GUILDHALL
FRATTON BRIDGE
MILTON
18 DOCKYARD
VIA ALBERT ROAD
ELM GROVE
GUILDHALL
ALEXANDRA PARK
VIA ELM GROVE
GUILDHALL
GUILDHALL
VIA TWYFORD AVENUE
COMMERCIAL ROAD
DOCKYARD
VIA NORTH END
GUILDHALL
COSHAM RAILWAY STN
VIA GUILDHALL
NORTH END
DOCKYARD
VIA TWYFORD AVENUE
GUILDHALL
COSHAM RAILWAY STN
VIA GUILDHALL
TWYFORD AVENUE

The service number 1 of the initial display is out of alignment to the left of the blind possibly to accommodate an A suffix which has been painted out. Such a 1A display would have been inappropriate for the intermediate points shown suggesting an incorrect specification.

The white blank final destination on two uppermost service 1 displays relate to the 21 July 1940 extension to North End.

The service numbers 2 and 4 next to the COSHAM RAILWAY STN. destination displays are out of alignment to the left of the blind and compressed to accommodate an A suffix which has been painted out.

It is unknown why the post-war service 13 and 14 displays were inserted after the 1 and 2s and prior to the 3 and 4s.

destination and three lines of intermediate points), was fitted immediately above the rear open platform entrance. On AEC 661Ts 16–24 this measured 31½in. by 14in. whereas that on 25–100 and BUT9611Ts 301–315 was somewhat smaller, measuring 24in. by 14in. The service number was not shown at this location.

There was a single line indicator box displaying the final destination inside the lower saloon at the top of the offside bay 5 window measuring 24in. by 6in. A similar box 30in. by 5in. was built into the vent panel immediately above the offside bay 5 window on BUT9611Ts 301–315. These boxes fell into disuse post war and were removed c. 1948–1949.

Service number and destination blinds

Pre-war blinds were identical whether the trolleybus was based at Eastney or North End Depot, the content and displays being changed at various times by stitching-in additional lengths of stencilled linen to accommodate additional or rerouted services, e.g. the amendments of 1 July 1946, or by "painting-out" information, e.g. the A suffixes. Black masking tape was

Pre-war side indicator blind (above platform)

VICTORIA ROAD
FRATTON ROAD
NORTH END
"RED LION" COSHAM

CLARENCE PIER
VIA NORTH END
COMMERCIAL ROAD
GUILDHALL

"RED LION" COSHAM
VIA GUILDHALL
COMMERCIAL ROAD
NORTH END

COSHAM RAILWAY STN
VIA GUILDHALL
COMMERCIAL ROAD
NORTH END

SOUTH PARADE PIER
VIA NORTH END
FRATTON ROAD
FAWCETT ROAD

"RED LION" COSHAM
VIA ELM GROVE
GUILDHALL
TWYFORD AVENUE

COSHAM RAILWAY STN
VIA ELM GROVE
GUILDHALL
TWYFORD AVENUE

SOUTH PARADE PIER
VIA TWYFORD AVENUE
GUILDHALL
ALBERT ROAD

"RED LION" COSHAM
VIA FAWCETT ROAD
FRATTON ROAD
NORTH END

COSHAM RAILWAY STN
VIA FAWCETT ROAD
FRATTON ROAD
NORTH END

EASTNEY
VIA KING'S ROAD
PALMERSTON ROAD
SOUTH PARADE PIER

continued

DOCKYARD
VIA MILTON
FRATTON BRIDGE
GUILDHALL

GUILDHALL
VIA MILTON
FRATTON BRIDGE
BRADFORD JUNCTION

EASTNEY
VIA GUILDHALL
FRATTON BRIDGE
MILTON

DOCKYARD VIA
SOUTH PARADE PIER
PALMERSTON ROAD
KING'S ROAD

DOCKYARD
VIA LAKE ROAD
GUILDHALL
PARK ROAD

COPNOR BRIDGE
VIA GUILDHALL
LAKE ROAD
NEW ROAD

FLOATING BRIDGE
VIA LAKE ROAD
GUILDHALL
HIGH STREET

COPNOR BRIDGE
VIA GUILDHALL
LAKE ROAD
NEW ROAD

EASTNEY
VIA GUILDHALL
BRADFORD ROAD
ALBERT ROAD

DOCKYARD
VIA MILTON
FRATTON BRIDGE
GUILDHALL

GUILDHALL
VIA MILTON
FRATTON BRIDGE
BRADFORD JUNCTION

continued

EASTNEY
VIA GUILDHALL
FRATTON BRIDGE
MILTON

DOCKYARD
VIA ALBERT ROAD
ELM GROVE
GUILDHALL

BRADFORD JUNCTION
VIA NORTH END
FRATTON ROAD

NORTH END
VIA FAWCETT ROAD
FRATTON ROAD

ALEXANDRA PARK
VIA ELM GROVE
GUILDHALL

GUILDHALL
VIA TWYFORD AVENUE
COMMERCIAL ROAD

DOCKYARD
VIA NORTH END
GUILDHALL

COSHAM RAILWAY STN
VIA GUILDHALL
NORTH END

DOCKYARD
VIA TWYFORD AVENUE
GUILDHALL

COSHAM RAILWAY STN
VIA GUILDHALL
TWYFORD AVENUE

S. PARADE PIER
VIA NORTH END
FRATTON ROAD
FAWCETT ROAD

This style of blind is believed to have been introduced in 1935 for use on AEC661T 16-24. The blind copied (in 1961) came from AEC661T 30 (a later delivery) and includes a number of later additions not least the very first display which omits a "via". Note the reluctance to abbreviate any location names.

Pre-war supplementary information and destination blind (front & rear)

PORTSMOUTH CORPORATION
RED LION COSHAM
COSHAM RAILWAY STN
CLARENCE PIER
SOUTH PARADE PIER
GUILDHALL
BRADFORD JUNCTION
FRATTON BRIDGE
NORTH END
ALEXANDRA PARK
ELM GROVE
KING'S ROAD
EASTNEY
WHITE HOUSE MILTON
DOCKYARD
COPNOR BRIDGE
COPNOR BRIDGE (ONLY)
GREEN LANE
FLOATING BRIDGE
PALMERSTON ROAD
FOOTBALL GROUND VIA FRATTON RD
BUCKLAND
KINGS THEATRE
SPECIAL
DEPOT
CIRCLE
FESTING ROAD
DOCKYARD VIA BUCKLAND
NORTH END VIA BUCKLAND
COSHAM VIA BUCKLAND
STRAND

This style of blind is believed to have been introduced in 1935–1936. The blind copied (in 1963) came from AEC661T 283 and includes a number of unpublished or unknown destinations:

Elm Grove; Buckland; Circle; Festing Road; Strand

applied to the glass front of the main indicator box covering approximately the uppermost location on the blind in June 1940 for security reasons. Although specifically intended to mask references to **DOCKYARD** this effectively covered all uppermost locations, the supplementary information blind immediately below being available to display non-sensitive destinations.

From January 1950 new blinds which differed according to whether the trolleybus was based at Eastney or North End Depot began to appear. This was a drawn-out process and it is possible that some of the vehicles withdrawn early retained pre-war screens until they were taken out of service.

Supplementary information/destination blinds
The display **PORTSMOUTH CORPORATION** ceased to be used in June 1940 for security reasons and was not officially used post-war.

Between 1940 and early post war this box was used to display non-sensitive destinations. Once the masking had been removed this position was used solely to display the final destination although in most cases trolleybuses continued to show their ultimate destination on the main service number and destination blinds too.

When appropriate, trolleybuses displayed paper stickers 'To and From the Show' or 'Circus' in the nearside driver's cab windscreen (both events being held on Southsea Common).

Post-war main indicator blind (front & rear) North End Depot

No.	Display
1	COSHAM NORTH END GUILDHALL OSBORNE ROAD
2	OSBORNE ROAD GUILDHALL NORTH END COSHAM
2	OSBORNE ROAD GUILDHALL NORTH END (ONLY)
3	COSHAM NORTH END FRATTON ROAD FAWCETT ROAD
4	FAWCETT ROAD FRATTON ROAD NORTH END COSHAM
4	FAWCETT ROAD FRATTON ROAD NORTH END (ONLY)
7	NEW ROAD FRATTON ROAD FAWCETT ROAD·STRAND OSBORNE ROAD
8	OSBORNE ROAD FAWCETT ROAD FRATTON ROAD·NEW RD COPNOR BRIDGE
9	COSHAM NORTH END GUILDHALL OSBORNE ROAD
9	VICTORIA ROAD FRATTON ROAD NORTH END COSHAM
10	COSHAM·N. END FRATTON ROAD VICTORIA ROAD OSBORNE ROAD
10	GUILDHALL NORTH END COSHAM
11	COPNOR BRIDGE NEW ROAD LAKE ROAD GUILDHALL
12	GUILDHALL LAKE ROAD NEW ROAD COPNOR BRIDGE
13	COSHAM·N. END FRATTON ROAD VICTORIA ROAD CIRCLE
14	CIRCLE VICTORIA ROAD FRATTON ROAD N. END·COSHAM
14	CIRCLE VICTORIA ROAD FRATTON ROAD NORTH END (ONLY)
15	COPNOR BRIDGE NEW RD·LAKE RD GUILDHALL HIGH STREET
16	GUILDHALL LAKE ROAD NEW ROAD COPNOR BRIDGE
19	COSHAM TWYFORD AVENUE GUILDHALL ALBERT ROAD
19	FRATTON BRIDGE GUILDHALL TWYFORD AVENUE ALEXANDRA PARK
19	FRATTON BRIDGE GUILDHALL (ONLY)
19	COSHAM TWYFORD AVENUE GUILDHALL
20	GUILDHALL FRATTON BRIDGE MILTON
20	ALBERT ROAD GUILDHALL TWYFORD AVENUE COSHAM
20	GUILDHALL TWYFORD AVENUE COSHAM

continued ☞

This style of blind was used on trolleybuses based at North End Depot.

Post-war main indicator blind (front & rear) BUT9611T Eastney Depot

No.	Display
5	CLARENDON ROAD S. PARADE PIER EASTNEY
5	CLARENDON ROAD S. PARADE PIER EASTNEY·MILTON COPNOR BRIDGE
6	COPNOR BRIDGE EASTNEY S. PARADE PIER CLARENDON ROAD
6	COPNOR BRIDGE MILTON EASTNEY
15	CLARENDON ROAD S. PARADE PIER EASTNEY·MILTON COPNOR BRIDGE
15	EASTNEY COPNOR BRIDGE CHICHESTER ROAD NORTH END
16	NORTH END CHICHESTER ROAD COPNOR BRIDGE EASTNEY
16	COPNOR BRIDGE EASTNEY S. PARADE PIER CLARENDON ROAD
17	GUILDHALL BRADFORD ROAD ALBERT ROAD
17	MILTON FRATTON BRIDGE GUILDHALL
18	GUILDHALL FRATTON BRIDGE MILTON
18	ALBERT ROAD BRADFORD ROAD GUILDHALL

This style of blind was used solely on BUT9611Ts based at Eastney Depot.

Note the display for service 15 and 16 including Clarendon Road added for an extension of these services to Dockyard which never materialised.

Post-war side indicator blind (above platform)

NORTH END
GUILDHALL
OSBORNE ROAD
S. PARADE PIER

NORTH END
COMMERCIAL ROAD
GUILDHALL (ONLY)

OSBORNE ROAD
GUILDHALL
NORTH END
COSHAM "RED LION"

OSBORNE ROAD
GUILDHALL
COMMERCIAL ROAD
NORTH END (ONLY)

NORTH END
FRATTON ROAD
FAWCETT ROAD
S. PARADE PIER

FAWCETT ROAD
FRATTON ROAD
NORTH END
COSHAM 'RLY STN'

FAWCETT ROAD
FRATTON ROAD
NORTH END (ONLY)

CLARENDON ROAD
S. PARADE PIER
EASTNEY
MILTON 'WHITE HOUSE'

EASTNEY
MILTON
COPNOR BRIDGE
COSHAM "RED LION"

EASTNEY
MILTON
COPNOR BRIDGE
COSHAM RLY STN (ONLY)

COPNOR BRIDGE
MILTON
EASTNEY (ONLY)
COPNOR BRIDGE

MILTON
EASTNEY
S. PARADE PIER

EASTNEY
S. PARADE PIER
CLARENDON ROAD
DOCKYARD

NEW RD·FRATTON RD
FAWCETT RD·STRAND
OSBORNE ROAD
CLARENCE PIER

OSBORNE ROAD
FAWCETT ROAD
FRATTON RD·NEW RD
COPNOR BRIDGE (ONLY)

OSBORNE RD·FAWCETT RD
FRATTON RD·NEW RD
COPNOR BRIDGE
GREEN LANE

continued

NORTH END
GUILDHALL
OSBORNE ROAD
CIRCLE

VICTORIA ROAD
FRATTON ROAD
NORTH END
COSHAM "RED LION"

NORTH END
FRATTON ROAD
VICTORIA RD·CIRCLE
OSBORNE ROAD

OSBORNE ROAD
GUILDHALL
NORTH END
COSHAM "RED LION"

NEW ROAD
LAKE ROAD
GUILDHALL
DOCKYARD

GUILDHALL
LAKE ROAD
NEW ROAD
COPNOR BRIDGE (ONLY)

GUILDHALL
LAKE RD·NEW RD
COPNOR BRIDGE
GREEN LANE

COSHAM·N. END
FRATTON ROAD
VICTORIA RD·CIRCLE
S. PARADE PIER

CIRCLE·VICTORIA RD
FRATTON ROAD
NORTH END
COSHAM RLY STN

CIRCLE
VICTORIA ROAD
FRATTON ROAD
NORTH END (ONLY)

CIRCLE
VICTORIA ROAD
NORTH END
COSHAM "RED LION"

CLARENDON ROAD
SOUTH PARADE PIER
EASTNEY·MILTON
COPNOR BRIDGE

COPNOR BRIDGE
CHICHESTER ROAD
NORTH END
ALEXANDRA PARK

NORTH END
CHICHESTER ROAD
COPNOR BRIDGE
EASTNEY

CHICHESTER ROAD
COPNOR BRIDGE
EASTNEY
SOUTH PARADE PIER

EASTNEY
SOUTH PARADE PIER
CLARENDON ROAD
DOCKYARD

continued

TWYFORD AVENUE
GUILDHALL
ALBERT ROAD
EASTNEY

FRATTON BRIDGE
GUILDHALL
TWYFORD AVENUE
ALEXANDRA PARK

FRATTON BRIDGE
GUILDHALL
(ONLY)

ALEXANDRA PARK
TWYFORD AVENUE
GUILDHALL (ONLY)

ALEXANDRA PARK
TWYFORD AVENUE
GUILDHALL
CLARENCE PIER

GUILDHALL
FRATTON BRIDGE
MILTON
EASTNEY

ALBERT ROAD
GUILDHALL
TWYFORD AVENUE
COSHAM RLY STN

GUILDHALL
TWYFORD AVENUE
ALEXANDRA PARK
COSHAM RLY STN

This style of blind was introduced in ca. 1953 and used on trolleybuses based at North End Depot. It contains displays for all services except 17 and 18.

Note the display for service 15 and 16 including Clarendon Road added for an extension of these services to Dockyard which never materialised.

Post-war supplementary information and destination blind (front & rear)

"RED LION" COSHAM
COSHAM RLY. STATION
CLARENCE PIER
S. PARADE PIER
GUILDHALL
BRADFORD JUNCTION
FRATTON BRIDGE
NORTH END
ALEXANDRA PARK
EASTNEY
"WHITE HOUSE" MILTON
DOCKYARD
COPNOR BRIDGE
COPNOR BRIDGE (ONLY)
GREEN LANE
PALMERSTON ROAD
FLOATING BRIDGE
FOOTBALL GND. VIA FRATTON
CIRCLE
STRAND
NORTH END VIA LAKE RD.
FARLINGTON

This style of blind was used on trolleybuses based at North End Depot.

Post-war side indicator blind (above platform) BUT9611T

GUILDHALL
S. PARADE PIER

GUILDHALL
COSHAM "RED LION"

FAWCETT ROAD
S. PARADE PIER

FAWCETT ROAD
COSHAM RLY STN

S. PARADE PIER
MILTON "WHITE HOUSE"

S. PARADE PIER
DOCKYARD

FRATTON BRIDGE
CLARENCE PIER

continued ☞

FRATTON BRIDGE
COPNOR BRIDGE

GUILDHALL
OSBORNE ROAD

FRATTON BRIDGE
COSHAM "RED LION"

FRATTON BRIDGE
OSBORNE ROAD

GUILDHALL
DOCKYARD

GUILDHALL
COPNOR BRIDGE

VICTORIA ROAD
S. PARADE PIER

continued ☞

VICTORIA ROAD
COSHAM RLY STN

VICTORIA ROAD
COSHAM RED LION

FLOATING BRIDGE

COPNOR BRIDGE

EASTNEY

DOCKYARD

MILTON "WHITE HOUSE"

continued ☞

TWYFORD AVENUE
GUILDHALL

ALEXANDRA PARK
TWYFORD AVENUE
COSHAM

CLARENCE PIER

GUILDHALL (ONLY)

NORTH END (ONLY)

This style of blind was fitted to the BUT9611Ts upon their entry into service but quickly fell into disuse (although retained until withdrawal). The blind was not amended for the 1953 or 1953 extensions as it had already fallen into disuse.

This view of AEC661T 277 at Cosham Railway Station in original (Livery 1) finish exemplifies the pre-war main indicator display. (R.D.H. Symons collection [photographer W.J. Haynes])

Beneath one of the gantry or double bracket arm support for which the Portsmouth trolleybus system was renowned 269 leaves the Guildhall behind it and travels west along Park Road to the Dockyard. (R.D.H. Symons collection [photographer C.W. Routh])

The driver of AEC661T 300 moves over into the right hand lane in preparation for turning out of Guildhall Square into Park Road. Note the CPPTD office on the Guildhall Square central island complete with four-faced clock gifted to the City in 1942 following the destruction of the Guildhall and its clock tower in January 1941. (Online Transport Archive [photographer D. Norman])

APPENDIX F

DEPOTS

Portsmouth's trolleybuses operated from two depots, both of which had been built during the tramway era and designed to suit rail-bound vehicles, that at North End having been completely rebuilt from its horse tram origins for the opening of the town's electric tramways in September 1901. Eastney had been built for trams and motorbuses, the trolleybuses subsequently taking over the tram depot portion.

Individual trolleybuses were allocated to a specific depot, although no indication of such was shown on the vehicles, and it was rare for a trolleybus to move from its "home" base. Each depot was responsible for running a group of services, in principle those to the north of the system being operated by North End and those to the east by Eastney, leading to vehicles often spending their entire working lives on the same group of services. In all cases trolleybuses returned daily to the "home" depot from which they had commenced service. Infrequently vehicles were transferred between the depots, usually following a repaint or rebuild. Official details of vehicle allocations are not known.

North End Depot

The Portsmouth Street Tramways Co. (PST) built a depot and stables on open land at the south end of Gladys Avenue, just off London Road, North End, backing on to housing in Cardiff Road to the west, Angerstein Road to the south and the Corpus Christi RC Church to the north. The depot served the PST line between North End and Floating Bridge, Old Portsmouth, which opened in September 1874.

Following municipalisation, the buildings were substantially demolished and expanded by the Corporation in preparation for electrification of the tramways, the southernmost buildings being retained and converted into the overhaul works whereas those to the north of the horse tramways entrance were demolished and replaced by the new tramcar running shed. This shed was a typical example of tramway architecture constructed with brick exterior walls having arched alcoves and matching tall windows on the east side, facing Gladys Avenue, a glass roof above the tram track access fan and a slate roof supported by light ironwork above the storage tracks. The building was 214ft long and 183ft wide, and capable of accommodating 113 tramcars, more than the entire fleet then envisaged. Access to the 16 parallel storage tracks equipped with the usual pits was by a single line from the street over a complex interlaced track fan inside the south end of the shed. The access track work in Gladys Avenue and the fan remained intact until removal in April–May 1954.

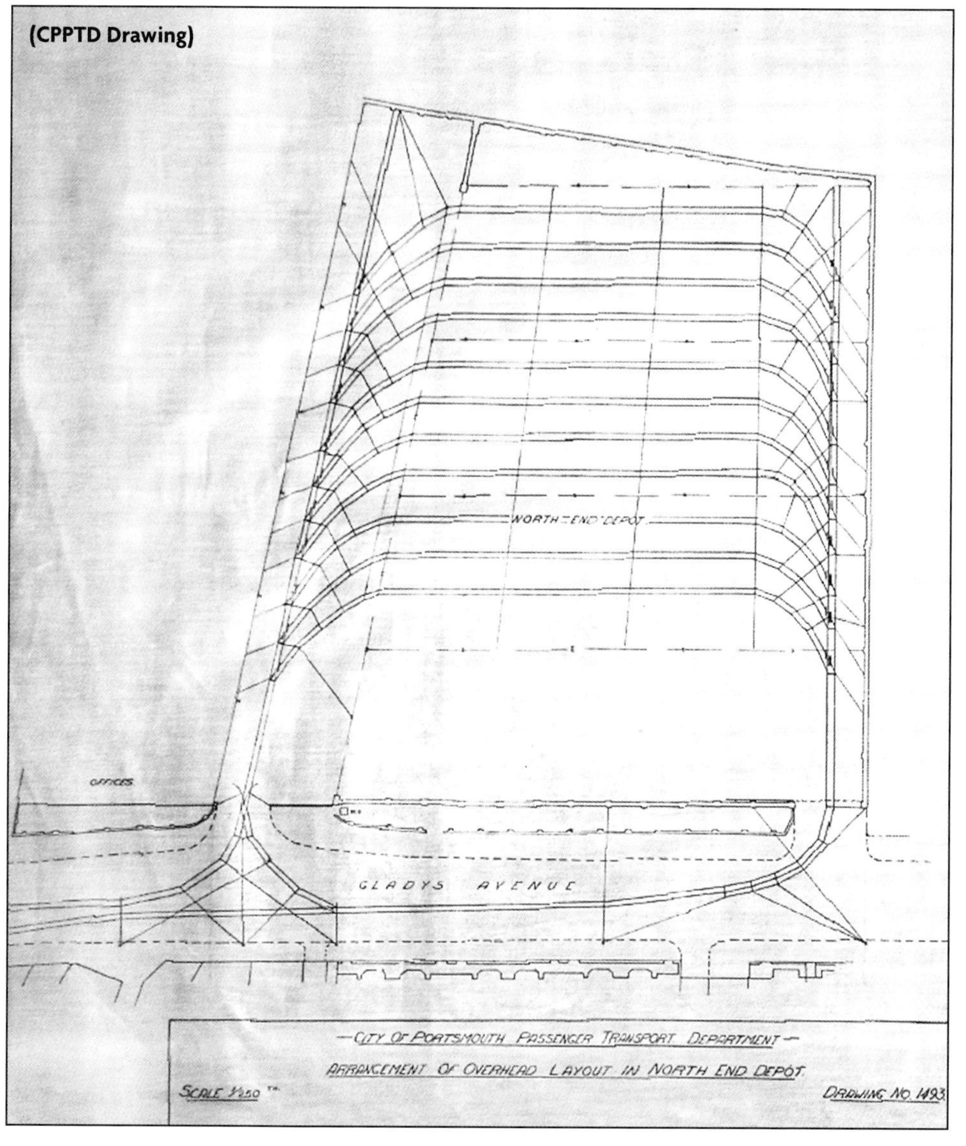

(CPPTD Drawing)

Maintenance shops, including two paint shops, were erected in winter 1902–03 immediately to the south, in a separate building 151ft long and 93ft wide, access to this being by a traverser, connected to the tracks in Gladys Avenue by a single line about 25 yards to the south of the running shed entrance.

When Eastney Depot opened in 1931 a number of trams and a greater number of motorbuses were re-allocated from North End thereby reducing empty mileage to the eastern routes and generally easing congestion in the running shed.

Work to prepare North End Depot for trolleybuses began in early 1934; however, the original overhead wiring layout within the running shed is not known. A reversing triangle was installed at the entrance from the outset enabling trolleybuses to reverse out into Gladys Avenue and this was used by short workings from South Parade Pier from October 1934. Committed to a policy of tramway conversion, it was decided in November 1934 to construct an additional doorway at its northeast corner facilitating unidirectional use, work being completed by March 1935. Henceforth the original southern doorway was used as the entrance and the new doorway as the exit. The reverser wiring was absorbed into the entry layout during August 1936.

Upon completion the running shed had 14 trolleybus lyes running from south-southeast to north-northwest aligned with Gladys Avenue, accessed by hand-operated facing frogs and arranged for unidirectional operation. There were stub sidings in the south west corner of the entrance area and in the northwest corner of the running shed. Total capacity, considering trolleybuses and motorbuses, was given as 138 in July 1949. There was no wired access to the paint shop, servicing bay or traverser.

In early 1959 a Februat B.4 vehicle washing machine was bought from The Equipment & Engineering Co. Ltd. and installed inside the running shed halfway along the rearmost lye. It is assumed that the machine could be used to wash both motorbuses and trolleybuses.

The entire fleet of prototype trolleybuses, 1–15, as well as the English Electric bodied AEC661Ts 16–24, were allocated to North End, this being the sole trolleybus depot at the time of their delivery. They remained there throughout their operating life.

Pre-war North End had the following trolleybus and service allocation:

Trolleybuses:	1–4	AEC661T
	5–7	Leyland TBD2
	8	Sunbeam MF2
	9	Karrier E4
	10	Sunbeam MF2
	11	Karrier E4
	12	AEC663T
	13	Sunbeam MS3
	14	Sunbeam MS3
	15	AEC663T
	16–24	AEC661T
	25–100	AEC661T – an unknown number of vehicles.

Services: 1, 2, 3, 3A, 4, 4A, 11, 12, 15, 16
Nos. 1–24 were not used on services 11, 12, 15 (i), 16 (i).

Post-war North End had the following trolleybus and service allocation:

Trolleybuses:	201–211, 213–224	AEC661T – in so far as the vehicle was licensed.
	225–300	AEC661T– an unknown number of vehicles.
	301–315	BUT9611T – by mid-1952, one vehicle.

The BUT9611Ts all entered service from North End and remained there for their first year or so operating on all the depot's services. Thereafter all but one were transferred to Eastney, one BUT9611T remaining allocated to North End, presumably to keep drivers familiar with this type of trolleybus. The last vehicle allocated was 302 which operated predominantly on services 7, 8.

Services: 1, 2, 3, 4, 7, 8, 9, 10, 11, 12, 13, 14, 15 (i), 16 (i)
19, 20 – one vehicle operated on this service, run jointly with Eastney Depot.
5, 6 – two vehicles operated on this service, run jointly with Eastney Depot from May 1952.
Nos 201, 202, 216, 218–220, 224 were not used on services 7, 8, 11, 12, 15 (i), 16 (i).

North End Depot closed to trolleybus operation on Saturday 2 December 1961, although it remained theoretically accessible to electric traction until 17 November 1962 when the trolley wires along Gladys Avenue to the junction with London Road were removed. Redundant trolleybuses were stored here prior to disposal until December 1963. The depot continued to operate motorbuses until closure, in connection with a service reduction, in November 1981. The buildings were demolished in March 1984 and the site is now occupied by houses named White Court after Mr A.W. White, one of the promoters of the Landport and Southsea Tramways Co. in 1863 and subsequently General Manager of the PST and later the Portsmouth & Horndean Light Railway.

AEC663T 215 with MCCW & F all metal body in North End Depot after its 1949 rebuilding and repainting. (Online Transport Archive [photographer G.F. Ashwell])

Eastney Depot

The expanded tramcar fleet and growing number of motorbuses meant that by the early 1920s North End Depot, as well as the subsidiary motorbus garages at Vivash Road, Fratton and Hester Road, Milton, was used to capacity and the search for a suitable site in the eastern part of the borough for a second depot began. A potential plot of land at the junction of Highland Road and Eastney Road, Eastney, was identified and negotiations for its purchase started in November 1925 although other sites continued to be considered. The Eastney Road plot as well as a 45ft frontage to Highland Road was purchased in summer 1927.

Tenders for different portions of the construction of Eastney Depot were invited at the end of October 1929. Messrs. A. & J. Main, as principal contractors, supplied and erected the steelwork and were generally responsible for the structure's completion, however, PCT direct labour was used wherever possible. This included excavation and site levelling for the foundations, laying the drains and reinforced concrete floor, as well as the preparations for the steel roof stanchions at depths from 4ft to 10ft. Tram tracks above the inspection pits were laid on the viaduct principle enabling maintenance staff to move easily from beneath one line of vehicles to the next without leaving the pits.

The depot complex covered some 3 acres at the south end of Eastney Road immediately to the north of where it made a crossroads with Highland Road, Cromwell Road and Henderson Road. The site was bordered by a Gospel Hall and housing on Methuen Road to the north, and the 'Highland Arms' and 'Mayflower' public houses, amongst other buildings, to the south. The tramway and later trolleybus running and repair sheds were at the east end with entrance and exit facing Eastney Road, there was a larger motorbus garage with a clear span of 120ft and a length of 200ft at the west end with access by way of Methuen Road, and the workshops, comprising paint shop, body building and repair shops, upholstery, machine and fitters' shop, armature and electric repairs, and blacksmiths, stores and foreman's offices, were between the two. Some 400 tons of steel were used for the skeleton of the main building, the roof being built in four ridges supported by four latticed girders with cantilever truss suspension.

There were six parallel storage tracks in the tramway running shed, three of which ran directly into the northbound Eastney Road line together with a further track which joined one of the three, and two giving access from the southbound Eastney Road line. The northern three lyes continued into the paint shop and the southern three into the body shop. There were a further two lyes in the overhaul shop accessed from the southernmost lye of the running shed. Eastney continued to run out trams until the final day of operation and, unable to find a buyer, many of the withdrawn cars were subsequently broken up there.

Until 1931 the undertaking's administrative offices were accommodated in the Guildhall (formerly known as the Town Hall). They then moved into a new purpose-built office building in Highland Road around the corner from the depot complex, constructed in a neo-Georgian style having brick front and side elevations, Portland stone dressings and main entrance, and Georgian-style windows. A large square three-faced clock hung out above the central first floor balcony which was surrounded by a portico. The stone balcony wall, above the main entrance, carried the title 'PORTSMOUTH CORPORATION TRAMWAYS' in raised metal capitals. Situated on the ground floor were an enquiry office, telephone switchboard, lost property and uniform stores, and offices for inspectors and the traffic superintendent. Grouped around a central circulation area was the cashier's department, including cashier's clerks, wages, cash counter, and strong room, and a separate ticket department. The administrative suite, made up of committee room, the general manager's office, a general office and stationery store, was on the first floor. The Tramways War Memorial was placed inside the main entrance.

CPPTD administrative offices Eastney. (National Tramway Museum [Tramway & Railway World])

Eastney Depot trolleybus shed. (National Tramway Museum [Tramway & Railway World])

An official opening ceremony was held on Thursday 21 January 1932 although the Eastney complex had been in use since 1 January 1932. The additional accommodation was long overdue with 117 tramcars and 80 motorbuses in stock whilst the North End repair facilities and machine shop had become inadequate. Henceforth major repairs and reconstruction, other than ordinary running repairs, could be concentrated under one roof at Eastney.

When reconstructed for trolleybus operation there was a single loop running around the circumference of the running shed providing trailing access into the northbound line in Eastney Road at the north east corner and trailing access into the southbound line at the southeast corner. Within this loop there were four disconnected sidings, the southernmost of which could be accessed by a hand-operated facing frog in the Eastney Road southbound line. There were two short stub

(CPPTD Drawing)

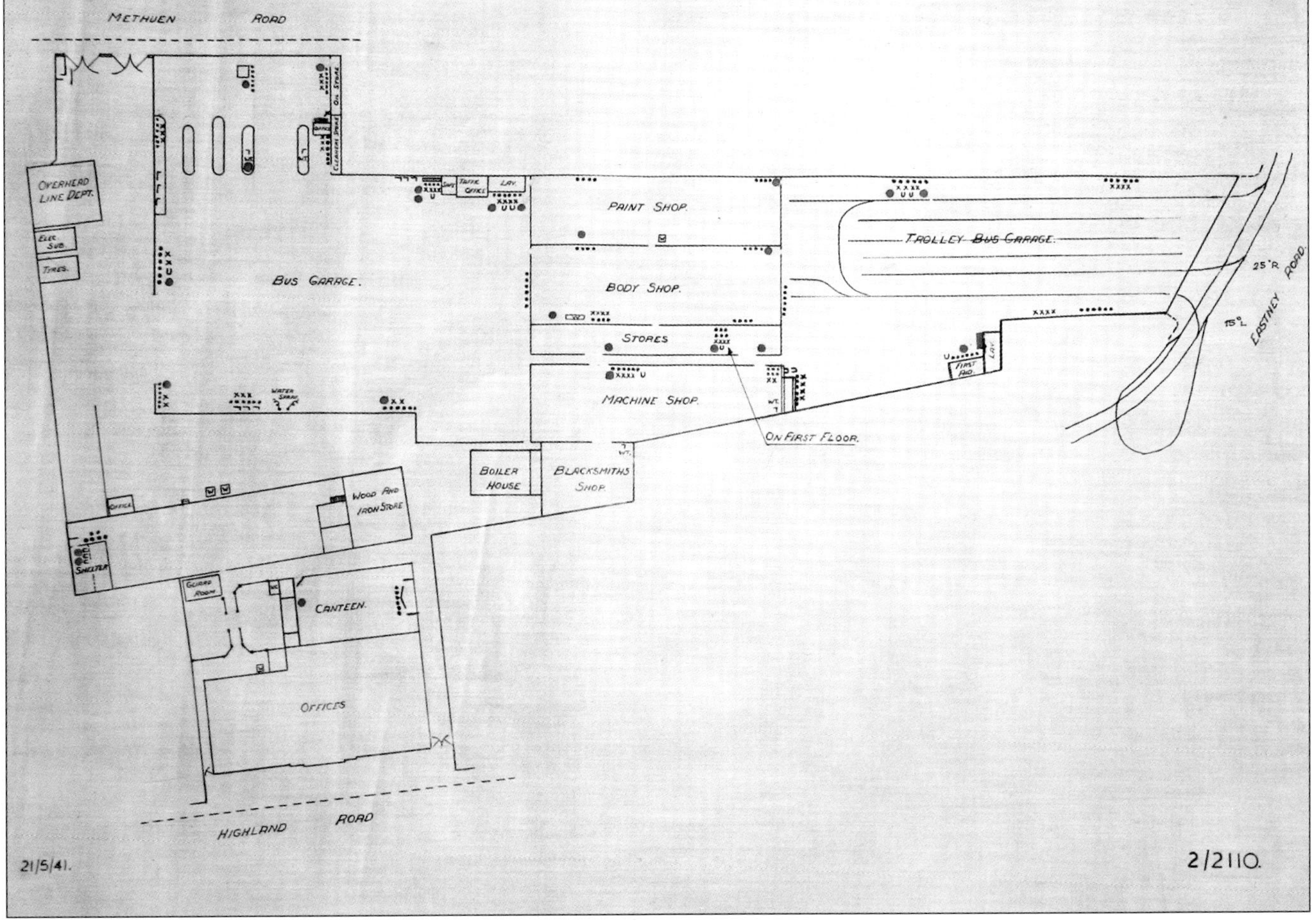

METHUEN ROAD
OVERHEAD LINE DEPT.
ELEC. SUB.
TYRES.
BUS GARAGE.
PAINT SHOP.
BODY SHOP.
STORES
MACHINE SHOP.
TROLLEY BUS GARAGE.
ON FIRST FLOOR.
BOILER HOUSE
BLACKSMITHS SHOP
WOOD AND IRON STORE
SHELTER
CANTEEN.
OFFICES
HIGHLAND ROAD
EASTNEY ROAD
21/5/41.
2/2110.

309 heads the trolleybus line-up at Eastney Depot on 21 July 1963. (T.V. Runnacles)

sidings in the south west corner of the running shed providing access to maintenance pits, and one in the northwest corner of the running shed. There was no wired access to the body shop. Total capacity, considering trolleybuses and motorbuses, was given as 107 in July 1949.

Although a Februat B.4 vehicle washing machine was installed in autumn 1959 it was located in the motorbus garage and not accessible to trolleybuses. It is assumed that trolleybuses continued to be washed manually.

In spring 1960 the trolleybus running shed to the east and the motorbus garage to the west were made into one. This involved relocating the body shop but no change to the trolleybus overhead layout.

Pre-war Eastney had the following trolleybus and service allocation:

Trolleybuses:	25–100	AEC661T – an unknown number of vehicles.
Services:	5, 6, 17, 18	

Post-war Eastney had the following trolleybus and service allocation:

Trolleybuses:	225–300	AEC661T – an unknown number of vehicles.
	301–315	BUT9611T – by mid-1952, 14 vehicles.
Services:	5, 6	jointly operated with North End Depot from May 1952.
	15, 16, 17, 18, 19, 20	jointly operated with North End Depot.

Eastney Depot continued to operate trolleybuses until 27 July 1963, the last day of electric traction in the city. Although withdrawn redundant trolleybuses had been stored in the depot yard since the mid-1950s as the fleet had been gradually reduced, following the final abandonment the last trolleybuses left Eastney within 24 hours. Since then, preserved trolleybuses have been housed in Eastney Depot. Motorbuses were operated until 1986, various modifications to the vehicular access being carried out in the interim, when the depot closed as a direct result of the department's compulsory privatisation.

The running shed and associated works at Eastney were demolished in April–May 1993; however, the undertaking's erstwhile headquarters passed to the Hampshire Constabulary becoming Southsea Police Station. Currently it is shown in the "Local List of Buildings of Architectural or Historical Interest".

Heading north past Eastney Depot on 21 July 1963, 313 having overtaken new OMO Leyland Leopard L1/Weymann motorbus 143 on trolleybus replacement service 15, passes beneath the exit wiring from the south side of the depot building. (T.V. Runnacles)

APPENDIX G

POWER SUPPLY AND GENERATION

One of the claimed economies of converting life-expired electric tramways to trolleybus operation was the continued use of the existing traction power supply system, with limited additional investment. Portsmouth Corporation's trolleybus network was no exception, the current supply arrangements being closely based on that built up in the first decade of the 20th century for the electric tramways. The trolleybuses like the trams before them received Direct Current (DC) electric power through overhead wires suspended above the route and supplied by underground cables from the power station and through local substations. A trolleybus system required two overhead wires, one of positive potential carrying current to the vehicle, and the other of negative potential returning the current and completing the connection. The trolley wire closest to the centre of the road was the positive wire. A tramway uses the running rails for its return connection.

Legislation required that the positive wire was interrupted every half mile, the sections each side of the insulating break being entirely separate from each other but connectable through switchgear placed in a cast iron roadside section pillar or a box mounted on a traction pole. Identical feeder pillars housed the cables from which the mains power supply was connected to the overhead wiring. Equipment in either pillar could be used to cut off power entirely in an emergency. The negative trolley wire was continuous but at points where negative feeder cables were connected the positive and negative feeds came either from the same pillar or there was a separate negative feeder pillar, which to the onlooker, was identical to a positive feeder pillar.

The distance from a power source reduced the available voltage (the so-called "voltage drop") and thus the maximum possible speed of a trolleybus, e.g. a current of 125 amps flowing to and from a trolleybus two miles from the supply point fell from 550 volts to 455 volts (approximate values). The greater rolling resistance of a rubber-tyred trolleybus, particularly over the street surfaces of the period, compared to that of the rail-bound tramcar, enhanced acceleration rates; more powerful traction motors and route extensions together placed greater demands on the power supply. Furthermore the electrical resistance of a negative trolley wire is around fifteen times that of a pair of steel tram rails. Once experience had been gained in operating the trolleybus system it was decided in the late 1930s to add a number of substations and feeders.

A typical trolleybus drawing away from rest will draw about 200 amps of current, which at a line voltage of 550 volts DC equates to 110 kW, but this drops off rapidly as the vehicle overcomes the initial rolling resistance and gains speed. In comparison a typical domestic electric heater element will use 1 kW or a 60–100 watt lamp bulb 0.06–0.1 kW, wattage being the amount of energy used, calculated by multiplying the voltage by the current flowing (in amperes). This is of course variable dependent on the rate of acceleration, any gradient and the passenger load. Pre-war averaged consumption of electricity per trolleybus measured at the substation busbars were considered to be about 2 kWh per mile, almost 50% greater than the trams they replaced. Each vehicle was equipped with an ampere hour meter but both average and individual returns were inconclusive, a monthly average reading from one trolleybus ranging between 1.5 and 1.87 kWh per mile.

Traction power needs increased in late 1950 with the arrival of the 15 BUT 9611Ts having 120hp motors and weighing in at 8 tons 4 cwt (compared with the AEC 661Ts of 1936–37 which were a ton lighter and had 80hp motors) whilst passenger loadings soared. Peak traction power requirements often occurred on a Saturday, then still a working or half working day in many businesses, when around lunchtime there would be a rush home, to the shops or to a major sporting event.

Power stations

Portsmouth Council decided in November 1889 that steps should be taken to generate electricity in the town and in 1892 received permission to construct a 200 volt Alternating Current (AC) single phase system to be supplied from a power station in St Mary Street (to the north west of High Street), Old Portsmouth. The site, which backed on to the Camber, a half-moon shaped inlet from Portsmouth Harbour where today's Isle of Wight vehicular ferries berth, was selected to enable coal for raising steam in the boilers to be easily imported by sea whilst sea water could be used for cooling the engines. The station, employing Ferranti dynamos, was commissioned in June 1894. The initial plant was made up of five Lancashire boilers each having a steaming capacity of 5,000 lb powering low speed engines coupled direct to two 200 kW alternators offering a combined output of 550 kW. A further 200 kW generator was installed by 1897. During the planning stage of the tramways' electrification it became evident that the town's power station would have insufficient capacity to additionally generate traction current whilst it was insufficiently central for the proposed network.

A suitable plot for a Tramways Department power station was found on Vivash Street, later renamed Vivash Road, Fratton, some 150 yards northwest of Fratton Bridge, and thus geographically practically in the middle of the planned system. Construction of the two main buildings, engine room and boiler house, laid out parallel to the street with the offices and stores at the north end, began in October 1900. The tramways power station opened in 1902 and supplied solely DC traction power.

The brick-built power-house was 142ft long, 100ft wide and 50ft high, with adjoining boiler room and a 155ft high chimney stack. There was the usual marble switchboard divided into 12 panels and this remained in use until the end of the trolleybus era. The tramways were fed by 14 feeders, the majority being laid in conduits although some were laid on the solid system, the longest being over 2½ miles in length and the shortest some 130 yards. Power was also supplied to the PHLR.

In 1921, in the aftermath of a coal strike which had seen one boiler at Vivash Road converted to oil-firing, the Council considered a merger of the Electricity and Tramways Departments. A decision was deferred; however, discussions continued aimed at reducing the cost of traction power. In the meantime the generating capacity at St Mary Street had reached 3,300 kW by 1914 and 5,800 kW by 1920. Coincidental with the retirement of the Tramways General Manager, it was decided that responsibility for the tramways traction power supply would pass to the Electric Lighting Committee, current being supplied at 0.8d per unit. Vivash Road power station closed on 30 March 1926 although steam was kept available for some months for use at busy times or in an emergency. In October 1926 the generating and steam plant was sold, and the majority of the buildings were taken over by the Cooperative Society who had a store nearby in Fratton Road. However, one corner was retained as a traction substation supplied from the Electricity Department's 5,600 volt AC network. Two 1,000 kW rotary converters and a 300 kW converter (the latter primarily to supply lighting power to North End Depot at night) were installed. As a DC substation, Vivash Road remained pivotal in the traction supply until the end of trolleybus operation in Portsmouth.

The St Mary Street site was extended in 1927 to accommodate the first 10,000 kW machine which was joined by a second in 1929. Camber Dock was opened that same year and linked to the power station by overhead conveyors across Gunwharf Road making supply by sea easier. Expansion of the plant continued, engulfing the whole area between Gunwharf Road, St George's Road and Warblington Street as Portsmouth increasingly supplied electricity to neighbouring towns and communities in Southern Hampshire. Two 300ft tall chimneys were built, providing one of the most recognisable features of the Portsmouth skyline.

The Electricity (Supply) Act 1926 foresaw a standardisation of the electricity supply throughout the UK through the establishment of a synchronised 132 kV/50Hz AC grid initially involving a collection of local grids, with emergency interlinks, covering most of England and later through a national grid. The implementation was entrusted to the Central Electricity Board (CEB) who began to construct a network of large generating plants and trunk connection to enable the National Grid to start operations in 1935. In April 1934 the Electricity Department entered into an agreement with the CEB whereby they would supply the CEB once its own needs had been met and the CEB would supply Portsmouth in case of breakdown. A year later the CEB took over the *de facto* operation of the Gunwharf Road power station and it became impossible to establish the cost of electrical energy based on the station's running costs.

By May 1935 generating capacity at Gunwharf Road had reached 32,500 kW whilst the boilers could produce 456,000 lbs of steam per hour and were capable of operating at a higher pressure and temperature to serve any extensions to the power station. There was sufficient space to lengthen the turbine house by up to 36ft providing enough space for up to three 30,000 kW turbo alternators across the 60ft wide building. The boiler house had been designed to accommodate six boilers of 50,000 lb per hour steaming capacity but when the first extension had been made it was found possible to install two boilers of 88,000 lb per hour. As the space for the last two boilers remained unoccupied it was decided to install those boilers and one 30,000 kW set immediately.

As the European situation continued to deteriorate in 1938 a trunk cable was laid from Gunwharf Road by way of the Dockyard's own power station to Wymering substation thereby providing an emergency electricity supply both to and from HM Dockyard. The cost was born by the government and proved its worth in 1941. In October 1938 the CEB directed the Electricity Department to install a further 30,000 kW turbo and two boiler units having a maximum continuous evaporating capacity of 150,000 lb per hour, to be operational by September 1941. In fact, capacity reached 92,000 kW with an output of 140 million units by 1939.

On 1 April 1948 the electricity supply industry was nationalised, the British Electricity Authority taking over responsibility for the operation of the nation's power stations and the "Grid", and the supply of electrical energy to the Area Boards. The City of Portsmouth Electricity Department became a sub-area of the Southern Electricity Board. Under the Electricity Act 1957 the Central Electricity Generating Board took over the British Electricity Authority's responsibilities.

In 1955 the Gunwharf Road Power Station generated 476 million units of electricity. At its peak the station was drawing 6.6 million gallons of sea water per hour from the Camber for condensing purposes; its own colliers, *Pompey Power* and *Pompey Light* delivered 172,000 tons of coal a year for the 13 boilers; the main turbine hall when re-built had dimensions of 429ft long, 65ft wide and 48ft high; and the ash bunkers could hold up to 600 tons of dry ash.

Power was supplied from the Gunwharf Power Station until the end of trolleybus operation but it was becoming increasingly outdated. In March 1977 it was disconnected from the grid and demolished between 1981 and 1983 to be replaced by domestic housing.

Feeder cables

A clear division of responsibilities was in place from 1926. The Portsmouth Corporation Electricity Department handled power generation and AC supply to defined substations whereas the Transport Department dealt with the onwards DC distribution to the street feeder pillars and trolleybus overhead wiring. This policy continued until the abandonment of trolleybuses in Portsmouth although the Electricity Department's responsibilities passed to their successors, the Southern Electricity Board, upon nationalisation.

The tramway system was fed from Vivash Road, Fratton, at 550 volts DC by means of 14 underground feeder cables, varying in length between over 2½ miles and about 400ft, insulated with vulcanised bitumen and laid primarily in conduits of vitrified stoneware by Dick, Kerr & Co. although some lengths were laid on the solid system, i.e. in troughing and surrounded by bitumen. The feeder cable network or "copper" (referring to the current-carrying metallic portion) was expanded during the trolleybus era to cope with increased energy demands, new routes and to provide improved redundancy, i.e. the ability to serve individual feeder points from different sources. This involved the provision of additional feeder points, e.g. 311 Fratton Road in September 1934, from existing DC feeder cables as well as the provision of substations (supplied with AC), e.g. St Ronan's Road, each with their own DC feeder cables and feeder points.

Ben Hall presented a paper to the MTTA Annual Conference 23–25 June 1937 in Portsmouth on the topic of converting tramways to trolley vehicle operation in which he admitted that at that time the traction power distribution network was still in transition with just a single source of supply. At that time there were 18 route miles of double track trolleybus lines with 85% of the traffic being carried within 1⅓ miles of Vivash Road. He considered that there was no single traffic centre, the routes being interlaced and intersecting one another, but there

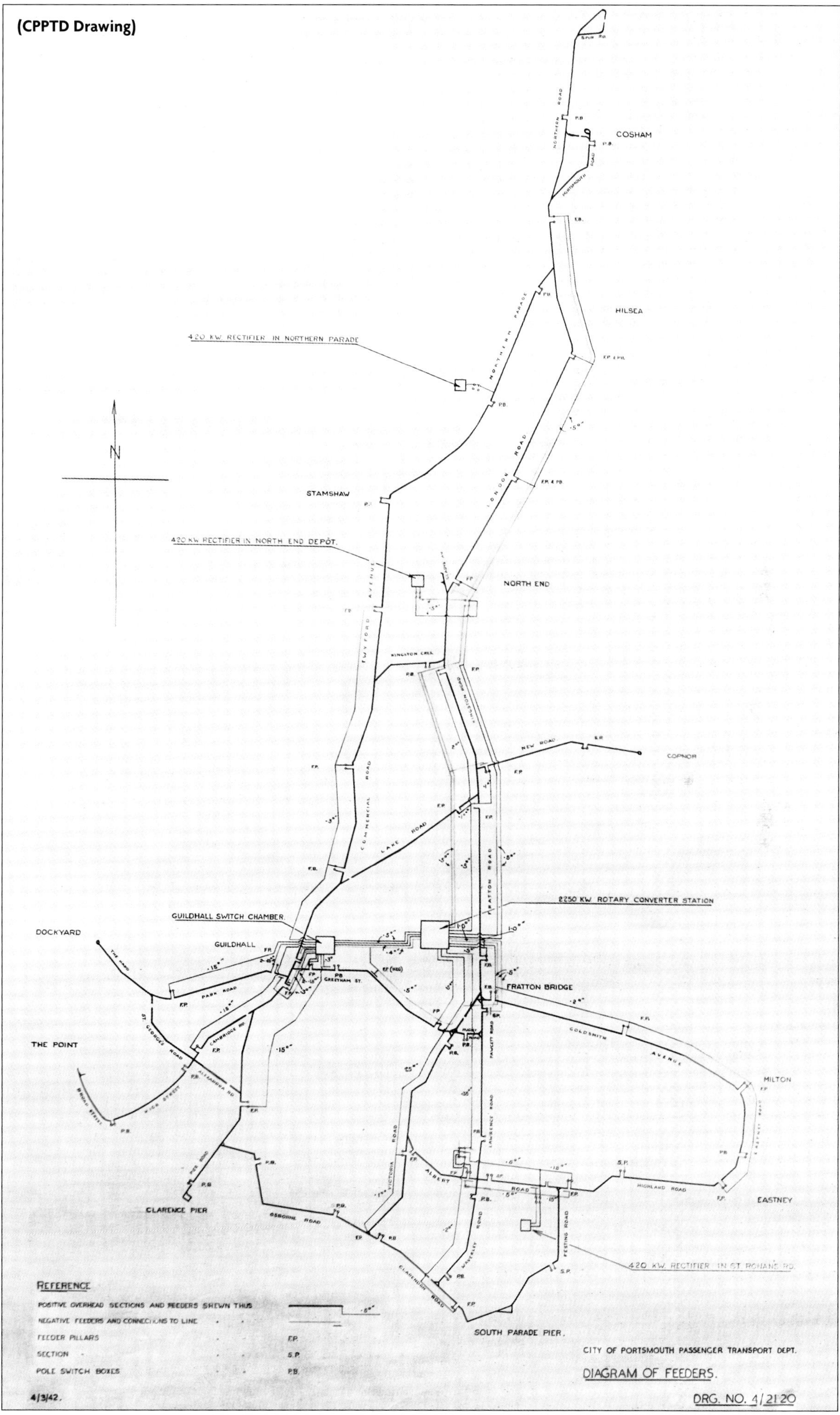
(CPPTD Drawing)
COSHAM
HILSEA
420 KW. RECTIFIER IN NORTHERN PARADE
N
STAMSHAW
420 KW. RECTIFIER IN NORTH END DEPOT.
NORTH END
COPNOR
2250 KW. ROTARY CONVERTER STATION
GUILDHALL SWITCH CHAMBER
DOCKYARD
GUILDHALL
FRATTON BRIDGE
THE POINT
HILTON
EASTNEY
CLARENCE PIER
420 KW. RECTIFIER IN ST. RONANS RD.
SOUTH PARADE PIER.
REFERENCE
POSITIVE OVERHEAD SECTIONS AND FEEDERS SHEWN THUS
NEGATIVE FEEDERS AND CONNECTIONS TO LINE
FEEDER PILLARS F.P.
SECTION S.P.
POLE SWITCH BOXES P.B.
CITY OF PORTSMOUTH PASSENGER TRANSPORT DEPT.
DIAGRAM OF FEEDERS.
4/3/42.
DRG. NO. 4/2120

were three fairly well defined areas, the traffic characteristics of which are as follows:

Area	Route miles	Percentage of traffic	Trolleybuses per route mile
Northern	8 (45%)	39%	3.9
South-western	4 (22%)	26%	5.3
South-eastern	6 (33%)	35%	4.7

This showed that the Vivash Road substation location was no longer ideal and too far from the Guildhall and Dockyard, the busiest district. The bulk of the traffic was in the south of Portsea Island with a comparatively long run to the north.

The existing feeder system had been inherited from the tramways and by 1937 only a temporary adaption to trolleybus needs had been made pending a decision on the installation of at least two new substations in the northern and south-eastern areas of the City. It was estimated that these stations would enable optimum trolleybus operation with very little addition to the existing tramway feeder copper. It was evident that more copper was required for trolleybus operation than trams and as a temporary solution some use of the disused tram track remaining in situ, albeit sometimes covered over, was made by bonding the negative wires to the rails. Such use was, for various reasons, confined to the northern and south-eastern parts of the system, and at that time he estimated that some 6 miles or about one third of the available track was so used. Nonetheless he was aware that the track would not remain permanently and that other power supply solutions were needed.

The voltage drop under a full summer load, based on an average current of 40 amps per trolleybus, revealed maximum drops as follows:

Cosham	120	Guildhall Switch House	60
Copnor	70	Dockyard	140
Eastney	100	Floating Bridge	140
South Parade Pier	70	Clarence Pier	120

The positive voltage drops were easily calculated, however the negative return, due to the rail bonding, was largely a matter of conjecture. The figures above showed that the south-western areas (Clarence Pier, Dockyard, Floating Bridge) suffered considerably, and that it was necessary to increase the copper between Vivash Road substation and the Guildhall Switch Chamber. As the negative cable was only 0.4 sq. in. in diameter at that time, much of the return current was carried by the negative wires along Bradford Road. This indicated the need of a substation near the Guildhall. The situation was confirmed by meter readings from trolleybuses in use after the initial conversion, when some 20 vehicles were in service, and again in 1936 when over 80 were in operation. The greater drop

TABLE B APPROXIMATE FEEDER & DISTRIBUTOR REQUIREMENTS.

SECTION	TRAFFIC		PRESENT TRAMWAY		INCREASE REQUIRED FOR TROLLEY BUSES			TROLLEY BUS REQUIREMENTS FOR NEW PLAN						
	APPROX MILES	Nº BUSES PER MILE PER TRACK	APPROX VOLTS DROP	COPPER TONS	APPROX VOLTS DROP	A COPPER TONS	B COPPER TONS	SUB-STATION	APPROX MILES	Nº BUSES PER MILE PER TRACK	NORMAL DROP	NORMAL TONS	USING RAILS DROP	USING RAILS TONS
COSHAM	3·5	2	120	37·5	100	52·8	44·8	NEW NORTH END SUB.	2	2	50	18·2	47	5·0
DERBY RD FEEDER									0·3		24	4·6	24	4·6
TWYFORD AVE, NORTHWARD									1·5	1·3	62	5·5	62	2·7
KINGSTON CR. FEEDER											21	0·8		0·4
COPNOR & LAKE RD *FEEDER*			70	1·6	60	4·8	4·8	DIRECT FROM FRATTON SUB.			60	4·8		2·8
FRATTON BRIDGE FEEDERS											21	13·7		13·7
EASTNEY *OR MILTON*	2·0	2	100	3·9	50	18·2	13·6		1·0	2	48	2·7	40	0·9
FAWCETT RD	1·0	1			34	1·4	-		·5	2	35	-		
VICTORIA RD	1·0	3	40	2·6	36	3·6	-		·5	4	42	-		
BRADFORD RD	1·0	3	65	2·0	36	3·6	-		·5	4	42	-		
ALBERT RD			50	2·9	29	16·8	16·8	NEW FESTING ROAD SUB.			8	3·6		1·8
HIGHLAND RD } FESTING RD			75	0·4	55	-	-		1·0	2	35	2·7		0·9
WAVERLEY RD	1·0	2	70	1·0	56	2·7	-		1·0	2	35	2·7		0·9
SOUTH PARADE PIER									1·5	2	42	7·3	30	2·8
FRATTON-GUILDHALL *FEED'R*			60	10·4	31	21·8	21·8	FROM FRATTON VIA GUILDHALL SW.			27	21·8	27	16·4
DOCKYARD	1·0	4	140	0·9	71	3·6	-		1·0	4	67	3·6	60	0·9
FLOATING BRIDGE	1·0	3	140	0·7	67	3·6	-		1·0	3	63	3·6	58	0·9
CLARENCE PIER	1·0	3	125	1·1	67	3·6	-		1·0	3	63	3·6	58	0·9
TWYFORD AVE.	2·5	1·6	80	3·5	98	20·9	7·3		1·0	2	54	2·7	46	0·9
TONS WT.				68·5		157·4	109·1					101·9		56·5

A. POS. SIDE ISOLATED IN HALF-MILE SECTIONS.
B. PROVISION FOR CONTINUOUS FEED THROUGH POS. TROLLEYS

(CPPTD)

and consequently lower efficiency led to increased ampere-hour (kWh) meter readings. Although the two observations could not be related to one another quantitatively, the apparent discrepancies in consumption figures are likely to have been primarily due to the distribution system.

There were already plans to install mercury-arc rectifier substations at North End and St Ronan's Road which would reduce these requirements to 100 tons. Bearing in mind that all the calculations were based on optimal power distribution with the maximum summer service, it would have been possible to disconnect the present system from the tram rails and carry on with little alteration to the feeders. On the other hand, it was evident that if the rails could remain and be effectively bonded to the negative trolley wires, only some 56 tons of distributor copper would be required, as shown in the table below. That the copper required could not be more than halved was due to the fact that regulations limited voltage drop in the rails to 7 volts. This figure was not likely to be exceeded in the case of the return to the new substations, but doubt existed in the neighbourhood of the Guildhall and the return to Vivash Road substation. It was thus advisable to retain certain negative feeders, as with the tramways before, and together with the reduced drop between the main substation and the Guildhall, the amount of copper was approximately halved.

Substations

Around the end of the 19th century DC was preferred for electric traction purposes because the speed of direct current motors and thus that of the vehicle could be simply controlled by varying the voltage applied to them. AC, however, was preferable to DC for power distribution and generation because power loss in transmission lines decreases significantly with higher voltages and during the tram and trolleybus era only AC could efficiently be transformed between voltages. Nonetheless electric power for Portsmouth's electric tramways was initially generated and distributed as DC by feeder cables to strategic locations along the routes throughout the town.

Once AC distribution was introduced it was necessary to find a means of converting this energy for use by DC traction motors. Initially a rotary converter, a large, rotating electromechanical device and basically a hybrid of a single winding AC motor and a DC generator (dynamo), was used to convert AC to DC. In Portsmouth, once Gunwharf Road had taken on responsibility for the traction supply, the rotary converters were located at Vivash Road. Thence DC traction current was transmitted in ducted underground cables to the trolleybus route where it would come up into a cast iron feeder pillar:

The complexity and size of rotary converters required regular attention and maintenance by skilled staff, and any loss of the incoming supply would cause protective switchgear to "drop out" requiring a manual restart. Thus from the late 1920s the need for additional or replacement equipment was met by the new technology of the mercury arc rectifier. In a rectifier substation, the incoming high voltage AC supply was first reduced by transforming to the correct input voltage of approximately 400 volts AC, and thence converted to a nominal 550 volts DC for the overhead line, whereas a rotary converter was an AC motor driving a DC generator that produced a DC current. A mercury arc rectifier had an efficiency of about 93–95%, dependent on load, compared to a rotary converter's efficiency of just over 90%.

The operation of mercury arc rectifiers (also known as *Cooper-Hewitt* or *Hewittic* rectifiers after their inventor, the American Peter Cooper Hewitt) was based on the discovery that an electric spark (arc) vaporises mercury contained in a steel tank into a vapour that can only conduct electric current in a single direction between the pool of mercury and a metal anode. AC was fed to the anodes of the octopus-like glass bulbs and an arc was set up between the anodes and a pool of mercury in the bottom of the bulb. Incoming current, alternating at a frequency of 50 cycles a second (the standard frequency of the National Grid supply) flashed 50 times per second between the anodes and the mercury-covered cathodes forming a virtually continuous arc. Multiple anodes were used, fed from a multiple-phase transformer, the arc jumping from the cathode pool to each anode in sequence. The arc glow changed in intensity as the number of trolleybuses moving increased or reduced, or even changed speed. There were three, six or even 12 transformer phases, each feeding one anode. Six and 12-phase systems used star-connected three-phase transformers with inter-phase transformers between the star common connections. In a six-phase rectifier there were six arms on each bulb each connected to a phase of the supply and thus the output was close to being a continuous current but with a slight ripple, that is, the actual voltage waxed and waned by about 20% of the nominal 550 volts DC at a frequency of 300 cycles (hertz). The windowless substation was filled with a ghostly greenish light, wavering slightly, the mercury bubbling constantly in the bulbs.

Construction was either a glass bulb cooled by an external fan or a steel tank of water for very large units with capacities above about 500 amps. To initiate the arc, an igniting electrode was dipped into the pool of mercury using an external electromagnet thereby drawing a small spark to ionise the mercury vapour, initiating the main arc. These substations had virtually no moving parts and made it practicable to open

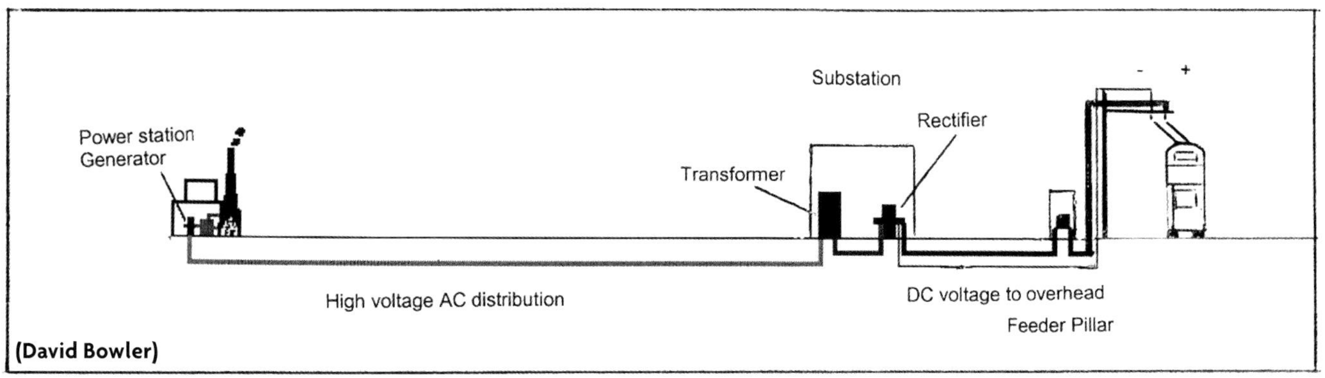

(David Bowler)

small substations along the route wherever power was needed. Control circuits within the mercury arc rectifier ensured that if no current at all was being taken from the overhead, the arc within the rectifier did not die out. Mercury arc rectifiers were used until the end of trolleybus operation.

The traction current was taken from the rectifiers to the switchboard busbars (bars of solid copper running the length of the rear of the board, their heavy rectangular section offering virtually no resistance to the current and enabling connections to the various switches to be solidly bolted to them). From the busbars, feeder cables went out to various parts of the system, each being connected to the busbars through a heavy-duty circuit breaker and isolating switch.

If the current exceeded a set value, its magnetic effect opened the automatic circuit breaker preventing excessive current from entering a cable and damaging it. A broken positive trolley wire would cut off current if the live ends made a good contact with earth; a de-wired trolley head might create a short circuit across the insulators of a frog or crossover, etc. The circuit breakers were equipped with time relays that automatically restored current after a pre-set period. If the fault was still present they re-opened. If this cycle of events occurred three times, on the fourth occasion the circuit breakers stayed open and an alarm sounded. It was then necessary to locate the fault and isolate the feeder concerned until it was safe to restore current.

A single source of traction power had sufficed for Portsmouth's tramways but by the end of 1936 difficulties had arisen in satisfying the increased energy needs of trolleybuses and distant route extensions solely from Vivash Road substation. In January 1937 the Electricity Department started work on providing additional traction power supplies to the northern suburbs and Southsea, these materialising as the North End and St Ronan's Road substations.

By the beginning of 1952, with the trolleybus system at its maximum extent, there were the following five substations in use all supplied by AC connections from Gunwharf Road Power Station:

Copnor Bridge

An additional substation, located between Copnor Road and the railway, immediately opposite the trolleybus turning circle at the east end of New Road, opened on 5 January 1952 to serve the extension along Copnor Road to Green Lane and those foreseen to Hilsea, Milton and Tangier Road.

Traction power was supplied to the following feeders (potential (+/-) shown where known):

- Copnor Road*, immediately to the north of the junction with New Road +/-
- Kingston Cross* +/-

*In conjunction with Vivash Road substation.

Fratton, Vivash Road

The former tramways power station was converted into both an AC domestic and industrial supply substation and a DC traction substation, both belonging to the Electricity Department. The Transport Department was only responsible up to the DC traction distribution board. Initially, Fratton was the sole source of trolleybus traction supply being equipped with two 1,000 kW and one 300 kW rotary converters. The equipment, distribution board and switchgear had no special technical features.

Traction power was supplied to the following feeders (feeder cable number, cable diameter and potential (+/-) shown where known):

- Albert Road*, junction with Lawrence Road (Vivash Road No. 8, 0.35 in.) +/-
- Albert Road Police Station, junction with Victoria Road South (Vivash Road No. 10, 0.25 in.) +
- Blackfriars Bridge, Blackfriars Road -
- Bradford Junction, east end of Blackfriars Road (Vivash Road No. 9, 0.5 in.) +/-
- The Circle, south end of Victoria Road South (Vivash Road No. 10, 0.1 in.) +
- Crystal Palace, north end of Fawcett Road between Fratton Bridge and Rugby Road (Vivash Road No. 13) +/-
- Eastney, south end of Eastney Road at Eastney Depot (Vivash Road No. 14, 0.2 in.) +
- Fratton Road (Vivash Road No. 13, 0.35) +/-
- Frogmore Road, Goldsmith Avenue (Vivash Road No. 14, 0.2 in.) +
- Gladys Avenue*** (Cosham auxiliary feeders 1 & 2, namely Vivash Road Nos 11 & 12, 0.5 in.) +/-
- Goldsmith Avenue, west end of Goldsmith Avenue (Vivash Road No. 14, 0.5 in.) +
- Guildhall Switch Chamber**** (4 feeders)
- Hilsea College** (London Road, 0.5 in.) +/-
- Kingston Cross (Vivash Road No. 7, 0.2 in.) +/-
- Lake Road, Fratton Road, (Vivash Road No. 7) +
- Lake Road Junction, north end of Fratton Road and east end of Lake Road, (Vivash Road No. 13, 0.5 in.) +/-
- Milton, north end of Eastney Road (Vivash Road No. 14, 0.2 in.) +
- New Road, west end (Vivash Road No. 7, 0.1 in.) +/-
- Ophir Road**, London Road, (Vivash Road Nos 11 & 12 auxiliary feeders, 0.5 in.) +/-
- Portsbridge** (Vivash Road Nos 11 & 12 auxiliary feeders, 0.5 in.) +/-
- St. Augustine Road* (Vivash Road No. 8, 0.15 in.) +/-
- St. Ronans Road Substation (Vivash Road No. 8, 0.5 in.) +/-
- Strand (Savoy Hotel)*, south end of Clarendon Road (Vivash Road No. 8, 0.2 in.) +
- Stubbington Avenue, London Road +/-
- Victoria Road South, junction with Albert Road (Vivash Road No. 10)

*In conjunction with St Ronan's Road Substation

**In conjunction with North End Substation

***Vivash Road Nos 11 & 12 which made up Cosham auxiliary feeders 1 & 2, were normally not on load, the switches at Vivash Road were kept out except when the supply from North End and Northern Parade failed.

****The four feeder cables from Vivash Road to the Guildhall Switch Chamber were:

No.1, 0.4 in. diameter
No.2, 0.4 in. diameter
No.3, 0.5 in. diameter
No.4, 0.5 in. diameter

and were distributed onwards from Guildhall Switchboard to supply the following locations:

Cambridge Junction, 0.15 in. diameter +
Charlotte Street, 0.3 in. diameter +
Greetham Street, 0.15 in. diameter +/-
Guildhall (Commercial Road), 0.2 in. diameter

Guildhall (Park Road), 0.15 in. diameter
Gunwharf (Park Road), 0.15 in. diameter +
Kings Road, 0.15 in. diameter +
Stanley Road, Twyford Avenue, 0.3 in. diameter
Sultan Road, Commercial Road, 0.3 in. diameter +

North End

An English Electric 420 kW steel tank cubicle-type mercury arc rectifier, stated to be for a line voltage of 560 volts and costing £1,308, was installed in North End Depot in 1938. The precise location is not known but it was probably adjacent to the yard situated to the south of the running shed entrance.

Traction power was supplied to the following feeders (potential (+/-) shown):

- Gladys Avenue +/-
- Hilsea College, London Road +/-
- Northern Parade, Kipling Road +/-
- Ophir Road, London Road +/-
- Portsbridge, London Road north of Hilsea Bastion junction +/-
- Stubbington Avenue, London Road +/-

All in conjunction with Northern Parade Substation

The feed north of Portsbridge to Cosham Railway Station and 'Red Lion' was solely by means of the overhead line.

Northern Parade

This substation was built on a small plot of land next to the Stamshaw RN Camp on the west side of Northern Parade just south of and opposite the junction with Wyllie Road.

Traction power was supplied to the following feeders (potential (+/-) shown):

- Gladys Avenue +/-
- Hilsea College, London Road +/-
- Northern Parade, Kipling Road +/-
- Ophir Road, London Road +/-
- Portsbridge, London Road north of Hilsea Bastion junction +/-
- Stubbington Avenue, London Road +/-

All in conjunction with North End substation.

St Ronan's Road

An English Electric 420 kW steel tank cubicle-type mercury arc rectifier for the DC traction supply, stated to be for a line voltage of 560 volts and costing £1,308, was installed in the existing Electricity Department substation, a single-story brick building on the east side of St. Ronan's Road just to the north of Old Bridge Road, in late 1938 or early 1939.

Traction power was supplied to the following feeders (potential (+/-) shown):

- Albert Road*, junction with Lawrence Road +/-
- St Augustine Road*, immediately to the east of Festing Road junction +/-
- St Ronan's Road*, Albert Road 120 yards west of Festing Road +/-
- Strand (Savoy Hotel)*, south end of Clarendon Road +

*In conjunction with Vivash Road substation.

This substation was converted into a private dwelling (50 St Ronan's Road) by the addition of a first floor extension, noticeably different from the original surviving construction. The architect won the 2009 Design Aware Best Adaptation Award of the Portsmouth Society.

A rectifier substation would have been added on Havant Road, Drayton, if the extensions on the mainland at Cosham had been built and a feeder cable from the existing Northern Parade substation to London Road, Hilsea laid in a conduit along Wyllie Road and Beechwood Road.

The AEC661T trolleybuses had regenerative braking, which fed current back into the overhead wires and subsequently to the substations. A rotary converter could absorb regenerated energy but a mercury arc rectifier presented, in effect, an open circuit. This resulted in an over voltage in the traction current supply which could damage other equipment connected to the supply (such as burning-out the high tension bulbs on adjacent trolleybuses) and much reduced braking on the trolleybus concerned if no other vehicles were drawing current in the section at the time.

It is not known if Portsmouth's substations were equipped with either ballast resistances, simulating the presence of another trolleybus, and relays to absorb any over-voltage created by vehicles regenerating, or by the use of automatic sectionalising switches at section breaks.

Electrical feeders

There were 39 feeders at the following locations:

Albert Road (i)	On the north side of Albert Road immediately to the east of its junction with Lawrence Road (feeding the junction and Lawrence Road)
Albert Road (ii)	On the north side of Albert Road immediately to the west of its junction with Lawrence Road (feeding Albert Road to the junction with Victoria Road South)
Albert Road Police Station (i)	On the south side of Albert Road immediately to the east of its junction with Victoria Road South
Albert Road Police Station (ii)	On the east side of Victoria Road South immediately to the south of its junction with Albert Road
Bradford Junction	On the south side of Blackfriars Road immediately to the west of Bradford Junction
Cambridge Junction (i)	On the west side of Cambridge Road immediately to the north of the crossroads with St George's Road (moved to St. George's Road upon the abandonment of the Floating Bridge route)
Cambridge Junction (ii)	On the north side of St George's Road immediately to the west of the junction with Cambridge Road (moved from south end of Cambridge Road upon the abandonment of the Floating Bridge route)
Charlotte Street (i)	On the west side of Commercial Road immediately to the north of Lake Road junction
Charlotte Street (ii)	On the west side of Commercial Road at its junction with Thomas Street

Circle (i)	On the west side of Victoria Road South immediately prior to its junction with Clarendon Road (moved to Clarendon Road upon the abandonment of the Victoria Road South route)
Circle (ii)	On the north side of Clarendon Road immediately to the west of its junction with Victoria Road South (moved from the south end of Victoria Road South upon the abandonment of that route)
Copnor Road	On the east side of Copnor Road immediately to the north of its junction with New Road East
Crystal Palace	On the east side of Fawcett Road at its north end between Fratton Bridge and Rugby Road
Eastney	On the west side of Eastney Road immediately to the south of the entrance to Eastney Depot
Fratton Road, Fratton Grove	On the east side of Fratton Road to the north of Fratton Grove
Frogmore Road	On the south side of Goldsmith Avenue opposite its junction with Frogmore Road
Gladys Avenue	On the east side of Gladys Avenue opposite North End Depot
Goldsmith Avenue	On the south side of Goldsmith Avenue at its west end immediately prior to the Fratton Bridge junction
Greetham Street	On the south side of Greetham Street a short distance east of Guildhall Square
Guildhall	On south side of Park Road to the west of Guildhall Square
Guildhall	On the west side of Commercial Road immediately to the south of Guildhall Square
Guildhall	On the west side of Guildhall Square immediately to the south of the Portsmouth and Southsea Station railway bridge
Gunwharf	On the south side of Park Road at its south end immediately prior to junction with Gunwharf Road
Hilsea College	On the west side of London Road opposite the junction with Old London Road
Kings Road	On the west side of Kings Terrace to the south of the junction with Alexandra Road
Kingston Cross	On the east side of Kingston Road immediately to the south of the junction with Kingston Crescent
Lake Road, Fratton Road	On the south side of Lake Road immediately to the west of its junction with Fratton Road
Lake Road Junction	On the west side of Fratton Road (outside 311 Fratton Road) immediately to the south of its junction with Lake Road
Milton	On the west side of Eastney Road at its north end by the junction with Essex Road
New Road	On the north side of New Road immediately to the east of the junction with Kingston Road
Northern Parade, Kipling Road	On the east side of Northern Parade at its junction with Kipling Road
Ophir Road	On the east side of London Road opposite its junction with Ophir Road
Portsbridge	On the west side of London Road by the entrance to Hilsea Lido some 250 yards north of Hilsea Bastion junction
St Augustine Road	On the north side of Highland Road immediately to the east of Festing Road junction
Stanley Road	On the west side of Twyford Avenue at its junction with Stanley Road
Strand (Savoy Hotel)	On the east side of Clarendon Road at its southern end to the north of the Savoy Hotel
Stubbington Avenue	On the east side of London Road at its junction with Stubbington Avenue, North End
Sultan Road	On the east side of Commercial Road at the junction with Sultan Road
Victoria Road South	Junction with Albert Road

It will be noted that there was solely one feeder point, at Copnor Bridge, immediately to the north of the junction with New Road, on the 1952 extension along Copnor Road and Milton Road. It was 1¾ miles to the next feeder at Portsbridge and about 1 mile to Milton 'White House' to the south. Rather long distances although not unmanageable in view of the combined frequency at peak hours on the busiest section between New Road and Chichester Road being a trolleybus every 3 minutes. Nonetheless former trolleybus driver Gordon Ferguson recalls that there were no sections of route in Portsmouth considered to be lacking in power.

Section insulators

A section insulator was an electrical break in the trolley wire that electrically isolated one section and its feeder from an adjoining section and its feeder. The resultant length of wire could be isolated by a section switch (contained in a feeder pillar, section pillar or pole box). The insulation on crossings at junctions was not used to provide insulation between positive overhead sections.

Legislation required that the electrical continuity of the positive wire be broken at least every half-mile by a switch that permitted the overhead wires on either side of the section insulator to be isolated in an emergency or connected to each other (the normal case). The same isolation equipment could

Having just passed beneath the St Augustine Road feeder in Highland Road, trolleybus 239 continues east around the Eastney "circle" and then back to Alexandra Park on a service 19 journey. (David Bowler collection [photographer's name not recorded])

be found in feeder and section pillars which could also fulfil the same functionality but were more expensive items than a less substantial pole-mounted switch box. Such boxes had to be inaccessible to pedestrians and were mounted 8–10ft off the ground on an adjacent traction pole. At these points a short length of the positive running wire was replaced by a non-conductive material and the electrical current carried over this break by a "bridge" that was linked by cables to the pillar or box. The opening of this switch isolated a section electrically.

The use of automatic sectionalising switches linking rectifier-fed sections with rotary converter-fed sections prevented overloads. Section ends could be identified by a cast iron pillar on the pavement nearby. The purpose of the isolation equipment inside, indistinguishable to the passer-by, was always intended to allow the overhead wires on either side of the section insulator to be isolated or fed from either end of the feeder cable. The same isolation equipment could be found in feeder pillars which could also fulfil the same functionality.

Section Insulators were situated at the following locations:

Albert Road, Festing Road junction
Alexandra Road
Pier Road
Cambridge Road, Commercial Road
Chichester Road, precise location not known
The Circle, Clarendon Road
Clarendon Road
Clarendon Road, Palmerston Road
Copnor Road, 'Coach and Horses' Hilsea
Copnor Road, Copythorne Road
Copnor Road, RAOC Rugby Camp
Copnor Road, Domum Road
Cosham, CPPTD private road
Eastney Road
Gladys Avenue, northern end
Gunwharf, St George's Road
The Hard, 'Keppel's Head'
Highland Road, Winter Road
Hilsea College, London Road
Kingston Crescent
Kipling Road, Northern Parade
Lake Road, Commercial Road
Lawrence Road, Norman Road
Milton Road, Hayling Avenue
Milton Road, Priorsdean Avenue
Milton Road, Velder Avenue
Milton 'White Horse', Gisor Road
New Road 'The Mermaid'
Northern Parade, Oakwood Road
Northern Road railway bridge
Northern Road, Spur Road
Ophir Road, London Road
Oyster Street, High Street
Portsmouth Road, Cosham
St Helens Parade, Cumberland House
Tipner, north end of Twyford Avenue
Victoria Road North, Bradford Junction north
Victoria Road North, Bradford Junction south
Waverley Road North
Waverley Road, The Strand
Western Parade, Southsea Terrace

Section pillars

Externally identical to feeder pillars, section pillars contained the necessary switches to connect or disconnect in various permutations the overhead trolley wires of adjacent sections fed from different sources. There was no connection to the underground feeder cables.

Section pillars were located at the following places:

Cumberland House, St Helens Parade
Crystal Palace, Fawcett Road (replaced with positive and negative feeder)
Highland Road, Winter Road (replaced with section insulator)
Hilsea 'Coach & Horses'
Milton 'White House', Milton Road immediately to the north of the junction with Goldsmith Avenue
'The Mermaid', east end of New Road, Copnor Bridge
Tipner, north end of Twyford Avenue (replaced with section insulator)

No limit was laid down on the number of trolleybuses which could operate on a given section at any one time but if several vehicles were all starting away at the same time, the line voltage fell and drivers learned to use their common sense. The vehicles' controls were designed to function at half the normal line voltage but problems developed if this fell below 400 volts, a common occurrence at peak hours. At times when few trolleybuses were operating, line voltage was accordingly high and high speeds could be obtained.

Key to Reference Codes used on Feeders and Sections Map

Ref. on map	Name and location	Side of road	Feeder Pillar +/-, +, -	Fed from	Direction(s) of Feed	Pole Switch Box +	Negative Feed -	Section Pillar +/-	Section Break	Balancing Cable	Notes
See Footnote 1	*See Footnote 2*	*See Footnote 3*		*See Footnote 4*	*See Footnote 5*				*See Footnote 6*		
A 1	**Guildhall** (south of Guildhall Square)	W	Yes	5	S	Yes	Yes		Yes		
A 2	**Greetham Street** (east of Guildhall Square)	S	Yes	3 & 9	E&W	Yes	Yes		Yes		
A 3	**Guildhall**, Railway Bridge	W	Yes	4	N				Yes		Removed post-war, possibly 1953 or 1957, when the feed at location AE 1 was moved.
AD 1	**Park Road**, Anglesea Road									Yes	
AD 2	**Guildhall**, Park Road	S	Yes	5	W	Yes	Yes		Yes		
AE 1	**CHARLOTTE ST.**, Commercial Road at Lake Road	W	Yes	4	N&S				Yes		Removed post-war, possibly 1953 or 1957, and replaced with the feed at location AE 2.
AE 2	**CHARLOTTE ST.**, Commercial Road at Thomas St	W	Yes	4	N&S				Yes		Replaced feeder pillars at locations A 3 and AE 1, possibly to make space (at AE 1) for bus stop shelters outside BHS store.
AE 3	**Lake Road**, Commercial Road								Yes		
AE 4	**SULTAN RD.**, Commercial Road	E	Yes	4	N&S				Yes		
AE 5	**STANLEY ROAD**, Twyford Avenue	W	Yes	4	N&S				Yes		
AE 6	**TIPNER**, Twyford Avenue	?						Yes	Yes		
AE 7	**Kipling Road**, Northern Parade	E				Yes			Yes		
AE 8	**NORTHERN PARADE**, Kipling Road	E	Yes	NP	N&S						
AE 9	**Northern Parade**, Oakwood Road	E				Yes			Yes		
AE 10	**Northern Parade**, Oakwood Road									Yes	
AF 1	**PIER ROAD**								Yes		
AF 2	**KINGS ROAD**, Kings Terrace	W	Yes	5	N&S				Yes		
AG 1	**Alexandra Road**, Kings Road								Yes		
AG 2	**Cambridge Road**, Commercial Road								Yes		Removed upon the abandonment of the Floating Bridge route.
AG 3	**CAMBRIDGE JUNC.**, Cambridge Road	W	Yes	5	N&S				Yes		Moved to location AG 6 when Floating Bridge route abandoned.

Ref. on map	Name and location	Side of road	Feeder Pillar +/-, +, -	Fed from	Direction(s) of Feed	Pole Switch Box +	Negative Feed -	Section Pillar +/-	Section Break	Balancing Cable	Notes
See Foot-note 1	*See Footnote 2*	*See Foot-note 3*		*See Foot-note 4*	*See Foot-note 5*				*See Foot-note 6*		
AG 4	**Cambridge Junction**, St. Georges Road	N	Yes	5	E&W						Located at AG 5 prior to Floating Bridge route abandonment.
AG 5	**OYSTER STREET**, High Street								Yes	Yes	Removed upon the abandonment of the Floating Bridge route.
AG 6	**Gunwharf**, St. Georges Road								Yes		
AH 1	**The Hard**, 'Keppel's Head'								Yes		On eastbound line only.
AH 2	**GUNWHARF**, south end Park Road	S	Yes	5	W				Yes		
C 1	**COACH & HORSES**, Copnor Road	N						Yes	Yes		
C 2	**RUGBY CAMP**, RAOC Copnor Road	W				Yes			Yes		
C 3	**DOMUM ROAD**, Copnor Road	W				Yes			Yes		
C 4	**COPYTHORNE ROAD**, Copnor Road	E				Yes			Yes		
C 5	**NEW ROAD EAST**, Copnor Road	E	Yes	7	N&S				Yes		
C 6	**Copnor Bridge**, opposite New Road	E					Yes				
C 7	**HAYLING AVENUE**, Milton Road	W				Yes			Yes		
C 8	**PRIORSDEAN AVENUE**, Milton Road	W				Yes			Yes		
C 9	**VELDER AVENUE**, Milton Road	E				Yes			Yes		
C 10	**WHITE HOUSE** Milton, Gisor Avenue	W						Yes	Yes		
CH 1	**CHICHESTER ROAD**	S				Yes			Yes		Details and location on Chichester Road not known.
GA 1	**LAKE RD.**, Fratton Road junction	S	Yes	7	S				Yes		
GB 1	**NEW RD.** (western end)	N	Yes	7	E		Yes		Yes		Also shown as NEW RD. JUNC.
GB 2	**THE MERMAID**, New Road	N						Yes	Yes		
GC 1	**Kingston Crescent** (mid-way)	S				Yes			Yes		
GC 2	**KINGSTON CROSS**, Kingston Road	E	Yes	7	N		Yes		Yes		
GL 1	**GLADYS AVE. N.** (northern end)	?				Yes			Yes		
GL 2	**GLADYS AVENUE**, North End Depot	E	Yes	7 & NP	N&S		Yes		Yes		Prior to the Gladys Ave extension the North End Depot feed was from Vivash Rd. No. 7 and thereafter from Northern Parade.

Ref. on map	Name and location	Side of road	Feeder Pillar +/-, +, -	Fed from	Direction(s) of Feed	Pole Switch Box +	Negative Feed -	Section Pillar +/-	Section Break	Balancing Cable	Notes
See Foot-note 1	*See Footnote 2*	*See Foot-note 3*		*See Foot-note 4*	*See Foot-note 5*				*See Foot-note 6*		
H 1	**Lawrence Road**, Norman Road	E				Yes			Yes		
HA 1	**Albert Road**, Festing Road	N	Yes	8	W&S				Yes		HA 1 was in position prior to installation of Festing Road overhead junction (1936) and feeder at location HE1.
HA 2	**Albert Road**, Festing Road	S				Yes			Yes		HA 2 replaced HA 1 after installation of Festing Road overhead junction (1936) and feeder at location HE1.
HA 3	**ST. RONAN'S ROAD**, Albert Road	S					Yes			Yes	
HA 4	**ALBERT RD.**, Lawrence Road east side	N	Yes	8	W				Yes		
HB 1	**STRAND**, Clarendon Road (north of Savoy Hotel)	E	Yes	8	E&W				Yes		Also shown as NORTH OF SAVOY HOTEL
HB 2	**Clarendon Road**, The Strand								Yes		
HB 3	**The Circle**, east of Victoria Road South	N				Yes			Yes		
HC 1	**Waverley Road**, south of Albert Road	E				Yes			Yes		
HC 2	**Waverley Road**, The Strand	E				Yes			Yes		
HD 1	**CUMBERLAND HOUSE**, St Helens Parade	S						Yes	Yes		
HE 1	**ST. AUGUSTINE RD.**, Highland Road	N	Yes	8	E&W		Yes		Yes		
M 1	**ALBERT RD. POLICE STATION**, Victoria Rd. South	E	Yes	10	S				Yes		
M 2	**CIRCLE**, Victoria Road South	W	Yes	10	N,E &W				Yes		See also M 3 and MA 1.
M 3	**The Circle**, west of Victoria Road South	N	Yes	10	E&W						The M 2 feed was relocated to immediately west of Victoria Road South after the abandonment of that route and the junction.
MA 1	**Clarendon Road**, east of Palmerston Road	N				Yes			Yes		Possibly removed when M 2 feeder at The Circle was resited to location M 3.
MA 2	**Western Parade**, Southsea Terrace	E						Yes	Yes		Until after 1943 this Section Pillar was only a Section Break.
MB 1	**ALBERT RD.**, Lawrence Road west side	N	Yes	8	W		Yes		Yes		
MB 2	**ALBERT RD. POLICE STATION**, west end Albert Rd	S	Yes	8	E				Yes		

Ref. on map	Name and location	Side of road	Feeder Pillar +/-, +, -	Fed from	Direction(s) of Feed	Pole Switch Box +	Negative Feed -	Section Pillar +/-	Section Break	Balancing Cable	Notes
See Footnote 1	*See Footnote 2*	*See Footnote 3*		*See Footnote 4*	*See Footnote 5*				*See Footnote 6*		
N 1	**Cosham Compound** (Cosham Railway Station)									Yes	Removed when Cosham Compound rebuilt in 1948.
N 2	**Cosham**, CPPTD Private Road								Yes		N 2 appears to have been added in 1956 when the southbound line in Northern Road was dismantled but seems to have been "bridged" in the latter days of trolleybus operation, possibly due to the removal of the Portsmouth Road (N 3) section break.
N 3	**Portsmouth Road**, north of Hawthorn Crescent	E				Yes			Yes		
N 4	**PORTSBRIDGE**, Hilsea Lido	W	Yes	NP	N&S		Yes		Yes		
N 5	**HILSEA COLLEGE**, London Road	W	Yes	NP	N&S					Yes	Northern feed.
N 6	**HILSEA COLLEGE**, London Road	W				Yes			Yes		Southern feed. Located one traction pole south of N 5.
N 7	**OPHIR RD.**, London Road	W	Yes	NP	N&S		Yes				Northern feed.
N 8	**OPHIR RD.**, London Road	W				Yes			Yes		Southern feed. Located one traction pole south of N 7.
N 9	**STUBBINGTON AV.**, London Road, North End	E	Yes	NP	N&S		Yes		Yes		Prior to the 1953 overhead reconstruction there were positive and negative feeds, and a section break at this location. This was changed to a single positive feed with section break. The Gladys Avenue Feeder Pillar (GL 2) was connected to this pillar.
	STUBBINGTON AV., London Road, North End	E	Yes	NP	N				Yes		
O 1	**Northern Road**, south of Spur Road								Yes		On Southbound line only.
O 2	**Northern Road**, north of railway bridge	W				Yes			Yes		
R 1	**BLACKFRIARS BRIDGE**, Blackfriars Road	W					Yes				
R 2	**BRADFORD JUNC.**, Bradford Road									Yes	
R 3	**BRADFORD JUNC.**, Bradford Road	S	Yes	9	E&W		Yes		Yes		
R 4	**VICTORIA ROAD NORTH**, south of Bradford Junc.	E				Yes			Yes		
R 5	**Victoria Road North**, south of Elm Grove	?				Yes			Yes		
R 6	**Rugby Road**	?					Yes			Yes	

Ref. on map	Name and location	Side of road	Feeder Pillar +/-, +, -	Fed from	Direction(s) of Feed	Pole Switch Box +	Negative Feed -	Section Pillar +/-	Section Break	Balancing Cable	Notes
See Foot-note 1	*See Footnote 2*	*See Foot-note 3*		*See Foot-note 4*	*See Foot-note 5*				*See Foot-note 6*		
S 1	**LAKE RD. JUNC.**, Fratton Road	W	Yes	13	N		Yes		Yes		
S 2	**FRATTON RD.**, Fratton Grove	E	Yes	13	N&S		Yes		Yes		
S 3	**Victoria Road North**, north of Bradford Junct.									Yes	
S 4	**Victoria Road North**, north of Bradford Junct.								Yes		
T 1	**GOLDSMITH AV.**, west end	S	Yes	14	E				Yes		
T 2	**Goldsmith Avenue**, Heidelburg Road									Yes	
T 3	**FROGMORE RD.**, Goldsmith Avenue	S	Yes	14	E&W				Yes		
TA 4	**MILTON**, Essex Road	W	Yes	14	N&S				Yes		
TA 5	**Eastney Road**					Yes			Yes		
TA 6	**EASTNEY**, south of Eastney Depot	W	Yes	14	N&S				Yes		Also fed Eastney Depot
TA 7	**Highland Road**, Winter Road	N						Yes	Yes		Until after 1943 this Section Pillar was only a Section Break.
TB 1	**CRYSTAL PALACE**, Fawcett Road	E	Yes	13	N&S		Yes		Yes		

Footnotes

Shading indicates "No"

1 The twin alpha codes relate to the CPPTD traction pole numbering system. The reference numbers relate solely to the Feeders and Sections Map. They do not represent pole numbers and were not used in any official capacity.

2 Names shown in CAPITALS were used within CPPTD to locate and map equipment. The precise wording on CPPTD plans has been used where known. *Additional information* shown in normal font is included to aid location on the maps.

3 Location of Piller on pavement or Box on pole:
N = North, E = East, W = West, S = South, ? = Not known

4 3 = Vivash Road No 3
4 = Vivash Road No 4
5 = Vivash Road No 5
7 = Vivash Road No 7 with Copnor Bridge Substation
8 = Vivash Road No 8 with St Ronan's Road Substation
9 = Vivash Road No 9
10 = Vivash Road No 10
13 = Vivash Road No 13
14 = Vivash Road No 14
NP = Combined Gladys Avenue and Northern Parade Substations

5 For each Feeder Pillar, the direction for which power was provided is shown by a letter / letters (Where a Section Break was included this might not be for both directions): N = North, E = East, W = West, S = South, ? = Not known

6 Section Breaks located close to a return loop in the overhead (e.g. The Hard) were provided only on one side of the road. Feeder Pillars were also Section Breaks (Section Insulators) except where there was a nearby Pole Box.

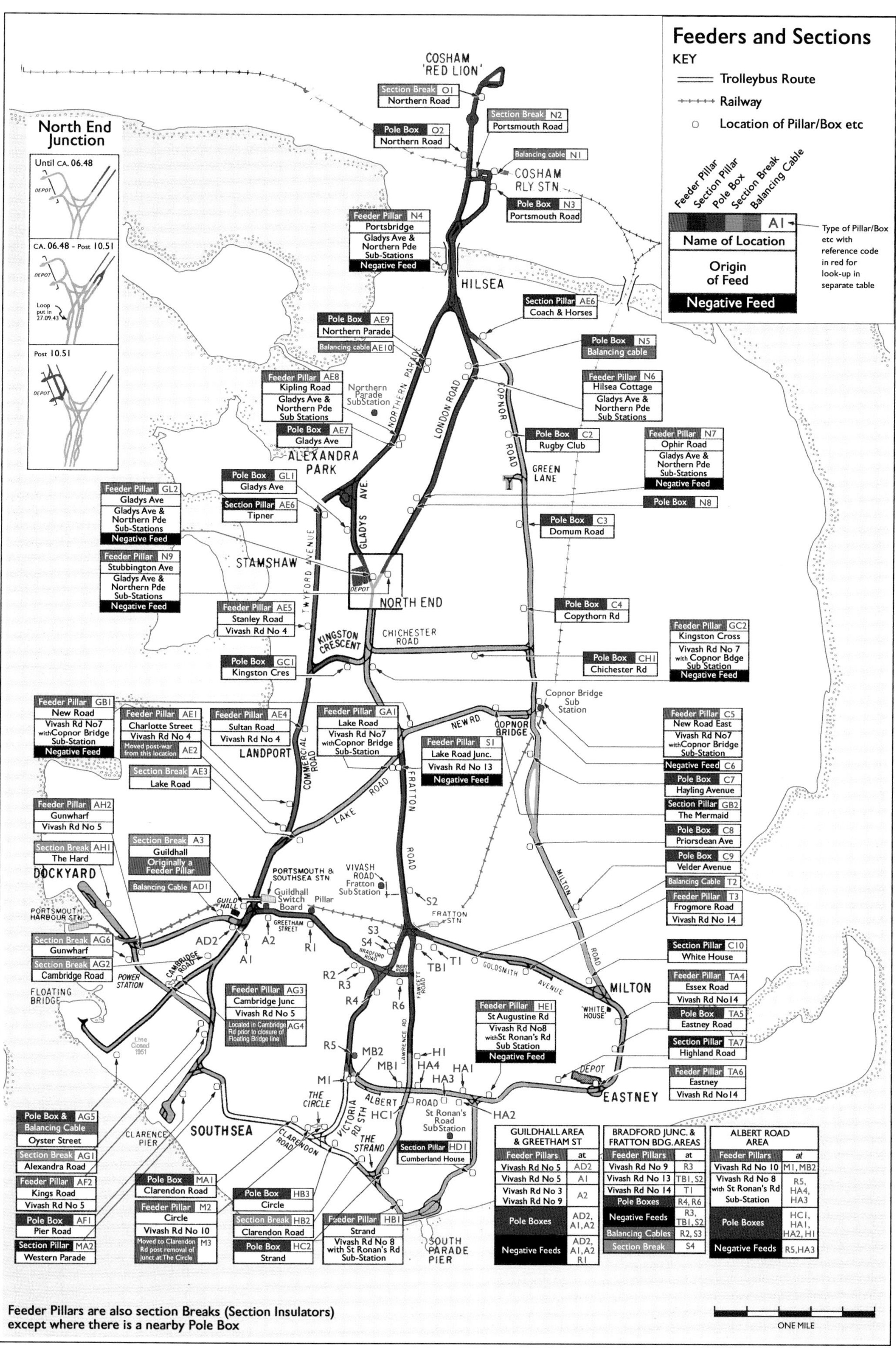

GUILDHALL AREA & GREETHAM ST	
Feeder Pillars	at
Vivash Rd No 5	AD2
Vivash Rd No 5	A1
Vivash Rd No 3 Vivash Rd No 9	A2
Pole Boxes	AD2, A1,A2
Negative Feeds	AD2, A1,A2 R1

BRADFORD JUNC. & FRATTON BDG. AREAS	
Feeder Pillars	at
Vivash Rd No 9	R3
Vivash Rd No 13	TB1, S2
Vivash Rd No 14	T1
Pole Boxes	R4, R6
Negative Feeds	R3, TB1, S2
Balancing Cables	R2, S3
Section Break	S4

ALBERT ROAD AREA	
Feeder Pillars	at
Vivash Rd No 10	M1, MB2
Vivash Rd No 8 with St Ronan's Rd Sub-Station	R5, HA4, HA3
Pole Boxes	HC1, HA1, HA2, H1
Negative Feeds	R5,HA3

Feeder Pillars are also section Breaks (Section Insulators) except where there is a nearby Pole Box

Regeneration

The wisdom of equipping the majority of Portsmouth's trolleybuses with regenerative braking has frequently been questioned considering the absence of any real gradients on the system. Ben Hall also addressed this at the 1937 MTTA Conference.

He prepared a simplified speed-time curve, assuming a constant rate of acceleration and braking up to and from a steady maximum speed, i.e. ignoring coasting and traffic conditions, the acceleration and maintenance of a steady speed being expressed in kWh units. The analysis assumed a 40% conversion efficiency by the traction motor on the rheostats and 82% off the rheostats, the latter figure applying whether the trolleybus was motoring or regenerating. A scheduled speed of 10 mph was assumed over a distance of ⅛ mile, corresponding to 8 stops a mile, each of 6 seconds duration. Acceleration and braking were taken at 3 mph per second (4.4ft per sec^2) and to allow for the effect of rotating parts, figures of 108 lb and 98 lb per ton per 1 mph per second were used for accelerating and braking respectively.

Consumption varied with the scheduled speed maintained, whilst the amount of regenerated energy depended upon the difference between the maximum speed attained and the minimum speed down to which regenerative braking was effective. The maximum speed, however, was not only dictated by the scheduled speed, but in practice was largely influenced by traffic conditions and the manner of driving. The minimum speed was a matter of design, but in the case of a compound motor was necessarily higher than the speed off the rheostats when motoring.

The analyses of energy consumption for various scheduled speeds (above) illustrated the relationship of the various factors through the following points:

(1) The degree of regeneration rose rapidly with increased scheduled speed.

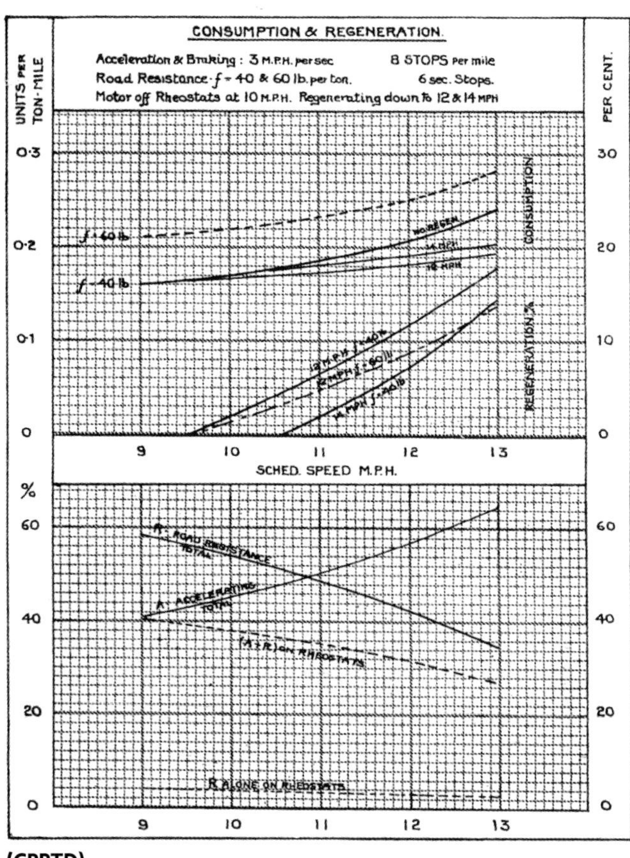

(CPPTD)

(2) Field control with a low full-field speed characteristic was desirable in order to get off the rheostats as quickly as possible.

(3) The above characteristics were also desirable for compound wound regenerative motors, the full-field speed curve being as flat as possible to allow a low minimum speed of effective braking.

(4) The analysis shown in the lower part of the table made it evident that any variation of road resistance had a greater effect at lower schedule speeds than at the higher ones where the period of acceleration predominated. During acceleration the portion due to road resistance was only a few per cent, so that increasing the road resistance from 40 to 60 lbs per ton increased consumption relatively more at a 9mph than at a 13 mph schedule, as shown by the dotted consumption curve.

(5) On the other hand during regeneration the resistance component of the energy returned was more or less constant at 13% irrespective of schedule speed. The net result of a higher road resistance on the percentage regeneration was shown by the dotted line.

(6) The main conclusion was that only a limited and variable amount of regeneration could be anticipated at scheduled speeds of 10–11 mph with more favourable results from increased scheduled speeds.

The other advantages of regeneration such as smoother braking, less wear and tear on brake linings, increased flexibility on running notches, and improvement on line voltage were available throughout the range of schedule speeds. In practice, other factors such as auxiliary equipment further influenced the results. A 1 kW motor generator set, at 60% efficiency, and a ¾hp compressor at 50% efficiency, required some 2.8 kW, but not continuously. This increased consumption by up to 3%. Due to the very short time during which regeneration took place, the effect of the auxiliaries, if operating, was negligible on the regenerated energy. Road resistance, varying from 60 to 90 lb per ton for macadam surfaces, and corners also had an influence. The curves in the table showed that an increase of 50% in the road resistance put up consumption by 18 to 32% according to schedule speed. The duration of a stop varied; the effect of a longer time on a given schedule was to increase consumption

The ampere-hour meters in the trolleybus driver's cab were only accurate within 5% and as they were calibrated for a fixed voltage their readings were liable to be high when recording motoring current and low when current was being returned. Moreover, their readings were subject to the line's loading conditions and this could vary greatly from moment to moment. In particular the voltage during regeneration was liable to fluctuate widely according to whether there was a load, i.e. other trolleybuses, inthe vicinity to absorb the energy. Such conditions could reduce regeneration by some 2%.

In conclusion Mr Hall pointed out that as so many different factors could influence a trolleybus journey it was not surprising that the quantitative results of regeneration were apparently small at moderate speeds. He had, however, endeavoured to show that results in normal service improved appreciably with the maintenance of higher schedule speeds. Substantial economies in returned current are increasingly difficult to obtain but combined with the other advantages even small savings due to regeneration were welcome.

APPENDIX H

OVERHEAD WIRING

The trolleybus overhead equipment installed in Spring 1934 for the initial, experimental conversion of the Southsea South Parade Pier – Cosham Railway Station route, just under 5 miles long, was erected by Clough, Smith & Co. Ltd., London SW1, specialist overhead line contractors. The extension beyond Southsea to Alexandra Park, Twyford Avenue, was constructed by Estler Bros, Victoria Docks, London E16. However the remaining tramway conversions and the Portsbridge – Cosham 'Red Lion' extension were again entrusted to Clough, Smith Ltd. The limited amount of overhead construction work thereafter was carried out entirely by the undertaking's own Overhead Line Department.

The trolleybuses were indeed the direct successors of their rail-bound predecessors in that they continued to use many items of tramway overhead equipment; in fact this was one of the economic arguments made for replacing trams with railless electric traction. The first electric tramway overhead equipment had been supplied and erected by Messrs. Macartney, McElroy & Co., of London, under a contract awarded on 18 December 1900. The trolley wire suspension was arranged to suit tramcars with fixed trolley heads, i.e. the wire was placed centrally over the track, and employed span wires in wide thoroughfares and bracket arms, predominantly of the single-arm type elsewhere. Many of these bracket arms retained ornate scrollwork until the conversion to trolleybus operation whilst the ornate cast bases bearing the coat of arms remained until the trolleybus era closed. The initial electric tramway overhead work featured double trolley wire throughout using OO B and S gauge hard drawn round copper wire with a breaking strain of 24 tons per square inch supplied in half mile sections and supported by galvanised steel span wires. However, by the early 1930s British Standard 23 trolley wire, size 3/0 or 4/0 was in use.

The conductor wires used by the trolleybuses were supported by cast metal ears consisting of two side plates which, by tightening clamping screws, gripped the lobe on top of the grooved wire. The positive wire was hung on the right in the direction of travel and the negative wire on the left for safety reasons, the positive wire suspension ears being initially painted red although this practice was discontinued later. On straight portions of overhead wiring these mechanical ears were 12in. long but post-war curved ears up to 24in. long, which tended to conform to the curvature under line tension thus avoiding acute changes in direction, were used, e.g. in Portsmouth Road, Cosham. Six-inch ears, originally intended solely to separate a span wire crossing above but not supporting a trolley wire, e.g. a frog anchor from a traction pole on the opposite side of the road that first diagonally crossed the pair of wires forming the route in the opposite direction, were also used amongst special work.

A supporting boss located midway along the length of the ear retained a screw-in moulded compound insulator, widely known as an "insulated bolt", which was itself retained in the hanger. Portsmouth also commissioned a "double pull-off" hanger with different length legs intended to compensate for the angle between the supporting span wire and the trolley wires.

By the mid-1930s a range of pre-assembled overhead fittings and in particular a single unit supporting both trolley wires (twin line hanger), an insulated spacer keeping the two wires the designated distance apart ensuring triple insulation between the wires, came onto the market. All trolleybus routes were equipped with trolley wires 24in. (2ft) apart, Portsmouth never employing the 18in. spacing used by many earlier trolleybus operators, and the trolley vehicles were equipped with under-running swivel head wheel collectors. Strain insulators were placed in span wires and catenaries to ensure triple insulation between positive and earth, and double insulation between negative and earth.

The route of the trolley wires was kept as straight as possible, minor deviations and irregularities of the kerb line being ignored to obtain a smooth run. It was assumed that the trolleybus would normally be running more or less beneath the route of the trolley wires and to avoid running with the trolley booms continually at a sideways angle the negative trolley wire was normally not strung more than 7ft from the kerb on roads up to 26ft wide, increasing to 11ft for roads between 39 and 45ft in width. A distance of 13ft was never exceeded. Wherever possible, curves were aligned so that the radius of the trolley wire was less than the route of the vehicle beneath, thereby minimising the risk of a dewirement.

Wherever both trams and trolleybuses were likely to work together for any length of time, separate trolleybus wiring was hung between the kerb and the tram overhead enabling trolley vehicles to "undertake" the trams. Where the trolleybus overhead equipment was supported by single bracket arms on each side of the road, short span wires were strung between the ends of each bracket arm supporting the tramway overhead line, e.g. London Road, Hilsea. From May 1936, as the conversion programme neared completion, trams and trolley vehicles began to share the same positive running wire.

Pre-war the overhead wiring layout, including crossings and junctions, was constructed on an individual basis from single line hangers and tramway style components, e.g. a left hand 25° facing junction would be made up of two single 25° left hand frogs and a 25° left hand insulated crossing with plain trolley wire in between. There appears to have been no preferred supplier of overhead equipment, although it may be noted that Estler Bros was the UK agent for Ohio Brass Co., Mansfield, USA, fittings at one time. In the mid-1930s British Insulated Cables Ltd. (BIC), whose equipment was manufactured at Prescot, Lancashire, began to introduce a range of pre-assembled overhead fittings in which rigid spacer bars linked the various parts and post-war they became the favoured supplier. Although The Anti-Attrition Metal Co. (AA), London SE15, by then licensed manufacturer and distributor of Ohio Brass fittings, continued to supply specific items and angles. In May 1945 BIC amalgamated with Callender's Cable & Construction Co. Ltd. of Belvedere, Erith, Kent, to become British Insulated Callender's Cables Ltd. (BICC).

In the case of span wire overhead construction, the galvanised steel supporting wire ran between traction poles planted, normally at the kerb, on each side of the road, and attached to the upper section of the pole beneath any street lighting attachment by a galvanised mild steel pole strap. MoT regulations required that the height of the trolley wire should not be less than 20ft above the surface of the road except under specified low bridges, e.g. Portsmouth Town Station Bridge, but to allow for sagging of the wires during hot weather a figure of 21ft was used in practice. Double insulation between the positive and negative trolley wires was provided by the hangers supporting the trolley wire (the primary insulation) and between the trolley wire and earth by the insulated bolt into the hanger and an insulator located either in the span wire or between the span wire and the retaining bracket (the secondary insulation). Wall-mounted rosettes, anchored in roadside buildings, could replace one or both traction poles. Span wire construction provided a flexible support to the trolley wire.

Where side bracket traction poles were employed the insulators supporting the trolley wire were carried by short lengths of span wire known as bowstrings thus providing the required double insulation between the positive trolley wire and earth, and also giving a degree of elasticity to the trolley wire support thereby increasing trolley wire life (rigid suspension inevitably caused wire fractures). Part of the weight of the arm, which normally would not exceed the recommended maximum length of 16ft, was taken by a tie-rod or rods.

In order to make further use of tramway traction poles Portsmouth adopted the cross tubular suspension or gantry system to support the increased weight of trolleybus overhead wiring. Various alternative methods of reinforcing traction poles had been tried, but none proved satisfactory. Where a cross tube was adopted as an alternative to a span or single bracket arm the traction poles were relieved of practically all stresses caused by a suspended load. Hence gantries could be adopted, and old and weakened poles retained or lightweight poles installed. The MoT granted approval for cross tubular suspension for spans of up to 40ft.

Simple span wire suspension inevitably sagged towards the centre of the road, which meant that the negative trolley wire hung slightly higher than the positive one; however, this offered no problem for the later slider trolley heads (also known as slipper heads). The difference in heights could be ameliorated by the availability of single line hangers in three forms, downwards, level and upwards. Use of an "up" and "down" hanger to support a pair of wires would bring a span wire incline of 1:10 into the horizontal. Latterly, a range of L-shaped twin-line hanger end fittings was introduced whereby the two trolley wires could be brought into uniform vertical alignment.

The initial costs of overhead equipment, excluding special work such as junctions, varied considerably, depending on the planned operating speed and geography of the route, a heavily curved section requiring proportionately more traction poles and bridle or pull-off span wires.

Despite the occasional need to move high loads through the city, e.g. to or from the Dockyard, no evidence has been found of any portion of overhead wiring designed with vertical "play" to enable the span to be lifted for them to pass.

During the tramway era wherever telephone wires crossed the road, thin guard wires were hung between higher-level spans, above and parallel to the trolley wires, to prevent a broken or sagging telephone wire coming into contact with the trolley wires. The introduction of trolleybuses in Portsmouth conveniently coincided with the move to place telephone lines underground in urban areas; however, where their lines continued to cross the road, the GPO substituted insulated wires removing the need for guard wires.

Trolleybus 312 prepares to turn right away from the sea front into Clarendon Road. The trailing (junction) frog at the west end of the parallel wiring leading from Southsea South Parade, Canoe Lake, turning circle can be seen two spans behind the trolleybus. (Tony Belton)

No evidence has been found of the use of protective netting hanging parallel to the trolley wires immediately above the footpath, as on some other trolleybus systems, at points where a swinging trolley pole could cause damage to nearby buildings and windows. This may be attributable to the high standard of overhead wiring work reducing the risk of de-wirements.

Unlike some other trolleybus systems Portsmouth did not employ any kind of markings or signs, whether at the side of the road, on the road surface or hanging from a span wire, to denote a frog, section breaker or other special work. Neither were strings of strategically placed "fairy lights" hung from the span wires to guide drivers through junctions or wide bends in fog.

There were overtaking or passing loops at a number of points on the system post-war, specifically Albert Road (King's Theatre) westbound, Clarence Pier (bus terminal), Cosham Railway Station (Cosham Compound) terminus, Cosham 'Red Lion' (Spur Road) terminus, Dockyard (The Hard), Goldsmith Avenue (Fratton Park) westbound, and Southsea South Parade Pier westbound. The loop at Albert Road fell into disuse by the early 1950s by which time theatre traffic could be handled by normal services and it was removed entirely, it is believed, in October 1954. The Goldsmith Avenue loop serving Portsmouth Football Club's home ground survived until March 1962 although it had not been used for many years, post-war sports extras being seemingly motorbus operated. The loop at Southsea South Parade Pier installed in about August 1948 was also removed in the early 1950s.

Trolley wire

In 1933, the Joint Committee on Overhead Line Equipment made up of specialists from members of the Municipal Tramways & Transport Association and the Tramways and Light Railways Association (the trade association of private tramways operators), recommended standardisation on a single profile of grooved trolley wire, British Standard (BS) 23 Revision 1, to gradually replace the various types then in use. In 1919 it had recommended a total of eight forms, four round and four grooved, each using 0 (1/0), 00 (2/0), 000 (3/0) and 0000 (4/0) wire, the suspension lobes being different in each case. The BS 23 Revision 1 profile accommodated suspensions that were not exactly vertical even when suspension ears projected beyond the wire diameter and did not disrupt the passage of V-shaped bronze trolley wheels, whether attached to fixed or swivel trolleyheads.

Portsmouth trams were equipped with fixed head trolleys until the conversion programme made it necessary for both trams and trolleybuses to use the same positive trolley wire. The vertical sides of swivelling sliding heads employing carbon inserts which started to appear on British trolleybuses from 1937 proved less accommodating and tended to foul the suspension ears around curves where horizontal centrifugal forces produced by the trolley poles reaching sideways thrust their trolley heads sideways. The vertical flanges could strike those protruding supports to produce a series of irritating "clonks" that resonated through the roof of the trolleybus and provided an audible indication of damage to the overhead infrastructure.

Portsmouth continued to use round section trolley wire until tramway abandonment, however, in preparation for the arrival of trolleybuses. Clough, Smith & Co., perhaps in co-operation with the undertaking's Overhead Line Department, designed a grooved 4/0 SWG wire with a higher and thus narrower width top lobe than specified in BS 23 Revision 1, which had reduced the suspension ear width to that of the wire diameter (0.426in.). Their modification kept the overall width of mechanical ears within the diameter of trolley wire (0.4568 in.) and reduced noise and sparks. Clough, Smith & Co. used this trolley wire, generally known as Portsmouth Section for all their work in the city, whilst Ben Hall referred to it as a "sugar loaf" section.

Worn trolley wheels were able to operate through ears on an even path, avoiding wear of the ears or the dishing of the trolley wire where it leaves the ear. Moreover being sparkless, there was no interference with wireless reception so far as the ears are concerned. A further advantage lay in the fact that the trolley wire had a collecting diameter equivalent to about 6/0 SWG; a valuable increase as laden trolleybuses of this period, weighing 12–13 tons, took starting currents in excess of 300 amps. Conductivity improved further when, during the course of 1939, Portsmouth experimented with sliding heads which provided a larger wire contact area than a trolley wheel, and then gave up using trolley wheels entirely.

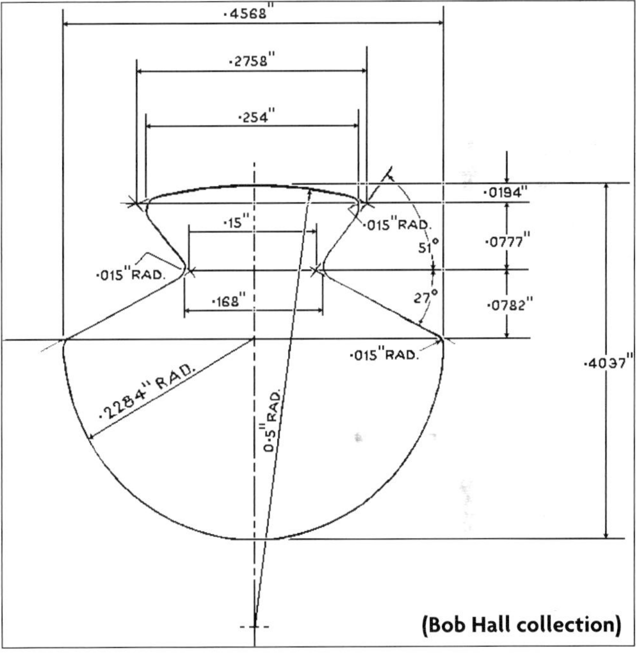

(Bob Hall collection)

Amongst others trolleybus operators, Cardiff, Manchester and Reading adopted the Portsmouth Section whilst interestingly Edinburgh Corporation Tramways, baulking at the likely cost of converting its overhead equipment to accept bow collectors, retained the traditional trolley poles and adopted carbon insert sliding heads using Portsmouth section trolley wire.

Both BIC and BICC referred to the Portsmouth Section by the abbreviation P. The CPPTD later adopted a modified profile, known, at least by BICC, as the Portsmouth Modified section and referred to by the abbreviation PM, as opposed to the two standard sections used by most trolleybus networks known SG (Standard Groove) or NS (New Standard). It is not know if those were formal industry terms but they were cast as identifying codes into the cast bronze end fittings for frogs, crossings and section insulators.

The BS23 (Revision 3) New Standard profile was issued in April 1949. This represented a direct development of, and improvement on, the Portsmouth profile whilst maintaining the principle of ensuring that a mechanical ear did not

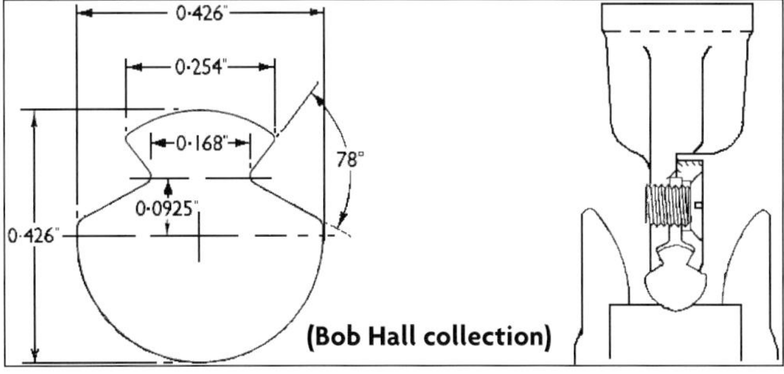

(Bob Hall collection)

protrude beyond the diameter of the wire. It embraced the principal groove dimensions but revised the cross-section to a circular profile. Revision 2 also acknowledged that high resistance bronze trolley wire had by then only specialised applications and deleted references to the alloy (copper or cadmium-copper being used henceforth), together with all mention of round wires. It withdrew all but 4/0 grooved wire for tramways and trolleybuses, and formalised the reduced lobe width that many undertakings had been using for more than a decade, in effect, placing undertakings still running under SG wire in the position of using a non-preferred section. Portsmouth never used SG or the later NS trolley wire, cf. Nottingham, which employed SG from its introduction but adopted NS for replacements, or Derby which, amongst many other operators, remained faithful to SG.

Traction poles

The tramway overhead wiring equipment was considerably lighter than that necessary for the trolleybuses, not least because it used just one rather than two trolley wires. The traction poles, supplied by Messrs Stewart and Menzies, Lanarkshire (a constituent company of Stewart & Lloyds Ltd.), were made from three-section solid-drawn mild steel tube, the sections being welded together under pressure, with ornamental collars over the joints. There were three weights, 8 cwt, 12 cwt and 16 cwt, the heavier poles being able to provide greater strength at locations such as curves, junctions or other special work, where the increased weight of the overhead wiring placed additional strains on its supports. Except for a limited number of centre poles in Guildhall Square, all the tramway traction poles were planted at the side of the road a maximum of 40yd apart.

The traction poles were ornamented with cast iron bases bearing the Corporation coat of arms, which provided some protection against collisions, cast iron ball or "urn" finials, wrought iron span wire strapping scrolls and side bracket arm scroll work. The majority of these poles remained in use until the end of the trolleybus era, albeit bereft of any dated Edwardian scrollwork (which in any case had proved difficult to maintain in the rust-provoking salt-laden atmosphere). Progressively, most of the cast iron bases also disappeared because they were susceptible to minor traffic accidents and heavy blows.

Where a new traction pole was planted, the standard on the Portsmouth trolleybus system was a 31ft heavy steel pole, 9½in. in diameter at the base, tapering initially to 8½in. and then again to 7½in. at the top but those manufactured after the early 1940s had fractionally larger dimensions of 9⅝, 8⅝in. and 7⅝in. respectively. They were manufactured by a variety of steel tube manufacturers and were not a specialist item. A variety of pole diameters and lengths, e.g. 33ft or 35ft, were available to again provide greater strength at locations where the increased weight of the overhead wiring placed additional strains on its supports. The lower 6ft of the traction pole was sunk into the ground, with a backwards rake to compensate for the weight of the overhead equipment, and the sunken portion embedded in concrete. Once the overhead wiring was complete its weight pulled that part of the pole above the surface into the vertical.

The conversion of the Southsea South Parade Pier – Cosham Railway Station route from tram to trolleybus operation, required the provision of separate trolleybus wires along roads which would in the main continue to be served by trams. Although the City Council had already adopted a policy of gradual tramway abandonment on 21 March 1933, it was expected that parallel operation of both modes of traction would continue for several years. As Portsmouth's trams were equipped with fixed trolley heads, their trolley poles could not follow the trolleybus positive trolley wire located closer to the kerb. This meant that it was necessary to suspend and maintain up to six trolley wires along much of the route, i.e. two tram positive conductor wires and two pairs of trolleybus conductor wires, which together with fittings imposed a weight of more than 350 lbs on each suspension point located every 40yd. As the roads were over 50ft wide in places it was initially difficult to meet the MoT's minimum trolley wire height of 20ft between points of suspension.

Despite the weight issue, the provision of so many conductors improved power distribution. In particular, the negative trolleybus wires paralleled the tram rails' negative return, offering a conductive cross-section equal to about 3½sq in. of copper – although the rail drop was not permitted to exceed 7 volts under these conditions.

The successful interface of a trolleybus trolley wheel or slider head with the conductor wire was primarily dependent upon maintaining the suspension ears vertical to the trolley head. It was accordingly decided that on the wider portions of the route each pair of trolleybus trolley wires would be suspended from bracket arms fixed to traction poles on each side of the road and to terminate the span wires supporting the single tramway trolley wires at bolts fixed into the ends of the bracket arms. This resulted in the trolleybus conductor wire ears being maintained in a vertical position by the bracket arm bowstrings although the tramway conductor wires were fractionally higher above the top of the rails.

As the conversion programme progressed it became increasingly unlikely that trams would continue to run along roads that had been equipped for trolleybus operation. In early May 1936 each tram was equipped with a swivelling trolley head which could follow the alignment of the trolleybus positive conductor wire even where this was at some distance from the centre line of the tram track. Henceforth separate tram positive conductor wires were rarely provided and the overhead equipment was reconfigured solely with the trolleybuses in mind, resulting in an increased number of tram de-wirements at the many temporary junctions and crossings with trolleybus overhead wiring. Tramway services were maintained throughout by preparing and erecting the new spans and suspensions during the day, running out the new wires during the night when the traction power could be switched off, and by finally removing redundant tramway conductor wires immediately prior to introducing the trolleybus service.

The Corporation decided to transfer the existing street lamps, suspended from the tramway span wires, to a second bracket arm fixed to the traction poles above the bracket arm or span wire supporting the trolleybus overhead equipment, alternately on each side of the road. At that time Portsmouth was experimenting with mercury vapour discharge lamps which ideally needed to be placed 25ft above the road. Given the widespread use of similar lamps throughout the city it was decided to standardise on 35ft long traction poles for use at all lightning positions, in essence half the number of poles erected.

During the initial conversions the top sections of many of the tramway traction poles were found to be badly corroded. They had been reinforced at an earlier date by a tube fixed internally to a steel disc which rested on a stud about 4ft from the top of the pole, the space in between being filled with concrete. In some cases the corrosion extended to the concrete reinforcement itself. It was found that the thickness of the bottom and middle sections of the oldest poles, then in use for over 30 years, was considerably greater than that of the later BS traction poles:

	Section in inches		
	Top	**Middle**	**Bottom**
Old light pole	¼	½	⅝
Old heavy pole	¼	½	⅞
BS medium pole	9/32	5/16	11/32
BS heavy pole	5/16	11/32	13/32

It was, however, found that the ornamental collars at the pole joints had originally been embedded in concrete, and when they were removed a non-corroded joint was exposed, and in many cases the original primer paint. This precaution had avoided much expensive pole renewal.

Owing to the greater thickness of the middle and bottom sections of the old pole over that of the new BS poles, it was decided to burn off 4ft 6 in. of the top section of the old poles, having an external diameter of 5½in., and to place around the remaining 1ft 6in. long spigot, extension tubes 5/16 in thick, and either 6ft 8in. or 10ft long to maintain the poles' existing length of 31ft, or to extend them to 33ft or 35ft respectively. Once these extension pieces had been fixed, the poles were filled with 3 to 1 concrete and reinforced with four ⅜in. diameter steel bars. The diameter of the top section of the finished pole was similar to that of the swaged portion of the middle section, and gave a uniform finish.

This treatment converted the erstwhile tramway traction poles (reportedly only light and heavy poles now remained in use) into poles exceeding even the then-new BS extra heavy poles in thickness, and when filled with reinforced concrete produced poles of exceptional strength. It was considered that if they were painted periodically they would last almost indefinitely.

It was decided as an experiment to test out five specially-designed concrete poles reinforced with high-tension steel bars at Cosham Railway Station turning circle. This location was selected as one experiencing the maximum strain to which traction poles on the system were likely to be subjected. The 33ft poles were designed to withstand a load of 2,825 lb applied 1ft 6 in. from the top of the pole, with the pole sunk 6ft into the ground, and with such a load to give a deflection not exceeding 9ins. They proved so successful in withstanding the load of the trolleybus trolley wires that the strain of an additional tramway loop was added. The poles were then subjected to a strain of over 3,400 lb; even then the maximum deflection was only 8¼in., compared with the BS extra heavy pole deflection of 6in. with a load of 2,750 lb.

A detailed examination was made of the 400 tramway traction poles along the initial route, necessitating the removal of all ornamental pole collars, to establish the extent of any corrosion. It was recognised that the size of pole and rake at each location had originally been selected to support one or two tramway trolley wires, whereas with the conversion a minimum of four trolleybus trolley wires and potentially, two tram trolley wires, now needed to be supported. It was decided where necessary to employ new BS medium and heavy poles, each 31ft, 33ft or 35ft in length. These new poles were used principally on the outside of curves, at junctions, at crossings and at terminal loops. Some of the existing 31ft poles which had been erected in recent years were increased in length to 33ft or 35ft by the addition of 2ft or 4ft extensions. Including the poles to be fitted with bracket arms or lighting brackets, and those to be removed, reinforced with concrete or re-raked, there were 15 alternative methods of dealing with each pole position. Finally, each pole position, classified as above, was plotted on detailed route plans.

Along one section of the route, where BS light poles had recently been planted, but where the road was insufficiently wide for two single bracket arms, one on each pavement, it was found that the poles were not strong enough to support six wires. Even on moderate curves the supporting span wires had to be strained up to a tension of over 1,300 lb. It was, therefore, decided as an experiment and to avoid replacing the poles with those of a heavier type, to substitute a steel tube for the span wire. This reduced the above strain on the poles to 440 lb at moderate curves, and to a dead load only on the straight. This form of construction, known as a gantry or double bracket arm, was examined by a MoT inspecting officer and approved for roads up to 36ft wide.

Single bracket arm construction was employed for narrow streets, and where two pairs of trolley wires had to be carried, each pair was supported on a separate flexible bowstring.

All positive section insulators, negative splicing ears, frogs and insulated crossings were of the BIC type, and

No. 286 of December 1936 heads east along Park Road towards Guildhall Square beneath gantry suspension alongside the electrified railway line (3-rail DC) that runs on an embankment from Portsmouth & Southsea Station to Portsmouth Harbour Station. (Tony Belton)

The offside trolley head of Leyland TBD2 206 receives attention. (D.A.P. Janes)

incorporated the latest improvements based on experience at other trolleybus systems. These fittings were designed so that the trolley wheel gradually ran upon its inside flanges as the wheel left the trolley wire and entered the fittings, and passed from the flanges to the wire on leaving the fittings. This design not only ensured smooth operation, but enabled the original section of the trolley wire below the point at which the wire entered the terminal clamp to be permanently retained.

Portsmouth never used the catenary suspension system, pioneered by Nottingham, for its span wire construction as by 1934 it had been found that when several trolleybuses were running close together the combined upward pressure from the trolley poles could raise the trolley wires sufficiently to touch the span wires above and cause a short circuit. However, where it was necessary to retain the tramway trolley wires temporarily or support the additional weight of insulated crossings, etc., a supplementary span wire, equipped with a short dropper, was strung at a higher level above the main span wire, as shown in some of the accompanying illustrations.

Having selected the nearside line at the auto frog some 50 yards behind, AEC661T 273 climbs over Fratton Bridge on its way to Clarence Pier. An example of a supplementary span wire and dropper is evident. (Tony Belton)

Clough, Smith prepared 10ft to 1in. plans of the 11 junctions to be constructed from which the most suitable layout, both from an engineering and traffic perspective, could be decided. The final version in each case was used as a basis for ordering the special work and for use by the on-site engineers. The suspension fittings, such as straight-line hangers, double and single pull-offs were designed to compensate for the sag of the supporting span wires, ensuring that the ears stood vertically with the trolley wheels.

Statutory regulations stipulated a maximum longitudinal span of 120ft and this separation was retained where existing tramway traction poles were reused. Along routes not previously traversed by trams shorter spans of 105ft became general to compensate for the increased weight aloft, whilst along curved sections of road where the trolley wire had to be pulled into a series of straights approximating to the desired curves, poles were more frequent. In such cases of stepped curvature the angle did not exceed 10° to reduce the risk of de-wirements. There was a considerable weight of equipment aloft: as an example the two pairs of trolley wires on a straight section between two traction poles, together with the supporting hangers and span wires, weighed about 235 lb whilst a post-war BICC electrically-operated turnout frog weighed in excess of 80 lb.

Traction poles, bracket arms and gantries were painted silver (officially aluminium) at infrequent intervals except for 2ft at the bottom of the pole (1ft if the cast iron base remained in place), any remaining ornamental collars at the pole joints, and the finial (ball or "urn") which were painted black. Until 1931 they had been painted battleship grey relieved with black bands and bases. Pre-war various arrangements of coloured horizontal bands around the poles indicated fare stages and stops.

A unique alpha-numeric code was stencilled on each traction pole with small black capital letters and numbers, painted about 12ft (exceptionally 6ft on the Floating Bridge – Commercial Road section) above the ground level so that a location could be pinpointed in case of a breakdown or emergency. Each route had an alphabetic code of one or two letters, and every traction pole was numbered consecutively with even and odd numbers used on opposite sides of the road. Although subject to confirmation it is believed that pole numbers on the outer side of a curve were given alphabetic suffixes to ensure that the pairing of pole numbers subsequently continued. Numbering ran in the direction shown in the list below.

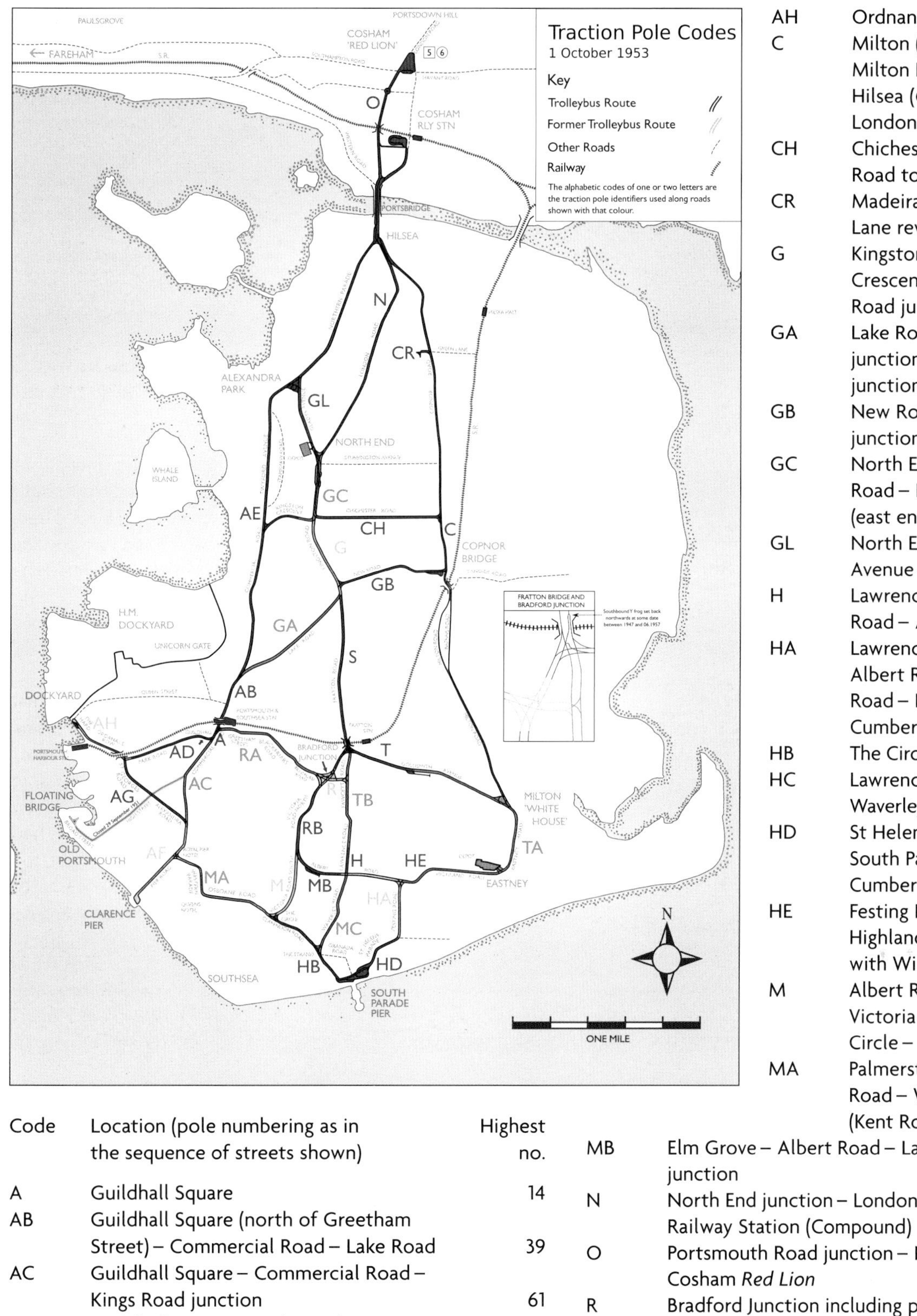

Code	Location (pole numbering as in the sequence of streets shown)	Highest no.
A	Guildhall Square	14
AB	Guildhall Square (north of Greetham Street) – Commercial Road – Lake Road	39
AC	Guildhall Square – Commercial Road – Kings Road junction	61
AD	Guildhall Square – Park Road	44
AE	Lake Road junction – Commercial Road – Kingston Crescent (west end)	262
	Kingston Crescent junction – Twyford Road – Northern Parade – Hilsea	262
AF	Kings Road junction – Royal Pier Hotel – Clarence Pier	85
	Royal Pier Hotel –Southsea Terrace as far as Kent Road	85
AG	St George's Road – Alexandra Road – Kings Road junction	140
	Floating Bridge – Old Portsmouth – Cambridge Road – Victoria Hall	140
AH	Ordnance Row –The Hard	47
C	Milton (*White House*) – Milton Road – Copnor Road – Hilsea (*Coach & Horses*, London Road junction)	292
CH	Chichester Road from London Road to Copnor Road	54
CR	Madeira Road (Green Lane reverser)	10
G	Kingston Road (Kingston Crescent junction – Lake Road junction)	58
GA	Lake Road (Kingston Road junction – Commercial Road junction)	49
GB	New Road (Kingston Road junction) – Copnor Bridge	54
GC	North End Depot – Kingston Road – Kingston Crescent (east end)	54
GL	North End Depot – Gladys Avenue – Northern Parade	37
H	Lawrence Road (Harold Road – Albert Road)	18
HA	Lawrence Road junction – Albert Road – Highland Road – Festing Road – Cumberland House	64
HB	The Circle – Clarendon Road	44
HC	Lawrence Road junction – Waverley Road – The Strand	27
HD	St Helen's Park Crescent – South Parade Pier – Cumberland House	61
HE	Festing Road junction – Highland Road, junction with Winter Road	34
M	Albert Road junction – Victoria Road South – The Circle – Palmerston Road	54
MA	Palmerston Road – Osborne Road – Western Parade (Kent Road)	53
MB	Elm Grove – Albert Road – Lawrence Road junction	30
N	North End junction – London Road – Cosham Railway Station (Compound)	226
O	Portsmouth Road junction – Northern Road – Cosham *Red Lion*	87
R	Bradford Junction including parts of Victoria Road North and Rugby Road	26
RA	Guildhall Square – Greetham Street – Bradford Junction	62
RB	Bradford Junction – Victoria Road North – Elm Grove	52
S	Lake Road junction – Fratton Road – Victoria Road North – Bradford Junction	89
T	Fratton Bridge – Goldsmith Avenue (Haslemere Road)	44
TA	Goldsmith Avenue (Haslemere Road) – Eastney – Highland Road (Winter Road)	144
TB	Fratton Bridge – Fawcett Road – Lawrence Road (Harold Road)	52

The coding system originated with the tramways and it was unusual for a pole to be re-numbered. Exceptions to this rule were briefly in 1934 when additional poles took on suffix letters. For example, new poles were planted outside the depot in Gladys Avenue and were initially coded GC1A, GC1B, GC1C, GC0, and GC00 to avoid re-numbering of other poles. However, these codes were subsequently changed, probably when the new exit was installed.

When a significant number of additional or replacement poles were required for tram to trolleybus conversion some re-numbering took place, plus many "N" poles in Cosham were re-numbered for tram changes and alterations to the "Compound". Subsequent additional poles took on a suffix letter (A, B, C).

Examples:
Clarence Pier terminus – final traction poles supporting the circle numbered AF 77 and 78.
Floating Bridge terminus – traction poles AG 4–11 supported the reversing triangle.

Single bracket arms could be found at many places on the Portsmouth system where the streets were deemed impractically wide for span wires, e.g. London Road, along roads having one-way wiring only, e.g. Baffins Road, or along dual carriageways, e.g. Portsbridge. Subject to the width of the road, side bracket arms could support two pairs of trolley wires, e.g. along Osborne Road where both outbound and inbound wires were supported by poles planted on one side of the road or the other, Victoria Road South, along Waverley Road where both outbound and inbound wires were supported by poles planted on the east side of the road. They were also used to provide additional support for frogs at some points, e.g. access to Eastney Depot from the north.

Single bracket arms were used on:
Baffins Road
Commercial Road
High Street, Old Portsmouth
Kings Terrace
London Road, Hilsea
New Road*
Northern Road, Cosham
Osborne Road*
Portsbridge* (northbound)
Portsbridge (southbound)
Rugby Road
Spur Road, Cosham
St George's Road
Victoria Road
Waverley Road
An asterisk (*) after the name of the roads listed above indicates that single bracket arms supported both pairs of wires on at least some parts of the road.

Portsmouth probably made greater use of gantries than any other British trolleybus operator and virtually all of them remained until abandonment of the respective route whereas other operators had tended to replace them with span wires requiring heavier traction poles after some years of use. There were many isolated gantries but lengths of these supports could be found in:
Albert Road
Blackfriars Road
Cambridge Road
Clarendon Road
Commercial Road
Eastney Road
Fratton Road, south of St. Mary's Church
Goldsmith Avenue
Greetham Street
Highland Road
Kings Terrace
Lake Road
Osborne Road
Park Road
St Helen's Parade
Southsea Terrace
Victoria Road North
Western Parade

Many traction poles were retained for street lighting purposes after trolleybus operation along the street concerned had ended, some staying in place for 20 or more years. Indeed one was still intact at Hilsea 'Coach & Horses' in early 2012.

Wall-mounted rosettes were infrequently used, the only known locations being:
Albert Road on Kings Theatre
Fratton Bridge on the bank at the corner of the junction between Fawcett Road and Victoria Road North
Fratton Road on Co-op building
Gladys Avenue, North End on east wall of depot building
Goldsmith Avenue on Talbot Hotel (corner of Francis Avenue)
Kingston Road on Oddfellows Hall
London Road, North End on Southdown office

Frogs

Strictly speaking a "frog" is an item of overhead equipment where a trolleybus trolley wheel or slider head diverged from a single conductor wire to two, or converged from two conductor wires into one. More generally a frog is considered to refer to all the items necessary to provide points or switches in the overhead wiring for a pair of trolley wires. Frogs were built up from metal castings with wooden beam insulation and runners instead of trolley wire, but to the same profile, where the positive and negative wires crossed. A pair of single line frogs, a leader and a companion; a centre crossing, where the wires crossed; extruded runners and insulating spacers, were needed to build up what is more commonly known as a frog. The insulating spacers that kept the trolley wires the required 24in. apart were either wood or two pairs of galvanised steel links, secured by pins, appearing like a large rivet, with a double-eye globe insulator between them to ensure the necessary triple insulation between positive and negative trolley wires, and between the positive trolley wire and earth.

The experimental trolleybus route between Cosham Railway Station and Southsea South Parade Pier required a minimum of frogs for depot access purposes. Hand-operated turnout frogs were installed at North End Junction enabling northbound vehicles running out of service to turn left into Gladys Avenue or when running out of the depot to turn left into the northbound London Road wiring. Operation of such frogs required the conductor to leave the rear platform and pull a handle, attached at a convenient height to a nearby traction pole, and connected by a wire cable to the frog mechanism when the trolleybus needed to follow a branch line or secondary route.

Once the tramway conversion programme got under way, the complex nature of the system involving frequent junctions, acknowledgement that the conductor's first priorities were to collect fares and ensure his passengers' safety, as well as increasing trolleybus and other traffic, encouraged the undertaking to adopt electrically-operated frogs. Hand-operated frogs were installed at places close to a bus stop, e.g. the turn out of Copnor Road northbound into Madeira Road, at lesser-used junctions, e.g. from Kingston Road southbound into New Road, and at terminal loops, e.g. The Hard, and these were retained throughout the life of the system. The hand-operated frogs installed in Portsmouth were of the pull and hold variety. There is no evidence that Portsmouth employed mechanically re-set hand-operated turnout frogs, where once pulled the handle could be released immediately, the frog remaining set for the branch line until the trolley head struck a small rubber roller at the side of the frog which unlatched the mechanism and allowed springs to return the frog to its normal position, set for the main line.

The trolley heads ran on their flanges through the frogs and crossing leading to vertical movement, resulting in the term "ramp-end". This both restricted speed and broke the carbon inserts when slider heads were adopted. In the late 1930s a range of standard assemblies for double-tongued 15° or 25° frogs with 17½° or 25° crossings employing less obtrusive "wire profile" fittings having reversible insulated running strips matching the profile of the trolley wire and retained by a "dumb-bell" insulator unit, became available. Combined with the use of slider heads these permitted higher speeds with little risk of de-wirement, 30 mph being achieved in tests when following the main line beneath turnout frogs. Trailing (junction) frogs were usually simple castings with no moving components, the heads running through on their flanges; however, they were also available with moving tongues for installation at locations where it was not easy to coast.

Electrically-operated frogs or "auto frogs", using similar technology to that employed by tramway automatic point turners, were introduced into the UK in about 1930 and were thus freely available by the time Portsmouth commenced its tramway conversion programme. It seems that the first such frog was installed in July 1935, although it only came into scheduled use on 3 November 1935, in the eastbound Southsea South Parade wiring enabling trolleybuses to continue into St Helen's Parade and Festing Road rather than turn south into the Canoe Lake turning circle which had acted as the terminus for all services since August 1934. Two more auto frogs followed in September 1935 at the junction of Commercial Road northbound and Kingston Crescent ('Air Balloon'), and at the junction of London Road southbound with Kingston Crescent (Kingston Cross). In October 1936 it was decided to install 16 auto frogs at various points of the system at a cost of £20 each plus installation. It was decided to standardise on the automatic frog setter devised by the Forest City Electric Co., Illinois, USA, and manufactured in the UK at that company's Stretford, Manchester, works. This required the installation of a transfer contact ahead of the frog with a restoring contact skate just beyond the frog to return it to the normal route (Forest City drawing F51882.1 of 1 March 1937 refers).

Portsmouth's auto frog operating policy was "power on for the branch" and "coast for straight on", i.e. power off for the main route, and normally coinciding with the insulated route along which a driver was required to coast with power off. Some 10 to 15yd before the frog, a skate, correctly known as a transfer or setting contact and appearing to the pedestrian rather like a bulky hanger, was fixed immediately above the positive trolley wire to energise the auto frog. As the trolleybus approached the transfer contact, a driver wishing to take the branch line would keep his foot on the power pedal, simultaneously controlling the vehicle's speed with the hand brake. The trolley wheel or slider head touched the transfer contact thereby bringing the frog operating solenoid momentarily into the traction motor circuit. If the trolleybus was drawing power, current passed from the positive wire, through the traction motor to the transfer contact, thence through the connecting cable to the frog setter operating relay installed in a traction pole mounted box about 8ft above the ground, which then sent current to the operating solenoid further up the pole and back to the overhead. If the driver wished to remain on the main line, he would coast under the transfer contact with his foot off the power pedal to ensure that no current was taken through the setter. The Forest City setter employed a powerful solenoid, contained in a somewhat smaller oblong metal box mounted on the traction pole adjacent to the overhead frog, exerting a pull of c. 80 lb (betraying its tramway origins) and worked a normal hand-operated frog, which could be operated or reset manually in case of failure, and lit a confirming indicator lamp.

Confirming indicator lights were built into the front panel of the auto frog setter operating relay, an aluminium painted oblong metal box with a gently curved top, to provide some protection against the elements, normally attached to the nearside traction pole closest to the frog. There was a sun visor, often flat-topped, immediately above the indicator lens. There was provision in the circuitry for a "repeater" light, which could be placed on another traction pole further ahead so as to be more clearly visible to the trolleybus driver, e.g. on the opposite side of the road. Two examples are known: for the auto frog in the southbound Waverley Road wiring at the Clarendon Road junction (The Strand), and for that in the northbound Commercial Road wiring at Guildhall Square for the turn into Greetham Street. No light was illuminated when a trolleybus coasted beneath the transfer contact to follow the main line, thereby confirming that the frog had not been inadvertently set. An amber light confirmed that the relay had moved to the required position setting the frog for the branch.

All auto frogs could also be worked as hand-operated frogs and were equipped with a grab handle for manual operation. Each relay box was equipped with a pull cord attached to the armature of the relay to allow it to be reversed, break the circuit to the operating solenoid and thus allow the frog to return to normal after an erroneous setting by the driver. If, when taking the branch line, the light went out before the trolley heads had cleared the frog or if the light did not go out after they had cleared the frog, the driver would stop and send his conductor back to pull the frog manually or pull the reset cord if the frog had not restored.

Each frog setter operating relay box had space for two lamps, each plugged into conventional bayonet sockets, and lenses, e.g. at the junction of Victoria Road southbound with Albert Road where there were two hooded amber-coloured lenses although solely the right one for service 13 illuminated, although in most cases the second lens was blanked off and no lamp bulb was present. Some boxes had a single rectangular aspect having a frosted glass screen upon which one or more black arrows were painted to indicate the direction in which the frog had been set, and with an anti-glare visor above.

The auto frog setter and, below, the operating relay with confirming indicator lights in the front panel, at the west end of Park Road. These related to frog 43 (see Facing (Turnout) Frogs map on page 299) at the east end of Ordnance Row. (Roger Funnell)

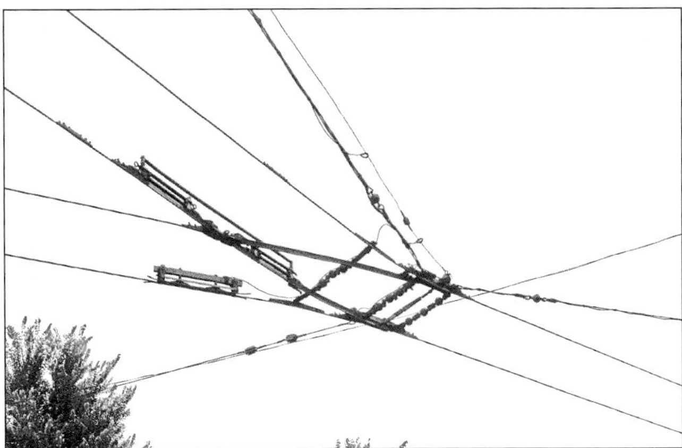

Auto frog and restoring contact (location unknown). (Roger Funnell)

Further evidence of whether or not the trolleys had taken the correct route was provided by the driver's de-wirement indicator, which would give a momentary audible signal when the trolley heads followed the "main line" or insulated route and passed under the insulated section of the frog.

The skate used as a restoring contact with the Forest City machine had a lightly-sprung contact strip suspended about half an inch above the positive wire of the branch line just beyond the frog. As the trolley head passed beneath, it came into contact with the contact strip thus sending a current at line voltage back to the frog setter relay. This reversed the relay and cut off current to the operating solenoid thus allowing the position of the frog to reset to the normal main line route.

Drivers were required to learn which auto frogs needed operating for each route as a part of their training, nonetheless it should be remembered that the driver was some 30ft in front of the trolley heads. The position of the transfer

The indicator lights for frog 24 are illuminated as 311 turns out of Highland Road into Festing Road at the Festing Hotel junction. (Roger Funnell)

contact provided sufficient distance to stop the trolleybus if a driver had failed to operate the frog or operated it in error. The conductor would then alight to set or re-set the frog manually for the appropriate direction, each auto frog installation also being equipped with a hand-operated cable pull. As road traffic continued to increase and turning lanes started to be painted on the road surface, where appropriate and practicable the Overhead Line Department introduced a policy of installing the transfer contact and frog further back from the road junction where the trolleybus' reduced speed passing beneath a frog might disrupt other vehicles, e.g. Copnor Road northbound junction with Chichester Road, northbound across Portsbridge for the junction between Northern Road and Portsmouth Road, and southbound at Military Road for the Hilsea 'Coach & Horses' junction between London Road and Copnor Road. The location was usually carefully co-ordinated with a point where the vehicle was travelling slowly just before or after a stop. This resulted in two parallel pairs of wires up to the turn itself allowing the trolleybus driver to concentrate on the surrounding traffic conditions and, where appropriate, select the correct traffic lane at the junction. It also allowed other trolleybuses to overtake in another traffic lane. This layout also gave the driver a last chance to avoid de-wirement should he or she have incorrectly gained the wrong wiring after the frog by manually transferring the trolley poles using the bamboo pole carried by every trolleybus, from one pair of wires to the other.

Former Trolleybus Driver Gordon Ferguson recalls that traffic conditions at busy junctions could make it very difficult to crawl forward without putting on power at the wrong moment and so setting an unwanted frog. Drivers sometimes switched over to their traction battery to move forward without operating the frog.

At some locations, e.g. in Waverley Road southbound at The Strand, and in Kings Terrace northbound for the Alexandra Road/Landport Terrace junction, electrically-operated reset frogs controlled by a push-button mounted on a convenient traction pole were in use. Controlled by the conductor, these operated at low voltage, working a relay, and the frog would mechanically reset once the trolley heads had passed beneath.

Frogs would normally not freeze due to the heating effect of current flowing in the wires however, despite liberal applications of an anti-freeze and glycerine mixture, early morning journeys could suffer and auto frogs might require manual operation.

During the war Mr Hall designed an asbestos shield to hang above feeders, frogs, junctions and section breakers to avoid the risk of any arcing or sparks being visible to enemy aircraft.

In normal use the solenoid would only be energised for a short while from when a bus passed the setting contact to when it activated the restoring skate. Coils burned out from time to time, perhaps due to a trolleybus having been forced to stop between the two contacts leaving the solenoid energised and heating up, or a malfunction of the reset contactor or circuit, and had to be replaced.

The frog setter comprised a rather crude "stick" relay (so called because when operated it stuck in that position until reversed by another electric current) used as a tramway point setter in an earlier era. It relied upon balance either side of vertical equilibrium to remain in place, rather than a

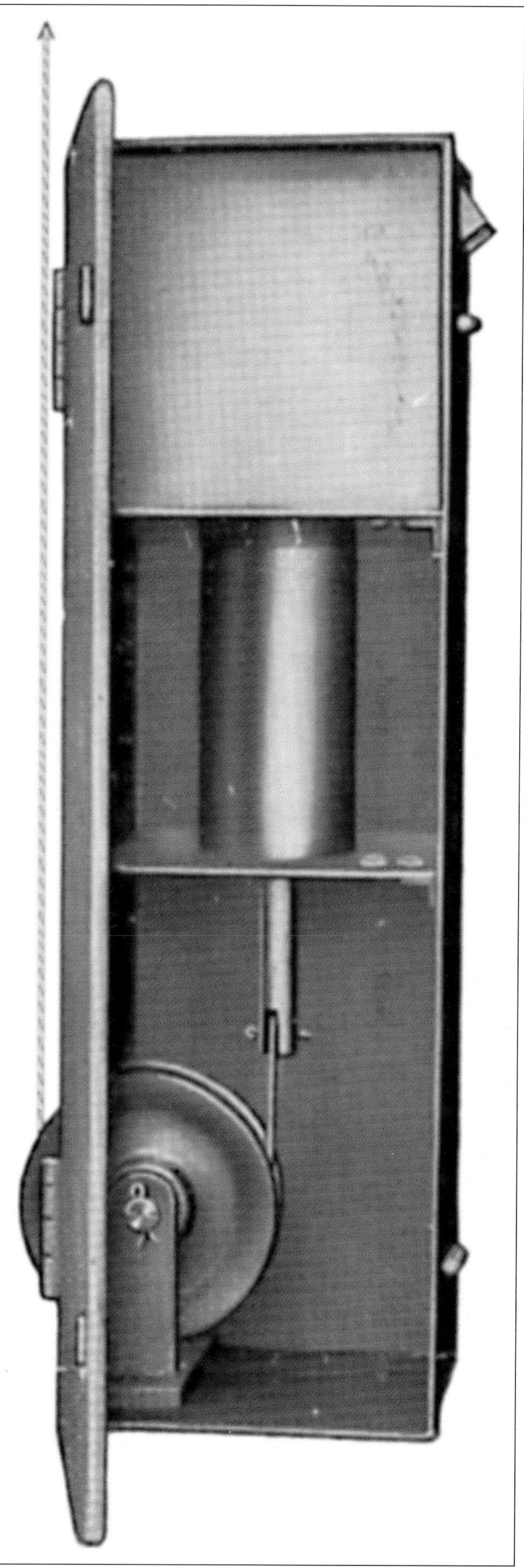

Pole mounted frog solenoid shown in the "at rest" position. Energising the coil drew the iron armature up into the centre of the coil thus pulling the cord attached to the frog. (Bob Hall)

Looking north along London Road, North End, from outside the Odeon Cinema. The passing loops for the separate Commercial Road and Fratton Road bus stops (accessed by frog 61 – see Facing (Turnout) Frogs map on page 299) as well as the overtaking line providing an uninterrupted link from Gladys Avenue to Chichester Road can be clearly seen. No. 278 heads south towards Southsea South Parade Pier. (David Bowler collection [photographer's name not recorded])

continuous current, and hence the box had to be mounted vertically. The armature was actually shaped like a sector of a circle and not as shown diagrammatically. Giving it added weight would result in a good contact at 7.

The restoring circuit included a 200W resistance and was presumably left in place. It may be that whereas the operating circuit included the pole-mounted solenoid there was no corresponding resistance in the restore circuit which therefore required one on the relay panel.

There was no resistor in the operating circuit, the resistance of coil A was enough to suit the situation bearing in mind that normally a current would only flow briefly in the circuit and because the resistance of the trolleybus circuitry provided limitation to the current flow.

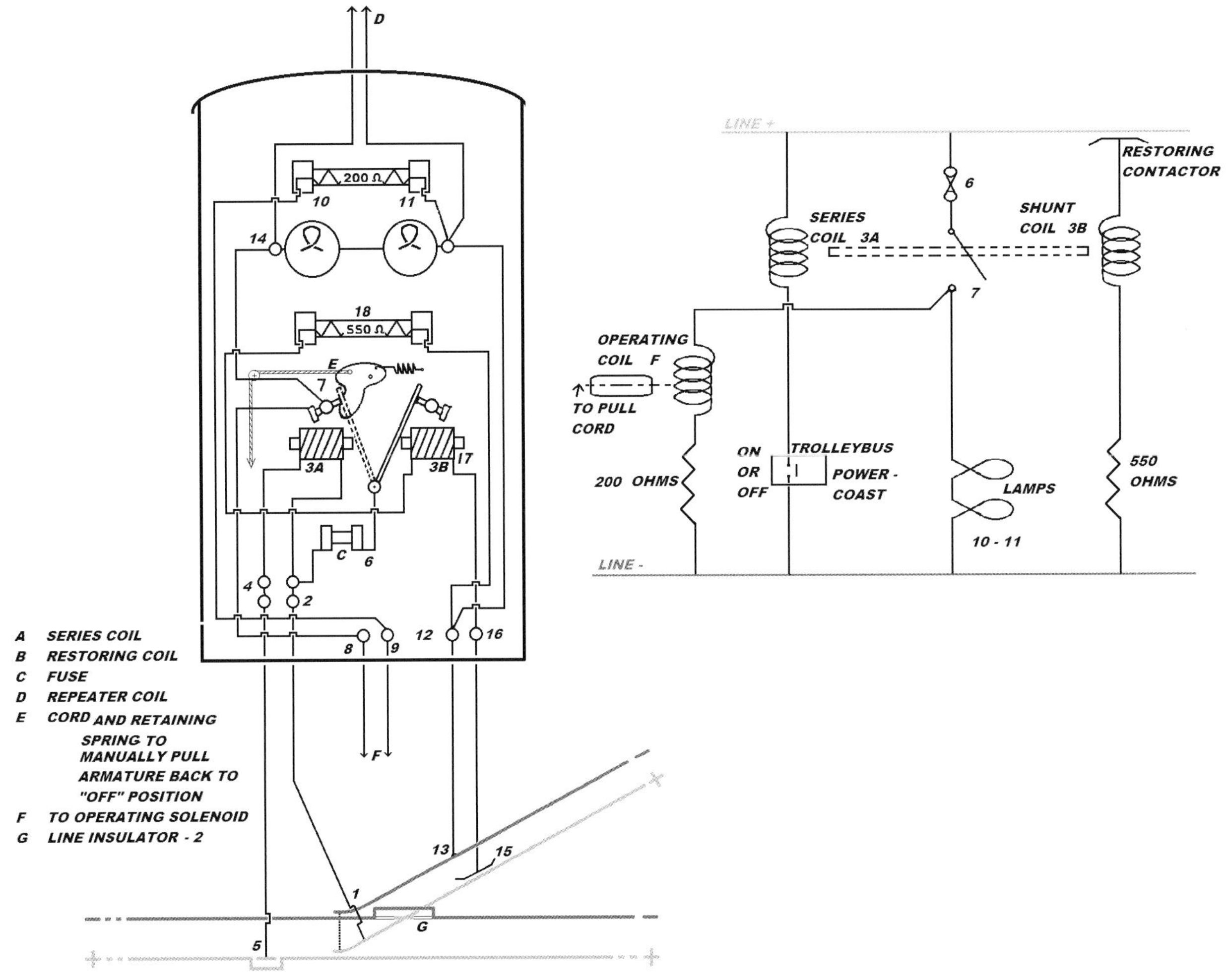

A SERIES COIL
B RESTORING COIL
C FUSE
D REPEATER COIL
E CORD AND RETAINING SPRING TO MANUALLY PULL ARMATURE BACK TO "OFF" POSITION
F TO OPERATING SOLENOID
G LINE INSULATOR - 2

FOREST CITY FROG SETTING RELAY PANEL **(Bob Hall collection)**

The operation of the frog setter was as follows:

When a trolleybus passed under the setting contact 5 with power on, current at line voltage was drawn through the circuit in the order 1 – 2 – 3 – 4 – 5 and thence through the traction motor of the vehicle to the negative line. As the trolleybus could be drawing some power all the time, e.g. for a motor generator or an air compressor, the resistance of coil A was presumably high enough to ensure that it only operated at the appropriate voltage.

The setting coil A, or 3, pulled the armature over, making contact at 7. Current flowed 1 – 2 – 6 – 7 – 8 and thus to the operating solenoid, returning 9 – 10 – 11 – 12 – 13. Although current would no longer be flowing through the operating circuit the armature stayed in the operating position simply by its own weight.

At the same time current flowed 7 – 14 – 11 – 12 – 13 causing the lamps to illuminate, thus indicating that the armature has been pulled over by coil A (or 3) and that (presumably) the frog has been operated. This type of auto frog did not prove the position of the frog tongues.

When a trolleybus operated the restoring contact skate current at line voltage passed 15 – 16 – 17 – 18 – 12 – 13. This operated the restoring coil B, pulling armature over to its normal position and opening contact 7.

The cord dangling from the bottom of the box and fixed to a cam made of insulating material was used to pull the live armature over manually should the frog fail to restore (or be switched in error). Whether there was any insulation or whether this relied on the cord keeping dry is not known. If the frog did not respond correctly and the route was not set for the branch the frog was worked as a normal pull frog and the operating handle and wire had nothing to do with the frog setter, passing behind the relay box.

Auto-frog locations and operating direction

The figure in parenthese on the first line in each case relates to the reference numbers on the accompanying map and table.

London Road/Northern Parade junction (Hilsea) southbound (8)
Operate for Northern Parade

London Road/Copnor Road junction (Hilsea) southbound (9)
Operate for Copnor Road

London Road (Hilsea) northbound, Northern Road/Portsmouth Road junction (7)
Operate for Portsmouth Road and Cosham Railway Station

Copnor Road/Chichester Road junction northbound (13)
Operate for Chichester Road

Copnor Road/New Road junction southbound (15)
Operate for Milton Road

Eastney Road (Milton) northbound, Goldsmith Avenue/Milton Road junction (19)
Operate for Goldsmith Avenue and Milton 'White House' turning circle

Highland Road/Festing Road junction ('Festing Hotel') westbound (24)
Operate for Festing Road

Southsea South Parade eastbound, St. Helen's Parade/Canoe Lake turning circle (27)
Operate for St Helen's Parade and Festing Road

Southsea South Parade westbound, passing loop at South Parade Pier loading point (29)
Operate for outside (overtaking) line

Clarendon Road/Waverley Road junction (The Strand) westbound (30)
Operate for Waverley Road

Waverley Road/Clarendon Road junction (The Strand) southbound (32)
Operate for Southsea South Parade Pier

Clarendon Road/Victoria Road South junction (The Circle) westbound (34)
Operate for Victoria Road South

Southsea Terrace westbound, Bellevue Terrace/Pier Road junction (Royal Pier Hotel) (36)
Operate for Pier Road and Clarence Pier

Bellevue Terrace southbound, Southsea Terrace/Pier Road junction (Royal Pier Hotel) (37)
Operate for Pier Road and Clarence Pier

Pier Road northbound, Bellevue Terrace/Southsea Terrace junction (Royal Pier Hotel) (38)
Operate for Bellevue Terrace

Clarence Pier, loading bay 1 (east)/loading bay 2 and 3 (west) (39)
Operate for loading bay 1

Kings Terrace northbound, Alexandra Road/Landport Terrace junction (41)
Operate for Landport Terrace and Guildhall

Commercial Road southbound, Cambridge Road/Hampshire Terrace (Victoria Hall) (42)
Believed to operate for Cambridge Road and Floating Bridge

Ordnance Row eastbound, Park Road/St George's Road junction (43)
Operate for St George's Road

Guildhall Square, Commercial Road southbound, Commercial Road/Greetham Street junction (46)
Operate for Greetham Street

Greetham Street westbound, Commercial Road junction (Guildhall Square) (47)
Operate for Commercial Road northbound

Guildhall Square, Commercial Road northbound, Commercial Road/Greetham Street junction (48)
Operate for Commercial Road northbound

Guildhall Square, Commercial Road southbound, Commercial Road/Park Road junction (49)
Operate for Commercial Road southbound

Commercial Road northbound, Lake Road junction (51)
Operate for Lake Road

Commercial Road northbound, Kingston Crescent ('Air Balloon') junction (52)
Operate for Kingston Crescent

Northern Parade northbound, Alexandra Park turning circle and Gladys Avenue (55)
Operate for Alexandra Park turning circle

Gladys Avenue southbound, North End, London Road junction (59)
Operate for Chichester Road "overtaking" wiring

London Road southbound, North End bus stops (61)
Operate for Commercial Road (via Kingston Crescent)

London Road northbound, North End, Gladys Avenue junction (64)
Operate for Gladys Avenue

Kingston Cross, London Road southbound, Kingston Road/Kingston Crescent junction (69)
Operate for Kingston Crescent

Kingston Road/New Road junction northbound (71)
Operate for New Road

Kingston Road/Lake Road junction southbound (72)
Operate for Lake Road

Victoria Road North northbound, Fratton Bridge, Goldsmith Avenue junction (73)
Operate for Fratton Road

Fratton Road southbound, Fratton Bridge, Victoria Road North/Fawcett Road junction (75)
Operate for Victoria Road North

Victoria Road North southbound, Bradford Junction, Bradford Road junction (79)
Operate for Victoria Road North

Bradford Road eastbound, Bradford Junction, Victoria Road North/Rugby Road junction (81)
Operate for Victoria Road North southbound and Albert Road

Reversers (reversing triangles)

Reversing triangles installed at the terminal point of a route were built up using two spring trail frogs, making reversal, in respect of the trolley booms, entirely automatic (a reversing triangle installed at an intermediate point, although no example occurred on the Portsmouth system. required, in addition, a crossover and a trail (junction) frog to re-join the through wiring).

As a vehicle entered the reversing triangle, the trolley wheels or sliding heads passing in the normal, "trailing" direction, pushed the frog tongues aside. Once the vehicle began its reversing manoeuvre, the wheels or heads reversing through the frog onto the triangle were automatically routed onto the "branch" and pushed through another spring trail frog at the apex. On leaving, again in the "trailing" position, they were automatically routed to the exit from the reversing triangle.

Reversing triangles were installed at:
Floating Bridge, Broad Street/East Street
Green Lane, Madeira Road/Compton Road
North End Depot, Gladys Avenue southern entrance October 1934–August 1936

Reversing triangles were proposed at various times at:
Farlington, Havant Road at Rectory Avenue, as the terminus of the extension from Cosham approved by the Portsmouth Corporation (Trolley Vehicles) Order Confirmation Act, 1948. The reverser would have been made up of a 25° left hand sprung trail frog, a 25° Y sprung trail frog and a crossover.

Nelson Square, off Park Road, proposed in late November 1936 to serve as the Guildhall terminus of services from the east and north. The reverser would have been made up of 25° left hand spring trail frog, a 25° left hand sprung facing frog and a 40° crossover. The single line in Nelson Square (in fact a street rather than a square in the usual sense), would have been about 100 yards long to provide parking for trolleybuses to wait out of service.

Paulsgrove, Jubilee Avenue at Portsdown Road, as the terminus of the extension from Cosham proposed in 1947 but

Fratton Bridge overhead wiring layout looking north to Fratton Road post 1960. (Roger Funnell)

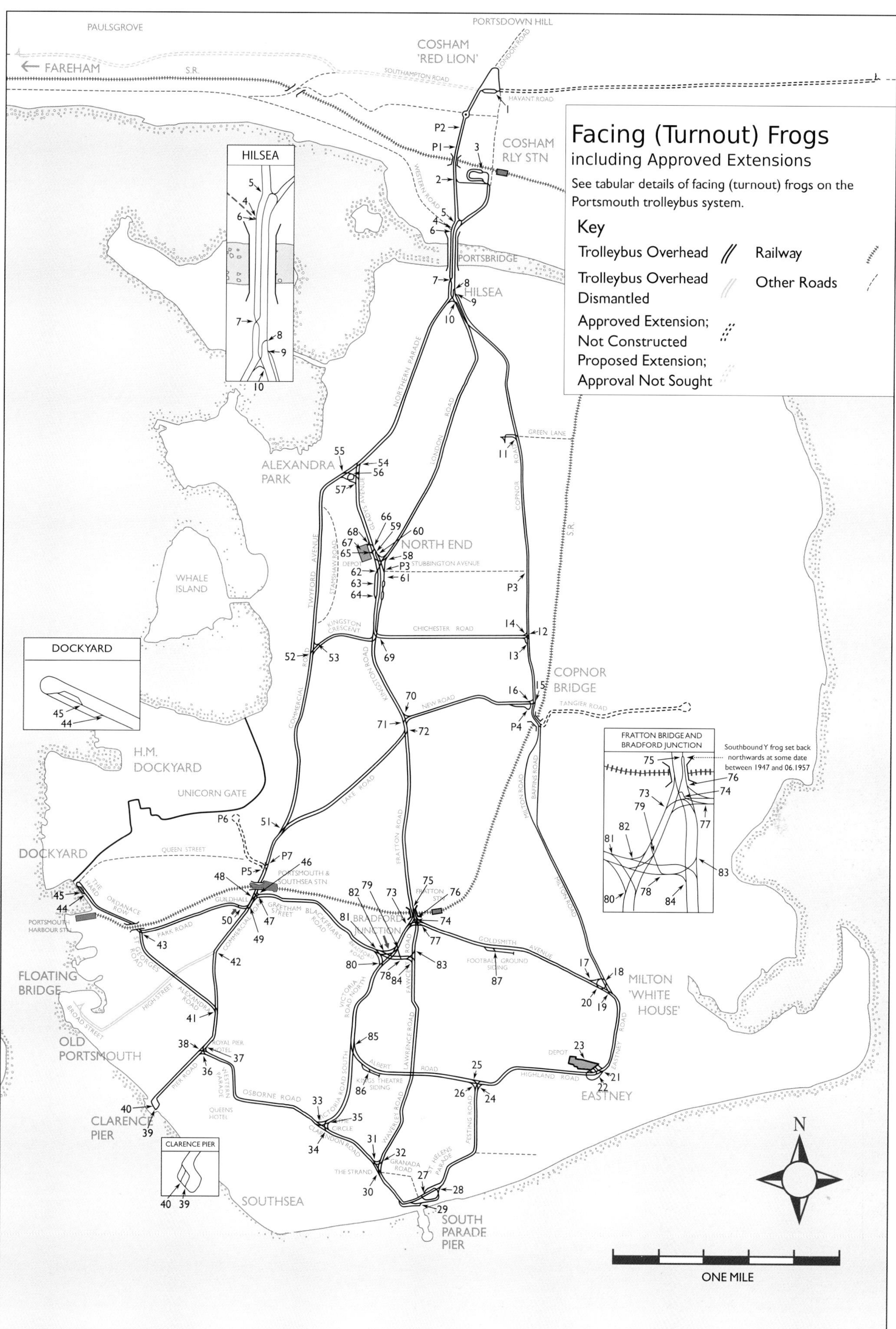
Facing (Turnout) Frogs
including Approved Extensions
See tabular details of facing (turnout) frogs on the Portsmouth trolleybus system.
Key
Trolleybus Overhead
Railway
Trolleybus Overhead Dismantled
Other Roads
Approved Extension; Not Constructed
Proposed Extension; Approval Not Sought
HILSEA
DOCKYARD
FRATTON BRIDGE AND BRADFORD JUNCTION
Southbound Y frog set back northwards at some date between 1947 and 06.1957
CLARENCE PIER
PAULSGROVE
PORTSDOWN HILL
COSHAM 'RED LION'
FAREHAM
COSHAM RLY STN
PORTSBRIDGE
HILSEA
ALEXANDRA PARK
WHALE ISLAND
NORTH END
COPNOR BRIDGE
H.M. DOCKYARD
UNICORN GATE
DOCKYARD
PORTSMOUTH & SOUTHSEA STN
BRADFORD JUNCTION
FRATTON STN
PORTSMOUTH HARBOUR STN
FLOATING BRIDGE
OLD PORTSMOUTH
MILTON 'WHITE HOUSE'
EASTNEY
CLARENCE PIER
SOUTHSEA
SOUTH PARADE PIER
N
ONE MILE

Details of Facing (Turnout) Frogs on the Portsmouth trolleybus system

Key to Map	Location *Sequence is clockwise around the City An asterisk (*) by the Key number denotes a Note below*		Route Options		Operation			Traction Pole		Dates		
			Left	Right	Default **L**eft or **R**ight	**S**kate or **B**utton or **P**ull	Angle (°) and direction of frogs	Wording on pole, setter box, etc. (where definitely known)	Pole Code	Frog installed	*Frog into scheduled use*	Frog removed
1*	**Cosham**	Spur Road, 'Red Lion'	Inside line	Outside line	**L**	**P**	25 Y	Pull for outside line	**O 79**	Post-Feb 1944	Post-Feb 1944	June 1963
2*		Northern Road (Sbnd)	Private Road	Northern Road	**L**	**P**	25 L		**O 16**	April 1942	3 May 1942	1956
3*		Railway Station (Compound)	Inside line	Outside line	**L**	**P**	25 Y	Pull for outside line	**N 223**	Aug 1948	26 Sep 1948	5 July 1963
4*	**Hilsea/Portsbridge**	London Road (Nbnd) at Western Road	Red Lion	Station	**L**	**P**	25 R		**N 167**	8 Aug 1936	1 Oct 1936	Nov 1936
5*		London Road (Nbnd) south of Northern Road	Red Lion	Station	**L**	**P**	25 R		**N 177**	Nov 1936	Nov 1936	Apr 1937
6*		London Road (Nbnd) at Western Road	Red Lion	Station	**L**	**S**	25 R		**N 164**	Apr 1937	Apr 1937	Mar 1939
7*		London Road (Nbnd) opposite Southdown Garage	Red Lion	Station	**L**	**S**	25 Y	Pull for Cosham Gate	**N 143A**	Mar 1939	Mar 1939	Aug 1963
8*		London Road (Sbnd)	London / Copnor Roads	Northern Parade	**L**	**B**	15 R	Pull for Northern Parade	**Bus Stop**	6 Oct 1935	3 Nov 1935	2 Aug 1961
9*		London Road (Sbnd)	Copnor Road	London Road	**R**	**S**	?? L	Pull for Copnor Road	**N 134**	1952	25 May 1952	July 1963
10*		London Road (Nbnd)	Northern Parade	Portsbridge	**R**	**P**	25 L		**N 117**	By Mar 1943	No scheduled use	12 April 1961
11	**Green Lane**	Copnor Road (Nbnd) at Madeira Road	Madeira Road	Hilsea	**R**	**P**	25 L	Pull for Madeira Road	**CR 1**	1951	6 Jan 1952	19 Sep 1963
12*	**Chichester Road/ Copnor Road**	Copnor Road (Sbnd) at Chichester Road	Copnor Bridge	Chichester Road	**L**	**P**	25 R	Pull for Chichester Rd.	**C 158**	Aug 1953	27 Sep 1953	May 1963
13*		Copnor Road (Nbnd) at Chichester Road	Chichester Road	Green Lane	**R**	**B**	25 L	Pull for Chichester Rd	**Bus Stop**	Aug 1953	27 Sep 1953	May 1963
14*		Chichester Road (Ebnd) at Copnor Road	Green Lane	Copnor Bridge	**R**	**P**	25 Y	Pull for Left Hand curve	**CH 63**	Aug 1953	27 Sep 1953	May 1963

Key to Map	Location *Sequence is clockwise around the City* *An asterisk (*) by the Key number denotes a Note below*		Route Options		Operation			Traction Pole		Dates		
			Left	Right	Default **L**eft or **R**ight	**S**kate or **B**utton or **P**ull	Angle (°) and direction of frogs	Wording on pole, setter box, etc. (where definitely known)	Pole Code	Frog installed	*Frog into scheduled use*	Frog removed
15	**Copnor Bridge**	Copnor Road (Sbnd) at New Road	Milton	New Road	**R**	**S**	17 R		**C 11 ?**	Nov 1951	6 Jan 1952	Oct 1963
16	**Copnor Bridge**	New Road (Ebnd) at Copnor Road	Green Lane	Turning Circle	**L**	**P ?**	25 Y	Pull for Turning Circle	**GB 5 ?**	Nov 1951	6 Jan 1952	June 1963
17*	**Milton**	Goldsmith Avenue (Ebnd) at 'White House' turning circle	Turning Circle	Eastney	**R**	**P**	25 L	Pull for Turning Circle	**TA 26**	11 Sep 1936	10 Nov 1936	15 June 1963
18*	**Milton**	Milton Road (Sbnd) at Goldsmith Avenue	Eastney	Turning Circle or Fratton Bridge	**L**	**P**	25 R	Pull for Turning Circle	**TA 4 ? or TA ??**	11 Sep 1936	1942	June 1963
19	**Milton**	Eastney Road (Nbnd) at Goldsmith Avenue	Fratton Bridge or Turning Circle	Copnor	**R**	**S**	15 R	Pull for Goldsmith Avenue	**TA 4 ? or TA ??**	1952	25 May 1952	June 1963
20	**Milton**	Goldsmith Avenue (Wbnd) at 'White House' turning circle	Fratton Bridge	Turning Circle	**L**	**P**	25 R	Pull for Turning Circle	**TA 4 ? or TA ??**	11 Sep 1936	10 Nov 1936	Nov 1963
21	**Eastney**	Eastney Road (Sbnd) at Depot	Highland Road or Turning Circle	Depot	**L**	**P**	25 R	Pull for Depot	**TA 96**	Nov 1936	10 Nov 1936	Nov 1963
22	**Eastney**	Eastney Road (Sbnd) at Cromwell Road	Turning Circle	Highland Road	**R**	**P**	15 L	Pull for Turning Circle	**TA 97**	1953	27 Sep 1953	Dec 1962
23	**Eastney**	Eastney Depot	There were three facing frogs inside the depot (one giving access from the Eastney Road Sbnd line to the loop around the building and two giving access to the overhaul area) and three unconnected sidings.							Nov 1936	Nov 1936	Feb-Oct 1964
24*	**Festing Road**	Highland Road (Wbnd) at Festing Road	Festing Road	Albert Road	**R**	**S**	25 L	Pull for Festing Road	**HA33A**	Oct 1936	10 Nov 1936	Dec 1963
25	**Festing Road**	Albert Road (Ebnd) at Festing Road	Highland Road	Festing Road	**L**	**??**	25 R		**HA 32**	Oct 1936	10 Nov 1936	Oct 1954
26	**Festing Road**	Festing Road at Albert Road (Nbnd)	Albert Road	Highland Road	**R**	**??**	25 Y		**HA 37**	Oct 1936	10 Nov 1936	Oct 1954
27*	**South Parade Pier**	South Parade (Ebnd) at private road (Canoe Lake)	Festing Road	Private Road	**R**	**S**	25 L	Pull for Festing Road	**HD 27**	July 1935	3 Nov 1935	Dec 1963
28*	**South Parade Pier**	St. Helens Parade (Wbnd) at private road (Canoe Lake)	Private Road	The Strand	**R**	**P**	25 Y		**HD 40**	Nov 1936	10 Nov 1936	Dec 1963
29*	**South Parade Pier**	South Parade (Wbnd)	Inside line	Outside line	**L**	**S**	25 L		**HD 22**	Post-Aug 1948	Post-Aug 1948	Post-Sep 1953

Key to Map	Location *Sequence is clockwise around the City* *An asterisk (*) by the Key number denotes a Note below*		Route Options		Operation			Traction Pole		Dates		
			Left	Right	Default **L**eft or **R**ight	**S**kate or **B**utton or **P**ull	Angle (°) and direction of frogs	Wording on pole, setter box, etc. (where definitely known)	Pole Code	Frog installed	*Frog into scheduled use*	Frog removed
30*	**The Strand**	Clarendon Road (Wbnd) at Waverley Road	The Circle	Waverley Road	**L**	**S**	25 R	Pull for Waverley Road	**HB ??**	Sep 1936	10 Nov 1936	Oct 1962
31*	**The Strand**	Clarendon Road (Ebnd) at Waverley Road	Waverley Road	S Parade Pier	**R**	**P**	25 L	Pull for Waverley Road	**HB 29**	Sep 1936	1 Sep 1939	Oct 1962
32*	**The Strand**	Waverley Road (Sbnd) at Clarendon Road	S Parade Pier.	The Circle	**R**	**B**	25 R		**Bus Stop**	Sep 1936	1 Sep 1939	Oct 1962
33	**The Circle**	Clarendon Road (Ebnd) at Victoria Road South	Victoria Road Sth	The Strand	**R**	**P**	25 L	Pull for Victoria Rd	**M 44 ?**	Sep 1936	1 Sep 1939	Oct 1960
34	**The Circle**	Clarendon Road (Wbnd) at Victoria Road South	Palmerston Road	Victoria Road South	**L**	**S**	25 R	Pull for Victoria Rd	**M 34**	Sep 1936	1 Jul 1946	Oct 1960
35	**The Circle**	Victoria Road South (Sbnd) at Clarendon Road	The Strand	Palmerston Road	**L**	**??**	25 L	Pull for Palmerston Rd	**M ??**	Sep 1936	1 Jul 1946	Oct 1960
36	**Royal Pier Hotel**	Southsea Terrace (Wbnd) at Pier Road	Clarence Pier	Kings Terrace	**R**	**S**	25 R	Pull for Clarence Pier	**AF 3 ?**	Aug 1936	1 Sep 1939	March 1962
37	**Royal Pier Hotel**	Bellevue Terrace (Sbnd) at Southsea Terrace	Palmerston Road	Clarence Pier	**L**	**S**	25 L	Pull for Clarence Pier	**AF 13 ?**	Aug 1936	1 Oct 1936	March 1962
38	**Royal Pier Hotel**	Pier Road (Nbnd) at Southsea Terrace	Bellevue Terrace	Palmerston Road	**R**	**S ?**	25 R		**AF 43**	Aug 1936	1 Sep 1939	March 1962
39*	**Clarence Pier**	Clarence Pier	Second/Third loading bays	First loading bay	**L**	**S**	25 R		**AF 77**	Spring 1937	9 May 1937	Feb 1962
40*	**Clarence Pier**	Clarence Pier	Third loading bay	Second loading bay	**L ?**	**P**	25 R		**AF 78**	Spring 1937	9 May 1937	Feb 1962
41*	**The Terraces**	Kings Terrace (Nbnd) at Alexandra Road	Gunwharf	Guildhall	**L**	**B**	25 L	Pull for Guildhall	**Bus Stop**	Sep 1936	10 Nov 1936	May 1962
42*	**The Terraces**	Commercial Road (Sbnd) at Cambridge Road (Victoria Hall)	Kings Terrace	Floating Bridge	**L ?**	**S ?**	25 Y		**AC 16**	Oct 1936	1 Nov 1936	late 1951
43	**Gunwharf and Dockyard**	Ordnance Row (Ebnd) at Park Road	Guildhall	St Georges Road	**L**	**S**	25 Y	Pull for St George's Road	**AH 10**	Oct 1936	10 Nov 1936	Sep 1963
44	**Gunwharf and Dockyard**	The Hard (Dockyard)	left hand line	centre or outside line	**R**	**P**	25 L	Pull for left hand line	**AH 31**	19 Sep 1936	1 Nov 1936	Jan 1964
45	**Gunwharf and Dockyard**	The Hard (Dockyard)	centre line	outside line	**L**	**P**	25 R	Pull for outside line	**AH 37**	19 Sep 1936	1 Nov 1936	Jan 1964

Key to Map	Location *Sequence is clockwise around the City* *An asterisk (*) by the Key number denotes a Note below*		Route Options		Operation			Traction Pole		Dates		
			Left	Right	Default **L**eft or **R**ight	**S**kate or **B**utton or **P**ull	Angle (°) and direction of frogs	Wording on pole, setter box, etc. (where definitely known)	Pole Code	Frog installed	*Frog into scheduled use*	Frog removed
46	**Guildhall**	Commercial Road (Sbnd) at Greetham Street	Greetham Street	Guildhall Square	**R**	**S**	25 Y	Pull for Greetham St.	**A 2**	Aug 1936	1 Oct 1936	April 1962
47*		Greetham Street (Wbnd) at Commercial Road	Guildhall Square	Commercial Road (northern part)	**L**	**S**	25 R	Pull for Twyford Ave.	**RA 1**	28 Oct 1936	10 Nov 1936	May 1962
48*		Guildhall Square (Nbnd) at Greetham Street	Commercial Road (northern part)	Greetham Street	**R**	**S**	15 R	Pull for Commercial Rd.	**A 11**	Aug 1936	10 Nov 1936	May 1962
49		Guildhall Square (Sbnd) at Park Road	Commercial Road (southern part)	Dockyard	**R**	**S**	15 R	Pull for straight line	**A 10**	18 Oct 1936	10 Nov 1936	May 1962
50		Park Road (Wbnd), Guildhall terminus	Dockyard	Turning Circle	**L**	**P**	25 R	Pull for Turning Circle	**AD 1A**	Sep 1942	Sep 1942	15 July 1963
51	**Commercial Rd & Twyford Ave**	Commercial Road at Lake Road (Nbnd)	Commercial Road (northern part)	Lake Road	**L**	**S**	25 Y	Pull for Lake Road	**AB 37 ?**	15 Oct 1936	1 Nov 1936	July 1961
52*		Commercial Road (Nbnd) at Kingston Crescent 'Air Balloon'	Twyford Avenue	Kingston Crescent	**L**	**S**	25 R		**AE 71**	Sep 1935	1 Aug 1936	Dec 1960
53*		Twyford Avenue (Sbnd) at Kingston Crescent	Kingston Crescent	Guildhall	**R**	**P**	25 L		**AE 92A**	After May1943	No scheduled use	by Jan 1961
54	**Alexandra Park**	Northern Parade (Sbnd) at Gladys Avenue	Gladys Avenue	Twyford Avenue	**R**	**P**	25 L		**AE 186**	Sep 1953	No scheduled use	Spring 1961
55		Northern Parade (Nbnd) at Alexandra Park	Hilsea	Bus terminus or Gladys Avenue	**L**	**S**	25 R		**AE 181**	June 1946	1 July 1946	Spring 1961
56		Alexandra Park bus terminus	Gladys Avenue	Turning Circle	**??**	**P**	25 R	Pull for Turning Circle	**AE 182**	Sep 1953	27 Sep 1953	Spring 1961
57		Gladys Avenue (Nbnd) at Alexandra Park bus terminus	Turning Circle	Hilsea	**R**	**P**	25 L		**GL 37 ?**	Sep 1953	27 Sep 1953	Spring 1961

Key to Map	Location *Sequence is clockwise around the City* *An asterisk (*) by the Key number denotes a Note below*		Route Options		Operation			Traction Pole		Dates		
			Left	Right	Default **L**eft or **R**ight	**S**kate or **B**utton or **P**ull	Angle (°) and direction of frogs	Wording on pole, setter box, etc. (where definitely known)	Pole Code	Frog installed	*Frog into scheduled use*	Frog removed
58*	**North End**	London Road (Sbnd) at Gladys Avenue	London Road	Gladys Avenue	**L**	**P**	25 R	Pull for Depot	**GC 11**	Post 1935	No scheduled use	Spring 1963
59*		Gladys Avenue (Sbnd) at London Road	London Road	Chichester Road	**L**	**B**	15 R	Pull for Chichester Rd	**Bus Stop**	1953	27 Sep 1953	Spring 1963
60		Gladys Avenue (Sbnd) at London Road	Cosham	London Road	**R**	**P**	25 L	Pull for Cosham	**GC 9**	May 1934	4 Aug 1934	March 1963
61*		London Road (Sbnd)	Commercial Road services bus stop	Fratton Road services bus stop	**L**	**S**	25 R		**GC 17**	June 1948	June 1948	March 1963
62*		London Road (Nbnd) – original	Gladys Avenue	Cosham	**R**	**P**	25 Y		**GC 16**	May 1934	4 Aug 1934	Aug 1953
63*		London Road (Nbnd) – passing loop	Inside line	Outside line	**L**	**P**	15 R		**GC 18A**	Sep 1943	27 Sep 1943	Aug 1953
64*		London Road (Nbnd) – replacement	Cosham	Gladys Avenue	**L**	**S**	15 R		**GC 18A**	Aug 1953	Aug 1953	March 1963
65*		North End Depot (Nbnd) at Gladys Avenue	Depot	Alexandra Park	**R**	**P**	25 L	Pull for Depot	**GC 6**	Sep 1953	27 Sep 1953	Nov 1962
66		North End Depot (Sbnd) at Gladys Avenue	North End Junc	Depot	**L**	**P**	25 R	Pull for Depot	**GC 3**	Aug 1936	4 Aug 1934	Nov 1962
67		North End Depot	There were eleven facing 25°R frogs inside the depot building							Aug 1936	Aug 1936	Nov 1962
68		North End Depot (exit from depot)	Alexandra Park	North End Junc	**R**	**P**	25 Y	Pull for Northern Parade.	Wording painted on depot wall.	Sep 1953	27 Sep 1953	Nov 1962
69*	**London Road and Kingston Road**	London Road, Kingston Cross (Sbnd) at Kingston Crescent	Kingston Road	Kingston Crescent	**L**	**S**	25 R		**GC 41A**	Sep 1935	1 Aug 1936	Nov 1961
70		Kingston Road (Sbnd) at New Road	New Road	Kingston Road	**R**	**P**	25 L	Pull for New Road	**G 37**	ca. 1945–46	No scheduled use	Feb 1963
71*		Kingston Road at New Road (Nbnd)	Kingston Road	New Road	**L**	**S**	25 R	Pull for New Road	**G 42**	24 Oct 1936	1 Nov 1936	Feb 1963
72		Kingston Road (Sbnd) at Lake Road	Fratton Road	Lake Road	**L**	**S**	25 R	Pull for Lake Road	**G 55 ?**	24 Oct 1936	1 Nov 1936	March 1962

Key to Map	Location *Sequence is clockwise around the City An asterisk (*) by the Key number denotes a Note below*		Route Options		Operation			Traction Pole		Dates		
			Left	Right	Default **L**eft or **R**ight	**S**kate or **B**utton or **P**ull	Angle (°) and direction of frogs	Wording on pole, setter box, etc. (where definitely known)	Pole Code	Frog installed	*Frog into scheduled use*	Frog removed
73*	**Fratton Bridge**	Victoria Road North (Nbnd) at Goldsmith Avenue	Fratton Road	Goldsmith Avenue or Fawcett Road	**R**	**S**	25 R		**S 74 ?**	June 1936	1 Sep 1939	Nov 1962
74		Victoria Road North (Nbnd) at Goldsmith Avenue	Goldsmith Avenue	Fawcett Road	**L**	**P ?**	15 R		**S 81 ?**	June 1936	No scheduled use	late 1940s
75*		Fratton Road (Sbnd)	Fawcett Road or Goldsmith Ave	Bradford Junction	**L**	**B**	25 Y		**Bus Stop**	June 1936	1 Sep 1939	Nov 1962
76*		Fratton Road (Sbnd) at Goldsmith Avenue	Goldsmith Ave	Fawcett Road	**R**	**P**	25 L	Pull for Milton	**S 71**	June 1936	No scheduled use	Nov 1962
77*		Goldsmith Avenue (Wbnd) at Fratton Road	Bradford Junction	Fratton Road	**L**	**P**	25 R		**S 75 ?**	June 1936	No scheduled use	Nov 1962
78*	**Bradford Junction**	Rugby Road (Wbnd) at Victoria Road North	Guildhall	Fratton Bridge	**R**	**P**	25 R	Pull for Guildhall	**R 17 ?**	10 May 1936	1946	early 1962
79*		Victoria Road North (Sbnd) at Bradford Road	Albert Road	Guildhall	**R**	**S**	25 R		**R 18 ?**	May 1936	1 Sep 1939	mid July 1963
80*		Victoria Road North (Nbnd) at Bradford Road	Guildhall	Fratton Bridge	**L**	**P**	25 Y		**R 25 ?**	10 May 1936	1 Sep 1939	Oct 1963
81*		Bradford Road (Ebnd) at Victoria Road North	Fratton Bridge or Rugby Road	Albert Road	**L**	**S**	25 Y	Pull for Albert Road	**R 2 ?**	10 May 1936	10 Nov 1936	Oct 1963
82*		Bradford Road (Ebnd) at Victoria Road North	Fratton Bridge	Rugby Road	**L**	**P**	25 Y		**R 11 ?**	10 May 1936	No scheduled use	Dec 1961
83	**Rugby Road**	Fawcett Road (Sbnd) at Rugby Road	Fawcett Road	Rugby Road	**L**	**P**	25 R	Pull for Rugby Rd	**TB 11**	April 1936	1946	Dec 1961
84		Fawcett Road (Nbnd) at Rugby Road	Rugby Road	Fratton Bridge	**R**	**P**	25 L	Pull for Rugby Rd	**TB 16**	April 1936	No scheduled use	Dec 1961

Key to Map	Location *Sequence is clockwise around the City* *An asterisk (*) by the Key number denotes a Note below*		Route Options		Operation			Traction Pole		Dates		
			Left	Right	Default **L**eft or **R**ight	**S**kate or **B**utton or **P**ull	Angle (°) and direction of frogs	Wording on pole, setter box, etc. (where definitely known)	Pole Code	Frog installed	*Frog into scheduled use*	Frog removed
85	**Albert Road**	Victoria Road (Sbnd) at Albert Road	Albert Road	The Circle	**L**	**P**	25 R	Pull for Victoria Rd	**RB 5 ? or M 1 ?**	23 Sep 1936	1 Sep 1939	early 1961
86*	**Albert Road**	Albert Road Kings (Wbnd) Theatre siding	Remainder of siding	Main Line	**L**	**P**	25 R	Pull for Main Line	**MB ??**	1945–46	No scheduled use	Oct 1954
87*	**Goldsmith Av**	Goldsmith Avenue (Wbnd) Football Ground siding	Remainder of siding	Main Line	**L**	**P**	25 R	Pull for Main Line	**T 44 ? or TA 1 ?**	Early post-war	No scheduled use	March 1962
	Facing Frogs foreseen in the post-war extension plans (not implemented)											
P1	**Cosham**	Northern Road (Nbnd) (Telephone Exchange)	Farlington	Red Lion or Paulsgrove			25 L					
P2	**Cosham**	Northern Road (Nbnd) (Post Office)	Paulsgrove	Red Lion			25 L					
P3*		Stubbington Avenue										
P4*	**Copnor Bridge**	New Road at Copnor Road (Ebnd)	Turning Circle or Green Lane	Tangier Road			25 R					
P6*	**Edinburgh Road**	Commercial Road (Nbnd)	Edinburgh Road	Commercial Road			15 L					
P7*	**Edinburgh Road**	Edinburgh Road (Ebnd)	Commercial Road Northbound	Guildhall			25 Y					
P8*	**Edinburgh Road**	Commercial Road (Sbnd)	Guildhall	Edinburgh Road			25 R					

General

Not all of the frogs detailed above were in situ at the same time. Generally the 1953 situation is listed (including pole numbers) unless specifically shown otherwise. Frogs installed temporarily enabling trams to use the trolleybus lines during 1934–36 are not included.

Frogs will have been used as soon as they were installed, for travel in the direction of the wire they replaced and for testing of the new facility, earlier than shown as "into scheduled use" which represents the date from which there was more than one direction in scheduled use.

During the early post-war years the original frogs and crossings incorporating wooden beams were progressively replaced with less obtrusive pre-assembled "wire section" equivalents.

The maximum number of facing frogs on the system, including those within depots was 94.

Automatic point controllers were introduced for Portsmouth trams in 1923 and were supplied by Forest City Company who also supplied the trolleybus "auto-frog" setters from 1936. All skate and push button operations also had a pull facility for emergencies, including a reset option. Where details of wording on poles, etc. are unknown a blank entry appears in the "wording on pole" column.

The Pole Code system of letters and numbers originated with the tram network and it was unusual for a pole to be renumbered. Exceptions to this rule were briefly in 1934 when additional poles took on suffix letters. For example, initially, in Gladys Avenue new poles outside the depot included **GC1A, GC1B, GC1C, GC0, GC00** to avoid renumbering of other poles but this was changed, probably when the new exit was installed.

When a significant number of additional or replacement poles were required for tram to trolleybus conversion some renumbering took place plus many "N" poles in Cosham were renumbered for tram changes and alterations to the "Compound". Subsequent additional poles took on a suffix letter (A, B, C).

Estler Brothers Ltd, during their 1934/35 installations, numbered all poles sequentially on their blueprints, e.g. pole **GC47** was shown as their pole code **405**.

Poles which were removed, stored and, later, reused in another part of the system were renumbered accordingly.

The pole code was stencilled in black capital letters, usually approx 12 ft above ground level (approx 6 ft on the Floating Bridge – Commercial Rd section).

"Pull" instructions were, generally, painted on the poles approximately 5 ft above ground and wording, including full stops (after Rd etc) is shown where known. Wording on poles etc for skate / button operations was "OPERATE FOR . . . (same as 'pull')" / "PUSH FOR . . . (same as 'pull'), respectively, and RESET.

Notes to specific frogs or junctions

1 The position of the original October 1936 overhead installation at this location suggests that a passing loop was already planned although it was 1944 before it was installed.

2 Wiring along the private road was authorised in January 1937 but not erected until April 1942, coming into use by service vehicles on 3 May 1942. There was no advertised service use of the southbound wiring in Northern Road south of the private road from that date, however, it is probable that journeys returning to depot continued to use the more direct link to Portsbridge.

3 The area immediately south of Cosham railway level crossing, known officially variously as Cosham Railway Gates or Cosham Railway Station, but unofficially as Cosham Compound, opened to trams on 27 February 1920 and to motorbuses from the late 1920s. It was used by trams and trolleybuses from 4 August 1934, the trolleybuses using a single line loop inside of the tramway loop. When trams ceased to serve Cosham Compound in October 1934 the redundant loop of tramway overhead was rewired for trolleybuses and became the main service line. The original inner line was retained as a passing facility and for use by specials with access by a 25°Y hand-operated frog, the operating handle being on pole N222 in the middle of the Compound. This remained until the entire areas was reconstructed, involving some pole renumbering, in September 1948.

4–6 The original frog at this junction was installed in August 1936. Construction of new traffic islands in November 1936 required the frog to be moved somewhat to the north resulting in trolleybuses turning right to Cosham Station having to hug the western kerb, i.e. left lane. It was moved back to the junction with Western Road in April 1937 and equipped for auto frog operation, the setter being fitted to pole N164, one of two new poles required for the new roundabout at this junction. The auto frog equipment was one of the 16 sets purchased in December 1936. Due to the heavy traffic in this area, in 1938 plans were prepared to move the auto frog further south to a point opposite SMS Hilsea Garage, the work being carried out in March 1939 in conjunction with the installation of a second parallel line of overhead across Portsbridge.

7 As an additional in-cab warning device to remind drivers to ensure that they were on the correct Cosham line, a short length of "dead" overhead line was installed (probably in March 1939) at pole **N157** near the northern end of Portsbridge, on the Cosham Station line.

8 Originally the frog was at pole **N134** but when the triangular island at the junction of London Road with Northern Parade was replaced by a roundabout in December 1936, the overhead layout was changed and the frog moved to pole **N130**. The auto frog setter was in place by early September 1936. The auto frog is assumed to have been skate operated. In March 1939 the frog and setter were moved back to pole **N136** and it is thought that press button operation was introduced at the same time. The press button was fixed to the "Commercial Rd" bus stop pole immediately to the north of pole **N136**.

9 Following the abandonment of trolleybus operation on services 3 and 4 on 17 September 1960 the default changed and the wording became "Pull for London Road". The skate was removed on 2 August 1961.

10 The hand-operated frog enabling trolleybuses to turn from the northbound London Road wiring into the southbound Northern Parade Wiring at Hilsea was provided solely for testing vehicles after maintenance at North End Depot. It was installed by March 1943.

12+14	Although the Chichester Road junctions were available for use from 21 August 1953 there is no evidence from the timetables that they were used prior to the introduction of services 15(ii) and 16(ii) by trolleybuses travelling to/from Green Lane before/after service (the timetables foresaw use of New Road which involved a battery turn from New Road into Kingston Road). It is not known if early morning untimetabled journeys used Christchurch Road to reach Green Lane during this short interim period. One late night service 6 journey, however, continued to operate from Cosham to Copnor Bridge and then via New Road back to North End Depot until 30 May 1954.
13	The auto frog setter was located on pole **C 155**.
17	No timetabled use of this frog has been found, however Football Ground specials turned back here after setting down at Fratton Park prior to returning to the siding in the westbound Goldsmith Avenue wiring.
18	The frog in the Milton Road southbound wiring was used by short journeys on services 1A and 2A from June or July 1942 as was frog 20 in the Goldsmith Avenue westbound wiring.
24	There was a circular "repeater" indicator light on the next pole (**HA33**).
27	The original LH hand operated frog was located immediately to the west of the turn into the Canoe Lake turning circle (private road) but was moved further west to pole **HD25** by September 1936. In August 1948 the frog was moved east to pole HD27 and equipped with auto frog equipment (skate operated).
28	The line through the Canoe Lake turning circle from the hand-operated frog in the St. Helens Parade westbound line was slewed to cross (instead of join) the original line in the private road in September 1953. It then made a loop to join the St. Helens Parade eastbound line immediately before the frog at pole **HD27**. The frog at pole **HD40** was removed in December 1963 as part of the removal of overhead although the loop had been removed 17/18 July 1963.
29	Passing loop installed ca August 1948 replacing a single line.
30+31	The auto frog was moved from the Clarendon Road westbound line to the eastbound line in September 1960 following the abandonment of trolleybus services 3 and 4.
32	The auto frog setter was located on pole **HC25**. A circular "repeater" indicator light was on the next pole (**HB25B**).
39+40	A simple single line turning circle following the track of the tramway turning circle was initially installed here in May 1936 pending changes to the road layout and construction of several loading bays (two sidings having been planned in April 1935). Work commenced in February 1937 necessitating installation of a temporary turning circle in two locations at different stages of the work in Pier Road in February-May 1937. Upon completion the overhead layout comprised two sidings through the loading bays within the loop which permitted roadside loading on the northwest side of the loop in front of the Esplanade Hotel pre-war (tourist shops and amusement arcades post-war).
41	The auto frog setter was located at pole **AC61**.
	Removed following the abandonment of trolleybus services 15(i) and 16(i), and closure of the Floating Bridge line (29 42September 1951).
47	This junction is believed to have been the first auto frog installation in Portsmouth although that in London Road, Hilsea (8) might have been the first used in service
48	Pre-war the default was Left but this changed, at some time, to Right. The auto frog setter and indicator light was fixed to pole **A11** and there was a circular, hooded "repeater" light on pole **A9** planted in the central island of Guildhall Square. A bamboo trolley retrieval pole hung on pole A9.
50	A turning circle in the width of Park Road was installed ca September 1942. Prior to this trolleybuses terminating here had turned using their traction batteries. There had been plans in November 1936 for a reverser into Nelson Square, a street (now disappeared) 100 yards further west on the south side of Park Road, with a long siding for trolleybus parking but this never materialised.
52	The 25° trail frog at this junction in the Twyford Avenue southbound line were replaced by a BIC 15° one with a 17.5° crossing over the eastbound Kingston Crescent line on 11 March 1951.
53	The frog in the southbound Twyford Avenue wiring at Kingston Crescent was installed for wartime emergency use, probably in the second half of 1943. Post-war it was used to enable vehicles on test to follow a circular route North End – Hilsea – Kingston Crescent – North End (see note to frog 10). From September 1953 vehicles on test could return to the depot from Alexandra Park along Gladys Avenue.
58	This frog and link was installed ca October 1935 for North End Depot access purposes. Prior to this link the early trolleybuses, which were not equipped with traction batteries, must have used the maximum deviation of their trolley poles and momentum to turn into Gladys Avenue. It is possible that the installation was held back to avoid complex crossings of the tramway overhead equipment here which remained in use until summer 1935.

59 The auto frog setter was fixed to pole **GC7**.

61 During June 1948 the southbound stops for Guildhall and Fratton services were separated and a passing loop (with a crossover halfway between poles **GC11 and 13**) was installed. This allowed trolleybuses on each set of services to pass each other and enabled short workings on Fratton services to start at the new stop. The frog was north of that for turning right into Gladys Avenue and north of the Stubbington Avenue (pole **N2**) road junction. At some date after October 1951, with the remaining "Guildhall" stop also moved south, the frog was moved to immediately south of the trail frog from Gladys Avenue (pole **GC17**) which then required two operating skates, one on the line from Cosham and another on the line from Gladys Avenue, to select which bus stop was to be served. The wording used on the operating box was "Operate for Commercial Road via Kingston Cres." At a later date, this wording was simplified from 7 lines of text to just 5.

62–64 A passing loop in the northbound wiring south of the junction with Gladys Avenue came into use on 27 September 1943. In September 1953, with the introduction of schedules services along Gladys Avenue (services 15(ii) and 16(ii)), the 25° Y frog at the north end of the passing loop was replaced by a crossing, and the junction moved south and incorporated into the loop.

65 Initially there was a single entrance/exit at the south end of North End Depot equipped with a 25° Y reverser into Gladys Avenue and a sprung 25° R for travel south. When the new (northern) exit overhead came into use in August 1936 the 25° R no longer needed to be sprung.

69 A "repeater" indicator light was on pole **GC45** which was outside the 'White Hart' public house.

71 Following the abandonment of trolleybus operation on services 3 and 4 on 17 September 1960 the default changed and the wording became "Pull for North End".

73 This auto frog setter had an illuminated vertical arrow instead of the normal left / right facing type. The auto frog equipment was removed in November 1962 although the frog remained in place for the power feed from Fratton Road.

75 The Y frog was originally located on Fratton Bridge (pole **S69**) before set back northwards post-war (between 1947 and 1957) to the bus stop and parallel wiring installed up to the road junction. The auto frog setter was on pole **S63**.

76+77 Used solely for Football Ground specials to/from Goldsmith Avenue and vehicle transfers between depots.

78 No timetabled use of this frog prior to 1946 (when short working on services 3 and 4A were first shown) has been found.

79+81 In September 1948 the City's Civil Engineer proposed a remodelling of the Bradford Junction road layout and plans were prepared to accommodate this with the trolleybus overhead but the road layout remained the same until after the demise of the trolleybuses.

80+82 A skate-operated auto frog was probably installed here prior to the abandonment of services 13 and 14 (26 January 1959).

86+87 In both of these sidings the only facing frog was (with a trailing frog on the main line) mid-way along the siding. There was a trailing frog at the western end of each siding.

Notes to proposed post-war extensions (none of which were constructed)

Due to the absence of parliamentary approval and possibly the incomplete nature of many of the roads to be traversed no detailed plans of the Wymering and Paulsgrove extension, except for the junctions at Cosham, were prepared. The planning for all the other proposed and approved extensions were complete, including the location of traction poles. The reversing triangles proposed for Paulsgrove, Jubilee Avenue at Portsdown Road, and at Farlington, Havant Road at Rectory Avenue, would have been made up of 25° R and L sprung and trail frogs.

P3 The Stubbington Avenue extension plan include a triangular junction at Copnor Road permitting turns in both directions whereas at the North End end access would have been limited to London Road to the south of the junction. No access to Gladys Avenue or Hilsea would have been possible. A more complex junction would have been unworkable, hence the decision to wire Chichester Road instead of Stubbington Avenue.

P4 A turning circle would have been hung above the existing Stanley Avenue motorbus turning point in Tangier Road.

P5–7 A turning circle would have been installed at the junction of Unicorn Road with Flathouse Road where the road widened in front of Unicorn Gate.

Key	Nbnd = Northbound	Ebnd = Eastbound	**?** = single question mark indicates the preceding information is assumed correct but remains uncertain
	Sbnd = Southbound	Wbnd = Westbound	**??** = double question marks indicates not known

for which parliamentary approval was not sought. The reverser would have been made up of a crossover, a 25° left hand sprung trail frog and a 25° right hand sprung trail frog.

The Strand, Eastern Villas Road, as one of two possible solutions to avoid trolleybuses traversing the sea front during the Second World War. This solution would have been located on the south side of Clarendon Road to the east of the junction with Waverley Road requiring vehicles to reverse out of Clarendon Park Road using a 25° right hand spring trail frog into Eastern Villas Road and then a 25° Y sprung facing frog to return to The Strand. The existing westbound wire to the east of Eastern Villas Road would have been temporarily tied-off at a new traction pole to the west of HB42A.

The Strand, Kenilworth Road, was the second of two possible solutions to avoid trolleybuses traversing the sea front during the Second World War. This scheme would have been located on the north side of Clarendon Road to the west of the junction with Waverley Road requiring vehicles to reverse out of Clarendon Road at pole HB22. This would have required six traction poles, a 25° right hand spring trail frog into Kenilworth Road, a 25° left hand spring trail frog from Kenilworth Road into Clarendon Road, a 25° Y hand-operated frog (the reverser was intended to be used by eastbound services arriving from The Circle and by westbound services arriving from Waverley Road, so provision was made for a "pull" in Kenilworth Road) and a crossover. This scheme was chosen in preference to that in Eastern Villas Road in May 1942; however, as the sea front was re-opened to trolleybuses in June 1942 the plan was dropped. The subsequent closure from April to June 1944 in preparation for "D-Day" was considered too short a period to warrant implementation of the scheme.

Traffic islands or roundabouts were installed at the following locations after the construction of trolleybus equipment at the junctions concerned:

Location	Date
Albert Road, at the junction with Victoria Road (reduction in size of existing island)	by 1955
Alexandra Road, at the junction with Cambridge Road, High Street and St George's Road (Cambridge Junction)	c. 1956
Commercial Road at its north end, 'Air Balloon' junction with Kingston Crescent and Twyford Avenue	1943
Northern Road, Cosham, at the junction with Southampton Road (now known as Medina Road) and Wayte Street	1930s
Roundabout at this same location enlarged	c. 1953
Northern Road, Cosham, at the junction with Spur Road and the new "Link Road" (now known as Southampton Road)	5 August 1957
Portsbridge, north side	December 1936
Portsbridge, south side	January 1937

Little used or unusual sections of overhead wiring and turning circles

Trolleybuses did not regularly use the following stretches of overhead wiring:

Albert Road, Kings Theatre, siding

A siding about 220 yards long was installed at an unknown date in the financial year 1945–46 in the westbound Albert Road wiring, commencing at the junction with Napier Road and continuing to a point just beyond Exmouth Road, to

No. 250 circumnavigates the roundabout built c. 1953 to replace an earlier small island at the junction of Northern Road with Medina Road (named Southampton Road until 1958 when the Link Road was completed throughout) and Wayte Street travelling south on 17 March 1963. Cosham Fire Station is on the corner of Northern Road and Wayte Street to the nearside of the trolleybus. (T.V. Runnacles)

provide parking for extra trolleybuses serving Kings Theatre, located on the east side of the Albert Road junction with Exmouth Road. There was no wired-in access from the east: trolleybuses were required to de-wire and replace their booms on the siding wires. Approximately halfway along the siding, opposite Chelsea Road, there was a 25° right hand pull frog enabling trolleybuses to leave the siding and rejoin the through westbound wiring beneath a 25° trailing frog. The siding continued, rejoining the Albert Road through wiring just beyond Exmouth Road beneath a 25° trailing frog.

It is believed that the siding was removed in October 1954.

Goldsmith Avenue Football Ground siding

A siding about 400 yards long was installed at an unknown date early post-war in the westbound Goldsmith Avenue wiring, commencing opposite Winter Road and continuing to a point just beyond Frogmore Road, to provide parking for extra trolleybuses serving the football ground in Fratton Park, 250 yards to the north. The layout was similar to that at the Albert Road, Kings Theatre, siding. There was no wired-in access from the east: trolleybuses were required to de-wire and replace their booms on the siding wires. Approximately halfway along the siding, opposite Ruskin Road, there was a 25° right hand pull frog enabling trolleybuses to leave the siding and rejoin the through westbound wiring beneath a 25° trailing frog. The siding continued, rejoining the Goldsmith Avenue through wiring just beyond Frogmore Road beneath a 25° trailing frog.

The siding was removed during the week ending 10 March 1962 and the trolley wires were used to replace the parallel main line wires which were in need of replacement at the time.

Milton 'White House' turning circle

A turning circle accessible from both the eastbound and westbound Goldsmith Avenue wiring was constructed around a traffic island at the junction of Goldsmith Avenue with Eastney Road and Milton Road, opposite the 'White House' public house. Work was completed on 11 September 1936; however, trolleybuses were only introduced along Goldsmith Avenue on 10 November 1936.

No timetabled journeys from the eastbound Goldsmith Avenue wiring ever terminated here. Football Ground specials probably used it after setting down at the Football Ground before returning to the siding in Goldsmith Avenue (westbound). The circle was available to trolleybuses from Eastney Road turning back before entering Eastney Depot; however, there were no timetabled journeys from this direction until summer 1942 when services 1A and 2A were extended to Milton 'White House' presumably primarily for turning purposes.

The turning circle remained in use until the final abandonment of the system. Until 27 July 1963 a weekday service 6 working, Monday–Saturday at 08.30am, and on Sunday mornings five workings started here, in all cases for the Dockyard.

Northern Road southbound (from 1942)

In May 1940 plans to widen the private road running east from Northern Road to the Cosham Railway Station terminus (Cosham Compound) were approved; however, due to wartime restrictions work only began in April 1942. All trolleybuses heading south from Cosham 'Red Lion' were diverted along the private road on 3 May 1942, and the southbound wiring along Northern Road from the private road to the Western Road

1950 BUT9611T 305 joins Milton Road at Milton 'White House' on its northbound journey to Cosham 'Red Lion'. In the upper left foreground the wires leaving the turning circle and joining Milton Road southbound can be seen. (Tony Belton)

Typically poised with driver's cab doors left open, 239 and 306 wait beneath their respective turning circles at Alexandra Park terminus (junction of Gladys Avenue with Northern Parade) on the final day of operations to this point (30 April 1960). (D.A.P. Janes)

roundabout fell into disuse. The disused wiring was removed in 1956.

Rugby Road

The 0.11 mile long section of interlaced track tramway in Rugby Road, which runs between Fawcett Road and Victoria Road North, was part of the Southsea South Parade Pier – Guildhall through route which followed Fawcett Road, Rugby Road, Bradford Road and Greetham Street. The tramway was abandoned in 1932 and the route was foreseen as offering potential for the initial experimental trolley vehicle service. This did not materialise and Rugby Road was not equipped with trolleybus equipment until May–June 1936 being officially accepted for service with the final tram to trolleybus conversions of November 1936.

In principle the wiring in Rugby Road allowed trolleybuses from Southsea The Strand to turn west out of Fawcett Road, cross Bradford Junction and continue into Bradford Road, and vice versa. It also enabled vehicles from Fratton Bridge and points north thereof to traverse the northern end of Fawcett Road before turning west into Rugby Road and then north into Victoria Road North at Bradford Junction, i.e. it provided a short-working turning circle from the north. Furthermore short-workings from Southsea South Parade Pier to Fratton Bridge via Fawcett Road could also turn back here until early post-war. Despite numerous requests over the years no through trolleybus service ever ran along Rugby Road and its use was limited to late evening short-workings of trolleybuses returning to North End Depot at the end of their duties.

The turning circle fell into disuse on 17 September 1960 with the withdrawal of trolleybus services 3 and 4 but all the Rugby Road wiring remained available for use until the week ending 8 December 1961 when all trolley wires, connections to other roads and bracket arms were removed.

Termini

Until the post-war period there were many examples of trolleybuses using their traction batteries on a regular basis at termini, not least due to the paucity of emergency or short-working turning points. Wired trolleybus terminal arrangements can be conveniently categorised as follows:

Turning circles on CPPTD private property

Alexandra Park (Gladys Avenue): In May 1939 a plot of Corporation land at the junction of Gladys Avenue with Northern Parade, opposite Alexandra Park, was cleared for use as a motorbus terminus. On 7 July 1941, as a fuel economy measure, trolleybuses took over the operation of workmen's services to and from the Dockyard and they turned at the Alexandra Park terminus by use of their traction batteries. In September 1942 or shortly thereafter a single line turning circle, accessible from the northbound wiring in Northern Parade, was installed.

In 1950, in connection with the extension along Gladys Avenue between North End Depot and Northern Parade, it was decided to install a turning circle superimposed on the existing one but accessible from Gladys Avenue. Work was completed in August 1953 and services 15 and 16 from the North End direction began to terminate at Alexandra Park on

Alexandra Park turning circles seen from the west side of Northern Parade (28 June 1956). (D.A.P. Janes [photographer G.A. Tucker])

27 September 1953. The layout involved an 80° crossover on the west side of the site where the wires arriving from Gladys Avenue northbound crossed the wires joining Northern Parade southbound. There was a trailing frog on the north side where the wires arriving from Gladys Avenue joined those arriving from Northern Parade northbound, followed immediately by a 25° right hand hand-operated frog enabling trolleybuses to either return to Northern Parade or join the Gladys Avenue southbound wiring. Thus vehicles from Northern Parade could cross the site and continue to North End Depot.

The turning circle fell into disuse on 30 April 1960 with the conversion of services 15 and 16 along Gladys Avenue, and 19 and 20 along Northern Parade to motorbus operation. The wiring remained intact until cut down in early March 1961.

Clarence Pier (bus station): An initial plan drawn in April 1935 proposed a teardrop shaped turning circle immediately in front of the entrance to Clarence Pier, similar to the existing tram track loop, but with two sidings accessed by 25° right hand frogs. By December 1935 this had been redesigned in connection with planned improvements to Clarence Esplanade. The revised layout foresaw a loop around the ornamental garden and public conveniences at the east end of the Esplanade, across the entrance to Clarence Pier and then the Esplanade Hotel, before rejoining Pier Road. Two sidings serving loading bays at an angle within the loop on CPPTD property immediately in front of the Pier were also included. Delays in constructing the new road layout made a temporary solution necessary if the tram to trolleybus conversion was not to be delayed and in May 1936 Clough, Smith & Co. were instructed to install a clockwise single line turning circle. This work was completed by end June 1936 although the terminus remained isolated from the growing system. On 1 October 1936 trolleybus services 1 and 2 between Clarence Pier Cosham 'Red Lion' commenced.

Road work only started at the beginning of 1937, the loading bays being completed in February 1937. Clough, Smith & Co. immediately started to erect overhead equipment for the terminal arrangements originally planned, necessitating a temporary turning circle in Pier Road. The full layout came into service on 9 May 1937 and involved a 25° right hand auto frog giving access to the first loading bay and then a 25° right hand hand-operated frog serving the second loading bay (the third was on the public carriageway in front of the Esplanade Hotel). No changes were made to this layout until after trolleybus services to and from Clarence Pier ceased on 2 December 1961, all wiring in the terminal area being cut down in February 1962.

Cosham Railway Station (Cosham Compound): A single line clockwise turning circle was installed within the tramway terminal loop on CPPTD property between the PHLR embankment and Portsmouth Road immediately to the west of Cosham Railway Station and level crossing in spring 1934. It came into service on 4 August 1934. At some stage between October 1934 and November 1935, probably after the end of the special tram services to and from Cosham in July 1935, a siding was installed on the east side of the turning circle parallel to Portsmouth Road. Access was by means of a 25° Y hand-operated frog at the northernmost point of the layout with a 25° left hand trail point at the south end a few yards south of the passenger waiting shelter.

Upon the completion of overhead wiring along the private road from Northern Road in April 1942 (brought into service

Clarence Pier bus station out of season was not the most welcoming point of the South Coast! The crew of AEC661T 273 relax in the lower saloon until time for their departure to Green Lane. (Tony Belton)

1934 AEC661T 204 with English Electric composite body and 1936 AEC661T 285 with Cravens all metal body, together with Leyland Titan TD4 motorbus 132, at Cosham Railway Station terminal loops prior to its 1948 reconstruction. (A.D. Packer)

3 May 1942) a 30° crossing was installed in the northbound line into the Compound and a 25° right hand trail frog in the southbound line at the junction with Portsmouth Road.

During summer 1948 the overhead wiring layout was redesigned. From September 1948 trolleybuses turned in an anti-clockwise direction and the siding was moved to the west side of the property with a 25° Y hand-operated frog on the northern periphery. The siding ended with a left hand trail frog parallel to the private road wiring which was itself joined just prior to the crossover with the northbound wiring and the junction with Portsmouth Road. This enabled all the trolleybus boarding points together with a re-positioned passenger waiting shelter to be located together on the southern periphery of the Compound.

The outer through wiring fell into disuse with the conversion of trolleybus services 19 and 20 to motorbus operation on 30 April 1960 and the remainder became redundant on 17 September 1960 when Cosham Railway Station ceased to be a trolleybus terminus; however, the entire overhead wiring layout remained aloft until June 1963 when dismantlement commenced. The line along the private road through the southern side of the property remained in use until the end of trolleybus operation in Portsmouth on 27 July 1963.

Southsea South Parade Pier (Canoe Lake): A single line turning circle to serve the experimental first trolleybus route was erected in spring 1934 above a purpose-built private road at the west end of the Canoe Lake Grounds which lay between St Helen's Parade and Southsea Esplanade about 200 yards to the east of Southsea South Parade Pier. It was brought into service on 4 August 1934.

Construction of an alternative trolleybus route between Southsea South Parade Pier and Cosham by way of St Helen's Parade, Festing Road, Bradford Junction and the Guildhall necessitated through wiring along St Helen's Parade. This was accomplished by installing a 25° left hand hand-operated frog in the eastbound line and a trailing frog in the wiring at the north end of the private road, which was thus used by all terminating and westbound trolleybuses. By September 1936 the facing frog had been set back some distance to the west and the westbound line from St Helen's Parade had been extended across the entrance of the private road to rejoin the exit wiring from the turning circle just east of the entrance to the Pier.

In August 1948 the eastbound facing frog was moved about halfway back to the north entrance of the private road and provided with an auto frog setter. At the same time or shortly thereafter a passing loop was installed in the westbound wiring in front of the entrance to the Pier accessed by a 25° left hand auto frog. The two parallel westbound wires merged in Clarendon Road just to the north of the junction with South Parade.

In or around September 1953 the trailing frog in the wiring at the north end of the private road was removed and replaced by a crossover enabling the line from St Helen's Parade westbound to turn back into the eastbound line immediately prior to the auto frog and thus creating two superimposed turning circles, one for trolleybuses from the east (used only by summer season short workings on services 5 and 6) and the other for those from the west.

The trailing frog in Clarendon Road where the passing loop and through westbound wiring merged was cut back some 50 yards onto South Parade at the beginning of September 1961.

Withdrawal of trolleybuses from services 3 and 4 on 17 September 1960 brought an end to frequent use of the turning circle from the west although the entire layout was retained and used by four early morning short workings of the 5 and 6 from and to the Dockyard. On 17 and 18 July 1963 the turning circle accessible from St Helen's Parade westbound was cut down, the remainder being removed on 3 December 1963.

In the width of the road

Dockyard Main Gate (The Hard): The terminal layout at The Hard, comprising two parallel loops on the west side of the road and a turning circle at the north end of the Hard immediately before the right-angle corner into Queen Street and in front of the Dockyard Main Gate, was approved in September 1935. The turning circle was strung on 19 September 1936 and the remaining wiring later in the month although it was not yet part of a contiguous route. The loop next to the kerb was accessed by a 25° left hand hand-operated frog, the central through line rejoining the loop immediately before the turning circle, and a loop towards the centre of the road accessed by a 25° right hand hand-operated frog and which

Consecutively numbered vehicles, AEC661T 300 (100) of 1937 and BUT9611T 301 of 1950, stand at Cosham Railway Station bus terminus following the reconstruction. The driver of 301 points out a feature of the frog providing access to the waiting loop. Both crew members have white summer season tops to their uniform caps whilst the driver sports a lightweight dust jacket. (Roy Marshall)

On The Hard trolleybus 299 leads an unidentified BUT9611T in the middle loop with another AEC661T, no. 282, at the kerb. There are apparently plans for a new Moss Bros. store on the bomb site behind the passenger waiting shelter. Their Portsmouth store opened in 1940 to serve the naval business and was promptly hit in a bombing raid. Business was conducted for some years after the Second World War from a wooden hut! (Roy Marshall)

also rejoined the central line prior to its junction with the kerbside line. Trolleybus services reached the Dockyard Main Gate on 10 November 1936.

There were various plans towards the end of the Second World War to construct a bus station on land to be reclaimed to the west of The Hard between Portsmouth Harbour Station and the Common Hard access to Gosport Ferry in an effort to combat increasing traffic congestion but the post-war financial stringencies prevented construction. It is unclear how the trolleybuses would have been affected. As a cheaper alternative four different schemes involving various arrangements of loop lines and loading bays either on east or west side of The Hard were investigated in November 1944 but nothing materialised.

Copnor Bridge (New Road): A simple, single line loop, initially in the width of New Road behind a semi-circular traffic island immediately to the west of its junction with Copnor Road was installed in June 1936. Drawings prepared in conjunction with the Portsmouth Corporation (Trolley Vehicles) Order Confirmation Act, 1948, show that the turning circle would have been retained in the middle of a triangular junction with Copnor Road. The wires turning south across Copnor Bridge would have provided access to and from Tangier Road which branches off to the east immediately after the bridge over the railway (Copnor Bridge). The westbound wires from the southern end of Copnor Road would have crossed and run parallel to the turning circle exit wires at the bus stop at the east end of New Road where trolleybuses took a layover. As the Tangier Road extension was not constructed solely a northwards junction with Copnor Road was installed in November 1951: the turning circle was retained unchanged but parallel wiring was installed at the New Road bus stop prior to a trailing frog.

Guildhall (Park Road): Having discounted proposals for a turning circle clockwise around the Victoria Statue located on a triangular site bounded by Commercial Road, Percy Street and Russell Street, accessible from the Commercial Road (both ends), Greetham Street and Park Street (but with no return into the southern part of Commercial Road) in September 1935, construction of a roundabout in Guildhall Square (Commercial Road) between the Guildhall and the Sussex Hotel accessible from all directions, possibly with a siding stub in Russell Street, was investigated but also rejected in late 1935. This led to proposals for a reversing triangle into Nelson Square off Park Street in late 1936 but nothing was constructed. As far as can be ascertained, all trolleybuses terminating at the Guildhall pre-war did so by making a "U-turn" in the width of Park Road by use of their traction batteries. In September 1942, or shortly thereafter, a rather tight turning circle was installed here with a 25° hand-operated right hand frog at the top of the private road leading into the Portsmouth & Gosport Gas Co. premises and a 25° left hand trail frog outside the Park Road side entrance to the Guildhall. Drivers were frequently unable to turn around with just one attempt.

Around traffic islands or at wide road junctions

Eastney (Highland Road): In connection with the Chichester Road and Gladys Avenue route extension a turning circle was constructed around a traffic island at the north end of Cromwell Road at its junction with Eastney Road and Highland

Heading north along Copnor Road 300 descends from Copnor Bridge past the turning circle at the east end of New Road on 24 March 1963. (T.V. Runnacles)

AEC661T 273 turns at Copnor Bridge on 15 June 1961. (A.D. Packer)

Parked cars made use of the Guildhall turning circle at the east end of Park Road a difficult manoeuvre. It seems unlikely that 289 will complete its turn at the first attempt (28 September 1962). (T.V. Runnacles)

Road, to serve as the southern terminus for the new services (15 and 16) from 27 September 1953. Access was by means of a 15° left hand hand-operated frog from the southbound Eastney Road line immediately opposite Eastney Depot. The turning circle remained intact upon conversion of services 15 and 16 to motorbus operation on 30 April 1960 but it remained available for use until 8 December 1962 when the facing and trailing frogs were removed, the remainder being cut down in February 1963.

Milton 'White House': A public house on the south side of Goldsmith Avenue gave its name to this turning circle around a traffic island at the junction of Eastney road, Goldsmith Avenue and Milton Road. The circle could be approached from the Goldsmith Avenue eastbound line using a 25° left hand hand-operated frog or the Milton Road northbound line using a 25° right hand hand-operated frog. Construction was completed 11 September 1936 and the turning circle was available to service vehicles from 10 November 1936 although as far as can be ascertained no scheduled services turned here. It is assumed that football specials from the Goldsmith Avenue direction used the turning circle immediately. Scheduled services and short workings from the Eastney direction began to terminate here from June or July 1942.

Construction of the Milton Road route extension in 1952 resulted in a double junction being installed on the eastern perimeter of the turning circle where it hung above the southbound lane of Milton Road and a new trail frog from the circle was inserted here. This layout remained aloft and available for use until the abandonment of trolleybus operation in Portsmouth.

Circular routing around a number of streets

Cosham 'Red Lion' (Northern Road, London Road, Spur Road): The northernmost terminus in Portsmouth was made up of a single line clockwise route following the streets mentioned above, the 'Red Lion' public house being built on the west side of the junction of London Road and Spur Road. A passing loop, accessible by a 25° Y hand-operated frog was installed in Spur Road in early 1944 to handle the increased number of services terminating here. This remained aloft and available for use until its removal on 6 June 1963.

Fratton Bridge (Fawcett Road, Rugby Road, Victoria Road North): The complex layout here can be best understood by reference to a map. It was possible for trolleybuses from the Fratton Road southbound line to turn back to the north by circumnavigating Fawcett Road, Rugby Road (westbound)

BUT9611T 312 waits in Spur Road, the nominal starting point for services from Cosham 'Red Lion', as a half-timbered Morris 1000 Traveller drives past. In the background the terminal loop wiring turning out of London Road is visible. Beyond the traffic lights Havant Road and the starting point of the authorised but un-built extension to Farlington can be seen. (Hugh Taylor collection [photographer's name not recorded])

and Victoria Road North (northbound) in that sequence. Until early post-war, trolleybuses from Fawcett Road and thus South Parade Pier could turn back using the link from Victoria Road North (northbound) into Fawcett Road (southbound), as could trolleybuses from the Bradford Road eastbound line. Apart from the link referred to above the entire layout remained intact, albeit increasingly disused by service journeys after 17 September 1960, until removal of the unused portions commenced in November 1962. The through wiring Bradford Road – Victoria Road North – Goldsmith Avenue remained available for use until the final abandonment of trolleybus operation in Portsmouth

Reversing triangles (reversers)

Green Lane: Although there were a number of suitable streets nearby for a one-way terminal loop around a block these would all have involved a considerable length of, probably non-revenue, overhead wiring. Nonetheless, it is unusual that a reversing triangle was installed at such a relatively late stage in British trolleybus history. The motorbus services replaced had also reversed at the same location. Installed in late 1951 the reversing triangle came into use on 6 January 1952 when trolleybus services 7, 8, 11 and 12 were extended from Copnor Bridge to Green Lane. The destination was a misnomer as the trolleybuses turned into a side street off Copnor Road opposite Green Lane.

Trolleybuses turned west out of Copnor Road into Madeira Road and came to a halt once they had passed the junction with Compton Road. They then reversed into Compton Road before turning back into Madeira Road. The reversing triangle consisted of a 25° right hand and a 25° Y frog, and crossover. It continued to be used by normal services until the withdrawal of services 7, 8, 11 and 12 on 2 December 1961 but continued to be used regularly for a service 5 short working at 6.0pm on Fridays only until 22 June 1963. The reversing triangle was dismantled on 9 September 1963.

In view of the different headways of services 7 and 11, there were thoughts of installing a passing loop on the north side of Madeira Road in order that trolleybuses could wait at the bus stop there once they had pulled out of Compton Road, thereby ensuring that they left in the correct sequence. This was never installed. Any trolleybus likely to delay the departure of the vehicle behind simply waited at the western extremity of the Madeira Road wires before reversing, leaving sufficient space for the next arrival to reverse and depart.

Old Portsmouth, Point (Floating Bridge): Trolleybuses approached northwards along Broad Street but terminated 100 yards short of the tram terminus and south of the tramway passing loop and stub which was at the top of the slipway leading on to the floating bridge or chain ferry to Gosport outside the 'Union Tavern' (now known as 'The Spice Island Inn') public house. Having unloaded in Broad Street, trolleybuses reversed into East Street, the last side street leading off Broad Street to the east before the slipway was reached, thereby avoiding any conflict with traffic queuing for the ferry. They then turned left back into Broad Street to wait at the boarding point.

The reversing triangle, made up of a 25° right hand spring trail frog and a 25° Y spring trail frog, was installed in October 1936 and came into use on 1 November 1936 when services 15 and 16 commenced. It is not known if the reversing triangle itself was damaged during the Second World War but in view of the intensive bombing in the area this is quite likely. Substantial reconstruction of the overhead equipment due to air-raid damage was necessary and by March 1943, but probably already from 6 July 1941, the layout had been changed whereby trolleybuses turned into East Street upon arrival at the terminus and then reversed into Broad Street requiring the addition of a crossover in the exit wiring.

The reversing triangle was dismantled in late 1951 following the abandonment of trolleybus service in Old Portsmouth.

Unfulfilled proposals

A number of drawings still survive showing traction pole location and overhead wiring layout proposals for routes or terminal arrangements that never materialised. These include:

Edinburgh Road and Unicorn Road, providing a link between Commercial Road and HM Dockyard Unicorn Gate.

Havant Road, between Spur Road, Cosham, and Farlington, Rectory Avenue.

Southampton Road, between Northern Road, Cosham, and the City Boundary at Portsdown Road, n.b. part of the then (October 1934) Southampton Road, now named Medina Road.

London Road (junction with Spur Road), Cosham, to Portchester Cross Roads along the proposed "Link Road" (today's Southampton Road) and Allaway Avenue through the expanding Paulsgrove and Wymering housing estates (May 1947).

London Road (junction with Spur Road), Cosham, to Paulsgrove (junction of Jubilee Avenue with Portsdown Road) along the proposed "Link Road" (today's Southampton Road), Allaway Avenue and Jubilee Avenue (August 1947).

Stubbington Avenue, along its entire length between Copnor Road and London Road (replaced by an alternative route along Chichester Road).

Tangier Road, Copnor Bridge to Stanley Avenue.

Overbridges

There were only two locations on the system where trolleybuses operated beneath railway overbridges (at all other points the routes were carried above the railway) and both required that the overhead wiring was positioned to the nearside of the road to maximise the available height required by the trolley poles.

Height clearances recorded were:

Ordnance Row (Portsmouth Harbour Station)	16ft 0in.
Commercial Road (Portsmouth & Southsea Station)	16ft 3in.

Beneath both bridges the trolley wire was attached to a T-iron suspended by porcelain insulators from wooden troughs, intended to catch the trolley in event of a de-wirement as contact with the girder work would almost certainly have damaged and/or ripped off a moving trolley head, attached to the underside of the bridge. There is no evidence of similar wooden troughing being generally attached to the roof girders inside the depots, although such troughs were provided over a distance of about 20ft immediately inside the entrance to Eastney Depot.

BUT9611T 307 passes carefully beneath the troughing under the railway bridge leading to Portsmouth Harbour Station at the east end of Ordnance Row a few yards before the junction for Park Road. An SMS Leyland Cheetah single-decker motorbus waits in St George's Square on the other side of the railway bridge. The St George's Road frog setter is visible just in front of the bracket arm. (Roy Marshall)

Vehicle equipment

The two current collectors on the roof of each trolleybus consisted of three main parts: the trolley base carrying the trolley boom and allowing the boom to swing in a horizontal plane and to rise under spring tension; the boom itself and, at the extreme end of the boom, the trolley head, which made contact with the under surface of the power conducting trolley wire. All three parts were insulated from each other, and the base was also insulated from the trolley gantry by bonded-rubber mountings provided to minimise the transmission of noise to the roof. Nonetheless, an abiding memory of Portsmouth trolleybuses was the thunderous roof noise whenever the vehicle passed beneath special work! Radio suppressor coils were mounted on the roof forward of the base on all Portsmouth's trolley vehicles. The trolley wheels were about 4in. in diameter.

The current was carried from the trolley head by a flexible cable running through the hollow trolley boom which narrowed to 1in. diameter at the trolley head end. The boom, a tapering steel tube was wrapped in black bitumen impregnated insulating tape to minimise the chance of it shorting the trolley wires in the event of a de-wirement. All vehicles were equipped with Brecknell Willis trolley bases having paired springs lying alongside the trolley boom. The vertical upward pressure of the trolley heads on the wire could be measured by hanging a scale from each boom and could be adjusted at the springs on the trolley base: it is not known what upward pressure was normally applied in Portsmouth.

During the course of 1939 the wheel collector swivel trolley heads were replaced throughout the fleet with slider heads, the entire unit comprising a steel "harp" (which fitted on to the end of the boom and was retained by two bolts) into which sat a swivelling gunmetal globe. On top of the globe there was a phosphor bronze (BICC) or steel (AA) slipper into which fitted a preformed carbon insert skid. The self-lubricating carbon inserts dramatically reduced trolley wire wear, in some cases almost doubling the "wire life", virtually removed the necessity to apply a conductive grease to the trolley wires, reduced the risk of dewirements, permitted higher operating speeds and eliminated the noise (particularly when wet) from the trolley wheels rotating at high speed.

The carbon inserts were inspected for damage and wear daily, an average life being around 800 miles but considerably less in wet or frosty weather. Frost or ice on the trolley wires interrupted conductivity resulting in control difficulties and a jerky ride as well as intense arcing which quickly damaged and wore the carbon insert. Thus, prior to the start of service on frosty mornings a trolleybus equipped with cast-iron inserts in each trolley head instead of the conventional carbon inserts would traverse all routes to remove frost and ice from the trolley wires. The cast-iron inserts were replaced with a normal carbon insert as soon as possible as their prolonged use would not only remove the frost but would also "shave" the trolley wire.

The Overhead Line Department

This department was housed to the rear of the Eastney Depot premises in a separate building near the Methuen Road entrance to the motorbus garage. There were 26 employees in 1938–39 but this had fallen to 20 by 1945–46 due to labour economies made during the war. In comparison the works had 274 and 241 employees respectively. Mr W.H. Radley was Overhead Line Superintendent from the commencement of trolleybus operations until his retirement, after 40 years service, on 31 August 1941.

The regular maintenance programme had to consider that normal wear and tear made the trolley wire thin where it led in and out of any rigid fitting. In order to remove and replace a worn or broken length of trolley wire, "come-along" clamps would be attached to the trolley wire, one each side of the section needing repair or replacement, and an unscrewed turnbuckle, i.e. an expanding screw with hooks at each end, would be hooked onto the rings attached to each clamp. The turnbuckle was progressively tightened thereby increasing the tension in the trolley wire on the "outer" side of the "come-along" clamps but creating looseness or sag between them. The section to be removed could then be cut out and a new length, with a joining or splicing ear at each end, inserted to a fixing clamp fastened to the trolley wire ends protruding from the "inner" side of the "come-along" clamps. Once the clamping screws within each splicing ear had been securely tightened to ensure mechanical and electrical connection and any kinks removed by the use of special straightening rollers, the tension in the wires would be adjusted to the appropriate figure for that location with a dynamometer or heavy duty spring balance. The turnbuckle would then be gradually opened, allowing the overhead wiring layout to return to its normal position, and the "come-along" clamps removed.

A similar procedure was followed to handle or remove longer distances of trolley wire or frogs. Dependent on the weight, the turnbuckle(s) would be tied off and secured to a traction pole(s) thereby retaining the length under tension. When the overhead wiring network was being dismantled, trolley wire could be dropped in 40-yard lengths and the span wires would either be taken down at the same time or left *in situ* and removed at a later date.

Span wires suffered no mechanical wear and tear, and were normally only replaced in conjunction with changes to the road layout or when they were life-expired, the biggest enemy being corrosion.

Occasional work such as layout alterations, the renewal of fittings and rewiring was done at night. Some worn parts of equipment such as crossings, frogs and trolleyheads, were reconditioned by the Department by building up using sifbronze welding.

Departmental vehicles

CPPTD, of necessity, had a number of non-passenger carrying vehicles to support their operations. Many of these were required for both the motor bus and trolleybus activities, e.g. cash and ticket vans, and towing vehicles, whereas others were dedicated to the trolleybus network, e.g. tower wagons. During the trolleybus era, the Overhead Line Department was the main user of the following vehicles:

Departmental Vehicles (Trolleybuses)

Fleet No. Original	Last	Reg. No.	Chassis	Chassis No.	Into Service	As	Converted	Into	Withdrawn	Sold
1		BK2978	Thornycroft J		1919	Motorbus	By 1934	Lorry	N/K	
4		BK2980	Thornycroft J		1919	Motorbus	By 1931	Tower wagon	1937	
7		BK2983	Thornycroft J		1919	Motorbus	By 1934	Tower wagon	N/K	
16	TW1	TP181	Dennis		1924	Motorbus	01.1933	Tower wagon	1953	
27		TP755	Dennis		1925	Motorbus	12.1932	Towing vehicle	01.1953	
30		TP758	Dennis		1925	Motorbus	03.1933	Lorry	N/K	
34	TW2	TP765	Dennis		1925	Motorbus	09.1932	Tower wagon	06.1952	
17	TW1	RV3411	Leyland TD2	2/2874	08.07.1933	Motorbus	06.1952	Tower wagon	1975	Preserved: Portsmouth City Museums
18	TW2	RV3412	Leyland TD2	2/2875	08.07.1933	Motorbus	11.1952	Tower wagon	1976	
74		RV720	Crossley Condor	90803	22.10.1931	Motorbus	1948	Breakdown recovery vehicle	1975	Preserved: Portsmouth City Museums
80		RV1143	Tilling Stevens E60A6			Motorbus	By 09.1944	Tree lopper	1952	
105		RV2000	Crossley Condor		1932	Motorbus	01.1953	Lorry	1961	
		WTP971	Bedford 90	CASV194415	01.02.1961	Van	N/A		1975	
		WRV399	Karrier Bantam	FD298-D74A2369	01.03.1961	Tipping lorry	N/A		1975	

Tower wagon 2 in Granada Road. (City of Portsmouth Archives)

1933 Leyland Titan TD2 Tower Wagon 1 (RV3411), formerly double-deck motorbus 17. This vehicle is preserved by Portsmouth City Museums Department. (City of Portsmouth Archives)

APPENDIX I
FARES, FARE TABLES AND TICKETS

Fares

At the beginning of the electric tramway era the routes were divided into penny (1d) stages with overlapping stages throughout, although the stages were not necessarily of equal length, e.g. the fare from Bradford Junction to Clarence Pier was 2d but from Bradford Junction to Floating Bridge was only 1d for a slightly greater distance. In 1904 it was stated that some 86% of passengers paid a penny fare. Many of the penny stages were successively extended in length and by 1908 only journeys between Cosham and Clarence Pier or Southsea South Parade Pier warranted a 3d fare. There was another round of stage extensions in May 1915 by which time the fare between the Town Hall and Eastney had fallen to 1d.

Packets of ten 1d tickets could be bought at a discount for 9d and used in multiples for 2d or 3d stages whilst children over 3 and under 12 years of age were charged 1d where the adult fare was 2d, and 2d where the adult fare was 3d. Workmen's fares were introduced in 1903 on the basis of 1d single and 2d return over sections for which the normal adult fare of 2d was applicable. They were subject to issuance and travel time restrictions.

Operating expenses rose rapidly after the First World War and fares were increased in 1920, the 1d fare rose to 1½d, the 2d to 3d, and the 3d to 4½d. In 1921 the 1½d and 3d fare stages were cut back to approximately the length of the former 1d and 2d stages prior to 1915 and workmen's fares were withdrawn. Only the post-war depression prompted a reduction in fares when in May 1922 the 1d fare was reintroduced and some halfpenny stages appeared. In 1928 a maximum fare of 3d was introduced.

The trolleybuses adopted a similar staged fares system, charges being based on a stage or portion of a stage. In principle the trolleybus fares were the same as those on the tram or motorbus services they replaced or paralleled between any two points. There is no evidence that transfer fares between points not linked by direct services, e.g. Floating Bridge – Southsea South Parade Pier, were offered between trolleybuses and other CPPTD services or, later when the Portsmouth Joint Transport Area was established, between trolleybuses and SMS motorbuses.

The Corporation were obliged by the Portsmouth Corporation Act 1930 to offer workmen's fares on the

TRAMWAY AND TROLLEY BUS SERVICES.

FARES AND STAGES.

SERVICE 1

"RED LION", COSHAM to CLARENCE PIER via LONDON ROAD, NORTH END, COMMERCIAL ROAD, and THE GUILDHALL.

SERVICE 2

CLARENCE PIER to "RED LION". COSHAM, via THE GUILDHALL, COMMERCIAL ROAD, NORTH END, and LONDON ROAD.

"Red Lion", Cosham 1												
1	Cosham Railway Gates 2											
1	1	Hilsea Bastion 3										
1½	1	1	Hilsea Barracks 4									
2	1½	1	1	North End Avenue 5								
2½	2	1½	1	1	North End Junction 6							
3	2½	2	1½	1	1	Kingston Cross 7						
3	2½	2	1½	1	1	1	"Air Balloon" 8					
3½	3	2½	2	1½	1	1	1	Sultan Road 9				
3½	3	3	2½	2	1½	1	1	1	Charlotte Street 10			
3½	3	3	3	2½	2	1½	1½	1	1	Guildhall 11		
3½	3	3	3	3	2½	2	2	1½	1	1	King's Rd. Junction 12	
3½	3	3	3	3	3	2½	2½	2	1½	1	1	Clarence Pier 13

Fare Tables for services 1 & 2 for the period October – December 1936

SERVICE 3

"RED LION", COSHAM, NORTH END, FRATTON ROAD, FAWCETT ROAD, SOUTH PARADE PIER, and then ALBERT ROAD, GUILDHALL, COMMERCIAL ROAD, TWYFORD AVENUE, NORTHERN PARADE to "RED LION", COSHAM.

SERVICE 4

"RED LION", COSHAM, NORTHERN PARADE, TWYFORD AVENUE, COMMERCIAL ROAD, GUILDHALL, ALBERT ROAD, SOUTH PARADE PIER and then FAWCETT ROAD, FRATTON ROAD, NORTH END to "RED LION", COSHAM.

"Red Lion", Cosham 1
1 Cosham Railway Gates 2
1 1 Hilsea Bastion 3
1½ 1 1 Hilsea Barracks 4
2 1½ 1 1 North End Avenue 5
2½ 2 1½ 1 1 North End Junction 6
3 2½ 2 1½ 1 1 Kingston Cross 7
3 2½ 2 1½ 1 1 1 New Road and Kingston Road Junction 8
3½ 3 2½ 2 1½ 1 1 1 Kingston Church 9
3½ 3 3 2½ 2 1½ 1½ 1 1 Fratton Bridge 10
3½ 3 3 2½ 2 2 1½ 1 1 1 Rugby Road 11
3½ 3 3 3 2½ 2 2 1½ 1 1 1 Fawcett Inn 12
3½ 3 3 3 2½ 2½ 2 1½ 1½ 1 1 1 Lawrence Road and Albert Road Junction 13
3½ 3 3 3 3 2½ 2½ 2 1½ 1½ 1 1 1 Strand 14
3½ 3 3 3 3 3 3 2½ 2 1½ 1½ 1 1 1 South Parade Pier 15
3 2½ 2 2 1½ 1½ 1 1 Festing Hotel 16
3 2½ 2½ 2 2 1½ 1 1 Lawrence Road and Albert Road Junction 1
3 3 2½ 2½ 2 1½ 1 1 Elm Grove 18
3 3 2½ 2½ 2 2 1 1 1 Bradford Road Junction 19
3 3 2½ 2 1½ 1½ 1 1 Blackfriars Road Bridge 20
3 3 3 2 2 1½ 1 1 1 Guildhall 21
3 3 2 2 1½ 1 1 1 Charlotte Street 22
3 2½ 2½ 2 1½ 1½ 1 1 Sultan Road 23
3 3 3 2½ 2 2 1½ 1 1 "Air Balloon" 24
3 3 3 2½ 2 2 1½ 1 1 1 Beresford Hotel 25
3 3 3 3 2½ 2½ 2 1½ 1 1 1 Wilson Road 26
3 3 3 3 2½ 2½ 2 1½ 1 1 1 1 Avenue Hotel 27
3 3 3 3 2½ 2½ 2 2 1½ 1 1 1 1 Alexandra Park 28
3 3 3 3 3 3 2½ 2 2 1½ 1½ 1 1 1 Doyle Avenue 29
3 3 3 3 3 3 3 2½ 2 1½ 1½ 1 1 1 1 Oakwood Road 30
3 3 3 3 3 3 3 3 2½ 2 2 1½ 1½ 1 1 1 Hilsea B'tion 31
3 3 3 3 3 3 3 3 3 2½ 2½ 2 2 1½ 1½ 1 1 Cosham Rly. Gates 32
3½ 3½ 3½ 3½ 3½ 3½ 3½ 3½ 3½ 3 3 2½ 2½ 2 1½ 1½ 1 1 "Red Lion", Cosham 33

Note.—The figures in Heavy Type represent Pence.

Fare Tables for services 3 & 4 for the period October – December 1936

trolleybuses although there was no such requirement on the motorbuses or trams. The introduction of workmen's fares was delayed until the tram to trolleybus conversion programme was almost complete due to the fear of reduced revenues. On 1 October 1936 workmen's fares were put into operation on all motorbus and trolleybus services on the following basis:

Return journey for	1d stage	Fare 1½d
	1½d stage	Fare 2½d
	2d stage	Fare 3d
	2½d stage	Fare 4d
	3d stage	Fare 4½d
	3½d stage	Fare 5d

Reduced workmen's fares were available to all passengers (there being no discrimination between, for example, workmen wearing overalls and others despite the wording of the Act) on journeys commencing before 8am Monday–Saturday except Good Friday and Christmas Day. The return portion of these tickets was available for return on any departure after 12 noon. There were no normal return fares.

An attempt to withdraw workmen's fares in 1940 for the duration of the war was refused by the MoWT and RTC. Whenever there was a general increase, workmen's fares increased in line with ordinary single fares with commensurate increases in the minimum workmen's return fare, e.g. in 1951 from 4d to 6d. In an effort to increase revenue the Corporation applied to the MoT to be relieved of their obligation to provide cheap fares for workmen on their trolley vehicle services and this was granted effective from 10 October 1954.

Although the last trolleybus in Portsmouth operated in July 1963, the 2p decimal currency pre-payment vouchers (Bell Punch tickets) introduced in 1971 bore the inscription "This Voucher will be accepted on any Southdown or Corporation 'bus or trolleybus as equivalent to cash to the value of 2p for the payment of a Bus Fare".

Bell Punch tickets

Initially trolleybus tickets were of the same Bell Punch numbered fare stage colour-coded type, with separate sets for each pair of services, as used on the trams. The conductor was equipped with a wooden rack holding pre-printed paper tickets, divided by value, under a spring and cancelling punch. The stage numbers instead of a geographical name were printed along the edges of the ticket with the undertaking's title or abbreviated title, and other information in a central column. Older ticket stock displayed the title "Portsmouth Corporation Trys.". The conductor used a cancelling punch to make a small round hole against the fare stage number where the passenger had started the journey whilst the fare paid indicated how far the passenger could travel. The cancelling punch recorded the number of holes punched on a secure register inside the machine whilst the small coloured circle of

3 **COSHAM RAILWAY GATES To SOUTH PARADE PIER** ***via*** **London Road, North End Junction, Kingston Road, Fratton Road, Fawcett Road, Waverley Road and Strand.**

4a **SOUTH PARADE PIER To COSHAM RAILWAY GATES** ***via*** **Strand, Waverley Road, Fawcett Road, Fratton Road, Kingston Road, North End Junction and London Road.**

Red Lion, Cosham 3
1½| Cosham Railway Gates 4
1½|1½| Hilsea Bastion 5
1½|1½|1½| Hilsea Barracks 6
2 |1½|1½|1½| North End Avenue 7
2½|2 |1½|1½|1½| North End Junction 8
3 |2½|2 |1½|1½|1½| Kingston Cross 9
3 |2½|2 |1½|1½|1½|1½| New Rd. & Kingston Rd. Junc. 10
3½|3 |2½|2 |1½|1½|1½|1½| Kingston Church 11
3½|3 |3 |2½|2 |1½|1½|1½|1½| Fratton Bridge 12
3½|3 |3 |2½|2 |2 |1½|1½|1½|1½| Rugby Road 13
3½|3 |3 |3 |2½|2 |2 |1½|1½|1½|1½| Fawcett Inn 14
3½|3 |3 |3 |2½|2½|2 |1½|1½|1½|1½|1½| Lawrence & Albert Rd.s.
3½|3 |3 |3 |3 |2½|2½|2 |1½|1½|1½|1½|1½| Strand [Junc. 15
3½|3 |3 |3 |3 |3 |3 |2½|2 |1½|1½|1½|1½|1½| S. Parade Pier 17

Fare Tables for services 3 & 4A applicable from March 1948

3a **ALEXANDRA PARK to EASTNEY** *via* **Twyford Avenue, Commercial Road, Guildhall, Bradford Junction and Goldsmith Avenue, then**

EASTNEY To COSHAM RAILWAY GATES *via* **Highland Road, Albert Road, Bradford Junction, Guildhall, Commercial Road, Twyford Avenue and Northern Parade.**

4 **COSHAM RAILWAY GATES To EASTNEY** *via* **Northern Parade, Twyford Avenue, Commercial Road, Guildhall, Bradford Junction, Albert Road and Highland Road, then**

EASTNEY To ALEXANDRA PARK *via* **Goldsmith Avenue, Bradford Junc., Guildhall, Commercial Road and Twyford Avenue.**

Alexandra Park 28
1½| Avenue Hotel 27
1½|1½| Beresford Hotel 25
1½|1½|1½| Air Balloon 24
1½|1½|1½|1½| Sultan Road 23
2 |1½|1½|1½|1½| Charlotte St. & Lake Rd Junc. 22
2 |2 |1½|1½|1½|1½| Guildhall 21
2½|2½|2 |2 |1½|1½|1½| Blackfriars Rd. Bridge 20
2½|2½|2 |2 |1½|1½|1½|1½| Bradford Rd. Junction 19
3 |3 |2½|2½|2 |1½|1½|1½|1½| Fratton Bridge 17
3 |3 |2½|2½|2 |1½|1½|1½|1½|1½| Talbot Road 16
3 |3 |3 |3 |2½|2 |1½|1½|1½|1½|1½| Frensham Road 15
3 |3 |3 |3 |2½|2 |1½|1½|1½|1½|1½|1½| Frogmore Road 14
4 |4 |3½|3½|3 |2½|2 |1½|1½|1½|1½|1½|1½| White House, Milton 13
4½|4½|4 |4 |3½|3 |2½|2 |2 |1½|1½|1½|1½|1½| Bransbury Road 12
4½|4½|4 |4 |3½|3 |2½|2 |2 |1½|1½|1½|1½|1½|1½| Eastney 11
4½|4½|4½|4½|4 |3½|3 |2½|2½|2 |2 |1½|1½|1½|1½|1½| Winter Road 10
4½|4½|4½|4½|4 |3½|3 |2½|2½|2 |2 |2 |1½|1½|1½|1½|1½| Festing Hotel 9
5 |5 |5 |5 |4½|4 |3½|3 |3 |2½|2½|2 |2 |1½|1½|1½|1½|1½| Lawrence Rd. & Albert Rd. Junc. 17
5½|5½|5½|5½|5 |4½|4 |3½|3 |3 |3 |2½|2½|2 |1½|1½|1½|1½|1½| Elm Grove 18
5½|5½|5½|5½|5 |4½|4 |4 |4 |3 |3 |2½|2½|2½|2 |2 |1½|1½|1½|1½| Bradford Road Junction 19
6 |6 |6 |6 |5½|5 |4½|4 |4 |3 |3 |3 |3 |3 |2½|2½|2 |1½|1½|1½|1½| Blackfriars Road Bridge 20
6½|6½|6½|6½|6 |5½|5 |4½|4½|4 |4 |3½|3½|3 |2½|2½|2 |2 |1½|1½|1½|1½| Guildhall 21
6½|6½|6½|6½|6 |5½|5 |4½|4½|4 |4 |4 |3½|3½|3 |3 |2½|2 |2 |1½|1½|1½|1½| Charlotte St. & Lake Road Junc. 22
7 |7 |7 |7 |6½|6 |5½|5 |5 |4½|4½|4 |4 |4 |3½|3½|3 |2½|2½|2 |1½|1½|1½|1½| Sultan Road 23
7½|7½|7½|7½|7 |6½|6 |5½|5½|5 |5 |4½|4½|4½|4 |4 |3½|3 |3 |2½|2 |2 |1½|1½|1½| Air Balloon 24
7½|7½|7½|7½|7 |6½|6 |5½|5½|5 |5 |4½|4½|4½|4 |4 |3½|3 |3 |2½|2 |2 |1½|1½|1½|1½| Beresford Hotel 25
7½|7½|7½|7½|7 |6½|6 |5½|5½|5 |5 |5 |4½|4½|4½|4½|4 |3 |3 |3 |2½|2½|2 |1½|1½|1½|1½| Wilson Road 26
7½|7½|7½|7½|7 |6½|6 |5½|5½|5 |5 |5 |4½|4½|4½|4½|4 |3 |3 |3 |2½|2½|2 |1½|1½|1½|1½|1½| Avenue Hotel 27
7½|7½|7½|7½|7 |6½|6 |5½|5½|5 |5 |5 |4½|4½|4½|4½|4 |3 |3 |3 |2½|2½|2 |2 |1½|1½|1½|1½|1½| Alexandra Park 28
7½|7½|7½|7½|7 |6½|6 |5½|5½|5 |5 |5 |4½|4½|4½|4½|4½|3 |3 |3 |3 |3 |2½|2 |2 |1½|1½|1½|1½|1½| Doyle Avenue 29
7½|7½|7½|7½|7 |6½|6 |5½|5½|5 |5 |5 |4½|4½|4½|4½|4½|3 |3 |3 |3 |3 |3 |2½|2 |1½|1½|1½|1½|1½|1½| Oakwood Road 30
7½|7½|7½|7½|7 |6½|6 |5½|5½|5 |5 |5 |4½|4½|4½|4½|4½|3 |3 |3 |3 |3 |3 |3 |2½|2 |2 |1½|1½|1½|1½|1½| Hilsea Bastion 31
7½|7½|7½|7½|7 |6½|6 |5½|5½|5 |5 |5 |4½|4½|4½|4½|4½|3 |3 |3 |3 |3 |3 |3 |3 |2½|2½|2 |2 |1½|1½|1½|1½| Cosham Rly. Gates **32**
8 |8 |8 |8 |7½|7 |6½|6 |6 |5½|5½|5½|5 |5 |5 |5 |5 |3½|3½|3½|3½|3½|3½|3½|3½|3 |3 |2½|2½|2 |1½|1½|1½|1½| Red Lion, Cosham **33**

Fare Tables for services 3A & 4 applicable from March 1948

paper punched out of the ticket was retained in the machine for accounting purposes. It also made an audible ring thus ensuring that a fraudulent conductor was not selling a used ticket. At the outer terminus the conductor would record the serial number of the first ticket of each denomination on the rack and enter this on the way sheet. This would be checked by inspectors, who would board vehicles at random, to ensure that the conductor was issuing tickets correctly and that passengers had paid the appropriate fare.

Although efficient and successful, the ticketing system was "administration-heavy", very slow, and required considerable manual dexterity and was therefore labour intensive.

Ticket colours and styles

The titles used variously on Bell Punch tickets during the trolleybus era were, "Portsmouth Corporation Tramways.", "Portsmouth Corporation Trys.", "PORTSMOUTH CORP'N TRAMWAYS", and from 1946 "PORTSMOUTH JOINT TRANSPORT AREA". Solely numerical fare stages were used (the use of geographical fare stages on tickets having been given up in 1927) and all printing was in black.

By the latter days of tramway operation and introduction of the first trolleybuses, tickets were coloured as follows:

Colour	*Denomination*	*Period*	*Comment*
Ordinary fares:			
Blue	1d		Almost 3in. long, believed 1¼in. wide
Blue	1½d		2¼in. long, believed 1¼in. wide
Buff	2d		Ditto
Green	2½d		Ditto
Yellow	3d		Ditto
Mauve	4d		Ditto
Rose	4½d		Ditto
Salmon	5d		Ditto
Grey	6d		Ditto
Exchange tickets:			
White	1d		Red band down centre of ticket
Blue	1½d		Ditto
Yellow	3d		Ditto

Prepaid 1d tickets or vouchers were sold at a discount in packets of 14 for a shilling, and prepaid 1½d tickets in packets of eight for 10½d and 16 for 1s 9d. They could be tendered separately or for higher fares. At the start of the trolleybus era the prepaid tickets were printed on pink paper with a red overprint "Pre-Paid". The conductor punched them at the appropriate fare stage, tore them in half, returned one half to the passenger, and kept the other half for accounting purposes. In order to cope with inflation, vouchers for different fare values printed on different colours of paper were progressively introduced, the following denominations being known: 1d pink, 2d blue or purple, 6d yellow.

The undertaking appears to have purchased tickets and vouchers for its punches from Bell Punch Co. Ltd., London, and Punch & Ticket Co., London N1, although latterly the printer's name was not always evident on the ticket.

Scholar's season tickets, valid for a school term, were available pre-war on a sliding scale dependent on the adult fare and the scholar's age, e.g. 1d adult fare for those under 14 years 7s 6d and for those 14–18 years 12s (rates applicable 1936–1940). In November 1940 the RTC approved introduction of a 4s monthly scholar's (under 14 years) season ticket.

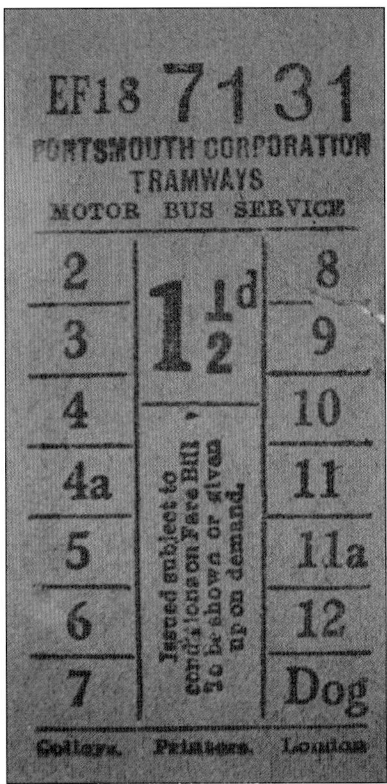

A 1½d Bell Punch style ticket punched to show that the passenger had started the journey at fare stage 6 (this example was used on a motor bus service)

TIM

Faster trolleybus service speeds compared to the trams left conductors with less time to collect fares and issue traditional Bell Punch tickets from a ticket rack particularly for short stage journeys within the city centre. Revenue was being lost whilst administrative costs were rising and furthermore by autumn 1936 many of the ticket punches were considered life expired. Trials were carried out with "Verometer" and Ticket Issuing Machines Ltd. (TIM) mechanical equipment, before it was decided in July 1937 to obtain 240 TIM machines and close the contact with the Bell Punch ticket suppliers for £51 10s, instead of buying 600 new punches at £3 each.

The TIM machines were provided to the undertaking without charge subject to a commitment to purchase the appropriate blank paper rolls upon which the tickets were printed, sufficient for 260,000 tickets, at a price of 7½d per thousand, per machine per annum for a period of 3 years. Thereafter the machines belonged to CPPTD and the price fell, typically to 3d per thousand tickets. A further 14 TIMS were acquired on the same basis in October 1938. Subsequently further TIM machines were purchased outright without any paper roll conditions; 50 were acquired in May 1940 at £14 10s each, 20 TIM Majors in June 1947 at £32 each to cope with the post-war expansion in services, 60 TIM III machines in February 1950 also at £32 each, and 50 TIM III machines in September 1951 to serve the extensions at £34 17s each. By 1943 it was considered that the ticket cancelling machines in use were no longer suitable and 250 Cooper Webb Jones "Downward-Cancelling" machines at 17s 6d each were ordered.

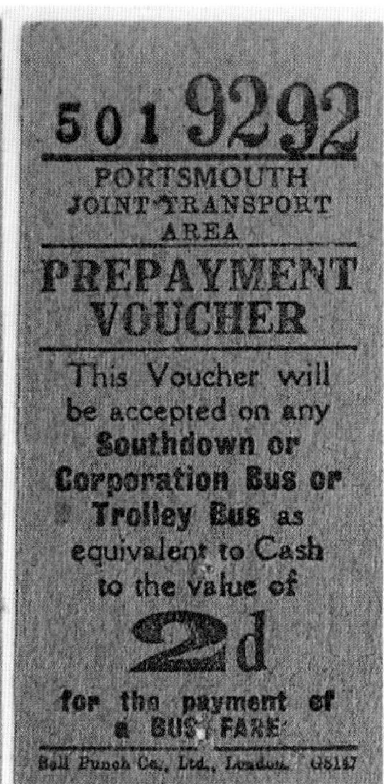

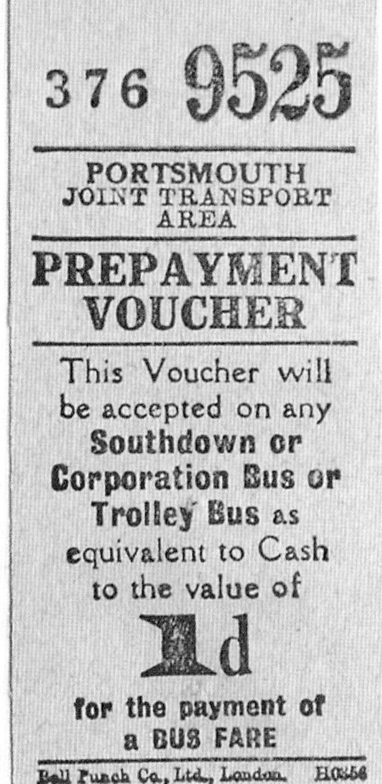

Examples of pre-payment vouchers from the post-1946 'Portsmouth Joint Transport Area' era. (Colin Page)

Following approaches from both TIM and the National Cash Register Co. Ltd. paper rolls with advertisements on the rear side were introduced on 1 March 1955. This reduced the cost from 138s to 128s per thousand rolls and was estimated to save the undertaking £150 pa.

The TIM had a dial that allowed the conductor to quickly choose the appropriate fare from 10 different values, the direction of travel and the fare stage boarded. The ticket was printed on plain roll of paper which also indicated the date of issue. The machine also recorded the number of fares issued for each value for administrative and control purposes. However, the TIM system could not cope easily with fare increases which, once all values were in use or were no longer used, required each machine to be equipped with new printing plates. In order to cope with the fare increases introduced on 11 April 1952, suitably modified TIM machines able to issue values up to 7d were introduced on services 3 and 4 during the course of that month. By June 1952 they were also in use on services 5, 6, 9, 10, 13 and 14.

Ticket colours and styles

Titles varied according to the date of manufacture of the machine and its printing plates, "C.P.P.T.D" on pre-war machines, and "C.P.P.T.D." on post-war machines having been observed. Tickets were 3⅛in by 1½in, in size.

The printing included a number of boxes or squares originally headed "STAGE BOARDED" on the left, "FARE PAID" showing the type of fare (ORD – Ordinary, WR – Workman's Return being printed to the left of the amount) and amount paid on the right, and in between at the base "SERVICE" showing the service number upon which the ticket was issued and "DATE". In the upper central area the undertaking's abbreviated title, machine number and the ticket sequence number was printed. The whole was contained in a rectangular frame with the customary legal disclaimer appearing outside the frame on the left.

Emergency "Duplex" tickets were also carried by conductors and used if the TIM machine broke down. These were pre-printed punch-type tickets displaying all the relevant wording, stage numbers, etc., but printed in two mirror imaged halves, separated with a vertical serration. The ticket was folded in half and punched once (being mirrored). The conductor tore the ticket in half down the serration and gave the right half to the passenger whilst retaining the left half for accounting purposes.

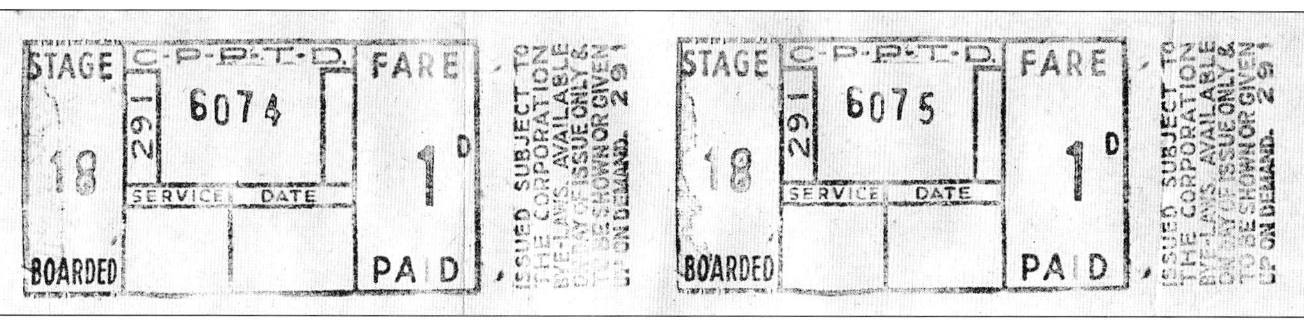

A CPPTD TIM ticket. This particular examples was issued on trolleybus no. 246 on 22 June 1963. (T.V. Runnacles)

SINGLE	RETURN	WKMN. RETURN	WKMN. RETURN	RETURN	SINGLE
Ak 3080			Ak 3080		
½d	EMERGENCY TICKET	3/-	3/-	EMERGENCY TICKET	½d
1d		2/-	2/-		1d
1½d		1/-	1/-		1½d
2d		11d	11d		2d
2½d		10d	10d		2½d
3d	CITY OF PORTSMOUTH PASSENGER TRANSPORT This portion to be handed in with receipts. Detailed instructions overleaf.	9½d	9½d	CITY OF PORTSMOUTH PASSENGER TRANSPORT This portion to be handed to Passenger. Conditions of issue, see overleaf.	3d
3½d		9d	9d		3½d
4d		8½d	8½d		4d
4½d		8d	8d		4½d
5d		7½d	7½d		5d
5½d		7d	7d		5½d
6d	P8320	6½d	6½d		6d

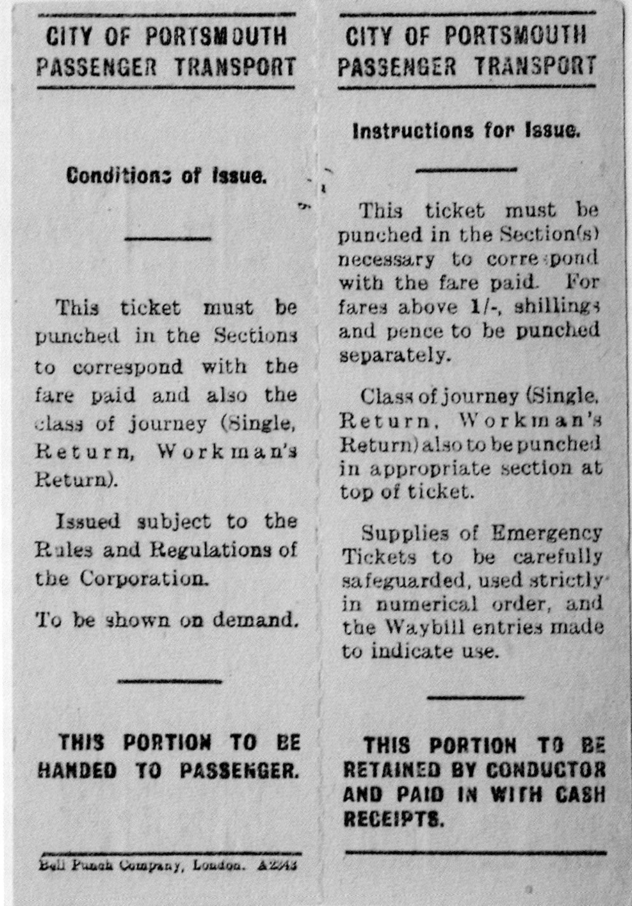

CITY OF PORTSMOUTH PASSENGER TRANSPORT

Conditions of Issue.

This ticket must be punched in the Sections to correspond with the fare paid and also the class of journey (Single, Return, Workman's Return).

Issued subject to the Rules and Regulations of the Corporation.

To be shown on demand.

THIS PORTION TO BE HANDED TO PASSENGER.

Bell Punch Company, London. A2243

CITY OF PORTSMOUTH PASSENGER TRANSPORT

Instructions for Issue.

This ticket must be punched in the Section(s) necessary to correspond with the fare paid. For fares above 1/-, shillings and pence to be punched separately.

Class of journey (Single, Return, Workman's Return) also to be punched in appropriate section at top of ticket.

Supplies of Emergency Tickets to be carefully safeguarded, used strictly in numerical order, and the Waybill entries made to indicate use.

THIS PORTION TO BE RETAINED BY CONDUCTOR AND PAID IN WITH CASH RECEIPTS.

Both halves (front and rear) of an emergency ticket. (Colin Page)

No other type of ticket machine was used on the trolleybuses although the Bell Bunch "Ultimate" system was introduced in 1958 on one-man operated (OMO) vehicles and then "Solomatics", the OMO fixed version of the portable "Ultimate" machine, in 1959–60.

On 3 March 1963 on its way south along Copnor Road BUT9611T 312 passes the impressive overhead "T" junction with Chichester Road. (T.V. Runnacles)

APPENDIX J

TIMETABLES AND PUBLIC INFORMATION

The pattern of trolleybus services varied little from the tramcar services they replaced and was heavily dependent on workmen's traffic to and from HM Dockyard and thus on the strategic relevance of the Royal Navy of the time. Naval rearmament began in the mid-1930s (in 1937 it was stated that 75% of the City's population depended directly or indirectly on the Services) and the Royal Navy was still the second largest navy in the world in the 1950s. So Portsmouth's trolleybuses benefited from a relatively stable load compared with other trolleybus operators who were subject to the economic vagaries of a single industry. In addition, there was an annual seasonal influx of holidaymakers to Southsea in a period when Britons holidayed at home.

By January 1939 early morning weekday (Monday to Saturday) trolleybuses to the Dockyard left Copnor on service 11 at 5.30am, 5.44am, 5.54am and then every 5 minutes until 6.54am; from Eastney on service 17 at 5.45am, 5.52am and then every 5 minutes until 7.07am; and from Milton at 5.56am and then every 5 minutes until 6.56am. The basic service to and from other points started from about 7am. In all cases services then ran at a regular 12 minute interval until around midday and then every 10 minutes until the close between 11.00 and 11.30pm. Additional special journeys, mainly to destinations outside the trolleybus network and which were not published in the city guide or later the timetable booklets, ran during peak hours. The Sunday service only commenced from about 9.30am and then ran at 12 minute intervals until the close.

Following the outbreak of the Second World War last motorbus and trolleybuses services were progressively curtailed to around 10pm and then in January 1943 to 9.00–9.30pm. Although first trolleybuses on Sundays were unaffected thereafter the frequency was reduced to every 30 minutes until after 2pm. Monday to Saturday off-peak frequencies were reduced from every 10 minutes to every 12 minutes.

Throughout the pre-war period although timetables specifically referred to Cosham 'Red Lion' Hotel, they did not specify Cosham Railway Station but continued to simply refer to Cosham for this point. In respect of services 3A and 4A, the "A" suffix was not shown in the timetables whilst the service number blinds of trolleybuses 1–15 did not include any numbers with suffixes. The earliest official recognition of the 3, 3A, 4, 4A arrangements was a one-day alteration on 3 September 1944. Only on 1 July 1946, with the issue of the first joint CPPTD/SMS timetable, were services advertised with the "A" suffix and Cosham Railway Station referred to, albeit as Cosham Railway Gates, as in the fare tables.

Trolleybuses 216–300 displayed COSHAM RAILWAY STN. or COSHAM RLY. STATION, depending on the ultimate screen and 201–215 continued to show simply COSHAM until equipped with new blinds in c. 1947 which carried COSHAM RLY. STN.

Interestingly, the May–June 1940 timetable shows that portions of motorbus services I and J were operated by trolleybus, namely on weekdays between North End and Palmerston Road via Fratton and via the Guildhall, and on Sundays between Cosham Railway Gates or North End and Southsea South Parade Pier via Fratton Road. On weekdays this service duplicated services 1 and 2 between Royal Pier Hotel and Cosham. The trolleybus-operated portions of service I and J were merged with trolleybus services 1 and 2 either on 5 July 1940 when the seafront was closed or on 21 July 1940.

As can be seen from the various extracts by the late 1940s weekday (Monday–Friday) schedules for most services had returned to a basic 12-minute service in the mornings and a 10-minute service in the afternoons with the same or even better frequency in the evenings, well-illustrating how people went out to entertainments during the trolleybus era. Many non-timetabled specials continued to operate during the peak hours, those following routes that were equipped with overhead wiring throughout being trolleybus operated until the system began to decline in the mid-1950s.

Fare and timetables

Throughout the electric tramway era the first and last journeys to and from key points on the route of travel, and the frequency or frequencies throughout the day, were, as in many other places, included in commercially-produced town or city guides. The Portsmouth undertaking did not publish its own public time or fare "tables" as such, although timetables appeared on the trams themselves from July 1902. This format continued unchanged following the introduction of trolleybus services, the booklets including brief information on places of interest, parks, theatres, etc., and the motorbus or trolleybus services that reached them, often with the applicable fare. This city guide format was still in use when publication ceased entirely in 1940 due to wartime security restrictions.

Although CPPTD prepared the fare and schedule data contained in the booklets, they preferred to invite tenders from specialist publishers or advertising agents for their printing and production. The arrangements varied somewhat over the years but it was assumed that the publishers would produce the timetable booklet free of charge and that their costs would be recovered from the charges for advertisements also included in the booklet. The entire print run passed to the Department for sale to the travelling public.

In April 1935 Messrs Pearl, Dean & Pearl, Ltd. successfully tendered to supply 10,000 timetable booklets annually, at a charge of £13 for including fare tables and a map of services, for five years, all other costs being covered by the advertising therein. They terminated the contract prematurely and from 1 October 1938 the Portsmouth firm of Charpentier & Co. supplied the 10,000 timetables subject to the Corporation guaranteeing six full pages of advertisements at £6 10s per page. This agreement continued until September 1940.

The booklets were correctly titled "OFFICIAL **TIME-TABLE** AND CITY GUIDE" and were published three times a year, corresponding approximately to the first 5 months of the year, the summer season, and the rest of the year. Timetable information for each service was based on a list of first and last departures from each origin or starting point on weekdays (Monday to Saturday during the trolleybus era) and Sundays, and the service interval throughout the day. The roads and streets traversed were shown in each case. In addition the booklet contained detailed early morning trolleybus services, special trolleybus services connecting with Sunday morning excursion trains, last trolleybuses from Portsmouth Station on Sunday evenings, relevant fare tables, regulations and a diagrammatic system map, as well as many advertisements. There was, however, no alphabetical list of places served. The booklets were available to the public free of charge.

As can be seen below the dimensions varied according to the publisher and between issues:

Date	*Publisher*	*Dimensions (approximate)*
April 1934	Magnet Advertising	5½ in. × 8⁵⁄₁₂ in.
August 1936	Pearl, Dean & Pearl	4⅙ in. × 5⁵⁄₁₂ in.
July 1937	Pearl, Dean & Pearl	4⅙ in. × 5½ in.
January 1939	Charpentier Ltd.	4¾ in. × 6 in.
April 1940	Charpentier Ltd.	4¾ in. × 5⅚ in.
July 1946	Joint Transport Services	4 in. × 6½ in.
1948	Joint Transport Services	4 in. × 5½ in.
1954	Joint Transport Services	4 in. × 6¾ in.
1962	Joint Transport Services	4 in. × 6⅚ in.

Larger size booklets appeared from May 1965.

The last timetable and city guide following the outbreak of the Second World War is believed to have appeared in April 1940 whilst a separate fare table booklet, printed by Coasby & Co. Ltd., Southsea, was dated March 1942. No further fare and timetable booklets whether accompanied by a city guide or not, appear to have been published until 1 July 1946 and information about service changes seems to have been limited to announcements in the local newspapers and notices in the vehicles.

These arrangements proved difficult to reintroduce after the war, the potential publishers arguing that it was unremunerative for them to produce the timetable and fares booklet free of charge, and receive no portion of the sales revenue. The first post-war timetable booklet to appear was that issued jointly with SMS concurrent with the launch of Portsmouth Area Joint Transport Services on 1 July 1946 with a period of validity from 1 July until 28 September 1946. Each trolleybus service timetable was clearly headed "Corporation Trolley Bus Service" followed by the service number. The pre-war practice of showing separate overviews of "Corporation Early Morning Special Services", "Corporation Special Dockyard Buses", etc., continued. Initially there were three issues annually, covering the first 5 to 6 months of the year, the summer season, and the rest of the year, respectively. As an economy the number of issues was reduced from 1948–49 to two issues, May–September and the rest of the year, respectively. The booklet was no longer free of charge but cost 3d.

In 1948 the Portsmouth Passenger Transport Committee asked their General Manager to consider including fare tables in the joint timetable booklets and increased publicity given to their sale, potentially at enquiry offices and from conductors. Nonetheless the fare tables remained in a separate booklet throughout the post-war period.

Prior to any timetable change detailed information was published in the local newspapers a few days beforehand and traffic notices appeared on the vehicles.

Groups of trolleybus services serving a series of roads or points were never combined into a single timetable, e.g. in the 1950s Southsea *The Strand* – Fratton Bridge – New Road was served by services 4 and 8 northbound and services 3 and 7 southbound, Guildhall – Fratton Bridge – Goldsmith Avenue – Eastney was served by services 18 and 20 eastbound and services 17 and 19 westbound; which did little to aid clarity when travellers unfamiliar with the city were seeking the service number of a trolleybus to their chosen destination. However, SMS did combine their timetables for some services, e.g. to Emsworth and Waterlooville, in addition to the individual service timetables. The Portsmouth Area Joint Transport Services timetables showed the name of every street traversed by each service in sequence whilst the heading of each fare and timetable clearly indicated whether it was a motorbus or trolleybus service.

By summer 1957 each issue contained a fold-out sheet affixed to the inside of the rear cover with a map of city service on one side and suburban services within the Joint Area on the other. Later issues had the maps bound into the booklet. An alphabetical list of places served accompanied by the relevant service numbers, was still absent.

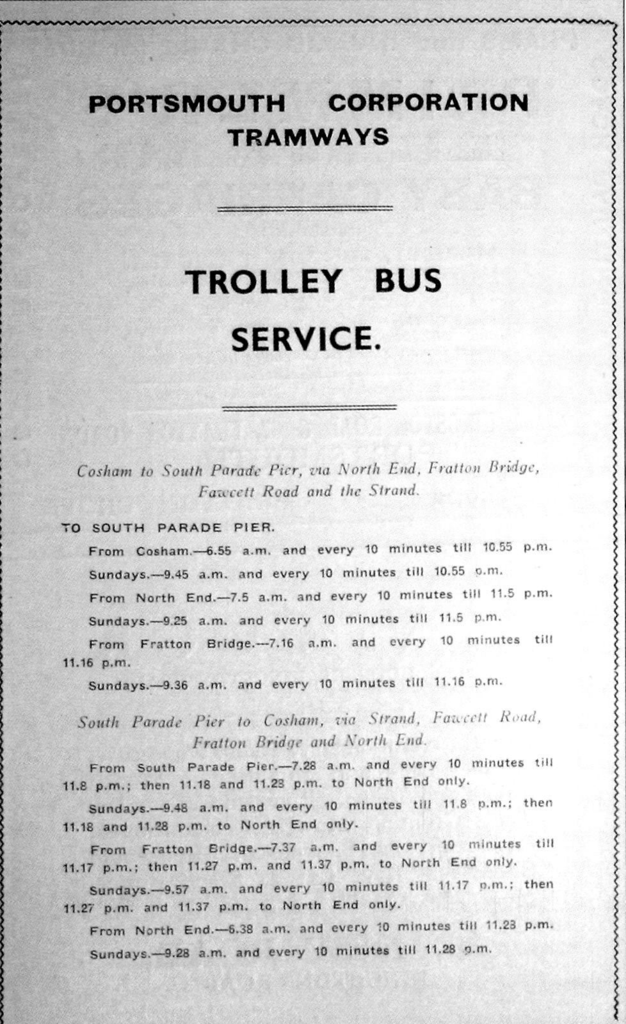

PORTSMOUTH CORPORATION TRAMWAYS

TROLLEY BUS SERVICE.

Cosham to South Parade Pier, via North End, Fratton Bridge, Fawcett Road and the Strand.

TO SOUTH PARADE PIER.

From Cosham.—6.55 a.m. and every 10 minutes till 10.55 p.m.

Sundays.—9.45 a.m. and every 10 minutes till 10.55 p.m.

From North End.—7.5 a.m. and every 10 minutes till 11.5 p.m.

Sundays.—9.25 a.m. and every 10 minutes till 11.5 p.m.

From Fratton Bridge.—7.16 a.m. and every 10 minutes till 11.16 p.m.

Sundays.—9.36 a.m. and every 10 minutes till 11.16 p.m.

South Parade Pier to Cosham, via Strand, Fawcett Road, Fratton Bridge and North End.

From South Parade Pier.—7.28 a.m. and every 10 minutes till 11.8 p.m.; then 11.18 and 11.28 p.m. to North End only.

Sundays.—9.48 a.m. and every 10 minutes till 11.8 p.m.; then 11.18 and 11.28 p.m. to North End only.

From Fratton Bridge.—7.37 a.m. and every 10 minutes till 11.17 p.m.; then 11.27 p.m. and 11.37 p.m. to North End only.

Sundays.—9.57 a.m. and every 10 minutes till 11.17 p.m.; then 11.27 p.m. and 11.37 p.m. to North End only.

From North End.—6.38 a.m. and every 10 minutes till 11.23 p.m.

Sundays.—9.28 a.m. and every 10 minutes till 11.28 p.m.

First timetable experimental trolleybus service, August 1934.

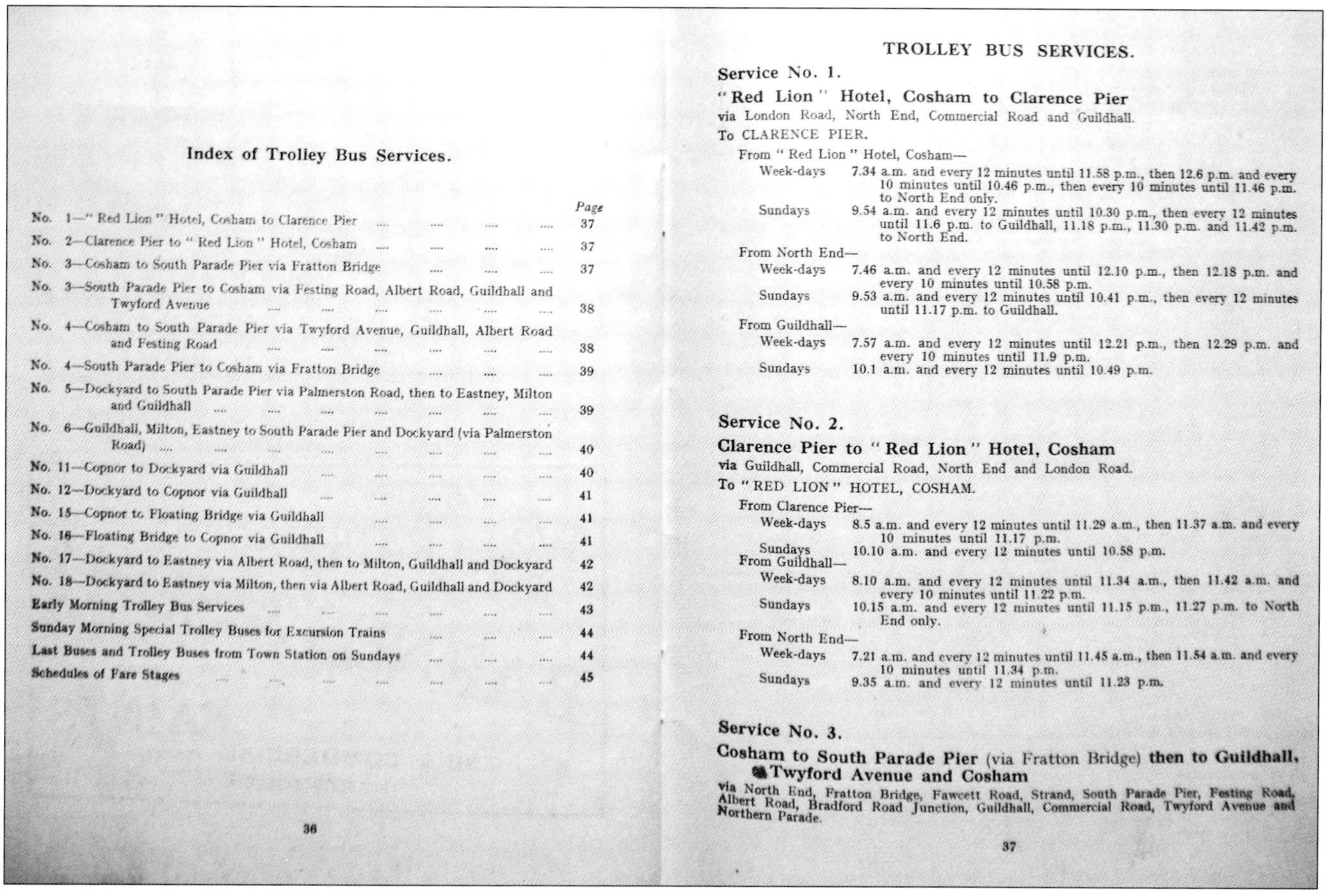

Index of Trolley Bus Services.

36

TROLLEY BUS SERVICES.

Service No. 1.

"Red Lion" Hotel, Cosham to Clarence Pier

via London Road, North End, Commercial Road and Guildhall.

To CLARENCE PIER.

From " Red Lion " Hotel, Cosham—

Week-days 7.34 a.m. and every 12 minutes until 11.58 p.m., then 12.6 p.m. and every 10 minutes until 10.46 p.m., then every 10 minutes until 11.46 p.m. to North End only.

Sundays 9.54 a.m. and every 12 minutes until 10.30 p.m., then every 12 minutes until 11.6 p.m. to Guildhall, 11.18 p.m., 11.30 p.m. and 11.42 p.m. to North End.

From North End—

Week-days 7.46 a.m. and every 12 minutes until 12.10 p.m., then 12.18 p.m. and every 10 minutes until 10.58 p.m.

Sundays 9.53 a.m. and every 12 minutes until 10.41 p.m., then every 12 minutes until 11.17 p.m. to Guildhall.

From Guildhall—

Week-days 7.57 a.m. and every 12 minutes until 12.21 p.m., then 12.29 p.m. and every 10 minutes until 11.9 p.m.

Sundays 10.1 a.m. and every 12 minutes until 10.49 p.m.

Service No. 2.

Clarence Pier to "Red Lion" Hotel, Cosham

via Guildhall, Commercial Road, North End and London Road.

To " RED LION " HOTEL, COSHAM.

From Clarence Pier—

Week-days 8.5 a.m. and every 12 minutes until 11.29 a.m., then 11.37 a.m. and every 10 minutes until 11.17 p.m.

Sundays 10.10 a.m. and every 12 minutes until 10.58 p.m.

From Guildhall—

Week-days 8.10 a.m. and every 12 minutes until 11.34 a.m., then 11.42 a.m. and every 10 minutes until 11.22 p.m.

Sundays 10.15 a.m. and every 12 minutes until 11.15 p.m., 11.27 p.m. to North End only.

From North End—

Week-days 7.21 a.m. and every 12 minutes until 11.45 a.m., then 11.54 a.m. and every 10 minutes until 11.34 p.m.

Sundays 9.35 a.m. and every 12 minutes until 11.23 p.m.

Service No. 3.

Cosham to South Parade Pier (via Fratton Bridge) **then to Guildhall, Twyford Avenue and Cosham**

via North End, Fratton Bridge, Fawcett Road, Strand, South Parade Pier, Festing Road, Albert Road, Bradford Road Junction, Guildhall, Commercial Road, Twyford Avenue and Northern Parade.

37

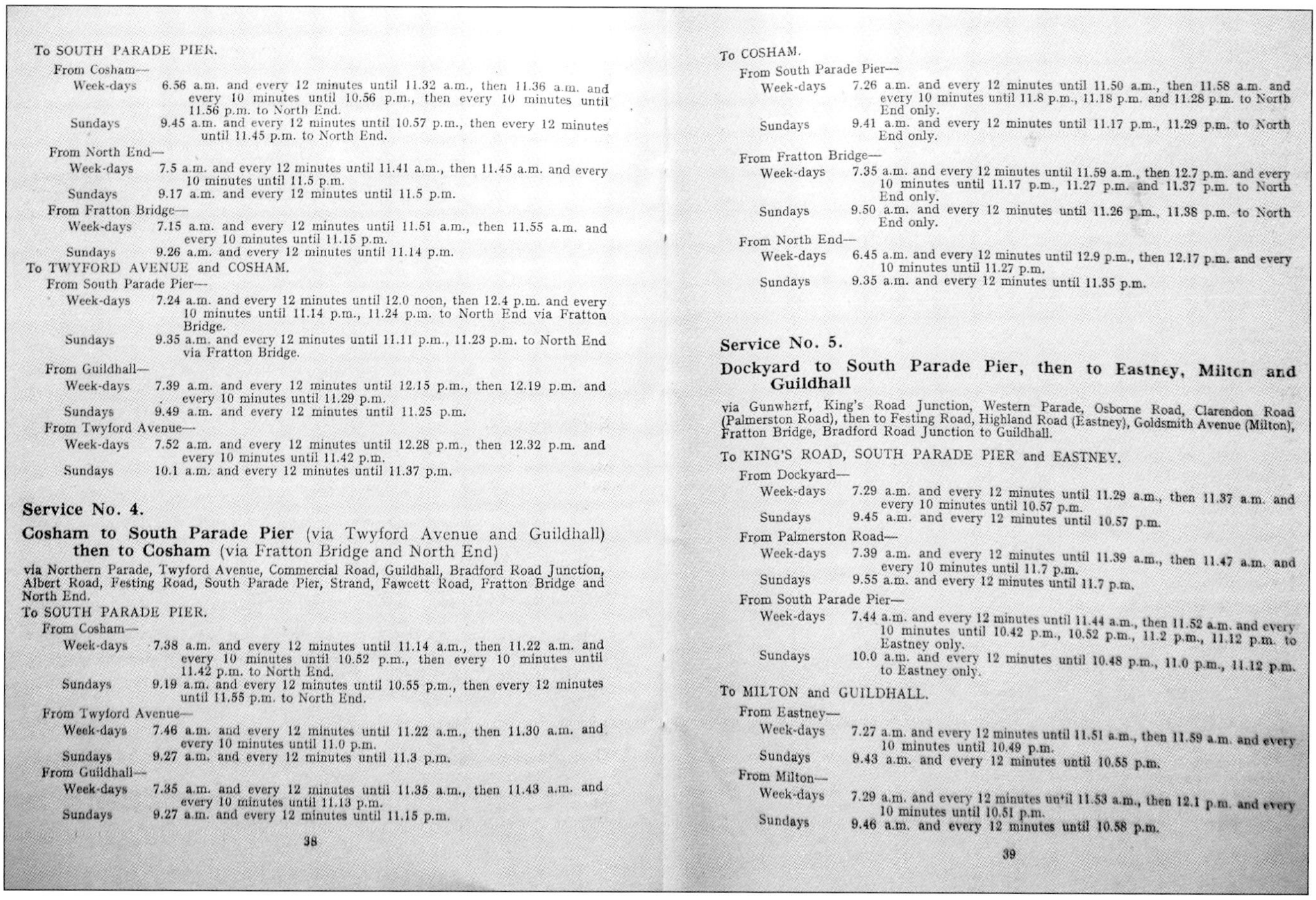

To SOUTH PARADE PIER.

From Cosham—

Week-days 6.56 a.m. and every 12 minutes until 11.32 a.m., then 11.36 a.m. and every 10 minutes until 10.56 p.m., then every 10 minutes until 11.56 p.m. to North End.

Sundays 9.45 a.m. and every 12 minutes until 10.57 p.m., then every 12 minutes until 11.45 p.m. to North End.

From North End—

Week-days 7.5 a.m. and every 12 minutes until 11.41 a.m., then 11.45 a.m. and every 10 minutes until 11.5 p.m.

Sundays 9.17 a.m. and every 12 minutes until 11.5 p.m.

From Fratton Bridge—

Week-days 7.15 a.m. and every 12 minutes until 11.51 a.m., then 11.55 a.m. and every 10 minutes until 11.15 p.m.

Sundays 9.26 a.m. and every 12 minutes until 11.14 p.m.

To TWYFORD AVENUE and COSHAM.

From South Parade Pier—

Week-days 7.24 a.m. and every 12 minutes until 12.0 noon, then 12.4 p.m. and every 10 minutes until 11.14 p.m., 11.24 p.m. to North End via Fratton Bridge.

Sundays 9.35 a.m. and every 12 minutes until 11.11 p.m., 11.23 p.m. to North End via Fratton Bridge.

From Guildhall—

Week-days 7.39 a.m. and every 12 minutes until 12.15 p.m., then 12.19 p.m. and every 10 minutes until 11.29 p.m.

Sundays 9.49 a.m. and every 12 minutes until 11.25 p.m.

From Twyford Avenue—

Week-days 7.52 a.m. and every 12 minutes until 12.28 p.m., then 12.32 p.m. and every 10 minutes until 11.42 p.m.

Sundays 10.1 a.m. and every 12 minutes until 11.37 p.m.

Service No. 4.

Cosham to South Parade Pier (via Twyford Avenue and Guildhall) **then to Cosham** (via Fratton Bridge and North End)

via Northern Parade, Twyford Avenue, Commercial Road, Guildhall, Bradford Road Junction, Albert Road, Festing Road, South Parade Pier, Strand, Fawcett Road, Fratton Bridge and North End.

To SOUTH PARADE PIER.

From Cosham—

Week-days 7.38 a.m. and every 12 minutes until 11.14 a.m., then 11.22 a.m. and every 10 minutes until 10.52 p.m., then every 10 minutes until 11.42 p.m. to North End.

Sundays 9.19 a.m. and every 12 minutes until 10.55 p.m., then every 12 minutes until 11.55 p.m. to North End.

From Twyford Avenue—

Week-days 7.46 a.m. and every 12 minutes until 11.22 a.m., then 11.30 a.m. and every 10 minutes until 11.0 p.m.

Sundays 9.27 a.m. and every 12 minutes until 11.3 p.m.

From Guildhall—

Week-days 7.35 a.m. and every 12 minutes until 11.35 a.m., then 11.43 a.m. and every 10 minutes until 11.13 p.m.

Sundays 9.27 a.m. and every 12 minutes until 11.15 p.m.

38

To COSHAM.

From South Parade Pier—

Week-days 7.26 a.m. and every 12 minutes until 11.50 a.m., then 11.58 a.m. and every 10 minutes until 11.8 p.m., 11.18 p.m. and 11.28 p.m. to North End only.

Sundays 9.41 a.m. and every 12 minutes until 11.17 p.m., 11.29 p.m. to North End only.

From Fratton Bridge—

Week-days 7.35 a.m. and every 12 minutes until 11.59 a.m., then 12.7 p.m. and every 10 minutes until 11.17 p.m., 11.27 p.m. and 11.37 p.m. to North End only.

Sundays 9.50 a.m. and every 12 minutes until 11.26 p.m., 11.38 p.m. to North End only.

From North End—

Week-days 6.45 a.m. and every 12 minutes until 12.9 p.m., then 12.17 p.m. and every 10 minutes until 11.27 p.m.

Sundays 9.35 a.m. and every 12 minutes until 11.35 p.m.

Service No. 5.

Dockyard to South Parade Pier, then to Eastney, Milton and Guildhall

via Gunwharf, King's Road Junction, Western Parade, Osborne Road, Clarendon Road (Palmerston Road), then to Festing Road, Highland Road (Eastney), Goldsmith Avenue (Milton), Fratton Bridge, Bradford Road Junction to Guildhall.

To KING'S ROAD, SOUTH PARADE PIER and EASTNEY.

From Dockyard—

Week-days 7.29 a.m. and every 12 minutes until 11.29 a.m., then 11.37 a.m. and every 10 minutes until 10.57 p.m.

Sundays 9.45 a.m. and every 12 minutes until 10.57 p.m.

From Palmerston Road—

Week-days 7.39 a.m. and every 12 minutes until 11.39 a.m., then 11.47 a.m. and every 10 minutes until 11.7 p.m.

Sundays 9.55 a.m. and every 12 minutes until 11.7 p.m.

From South Parade Pier—

Week-days 7.44 a.m. and every 12 minutes until 11.44 a.m., then 11.52 a.m. and every 10 minutes until 10.42 p.m., 10.52 p.m., 11.2 p.m., 11.12 p.m. to Eastney only.

Sundays 10.0 a.m. and every 12 minutes until 10.48 p.m., 11.0 p.m., 11.12 p.m. to Eastney only.

To MILTON and GUILDHALL.

From Eastney—

Week-days 7.27 a.m. and every 12 minutes until 11.51 a.m., then 11.59 a.m. and every 10 minutes until 10.49 p.m.

Sundays 9.43 a.m. and every 12 minutes until 10.55 p.m.

From Milton—

Week-days 7.29 a.m. and every 12 minutes until 11.53 a.m., then 12.1 p.m. and every 10 minutes until 10.51 p.m.

Sundays 9.46 a.m. and every 12 minutes until 10.58 p.m.

39

January–May 1939. CPPTD Timetable.

Corporation Trolley Bus Service 3	COSHAM (Railway Gates) — SOUTHSEA (South Parade Pier) Via London Road, North End Junction, Kingston Road, Fratton Road, Fawcett Road, Waverley Road and Strand.	Corporation Trolley Bus Service 3

WEEKDAY SERVICE

Cosham *Railway Gates*	6‡57	7‡ 9	7‡21	7 33	7 45	7 57	8 9	8 21	8 33	8 45	8 57	9 9	9 21	9 33	9 45	9 57	10 9	1021	1033
North End *Junction*	7 6	7 18	7 30	7 42	7 54	8 6	8 18	8 30	8 42	8 54	9 6	9 18	9 30	9 42	9 54	10 6	1018	1030	1042
Fratton Bridge	7 15	7 27	7 39	7 51	8 3	8 15	8 27	8 39	8 51	9 3	9 15	9 27	9 39	9 51	10 3	1015	1027	1039	1051
Southsea *South Parade Pier* ...	7 23	7 35	7 47	7 59	8 11	8 23	8 35	8 47	8 59	9 11	9 23	9 35	9 47	9 59	1011	1023	1035	1047	1059

Cosham *Railway Gates*	1045	1057	and at the	9	21	33	45	57		10 9	1021	1033	1045	1057	11 9	1116	1128
North End *Junction*	1054	11 6	following	18	30	42	54	6	until	1018	1030	1042	1054	11 6	1118	1125	1137
Fratton Bridge	11 3	1115	minutes past	27	39	51	3	15		1027	1039	1051	11 3	1115	1127	...	...
Southsea *South Parade Pier* ...	1111	1123	each hour	35	47	59	11	23		1035	1047	1059	1111	...	...	...	...

SUNDAY SERVICE

Cosham *Railway Gates*	8 15	8 45	9 15	9 30	9 45	10 0	1015	1030	1045	11 0	1115	1130	1145	12 0	1215	1230	1245	1257	1 9	1 21
North End *Junction*	8 24	8 54	9 24	9 39	9 54	10 9	1024	1039	1054	11 9	1124	1139	1154	12 9	1224	1239	1254	1 6	1 18	1 30
Fratton Bridge	8 33	9 3	9 33	9 48	10 3	1018	1033	1048	11 3	1118	1133	1148	12 3	1218	1233	1248	1 3	1 15	1 27	1 39
Southsea *South Parade Pier* ...	8 41	9 11	9 41	9 56	1011	1026	1041	1056	1111	1126	1141	1156	1211	1226	1241	1256	1 11	1 23	1 35	1 47

Cosham *Railway Gates*	1 33	1 45	1 57	and at the	9	21	33	45	57		10 9	1021	1033	1045	1057	11 9	1116	1128
North End *Junction*	1 42	1 54	2 6	following	18	30	42	54	6	until	1018	1030	1042	1054	11 6	1118	1125	1137
Fratton Bridge	1 51	2 3	2 15	mins. past	27	39	51	3	15		1027	1039	1051	11 3	1115	1127	...	...
Southsea *South Parade Pier* ...	1 59	2 11	2 23	each hour	35	47	59	11	23		1035	1047	1059	1111	...	...	...	...

‡—Starts from Cosham *Red Lion* 3 minutes earlier.

For Early Morning journeys, see pages 65-70, 75-77.

Service 3, Winter 1953 Timetable.

Corporation Trolley Bus Service 4	SOUTHSEA (South Parade Pier) — COSHAM (Railway Gates) Via Strand, Waverley Road, Fawcett Road, Fratton Road, Kingston Road, North End Junction and London Road.	Corporation Trolley Bus Service 4

WEEKDAY SERVICE

Southsea *South Parade Pier*	7 14	7 26	7 38	7 50	8 2	8 14	8 26	8 38	8 50	9 2	9 14	9 26	9 38	9 50	10 2	1014	1026	1038	1050	11 2	1114
Fratton Bridge	7 22	7 34	7 46	7 58	8 10	8 22	8 34	8 46	8 58	9 10	9 22	9 34	9 46	9 58	1010	1022	1034	1046	1058	1110	1122
North End *Junction*	7 31	7 43	7 55	8 7	8 19	8 31	8 43	8 55	9 7	9 19	9 31	9 43	9 55	10 7	1019	1031	1043	1055	11 7	1119	1131
Cosham *Railway Gates* ...	7 40	7 52	8 4	8 16	8 28	8 40	8 52	9 4	9 16	9 28	9 40	9 52	10 4	1016	1028	1040	1052	11 4	1116	1128	1140

Southsea *South Parade Pier*	1126	1138	1150	and at the	2	14	26	38	50		10 2	1014	1026	1038	1050	11 2	...	1114	...
Fratton Bridge	1134	1146	1158	following	10	22	34	46	58	until	1010	1022	1034	1046	1058	1110	1118	1122	1130
North End *Junction*	1143	1155	12 7	mins. past	19	31	43	55	7		1019	1031	1043	1055	11 7	1119	1127	1131	1139
Cosham *Railway Gates* ...	1152	12 4	1216	each hour	28	40	52	4	16		1028	1040	1052	11 4	1116	1128	...	...	...

SUNDAY SERVICE

Southsea *South Parade Pier*	...	...	8 45	...	9 15	...	9 45	10 0	1015	1030	1045	11 0	1115	1130	1145	12 0	1215	1230	1245	1 0	1 14
Fratton Bridge	...	...	8 53	...	9 23	...	9 53	10 8	1023	1038	1053	11 8	1123	1138	1153	12 8	1223	1238	1253	1 8	1 22
North End *Junction*	8 2	8 32	9 2	9 17	9 32	9 47	10 2	1017	1032	1047	11 2	1117	1132	1147	12 2	1217	1232	1247	1 2	1 17	1 31
Cosham *Railway Gates* ...	8 11	8 41	9 11	9 26	9 41	9 56	1011	1026	1041	1056	1111	1126	1141	1156	1211	1226	1241	1256	1 11	1 26	1 40

Southsea *South Parade Pier*	1 26	1 38	1 50	and at the	2	14	26	38	50		10 2	1014	1026	1038	1050	11 2	...	1114	...
Fratton Bridge	1 34	1 46	1 58	following	10	22	34	46	58	until	1010	1022	1034	1046	1058	1110	1118	1122	1130
North End *Junction*	1 43	1 55	2 7	mins. past	19	31	43	55	7		1019	1031	1043	1055	11 7	1119	1127	1131	1139
Cosham *Railway Gates* ...	1 52	2 4	2 16	each hour	28	40	52	4	16		1028	1040	1052	11 4	1116	1128	...	...	...

For Early Morning journeys, see pages 65-70, 75-77.

Service 4, Winter 1953 Timetable.

Trolleybus Service frequencies 1948 (minutes)

Service	AM	PM	Evenings
1A/2A	12	10	6
3/4A	12	10	6
3A/4	10	10	10
5/6	10	10	10
7/8	12	10	12
9/10	12	10	–
11/12	7½	7½	7½
13/14	12	10	12
15/16 (i)	15	15	15
17/18	10	10	12

Supplementary timetable leaflets were issued for every Bank Holiday and special events detailing the amended traffic arrangements on each day within the period of application.

Running times varied little during the life of the system, most changes taking place during the early years of the system as operations settled down:

	Summer 1937	*1953*
Cosham 'Red Lion' – North End	12	12*
Cosham Railway Station – North End	8	9
Dockyard – Palmerston Road	10	9
Guildhall – Milton 'White House'	12	10
Guildhall – Copnor Bridge	13	12

*By 1953 this journey was via Cosham Railway Station, involving one additional stop.

By the late 1920s passenger waiting shelters had been installed at the more important tram stops including Cosham Railway Station, Dockyard, Eastney, Greetham Street, Guildhall Square, Kings Road, Milton, St Mary's Church, St Mary's Road, Twyford Avenue and in Western Parade. In all cases timetables and a map of services were displayed inside them. From August 1936 Frank Mason & Co. Ltd. supplied metal timetable frames for use in the shelters, paying 10s p.a. per frame for the right to display advertisements in the frames; however, this arrangement ended soon after the outbreak of war.

Clocks

Good time-keeping was considered to be of the greatest importance and the Transport Department erected clocks at various locations:

Alexandra Park, on traction pole AE182 in the northern corner of the turning circle area.

Bradford Junction, inside the passenger waiting shelter on the west side of the central island.

Clarence Pier, on traction pole AF80.

Copnor Bridge, above the entrance to the passenger waiting shelter on the east side of the bridge approach.

Cosham 'Red Lion', on a lamp post on the north side of Spur Road opposite trolleybus stop.

Cosham Railway Station, on a separate pole in Portsmouth Road facing the Compound (pre 1948).

Dockyard, on traction pole AH38 at the corner of Clock Street opposite the trolleybus layover point.

Eastney, inside the passenger waiting shelter adjacent to Eastney Depot south wall.

Green Lane, inside the passenger waiting shelter opposite Madeira Road.

Guildhall, a four-faced clock on top of the CPPTD kiosk on the Guildhall Square central island was installed in 1942 following destruction of the Guildhall and its clock tower in January 1941. The clock was removed when the kiosk was moved to the north corner of Greetham Street (by which time the Guildhall clock tower had been reinstated).

King's Terrace, inside the passenger waiting shelter on the west side of the road.

Milton 'White House', inside the passenger waiting shelter on the south side of Goldsmith Avenue.

North End junction, on a traction pole on west side of London Road (near the stop for services to Cosham).

Southsea, South Parade Pier, attached to the pier entrance on its east side close to the original trolleybus terminus.

Recorder clocks, which provided a permanent record of a timely departure or a delay incurred en route by stamping the departure or passing time on a card held by the conductor, were not used in Portsmouth.

Stop signs

Pre-war various arrangements of coloured horizontal bands around the poles indicated fare stages and stops. Two broad red bands about 1ft deep and 1ft apart indicated a compulsory stop; in some cases ALL BUSES STOP HERE was stencilled in black capitals between the bands (one word above the other, BUSES being in larger lettering than the rest of the wording). There appears to have been no general use of bus stop flags; however, street views of the period show examples of two similar designs, one with a cross in the centre of the circle surrounded by illegible small writing, perhaps REQUEST STOP, and the other with a solid spot and no writing.

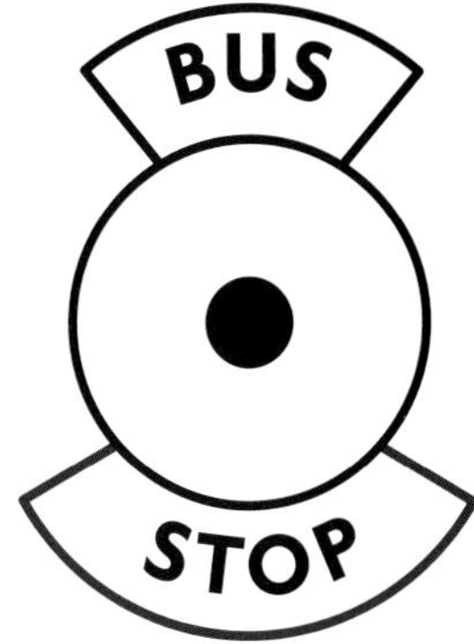

More important stops, such as those equipped with queuing barriers, displayed rectangular stop signs hanging at right angles from separate supporting tubular poles which were painted silver with a small red ball finial. The signs were headed CITY OF PORTSMOUTH PASSENGER TRANSPORT DEP[T]. in two lines with BUS STOP beneath, lettered in black on a white background. Beneath, SERVICES with the service number below, and side by side a list of the main stops served by the service concerned, lettered and numbered in white on a black background.

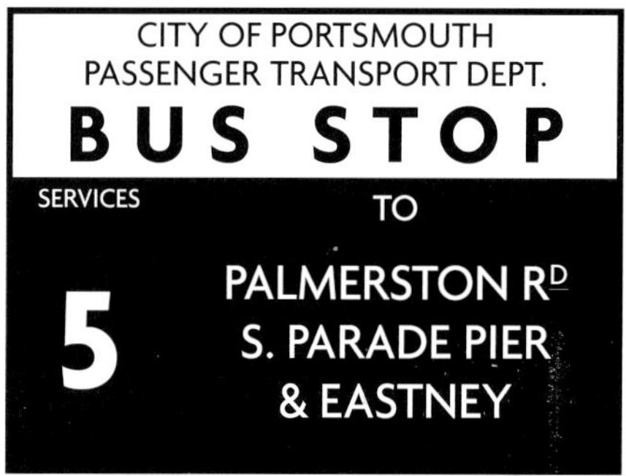

Post war rectangular stop flags displayed BUS STOP with FORM QUEUE THIS SIDE or FORM QUEUE OTHER SIDE beneath, lettered and framed in black on a white background.

More important stops were equipped with larger rectangular stop flags displayed BUS STOP, FORM QUEUE THIS SIDE or FORM QUEUE OTHER SIDE side by side, with SERVICE (some displayed ROUTE or had no heading at all) indicating the service number(s) serving the stop, and a list of the most important subsequent locations served by each service, beneath and again side by side, lettered, numbered and framed in black on a white background.

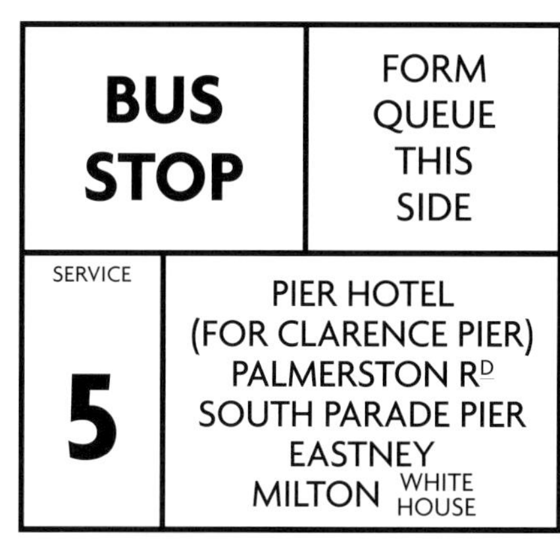

A separate sign above or beneath the main flag indicated FARE STAGE, lettered in black capitals on a yellow background, was added from the late 1950s where required.

Both styles of post war flags were affixed to traction poles or separate supporting tubular poles which were painted silver with a small red ball finial, as deemed appropriate.

Peak vehicle requirement

The Annual Report shows that by 1937 the winter timetable required 46 trolleybuses on weekdays off-peak and 62 at peak times. On Saturdays these figures rose to 66 trolleybuses off-peak and 95 in the afternoons to accommodate football traffic. The summer timetable required 63 trolleybuses on weekdays off-peak and 79 at peak times. On summer Saturdays 82 trolleybuses were required, this figure rising to 99 on Bank Holidays and Navy Days. This would have been a remarkable achievement considering that the CPPTD fleet at the time consisted of 100 trolleybuses (and 137 motorbuses) of which only 99 were licensed that summer (287 being de-licensed) thus it must be assumed that motorbuses were substituted for some of the extra journeys. The break-down between Eastney and North End Depots is not known.

Weekday peaks during the trolleybus era can be defined as relating approximately to Monday–Saturday 6.00am–9.00am, Monday–Friday 3.30pm–6.00pm and Saturday 12.00pm–6.00pm. The Dockyard ceased working on Saturdays in about 1952 commensurately reducing the Saturday vehicle requirement.

The 1946 winter timetable required a maximum of 74 trolleybuses although the average number in service on any day in April 1946 was shown as 69. The fact that by late 1940 trolleybuses 201–224 were taken out of service for the duration of the war, apparently without causing the department any difficulties in handling the increased traffic, brings these figures into perspective. The summer timetable required 74 trolleybuses on weekdays off-peak. As remarked elsewhere, much of the trolleybus era was characterised by a surplus of vehicles, usually de-licensed whereas, in general, trolleybus operators calculated with an allowance of around 10% for engineering spares.

There were 70 trolleybuses on the road for the August 1957 Bank Holiday and Navy Days weekend, it being noted that there were no further serviceable trolleybuses available.

By 17 May 1961 only 43 trolleybuses were available for service and by December 1961, with trolleybus operations contracted to services 5, 6 and 17, 18, only 20 trolleybuses were required at peaks, including specials, with 24 vehicles remaining in stock.

In addition to some improved frequencies shown in the public timetables, e.g. the frequency of services 11 and 12 increased to 6 minutes between 3.45pm and 6.00pm, the following trolleybus specials are known to have operated:

– Guildhall – Royal Pier Hotel – Southsea *South Parade Pier* – Festing Hotel – Eastney
Believed to have operated eastbound only.

5 Dockyard *Main Gate* – Royal Pier Hotel – Southsea *South Parade Pier* – Festing Hotel – Eastney – Milton *'White House'* – Copnor Bridge – Green Lane (only)
Fridays only, scheduled to reach Green Lane at 6.00pm after which the trolleybus returned to Eastney Depot.

17 Guildhall – Bradford Junction – Festing Hotel – Eastney – Milton *'White House'* – Bradford Junction – Guildhall
Unidirectional circular service (anti-clockwise) worked in conjunction with service 18.

Bus stop sign – Milton 'White House' (Roger Funnell)

18 Guildhall – Bradford Junction – Milton *'White House'* – Eastney –Festing Hotel – Bradford Junction – Guildhall
Unidirectional circular service (clockwise) worked in conjunction with service 17.

The majority of specials serving the Dockyard Outmuster were motorbus operated, most vehicles continuing thereafter to the airport to serve the Outmuster there, which was deliberately scheduled a little later in the day. Trolleybuses always played a subsidiary role in handling the Dockyard Outmuster specials.

Duty sheets

Way sheets were issued to the conductor together with his or her ticket machine. They showed the content of each duty, timings and specified whether a trolleybus was to be taken from the depot or relieved "on the road" and on which service, etc. The conductor was responsible for time-keeping by ensuring that there was no early departure from a timed stop. Trolleybus drivers were required to "sign on" for work 10 minutes before the allocated duty was scheduled to leave the depot in order that they had sufficient time to check the vehicle for any defects. At the start of duty conductors also had to "sign on" 10 minutes before they were due to leave the depot to collect their ticket machine, ticket box and way sheet. When a conductor started or finished duty "on the road", e.g. Alexandra Park or Copnor Bridge rather than at a depot, there was an allowance of time paid to permit them to collect their equipment from the depot and make their way to the relieving point or return to the depot and cash up their takings. Drivers starting or finishing "on the road" were paid from the time they were scheduled to take the vehicle over or until their scheduled relief time. When running into the depot drivers had a 5-minute allowance to park their trolleybus and conductors a 10-minute allowance to cash up their takings.

Running cards or similar were not issued to the driver or displayed anywhere on the trolleybus.

Crew changeover points

Copnor Bridge	Services 7, 8,	
Copnor Bridge	Services 11, 12	Note 1
Eastney Depot	Services 5, 6,	Note 2
Eastney Depot	Services 15, 16, 17, 18	
Eastney Depot	Services 19, 20	Note 3
North End Junction	Services 3, 4, 13, 14	

Notes:

1. Some duties changed at Guildhall Square.
2. Those duties operated by North End changed at Copnor Bridge.
3. Those duties operated by North End changed at Alexandra Park.

Just to the north of Guildhall Square AEC661T 298 climbs from beneath the Portsmouth & Southsea Station Railway Bridge over Commercial Road on a service 11 journey from Green Lane. An Austin Cambridge motor car pulls out behind the trolleybus and a Triumph Herald passes in the northbound carriageway. Brickwood's wares and their sunshine sign could be found through much of South England, stretching from Sussex to Dorset and north towards London, until the early 1970s when they were acquired by Whitbreads. Brewing at Queen Street, Portsmouth, ceased in 1983. (Tony Belton)

Following the addition of the small recessed window above the driver's windscreen AEC661T/English Electric 4 is seen heading south along Northern Parade past the Oakwood public house, now a Cooperative store, and St. Francis Church. (photographer's name not recorded)

APPENDIX K

ENTHUSIASTS' TOURS

The following enthusiasts' tours of the Portsmouth trolleybus system are known to have taken place:

Date	Vehicle	Hirer	Comment
Late 1940s	265	S.E. Harrison	Details not known
5 October 1947	210	Details not known	Details not known
22 July 1956	210	Southern Counties Touring Society	Free of charge
7 September 1957	241	Trolleybus Society (S.E. Harrison)	
3 July 1960	304	Southern Counties Touring Society	
7 April 1963	174	Southern Counties Touring Society	Last use of 5/6 turning circle at Southsea South Parade Pier

On 5 October 1947 Sunbeam MF2 210 stands at the south end of Gladys Avenue, with the tram tracks leading into North End Depot (on the left) still evident, on an enthusiasts' tour. (A.D. Packer)

On 5 October 1947 a group of enthusiasts toured the trolleybus system in Sunbeam MF2 210, seen here in Broad Street prior to turning into East Street at the Floating Bridge, Old Portsmouth reverser. (A.D. Packer)

APPENDIX L

LEGISLATION

Trolleybuses in the UK were essentially regulated in the same manner as their predecessors, the trams, and treated as light railways. This necessitated that a Bill be promoted in Parliament and an Act secured for the construction of a new trolleybus system or the conversion of an existing tramway to trolleybus operation.

This Appendix contains the relevant paragraphs of the Acts of Parliament relating to trolleybus operation in Portsmouth including that for the Joint Agreement with Southdown Motor Service. No relevant local Byelaws have been identified.

Certain paragraphs of the 1930 and 1946 Acts not directly related to the trolleybus network and its operation have been omitted for brevity in so far that this does not negatively affect comprehensibility.

Note: These extracts use the same grammar, spelling and style as the original documents. In view of the complex and dated terminology used in the original text.

---

20 GEO. 5.
Portsmouth Corporation Act, 1930

CHAPTER lii.

An Act to empower the lord mayor aldermen and citizens of the city of Portsmouth to acquire lands compulsorily and to establish thereon an aerodrome undertaking to confer powers upon them with respect to their tramways and electricity undertakings and for other purposes.

[15th April 1930.]

WHEREAS the city of Portsmouth (in this Act referred to as "the city") is a county borough within the meaning of the Local Government Act 1888 and is subject to the jurisdiction of the lord mayor aldermen and citizens of the city (in this Act referred to as "the Corporation"):

And whereas it is expedient that the Corporation should establish within the city an aerodrome and works and conveniences associated therewith and should be empowered to acquire lands for those purposes:

And whereas the Corporation are the owners of a system of tramways within the city and it is expedient that they should be empowered to substitute trolley vehicles on the routes thereof as by this Act provided:

And whereas it is expedient that further powers should be conferred upon the Corporation with respect to their tramway and electricity undertaking:

And whereas estimates have been prepared by the Corporation in relation to the purchase of lands and for the purposes of the aerodrome undertaking of the Corporation in respect of which they are by this Act authorised to borrow money and such estimates amount to one hundred and forty-two thousand pounds:

And whereas the several works included in such estimates are permanent works and it Is expedient that the cost thereof should be spread over a term of years as by this Act provided:

And whereas it is expedient that the other provisions contained in this Act should be enacted:

And whereas a plan of the lands by this Act authorized to be acquired and a book of reference to such plan containing the names of the owners and lessees or reputed owners and lessees and of the occupiers of the said land were duly deposited with the clerk of the peace for the county of Southampton which plan and book of references are in this Act respectively referred to as the deposited plan and book of reference:

And whereas the purposes of this Act cannot be effected without the authority of Parliament:

And whereas in relation to the promotion of the Bill for this Act the requirements of the Borough Funds Acts 1872 and 1903 have been observed:

May it therefore please Your Majesty that it may be enacted and be it enacted by the King's most Excellent Majesty by and with the advice and consent of the Lords Spiritual and Temporal and Commons in this present Parliament assembled and by the authority of the same as follows:—

PART I.
PRELIMINARY.

1. This Act may be cited as the Portsmouth Corporation Act 1930.

2. This Act is divided into Parts as follows;—
   Part I.—Preliminary.
   Part II.—Lands.
   Part III.—Aerodrome undertaking.
   Part IV.—Trolley vehicles &e.
   Part V.—Electricity.
   Part VI.—Finance.
   Part VII.—Miscellaneous.

3. The Lands Clauses Acts {except section 127 of the Lands Clauses Consolidation Act 1845) so far as the same are applicable to the purposes of and are not inconsistent with the provisions of this Act are hereby incorporated with and form part of this Act:

   Provided that the bond required by section 85 of the Lands Clauses Consolidation Act 1845 shall be under the corporate seal of the Corporation and shall be sufficient without the addition of the sureties mentioned in that section.

4. Subject to the provisions of this Act and unless the subject or context otherwise requires the subject or context otherwise requires the several words and expressions to which by the Acts incorporated with this Act and by the Public Health Acts meanings are assigned shall in this Act have in relation to the relative subject-matter the same respective meanings And in this Act—

   "The city" means the city of Portsmouth;

   "The Corporation" means the lord mayor aldermen and citizens of the city:

   "The council" means the council of the city;

   "The Minister" means the Minister of Health;

"The town clerk" and "the treasurer" mean respectively the town clerk and the treasurer of the city and respectively include any poison duly appointed by the Corporation to discharge the duties of any such officers:
"The Act of 1898" means the Portsmouth Corporation Tramways Act 1898;-
"The Order of 1900" means the Portsmouth Corporation Tramways Order 1900;
"The Act of 1920" means the Portsmouth Corporation Act 1920;-
"The Land Clauses Acts" means those Acts and the Acquisition of Land (Assessment of Compensation) Act 1919;
"The arbitrator" means the arbitrator to whom any question of disputed compensation is referred under the provisions of this Act;
"The Public Health Acts" means the Public Health Act 1875 and the Acts amending and extending the same;
"The aerodrome undertaking" means the aerodrome undertaking of the Corporation as from time to time authorised including any subsidiary business connected therewith;
"The tramway undertaking" means the tramway undertaking of the Corporation as from time authorised;
"Trolley vehicle" means a mechanically propelled vehicle adapted for use without rails upon roads and moved by electrical power transmitted thereto from some external source;
"Road authority" means with reference to any road or part of a road over which any proposed trolley vehicle service will pass the authority company or person charged with or liable to contribute to the maintenance of such road or part of a road;
"The electricity undertaking" means the electricity undertaking of the Corporation as from time to time authorised;
"The electricity limits" means the limits within which the Corporation are from time to time authorised to supply electricity;
"Daily penalty" means a penalty for every day on which any offence is continued after conviction;
"The general rate fund" and "the general rate" mean respectively the general rate fund and the general rate of the city;
"Statutory security" means any security in which trustees are for the time being by or under any Art of Parliament passed or to be passed authorised to invest trust money and any mortgage bond debenture debenture stock stock or other security authorised by or under any Act of Parliament passed or to be passed of any county council or municipal corporation or other local authority as defined by section 34 of the Local Loans Act 1875 but does not include annuities rentcharges or securities transferable by delivery or any securities of the Corporation;
"Statutory borrowing power" means any power whether or not coupled with a duty of borrowing or continuing on loan or re-borrowing money or of redeeming or paying off or creating or continuing payment of or in respect of any annuity rentcharge rent or other security representing or granted in lieu of consideration money for the time being existing under any Act of Parliament public or local passed or to be passed or under any Provisional Order confirmed by Act of Parliament passed or to be passed or under any order or sanction of any Government department made or given or to be made or given by authority of any Act of Parliament passed or to be passed; and
"Revenues of the Corporation" includes the revenues of the Corporation from time to time arising from any land undertakings or other property for the time being of the Corporation and the rates or contributions leviable by or on the order or precept of the Corporation.

Part IV.
Trolley Vehicles &c.

20.—(1) The Corporation may provide (but shall not manufacture) maintain and equip trolley vehicles and may work the same along any street or road in the city in which they are at the passing of this Act authorised to construct or work tramways and with the consent of the Minister of Transport in any other street or road so far as may be necessary for turning the vehicles.
(2) Provided that-

(a) Before equipping any trolley vehicle route to include a turning point or before arranging for a new turning point on any route the Corporation shall submit plans of the turning point to the Minister of Transport for approval;

(b) No turning point shall be fixed upon any road or street belonging to or maintained by a railway company without the consent in writing of such company which consent shall not be unreasonably withheld.

(3) As from the date upon which and so long as a service of trolley vehicles is provided by the Corporation in lieu of a tramway service upon the route of any of their tramways the revenue of the tramway undertaking shall (to such extent as the Corporation may from time to time by resolution determine) cease to be charged with any expenses incurred by the Corporation upon or in connection with the maintenance and repair of roads along the route or routes upon which such service of trolley vehicles is provided under any statutory enactment relating to that undertaking but nothing in this subsection shall relieve the Corporation of any liability attaching to them in respect of such maintenance repair.
21.—(1) The Corporation may in under or over the surface of the streets or roads along or adjoining those along which they are authorised to run trolley vehicles or in which if may be necessary so to do in order to connect the apparatus and equipment for working such vehicles with any generating station place erect and maintain all necessary and proper standards brackets conductors mains cables wires posts poles and any other necessary or convenient apparatus and equipment for the purpose of working the trolley vehicles by electrical power and may for that purpose subject to the provisions contained in Part II of the Tramways Act 1870 and in this part of this Act open and break up any such street or road and any sewers drains water or gas pipes tubes wires telephonic and telegraphic apparatus therein or thereunder and may supply electrical energy for the purpose of working the trolley vehicles Provided that no post or other apparatus shall be erected on the carriageway except with the consent of the Minister of Transport.
(2) Nothing in this section shall extend to or authorise any interference with any works of any undertakers within the meaning of the Electricity (Supply) Acts 1882 to 1928 to which the provisions of section 15 of the Electric Lighting Act 1882 apply except in accordance with and subject to the provisions of that section.

{3} The Corporation may also adapt and use for the purpose of working trolley vehicles any apparatus and equipment already provided by them for working tramways in streets or roads along which they are or may be authorised to run trolley vehicles.
(4) In this section the expression "generating station" has the meaning assigned to it by section 25 of the Electric Lighting Act 1909.
22. Subject to the provisions of this Act the Corporation shall have the exclusive right of using any apparatus provided erected or maintained by them for the purpose of working the trolley vehicles and any person (except by agreement with the Corporation) using the said apparatus shall for every offence be liable to a penalty not exceeding twenty pounds.

Paragraphs 23–24 omitted

25.—(1) The trolley vehicles and the electrical equipment thereof used under the authority of this Act shall be of such form construction weight and dimensions as the Minister of Transport may approve and no trolley vehicle shall be used by the Corporation which does not comply with the requirements of the said Minister.
(2) Before applying to the Minister of Transport for his approval of the weight of any trolley vehicle to be used upon any road which crosses a bridge belonging to or repairable by a railway company the Corporation shall give to such railway company notice of the weight of the trolley vehicles proposed to be used by them and the said Minister shall consider and determine after such inquiry as he may think fit any objections which may be submitted by the railway company to him on the ground that the strength of such bridge is insufficient to carry trolley vehicles of such weight Provided that notice of such objections shall be forwarded by such railway company to the Corporation at the same time as the same are submitted to the said Minister.
26. The following provisions shall apply to the use of electrical power under this Act unless such power is entirely contained in and carried along with the trolley vehicles:—
(1) The Corporation shall employ either insulated returns or uninsulated, metallic returns of low resistance:
(2) The Corporation shall take all reasonable precautions in constructing placing and maintaining their electric lines and circuits and other works of all descriptions and also in working their trolley vehicle undertaking so as not injuriously to affect by fusion or electrolytic action any gas or water pipes or other metallic pipes structures or substances or to interfere with the working of any wire line or apparatus from time to time used for the purpose of transmitting electrical power or of telegraphic telephonic or electric signalling communication or the currents in such wire line or apparatus:
(3) The electrical power shall be used only in accordance with the mechanical power regulations and in such regulations provisions shall be made for preventing funion or injurious electrolytic action of or on gas or water pipes or other metallic pipes structures or substance* and for minimising as far as is reasonably practicable injurious interference with the electric witch lines and apparatus of other parties and the currents therein whether such lines do or do not use the earth as a return:
(4) The Corporation shall be deemed to take all reasonable and proper precautions against interference with the working of any wire line or apparatus if and so long as they adopt and employ at the option of the Corporation either such insulated returns or such uninsulated metallic returns of low resistance and such other means of preventing injurious interference with the electric wires lines and apparatus of other parties and the currents therein as may be prescribed by the mechanical power regulations and in prescribing such means the Minister of Transport shall have regard to the expense involved and to the effect thereof upon the commercial prospects of the undertaking:
(5) The provisions of this section shall not operate to give any right of action in respect of injurious interference with any electric wire line or apparatus or the currents therein unless in the construction erection maintaining and working of such wire line and apparatus all reasonable and proper precautions including the use of an insulated return have been taken to prevent injurious interference therewith and with the currents therein by or from other electric currents:
(6) If any difference arises between the Corporation and any other party with respect to anything in this section such difference shall unless the parties otherwise agree be determined by the Minister of Transport or at his option by an arbitrator to be appointed by him and the costs of such determination shall be in the discretion of the said Minister or of the arbitrator as the case may be:
(7) The Corporation using electrical power contrary to the provisions of this Act or of the mechanical power regulations shall for every such offence be subject to a penalty not exceeding ten pounds and also if a continuing offence to a further penalty not exceeding five pounds for every day during which the offence continues after conviction thereof Provided always that whether any such penalty has been recovered or not the Minister of Transport if in his opinion the Corporation in the use of electrical power under the authority of this Act have made default in complying with the provisions of this Act or the mechanical power regulations may by order direct the Corporation to cease to use electrical power and thereupon the Corporation shall cease to use electrical power and shall not again use the same unless with the authority of the said Minister and in every such case that Minister shall make a special report to Parliament notifying the making of such order:
(8) The expression "Corporation" in this section includes licensees and any person owning working or running carriages over any of the trolley vehicle routes.

Paragraphs 27–30 omitted

31. Every artisan mechanic or daily labourer travelling on the trolley vehicles for the purpose of going to his work before eight a.m. on any day of the week except Sunday Christmas Day and Good Friday and returning therefrom not earlier than twelve noon on the same day shall for each such double journey be charged a fare not exceeding the fare which the Corporation for the time being charge for each such single journey.
32.—(1) If at any time hereafter the Corporation desire to provide maintain equip and use trolley vehicles upon any road (within the city) as defined by the Tramways Act 1870 (other than the streets and roads along and upon which they are by this Act authorised to use trolley vehicles) they may make application to the Minister of Transport and that Minister is hereby empowered to make a Provisional Order authorising the use by the Corporation of trolley vehicles subject to such

conditions and restrictions (if any) as he may think fit upon any road or roads to which such application relates and containing such incidental provisions as the said Minister may deem expedient and subject to the terms of the Provisional Order the provisions of this Act shall apply as if the use of trolley vehicles upon such road were authorised by this Act.

(2) No such application shall be entertained by the Minister of Transport unless the Corporation shall—

(a) have published once in each of two successive weeks in the months of October or November notice of their intention to make such application in some newspaper or newspapers circulating in the city ;

(b) have also published such notice once in the months of October or November in the London Gazette;

(c) have posted for fourteen consecutive days in the months of October or November in conspicuous positions in each of the roads to which such application relates a notice of their intention to make such application; and each such notice shall state the time and method for bringing before the said Minister any objections to the grant of such application.

(3) The Minister of Transport may and he is hereby empowered to prescribe the procedure with respect to any application for a Provisional Order under this section.

(4) The Minister of Transport shall consider any such application and may if he thinks fit direct an inquiry to be held in relation thereto or may otherwise inquire as to the propriety of proceeding upon such application and he shall consider any objection to such application that may be lodged with him in accordance with the prescribed procedure and shall determine whether or not it is expedient and proper that the application be granted either with or without addition or modification or subject or not to any restriction or condition.

(5) In any case where it shall appear to the Minister of Transport expedient that the application be granted he may settle and make a Provisional Order authorising the same and shall as soon as conveniently may be thereafter procure a Bill to be introduced into either House of Parliament for an Act to confirm the Provisional Order which shall be set out at length in the schedule to the Bill and until confirmation with or without amendment by such Act of Parliament a Provisional Order under this Act shall not have any operation.

(6) If while any such Bill is pending in either House of Parliament a petition is presented against any Provisional Order comprised therein the Bill so far as it relates to the Order petitioned against may be referred to a select committee and the petitioner shall be allowed to appear and oppose as in the case of a Bill for a special Act.

(7) The Act of Parliament confirming a Provisional Order under this Act shall be deemed a public general Act.

(8) The making of a Provisional Order under this section shall be prima facie evidence that all the requirements of this section in respect of proceedings required to be taken previously to the making of such Provisional Order have been complied with.

(9) Any expenses incurred by the Minister of Transport in connection with the preparation and making of any such Provisional Order any expenses incurred by the said Minister in connection with any inquiry under this section shall be paid by the Corporation.

Paragraphs 33–34 omitted

35. All subsisting regulations and byelaws relating to the tramways of the Corporation made in pursuance of the Tramways Act 1870 or of any other statutory enactment so far as the same are applicable shall with the necessary modifications apply to the trolley vehicles provided by the Corporation in pursuance of this Act.

36. Subject to the provisions of the Act the trolley vehicle undertaking authorised by this Act shall form part of the tramway undertaking.

37. The Corporation may if they think fit convey on their tramcars trolley vehicles and omnibuses dogs in the care of passengers the charge for any such dog to be a sum not exceeding the fare payable by the passenger.

38. The Corporation may run through tramcars along the route of any of the tramways of the Corporation or any specified portion thereof or through trolley vehicles or omnibuses along any route on which the Corporation are for the time being authorised to run trolley vehicles or omnibuses and such tramcars trolley vehicles and omnibuses shall be distinguished from other tramcars trolley vehicles and omnibuses in such manner as may be directed by the Corporation and they may demand and take for every passenger by such tramcars trolley vehicles and omnibuses a fare or charge not exceeding the maximum fare or charge authorised or chargeable for and in respect of the whole of such route or the whole of the portion thereof traversed by any such tramcars trolley vehicles and omnibuses Provided that during the running of such through tramcars trolley vehicles and omnibuses the Corporation shall maintain a reasonably sufficient ordinary service of tramcars trolley vehicles or omnibuses as the case may be:

Provided also that this section shall so far as it relates to motor vehicles (other than tramcars and trolley vehicles) carrying passengers for hire or reward at separate fares or motor vehicles (other than tramcars and trolley vehicles) carrying passengers for hire or reward and adapted to carry eight or more passengers cease to have effect on the passing during the present session of Parliament of any general Act relating road traffic.

39. The Corporation shall perform in respect of any trolley vehicles provided by them under this Act such services in regard to the conveyance of mails are prescribed by the Conveyance of Mail Act 1893 in the case of a tramway to which that Act applies.

Paragraphs 40–42 omitted

43. The Corporation may appoint the stations and places from which their omnibuses shall start or at which they may stop for the purpose of taking up and setting down passengers and may fix the time during which such omnibuses shall be allowed to remain at any such station or place:

Provided that this section shall cease to have effect on the passing during the present session of Parliament of any general Act relating to road traffic.

44.—(1) The Corporation may attach to any lamp-post pole standard or other similar erection erected on or in the highway on or near to any of the tramways of the Corporation or any of their trolley vehicle or omnibus routes signs or directions indicating the position of stopping places for tramcars trolley vehicles and omnibuses Provided that in cases where the Corporation are not the owners of such lamp-post pole standard or similar erection they shall give notice in writing of their intention to attach thereto any such sign or direction and shall make compensation to the owner for any damage or injury occasioned to such lamp-post pole standard or similar erection by such attachment and the Corporation shall indemnify the said owner against any claim for damage occasioned to any person or property by or by reason of such attachment.

(2) Nothing in this section shall be deemed to require the owner to retain any such lamp-post pole standard or similar erection when no longer required for his purposes.

(3) The Corporation shall not attach any such sign or direction to any pole post or standard belonging to the Postmaster-General except with his consent in writing or belonging to any local or road authority except with the consent of the authority in writing.

(4) The Corporation shall not attach any such sign or direction to any lamp-post pole standard or other similar erection belonging to the Southern Railway Company or to the Portsmouth Gas Company or to the Central Electricity Board respectively without the consent in writing of such company or board which consent in the case of the said gas company shall not he unreasonably withheld.

45. The Corporation shall keep the accounts in respect of the tramway undertaking so as to show separately (so far as may be reasonably practicable) the receipts and expenditure in regard to *(a)* the tramways *(b)* the trolley vehicles and *(c)* the omnibuses which the Corporation are empowered to provide and run and in such accounts capital shall he distinguished from revenue.

46. The Corporation shall in every year within three months after the close of their financial year or such longer period as the Minister of Transport may allow furnish to the Minister of Transport a copy of the annual accounts of the tramway undertaking.

Paragraphs 47–48 omitted

25 & 26 GEO. 5.
Portsmouth Corporation (Trolley Vehicles) Order Confirmation Act, 1935

CHAPTER xlv.

An Act to confirm a Provisional Order made by the Minister of Transport under the Portsmouth Corporation Act 1930 relating to Portsmouth Corporation trolley vehicles.

[10th July 1935.]

WHEREAS under the authority of section thirty-two of the Portsmouth Corporation Act 1930 the Minister of Transport has made the Provisional Order set out in the schedule to this Act annexed:

And whereas a Provisional Order made by the Minister of Transport under the authority of the said section is not of any validity or force whatever until the confirmation thereof by Act of Parliament:

And whereas it is expedient that the Provisional Order made by the Minister of Transport under the authority of the said section and set out in the schedule to this Act annexed be confirmed by Act of Parliament:

Be it therefore enacted by the King's most Excellent Majesty and with the advice and consent of the Lords Spiritual and Temporal and Commons in this present Parliament assembled and by the authority of the same as follows:-

1. This Act may be cited as the Portsmouth Corporation (Trolley Vehicles) Order Confirmation Act 1935.

2. The Order set out in the schedule to this Act shall be and the same is hereby confirmed and all the provisions thereof in manner and form as they are set out in the said schedule shall from and after the passing of this Act have full force and validity and the date of the same shall be the date of the passing of this Act.

SCHEDULE

PORTSMOUTH CORPORATION (TROLLEY VEHICLES)

Provisional Order authorising the lord mayor aldermen and citizens of the city of Portsmouth to use trolley vehicles upon certain routes in the city of Portsmouth.

1.—(1) This Order may be cited as the Portsmouth Corporation (Trolley Vehicles) Order 1935.

(2) The Portsmouth Corporation (Trolley Vehicles) Act 1930 and this Order may be cited together as the Portsmouth Corporation (Trolley Vehicles) Act and Orders 1930 and 1935.

2. In this Order the following expressions have unless the subject or context otherwise requires the meanings hereinafter assigned to them (namely): —

"The Act of 1930" means the Portsmouth Corporation Act 1930;

"The city" means the city of Portsmouth;

"The Corporation" means the lord mayor aldermen and citizens of the city;

"The Minister" means the Minister of Transport;

"Trolley vehicle" has the meaning assigned to it by section 4 (Interpretation) of the Act of 1930.

3. The Corporation may use trolley vehicles upon the following route in the city: —

Route No. 1 (6 furlongs 8.18 chains or thereabouts in length) commencing in Twyford Avenue at the terminus of the existing tramway therein proceeding along Northern Parade to and terminating at its junction with London Road;

Route No. 2 (7 furlongs or thereabouts in length) commencing at the junction of Portsmouth Road (Cosham) with Northern Road (Cosham) proceeding along Northern Road (Cosham) to its junction with London Road (Cosham) and along London Road (Cosham) to its junction with Spur Road and along Spur Road to and terminating at its junction with Northern Road (Cosham) :

Provided that—

(a) before equipping any trolley vehicle route to include a turning point or before arranging for a turning point on any route the Corporation shall submit plans of the turning point to the Minister of Transport for approval;

(b) no turning point shall be fixed upon any road or street belonging to or maintained by a railway company without the consent in writing of such company which consent shall not be unreasonably withheld;

(c) If the Corporation shall not have commenced to use trolley vehicles upon each of the routes authorised by this Order within five years from the passing of the Act confirming this Order, or such extended time as the Minister of Transport may upon the application of the Corporation allow the powers conferred by this Order shall so far as they relate to the use of trolley vehicles upon the route upon which the Corporation shall not have commenced to use trolley vehicles cease to be exerciseable.

4. The provisions of Part IV (Trolley vehicles &c.) of the Act of 1930 as amended by the Road Traffic Act 1930 and of

the enactments incorporated therewith or applied thereby in so far as those provisions relate to trolley vehicles and are applicable to and not inconsistent with or rendered unnecessary by the provisions of this Order shall apply to the trolley vehicles and routes referred to in and authorised by this Order in like manner as they apply to the trolley vehicles and routes authorised by the said Part IV.

5.—(1) The Corporation may from time to time independently of any other borrowing power borrow at interest for and in connection with the purposes mentioned in the first column of the following table the respective sums mentioned in the second column of the said table and they shall pay off all moneys so borrowed within such periods as the Corporation may determine not exceeding those respectively mentioned in the third column of the said table (namely):—

Purpose Repayment	Amount	Period for
(a) The provision of trolley vehicles.	£8,200	Ten years from the date or dates of borrowing.
(b) The provision of trolley vehicle equipment and the construction of other works necessary for working trolley vehicles along the route authorised by this Order.	£5,300	Fifteen years from the date or dates of borrowing.
(c) The payment of the costs charges and expenses of this Order.	The sum requisite	Five years from the confirmation of this Order.

(2) For the purposes of subsection (2) of section 63 (Power to borrow and repayment of borrowed moneys) of the Act of 1930 as modified by section 197 of the Local Government Act 1933 the purposes of this Order shall be deemed to be purposes of the tramway undertaking of the Corporation.

(3) The provisions of this section shall not limit the powers conferred upon the Corporation by section 149 (Power to use one form of mortgage for all purposes) of the Portsmouth Corporation Act 1920.

6. The provisions of section 250 (Procedure &c. for making byelaws) of the Local Government Act 1933 shall not apply in respect of byelaws to be made under section 46 (Byelaws by local authority Promoters may make certain regulations) of the Tramways Act 1870 or under section 69 (Shelters or waiting rooms and barriers) of the Portsmouth Corporation Act 1920.

7. The Minister of Transport may hold such inquiries he may consider necessary in regard to the exercise of powers conferred upon him or the giving of consents under this Order and section 290 of the Local Government Act 1933 shall apply accordingly.

8. All costs charges and expenses of and incidental to preparing, and obtaining and confirming of this Order or otherwise incurred in relation thereto as taxed by the taxing officer of the House of Lords or of the House of Commons shall be paid by the Corporation.

11 & 12 GEO. 6.
Portsmouth Corporation (Trolley Vehicles) Order Confirmation Act, 1948.

CHAPTER xxiv.

An Act to confirm a Provisional Order made by the Minister of Transport under the Portsmouth Corporation Act 1930 relating to Portsmouth Corporation trolley vehicles.

[30th July 1948.]

WHEREAS under the authority of section thirty-two of the Portsmouth Corporation Act 1930 the Minister of Transport has made the Provisional Order set out in the schedule to this Act annexed:

And whereas a Provisional Order made by the Minister of Transport under the authority of the said section is not of any validity or force whatever until the confirmation thereof by Act of Parliament:

And whereas it is expedient that the Provisional Order made by the Minister of Transport under the authority of the said section and set out in the schedule to this Act annexed be confirmed by Act of Parliament:

Be it therefore enacted by the King's most Excellent Majesty by and with the advice and consent of the Lords Spiritual and Temporal and Commons in this present Parliament assembled and by the authority of the same as follows:—

1. The Order set out in the schedule to this Act annexed shall be and the same is hereby confirmed and all the provisions thereof in manner and form as they are set out in the said schedule shall from and after the passing of this Act have full force and validity and the date of the same shall be the date of the passing of this Act.

2. This Act may be cited as the Portsmouth Corporation (Trolley Vehicles) Order Confirmation Act 1948.

SCHEDULE

PORTSMOUTH CORPORATION.

Order authorising the lord mayor aldermen and citizens of the city of Portsmouth to use trolley vehicles upon certain routes in the city of Portsmouth.

1.—(1) This Order may be cited as the Portsmouth Corporation (Trolley Vehicles) Order 1948.

(2) The Portsmouth Corporation (Trolley Vehicles) Act and Order 1930 and 1935 and this Order may be cited together as the Portsmouth Corporation (Trolley Vehicles) Act and Orders 1930 to 1948.

2. In this Order the following expressions have unless the subject or context otherwise requires the meanings hereinafter assigned to them (namely):—

"The city" means the city of Portsmouth;

"The Corporation" means the lord mayor aldermen and citizens of the city;

"The Act of 1930" means the Portsmouth Corporation Act 1930;

"Trolley vehicle" has the meaning assigned to it by section 4 (Interpretation) of the Act of 1930.

3. The Corporation may use trolley vehicles upon the following routes in the city:—

Route No. 1. (1 mile 7 furlongs 0.45 chains or thereabouts in length) commencing at the junction of Havant Road London Road and High Street (Cosham) proceeding along Havant Road to and terminating at a point 2 chains east of its junction with Rectory Avenue;

Route No. 2. (2 miles 7 furlongs 9.31 chains or thereabouts in length) commencing at the junction of Milton Road Eastney Road and Goldsmith Avenue proceeding along Milton Road to and over Copnor Bridge thence proceeding along Copnor Road to and terminating at its junction with London Road;
Route No. 3. (2 furlongs 2.27 chains or thereabouts in length) commencing by a junction with Route No. 2 authorised by this Order at the southern junction of Baffins Road and Milton Road proceeding along Baffins Road to and terminating by a junction with Route No. 2 authorised by this Order at the northern junction of Baffins Road and Milton Road;
Route No. 4. (3 furlongs or thereabouts in length) commencing in Gladys Avenue at the terminus of the existing trolley vehicle system proceeding along Gladys Avenue to and terminating at its junction with Northern Parade;
Route No. 5. (5 furlongs 2.4 chains or thereabouts in length) commencing at the junction of London Road and Stubbington Avenue proceeding along Stubbington Avenue to and terminating by a junction with Route No. 2 authorised by this Order in Copnor Road at a point therein opposite Burrfields Road;
Route No. 6. (5 furlongs 3.9 chains or thereabouts in length) commencing by a junction with Route No. 2 authorised by this Order in Milton Road at a point 3 chains south-east of the centre of Copnor Bridge proceeding along Milton Road and Tangier Road to and terminating at a point therein 4.54 chains east of its junction with Stanley Avenue;
Route No. 7. (2 furlongs 3.77 chains or thereabouts in length) commencing at the junction of Commercial Road and Edinburgh Road proceeding along Edinburgh Road and Unicorn Road to and terminating at its junction with Flathouse Road:
Provided that—

(a) before equipping any trolley vehicle route to include a turning point or before arranging for a new turning point on any route the Corporation shall submit plans of the turning point to the Minister of Transport for approval;

(b) if the Corporation shall not have commenced to use trolley vehicles upon each of the routes authorised by this Order within five years from the passing of the Act confirming this Order or such extended time as the Minister of Transport may upon the application of the Corporation allow the powers conferred by this Order shall so far as they relate to the use of trolley vehicles upon the route upon which the Corporation shall not have commenced to use trolley vehicles cease to be exerciseable.

4. The provisions of Part IV (Trolley vehicles &c.) of the Act of Application of 1930 as amended by the Road Traffic Act 1930 and of the enactments incorporated therewith or applied thereby in so far as those provisions relate to trolley vehicles and are applicable to and not inconsistent with or rendered unnecessary by the provisions of this Order shall apply to the trolley vehicles and routes referred to in and authorised by this Order in like manner as they apply to the trolley vehicles and routes authorised by the said Part IV.

5.—(1) The Corporation may from time to time independently of any other borrowing power borrow at interest for and in connection with the purposes mentioned in the first column of the following table the respective sums mentioned in the second column of the said table and they shall pay off all moneys so borrowed within such periods as the Corporation may determine not exceeding those respectively mentioned in the third column of the said table (namely):—

Purpose	Amount	Period for repayment
(a) The provision of trolley vehicles	£80,000	Ten years from the date or dates of borrowing
(b) The provision of trolley vehicle equipment and the construction of other works necessary for working trolley vehicles along the routes authorised by this Order.	£37,000	Fifteen years from the date or dates of borrowing
(c) The payment of the costs charges and expenses of this Order	The sum requisite	Five years from the confirmation of this Order

(2) For the purposes of subsection (2) of section 63 (Power to borrow and repayment of borrowed moneys) of the Act of 1930 as modified by section 197 of the Local Government Act 1933 the purposes of this Order shall be deemed to be purposes of the tramway undertaking of the Corporation.

(3) The provisions of this section shall not limit the powers conferred upon the Corporation by section 149 (Power to use one form of mortgage for all purposes) of the Portsmouth Corporation Act 1920.

6. It shall not be lawful to exercise the powers of borrowing conferred by this Order (other than the power of borrowing to pay the costs charges and expenses of this Order as hereinafter defined) otherwise than in compliance with the provisions of the Local Authorities Loans Act 1945 or of any order for the time being in force made under section 1 of the Borrowing (Control and Guarantees) Act 1946.

7. The provisions of section 250 (Procedure &c. for making byelaws) of the Local Government Act 1933 shall not apply in respect of byelaws to be made under section 46 (Byelaws by local authority Promoters may make certain regulations) of the Tramways Act 1870 or under section 69 (Shelters or waiting rooms and barriers) of the Portsmouth Corporation Act 1920.

8. The Minister of Transport may hold such inquiries as he may consider necessary in regard to the exercise of any powers conferred upon him or the giving of consents under this Order and section 290 of the Local Government Act 1933 shall apply accordingly.

9. All costs charges and expenses of and incidental to the preparing and obtaining and confirming of this Order or otherwise incurred in relation thereto as taxed by the taxing officer of the House of Lords or of the House of Commons shall be paid by the Corporation.

15 & 16 GEO. 6 & 1 ELIZ. 2
Portsmouth Corporation (Trolley Vehicles) Order Confirmation Act, 1952

CHAPTER xxiii.

An Act to confirm a Provisional Order made by the Minister of Transport under the Portsmouth Corporation Act 1930 as amended by the Portsmouth Corporation Act 1946 relating to Portsmouth Corporation trolley vehicles.

[1st August 1952.]

WHEREAS under the authority of section thirty-two of the Portsmouth Corporation Act 1930 as amended by section eight of the Portsmouth Corporation Act 1946 the Minister of Transport has made the Provisional Order set out in the schedule to this Act annexed:

And whereas a Provisional Order made by the Minister of Transport under the authority of the said section as so amended is not of any validity or force whatever until the confirmation thereof by Act of Parliament:

And whereas it is expedient that the Provisional Order made by the Minister of Transport under the authority of the said section as so amended and set out in the schedule to this Act annexed be confirmed by Act of Parliament:

Be it therefore enacted by the Queen's most Excellent Majesty by and with the advice and consent of the Lords Spiritual and Temporal and Commons in this present Parliament assembled and by the authority of the same as follows:—

1. The Order set out in the schedule to this Act annexed shall be and the same is hereby confirmed and all the provisions thereof in manner and form as they are set out in the said schedule shall from and after the passing of this Act have full force and validity and the date of the same shall be the date of the passing of this Act.

2. This Act may be cited as the Portsmouth (Trolley Vehicles) Order Confirmation Act 1952.

SCHEDULE

PORTSMOUTH CORPORATION (TROLLEY VEHICLES)

Provisional Order authorising the lord mayor aldermen and citizens of the city of Portsmouth to use trolley vehicles upon an additional route in the city of Portsmouth.

1.—(1) This Order may be cited as the Portsmouth Corporation (Trolley Vehicles) Order 1952.

(2) The Portsmouth Corporation (Trolley Vehicles) Act and Orders 1930 to 1948 and this Order may be cited together as the Portsmouth Corporation (Trolley Vehicles) Act and Orders 1930 to 1952.

2. In this Order the following expressions have unless the subject or context otherwise requires the meanings hereinafter assigned to them (namely): —

"The Act of 1930" means the Portsmouth Corporation Act1930;

"The city" means the city of Portsmouth;

"The Corporation" means the lord mayor aldermen and citizens of the city

"The Minister" means the Minister of Transport;

"Trolley vehicle" has the meaning assigned to it by section 4 (Interpretation) of the Act of 1930.

3. The Corporation may use trolley vehicles upon the following route in the city: —

Route No. 1 (5 furlongs 4.09 chains or thereabouts in length) commencing at the junction of London Road and Chichester Road proceeding along Chichester Road to and terminating at its junction with Copnor Road:

Provided that—

(a) before equipping the trolley vehicle route to include a turning point or before arranging for a new turning point on the route the Corporation shall submit plans of the turning point to the Minister for approval

(b) if the Corporation shall not have commenced to use trolley vehicles upon the trolley vehicle route authorised by this Order within five years from the passing of the Act confirming this Order or such extended time as the Minister may upon the application of the Corporation allow the powers conferred by this Order shall cease to be exercisable.

4.—(1) Subject to the provisions of this Order the Corporation may from time to time independently of any other borrowing power borrow at interest for and in connection with the purposes mentioned in the first column of the following table the respective sums mentioned in the second column of the said table and they shall pay off all moneys so borrowed within such periods as the Corporation may determine not exceeding those respectively mentioned in the third column of the said table (namely): —

Purpose Repayment	**Amount**	**Period for**
(a) The provision of trolley vehicle equipment and the construction of other works necessary for working trolley vehicles along the route authorised by this Order.	£3,200	Fifteen years from the date or dates of borrowing.
(b) The payment of the costs charges and expenses of this Order.	The sum requisite	Five years from the confirmation of this Order.

(2) The provisions of Part IX of the Local Government Act 1933 so far as they are not inconsistent with this Order shall extend and apply to money borrowed under this section as if it were borrowed under Part IX of that Act and the period fixed for the repayment of any money borrowed under this section shall as respects that money be the fixed period for the purpose of the said Part IX.

(3) In the application of the said provisions of the Local Government Act 1933 to the borrowing of any further money for the purposes of this Order the Minister shall be the sanctioning authority.

(4) The provisions of this section shall not limit the powers conferred upon the Corporation by section 149 (Power to use one form of mortgage for all purposes) of the Portsmouth Corporation Act1920.

5. It shall not be lawful to exercise the powers of borrowing conferred by this Order otherwise than in compliance with the provisions of the Local Authorities Loans Act 1945 or of any order for the time being in force made under section 1 of the Borrowing (Control and Guarantees) Act 1946.

6. The Minister may hold such inquiries as he may consider necessary in regard to the exercise of any powers conferred upon him or the giving of consents under this Order and section 290 of the Local Government Act 1933 shall apply accordingly.

7. This Order shall be deemed to be an enactment passed before and in force at the passing of the Town and Country Planning Act 1947 for the purposes of subsection (4) of section 13 and subsection (1) of section 118 of that Act.

8. All costs charges and expenses of and incidental to the preparing and obtaining and confirming of this Order or otherwise incurred in relation thereto as taxed by the taxing officer of the House of Lords or of the House of Commons shall be paid by the Corporation.

9 & 10 GEO. 6.
Portsmouth Corporation Act, 1946

CHAPTER xxxix

An Act to authorise agreements between the Portsmouth Corporation and Southdown Motor Services Limited for the provision and working in co-ordination of passenger road transport by the said Corporation and the said company to empower the said Corporation to borrow money and for other purposes.

[26th July 1946]

WHEREAS the city of Portsmouth (hereinafter referred to as "the City") is a county borough under the government of the lord mayor aldermen and citizens of the city (hereinafter referred to as "the Corporation"):

And whereas the Corporation under powers conferred by the Portsmouth Corporation (Trolley Vehicles) Act and Order 1930 and 1935 are the owners of and are working services of trolley vehicles within the city and by virtue of the Portsmouth Corporation Act 1920 and the Road Traffic Acts 1930 to 1937 are empowered to run and are running services of public service vehicles within the city:

And whereas Southdown Motor Services Limited (hereinafter referred to as "the company") under powers conferred by the Road Traffic Acts 1930 to 1937 provide and run services of public service vehicles within and without the city:

And whereas it is expedient that the Corporation and the company be empowered to enter into agreements with respect to (inter alia) the provision and working in coordination of passenger road transport provided or to be provided by the parties within and without the city:

And whereas the Corporation and the .company have entered into an agreement for the working in co-ordination of services of public service vehicles and trolley vehicles and it is expedient that the said agreement be confirmed and made binding on the parties thereto as in this Act provided:

And whereas it is expedient that the other provisions of this Act be enacted:

And whereas the purposes of this Act cannot be effected without the authority of Parliament:

And whereas in relation to the promotion of the Bill for this Act the requirements of Part XIII of the Local Government Act 1933 have been observed:

May it therefore please Your Majesty that it may be enacted and be it enacted by the King's most Excellent Majesty by and with the advice and consent of the Lords Spiritual and Temporal and Commons in this present Parliament assembled and by the authority of the same as follows: —

1. This Act may be cited as the Portsmouth Corporation Act 1946.

2. In this Act unless the subject or context otherwise requires—

"The Corporation" means the lord mayor aldermen and citizens of the city of Portsmouth;

"The company" means Southdown Motor Services Limited and includes their successors and assigns;

"The scheduled agreement" means the agreement dated the twenty-fourth day of May nineteen hundred and forty-six and made between the Corporation of the one part and the company of the other part of which a copy is set forth in the schedule to this Act;

"Public service vehicle" and "trolley vehicle" have the same respective meanings as in the Road Traffic Acts 1930 to 1937;

"The Act of 1933" means the Local Government Act1933;

"The Minister" means the Minister of Transport.

3. (1) An agreement entered into between the Corporation and the company under subsection (2) of section 105 (Working and other agreements) of the Road Traffic Act 1930 may make provision with respect to all or any of the following matters in addition to the matters referred to in that section:-

(a) The working maintenance and management of any service of trolley vehicles which the Corporation are authorised to use;

(b) The provision by either party to the agreement or the hiring by either party to the other party of trolley vehicles lands buildings apparatus and other property for the purposes of any service of trolley vehicles to which the agreement relates and the working user maintenance and management thereof;

(c) The supply of motive power for working any service of trolley vehicles to which the agreement relates;

(d) The interchange accommodation conveyance transmission and delivery of traffic arising on or coming from or destined for any service of public service vehicles or trolley vehicles provided by either of the parties to the agreement;

(e) The constitution of a joint committee to provide manage control or operate or to supervise the provision management control or operation of the services of public service vehicles or trolley vehicles to which the agreement relates;

(f) The fixing payment collection and apportionment of the fares and charges and other receipts arising from any service of public service vehicles or trolley vehicles provided by either of the parties to the agreement.

(2) The Corporation shall not manufacture any trolley vehicle for the purposes of any such agreement as aforesaid.

4. The scheduled agreement is hereby confirmed and made binding upon the Corporation and the company and effect may and shall be given thereto accordingly subject to such modifications (if any) as may from time to time be agreed between the Corporation and the company in writing under their respective common seals.

Paragraphs 5–8 omitted

9. (1) The trolley vehicles of the Corporation or the company shall not be deemed to be stage carriages for the purposes of sections 13 to 15 of the Railway Passenger Duty Act 1842 but for the purpose of calculating the number of passengers in excess of the seating capacity that may be carried thereon shall be deemed to be public service vehicles.

(2) Subsection (1) of section 23 (Vehicles not to be deemed light locomotives or motor cars) of the Portsmouth Corporation Act 1930 is hereby repealed.

Paragraph 10 omitted

11. Any trolley vehicles provided on any route by the company under the powers of this Act shall be used subject to the provisions of the Portsmouth Corporation (Trolley Vehicles) Act and Order 1930 and 1935 applying to that route and any existing byelaw or regulation made by the Minister or the Corporation applying to the trolley vehicles of the Corporation on that route shall apply to any trolley vehicles used by the company on that route as if the company were named therein as well as the Corporation:

Provided that—

(a) If the company are of the opinion that any such existing byelaw or regulation should not apply to trolley vehicles used by the company on any route the company may before commencing to use trolley vehicles on that route make a representation to that effect to the Minister and the Minister after considering the representation and any observations of the Corporation thereon may direct that the byelaw or regulation mentioned in the representation should not apply to trolley vehicles used by the company on that route or should apply subject to modifications; and

(b) If the Minister or the Corporation propose to make under the Portsmouth Corporation (Trolley Vehicles) Act and Order 1930 and 1935 any new byelaws or regulations applying to trolley vehicles used by the Corporation on any route then (i) the Minister or the Corporation (as the case may be) shall give notice to the company of the intention to make such new byelaws or regulations (ii) the company may within one month after the receipt of such notice make a representation to the Minister that such proposed new byelaws or regulations or some of them should not apply to trolley vehicles used by the company on the same route and (iii) if any such representation be duly made the Minister after considering the representation and any observations of the Corporation thereon may direct that the byelaws or regulations mentioned in the representation or some of them should not apply to trolley vehicles used by the company on that route or should apply subject to modifications.

Paragraphs 12–14 omitted

The SCHEDULE referred to in the foregoing Act.

This Agreement made this twenty-fourth day of May nineteen hundred and forty-six between the Lord Mayor Aldermen and Citizens of the city of Portsmouth (hereinafter referred to as "the Corporation" and "the city" respectively) of the one part and Southdown Motor Services Limited whose registered office is situate at 5 Steine Street Brighton in the county of Sussex (hereinafter referred to as "the Company") of the other part.

WHEREAS under powers conferred by the Portsmouth Corporation (Trolley Vehicles) Act and Order 1930 and 1935 the Corporation are the owners of and are working a system of trolley vehicles within the city and by virtue of the Portsmouth Corporation Act 1920 and the Road Traffic Acts 1930 to 1937 are empowered to run and are running services of public service vehicles within the city:

And whereas the Company are providing services of stage carriages and express carriages both within and without the city:

And whereas the Corporation and the Company have power under subsection (2) of section 105 of the Road Traffic Act 1930 to make and carry into effect agreements for the management working and maintenance of any service of public service vehicles which either of them is for the time being authorised to run in the city or in any district on any road in which the Corporation are for the time being authorised to run such vehicles and to make provision with respect to all or any of the matters mentioned in subsection (3) of that section:

And whereas the Corporation are promoting a Bill in the present session of Parliament to empower the Corporation and the Company by any agreement entered into between them under subsection (2) of section 105 of the Road Traffic Act 1930 to make provision with respect to all or any of the following matters in addition to the matters referred to in that section:—

(a) The working maintenance and management of any service of trolley vehicles which the Corporation are authorised to use;

(b) The provision by either party to the agreement or the hiring by either party to the other party of trolley vehicles lands buildings apparatus and other property for the purposes of any service of trolley vehicles to which the agreement relates and the working user maintenance and management thereof;

(c) The supply of motive power for working any trolley vehicle services to which the agreement relates;

(d) The interchange accommodation conveyance transmission and delivery of traffic arising on or coming from or destined for any service of public service vehicles or trolley vehicles provided by either of the parties to the agreement;

(e) The constitution of a joint committee to provide manage control or operate or to supervise the provision management control or operation of the services of public service vehicles or trolley vehicles to which the agreement relates;

(f) The fixing payment collection and apportionment of the fares and charges and other receipts arising from any service of public service vehicles or trolley vehicles provided by either of the parties to the agreement:

And whereas the Corporation and the Company are agreed that it is expedient in the public interest that arrangements should be made for the working in co-ordination of the services of public service and trolley vehicles now or from time to time provided by the Corporation or the Company within the city and neighbouring districts and for the constitution for that purpose of a joint committee with such powers and duties as are more particularly hereinafter defined:

Now therefore it is hereby agreed by and between the Corporation and the Company as follows:—

Part I.

Definitions.

1. In this agreement unless the context otherwise requires—

(i) "the agreed area" means the area bounded by the red line shown on the map which has been agreed by the Corporation and the Company and for the purpose of identification signed in duplicate by Victor Blanchard (the town clerk of the city) for the Corporation and Alfred Edward Cannon (the managing director of the Company) for the Company and a copy of which on a reduced scale is hereto annexed;

(ii) "the additional routes" means the roads marked by broken red lines on the said map;

(iii) "the appointed day" means the 1st day of July 1946 or such other date as may be agreed between the Corporation and the Company;

(iv) "the combined services" means the services whether of public service vehicles or trolley vehicles from time to time provided by the Corporation and the Company or either of them pursuant to clause 2 but does not include so much of any such service as is in accordance with clause 11 to be deemed to be a separate service provided by the Company;

(v) "the initial services" means the services referred to in paragraph (i) of clause 2;
(vi) references to the services of either party shall be construed as references to such of the combined services as are from time to time to be provided or operated by that party including any journeys to be operated by that party as part of any of the combined services which is to be provided or operated by the parties jointly;
(vii) "excepted service" means—
(a) a service of stage carriages or express carriages operated over a route partly inside and partly outside the agreed area—
on which the single or return fare charged for a journey between any two points within the agreed area or for a journey partly within the agreed area exceeds by not less than 50 per centum the lowest single or return fare (as the case may be) charged on any of the combined services for a journey (whether by the same or any other route) between those points or for the part of the journey within the agreed area (as the case may be); or
on which no passenger may under the road service licence authorising the service be both taken up and set down within the agreed area on one and the same journey; or
which is for the purpose of reaching a convenient terminal point or stand operated within the agreed area for a distance not exceeding half a mile from the boundary of that area or to a point within the area coloured brown on the agreed map; and
(b) any excursion or tour;
(viii) "miles run" means miles run or to be run on the combined services by vehicles operated by the Corporation or the Company (as the case may be) and includes miles run by any duplicate or relief vehicle so operated but does not include any dead miles and "the total miles run" means the aggregate of the miles run by the Corporation and the miles run by the Company;
(ix) "the Corporation's share" means 57 per centum and "the Company's share" means 43 per centum and "in the agreed share" has a corresponding meaning;
(x) "the joint committee" means the committee to be constituted as hereinafter provided;
(xi) "agreed or determined" means agreed by the parties hereto or decided by the joint committee or determined by arbitration under clause 36;
(xii) "quarter" means a period of three consecutive months ending on the 31st day of March the 30th day of June the 30th day of September or the 31st day of December in any year;
(xiii) "financial year" means a period of twelve consecutive months ending on the 31st day of March in any year;
(xiv) "the Bill" means the Bill which the Corporation are promoting as hereinbefore recited; and
(xv) "public service vehicle" "stage carriage" "express carriage" "contract carriage" "trolley vehicle" "road service licence" "public service vehicle licence" and "certificate of fitness" have the same meanings respectively as in the Road Traffic Acts 1930 to 1937 but "road service licence" and "public service vehicle licence" include respectively a permit issued under the Emergency Powers (Defence) Road Vehicles and Drivers Order 1943 (or any earlier order made under Regulation 72 of the Defence (General) Regulations 1939) authorising the provision of a road service and a permit issued under that order in lieu of a public service vehicle licence.

Part II.

The combined services.

2. The following services of trolley vehicles or public service vehicles shall subject to and in accordance with the provisions hereafter contained be provided and operated on or after the appointed day under the direction of the joint committee (namely): —
(i) such services (hereinafter referred to as " the initial services ") whether of trolley vehicles or public service vehicles as may be agreed or determined to be necessary or desirable in the public interest in substitution for the services of trolley vehicles or public service vehicles provided by the Corporation or the Company immediately before the appointed day along any route within the agreed area or along the whole or any part of any of the additional routes other than any excepted service; and
(ii) such services whether of trolley vehicles or public service vehicles along any route within the agreed area or along the whole or any part of any of the additional routes as may on or at any time after the appointed day be agreed or determined to be necessary or desirable in the public interest whether in substitution for or in addition to all or any of the initial services.
3. The services from time to time to be provided and operated as art of the combined services by the Corporation and the Company respectively or by the parties jointly shall from time to time be agreed : determined but the combined services shall be so allocated as—.
(a) to ensure efficiency and economy in operation;
(b) to give effect to any agreement which may be made between the Corporation and the Company relating to the allocation of the combined services or the division of the. total miles run during the financial year ending on the 31st day of March 1947 and any of the next following financial years; and
(c) to secure that subject to any such agreement the miles run during each financial year will subject to clause 18 be run by the Corporation and the Company respectively as nearly as may be in the agreed shares.
4. Subject as regards any service of public service vehicles to the grant of the necessary road service licence or to the conditions attached to any road service licence for the time being in force in respect of the service each of the parties shall at all times unless prevented by any strike or other emergency or any other cause outside its control operate its services efficiently and so as to comply with its obligations and duties under this agreement.
5. Subject to clause 6 each of the parties shall from time to time provide such public service vehicles and trolley vehicles equipment and apparatus (including spare vehicles equipment and apparatus) garages depots and other property as may be necessary or desirable to enable that party to provide and operate its services efficiently and otherwise to carry out efficiently its duties and obligations under this agreement and in particular shall keep all such vehicles clean and in good running order and condition Provided that save and subject as otherwise agreed between the parties hereto neither party shall be under obligation to provide any station passenger shelter or other facilities wholly or mainly for the convenience of passengers or intending passengers on the combined services or any of them or accommodation for the turning standing or parking of vehicles on any of those services.

6. The Corporation shall also from time to time provide all such plant apparatus and equipment as may from time to time be necessary or desirable for or in connection with the efficient working of the trolley vehicle services from time to time forming part of the combined services and if it shall be agreed or determined that any of such trolley vehicle services shall be provided and operated by the Company the Corporation shall upon and subject to such terms and conditions as may from time to time be agreed or determined—

(a) grant to the Company the right to use the apparatus and equipment of the Corporation so far as necessary for the working of the service or services of trolley vehicles to be provided and operated by the Company; and

(b) supply to the Company such electricity and afford to the Company such facilities as may be necessary in or for the purpose of working of such service or services.

7. Each of the parties shall employ all officers and servants from time to time necessary for the efficient management operation maintenance or supervision of its services or the vehicles from time to time used by that party on any of those services.

8. No public service vehicle or trolley vehicle not in use on the appointed day shall be used by either of the parties on any of the combined services which is not of a type previously agreed or determined to be suitable In particular unless previously otherwise so agreed or determined single-decked vehicles (whether public service vehicles or trolley vehicles) shall not be used by either of the parties on any of the combined services except any of the initial services provided in substitution for a service on which single-decked vehicles shall have been used immediately before the appointed day.

9. The Corporation's passenger transport manager and the Company's general manager shall as often as may be required meet to consider questions arising in relation to matters falling within any of the categories specified in subclause (2) of clause 31 or any other matters concerning the operation of the combined services In the event of disagreement on any such question either the Corporation's passenger transport manager or the Company's general manager may refer the question to the joint committee.

10. Each of the parties shall make such arrangements and give such instructions to its respective officers and servants as may from time to time be required to ensure that the officers and servants of each of the parties engaged in inspecting and regulating any part of the combined services when on the road shall co-operate with the officers and servants of the other party similarly engaged to secure efficient joint operation and shall have access to and powers of inspection upon any vehicles provided by either of the parties when on the road.

11. (1) The Company shall be at liberty to operate to and from points outside the agreed area any of the combined services for the time being operated by the Company and to make connections between or otherwise co-ordinate any of the combined services so operated by the Company with any other service or services operated by the Company or any other person outside the agreed area.

(2) If any of the combined services shall at any time be operated by the Company to and from points outside the agreed area then—

(a) any part of that service for the time being operated outside the agreed area (except any part of the service for the time being operated pursuant to clause 2 along the whole or any part of any of the additional routes) shall for the purposes of this agreement be deemed to be a separate service provided by the Company and not part of the combined services and accordingly none of the provisions of this agreement shall in any way apply to that part of that service;

(b) the miles run within the agreed area on that service by the vehicles operated by the Company shall from time to time be agreed or determined; and

(c) the Company shall bring into account such sums as may from time to time be agreed or determined fairly to represent the proportion of—

(i) the fares and charges received by the Company in respect of the carriage of passengers or accompanied luggage or animals on that service on journeys partly within and partly without the agreed area; and

(ii) any sums so received under arrangements for the through booking of passengers by that service and any other service; properly attributable to the part of such journeys within the agreed area.

12. (1) Neither of the parties shall on or after the appointed day—

(a) discontinue (save in consequence of any strike or other emergency or any other cause outside the control of the party) any of the combined services or operate any new service (whether of public service vehicles or trolley vehicles) within the agreed area or make any alteration in the route or timetable or any of the fares charged upon any of the combined services or seek power or authority to operate any such new service or make any such alteration unless the discontinuance or operation of such service or such alteration (as the case may be) shall previously have been agreed or determined; or

(b) operate or be directly or indirectly concerned or interested in the operation of any road passenger services within the agreed area otherwise than as part of the combined services in accordance with this agreement:

Provided that the Company may operate or be concerned or interested in the operation of contract carriages or any excepted service it shall not operate as part of any excepted service (not being an excursion or tour) any duplicate or relief vehicle solely for the purpose of carrying passengers to or from any point within the present boundary of the city from or to any other point within the agreed area.

(2) Nothing in this agreement shall be construed as prohibiting the Corporation from seeking power or authority to operate contract carriages or any excepted service but this provision shall not in any way restrict or prejudice the Company in objecting to or otherwise opposing the grant to or exercise by the Corporation of any such power or authority.

Paragraphs 13–15 omitted

Part III.

Division of receipts and accounts.

16. (1) All fares and charges received by either of the parties in respect of the carriage of passengers or accompanied luggage or animals within the agreed area on any of the combined services shall be brought into account by that party.

(2) If either of the parties shall enter into arrangements for the through booking of passengers by any of the combined services and any service operated by any other person that

party shall further bring into account under this clause any sums from time to time received under those arrangements in respect of the carriage of passengers or accompanied luggage or animals on any of the combined services within the agreed area.

(3) Each of the parties shall be entitled to retain for its own benefit all other receipts from its transport undertaking including receipts in respect of unaccompanied luggage or animals parcels or other goods carried or property found on the vehicles from time to time operated by it or advertisements on its vehicles or on tickets issued by it.

17. All fares charges and other sums to be brought into account by either of the parties under clause 16 or by the Company under paragraph (c) of subclause (2) of clause 11 shall be divisible between the parties in the agreed shares.

18. (1) If it shall be agreed or determined that the miles run by the Corporation or the Company during any quarter in any financial year and the miles run by that party during the other quarters in the same financial year will as nearly as may be estimated be less in the aggregate than the Corporation's share or the Company's share (as the case may be) of the total miles run during that financial year then the miles run by that party during any subsequent quarter or quarters in that financial year shall be increased so far as may be agreed or determined to be both necessary to eliminate the deficiency and practicable.

(2) If the miles run by the Corporation or the Company during any quarter shall exceed the Corporation's share or the Company's share (as the case may be) of the total miles run during that quarter then the Company or the Corporation (as the case may be) shall pay or allow to the other party a sum at the rate of 1s. 7d. per mile (or such other rate as may from time to time be agreed or determined to be reasonable having regard to any variation in all or any of the other party's costs of operation) for each mile run by the Corporation or the Company (as the case may be) during that quarter in excess of that party's share of the total miles run during that quarter.

(3) This clause is subject to any agreement which may be made between the Corporation and the Company relating to the allocation of the combined services or the division of the total miles run during the financial year ending on the 31st day of March 1947 and any of the next following financial years.

19. If pursuant to clause 2 it shall be agreed or determined to be necessary or desirable to provide and operate any of the combined services along the whole or any part of any of the additional routes then for the purpose of ascertaining—

the fares charges and other sums to be brought into account by either party under clause 16 in respect of that service or the proportion of any such fares charges or other sums to be brought into account by the Company under paragraph (c) of subclause (2) of clause 11 or the miles run on that service within the agreed area or on the combined services; that route or the part thereof over which the service shall be so operated shall so long as the service continues to be so operated be deemed to be within the agreed area.

Paragraph 20 omitted

21. (1) Each of the parties shall out of its own funds discharge all expenses of acquiring providing operating or maintaining its own vehicles garages depots and other properties used in connection with the combined services or any part thereof and all salaries wages compensation superannuation and similar payments and all other liabilities whatsoever in relation to its transport undertaking and the use of its vehicles and shall at all times keep the other party indemnified in respect thereof.

(2) In particular and without prejudice to the generality of subclause (i) of this clause each party shall keep the other indemnified—

(a) against all claims for accident (whether fatal or otherwise) delay detention loss or injury of or to any person whether passenger employee or third party or for loss delay detention of or damage to any property which shall arise out of the use of any vehicle operated by the first-mentioned party and whether or not such claims shall arise under any ticket issued or contract for the carriage of passengers made by the other party and against all costs charges and expenses in connection with any such claim;

(b) against all fines and penalties incurred by such other party in consequence of any breach of the conditions of a road service licence held by the parties jointly which may have arisen from the act or omission of the first-mentioned party and against any losses and expenses sustained by such other party in consequence of such licence being revoked or suspended by reason or on account of such breach:

Provided that this clause shall not apply to claims arising out of any accident in which a vehicle operated by either party and a vehicle operated by the other party shall both have been involved or out of any accident occurring to a vehicle operated by either party by reason of the manner in which a vehicle operated by the other party shall have been used.

22. (1) Each of the parties shall keep proper accounts and records relating to the tickets issued and the miles run on its services and the fares charges and other sums to be brought into account under this agreement by the parties respectively.

(2) Each of the parties shall at the end of each of their respective working weeks deliver to the other party a statement showing the number of tickets issued on the vehicles the total revenue received in respect of those tickets and the miles run on each of its services during that week.

(3) Each of the parties shall at all reasonable times and after reasonable notice produce to the authorised representatives of the other party the relevant accounts waybills and other records kept as aforesaid and afford to such representatives such facilities for inspecting and taking copies of or extracts from such accounts and records and .such information relating thereto or to any entry therein as the other party or its authorised representatives may reasonably require.

23. (1) Each of the parties shall as soon as practicable after the end of the quarter current at the appointed day and of each subsequent quarter prepare and deliver to the other party a statement in respect of that quarter and as soon as practicable after the end of the financial year current at the appointed day and of each subsequent financial year each of the parties shall deliver to the other party a final statement in respect of that year prepared and certified as correct by the auditors for the time being of the Corporation or the Company as the case may be. As soon as statements for any quarter or financial year shall have been prepared as aforesaid an account for that quarter or a final account for that year (as the case may be) shall be taken between the parties in manner hereinafter provided.

(2) *(a)* Every statement to be delivered by either party to the other shall be in such form and contain such particulars as may

from time to time be agreed or determined to be appropriate to show—

(i) the miles run by the accounting party during the quarter or financial year to which the statement relates;

(ii) the fares charges and other sums to be brought into account by the accounting party in respect of the period to which the statement relates; and

(iii) any sum recoverable by the accounting party from the other party under clause 20 in respect of that period.

(b) Every account to be taken as aforesaid between the parties in respect of any quarter or financial year shall show the like particulars as regards each party in respect of the period to which the account relates and also—

(i) the total miles run during that period;

(ii) any sums payable or allowable by either party to the other under clause 18 in respect of that period; and

(iii) the sum payable by either party to the other in respect of that period to give effect to clause 17 after allowing for any sums as allowable by or recoverable from either party under clause 18 or 20 in respect of that period.

(c) Every such statement or account shall be in such form and contain such particulars as may from time to time be agreed or determined to be appropriate for the purposes of this agreement.

(3) Any sum found on the taking of the account between the parties in respect of any quarter to be payable by either party to the other shall be paid forthwith on the completion of that account but subject to any correction or adjustment which may be found necessary on the taking of the final account between the parties for the financial year and any balance due from either party to the other in consequence of any such correction or adjustment shall be paid on the completion of that final account.

(4) The quarterly and annual accounts to be taken between the parties shall be taken and settled by the treasurer or other responsible officer of the Corporation and the chief accountant or other responsible officer of the Company Provided that if the taking or completion of any such account shall by reason of any default or unreasonable delay on the part of either of the parties or their respective officers be prevented or delayed for one month after that party shall have been required by notice in writing given by the other party to proceed with the taking of such account that account may be taken and completed by the other party and when so taken and completed shall be binding on both parties.

Part IV.

The joint committee.

24. (1) As soon as practicable after the execution of this agreement a joint committee shall be constituted and shall consist of six members of whom three shall be members of the city council from time to time nominated to the committee by the Corporation and three shall from time to time be nominated to the committee by the Company.

(2) Each of the parties may from time to time nominate three persons to act as reserve members of the joint committee A reserve member so nominated by either party may attend and vote at any meeting of the joint committee in place of any member of the committee nominated by the same party who shall be absent from that meeting but subject to clause 29 a reserve member shall not otherwise be entitled to attend or vote at any meeting of the joint committee.

(3) A member or reserve member of the joint committee shall remain in office until his office shall be vacated by his death or resignation or his nomination shall be revoked by the party by whom he shall have been nominated.

(4) On any member or reserve member ceasing to be a member of the joint committee the party who shall have nominated that member shall forthwith nominate another person as a member or reserve member (as the case may be) in his place.

(5) Every nomination of a member or reserve member of the joint committee and every revocation of any such nomination shall be made by notice in writing given by the Corporation or the Company (as the case may be) to the other party.

25. (1) At their first meeting and also at their first meeting after the 9th day of November in the year 1947 and every subsequent year the joint committee shall elect one of their members as chairman and another of their members as vice-chairman and the members so elected shall subject as hereinafter provided hold office until the close of the meeting in the following year at which a chairman and vice-chairman are to be so elected.

(2) The chairman and the vice-chairman shall each be elected in alternate years from the members nominated by the Corporation and from the members nominated by the Company but so that both of them shall not in any year be elected from the members nominated by the same party.

(3) If at any meeting of the joint committee at which the chairman or vice-chairman is to be elected there shall be an equality of votes between two candidates qualified in accordance with this clause and proposed for election at that meeting it shall be decided by lot which of the two candidates shall be chairman or vice-chairman (as the case may be).

(4) If the chairman or vice-chairman of the joint committee shall cease to be a member of the joint committee or shall resign his office as chairman or vice-chairman the joint committee shall at their next meeting elect as chairman or vice-chairman (as the case may be) in his place one of their members nominated by the party by whom the member so ceasing to be a member or resigning shall have been nominated and the member so elected shall hold office until the close of the meeting at which the member so ceasing to be a member or resigning would have vacated office if he had not so ceased to be a member or resigned.

(5) The chairman for the time being of the joint committee or in his absence the vice-chairman for the time being shall preside at all meetings of the joint committee Provided that if neither the chairman nor vice-chairman shall be present at any meeting within fifteen minutes after the time appointed for holding the meeting the members present may elect as chairman of that meeting one of their number nominated by the party by whom the chairman shall have been nominated.

26. (1) The quorum for the transaction of business shall be four members of whom two shall be persons nominated as such by the Corporation and two shall be persons nominated as such by the Company.

(2) Subject to subclause (4) of this clause questions arising at any meeting of the joint committee shall be decided by a majority of the votes of the members present and voting.

(3) Each member shall have one vote and in case of an equality of votes the chairman shall not have a second or casting vote.

(4) If any question arising at any meeting of the joint committee shall be decided against the vote of more than

one Corporation member or more than one Company member that decision shall not be binding but the question shall be adjourned for further consideration at a subsequent meeting of the joint committee and if at that meeting the joint committee shall on that question again be unable to reach a binding decision the question may be referred to arbitration under clause 36.

(5) The members for the time being of the joint committee may act notwithstanding any vacancy on the committee and all acts done at any meeting of the joint committee shall notwithstanding that it shall be afterwards discovered that there was some defect or irregularity in the nomination of any person acting as a member at that meeting or that any such person was not qualified so to act be as valid as if every such -person had been duly nominated and was qualified as a member.

(6) Subject to the provisions of this and the preceding clause of this agreement the joint committee may meet for the dispatch of business at such place in the city or elsewhere adjourn and otherwise regulate their meetings and proceedings as they may from time to time determine.

(7) In this clause unless the context otherwise requires "member" includes a reserve member.

Paragraphs 27–30 omitted

31. (1) The joint committee may consider and decide any questions from time to time arising in relation to matters falling within any of the categories specified in subclause (2) of this clause and shall consider and may decide any such questions from time to time referred to the joint committee by either of the parties or by the Corporation's passenger transport manager or the Company's general manager and any other questions from time to time referred to the joint committee by both of the parties hereto.

(2) The joint committee may under subclause (1) of this clause consider and decide questions arising in relation to matters falling within any of the following categories (namely):—

(a) the variation of the route or time-table of or the fares charged on any of the combined services;

(b) the discontinuance whether temporarily or otherwise of any of the combined services;

(c) the commencement of any new service (whether of public service vehicles or trolley vehicles) along any route within the agreed area or any of the additional routes as part of the combined services and the routes and time-table of and the fares to be charged on such service;

(d) the introduction of new fares on any of the combined services;

(e) the alteration of any existing fare stage points or the introduction of any new fare stage points on any route for the time being served by any of the combined services;

(f) the type of vehicles used or proposed to be used on any of the combined services;

(g) the form of tickets from time to time issued or available on the combined services or any of them the availability of tickets issued by either party or any particular class or classes of tickets so issued on vehicles operated on any of the combined services by the other party and the conditions upon which any such tickets are issued or available;

(h) the services or journeys from time to time to be operated by each of the parties to give effect to the provisions hereinbefore contained and the transfer of particular services or journeys from one of the parties to the other if and so far as necessary to adjust the number of miles run by each of the parties;

(i) the rate at which payments or allowances to be made under clause 18 should be calculated; and

(j) the method to be adopted in calculating the proper proportion to be brought into account by the Company under paragraph (c) of subclause (2) of clause n of any fares charges or other sums received by the Company in respect of the carriage of passengers or accompanied luggage or animals on journeys partly within and partly without the agreed area.

(3) The joint committee may further consider and make recommendations to the parties in relation to the provision of stations passenger shelters stop signs and other physical assets for use for the purposes of or in connection with the combined services or any of them but any recommendations so made shall not constitute a decision of the joint committee to which clause 32 applies and subclause (4) of clause 26 shall not apply to any question arising upon or in relation to the making of any such recommendation.

32. Every decision of the joint committee shall forthwith be communicated by the secretary of the joint committee to each of the parties and each of the parties shall give effect to any such decision as soon as practicable after it shall have been so communicated and in particular shall use its best endeavours as soon as practicable to obtain any road service licence or variation in the conditions attached to any road service licence and any statutory or other powers consent or authority which may be necessary to authorise that party to give effect to the decision.

Part V.
Miscellaneous.

Paragraphs 33 omitted

34. (1) Subject to clause 38 this agreement shall remain in force until determined by either party pursuant to subclause (2) of this clause and thereupon this agreement except and subject to clause 35 shall cease to have effect but without prejudice to any claim by either party against the other in respect of any antecedent breach of any of the provisions herein contained.

(2) Either of the parties may by giving to the other party not less than twelve months' previous notice in writing determine this agreement on the 31st day of March 1967 or any subsequent year and if an order shall be made or an effective resolution passed for the winding up of the Company except for the purposes of amalgamation or reconstruction the Corporation may thereupon by giving notice in writing to the Company forthwith determine this agreement.

Paragraph 35 omitted

36. Any dispute or difference arising between the parties as to the construction or effect of this agreement or any of the provisions therein contained or as to the rights duties or liabilities of either of the parties thereunder (including any dispute or difference upon or in relation to any account to which clause 23 relates and any question on which the joint committee shall be unable to reach a binding decision and which is not pursuant to subclause (4) of clause 26 required

to be adjourned for further consideration at a subsequent meeting of the committee) shall in default of agreement between the parties be referred on the application of either party to and determine! by a sole arbitrator agreed between the parties or in default of agreement nominated at the request of either party by the president for the time being of the Law Society and any such reference shall be deemed to be a submission to arbitration within the meaning o the Arbitration Acts 1889 to 1934 or any statutory re-enactment or modification thereof for the time being in force.

37. This agreement shall be added as a schedule to the Bill and a clause shall be inserted in the Bill to provide for the confirmation thereby of this agreement and to make it binding on the parties.

The Corporation shall use their best endeavours to obtain the approval of Parliament to this agreement and its confirmation by the Bill during the present session of Parliament and the Company shall support the Corporation in obtaining such approval and confirmation.

38. This agreement is conditional upon its being approved by Parliament and confirmed during the present session of Parliament subject to such alterations as Parliament may think fit to make therein Provided that if either House of Parliament shall make any material alteration in this agreement or in the Bill and either of the parties hall before the third reading of the Bill in the Second House give notice in writing to the other party to rescind this agreement then in that event or in the event of this agreement not being approved and confirmed as aforesaid during the said session this agreement and everything herein contained shall forthwith become null and void.

In witness whereof the parties hereto have caused their respective common seals to be hereunto affixed the day and year first above written.

The common seal of the Lord Mayor Aldermen and Citizens of the City of Portsmouth was hereunto affixed in pursuance of a resolution passed at a meeting of the council duly convened and held

V. BLANCHARD
Town Clerk.

The common seal of Southdown Motor Services Limited was hereunto affixed in the presence of

A. E. CANNON
Director.

L. G. HOPKINSON
Secretary.

APPENDIX M
PERSONALITIES

Archibald William Fielder

A native of Portsmouth, Mr Fielder joined Portsmouth Corporation Tramways as a motorbus conductor in 1925, subsequently driving trams and motorbuses. He was appointed Timekeeper in 1929, then Inspector and Depot Inspector. In October 1941 he was appointed Schedules Clerk upon the death of the incumbent and having reached the top of the grade as Traffic Clerk in 1944, he was promoted to Senior Schedule and Traffic Clerk in 1945. He became Assistant Traffic Superintendent in February 1946

On 1 January 1948 Mr Fielder was appointed Traffic Superintendent, the position that he held at the time of the final trolleybus abandonment. Having devoted the vast majority of his professional life to CPPTD he was promoted to General Manager upon the retirement of Mr Simmonds and held the post from 1965 until delayed retirement in February 1968.

Mr Fielder was the National Honorary Treasurer of the Institute of Traffic Administrators, and Secretary and Treasurer of the Hants and Isle of Wight centre of the Institute.

Ben Hall

One of two children from the marriage of Herbert Hall, a cashier and bookkeeper, and his wife Louisa, Benjamin Hall (always known as Ben) was born in spring 1885 at Huddersfield, West Yorkshire. He was educated at Huddersfield College and later at the Huddersfield Technical Institute. In 1901 he entered an electrical and mechanical engineering apprenticeship in the local textile industry before being articled in 1903 to Huddersfield Corporation Tramways for a further three years administrative training in every section of the undertaking.

In 1907 he was appointed Rolling Stock Engineer at Huddersfield and then in 1911 Electrical and Mains Engineer before moving to Chatham & District Light Railways Co. as Engineering Superintendent in 1914. In August 1918 he returned to the West Riding of Yorkshire as Deputy Borough Engineer and Tramways Manager at Keighley where he gained his first experience with trolley vehicles operating on the Cedes-Stoll system. He only stayed at Keighley until April 1919 when he was appointed Works Manager to Wigan Corporation Tramways and Motors Department. He was promoted General Manager and Engineer at Wigan with responsibility for a fleet of 79 trams and nine motorbuses in September 1919.

In March 1921 he was appointed General Manager and Engineer of Halifax Corporation Tramways where he remained until his appointment at Portsmouth. During his 5 years at Halifax he was responsible for modernising the system generally, relaying much of the track and placing several Cardan shaft-driven cars of his design in service. Three single-deck trolley vehicles were also operated in Halifax. Ben Hall started work at Portsmouth in the combined post of Manager and Engineer towards the end of March 1926, taking over from William Spaven, who had managed the undertaking since 1902, upon his retirement on 24 June 1926. Ben Hall's experiences in Halifax stood him in good stead for the Portsmouth tramway modernisation programme and in particular his innovative design of tramcar 1, seen as the prototype for a new fleet.

Despite his long managerial career and high reputation in the passenger transport industry there is no evidence that Ben Hall was ever associated with any of the professional institutions normally considered to be essential to senior management during the first half of the twentieth century.

Socially, Ben Hall became renowned for his overtures on his tin whistle. The TGWU invited him to a farewell dinner to mark their long relationship in January 1951 at which he was presented with a model of motorbus 199 made in the workshops of Reading & Co. Ltd., the local Portsmouth bodybuilder.

In 1909 he married Gertrude Holden and together they had one child, a daughter Kathleen Louise. Upon his retirement, he and his wife moved to southeast Surrey where Gertrude died in 1955 and Ben in spring 1968.

Ben Hall. (City of Portsmouth Archives)

Harry Charles Simmonds, A.M.Inst.T.
Born in 1900, H.C. Simmonds started his working life as an apprentice at the Royal Ordnance Factories Woolwich in 1914, his apprenticeship being interrupted from 1917 to 1919 by service in HM Forces.

In 1922 he joined the staff of Woodyatts Garages of Southend-on-Sea moving in 1923 to the Southend-on-Sea Corporation Electric Light and Light Railways Department where he rose to the position of Garage Foreman.

In 1937 he secured the post of Works Superintendent with Cleethorpes Corporation Transport where he supervised the tram to trolleybus conversion programme.

In June 1942 he joined Portsmouth Corporation Transport as Chief Assistant Engineer under Ben Hall being promoted in February 1945 to the newly created post of Deputy Manager and Engineer. In 1951 he was appointed to succeed Ben Hall. He became a Freemason shortly after moving to Portsmouth and was a Governor of the Royal Masonic Hospital London.

He retired in June 1965 to his home in Waterlooville and died on 3 July 1967 leaving a daughter.

Alderman Sir John Timpson. (Transport World)

Alderman Sir John Timpson, KBE, ORS, KST (Japan), JP
Son of a Dockyard worker from Fratton and one of a family of ten, John Timpson started work at 7 years of age, was apprenticed at nine and entered the Dockyard at 17, remaining there for 12 years in the decorating department of the painters shop. He left the Dockyard and set up business as a decorator in 1891.

He entered public life in 1901 and in 1907 became Town Councillor for the Mile End Ward which he represented until 1923 when he entered the Aldermanic Bench. He was honoured by the Japanese Emperor when the Crown Prince visited Portsmouth with the Japanese Fleet in 1921. During 30 years on the Council he served three years as Mayor during the difficult years after the First World War.

He devoted much time to the tramways and transport undertaking, as Vice Chairman of the Tramways Committee from 1907 and Chairman from 1915 until 1936 overseeing the transition from trams to trolleybuses. John Timpson was a Member of the National Joint Industrial Council for the Tramways Industry where he was renowned for his abilities as an arbitrator and for his impartial judgement. He was a prominent Freemason.

John Timpson never forgot his humble background and bought the family home in Fratton later in life to keep as a memorial. On one occasion, in an effort to avoid any unpleasantness, he introduced some of the large number of unemployed to the then Prince of Wales (later Edward VIII) when he passed through the City on his return from the USA. It was the Prince who recommended him for a knighthood.

Married some 55 years, he died at his family home in Cowplain on 19 October 1937 aged 75.

APPENDIX N

BIBLIOGRAPHY

Title	Author	Publisher	Date	ISBN number
Books, Brochures and Pamphlets				
British Trolleybuses 1911–1972	Geoff Lumb	Ian Allan Publishing	1995	0 7110 2347 6
Fares Please	Eric Watts	Milestone Publications	1987	0 9038 5298 5
Fleet History City of Portsmouth Passenger Transport Department 1901–64	J.H. Jones	Worthing Historic Commercial Vehicle Group	1964	–
Great British Tramway Networks	W.H. Bett & J.C. Gillham	Light Railway Transport League	1962	–
History of the British Trolleybus	Nicholas Owen	David & Charles	1974	0 7153 6370 0
Pontypridd Trolleybuses	David R.H. Bowler	Adam Gordon	2014	978 1 874422 976
Portsmouth City Transport 1840–1977	A.F. Milton & L.T.A. Bern	Published by the authors	1977	
Portsmouth Corporation Tramways 1896–1936	Edwin Course	Portsmouth City Council, The Portsmouth Papers (No. 45)	1986	0 901559 66 0
Portsmouth Tramways	Martin Petch	Middleton Press	1996	1 873793 72 3
Portsmouth Trolleybuses	Barry Cox	Middleton Press	2001	1 901706 73 7
Trackless to Trolleybus	S. Lockwood	Adam Gordon	2011	978 1 874422 860
Tramways of Portsmouth	S.E. Harrison	Light Railway Transport League	1954	–
The Tramways of the South Coast	J.C. Gillham & R.J.S. Wiseman	Light Rail Transit Association	2004	0 948106 30 1
The Trolleybuses of Portsmouth	D.A.P. Janes & R.G. Funnell	Reading Transport Society	1969	–
Trolleybus Trails	J. Joyce	Ian Allan Ltd	1963	–
The Ultimate Review		Transport Ticket Society	1967	–
Under Two Liveries	Harold Brearley & David T. Beach	West Riding Transport Society	1970	–

Newspapers

Portsmouth Evening News

Southern Daily Mail

Professional Periodicals

Bus & Coach

Electric Railway, Bus and Tram Journal

Tramway and Railway World

The Transport World

Enthusiasts' Magazines and Periodicals	Publisher	Date
Buses	Ian Allan Ltd.	1968–date
Buses Illustrated particularly issue 115, October 1964.	Ian Allan Ltd.	1949–67
National Trolleybus Association Newsletter	National Trolleybus Association	1963–67
Reading Transport Society Newsletter	Reading Transport Society	1961–71
Trolleybus (Journal/Magazine of the British Trolleybus Society)	British Trolleybus Society	1971–date
Trolleybus Society Newsletter	Trolleybus Society	1954–55
Trolleybus Magazine	National Trolleybus Association	1963–date

Others

Acts of Parliament

Minutes of the City of Portsmouth Electricity Committee — Copies held at the Portsmouth Record Office

Minutes of the City of Portsmouth Tramways Committee — Copies held at the Portsmouth Record Office

Minutes of the City of Portsmouth Passenger Transport Committee — Copies held at the Portsmouth Record Office

City of Portsmouth Passenger Transport Department: particulars of the trolley vehicle fleet

Surviving Records of the City of Portsmouth Passenger Transport Department — Copies held at the Portsmouth Record Office

BUT9611T 307 running south along Portsmouth Road, Cosham, approaches the roundabout at the junction with Northern Road on 11 May 1963. (T.V. Runnacles)

283 joins The Hard, terminal point for the Dockyard services, and passes the well-known Keppel's Head Hotel (built in 1779 and named after Admiral Keppel, First Lord of the Admiralty during the latter years of the American War of Independence) with its indicator blinds already set for the next journey. Note the railway signal box in the right hand background located at the throat of Portsmouth Harbour Station. (R.D.H. Symons)

APPENDIX O

STATISTICS

PORTSMOUTH MILEAGE & PASSENGERS

Year Ending	Trams		Trolleybus		Motorbus	
March	Mileage	Passengers	Mileage	Passengers	Mileage	Passengers
1934	3,134,349	31,762,638	–	–	2,655,593	28,111,546
35	2,525,420	25,630,509	243,122	2,566,576	3,176,507	31,781,433
36	1,807,800	19,516,612	567,685	6,196,798	3,654,580	35,960,327
37	859,839	9,098,036	1,543,874	15,603,291	3,601,277	35,199,192
38	–	–	2,479,517	25,796,330	3,655,593	35,775,244
39			2,520,907	27,821,366	3,425,878	34,753,599
40			2,589,856	31,786,976	2,808,295	29,500,725
41			2,145,959	25,240,072	2,259,194	21,875,963
42			2,405,132	26,295,590	2,305,352	25,204,679
43			3,004,596	32,306,415	1,913,732	20,577,086
44			2,257,979	33,963,131	1,828,569	18,837,738
45			2,308,548	37,957,528	1,891,489	21,061,974
46			2,851,297	43,270,359	2,621,309	28,908,970
47			3,858,779	48,632,062	3,220,821	32,413,424
48			3,802,269	47,129,757	3,759,094	38,016,299
49			3,662,723	45,328,398	4,198,711	42,477,726
50			3,149,238	40,709,444	4,425,661	44,894,404
51			2,815,513	36,649,344	4,562,095	45,347,630
52			2,791,546	36,001,147	4,619,092	45,595,965
53			3,017,595	35,210,966	4,341,195	37,945,218
54			2,879,330	34,575,592	4,133,125	36,996,022
55			2,745,980	33,045,592	4,048,670	36,137,189
56			2,730,613	31,269,285	4,189,314	35,446,247
57			2,661,633	30,311,509	4,114,116	35,386,924
58			2,680,389	28,018,594	3,969,184	31,986,738
59			2,625,468	26,398,256	3,834,864	30,001,310
60			2,440,279	21,264,380	3,934,849	34,098,285
61			1,534,932	15,508,813	4,713,283	38,686,219
62			1,160,120	11,794,224	5,140,476	41,399,900
63			812,074	7,941,766	5,434,474	43,517,174
64			227,940	2,260,853	6,035,763	49,101,367

Note: for the year ending 31 March 1935, figures for trams and motorbuses relate to the full 12 month period; figures for trolleybuses reflect 4 August 1934–31 March 1935.

PORTSMOUTH TROLLEYBUS & MOTORBUS COMPARATIVE STATEMENT

	1934–35						1935–36						1936–37					
	TRAMS		TROLLEYBUSES		MOTORBUSES		TRAMS		TROLLEYBUSES		MOTORBUSES		TRAMS		TROLLEYBUSES		MOTORBUSES	
	Amount	Per Mile	Amount	Per Mile	Amount	Per Mile	Amount	Per Mile	Amount	Per Mile	Amount	Per Mile	Amount	Per Mile	Amount	Per Mile	Amount	Per Mile
Traffic Expenses	64,125	6.094	6,104	6.026	71,342	5.39	47,311	6.281	12,408	5.246	84,078	5.521	22,213	6.2	38,847	6.039	85,465	5.696
General Expenses	14,330	1.362	1,641	1.62	14,503	1.096	11,025	1.464	4,179	1.767	15,885	1.043	5,432	1.516	11,711	1.821	17,168	1.144
Licences	354	0.034	846	0.835	10,426	0.788	344	0.046	1,601	0.677	9,668	0.635	201	0.056	5,351	0.832	9,076	0.605
Maintenance & Repairs	29,487	2.802	1,608	1.587	29,697	2.244	21,203	2.815	3,747	1.584	31,672	2.08	11,232	3.135	11,622	1.807	34,304	2.286
Power	8,755	0.832	1,018	1.005	19,999	1.511	6,640	0.882	2,414	1.021	25,342	1.664	3,401	0.949	7,396	1.15	25,897	1.726
Pensions	4,259	0.405	395	0.39	3,418	0.258	3,177	0.422	824	0.348	3,816	0.251	1,678	0.468	2,561	0.398	4,572	0.305
Total Revenue Expenses	121,310	11.529	11,612	11.463	149,385	11.287	89,700	11.908	25,173	10.642	170,461	11.194	44,157	12.325	77,488	12.046	176,482	11.761
Passengers	123,318	11.719	15,401	15.203	187,543	14.17	97,525	12.947	36,541	15.448	211,634	13.898	49,596	13.843	94,987	14.766	220,475	14.693
Advertising	17	0.002	122	0.12	816	0.062	1,328	0.176	447	0.189	2,061	0.135	393	0.11	959	0.149	2,030	0.135
Miscellaneous	312	0.03	11	0.011	135	0.01	257	0.034	38	0.016	245	0.016	84	0.023	151	0.023	352	0.023
Total Income	123,647	11.751	15,534	15.335	188,494	14.242	99,110	13.158	37,026	15.653	213,940	14.05	50,073	13.976	96,097	14.939	222,857	14.852
GROSS SURPLUS (+) or DEFICIT (-)	+2,337	0.222	+3,922	3.872	+39,108	2.955	+9,410	1.249	+11,853	5.011	+43,479	2.855	+5,916	1.651	+18,609	2.893	+46,375	3.091
Bank Interest rcvd	1,795	0.171	-	-	+680	0.051	+227	0.03	+290	0.123	+1,057	0.069	+165	0.046	+518	0.081	+1,290	0.086
Capital charges	25,144	2.39	2,668	2.634	27,041	2.043	18,895	2.508	6,484	2.741	31,765	2.086	17,852	4.983	17,574	2.732	35,641	2.375
Revenue Contributions													-	-	692	0.108	470	0.031
Income Tax	-	-	-	-	3,487	0.263	-	-	425	0.18	3,141	0.206	-	-	-	-	-	-
NET SURPLUS (+) or DEFICIT (-)	-21,012	-1.997	+1,254	1.238	+9,260	0.7	-9,258	-1.229	+5,234	2.213	+9,630	0.632	-11,771	-3.286	+861	0.134	+11,554	0.77

	1937–38				1938–39				1939–40				1940–41				1941–42			
	TROLLEYBUSES		MOTORBUSES		TROLLEYBUSES		MOTORBUSES		TROLLEYBUSES		MOTORBUSES		TROLLEYBUSES		MOTORBUSES		TROLLEYBUSES		MOTORBUSES	
	Amount	Per Mile	Amount	Per Mile	Amount	Per Mile	Amount	Per Mile	Amount	Per Mile	Amount	Per Mile	Amount	Per Mile	Amount	Per Mile	Amount	Per Mile	Amount	Per Mile
Traffic Expenses	62,510	6.051	90,417	5.936	66,948	6.374	90,581	6.346	72,673	6.735	79,377	6.784								
General Expenses	18,414	1.782	17,784	1.168	16,746	1.594	13,901	0.974	17,035	1.579	12,286	1.05								
Licences	8,303	0.804	11,027	0.724	8,129	0.774	9,716	0.681	7,366	0.683	7,928	0.678								
Maintenance & Repairs	20,631	1.997	35,683	2.343	19,681	1.874	32,797	2.298	16,403	1.52	26,069	2.228								
Power	13,636	1.32	23,341	1.532	15,429	1.469	23,444	1.642	18,802	1.742	19,122	1.634								
Pensions	4,662	0.451	5,922	0.389	4,911	0.468	6,150	0.431	5,328	0.494	5,758	0.492								
Total Revenue Expenses	128,156	12.405	184,175	12.092	131,845	12.552	176,589	12.371	137,607	12.752	150,540	12.865								
Passengers	156,057	15.105	222,784	14.626	164,873	15.697	215,288	15.082	188,977	17.512	188,220	16.085								
Advertising	1,370	0.133	2,518	0.165	1,283	0.122	2,139	0.15	1,640	0.152	2,315	0.198								
Miscellaneous	248	0.024	366	0.024	282	0.027	360	0.025	402	0.037	431	0.037								
Total Income	157,675	15.262	225,668	14.816	166,439	15.846	217,787	15.257	191,020	17.702	190,966	16.32								
GROSS SURPLUS (+) or DEFICIT (-)	+29,519	2.857	+41,494	2.724	+34,594	3.293	+41,198	2.886	+53,413	4.95	+40,426	3.455								
Bank Interest rcvd	+830	0.08	+1,166	0.077	+798	0.076	+1,016	0.071	+896	0.083	+968	0.083								
Capital charges	31,904	3.088	34,286	2.251	39,563	3.767	21,105	1.479	38,815	3.597	21,293	1.82								
including Revenue Contributions	395	0.038	250	0.016	712	0.068	332	0.023	114	0.011	2,174	0.186								
ARP	-	-	-	-	-	-	-	-	1,494	0.138	1,567	0.134								
NET SURPLUS (+) or DEFICIT (-)	-1,555	-0.151	+8,374	0.55	-4,528	-0.431	+21,263	1.49	+13,886	1.287	+16,360	1.398								

	1942–43				1943–44				1944–45				1945–46				1946–47			
	TROLLEYBUSES		MOTORBUSES		TROLLEYBUSES		MOTORBUSES		TROLLEYBUSES		MOTORBUSES		TROLLEYBUSES		MOTORBUSES		TROLLEYBUSES		MOTORBUSES	
	Amount	Per Mile	Amount	Per Mile	Amount	Per Mile	Amount	Per Mile	Amount	Per Mile	Amount	Per Mile	Amount	Per Mile	Amount	Per Mile	Amount	Per Mile	Amount	Per Mile
Traffic Expenses	78,375	6.26	65,826	8.255					77,571	8.064	64,366	8.167	95,503	8.039	89,599	8.203	138,796	8.633	117,730	8.773
General Expenses	28,461	2.273	17,588	2.206					30,256	3.145	20,334	2.58	31,214	2.627	23,058	2.111	38,163	2.374	25,818	1.924
Licences	6,811	0.544	8,057	1.01					6,575	0.684	8,743	1.109	6,435	0.542	8,574	0.785	7,485	0.466	8,352	0.622
Maintenance & Repairs	22,032	1.76	26,155	3.28					27,795	2.89	30,981	3.931	36,484	3.071	35,945	3.291	48,415	3.011	46,861	3.492
Power	26,355	2.105	19,334	2.425					28,125	2.924	19,976	2.535	26,637	2.242	25,950	2.376	34,775	2.163	29,613	2.207
Pensions	6,846	0.547	5,649	0.708					9,650	1.003	7,908	1.003	9,503	0.8	8,737	0.8	11,870	0.738	9,908	0.738
Total Revenue Expenses	168,880	13.49	142,609	17.885	167,315	17.784	141,731	18.602	179,972	18.71	152,307	19.325	205,776	17.321	191,863	17.566	279,505	17.384	238,281	17.756
Passengers	233,989	18.69	148,548	18.629					275,970	28.69	171,868	21.807	312,191	26.278	229,664	21.027	360,969	22.451	254,969	18.999
Advertising	800	0.064	1,571	0.197					684	0.071	2,100	0.266	593	0.05	3,363	0.308	706	0.044	4,538	0.338
Miscellaneous	380	0.03	313	0.039					380	0.04	311	0.039	191	0.016	176	0.016	274	0.017	228	0.017
Total Income	235,169	18.785	150,432	18.866	248,397	26.402	156,457	20.535	277,034	28.801	174,279	22.113	312,975	26.344	233,203	21.351	361,949	22.512	259,735	19.354
GROSS SURPLUS (+) or DEFICIT (-)	+66,289	5.295	+7,823	0.981	+81,082	8.618	+14,726	1.933	+97,062	10.091	+21,972	2.788	+107,199	9.023	+41,340	3.785	+82,444	5.128	+21,454	1.599
Bank Interest rcvd	+1,092	0.087	+901	0.113	+551	0.059	+446	0.059	+921	0.096	+755	0.096	+495	0.042	+455	0.042	nil	-	nil	-
Capital charges	27,235	2.175	3,989	0.5	24,998	2.657	3,401	0.446	22,386	2.327	2,293	0.291	16,660	1.402	2,366	0.217	5,903	0.367	2,096	0.156
Revenue Contributions	693	0.055	309	0.039	222	0.024	591	0.078	1,550	0.161	2,190	0.278	nil	-	nil	-	+589	0.037	291	0.022
Stores	721	0.058	595	0.075	-	-	-	-	-	-	-	-	-	-	-	-	-	-	-	-
ARP	1,135	0.091	935	0.117	2,377	0.253	1,925	0.253	1,151	0.12	943	0.12	42	0.004	38	0.003	+32	0.002	+27	0.002
NET SURPLUS (+) or DEFICIT (-)	+37,597	3.003	+2,896	0.363	+54,036	5.743	+9,255	1.215	72,895	7.578	17,301	2.195	90,992	7.659	39,390	3.606	+77,162	4.799	+19,094	1.423

	1947–48				1948–49			
	TROLLEYBUSES		MOTORBUSES		TROLLEYBUSES		MOTORBUSES	
	Amount	Per Mile	Amount	Per Mile	Amount	Per Mile	Amount	Per Mile
Traffic Expenses	147,489	9.31	148,167	9.46	150,032	9.831	174,238	9.96
Joint Services (SMS)	2,179	0.138	2,077	0.133	283	0.019	324	0.019
General Expenses	45,693	2.884	32,530	2.077	46,880	3.072	38,040	2.174
Licences	7,497	0.473	7,658	0.489	7,887	0.517	9,212	0.527
Maintenance & Repairs	50,292	3.174	62,058	3.962	57,786	3.786	64,304	3.676
Power	35,867	2.264	34,777	2.22	38,862	2.546	38,909	2.224
Pensions	13,203	0.833	13,053	0.833	14,369	0.942	16,472	0.942
Total Revenue Expenses	302,220	19.076	300,320	19.174	316,099	20.712	341,499	19.52
Passengers	343,095	21.656	298,853	19.08	333,217	21.834	337,645	19.3
Advertising	3,070	0.194	3,068	0.196	2,819	0.185	2,827	0.162
Miscellaneous	994	0.063	5,439	0.347	1,260	0.083	8,424	0.482
Joint Services (SMS)	9,495	0.599	7,796	0.498	1,125	0.074	1,289	0.074
Transfer from reserves, etc.	5,104	0.322	5,838	0.373	6,237	0.409	5,009	0.286
Total Income	361,758	22.834	320,994	20.494	344,658	22.584	355,194	20.303
GROSS SURPLUS (+) or DEFICIT (-)	+59,538	3.758	+20,674	1.32	+28,559	1.871	+13,695	0.783
Interest received	+1,154	0.073	+1,142	0.073	+594	0.039	+681	0.039
Capital charges	5,515	0.348	2,204	0.141	-5169	-0.339	2,667	0.152
Revenue Contributions	1,318	0.083	36	0.002	-1361	-0.089	2,238	0.128
Others	-	-	-	-	+3474	0.228	3,982	0.228
NET SURPLUS (+) or DEFICIT (-)	+53,860	3.4	+19,576	1.25	+26,098	1.71	+13,453	0.769

	1949–50				1950–51				1951–52			
	TROLLEYBUSES		MOTORBUSES		TROLLEYBUSES		MOTORBUSES		TROLLEYBUSES		MOTORBUSES	
	Amount	Per Mile	Amount	Per Mile	Amount	Per Mile	Amount	Per Mile	Amount	Per Mile	Amount	Per Mile
Traffic Expenses	130,221	9.924	185,334	10.051	135,211	11.526	206,446	10.861	149,402	12.845	231,202	12.013
Joint Services (SMS)	241	0.018	339	0.018	311	0.027	503	0.026	165	0.014	274	0.014
General Expenses	45,405	3.46	43,825	2.377	33,870	2.887	32,006	1.684	26,065	2.241	31,445	1.634
Licences	6,988	0.533	10,769	0.584	6,436	0.549	10,737	0.565	6,632	0.57	10,009	0.52
Maintenance & Repairs	53,326	4.064	67,703	3.671	45,088	3.843	72,929	3.837	50,534	4.345	72,402	3.762
Power	33,689	2.567	42,651	2.313	30,763	2.622	67,828	3.568	35,463	3.049	83,258	4.326
Pensions	13,096	0.998	18,404	0.998	11,700	0.997	18,959	0.997	11,061	0.951	18,291	0.95
Total Revenue Expenses	282,966	21.565	369,025	20.012	263,379	22.451	409,408	21.538	279,322	24.014	446,881	23.219
Passengers	298,621	22.758	363,633	19.72	259,230	22.097	371,349	19.536	291,709	25.079	432,370	22.465
Advertising	3,157	0.241	3,380	0.183	2,440	0.208	3,716	0.195	2,456	0.211	4,145	0.215
Miscellaneous	944	0.072	10,684	0.579	832	0.071	9,376	0.493	1,022	0.088	9,715	0.505
Joint Services (SMS)	-1,944	-0.148	-2,367	-0.128	144	0.012	234	0.012	-9,226	-0.793	-15,266	-0.793
Transfer from reserves, etc.	1780	0.136	1637	0.089	-	-	-	-				
Total Income	302,558	23.058	376,967	20.443	262,646	22.388	384,675	20.237	285,961	24.585	430,964	22.392
GROSS SURPLUS (+) or DEFICIT (-)	+19,592	1.493	+7,942	0.431	-733	-0.062	-24,733	-1.301	+6,639	0.571	-15,917	-0.827
Interest received	+298	0.023	+419	0.023	+41	0.003	+67	0.004	+41	0.004	+68	0.004
Capital charges	-4225	-0.322	-17256	-0.936	7,499	0.639	28,725	1.511	11,084	0.953	27,974	1.453
Revenue Contributions	1,218	0.093	2,674	0.145	745	0.064	935	0.049	1,921	0.165	426	0.022
Others	-	-	-	-	-	-	-	-	-	-	-	-
NET SURPLUS (+) or DEFICIT (-)	+14,447	1.101	-11,5694	-6.274	-8,936	-0.762	-54,326	-2.858	-6,325	-0.544	-44,249	-2.299

	1952–53				1953–54				1954–55				1955–56				1956–57			
	TROLLEYBUSES		MOTORBUSES		TROLLEYBUSES		MOTORBUSES		TROLLEYBUSES		MOTORBUSES		TROLLEYBUSES		MOTORBUSES		TROLLEYBUSES		MOTORBUSES	
	Amount	Per Mile	Amount	Per Mile	Amount	Per Mile	Amount	Per Mile	Amount	Per Mile	Amount	Per Mile	Amount	Per Mile	Amount	Per Mile	Amount	Per Mile	Amount	Per Mile
Traffic Expenses	147,044	11.695	194,811	10.770	144,968	12.084	191,204	11.103	147,776	12.916	198,080	11.742	159,740	14.040	221,848	12.709	163,892	14.778	227,254	13.257
Joint Services	95	0.007	137	0.008	137	0.011	197	0.012	176	0.015	259	0.015	159	0.014	244	0.014	108	0.010	167	0.010
Servicing Vehicles & Routes	18,002	1.432	29,236	1.616	13,962	1.164	227,769	1.322	12,793	1.118	21,864	1.296	14,101	1.239	24,291	1.392	15,221	1.373	26,553	1.549
Licences	6,414	0.510	10,958	0.606	39,161	3.263	84,038	4.880	38,220	3.340	80,823	4.791	40,976	3.602	82,977	4.754	42,128	3.798	88,714	5.175
Maintenance & Repairs	58,621	4.663	68,989	3.814	53,781	4.483	63,946	3.713	55,914	4.887	63,945	3.791	64,099	5.634	63,248	3.623	57,544	5.189	72,449	4.226
Power	39,274	3.124	92,801	5.130	6,126	0.511	11,714	0.680	5,732	0.501	11,705	0.694	5,860	0.515	11,877	0.680	5,823	0.525	12,703	0.741
General	25,278	2.010	20,519	1.134	24,929	2.078	20,568	1.194	24,732	2.162	20,778	1.232	25,900	2.276	22,431	1.285	17,936	1.617	25,961	1.515
Pensions	26,921	2.141	37,728	2.086	27,804	2.318	37,164	2.158	27,772	2.427	38,025	2.254	29,312	2.576	41,612	2.384	31,237	2.817	44,362	2.588
Total Revenue Expenses	321,649	25.582	455,179	25.164	310,869	25.912	431,600	25.062	313,115	27.366	435,479	25,815	340,147	29.896	468,528	26.841	333,889	30.107	498,163	29.061
Passengers	369,821	29.413	453,314	25.061	357,528	29.801	450,169	26.140	341,046	29.808	455,286	26.988	345,379	30.356	505,596	28.965	366,276	33.027	544,691	31.775
Joint Services	-11,480	0.913	-14,017	0.775	123	0.010	176	0.010	121	0.010	178	0.011	118	0.010	181	0.010	118	0.011	182	0.011
Advertising	1,996	0.159	3,767	0.208	2,306	0.192	4,240	0.246	2,438	0.214	4,379	0.260	2,773	0.244	4,698	0.27	2,972	0.268	5,959	0.348
Miscellaneous	1,627	0.129	10,320	0.567	806	0.068	769	0.045	709	0.061	611	0.036	728	0.064	625	0.035	770	0.069	680	0.039
Total Income	361,964	28.788	453,384	25.065	360,763	30.071	455,354	26.441	344,314	30.093	460,454	27.295	348,998	30.674	511,100	29.280	370,136	33.375	551,512	32,173
GROSS SURPLUS (+) or DEFICIT (-)	40,315	3.206	1,795	0.099	49,894	4.159	23,754	1.379	+31,199	+2.727	+24,975	+1.480	+8,851	+0.778	+42,572	+2.439	+36,247	+3.268	+53,349	+3.112
Bank Interest rcvd	+64	0.005	+45	0.002	+299	0.025	+429	0.025	+732	0.064	+1,080	0.064	+1,130	0.099	+1,733	0.099	+1,509	0.135	+2,331	0.136
Capital charges	12,661	1.007	29,118	1.61	13,147	1.096	41,531	2.412	13,707	1.198	28,142	1.668	13,152	1.156	19,653	1.126	12,717	1.147	32,298	1.884
including Revenue Contributions including Income Tax	2,840	0.226	606	0.034	827	0.069	796	0.046	2,055	0.18	3,031	0.18	1,603	0.141	2,459	0.141	1,377	0.124	9,858	0.575
NET SURPLUS (+) or DEFICIT (-)	24,549	1.952	-31,920	-1.765	+37,194	3.1	-16,730	-0.971	+16,169	1.413	-5,118	-0.303	-4,774	-0.42	+22,193	1.271	+23,662	2.134	+13,524	0.789

	1957–58				1958–59				1959–60				1960–61				1961–62			
	TROLLEYBUSES		MOTORBUSES		TROLLEYBUSES		MOTORBUSES		TROLLEYBUSES		MOTORBUSES		TROLLEYBUSES		MOTORBUSES		TROLLEYBUSES		MOTORBUSES	
	Amount	Per Mile	Amount	Per Mile	Amount	Per Mile	Amount	Per Mile	Amount	Per Mile	Amount	Per Mile	Amount	Per Mile	Amount	Per Mile	Amount	Per Mile	Amount	Per Mile
Traffic Expenses incl. Pensions	200,467	17.95	268,755	16.25	202,268	18.49	267,550	16.744	191,994	18.882	281,000	17.140	138,139	21.599	363,732	18.521	110,333	22.825	409,564	19.122
Joint Services	129	0.012	190	0.011	+28	0.003	+41	0.003	82	0.008	133	0.008	48	0.007	146	0.007	44	0.009	196	0.009
Servicing Vehicles & Routes	20,951	1.876	34,353	2.077	19,981	1.827	32,934	2.061	16,661	1.639	30,576	1.865	10,363	1.620	35,420	1.804	8,525	1.764	38,588	1.802
Power	46,004	4.119	82,431	4.984	46,187	4.222	76,287	4.774	41,118	4.044	78,420	4.783	30,664	4.795	92,406	4.705	25,693	5.315	103,431	4.829
Maintenance & Repairs	55,762	4.993	88,738	5.366	51,485	4.706	77,232	4.833	51,400	5.055	66,877	4.079	32,711	5.115	70,986	3.615	24,168	0.500	79,847	3.728
Licences	5,885	0.527	13,215	0.799	5,545	0.507	11,935	0.747	1,881	0.185	5,046	0.308	1,296	0.203	5,624	0.286	944	0.195	5,808	0.271
General Expenses	21,755	1.948	30,481	1.843	22,428	2.05	30,663	1.919	23,245	2.286	34,925	2.130	15,670	2.450	41,273	2.102	10,730	2.220	47,949	2.239
Welfare	348	0.031	497	0.03	241	0.022	339	0.021	336	0.033	527	0.032	231	0.036	664	0.034	296	0.061	1,224	0.057
Total Revenue Expenses	351,301	31.455	518,660	31.361	348,107	31.821	496,899	31.098	326,717	32.132	497,504	30.345	229,122	35.825	610,251	31.074	180,733	37.389	686,607	32.057
Passengers	372,604	33.363	533,740	32.273	381,113	34.838	534,634	33.459	363,912	35.790	552,971	33.729	234,863	36.722	692,915	35.283	187,223	38.732	774,875	36.178
Joint Services	121	0.011	178	0.011	122	0.011	177	0.011	115	0.011	184	0.011	75	0.012	231	0.012	59	0.012	263	0.012
Advertising	3,223	0.289	6,167	0.373	3,244	0.297	6,035	0.378	2,937	0.289	6,534	0.398	2,890	0.452	6,896	0.351	2,725	0.564	7,846	0.366
Miscellaneous	686	0.061	549	0.033	630	0.057	860	0.054	691	0.068	744	0.045	477	0.075	858	0.044	405	0.083	904	0.042
Total Income	376,634	33.724	540,634	32.69	385,109	35.203	541,706	33.902	367,655	36.158	560,433	34.183	238,305	37.261	700,900	35.690	190,412	39.391	783,888	36.598
GROSS SURPLUS (+) or DEFICIT (-)	+25,333	2.268	+21,974	1.329	+37,002	+3.382	+44807	+2.804	+40,938	+4.026	+62,929	+3.838	+9,183	+1.436	+90,649	+4.616	+9,679	+2.002	+97,281	4.541
Interest received	+2,465	0.221	3,650	0.221	+2,691	+0.246	+3,931	+0.246	+1,702	+0.167	+2,743	+0.167	+1,164	+0.182	+3,575	+0.182	+1,000	+0.207	+4,430	+0.206
Capital charges	12,648	1.132	34,178	2.067	10,914	0.998	38,903	2.434	9,417	0.926	41,257	2.516	7,728	1.208	45,889	2.336	2,036	0.421	31,837	1.486
NET SURPLUS (+) or DEFICIT (-)	+15,150	1.357	-8,554	-0.517	+28,779	+2.630	+9,835	+0.616	+33,223	+3.267	+24,415	+1.489	+2,619	+0.410	+48,335	+2.462	+8,643	+1.788	+69,874	+3.261

	1962–63				1963–64			
	TROLLEYBUSES		MOTORBUSES		TROLLEYBUSES		MOTORBUSES	
	Amount	Per Mile	Amount	Per Mile	Amount	Per Mile	Amount	Per Mile
Traffic Expenses incl. Pensions	77,266	22835	453,630	20.033	21,828	22.983	525,306	20.888
Joint Services	32	0.009	214	0.009	-	-	-	-
Servicing Vehicles & Routes	5,662	1.674	44,023	1.944	1,468	1.546	46,701	1.857
Power	17,561	5.190	109,629	4.843	5,166	5.439	122,671	4.878
Maintenance & Repairs	19,024	5.622	93,343	4.122	4,532	4.772	97,263	3.867
Licences	688	0.204	6,458	0.285	200	0.210	7,061	0.281
General Expenses	9,256	2.735	52,580	2.322	3,894	4.100	83,781	3.331
Welfare	243	0.072	1,614	0.071	63	0.066	1,880	0.075
Total Revenue Expenses	129,732	38.341	761,491	33.629	37,151	39.116	884,663	35.177
Passengers	134,654	39.796	846,053	37.363	41,610	43.812	986,646	39.232
Joint Services	42	0.012	280	0.012	-	-	-	-
Advertising	2,184	0.645	7,967	0.352	416	0.437	9,701	0.385
Miscellaneous	142	0.042	827	0.037	17	0.018	819	0.033
Total Income	137,022	40.495	855,127	37.764	42,043	44.267	997,166	39.650
GROSS SURPLUS (+) or DEFICIT (-)	+7,290	+2.154	+93,636	+4.135	+4,892	+5.151	+112,503	+4.473
Interest received	+675	+0.200	+4,516	+0.199	+231	+0.243	+6,109	+0.243
Capital charges	1,326	0.392	59,783	2.640	914	0.962	59,762	2.376
NET SURPLUS (+) or DEFICIT (-)	+6,639	+1.962	+38,369	1.694	+4,209	+4.432	+58,850	+2.340

Note:
Figures for 1940–1941 & 1941–1942 were not published due to wartime security restrictions.
Figures for 1943–1944 were incompletely published due to wartime security restrictions.

APPENDIX P

CONSULTANT'S REPORT

Continuing opposition to the Passenger Transport Committee's proposals for trolleybus abandonment led to independent consultants, Harold Whitehead & Partners Ltd., being appointed in November 1958 to review the Corporation's passenger transport policy. The terms of the consultancy contract were:

(1) To examine the present and future financial and economic aspects of the undertaking as a whole and of motor buses and trolleybuses individually.
(2) To make recommendations on any additions or withdrawals of motorbuses or trolleybuses (and equipment) that may be necessary to provide the most economical undertaking consistent with an adequate service to the public.
(3) To examine the operation of the joint agreement with SMS to determine the advantages or disadvantages to the Corporation, and to make recommendations on any alterations in its operation (consistent with the agreement itself) which may be necessary to provide greater benefit to the Corporation.
(4) To recommend the most profitable line of action open to the Corporation when the existing agreement with SMS expires.
(5) To report or recommend on any matter which they feel may have a bearing on the future efficient operation of the Corporation Transport Undertaking.

The consultant's report was presented to the Passenger Transport Committee on 1 September 1959 and is given in its entirety below.

CITY OF PORTSMOUTH

PASSENGER TRANSPORT DEPARTMENT

REPORT ON

I THE FUTURE OF THE TROLLEY BUS SYSTEM

II THE CO-ORDINATION AGREEMENT WITH SOUTHDOWN MOTOR SERVICES LTD.

Harold Whitehead & Partners Ltd, Chandos Court, Carton Street, London, S.W.1,

July 1959.

CONTENTS

INTRODUCTION
1. The issues with which this report is concerned are those epitomised in our preliminary survey of January 1959 as

I The future use to be made of trolley buses, bearing in mind the need to maintain an adequate and economical Transport undertaking

II The balance of advantage resulting from the agreement with Southdown Motor Services, and hence the desirability of renewing it, with or without amendment, after its expiry.

2. We embarked upon our investigation accepting that it appears generally agreed that in view of the age of much of the equipment and of nearly 80% of the vehicles (57 out of

72 date from 1937 or earlier), this is the appropriate time to consider the future of the trolley bus system.

3. We have had access to all the Corporation records, documents and files for which we have asked; the willing co-operation of officers in the departments of the Town Clerk, the Borough Treasurer, Transport, the City Engineer, City Development, Health and Police, and also of Southdown Motor Services and Mr. S.D. Herington of Sydney Morse & Co.; discussion with the Joint Committee of Local Ratepayers and Portsmouth Trades Council, with the Secretary of the Chamber of Commerce, and also with the Transport Managers of nine other municipalities and a transport consultant with experience of operating trolley buses. We have-received information from the Electrical Development Association, the British Medical Association, the National Smoke Abatement Society*, U.N.E.S.C.O. and from various transport journals.

4. The questions at issue are considered solely in the light of the conditions now prevailing in the City of Portsmouth and the hinterland which constitutes the Co-ordinated Area, and as they seem likely to evolve during the next twenty years or so. Nevertheless we have been careful to inform ourselves of the conditions elsewhere so as to be able to profit by the experience of others.
* Now *(sic)* the National Society for Clean Air.

OUR CONCLUSIONS

5. After careful consideration of all the information available to us we have reached the following conclusions.

I

6. Having regard to the present and anticipated future situation in the City of Portsmouth and the adjacent area of co-ordination during the next twenty years or so, the decision of the Corporation Transport Committee gradually, and as found expedient, to abandon trolley buses is sound.

7. By so doing a flexibility will be achieved which will enable the services and routing to be adapted readily to changing demands.

8. At the end of the period a new situation will have evolved when it might be expedient to reconsider the whole matter. In our view it is likely that by that time new means of propulsion will be available without the respective disadvantages of both diesel buses and trolley buses.

II

9. A co-ordination agreement covering operations over the whole area is necessary.

10. In our opinion the present agreement is a satisfactory one and should be continued. We would not seek to change any material aspect of it.

11. We would add that under Clause 4 of the Portsmouth Corporation Act 1946, the two parties are given wide freedom to make such modification of the terms as may at any time be agreed between them. Consequently it will not be necessary to draft an entirely new agreement in order to enable the co-ordination to be adapted to new circumstances.

12. In the remainder of this report we give our reasons for these conclusions.

PART 1

THE FUTURE OF THE TROLLEY BUS SYSTEM

1 THE ORIGIN OF THE PROPOSAL TO ELIMINATE TROLLEY BUSES

13. Early in 1956 the question of one-way traffic in Twyford Avenue and Stamshaw Road was under consideration. At the special joint sub-committee of February 16th the principle of one-way traffic was approved. During the discussion the Chairman of the Passenger Transport Committee stated that he would be reluctant to recommend the transfer of trolley bus equipment to Stamshaw Road on the score of cost and because, in his personal opinion, "so far as Portsmouth was concerned, the operation of trolley buses had become obsolescent". The committee recommended to the Passenger Transport Committee "that the use of trolley buses in Twyford Avenue be discontinued and that the existing route be served by liquid fuel buses".

14. Following upon this joint committee the Deputy General Manager prepared a memorandum to the General Manager and Engineer, expressing the view "that with the altered circumstances following co-ordination with the Southdown Motor Services, whereby we became interested in operation extending over an area of 127 square miles operating to north, east and west of Cosham as opposed to operations confined to points south of Spur Road, Cosham, and within an area of 10 square miles, serious consideration should be given to the introduction of Motor Buses in lieu of Trolley Buses operating on the north and south routes". And later, "having regard to the peculiarities of the traffic operation and the fact that the trolley fleet has deteriorated, necessitating considerable replacement or re-building, it would appear an opportune time for your Committee to consider future policy".

This memorandum would appear to be the initiating document of the future discussion. Although the memorandum makes a passing reference to the cost of erecting overhead equipment to cover the "many streams of operation beyond Cosham", its theme is essentially that of traffic considerations, not that of cost.

15. We think it unfortunate that so much of the subsequent controversy centred on cost rather than on a broad view of the traffic requirements to be anticipated during the next 20–25 years.

TOTAL OPERATING COSTS OF MOTOR BUSES AND TROLLEY BUSES

(i) Costs in 1956 and 1959

17. The Manager's and Treasurer's Report dated 25th July, 1956 dealt with the implications of gradual abandonment of the trolleybus system and the substitution of motor buses. Attached to this was a schedule comparing the operating costs of motor buses with trolley buses assuming that the whole system were either the one or the other. It was stated that the motor buses were cheaper to operate than the trolley buses when account was taken of providing and maintaining overhead equipment for the trolley system.

The total costs were given as:-

Motor buses	30.714	pence per vehicle mile
Trolley buses	32.550	" " " "
Trolley buses higher by	1.636	" " " "

18. As there have been many changes in expenditure levels since 1956 we asked the Treasurer's Department to prepare similar costs for 1959 conditions which are as follows:-

Comparative Costs Based on 1959 Conditions
Per Vehicle Mile

	Motor Buses d.	Trolley Buses d.
Traffic Operation	17.451	17.446
Servicing Vehicles and Routes	2.052	1.840
Power	4.775	4.222
Repairs Maintenance	3.886	3.534
Licenses for Passenger Vehicles	0.225	0.225
Management and General Expenses	1.892	1.897
Welfare, Medical	0.022	0.022
Overhead Equipment Repairs and Rates	–	1.254
Operating Cost	30.303	30.440
Loan Charges		
Vehicles	3.406	4.318
Overhead Equipment	–	0.825
TOTAL COST	33.809	35.583

Trolley buses higher by 1.874

19. We have examined the operation costs as shown above and we have discussed them with officials of the Corporation. We are satisfied that these costs have been prepared on a sound basis and that the apportionment of expenditure between the two forms of transport is reasonable for the purpose of showing costs of operating under identical route conditions.

(ii) Comments on Certain Items of Cost

(a) Loan charges

20. The loan charges for vehicles shown above are calculated on the basis that the estimated current replacement cost of a vehicle, together with the cost of interest on the loan required to finance it, is written off in revenue costs over the period of years during which the borrowed money is repayable. For motor buses this period is 12 years and for trolley buses 14. These loan repayment periods are, we understand, fixed by the Ministry of Transport. We consider the Ministry's ratio between the repayment periods for a motorbus and that for a trolley bus must be accepted. The actual period of repayment however seems far too short to be used for writing off the asset having regard to the operating experience of Portsmouth.

(b) Interest

21. Although we are of the opinion that in ordinary business circumstances interest payable on borrowed money should be considered as an appropriation of profit and should not form part of costs we appreciate that in the case of a Municipal Corporation a method of financing the transport department's assets is through the use of loans repayable over a fixed term of years as laid down by government department. As the cost of interest can be directly related to the cost of individual assets we are prepared to accept the official approach that interest does form an element in the cost for the purpose of comparison of the expense of operating the two types of vehicles. Accordingly we have shown separately in our costs the interest payable an borrowed money, but we have spread the total cost of interest over the period of asset life we have adopted for depreciation, on this basis therefore the interest is in effect an addition to the purchase cost of the assets,

(c) Depreciation

22. In industrial and commercial undertakings the cost of capital equipment is usually written off over the expected life of the asset in question. The period of life adopted is, of course, calculated according to the experience of operating similar assets, combined with a consideration of the policy of repairs maintenance to be adopted. It should also have some regard to the expectation of obsolescence which could arise and affect the normal physical life of the asset.

23. Following normal business practice we propose that our costs for purpose of comparison should include the depreciation on vehicles related to a normal expectation of life usage. For this purpose we have adopted 18 years for a motor bus and 21 years for a trolley bus. We cannot be sure whether these periods of usage are acceptable to all parties and they are probably conservative. They do in any case maintain a ratio between motor buses and trolley buses similar to that adopted by the Ministry of Transport for the repayment of loan. A slightly longer term than those we have used would not substantially affect the cost shown.

24. Officials of the Transport Department are of the view that new poles for overhead equipment are unlikely to last as long as the old ones: the poles available are of inferior quality to those originally installed, and they have estimated a life of approximately 25 years. Whether or not this estimate is too conservative, we consider it would not be prudent to compare costs based on a longer period. Accordingly we have used 25 years for calculating depreciation of overhead equipment. We have, however, also illustrated the effect if the life were 50 years, as this latter period is more closely related to the experience of the existing installation.

25. The depreciation included in our figures below is related to the current cost of new vehicles and equipment as there does not appear to be any other fair basis of cost comparison of operating the two types of vehicles. The interest charge is the amount payable during the loan period spread over the same period as adopted for depreciation calculations.

(d) Maintenance – Capital items

26. In the figure included in our comparative costs shown hereunder we have increased the Treasurer's repairs expenditure (based on an average of 10 years) to include some items which were charged to capital account* and which in our view could be considered as revenue maintenance outlay. We have also made an adjustment to bring these costs into line with 1959 expenditure levels.

* The principal item was the purchase of 9 double-deck bus bodies at a cost of £19,890.

(iii) Comparison of Costs using Adjusted Figures

The comparison of total costs, based on the 1958/59 figures, but taking into account the adjustments discussed in the foregoing paragraphs, is:-

Per Vehicle Mile

	Motor Buses d.	Trolley Buses d.
Operating Costs (as paragraph 18)	30.303	30.440
Additions to Maintenance and Allowance for Revised Expenditure Level (paragraph 26)	1.170	0.825
Adjusted Operating Cost	31.473	31.265
Depreciation of		
Vehicles	1.809	2.224
Overhead Equipment	–	0.604

Loan Charges		
Vehicles	0.461	0.655
Overhead Equipment	–	0.189
TOTAL COST	33.743	34.937

If expenditure on overhead equipment were spread over 50 years, the costs for depreciation and interest would be:

Depreciation	0.302
Interest	0.094

28. The foregoing comparison of the 1958/9 figures shows that the trolley buses cost 34.937d. per mile as compared with the motor buses at 33.743d. per mile, a difference in favour of the motor bus of 1.194d. per mile or, on the basis of the 1958/9 trolley bus mileage, approximately £13,000 per annum.

29. Although our adjusted figures show a smaller difference between trolley buses and motor buses than those given in section (i), it will be seen that the total cost per mile for trolley buses is still higher than motor buses. Expenditure on the overhead equipment for the trolley system is, therefore, an important element of cost both as regards maintenance and capital. No similar outlay arises in the case of motor buses which, being self-contained for motive power, do not require such a specialised road service capital outlay.

(iv) General

30. We would mention that the annual accounts for the transport undertaking are made up separately for motor buses and for trolley buses in order to comply with approved procedure. They are not, however, suitable for making comparisons of profitability between the two forms of transport as they cover all the different routes served and they do not provide information which enables a comparison to be made of operations on identical routes. Profits are only suitable for comparison in so far as they arise on exactly similar routes and such information is not available.

31. In the published accounts, the cost of debt charges as between motor buses and trolley buses is not comparable because these figures are applicable to mixed sums of outstanding debt and are not written off in direct relationship to the estimated useful life of the assets.

32. The overall income from the public road transport would, in principle, be the same whichever form of transport were used, as the public would, in the main, travel on whichever of the two were provided. Thus the important factor in the economy is the total cost per vehicle mile. According to the information we have obtained it does appear that taking into account all capital equipment the bus is cheaper to operate than the trolley.

TRAFFIC CONSIDERATIONS – THE MAIN BASIS OF OUR CONCLUSION

33. An admitted, and, in our opinion, the greatest objection to trolley buses is that they are route-bound and inflexible. This drawback may be of minor importance in a town in which the pattern of transport demand and the bus routes are well established but, nevertheless, inconvenience arises when special occasions or road works require temporary diversion of traffic. Moreover, even in towns where the pattern of transport seems well established, changes do occur in the course of time.

34. In the case of Portsmouth a number of special circumstances must be considered:
– the effect of decline in the number of passengers carried,
– the unpredictable changes in demand due to changes in the weather, which particularly affect a holiday resort,
– the widespread destruction during the war,
– the movement of population within and beyond the City boundaries,
– the development of new industrial areas,
– the development plans for City improvement.

35. We discuss first the present position before bringing into consideration the shift of population and the long term plans for City development.

(i) The Present Position – The Effect of Falling Traffic

36. The trolley bus routes are largely based on the original tram routes which were designed to serve a self-contained city. The question of extension of routes beyond the City boundary had not arisen; indeed there were statutory limitations to the effect that Portsmouth services could not extend beyond Cosham (this limitation still exists and route extensions can be made only by agreement with the Southdown Company). For present conditions the trolley bus routes appear to us to be complicated and to have an unduly large number of corners, frogs and crossovers,* which involve both increased capital cost and slower running.** Critics of the Transport Department have claimed that "re-arrangement of services is long overdue".***

37. Small re-arrangements of routes have been made from time to time which in total have had considerable effect in adapting the services to new needs. With falling traffic, however, more general review of services will be expedited. The rate of decline in the number of passengers carried within the coordinated area in recent years has increased from 1.2 to 2.5% for the years ending March, 1954, 1955 and 1956; to 3.5% in 1957; and 8.5% in 1958;**** and 4.3% in 1959. There is reason to suppose that the decline has been rather greater on the City routes.

(a) North – south routes

38. As regards the main north-south routes, Commercial Road, Fratton Road and Copnor Road, the effect of the decline has been that the buses from beyond Cosham are able to deal with the local City demand, gradually rendering the more or less direct north -south town routes terminating at or below Cosham (G/H, 3/4, 5/6 and 19/20) largely redundant. These latter routes are mainly served by trolley buses and these are, therefore, primarily affected: if they had all been bus routes the effect would have been the same. The necessary adjustment cannot reasonably be made by reducing the number of longer distance buses since, beyond Cosham, these fan out to give the minimum reasonable service to outer areas.

39. There is the conceivable alternative of providing a transfer station at, say, Cosham where the country buses would terminate. Such a proposal would raise serious problems in the working of the Co-ordination Agreement. The Southdown buses would need either to terminate at the station or to run through the City on a limited stop or protective fare basis.

* Excluding the depots, there are 224 frogs and crossovers and 11 turning circles.

** The speed limit at corners and junctions has been raised from 5 to 8 miles per hour, but in practice drivers take such points very cautiously for fear of dewirements.
*** Letter to Town Clerk from G. Kingsford, 28th January, 1959.
**** The year 1957/8 was affected by the Southdown strike, but the total fall from 1956/7 to 1958/9 was 12.4%.

The Southdown Company would undoubtedly resist any proposal to terminate their services at Cosham or some other transfer station and, in view of their long established right to operate into Southsea, we feel sure that the Traffic Commissioners would support them, though this issue has not been put to the test recently. If, on the other hand, the Southdown buses were to run non-stop or even limited-stop to Southsea, having shed some of their passengers at a transfer station, they would be running in the City with empty seats, while City local services would be running on the same routes (probably also with empty seats). This would obviously involve waste mileage for which the travelling public must pay and also increase the congestion in the City streets. Indeed, it was this sort of situation which necessitated the co-ordination agreement in the first instance.

40. These traffic considerations would apply no less forcibly in respect of long-distance Corporation buses. If they serve every stop within the City, with declining traffic, they will increasingly be able to cope with the local demands during normal periods. If on the other hand, they ran express through the City, passengers would have to transfer, and additional vehicles would be needed to serve the intermediate stops. Moreover passenger transfer takes time and even though this may be a matter of two or three minutes only, it is, for the vehicle, additional lay over time which would otherwise be employed in running.

41. It is, of course, realised that at peak periods and on special occasions short working could be introduced to deal with inequality of demand over some portion of the route, but this gives no case for services operating only to a transfer station in the nearer outskirts of the City.

42. We do not think people, especially those who travel daily from and to the near housing estates beyond Cosham, would like changing. Having secured a seat at the start of their journey inwards, they might find themselves queuing for the continuation bus. On the outward journey they might have to wait before continuing their journey on a less frequent service, and a wait at the transfer station would be more resented than the same waiting period at the beginning of their journey after which, having obtained a seat, they know they will be undisturbed until the end of their journey.

43. A further consideration from the passengers' point of view is that with the rate of fare graded according to distance they would have to take two tickets which would cost more than a single ticket for the whole journey. This would be particularly resented by those travelling from points not far from the transfer station.

44. The foregoing argument is valid for both motor buses and trolley buses, but whereas there is the alternative of extending the motor bus routes, the practicability of doing so with trolleybuses is limited. It is inconceivable that they should be extended to all the outer destinations and wherever they terminated intermediately in the north-easterly area the questions of transfer or of duplication would arise. We would agree that were the general case for retention of trolley buses established, their extension to Paulsgrove would be reasonable.

(b) East – west traffic south of Portsbridge

45. South of Portsbridge there are 6 services entirely within the City (O/P, G/H, 7/8, 11/12, 15/16 and 17/18) which provide the bulk of the east-west service. Route C/D makes two cross-town traverses before alternate buses turn north to leave the island by Eastern Road. The falling traffic will increasingly be met by using single-deck one-man buses. Consequently there will be diminished utilisation of east – west trolley bus equipment just as is occurring in the case of the north-south routes, though for a slightly different reason – a reduction is required of capacity per journey instead of a transfer of traffic to long distance vehicles.

(ii) Short Running

46. Apart from the interruption or diversion of services occasioned by road works and special events which can be anticipated, but in which trolley buses present particular difficulties*, Portsmouth and Southsea, as a holiday resort, has the problem of the unpredictability of traffic demands under varying weather conditions. It is for this reason that many of the service timetables are the same summer and winter. The timetable gives the minimum services, but these are supplemented as and where required. Such augmentation presents no great problem if the whole route is involved, but in practice the unpredicted need is likely to arise on parts of a route only, as, for example, between the town centre and the front. It is impossible to provide for ad hoc turn round of trolley buses at any point and in practice such short running on trolley bus routes is done by buses.
* A particular, but admittedly minor, disadvantage of trolley buses is that in the case of road works involving the temporary or permanent re-siting of the trolley poles and wiring, additional cost is involved, and it is a cost which does not qualify for the 75% road grant, even though the main job may do so.

47. An analysis of such augmentation by buses during the week 4th to 10th August, 1957 showed:-

Total trolley bus miles run	60,624 miles
Augmentation by motor buses over short sections of trolley bus routes	7,809 miles

Thus the trolley buses were supplemented by motor buses to the extent of nearly 13%. We are informed that if trolley buses alone had been used, reversing at their nearest turning points, the supplementary mileage would have been about doubled, this further additional mileage being largely waste. Under these circumstances the total trolley bus mileage would have been about 76,000, of which 10% would have been largely waste.

48. There is also the practical consideration that if, as is usual at such times, the crowd is moving mainly in one direction, motor buses can make a quick return journey "out of service". This is impossible with trolley buses which are route bound by the vehicles in front of them. Consequently more trolley buses would be needed than motor buses.

(iii) Special Peak Travel

49. Apart from the morning and evening peak traffic on the normal routes, Portsmouth has the special problem of the in and out muster at the Dockyard and at the newer industrial estate adjacent to the airport.

50. The Dockyard Main Gate presents no problem since it is the normal terminus of 1 motor bus and 3 trolley bus routes and is also served by bus route C/D. The peak traffic is met by 8 buses and 7 trolley buses, the latter operating on the 3 normal and on 2 special routes.

51. The Marlborough and Unicorn Gates, however, where the greatest number of people must be catered for, are on roads which do not call for any regular service through the day. The local residential area is adequately served by the C/D bus along Queen Street. The peak demand at these gates is met by 30 Corporation and 8 Southdown buses. Thirteen of the Corporation buses run on to 4 trolley bus routes, but to cater for these two movements a day would not justify trolley bus equipment, particularly as the arrangements for manoeuvring the trolley buses would be complicated and expensive.

52. Apart from the C/D bus on Eastern Road, the airport approach road does not call for regular passenger service during the day and is not appropriate for trolley bus equipment. The peak demand is met by 27 Corporation buses and 1 Southdown bus, and it is to be noted that, taking advantage of the half hour difference in working times the Corporation buses are the same ones which have first handled the outmuster from Unicorn Gate. (The other 3 buses have a longer journey and are not available for the airport traffic).*

53. If the Marlborough and Unicorn Gates were served by trolley buses, 13 would be needed and these would be useless for handling the airport peak. Consequently 13 other buses would need to be brought into service for this one movement and the total special peak traffic would require 43 Corporation vehicles instead of the present 30.

54. It is evident that trolley buses have no advantage to offer in dealing with this special traffic.

55. In view of the fact that only 9 Southdown buses are used to serve the special peak traffic we have been discussing, it should be noted that the Southdown Company caters for the whole of the corresponding traffic on Portsdown Hill and elsewhere in the coordinated area. Comparable figures for the total number of peak time additional vehicles in mid-June 1959 were:-

	Corporation	Southdown
Vehicles on normal service	98	67
Peak time specials	76	48
Total vehicles	174	115
Peak specials proportion	44%	42%

* We think the Transport Management are to be complimented upon the ingenuity and efficiency with which these two movements are effected with only a half hour interval between them.

(iv) The Movement of Population

56. The following table gives estimates of the population of the co-ordinated area.

	1949 (,000)	1958 (,000)	1971 (,000)
Area excluding Portsmouth			
Havant with Hayling	31	63	108
- increase %	103%	70%	
Porchester to Fareham	27.7	(33)	36
- increase %	19%	10%	
Petersfield UDC & RDC	26.4	28.6	(29)
- increase %	8%	3%	
Droxford RDC	19.4	20.7	(21)
- increase %	7%	3%	
Total excluding Portsmouth	104.5	145.3	194
- increase %	39%	34%	
Portsmouth (incl. Services)	240	223	203
- decrease	7%	9%	
Co-ordinated Area	344	368	397
- increase %	7%	8%	
Portsmouth - % of total	70%	61%	51%

Note The data except for the figures in () were supplied by the City Development Department.

57. The trend after 1971 is a matter of speculation. It seems likely that the population of the hinterland will continue to increase, probably at a decreased rate. Assuming no boundary changes, the population of the City is expected to stabilise except for the possibility of some new housing on sites released by the Admiralty and on the present site of the airport etc.

58. From the figures quoted above it is evident that within the next dozen years there will be an increased demand for long distance transport, while the decline of local traffic within the City is expected to continue. This decline will be in addition to that due to increasing use of private motor cars and motor cycles. This combination of additional fall in traffic and increase in long distance services will expedite the time when the latter will render redundant normal south-north services terminating at or south of Cosham.

(v) City Development

59. Formerly the economy of Portsmouth was based on the Dockyard and very largely therefore on the southern half of the west side of the island. At that time it was less customary for women to go out to work and there was no great call for industries to employ them. Today that position has entirely changed and efforts are made to balance the labour market by introducing light industries and there is a growing industrial estate in the northeast corner of the island. This has naturally led to some reorientation of public transport.

60. The devastation of war and the natural increase in population have together led to considerable movement of population within the City, notably to the areas east and west of Cosham, from Farlington to Paulsgrove; and beyond the City boundary, especially to the north and north-west of Havant. The population within the City north of Portsbridge has increased from rather more than 20,000 to perhaps 45,000 and that of Havant and Hayling has doubled to 63,000 between 1949 and 1958.

61. Under the development plan the population of the City is expected to fall to about 203,000 by 1971, but even so there is little space available for re-housing. The Admiralty may release the Victoria, Duchess of Kent and Clarence Barracks which would give housing space for about 1,500 people and there is the possibility of a similar area in Hilsea becoming available. There must therefore be a large over-spill elsewhere, but where is at present uncertain.

62. The Leigh Park estate is expected to be fully developed by 1963 and the City Development Department advocates new housing estates in the area north and west of Waterlooville to take 20,000 people. The County Authorities would like to restrict the growth of Havant and Waterlooville in favour of enlarging existing communities further afield in the green belt area. The Hampshire Green Belt Inquiry, now sitting, may lead to a Ministerial decision on this issue.

63. Apparently the County Authorities might prefer Portsmouth to incorporate Hayling Island and provide housing there, rather than to further expand the already considerable population in the Havant and Waterlooville area. This would allow an attractive extension of the sea front to a terrain of sands and dunes and to Chichester Harbour. A bridge over Hayling Ferry already forms part of the approved development plan. We understand, however, that the site preparation for housing (drainage, water supply etc.) would be very expensive; and, in any case, the bridge was planned to follow other road developments and its erection was not envisaged before 15 to 20 years. Housing space will be required earlier. It seems probable that Portsmouth will take in Hayling Island sooner or later and, if soon, the bridge plan might be advanced.

64. If population expansion is directed to the north and west of Waterlooville, the effect will be still further to increase the north-south bus services into the city, accelerating the redundancy of north-south services limited to the City. If Hayling Island is developed a new main route into the City from the east will be created. In both cases the pattern of transport would be changed and in neither case would it be expedient to use trolley buses for the new traffic.

65. Within the City, a consequence of war damage has been some re-distribution of shopping areas. Kings Road and Elm Grove are now mainly residential and the shopping area round Palmerston Road has been further developed. When the Commercial Road shopping area was damaged some businesses moved to North End and though some returned to Commercial Road as soon as they could, North End has continued as a main shopping area especially for people from Hilsea and beyond. There are now more shops than before in Copnor Road, but rather fewer in Fratton Road and Kingston Road while a small shopping area has sprung up east of the railway in Tangier Road. These changes may not amount to a major shift of the shopping centres of gravity, but they do represent some movement north and east and indicate some change in the direction in which people will travel.

66. Under the development plan a number of road changes are projected and some of these, especially of the second (6–20 years) period of the plan, will have a significant effect on the pattern of traffic.

67. There are still some 5¼ route miles of tram track to be taken up during the next 6 to 8 years, and within this period several roads are to be widened, e.g. a short length of Commercial Road, Arundel Street, Palmerston Road and Twyford Avenue. Wherever trolley bus routes are involved such road works will involve some public inconvenience due to the inflexibility of trolley buses.

68. The changes to be made during the second period of the plan concern both north-south and east-west roads.

The North-South projects include:
– a by-pass of Commercial Road by a new Dockyard loop road via Anglesea Road to the Dockyard Main Gate and via St. Michaels Road to the Victoria Hall,
– widening Burgoyne Road to provide a direct main traffic access from Fratton Bridge to the Front,*
– re-aligning Copnor Bridge to ease traffic flow.

The original plan provided for a main traffic route via Prince Albert Road and Street from Milton Road to Eastern Parade. This was not approved at the time, but it is understood the matter is likely to be re-opened.
– extension of Eastern Road across Milton Lake to Eastney Esplanade,
– a further long term project, not covered by the present plan, would, if adopted, provide for a western outlet corresponding to Eastern Road, from Twyford Avenue and Alexandra Park across the harbour to Southampton Road.

The effect of these projects will be to establish new main, and in most cases more direct, routes from the north to the sea front, routes to which the public transport services must be adapted.

69. The East-West projects include,
– making a main route linking the civic centre via Greetham Street, Goldsmith Avenue and the Old Canal to the projected extension of Easter Road and, in due course, beyond to the projected Hayling Bridge,
*When the time comes to replace the South Parade Pier in perhaps 20 years' time, the new pier may be built opposite Burgoyne Road.

Some of this work In Greetham Street and Goldsmith Avenue is planned to be done in the next few years. The new road to link these two streets may come much later.
– extension of Stubbington Avenue along: Burrfield's Road across the railway to Eastern Road,
– possible extension of Rat Lane across the railway to serve industrial development in the vicinity of the airport and linking with Eastern Road,
– also the re-alignment of Copnor Bridge will ease the way for traffic between New Road and Tangier Road.

The obvious consequence of providing these main cross roads will be the re-organisation of public transport so as to make the best use of them. In particular the Greetham Street – Old Canal project will be of great importance if the City acquires Hayling Island since it will provide a direct route from Hayling Bridge to the town centre and to the Dockyards.

(vi) Summary of Traffic Considerations and Conclusion

70. Summarising the foregoing discussion of traffic considerations it is evident that:

1. At the present time the trolley buses cannot provide the flexibility required, especially in a holiday resort, to meet the unpredictable fluctuations in demand due to varying weather conditions, or the dislocation caused by special events.

2. Falling traffic and expansion of services to new populations beyond the City boundary will combine to make all in-city north-south services normally redundant.
3. During the period of City reconstruction and development traffic diversions will be desirable or sometimes necessary. Under such conditions trolley buses increase inconvenience and to some extent cost.
4. During this period new roads will gradually become available for public transport and, in so far as this is by motor buses, routes can progressively be re-organised.
5. By the time the present City plan is completed, in 15 to 20 years, the combined effect of falling traffic, expansion of population, development of light industries and the provision of new roads will have been to create a new pattern of public transport demand and opportunity.

71. During the next 20 years the conditions in Portsmouth will be such that complete freedom to experiment and to reorganise the public transport routes will be of the utmost value. By the end of that time the new pattern of requirements will have emerged. By that time, also, it is more than possible that new power units will have been developed without the respective disadvantages of both diesel buses and trolley buses.

72. Since, therefore, a decision must be made now either gradually to renew the trolley bus system and fleet, or gradually to abandon it, we believe the decision of the Transport Committee to adopt the latter course was wise.

4.

OTHER FACTORS CONSIDERED

73. In our opinion the major factors determining the decision as to the retention or abandonment of the trolley buses are those discussed above, namely
- operating and overall costs,
- traffic considerations.

A number of other factors have been considered, however, and some of these are briefly discussed below.

(i) Air Pollution

74. Air pollution is a matter which is rightly causing great concern in the present day and it is recognised that much of it is caused by the exhaust from road vehicles especially in the larger towns. We doubt, however, whether such anxiety need be very great in Portsmouth. The City is practically surrounded by water: there are no topographical obstacles to the free flow of the regular land and sea breezes: it is subject at times to sea fog, but we are informed that smog is practically unknown. The City Authorities have felt no need for a policy on pollution by diesel exhaust and we note that the new Cleansing Department vehicles and the new ambulances are diesel driven.

75. It is known that under certain circumstances (over-rich mixture and imperfect combustion) diesel exhaust contains cancer-producing agents, notably 3:4 benzpyrene, but smoke is produced at the same time, and "diesel smoke is unnecessary and could certainly be reduced if the machines were properly controlled".* Mr. J.R. Nicholson-Lailey, the Chairman of the Science Committee of the British Medical Association, reported that the Science Committee and the Council "had been unable to produce scientific evidence that a properly controlled and driven diesel engine was the danger it had been alleged to be".* That matter is in the hands of the owners of the vehicles and of the police. Exhaust analyses of public transport vehicles in London, Derby, Reading and Cardiff have revealed no significant amounts of 3:4 benzpyrene or of products known to be harmful.

76. The increase in lung cancer is rightly a matter for anxiety, but diesel exhaust fumes do not appear to be a main cause. Figures relating the incidence of lung cancer to the increase in the number of diesel vehicles appear to overlook the fact that cancer takes some 10 to 15 years to "incubate"; and a dozen years ago there were comparatively few diesels on the roads,

77. In fact it would seem that the petrol engine is more, and more immediately, harmful than the diesel engine. The latter produces sulphur compounds and aldehydes which are irritants; and it may produce more 3:4 benzpyrene than the petrol engine if badly controlled, but this is made obvious by the emission of smoke. The petrol engine exhaust may be invisible, but none the less toxic. It raises no sulphur problem but it emits 3:4 benzpyrene and nitrogen, oxygen, chlorine and bromine compounds which are bronchial and lung irritants, and also toxic tetra ethyl lead derivatives.

78. In any case out of the 5 million vehicles on the roads of Great Britain in 1957 only 1.5% were buses and coaches, while nearly 4 million were cars and taxis almost entirely petrol driven. In Portsmouth there are some 30,000 licensed vehicles and the number of trolley buses and motor buses (including Southdown) in normal service is rather less than 1%, or of trolley buses alone, less than ¼%.

*B.M.A. Annual Representative Meeting, July 1956.
Dr. R. Cove-Smith urged stricter observance of the existing law in respect of exhaust fumes. The motion was carried. The debate continued on lung cancer, Mr. J.R. Nicholson-Lailey summed up. No further vote was taken.

79. While the question of air pollution is highly important there must be some sense of proportion in considering any particular type of vehicle. Nevertheless the absence of any exhaust is a factor in favour of the trolley bus, and one which should be given very considerable weight in some areas even though it is one of much less importance in a seaside town like Portsmouth.

(ii) Considerations Relative to Oil and Electricity

80. One may well believe that as a national policy, limitation of our dependency upon oil has much to commend it, but the present position is in conformity with Government policy and local government authorities should doubtless be expected to accept it as such.

81. Since 1952 the cost of oil has fluctuated, but the price trend has tended to be very slowly downward. This may continue for the immediate future, but in the long run we expect prices will rise at least pro rata to any general increase in prices: and later due to diminution of supplies. The tax of 2s 6d per gallon is severe (costing the Corporation £52,000 in the year 1958/9). The fate of the tax is speculative: it is a political rather than an economic question. When it is considered, however, that transport enters into the cost of all goods and that the railways are already exempt from the tax, it seems not unlikely that some concession may be made to road transport in order to steady the cost of living should it show any tendency to

rise, but we think its entire removal unlikely. The Chambers of Commerce have advocated a reduction of 6d. per gallon and have felt it would be unrealistic to ask for more. A reduction of 6d. would lower the cost per bus mile by about 0.66d. and it would not need much more than that to give diesel buses a decisive advantage over trolley buses in respect of running costs.

82. The cost of electricity has risen fairly steadily over the past ten years, but in 1958/9 it was still cheaper than oil by about 0.55d. per vehicle mile. The immediate future of the price of electricity is uncertain: a continued slow rise would be expected, but it has been suggested that surplus stocks of coal should be sold to power stations at cut prices. As the atomic power programme gets under way the cost of generation is likely to be more stabilised. Perhaps, at first, slightly above the present cost, but later falling by some 15% or even 20% as more reactors are brought into use. Since the cost of fossil fuels will almost certainly rise with increasing scarcity, in the long term electricity is likely to be significantly the cheaper form of energy. By that time, moreover, it is possible, perhaps probable, that new electric power units will be available for transport vehicles which will be independent of external transmission.

83. It is difficult to draw a positive conclusion as to the more economical source of energy for the next few years, but perhaps the prospects are slightly in favour of oil.

(iii) Comfort, Vibration and Silence

84. The motor bus and trolley bus can offer substantially the same seating comfort, but in respect of vibration and silence the trolley bus is superior.

85. Even so it must be recognised that the modern motor bus is relatively quiet and free from vibration even when accelerating, so long as it is new and well maintained. Later in the life of the vehicle, gear and exhaust noise will tend to increase much more than the noise of an old trolley bus, the difference being perhaps more apparent to the residents on the route than to the passengers. In practice moreover comfort, vibration and silence are all dependent upon the road surface; and on bad roads there is little to choose between the types of vehicle.

86. On the whole, however, these factors are in favour of the trolley bus.

(iv) Power, Speed and Safety

87. The capacity of the trolley bus motor to take heavy overload and to do so quietly, is an advantage where there are steep hills, but there are none on the Portsmouth trolley bus routes.

88. This reserve of power affords rapid acceleration which gives the trolley bus an advantage on a straight run, especially where stops are frequent. In practice, however, especially where routes are complicated, as in Portsmouth, the advantage given by rapid acceleration is lost by the need to take corners, crossings and frogs slowly.

89. The motor bus has the higher maximum speed, but except in open country, where one would not expect to find trolley buses, the point is academic. In city streets the average speed is determined by other considerations – the general rate of traffic flow; the number of stops; and the time needed to collect fares. In Portsmouth, as is usual elsewhere, motor buses and trolley buses on the same route run to the same schedules; and for both types of vehicle the average speed ranges from about 9 to 13 miles per hour according to route conditions.

90. The high acceleration and rapid braking as compared with that of ordinary traffic seems to give the trolley bus increased liability to accident. An analysis of the police records of reported accidents between vehicles within the City during the past 6½ years, and taking into account the total number of trolley buses and motor buses (including Southdown) respectively on the roads, shows that trolley buses were involved in rather more than half as many again as motor buses. There are no corresponding records of accidents to persons, except fatal ones which were too few to be conclusive. However the Transport Committee analyses of accidents during 1957/8 and 1958/9 show a very few* more boarding and alighting accidents for trolley buses than for motor buses though there are more of the latter in normal use.

91. On balance we find very little to choose as to power, speed and safety between the two types of vehicle under the conditions which prevail in Portsmouth.

(v) Ease of Driving

92. We have discussed with several experienced drivers the merits of the two types of vehicle from the driver's point of view. In every case preference was definitely in favour of the motor bus.

93. We recognise that these drivers all handled both types of vehicle and they may have been bus men first and trolley men second. Therefore they may not all have achieved the fullest technique of handling trolley buses especially as regards their speed control and braking system. But with a relatively small fleet, such as Portsmouth has, it is not practicable to confine all the drivers to one type of bus only. That is indeed one of the disadvantages of having a mixed fleet.

*The difference over the two years is about 2% of the total.

94. The views expressed were:

– The motor bus is physically the more tiring, but more interesting.

– The motor bus driver has more opportunity for variety, special journeys etc.

– The motor bus driver's licence covers also his own motor cycle or car.

– The trolley bus gives more nervous strain. Whereas the motor bus driver can keep his eye on the road, the trolley bus driver must drive "on the road and on the wires". In particular he has to be careful not to run out of reach of his wires when cornering, switching or pulling out. When manoeuvring in difficult traffic he needs to give full attention to the road, but must at the same time maintain position relative to the wires.

– In case of dewirement there is no warning to following traffic, but the trolley bus must stop immediately. Otherwise, at the best he may run out of reach of the wires, or at the worst cause a short circuit and widespread dislocation.

(vi) General Comment

95. We have made no attempt to weigh against each other the factors discussed in this chapter of our report. Under the conditions prevailing in Portsmouth, in our opinion none of them are of over-riding importance.

THE CO-ORDINATION AGREEMENT

1. RETROSPECT

96. The Road Traffic Act of 1930 confirmed existing operators in the possession of the public transport routes they had exploited. The Southdown Motor Bus Company had operating rights through Portsmouth to Southsea but the Corporation routes were protected by higher fares on the Southdown buses. The rights of the Corporation were limited to the area south of Cosham Red Lion.

97. This was the position in 1934 when the Southdown Company successfully opposed extension of the City services beyond Cosham to the City boundaries.

98. The question of the extension of the City services was again being put to the test in 1939, but the war intervened and under the Defence of the Realm regulations the Corporation were allowed to run buses to Farlington, but without prejudice to the post-war position.

99. Meanwhile the movement of population out of the City reduced transport needs and the Corporation had more vehicles than were needed, while the Southdown Company – their fleet depleted by requisitioning and also having special commitments – could not provide service to the new dormitory areas. Co-operation between the Corporation and the Company started at this time, vehicles of the former being hired to the latter. The cooperation continued after the war when shortage of staff made it impossible for the Corporation to meet the transport demand.

100. It is very doubtful whether after the war the Traffic Commissioners would have countenanced a return to the earlier wasteful competition and it was to the interest of both parties that the terms of their co-operation should be codified. The present Agreement came into effect on 24th May 1946 for 21 years until 31st March 1967.

2. EQUITY OF THE AGEEMENT

101. The actual form of the Agreement is based upon that of Plymouth, but the general basis of the co-ordination is very much the same as that of other agreements elsewhere in the country. According to the circumstances of different areas the division of revenues differs and opinions may vary as to the equity of the division.

(i) The Requirements of Co-ordination

102. It must be recognised that in the matter of public transport a municipality does not stand alone. There is always a hinterland from which people travel to the centre and the population of the hinterland – especially "dormitory" population- exists largely because there is such a centre which affords occupation and facilities for shopping, entertainment etc. This involves transport routes fanning out from the centre to surrounding districts.

103. It is inevitable that some routes will be more profitable than others; and likely that those within the town will have the highest revenues. Adequate service must be provided, as a social obligation, over the whole area and taking the area as a whole therefore it is reasonable to expect the revenues from busy routes to support the less profitable ones.

104. On the other hand, although there are known differences between town and country routes, for any particular type of vehicle* the cost per vehicle mile of any route is, broadly speaking, very much the same regardless of the revenue and of the frequency of service.

105. Consequently once the division of revenue has been agreed it does not matter which of the parties operates any particular service, provided only that the total effort put out by each party is near enough in the same proportion as the revenue received. That is the "agreed shares" should apply both to revenues and to the mileage operated.

* This does not apply to trolley buses for which overhead equipment is required according to the length of the route, and the incidence of the capital charges is proportional to the frequency of the service.

(ii) The Equity of the Agreed Shares

106. We have been unable to establish an actuarial yardstick by which the fair division of revenues can be derived as the result of arithmetical calculation since practical considerations arise which are not susceptible to numerical measurement.

For example:-

- The Southdown Company have established and confirmed rights to operate services through Portsmouth to Southsea, even though they had formerly to submit to restrictive fares.
- The Corporation have no rights to operate services beyond Cosham Red Lion, not even so far as the present City boundary, and can do so only with the consent of the Southdown Company.
- It is mainly due to the existence of Portsmouth that there is a transport demand on anything like the present scale, from the hinterland within the co-ordination area.
- A considerable and increasing proportion of the population of the hinterland is due to over-spill from the City.

107. Bearing the above considerations in mind it is nevertheless reasonable to assume that transport service is required to some degree in proportion to population.

108. Before the war the City probably accounted for 85% or more of the population in the present area of co-ordination. During the war the proportion fell sharply –

by 1949, to 70% of the total
by 1958, to 61% of the total

and it is estimated it will be about 50% in 1971.

109. Before the war the Corporation Transport Services, i.e. within the statutory limit at Cosham, provided some 58% of the mileage and collected over 67% of the revenue. After the war these figures had fallen to nearly 48% and 50% respectively, but at that time conditions were exceptional owing to shortage of staff. Consequently, in order to arrive at a mutually acceptable division, the Corporation Transport Committee and the Southdown Company each estimated the services they would expect to run under competitive conditions in 1946/7. These estimates gave the ratio of 57:43, which was adopted for the agreement.

110. Perhaps the Corporation proportion was rather on the low side, if the respective populations are taken into account, but allowance must be made for the established rights of the Southdown Company to some share in the City traffic. The actual division could only be settled by negotiation. Whether the Corporation could and should have obtained better term

is futile argument today and any greater share might have been at the cost of amity.

111. In effect the Agreement assumes equal reward for equal effort. The City services are, however, the more remunerative and as long as the Corporation operates a preponderance of high revenue routes, more revenue will be paid into the pool than is received from it. This is an inevitable corollary of treating the whole co-ordinated area as a single transport system. Decline of the internal city traffic along with the outward spread of population and industrial development outside the city will change the balance and, in our opinion, will have the effect of rendering the terms of the Agreement more favourable to the Corporation.

(iii) Excess Miles Payment

112. Under the Agreement the two parties share the mileage operated in the agreed proportions and since it is impracticable to control the mileage exactly week by week, it is agreed that any disparity during one quarter shall be adjusted during the next. Even so, the control cannot be so exact as to avoid marginal differences. Consequently the Agreement also provides for the payment to the party which exceeds its quota, of a sum representing the cost of operating the additional miles.

113. It is important that the adjustment of mileage operated should be as close as possible. Otherwise questions would arise as to the equity of payments for excess mileage, the operating cost of which cannot be exactly known (also the average cost per vehicle mile is not the same for both the Corporation and the Company). Under the Agreement the excess mileage payment can be revised when required and in theory this should perhaps have been done as the cost of operation increased. In fact, it remained at 1/7 until 1958, but it has since been raised twice.

114. In practice, however, the agreed mileage division is very closely achieved. 1958/9 was by far the worst year in this respect since 1949. Even so the excess (run by the Corporation fleet) was only 0.023% of the total miles run by the combined services and the payment was only £313 – an entirely negligible sum compared with the total revenues.

115. Indeed the excess miles payment is so trivial that we wonder whether the cash adjustment could not be done only once a year – or even be forgotten altogether.

3. THE RESULTS OF CO-ORDINATION

116. So long as protective fares were in operation, Southdown buses ran within the City with empty seats, while Corporation buses were carrying passengers, at ordinary fares, to Cosham where they transferred to the Southdown buses for the further outward journey. By co-ordination waste mileage has been reduced by at least 800,000 to 900,000 miles a year while maintaining an adequate service to the public. For example, in spite of the reduction in the miles operated between Cosham, North End and Commercial Road, the number of buses available at ordinary fares was doubled.

117. At the same time the Corporation Services have been able to extend beyond Cosham into the surrounding country and in this way to share in the transport of the city's overspill population. The extent to which this has been done is shown by the following figures.

Miles run by Corporation Vehicles

Year (ending March 31st)	1946	1252	1251
Total miles run – million	5.32	7.18	6.36
Estimated miles beyond Cosham – normal services only – thousand	145	773	928
Estimated miles beyond Cosham – normal services only – % of total	2.7	10.8	14.6

118. The economies due to reduced mileage have helped to meet rising costs and have delayed applications for fare increases. The public have therefore enjoyed an adequate, and in some cases, better service at less cost than would otherwise have been possible.

119. We have noted that in practice the co-ordination is effected on an amicable basis and that both the Corporation and the Southdown Company managers are satisfied with it.

4. SUMMARY AND CONCLUSION AS TO THE CO-ORDINATION AGREEMENT

120. We have noted that:-

(1) The Southdown Company has established running rights within the City.

(2) There is a statutory limit to the freedom of the Corporation to operate passenger transport service, which may not run beyond Cosham without consent of the Southdown Company.

(3) The City Transport Committee and the Company were already co-operating before the present Agreement was made. It was, and is, in the interest of both parties that coordination should be codified. A return to earlier competitive working is unthinkable.

(4) In the matter of public transport a municipality does not stand alone: it serves and is served by a wider area, which is rightly to be considered as a single transport unit.

In such an area the high revenue routes (usually the City ones) must be expected to give some support to such less remunerative services as it is necessary to provide in the public interest.

(5) The present Agreement appears to us to be equitably framed and its terms will tend to be increasingly favourable to the Corporation. Nevertheless so long as the Corporation operates a preponderance of high revenue routes, more will be paid into the pool than is received from it.

(6) Co-ordination has achieved considerable economies in mileage and in the cost of providing public service, and has enabled such service to be given at lower fares than would otherwise have been possible.

(8) Under the Agreement the co-operation between the Corporation Transport Committee and the Southdown Company is amicable and there is full freedom to effect such improvements in the services as may become practicable.

121. We conclude therefore that the present Agreement is a satisfactory one and should be continued. We would not seek to change any material aspect of it.

122. We would add that under Clause 4 of the Portsmouth Corporation Act 1946 the two parties are given wide freedom to make such modification to the agreement as may at any time be agreed between them. Consequently it will not be necessary to draft an entirely new agreement in order to enable the co-ordination to be adapted to new circumstances.

4. The scheduled agreement is hereby confirmed and made binding upon the Corporation and the company and effect may and shall be given thereto accordingly subject to such modifications (if any) as may from time to time be agreed between the Corporation and the company in writing under their respective common seals.

Swooping down from the railway bridge into Copnor Road 233 runs out of service beneath the junction and past the erstwhile Copnor Bridge turning circle on 23 June 1963, two days after its official date of withdrawal! (T.V. Runnacles)

APPENDIX Q

SOUTHDOWN IN PORTSMOUTH & CO-ORDINATION

There is little doubt that the natural development of the Portsmouth trolleybus network and indeed the City's own motorbus services was stifled by the efforts of Southdown Motor Services and their successful use of the legislation in place at the time. The City's island location assisted the company in its efforts nonetheless the Transport Department seems to have manoeuvred itself into a more disadvantageous position than other municipal transport undertakings in relation to the neighbouring rural motorbus operator. A review of the relationship with Southdown and the various co-ordination agreements is thus an essential part of the history of the trolleybus in the City of Portsmouth.

Scheduled motorbus services into Portsmouth appear to have been introduced on 12 October 1907 when the Sussex Motor Road Car Co. Ltd. started a thrice-daily service between Bognor Regis and Portsmouth via Chichester, Emsworth and Havant. Journeys started and terminated outside their agents' offices, Frank Bartlett's travel agency at 67 Commercial Road one block south of the Town Hall. Due to a lack of business, permission was sought from Portsmouth Council to run two of the four buses used on the route within the town boundaries and an Edinburgh Road – Arundel Street – Fratton Bridge – Goldsmith Avenue – Eastney Barracks service commenced in December 1907. Services along South Parade between Clarence Pier and Eastney started in spring 1908 and in late 1908 a route to Portsdown and Hambledon was introduced. All services in the Portsmouth area ceased in autumn 1908 as there was insufficient revenue to pay the rent for their garage in Rudmore Lane and the entire company was liquidated at the end of the year.

Much of the expertise and some of the equipment passed to a new company, Worthing Motor Services Ltd., formed in March 1909; however, no interest was shown in expanding westwards to Portsmouth. As war on the Continent became imminent the military authorities began to requisition suitable motor bus chassis and the south coast operators, having lost much of their rolling stock, endeavoured to maintain services by a policy of mutual cooperation and support. This lead to the amalgamation on 1 April 1915 of Worthing Motor Services Ltd. with London & South Haulage Co. Ltd. and the country routes of the Brighton, Hove & Preston United Omnibus Co. Ltd. (the urban operations passed to Thomas Tilling Ltd. which was subsequently renamed as the Brighton Hove & District Omnibus Company Ltd.) into a single company, incorporated on 2 June 1915, Southdown Motor Services Ltd. (SMS) based in Brighton.

In May 1915 the new company purchased the Bognor charabanc business of Arthur Davies together with his unutilised licence for a stage carriage service to Portsmouth. Despite wartime restrictions SMS introduced a thrice-daily service between Bognor Pier and Portsmouth Town Hall on 4 April 1916; however, as a result of both Westhampnett RDC and West Sussex County Council demanding a wayleave for use of the roads under their jurisdiction the service was withdrawn on 31 October 1916.

Once the war was over SMS expanded rapidly. The Bognor and Portsmouth service, designated as service number 31, was reintroduced and extended eastwards to Worthing on 18 October 1919 with a further extension to Brighton on 29 March 1920. Portsmouth's Watch Committee, as the licensing authority for motor buses and services within the town boundaries until the Road Traffic Act 1930, stated that a fare of 6d between the Town Hall and Cosham must be charged to avoid competition with the Corporation Tramways, however, there is no evidence that this condition was enforced by any kind of written agreement.

Growing congestion around Portsmouth Town Hall led to a decision on 12 April 1921 that motor buses should stand in Edinburgh Road, however, SMS asked if they could stand next to the railway goods yard entrance (between Portsmouth & Southsea Station and Greetham Street, opposite the Town Hall). Instead they were granted permission to stand in the short road between Cambridge Road and Hampshire Terrace facing the south end of Victoria Hall and in Park Road. Outbound, loading was permitted in Town Hall Square. On inbound journeys SMS were allowed to stop near the railway goods yard entrance and in Russell Street. SMS vehicles were parked at various sites nearby until, in 1923, the company opened its own premises in Hyde Park Road.

By April 1922, in addition to Portsmouth Corporation Tramway's own motor buses, the following "country" operators were plying for hire in the Borough:

- Mr Fry, London Road, Portsmouth, ran a regular service to Hambledon and Westbourne, offering 2d fares stages, i.e. from Unicorn Road to North End and from Dockyard to Town Hall, between Drayton and the Dockyard.
- Mr E. Byng, Belgrave Street, Portsmouth, ran a special service between the Municipal College and Fratton Park at 6d single for football matches.
- Southdown Motor Services Ltd. ran regular services to Bognor, Brighton, Fareham and Worthing offering a 6d fare between the Victoria Hall and Cosham.
- Mr. Frank Plater, Southsea Tourist Co. Ltd., Southsea Terrace, Portsmouth, ran regular services between Southsea South Parade Pier and Horndean, offering 3d fares from Cosham to North End, and from North End to South Parade Pier.
- Furthermore, Messrs Brook, Hewett, Masters, and Salman, separately all ran special services between the Municipal College and Fratton Park at 6d single for football matches.

All the operators of regular services stated that they did not offer fares for travel within the Borough boundaries. However, the MoT informed the Portsmouth Town Clerk that in their view a local authority had no power to attach conditions to licences, fares, etc. although they might seek a written undertaking from operators that they would not pick up local passengers on tramway routes.

In September 1921 SMS introduced a service between Portsmouth and Fareham, extending this to Southampton in June 1922. As this extension paralleled a Hants & Dorset Motor Services Ltd. (H&D) route, at the end of November 1922 H&D and SMS introduced a jointly-operated service between Southampton and Portsmouth. Matters were no doubt eased by the fact that W.F. French was Chairman of both companies. SMS introduced a Portsmouth – Winchester service on 1 January 1923, this also becoming jointly operated with H&D from April 1923. As a condition of licensing these services Portsmouth Corporation required that a 6d minimum fare should apply within its boundaries, but in 1925 this policy was relaxed and both operators were able to charge 1d fares on the stages between the Victoria Hall, Commercial Road (located at the junction with Cambridge Road and probably the first cinema in Portsmouth) and the Air Balloon public house (just south of Kingston Crescent), Royal Hospital (Landport) and North End, North End and Copsey's Siding (junction with Old London Road, Hilsea), Hilsea Post Office and Cosham and Cosham to First Avenue Wymering paralleling tram service A (Clarence Pier – Cosham) as far as Cosham. The joint operation of through journeys ceased on 28 February 1926 with both companies terminating at Fareham although through fares remained available.

Although Portsmouth Corporation trams had operated along the Portsmouth and Horndean Light Railway (PHLR) as far north as the end of the double track on Portsdown Hill, opposite the north end of Widley Road, at various times between March 1903 and 30 June 1907, until the 1920s PHLR cars had never operated a through service into Portsmouth.

Prompted by competition from Southsea Tourist Co. Ltd. motor buses, the PHLR was able to negotiate a through running agreement removing the need for passengers to change cars at Cosham. Through services between Portsmouth Town Hall and Horndean Causeway, travelling along Commercial Road, Kingston Crescent and London Road, commenced on 1 August 1924. The service was extended across Guildhall Square along Commercial Road, the Terraces, Western Parade and Osborne Road to Palmerston Road crossroads for the Christmas period in 1924, 1925 and again in 1926. In 1925 the PHLR ran a through service to/from Clarence Pier on summer Bank Holidays. The 1926 Christmas extension continued until 19 April 1927 when cars were further extended to Southsea South Parade Pier on a permanent basis. The PHLR cars were rerouted between North End and the Town Hall via Kingston Road and Lake Road on 30 March 1931. There was a tram every 15 minutes with extras between Cosham and Horndean. Through passengers required separate tickets for the PHLR and the Portsmouth Corporation Tramway (PCT) portions of their journey, all receipts within the city boundary passing to the Corporation less working expenses. This also applied to the fares for local passengers in Portsmouth who could also be carried.

On 1 March 1925 SMS acquired the Southsea Tourist Co. Ltd. which, in addition to excursions from North End, Portsmouth and Southsea, had introduced scheduled services in about 1920 between Southsea South Parade Pier and Waterlooville, Horndean, Petersfield and Butser, leaving Portsmouth along Fratton Road and North End, and thus competing with the PHLR for much of the way.

On 12 July 1925 PCT extended their South Parade Pier and Cosham Railway Station via Copnor Road motor bus service H to the New Inn, Drayton, with a penny fare between Cosham Railway Station and the New Inn against the 2d fare charged by SMS on their 31 Portsmouth – Brighton service, which by now was running every 30 minutes, between these same two points. Although they had benefited from the removal of the minimum fare ruling SMS found this unacceptable and on 23 July 1925 they reduced their Copnor Railway Station – New Inn, Drayton fare to match that of PCT and cut all their fares within the boundaries to the applicable tram fares. On the same date SMS introduced a half-hourly service between Southsea South Parade Pier and Emsworth via Fratton Road running alternately with the 31. The network and frequencies of SMS services to/from Portsmouth had now grown to provide PCT with severe competition and by this date comprised the following services:

31 Portsmouth Victoria Hall – North End – Cosham – Bognor/Worthing/Brighton
via Commercial Road, Guildhall Square, Commercial Road, Kingston Crescent.

33 Portsmouth Victoria Hall – North End – Cosham – Fareham – Southampton
via Commercial Road, Guildhall Square, Commercial Road, Kingston Crescent.

36 Portsmouth Victoria Hall – North End – Cosham – Fareham – Winchester
via Commercial Road, Guildhall Square, Commercial Road, Kingston Crescent.
(hourly short workings on services 33/36 ran between Southsea South Parade Pier and Fareham via South Parade, Clarence Parade, Palmerston Road, Kent Road, Southsea Terrace, Bellevue Terrace, Jubilee Terrace, Kings Terrace, Landport Terrace, Hampshire Terrace and thence as the main service).

41 Southsea South Parade Pier – Theatre Royal – North End – Cosham – Horndean
via South Parade, Palmerston Road, Kent Road, Southsea Terrace, Bellevue Terrace, Jubilee Terrace, Kings Terrace, Landport Terrace, Hampshire Terrace, Commercial Road, Guildhall Square, Commercial Road, Kingston Crescent.

42 Southsea South Parade Pier – Theatre Royal – North End – Cosham – Petersfield via South Parade, Clarence Parade, Palmerston Road, Kent Road, Southsea Terrace, Bellevue Terrace, Jubilee Terrace, Kings Terrace, Landport Terrace, Hampshire Terrace, Commercial Road, Guildhall Square, Commercial Road, Kingston Crescent.

44 Southsea South Parade Pier – Fratton Road – North End – Cosham – Emsworth
via South Parade, Clarence Parade, Palmerston Road, Clarendon Road, The Circle, Victoria Road.

It soon became evident that on services paralleling tram routes SMS were using the same stops and charging the same fares as PCT, indeed the police reported that SMS was charging 2d to North End, the tram fare being 2½d, and that the conductors were touting for passengers. Alderman Sir John Timpson, Chairman of the Tramways Committee addressed a joint Subcommittee of the Portsmouth Tramways and Watch Committees on 7 November 1925. He pointed out that there were no written conditions on fares only a verbal undertaking and that the Watch Committee as Licensing Authority did not consult with the Tramways Committee when licensing vehicles to run along routes already served by trams.

On 22 June 1926 the Tramways Committee suggested that specified routes, stopping places, approved timetables and annual licences should apply to motor buses plying for hire in Portsmouth. Furthermore licensed operators must charge a minimum fare of 2d in excess of any fare charged on the Corporation trams or motor buses for every passenger carried over any stage or stages of the route served by the

Corporation who is picked up in the City or within 440 yards of the City Boundary, and vice versa. The Watch Committee met SMS representatives, led by their Traffic Manager, Douglas Mackenzie, on 2 July 1926. He admitted that the Southsea Tourist Co. had initially charged fares 6d above the applicable Corporation tram fares and that this excess was subsequently reduced, first to 3d and then, as a result of complaints about the different charges, dropped altogether. SMS would accept a 1d excess, however, if the Corporation now insisted on a 2d excess fare they would appeal to the MoT. The Watch Committee resolved that any renewal of the SMS licences would be subject to the 2d excess fare and all the other conditions shown above.

SMS lodged an appeal with the MoT under Section 14 (3) of the Roads Act 1920, against the Corporation's decision and in February 1927 the Chairman and Vice-Chairman of the Watch Committee, the Town Clerk and Alderman Sir John Timpson met Sir Henry Maybury, Director-General of Roads, at the MoT. The Corporation capitulated on the level of the excess fare and made another proposal to SMS in April 1927 but the company remained dissatisfied and submitted a counter-proposal to the MoT. On 13 June 1927 the Tramways Committee Chairman, the Watch Committee Chairman, the Tramways General Manager Ben Hall and the Chief Constable met Sir Henry Maybury, as arbiter, and representatives of SMS.

After a one week adjournment the following, in which it will be noted the Corporation gave up any hope of a monopoly within the City Boundaries beyond Cosham Railway Station, was agreed:

1. *The Company shall not while operating on the Portsmouth side of the City Boundary at Drayton, the George Hotel on Portsdown Hill, or the junction of the Southampton and Western Roads, charge any fare less than 6d for any passenger to be carried to or from any point south of Cosham Railway Station.*
2. *The Corporation will not operate any service by tramway or omnibus north of Cosham Railway Station except that they may continue the through running arrangement at present existing as to the tramcars with the Portsmouth and Horndean Light Railway Company and the operation of motor omnibuses between the City and the George Hotel, Portsdown Hill, in accordance with the provisions of Section 66 of the Portsmouth Corporation Act 1920.*
3. *Notwithstanding the provisions of Clauses 1 and 2 hereof, the Company may prior to 8 am continue to run a service of workmen's buses between Drayton and the Dockyard at the existing fare of 6d return, and also to carry workmen between Bradford Road Junction and Hilsea on the two buses leaving Bradford Road Junction at 5 am and 6 am respectively, at fares not less than those charged by the Corporation to ordinary tramway passengers. Provided always that the Corporation may, if they see fit, run the like service of workmen's buses subject to an arrangement with the Company so as to avoid duplication of services.*
4. *The Company's vehicles shall only be run upon the routes specified in the licences or such other routes as may be approved by the Watch Committee from time to time.*
5. *The Company's vehicles shall not stop for picking up or setting down passengers at points or places which by reason of traffic or safety considerations the Watch Committee from time to time may consider unsuitable.*
6. *The vehicles shall be run only in accordance with the time table to be deposited with the Watch Committee, and the full service of the deposited time table shall be regularly maintained.*
7. *On each journey in the City the vehicles shall run to or from the City Boundary and as provided by the time table, and a statement of the fares charged shall be exhibited in a conspicuous position and easily legible on each omnibus.*
8. *No charabanc shall at any time be substituted for a motor omnibus run by the Company within the City Boundaries.*
9. *Either party shall be at liberty to determine this agreement by giving to the other not less than three months' previous notice in writing, expiring with the date of expiration of the licences granted to the Company* in accordance herewith.

In addition the estimated number of vehicles to be licensed was increased to 100 although this did not necessarily mean that they would all be in use.

After the meeting SMS added that they were willing either to withdraw season tickets or increase the charge for such tickets, as preferred by the Portsmouth Watch Committee. By 6 July 1927 agreement was reached on season tickets, children's fares and workmen's buses, as well as two routes to Southsea South Parade Pier namely by way of The Terraces, Western Parade, Clarence Parade and South Parade, or alternately Victoria Road North, Victoria Road South, the Circle, Lennox Road and South Parade.

SMS were granted licences from 18 July 1927 which would expire 1 May 1928, and all other bus operators into City were required to accept the same conditions. Although the disagreement was over SMS had secured a highly remunerative foothold in the growing developments to the north of Portsea Island and in the same move put a strait-jacket on Portsmouth Corporation's own transport plans. This would greatly influence the dimensions of the later trolleybus network.

By September 1927 the Palmerston-Osborne and Clarendon Roads Traders' Association asked that SMS buses be allowed to revert to travelling along Palmerston Road and this concession was granted, initially for 6 months, subject to no changes to the frequencies.

On 18 July 1927 PCT replaced the alphabetical codes of their tram services with numbers and introduced numbered fare stages which may have led to some fare reductions. SMS feared that these reductions would reduce the number of passengers that they carried within the city boundaries, and on 21 October 1927 they asked for changes to the Agreement to promote co-ordination between the Company and the Corporation, and permit adjustment to their fares in relation to those charged by the Corporation. The Corporation was prepared to reduce the fares in question to their former level, however, at a meeting between the Joint Sub-Watch and Tramways Committee and SMS on 26 January 1928 the company stated that they did not wish to retain the higher fares levels. Discussion then centred on a reduction of the minimum fare stipulated in the Agreement from 6d to 5d, and a reduction of the SMS fares between Drayton and Cosham.

Ben Hall felt that this reduction would not adversely affect the Corporation's receipts to any great extent but went as far as to suggest that PCT might take over SMS operations from the point that they entered the City Boundary similar to the agreement existing with the Portsdown & Horndean Light Railway where separate tickets were issued for that part of the passenger's journey north of Cosham an south thereof. And thus on 4 May 1928 the Subcommittee recommended that a reduction of the minimum fare of SMS south of Cosham

Railway Gates from 6d to 5d on condition that they reduced their fare from Drayton to the Cosham Railway Station Gates from 2d to 1d. SMS sent holding reply as they wished to see what effect favourable weather conditions would have on their revenues (they seem to have never responded on this). It will be noted that this was the first occasion that Cosham Railway Station Gates was referred to as the "fare boundary location" in negotiations between the Corporation and SMS.

In order to cope with the huge crowds expected at the Schneider Trophy seaplane speed contest based at Cowes, held on 7 September 1929, and following a course across Southsea between turning points off Calshot and Hayling Island, co-operation between PCT and SMS was a necessity. There were an estimated 1.5 million spectators.

On 8 October 1929 a renegotiated agreement between the Corporation and SMS was announced effective from 1 January 1930. The undertakings agreed to co-ordinate their timetables with SMS motorbuses charging the applicable tram fare and issuing tickets printed by the Corporation. All revenue earned within the city boundary passed to the Corporation and SMS was paid an agreed amount per bus mile operated which reflected the company's working expenses per bus mile each year. Transfer and season tickets were to be continued and the fares charged on Southdown buses fixed by the Tramways General Manager.

The agreed boundary points for fare protection purposes were deemed to be Paulsgrove House on Portchester Road (today's M27 bridge across Southampton Road); the New Inn, junction of Drayton Lane with Havant Road, Drayton; and the George Inn, London Road, Portsdown (just south of the crossroads with Portsdown Hill Road). These points were entitled Stage 0 under the numbered fare stage system introduced on 18 July 1927, Cosham *Red Lion* being Stage 2 and Cosham Railway Station Stage 3. For journeys within the city boundary SMS issued Corporation tickets headed "Portsmouth Corporation and Southdown Motor Services, Joint Services". The agreement was renewed after one year

The Portsmouth Corporation Tramways Committee found themselves in a quandary as the date of renewal of the agreement with SMS approached. On 8 July 1931 it was decided that an arrangement should be made whereby protective fares in excess of those charged on the Corporation trams and buses, should be charged on SMS buses operated within the city and within a distance of a ¼ mile from the city boundaries. At a meeting on 17 July 1931 Mr Mackenzie stated that SMS would accept the protective fares suggested on their buses south of Cosham Railway Station Gates but if the Corporation insisted on running to the city boundaries the Company would approach the Traffic Commissioners (RTC).

The Town Clerk pointed out that City Boundaries were likely to be extended and asked if SMS would accept the Corporation running buses to a reasonable distance from the new boundaries based on the same mileage which the Company suggest they should now be allowed to run within the City Boundaries. SMS agreed to consider this proposal.

At the Tramways Committee Meeting the following day the General Manager stated that he felt it would be uneconomic for PCT to run services to the city boundaries. Negotiations with SMS continued on the basis of protective fares within the city south of Cosham Railway Station Gates together with a payment in respect of passengers carried on SMS vehicles or bus miles run between Cosham Railway Station Gates and the city boundaries. By mid August 1931 SMS agreed to protective fares at 2d above those on Corporation vehicles but would not accept that a payment should be made to secure that the Corporation did not commence operations in that part of the city already served by SMS. The Subcommittee adhered to their previous decision as SMS was gaining a monopoly north of Cosham Railway Station Gates and this remained the only point of contention with the Company. SMS went on to pointed out that the previous agreements had all been short-lived (1 year) and that they needed some security of tenure, Mr Mackenzie suggesting 21 years something that the Corporation would not agree to.

On 13 November 1931, Southdown appealed to the RTC against eight licence applications by Portsmouth Corporation and had nine of theirs objected to by the municipality. A compromise solution was reached, effective 14 December 1931, whereby no PCT motor buses ran north of Cosham Railway Station Gates although SMS made no special payments for this pseudo-monopoly, whilst the Corporation removed their objections to SMS working within the city on condition that protective fares, on a sliding scale of 1d–2d in excess of the Corporation fares, were reintroduced. This gave the Corporation a degree of protection and reduced the risk of SMS's long-distance passengers being crowded-out by short stage passengers in Portsmouth. Despite a protracted argument in 1934, this arrangement remained in force until 1946. Other motor bus operators running into the city still had to charge 6d excess but these were progressively acquired by SMS, the company having secured a monopoly of stage-carriage traffic between Portsmouth and the surrounding countryside by September 1935.

Withdrawal of the last regular Corporation Tramways service to Cosham on 1 October 1934 meant that the PHLR, owned by the Provincial Tramways Company's Hampshire Light Railway (Electric) Co. Ltd., would soon be unable to operate further south than the Interchange Platform adjoining Cosham Railway Station. On 8 October 1934 PHLR gave 3 months' notice of their intention to end their through-running agreement and in mid-November 1934 the RTC granted SMS a temporary licence, valid until 31 March 1935, for increasing their services to replace the trams. The temporary nature of this licence was intended to give the Corporation a period of grace to consider whether or not they wished to acquire that part of the Light Railway that was within the City Boundary as provided for in the Horndean Light Railway Order. The tramway company's goodwill was bought by SMS whose motor buses replaced the trams on 10 January 1935 thereby reintroducing through services to and from Portsmouth (SMS service 41) and on 15 January 1935 the Portsmouth Tramways Committee recommended not to exercise their purchase option thereby losing an opportunity to serve areas north of Cosham Railway Station Gates.

In February 1935 SMS and the Tramways Committee discussed the City's application to the MoT for an Order to operate trolley vehicles to the city boundaries. SMS agreed to withdraw their opposition to the running of trolley vehicles to Cosham "Red Lion" if the Corporation withdrew their application in respect of the routes to the City Boundaries to the east, west and north, the 3½d fare to the "Red Lion" to be retained on the trolley buses. On 19 February 1935 the Tramways Committee recommended that the Council should accept these conditions.

Apart from occasional skirmishes Portsmouth Corporation and Southdown cooperated through the 1930s and the company's operations grew so large that, in 1934, an impressive new garage-cum-coach station was opened at Hilsea. In June

1939 however SMS applied to the Traffic Commissioner for a licence to operate a service from Portsdown Hill (North) Housing Estate, i.e. to the north of Cosham Railway Station Gates, and the, by then, Passenger Transport Committee resolved to make a similar application to operate this service. The hearing was adjourned due to the developments on Mainland Europe.

The outbreak of war led to a rapid evacuation of civilians from the vicinity of the major naval base; the amount of traffic on Portsea Island itself fell whilst "country" services from the surrounding areas were overcrowded with people dispersed from the City.

The Traffic Commissioner considered that SMS was not coping with traffic demands to and from the outlying districts at peak times and in December 1940 asked CPPTD and SMS to seek a remedy, without success. A further request led to suggestions that SMS could augment its peak hour services northwards over Portsdown Hill by extending Waterlooville journeys to Cowplain. The Traffic Commissioner then summoned CPPTD and SMS to a meeting on 21 March 1941 at which he stated that if agreement was not reached he would simply give instructions as to what had to be done. This led to SMS using at least 10 CPPTD double-deck motorbuses for an experimental 2 month period subsequently extended to for six month, then to 30 September 1942 and finally until 31 March 1943.

In March 1945 SMS advised that they wished to increase their out-district services within the City and following a meeting with a Special Committee of the Passenger Transport Committee any objections were withdrawn subject to SMS reducing their mileage operated by duplications within the City and adjacent area by an amount as near as possible to that which would be imposed by the Company's reintroduction of their basic pre-war headways affected. The Regional Traffic Commissioner commented that the CPPTD and SMS should consider a co-ordination scheme for the City and surrounding areas. As a direct consequence of the war, a large proportion of the city's population had left the urban area of Portsea Island and this migration was expected to continue as damaged or poor quality dwellings were demolished. This had left CPPTD with less traffic than in the past but increased loads on SMS country services from the outer districts. Mr Hall, the Portsmouth General Manager, investigated similar schemes in other towns and cities.

Negotiations centred on a division of mileage and revenues, taking into account the conditions that had existed prior to the war, the likelihood of the evacuated population returning to Portsea Island and housing developments in the SMS area on the mainland. By now there were some 33 journeys an hour in both directions to and from the City of which 15 terminated at the Theatre Royal, immediately to the south of the Guildhall, and the remainder continued to Southsea. SMS insisted in November 1945 that they were not prepared to give up mileage which they were then running in order to enable the Corporation to run a certain percentage of the mileage. In respect of the duration of the agreement, SMS sought 21 years whereas Portsmouth wanted just 5 years.

Agreement was reached to co-ordinate services for 21 years within an area bounded by Fareham, Petersfield and Emsworth, the Corporation to operate 57% of the mileage, receiving 57% of receipts, and Southdown to operate and receive 43%. As the CPPTD trolleybus system was involved this required the promotion of an Act in parliament, the Portsmouth Corporation Act, 1946. In early June 1946 SMS wrote to terminate the Wartime Operating Agreement effective 30 June 1946. The co-ordination agreement, marketed as the Portsmouth Area Joint Transport Services, was introduced on 1 July 1946 and outlived the trolleybuses, continuing until deregulation in 1986. The pooling arrangements sometimes led to motorbuses from one operator being put onto services of the other usually towards the end of each financial year, but sometimes for longer periods, in order to achieve the agreed mileage. This proration included the cost of providing passenger waiting shelters, maintenance and rental, however each operator remained responsible for the provision and maintenance of vehicles, staff, equipment, depots, offices, etc. A Joint Transport Committee, comprising six members, three from each operator, was set-up to co-ordinate operational issues including publication of a single timetable and fare table as well as applications for fare increases.

SMS immediately adopted the same fares as the Corporation between Kingston Cross and Southsea via either Commercial Road or Fratton Road but retained the protective fares for journeys to and from points between Kinston Cross and Cosham until 17 May 1947. CPPTD adopted SMS conditions for the issue of adult, children's, scholars and season tickets whilst CPPTD conditions prevailed for workman's fares. SMS adopted the CPPTD minimum fare of 1½d over common sections of the Corporation's services east and west of Cosham "Red Lion".

In June 1951 the Joint PTC recommended that the Corporation should approach the Public Transport Association and MPTA with a view to making representations that the MoT's powers in relation to trolleybus fares should be vested in the Licensing Authority, however as this would require legislation nothing further was done.

The Co-ordination Agreement remained a thorn in the side of all those supporting trolleybus retention from the mid-1950s particularly as the partial replacement of some services was made by SMS motorbuses. By 1953 CPPTD trolleybus services 1, 1A, 2, 2A, 9, 10 were withdrawn. The replacement services were extended (something that would not have been previously easily possible) and in some cases jointly operated with SMS whilst in the case of trolleybus services 9 and 10 parts of the route were covered by rerouting longer SMS services. It also permitted a flexible approach to traffic demands for example when at the end of 1959 some SMS services were rerouted from Commercial Road to Fratton Road during the evening reducing service gaps and resulting in a more even spacing of the Fratton Road services.

Looking back on the first decade of the Portsmouth Area Joint Transport Services both operators considered that it had led to considerable economies which had enabled many of the increased costs of the late 1940s to be absorbed without fare increases. The public had benefitted from the knowledge that they could board any service going to their chosen destination, whether a CPPTD or an SMS vehicle, and pay the same fare. The frequency of trolleybus services to and from Cosham had however been reduced as SMS out-district services were able to carry the local traffic.

The 1959 consultants report into the Corporation's passenger transport policy could find no fault with the Co-ordination Agreement from an economic perspective. See Appendix Q, section II.

In 1967, after the trolleybus abandonment, the Agreement was renewed with a number of changes including mileage balancing which was henceforth effected by financial adjustment, for a further ten year period. A further renewal took place in 1977 but was overtaken by deregulation in 1986.